FROM GOETHE
TO GUNDOLF

From Goethe to Gundolf

Essays on German Literature
and Culture

Roger Paulin

https://www.openbookpublishers.com

© 2021 Roger Paulin

This work is licensed under a Creative Commons Attribution 4.0 International license (CC BY 4.0). This license allows you to share, copy, distribute and transmit the text; to adapt the text and to make commercial use of the text providing attribution is made to the authors (but not in any way that suggests that they endorse you or your use of the work). Attribution should include the following information:

Roger Paulin, *From Goethe to Gundolf: Essays on German Literature and Culture.* Cambridge, UK: Open Book Publishers, 2021, https://doi.org/10.11647/OBP.0258

Copyright and permissions for the reuse of many of the images included in this publication differ from the above. Copyright and permissions information for images is provided separately in the List of Illustrations. In order to access detailed and updated information on the license, please visit, https://doi.org/10.11647/OBP.0258#copyright

Further details about CC-BY licenses are available at, https://creativecommons.org/licenses/by/4.0/

All external links were active at the time of publication unless otherwise stated and have been archived via the Internet Archive Wayback Machine at https://archive.org/web

Updated digital material and resources associated with this volume are available at https://doi.org/10.11647/OBP.0258#resources

Every effort has been made to identify and contact copyright holders and any omission or error will be corrected if notification is made to the publisher.

ISBN Paperback: 9781800642126
ISBN Hardback: 9781800642133
ISBN Digital (PDF): 9781800642140
ISBN Digital ebook (epub): 9781800642157
ISBN Digital ebook (mobi): 9781800642164
ISBN Digital (XML): 9781800642171
DOI: 10.11647/OBP.0258

Cover photo and design by Andrew Corbett, CC-BY 4.0.

Contents

Foreword		ix
GOETHE AND SCHILLER: GOETHEZEIT		xi
1.	Goethe: *Die Leiden des jungen Werthers*	1
2.	Goethe and Stolberg in Italy: The Consequences for Romantic Art	25
3.	Schiller: *Wallenstein*	45
4.	Laocoon, Dante, Shakespeare, August Wilhelm Schlegel and the Overcoming of Tragedy	59
5.	Adding Stones to the Edifice: Patterns of German Biography	79
6.	Kleist's Metamorphoses. Some Remarks on the Use of Mythology in *Penthesilea*	95
7.	Goethe, the Brothers Grimm and Academic Freedom	123
ROMANTICISM		145
8.	Fairy Stories for Very Sophisticated Children: Ludwig Tieck's *Phantasus*	147
9.	Gundolf's Romanticism	161
NINETEENTH CENTURY		177
10.	Some Remarks on the New Edition of the Works of Wilhelm Müller	179
11.	Heine and Shakespeare	207
12.	The 'Schillerfeier' of 1859 and the 'Shakespearefest' of 1864. With Some Remarks on Theodor Fontane's Contributions	223
13.	Under the Horse's Tail: The Poets, Statuary and the Literary Canon in Nineteenth-Century Germany	245

POETRY 269

14. Friedrich Gottlieb Klopstock: 'Der Zürchersee' 271
15. Annette von Droste-Hülshoff 293
16. Rilke: Duino Elegy Ten: *In memoriam Leslie Seiffert, 1934–90* 313

BOOKS 337

17. Julius Hare's German Books in Trinity College Library, Cambridge 339

Bibliography 365
List of Illustrations 389
Index 393

Foreword

These essays are a selection of my research papers and public lectures over a period of nearly forty years. They represent my major interests — Romanticism, and the reception of Shakespeare in Germany — but also excursions into other areas that have caught my imagination. I have always taught across a broad spectrum of German literature, and these essays reflect that scope. With three exceptions, they have all appeared in scholarly journals or collected volumes, between 1982 to 2010. Most have been subject to some reformulation, but their substantial arguments have not been changed. I have taken the opportunity to correct some errors and to add references to more recent scholarship.

This collection draws on pieces which were in the true sense 'occasional', and others which arose out of my major research interests. Those in the former category include the chapter on Kleist (Chapter 6), inspired by Charles Tomlinson's Clark Lectures in Cambridge and very much an early 'one-off'; while the chapter on Academic Freedom (Chapter 7), my Inaugural Lecture in Cambridge in 1990, pertinent then, still retains its relevance today. Several chapters reflect my abiding love of poetry in all its forms and my pleasure in teaching it. They are all based on public lectures given in Cambridge (Klopstock, Chapter 14; Werther, Chapter 1; Wallenstein, Chapter 3; Annette von Droste-Hülshoff, Chapter 15; Rilke's Tenth Elegy, Chapter 16). My interest in Romanticism, its origins and its pervasive influence, is displayed in the chapters on Goethe and Stolberg (Chapter 2), Fairy Stories (Chapter 8) and Gundolf (Chapter 9). They cover concerns not always central to present-day Romantic studies. Chapter 4 is a brief but in-depth study of an aspect of August Wilhelm Schlegel, that cosmopolitan writer of whom I wrote a biography in 2016. Similarly, Heine and Shakespeare (Chapter 11) and the 'Schillerfeier' (Chapter 12) look at detailed issues in Shakespeare's reception in Germany that arose in the composition of my monograph on the same subject (2003). The link between the lives of the poets, their commemoration and the literary canon, has always been an interest of mine: 'Adding Stones to the Edifice' (Chapter 5) examines the German biographical tradition, Wilhelm Müller (Chapter 10) serves to illustrate the problems of a 'minor' poet, and 'Under the Horse's Tail' (Chapter 13) looks at the public memorialization of the poets. My chapter on Julius Hare's books in Trinity College Library (Chapter 17) tells of the treasures of German literature to be found there and records my lasting love of books in all forms, however obscure or recondite.

The translations are my own, unless otherwise indicated.

I wish to record my gratitude to my friend and colleague Peter Hutchinson, who was responsible for commissioning and originally publishing five of these pieces.

I have been encouraged in this endeavour by the example of my late friend and colleague, Hugh Barr Nisbet, whose dedication to scholarship — and whose stoicism in adversity — I here acknowledge.

The Managers of the Schröder Fund, Department of German, University of Cambridge, made a generous grant towards the production of this book.

I wish to record my thanks to all at Open Book Publishers who have seen this book through to its completion, not least their patience and forbearance with an author whose IT literacy leaves much to be desired.

GOETHE AND SCHILLER:
GOETHEZEIT

Fig. 1 James Hervey, *Meditations and Contemplations* (London: J. Goodwin, 1812).

1. Goethe

Die Leiden des jungen Werthers

Goethe and the Novel

Only superlatives will do for *Werther*. For Thomas Mann, for instance, it remains 'ein Meisterwerk'.[1] For this and other modern masters of the theme of death such a reaction might come more from literary mediation than through direct access. For earlier generations, however, it came straight from the experience of the heart. *Werther* concentrates many of the aspirations and strivings of the *Sturm und Drang* ('Storm and Stress') and is its finest literary expression. It is the textbook from which the German Romantics learn their *Weltschmerz* ('melancholy'). Their European counterparts in *mal du siècle* can create Adolphe, René, Ortis or Manfred[2] because Werther has shown the way. At home, a succession of tragic heroes, Bonaventura, Roquairol and Danton,[3] can pronounce on the futility of existence with an eloquence lent by the earlier model. Yet against such specific literary influence one must set the sheer importance of the text for the whole of German literature — and for Johann Wolfgang Goethe himself as its representative. It is the first

---

1 'A masterpiece'. For a selection of modern reactions to Werther see Johann Wolfgang Goethe, *Die Leiden des jungen Werther. Ein unklassischer Klassiker. Neu herausgegeben und mit Dokumenten und Materialien, Wertheriana und Wertheriaden*, ed. by Hans Christoph Buch, Wagenbach Taschenbücher 898 (Berlin: Wagenbach, 1982), 248–51. This chapter was originally published as the Introduction to Goethe, *Die Leiden des jungen Werthers*, ed. by Roger Paulin (London: Bristol Classical Press, 1993), vii-xxvi.
2 Benjamin Constan*t*, *Adolphe* (1816), François-René de Chateaubriand, *René* (1802), Ugo Foscolo, *Ultime lettere di Jacopo Ortis* (1816), Lord Byron, *Manfred* (1817).
3 Heroes in, respectively, Jean Paul, *Titan* (1800–03), [Ernst August Friedrich Klingemann], *Die Nachwachen des Bonaventura* (1805), Georg Büchner, *Dantons Tod* (1835).

© 2021 Roger Paulin, CC BY 4.0   https://doi.org/10.11647/OBP.0258.01

German novel to gain international fame, and nothing Goethe or any other German writes in this mode will catch Europe's attention again for well over a century. It is Goethe's only novel to sustain narrative breath from start to finish. It is his only true tragedy. It might even be said that the young man of twenty-four wrote nothing better. The fame and scandal it attracted to his name, while not inhibiting his creativity, certainly did stamp him in the eyes of many as the author of just one book and as such was an encumbrance and an embarrassment in his middle years — 'ein Unheil, was mich bis nach Indien verfolgen würde'.[4] But by 1824, fifty years after the first printing and in the year of his poem 'An Werther', Goethe — now well over seventy — cannot help admitting that 'Es sind lauter Brandraketen!',[5] that the novel still packs an explosive charge. There is pride here at having written *Werther* at twenty-four, and by implication, at having been a celebrity ever since.

Goethe claimed in a conversation with Johann Peter Eckermann early in 1824 that he had read the novel only once since its first appearance, presumably for the revisions carried out from 1782 onwards. However that may be — and there is no reason necessarily to doubt him — Goethe certainly had little to say about his most famous work until drawn in 1808 by no less an interlocutor than Napoleon Bonaparte. And it was a combination of real circumstances and the reflexion on circumstances once real, that caused him to return again to the work and its implications. The suicide of the stepson of his friend Carl Friedrich Zelter in 1812 brings back the memory of *taedium vitae*. It was that surfeit of life, that had once gripped his vitals, in the experience leading up to *Werther*, and that he had escaped ('den Wellen des Todes [...] entkommen').[6] The reflexion on his own life, as his autobiography *Dichtung und Wahrheit / Poetry and Truth* enters into its 'Werther phase' in 1813, causes him to pause for thought on how it may have been and now seemed. There could of course be no question of stating how it actually was, but a disparate and confused set of events could now be stylized into the

---

4   'A misfortune that might pursue me as far as India'. All Goethe quotations are taken where possible from Goethe, *Der junge Goethe. Neu bearbeitete Ausgabe in fünf Bänden*, ed. by Hanna Fischer-Lamberg, 5 vols (Berlin: De Gruyter, 1963–74) (*DjG*), and Goethe, *Goethes Werke. Hamburger Ausgabe*, ed. by Erich Trunz et al., 14 vols (Hamburg: Wegner, 1948–60) (*HA*); here, *HA*, VI, 530. The text *of Werther* is that of the first edition of 1774.
5   'Fireworks, the lot of them'. *HA*, VI, 534.
6   'Escaped from the waves of death'. *HA*, VI, 534.

coherent whole that is conditional on reflective maturity. To protect the integrity of a life so portrayed, Goethe warned against 'zerrupfen und die Form zerstören',[7] an injunction to respect both *Werther* the work of art and the account of its genesis. Later generations of commentators, armed with more factual evidence than Goethe during his lifetime was willing to surrender, do well to remember this warning. But if it is the novel that we wish to understand and appreciate better, the biographical background should enhance rather than detract from it.

Yet care is needed in linking life and work too closely. In writing *Werther* in the epistolary mode, Goethe was obeying urges that were certainly more literary than personal. Among the extraordinary collection first edited over a century ago as *Der junge Goethe*, there is the opening of a fragmentary *Roman in Briefen/Novel in Letters*. No longer attributed to Goethe, it dates from 1770–71, Goethe's Strasbourg interlude. Its theme of a love just ended and the heart's 'Wallendes Sehnen nach Etwas'[8] suggest an early draft of *Werther*, or rather of that shadowy web of relationships in the novel's first page or two, abandoned once it finds its true tone and style. Above all, it indicates that Goethe's novel-writing is not 'naïve', in the sense that he is fully aware of a current European fashion. He had already displayed an ambition sufficient not only to sum up Shakespeare's world in his *Zum Schäkespear's Tag/On Shakespeare's Day* but also to write the Shakespeareanizing *Götz von Berlichingen*; he would not regard the presence of Samuel Richardson's or Jean-Jacques Rousseau's epistolary novels as an impediment to fiction-writing. The mode was now so popular that its debasements — those 'Miß Jennys'[9] that once occupied Lotte's few leisure hours — were almost as well-known as its high achievements. The epistolary novel appeals for its very ability to present character, motives and heart's stirrings as spontaneous and genuine but yet also morally structured. The *Roman in Briefen* — two letters and a few fragments — seems to conform to that pattern. It is at any rate not yet moving towards the device that gives *Werther* its uniqueness: the absence of replies. For by denying

---

7   'Unpicking and ruining the form'. *HA*, IX, 592.
8   'Waves of longing for something'. The fragment is still attributed to Goethe by Ernst Beutler in Goethe, *Sämtliche Werke. Artemis-Gedenkausgabe*, ed. by Ernst Beutler, 18 vols (Munich: dtv, 1977), and it is quoted here after that edition, IV, 263.
9   Cf. *DjG*, IV, 116.

Werther's correspondents the chance to articulate a counter-position, Goethe seems to present Werther's heart as the sole moral reference and arbiter, overriding others' qualifications or tiresome interjections. Thus it is that Werther's style and presentation, this view of himself and others, are the only ones 'in character', and as such they seize us.

Wetzlar

'Und doch muss man einmal erfahren dass Mädgen — Mädgen sind'.[10] Were these words of the *Roman in Briefen* by Goethe, they would suggest a young man of great talent but considerable emotional instability and egoism. His callous abandonment of Friederike Brion in Strasbourg in 1771 is witness to this. Yet Strasbourg had also stood for legal studies and not just for the heart or letters. At his father's insistence the young doctor of law was now to gain further legal experience at the 'Reichskammergericht' in Wetzlar.[11] It was following family tradition, to convey some of that same professional solidity to yet another generation. Despite Joseph II's reforms, this imperial appeal court was still a circumlocution office, one of those tottering institutions of the old regime waiting only for Napoleon to give it the final push. In 1772, however, delegations from the various sovereign states within the Holy Roman Empire were still representing their interests there; it made Wetzlar the town into a place where the aristocracy, the bourgeoisie and the people — all knowing their stations — came together and kept apart. In all this, Goethe was a free agent, but he soon found social contact with young men of his own age: Johann Christian Kestner, a secretary with the Hanoverian delegation, Karl Wilhelm Jerusalem from Brunswick, even a fellow-poet, Friedrich Wilhelm Gotter from Gotha. From May to September 1772, Goethe's pursuits were hardly juridical; he was a member of a burlesque order of chivalry where he bore the name of 'Götz', and he enjoyed numerous visits — more than would prove decorous — in the Buff household. Kestner was engaged to Charlotte Buff, the nineteen-year-old daughter of the estate-manager of the 'Deutschordenshof',[12] who, after the recent death of her mother,

---

10 'And still one has to learn that girls — are girls'. *Artemis-Gedenkausgabe*, IV, 265.
11 Imperial Appeal Court.
12 Property belonging to the German Order.

was caring for her eleven brothers and sisters. Kestner had every reason to observe this young man, 'in allen seinen Affecten heftig', 'Aller Zwang ist ihm verhaßt', 'Er liebt die Kinder',[13] '*bizarre*'. At a ball given in the nearby village of Volpertshausen on June 9, 1772, 'Dr Goede' danced with Charlotte and promptly fell in love. It took him some months before he faced the fact that he was very much in the way. He departed precipitately on September 11, without a formal leave-taking from either Kestner or Lotte. Returning on foot to Frankfurt, he spent some time with the La Roche family near Ehrenbreitstein: Sophie von La Roche's novel *Geschichte des Fräuleins von Sternheim/The History of Mademoiselle de Sternheim* (1771), with its story of court intrigue and virtue preserved, had made her a celebrity. But Goethe was attracted to their daughter Maximiliane. She however was already promised to the Frankfurt merchant Peter Brentano. Goethe returned abruptly to Frankfurt, which was to be his base for the next eighteen months. On October 30, Karl Wilhelm Jerusalem shot himself in Wetzlar with pistols borrowed from Kestner. As Goethe was to learn in a long account from Kestner, an impossible attachment to a married woman had been but the last in a series of personal calamities that had befallen him. On April 4, 1773, Kestner and Lotte were married; in January 1774, it was Maxe von La Roche and Peter Brentano's turn. From February to May, 1774, Goethe was occupied with writing his novel, which Weygand in Leipzig published in September as *Die Leiden des jungen Werthers.*

The Question of Autobiography

These raw facts produce at a basic level a series of coincidences with the text of the novel. Goethe's first readers were aware of this and Goethe knew that they knew. Thus began the most tiresome aspect of study of this novel, to explore:

> Ob denn auch Werther gelebt? ob denn auch alles fein wahr sei?[14]

as a manuscript variant of Goethe's own *Römische Elegie* II of 1795 puts it.

---

13   'Violent in all his feelings'; 'Detests all constraint'; 'Loves children'. *Goethe in vertraulichen Briefen seiner Zeitgenossen*, ed. by Wilhelm Bode, 3 vols (Berlin: Aufbau, 1979), I, 36.
14   'Did Werther really exist? Was it all really true?' *HA*, I, 492, VI, 530.

Kestner, who had every reason to believe that he was the Albert of the original, was not long in informing Goethe that he was 'schlecht erbauet'[15] by the novel and its mixture of fact and fiction, at the way real persons had been 'prostituirt'.[16] Yet Kestner was magnanimous: for Goethe, only a matter of weeks after the novel's publication, was already complaining to him of the 'Verdacht, Missdeutung pp. im schwäzzenden Publikum', that 'Heerd Schwein'.[17] But that 'herd of swine' contained many of the soulful fraternity, those who read from the heart and expected the heart to ratify as true any specific or identifiable reference. It embraced others, notably Gothold Ephraim Lessing, for whom the overt associations of Jerusalem's suicide — not to speak of a copy of *Emilia Galotti* open on the desk — were a travesty of all that his young friend had stood for. His letter to Johann Joachim Eschenburg of October 26, 1774 has become famous:

> ja, wenn unseres J[erusalem]s Geist völlig in dieser Lage gewesen wäre, so müßte ich ihn fast —verachten. Glauben Sie wohl, daß je ein römischer oder griechischer Jüngling sich so und darum das Leben genommen? Gewiß nicht. Die wußten sich vor der Schwärmerey der Liebe ganz anders zu schützen; [...] Solche kleingrosse, verächtlich schätzbare Originale hervorzubringen, war nur der christlichen Erziehung vorbehalten, die ein körperliches Bedürfniß so schön in eine geistige Vollkommenheit zu verwandeln weiß.[18]

Goethe faced the danger of his novel becoming a mere *roman à clef*. More seriously, however, he might be seen as ghoulishly creating fiction out of the real circumstances of a young man now dead and no longer able to defend himself. The first, and the added suspicion that the novel reflected Goethe's own views ('ich fürchte, viele werden glauben,

---

15 'Highly displeased'.
16 'Travestied'. *DjG*, IV, 381.
17 'Suspicion, distortion etc. among my chattering readers', 'herd of swine'. *DjG*, IV, 255.
18 'Yes, if our Jerusalem's mind had been in that state, then I would just about have to — despise him. Can you imagine a Roman or Greek youth taking his life for this cause in such a fashion? Of course not. They knew of other ways of protecting themselves against the flights of love. [...] Only a Christian upbringing could produce such puny and contemptible types, adept at changing a physical need into a perfection of the mind'. *Goethe in vertraulichen Briefen*, I, 74.

daß Goethe selbst so denkt'),[19] would not outlive initial reactions to the work. The second would not go away quite so easily. For Goethe had requested from Kestner a full and circumstantial account of Jerusalem's last days[20] and had made extensive use of it in the novel. Genius is not fastidious. Perhaps Goethe's stress in his later account in *Dichtung und Wahrheit* (Part Three, Book 13) on the symbolic unity of the work and the impossibility of unravelling the strands of fact and fiction, is designed partly to play down his own involvement in all these events. The atmosphere of *taedium vitae* described there, has, he claims, been induced more by literature than by real life — by the brooding, melancholic or elegiac poetry of English provenance, into which both novel and remembered experience may be integrated. Instead of a detailed account of Jerusalem's circumstances, we have a stanza from Thomas Warton's poem 'The Suicide',[21] a 'case' that is typical and non-specific. Autobiographical truth, as he wrote in a letter of 1830, stood for 'das eigentlich Grundwahre',[22] not objective reality. Thus Goethe can claim that it was Jerusalem's suicide that first caused the plan of *Werther* to 'freeze' into place as a 'solide Masse'.[23] It was, however, to be well over a year, after the further distress of the marriages of Lotte and Maxe, that he was to sit down and, as it were, write *Werther* out of his system. Yet the suicide of Jerusalem did, perhaps in another sense, provide the germ of the novel. On hearing of this shocking event, Goethe wrote the following letter to Kestner in early November 1772:

> Der unglückliche Jerusalem. Die Nachricht war mir schröcklich und unerwartet, es war grässlich zum angenehmsten Geschenck der Liebe diese Nachricht zur Beylage. Der unglückliche. Aber die Teufel, welches sind die schändlichen Menschen die nichts geniessen denn Spreu der Eitelkeit, und Götzen Lust in ihrem Herzen haben, und Götzendie[n]st predigen, und hemmen gute Natur, und übertreiben und verderben die Kräffte sind schuld an diesem Unglück an unserm Unglück hohle sie der Teufel ihr Bruder. Wenn der verfluchte Pfaff sein Vater nicht schuld ist

---

19 'I fear that quite a few will believe Goethe himself thinks this way'. *Goethe in vertraulichen Briefen*, I, 85.
20 *DjG*, IV, 351–56.
21 *HA*, IX, 583.
22 'The basic underlying truth'. Quoted in Goethe, *Sämtliche Werke, Briefe, Tagebücher und Gespräche*, ed. by Dieter Borchmeyer et al., 40 vols (Frankfurt am Main: Deutscher Klassiker Verlag, 1985–98), II, 2, 209.
23 *HA*, IX, 583.

so verzeih mirs Gott dass ich ihm Wünsche er möge den Hals brechen wie Eli. Der arme iunge! wenn ich zurückkam vom Spaziergang und er mir begegnete hinaus im Mondschein, sagt ich er ist verliebt. Lotte muss sich noch erinnern dass ich drüber lächelte. Gott weis die Einsamkeit hat sein Herz untergraben, und — seit sieben jahren kenn ich die Gestalt, ich habe wenig mit ihm geredt, bey meiner Abreise nahm ich ihm ein Buch mit das will ich behalten und sein Gedencken so lang ich lebe.[24]

Kestner's long reply was written in response to this impulsive note. Whereas Kestner's letter adopts a uniform, almost forensic tone in both report and commentary, Goethe's is notable for the way in which levels of style succeed and overlay each other. It is the characteristic style of the young Goethe's letters. There are two distinct reactions to the imperative question: why? The first seizes on those whose vanity and idolatry — biblical words — have corrupted human nature, a Rousseauistic response overlaid with the vocabulary and tone of Martin Luther's Bible. But if they were not the offenders, then Jerusalem's theologian father was, and, searching the scriptures for a terrible example, Goethe wishes on him the fate of the high priest Eli, whose 'neck brake' when he fell at hearing of the deaths of his sons (1 Samuel 4:18, AV). But then perhaps personal experience, in both Leipzig and Wetzlar, may confirm a further reason for the tragedy. Goethe diagnoses a condition: solitary walks in the moonlight, something which the medicine of the century would have called 'melancolia errabunda', here with the special manifestation of *solitude*. The phrase 'die Einsamkeit hat sein Herz untergraben' recurs in another letter from about the same time, and it recalls the letter in *Werther* of August 18 in Part One, in which the experience of solitude amid God's creation, once the source of well-being and exaltation, in the contemplation of a well-ordered harmony, has become one great open grave, the scene of universal Moloch-like

---

24 'Poor unhappy Jerusalem. The news was terrible, unexpected, an awful postscript this news was to your so pleasant gift of love. Poor unhappy lad. But the devils, the scoundrels whose whole sustenance is the chaff of vanity and who make lust their heart's idol, and preach idolatry, and keep back the goodness of nature and push our forces to extremes and pervert them, are to blame, the devil take them their brother. If his damned parson of a father isn't to blame then God forgive me if I wish he'd break his neck like Eli. The poor lad! When I used to come back from my walk and I met him out there in the moonlight, I said he's in love. Lotte must remember that I found it amusing. God knows solitude has undermined his heart — and I have known this person for seven years, spoken but little with him, when I left I borrowed a book from him, I will keep it and his memory as long as I live'. *DjG*, III, 7.

destruction: 'Mir untergräbt das Herz die verzehrende Kraft, die im All der Natur verborgen liegt'.[25] Does Goethe, in his first, unrehearsed reaction to the news, sense that here was also the stuff of a good novel? The question has been asked, and must be asked again. It may have been the reason for his request from Kestner for more details, some of which actually go verbatim into the text of the novel. Genius is unsentimental and does not draw life and art into neat partitions. Even if Goethe was not planning a novel, let alone writing one, there is already some of the stuff of the novel in the above letter: the biblical style, interspersed with the colloquial, the abrupt transitions, the sentences that do not finish. In the novel, they are conscious devices, symptomatic of one whose heart is indeed consumed and undermined by total solitude. More than that one cannot say.

Another whole series of later statements by Goethe must also be considered. It had been his purpose, he claims, to remain alive in order to leave an account of how it actually was. His creative urge proved to be sufficiently robust to resist the enticements of self-inflicted death and was the 'Talent, das in mir steckt'[26] that kept him going through the vicissitudes of life. It is the reverse side of his awareness of being the favourite of the gods, the happy man: instead, he is the one chosen to survive, like Job's servant ('Herr, alle Deine Schafe und Knechte sind erschlagen worden, und ich bin allein entronnen, Dir Kunde zu bringen'),[27] like the pelican ('Das ist auch so ein Geschöpf, [...] das ich gleich dem Pelikan mit dem Blute meines eigenen Herzens gefüttert habe'),[28] or best-known of all, 'An Werther' (1824):

> Noch einmal wagst du, vielbeweinter Schatten,
> Hervor dich an das Tageslicht,
> Begegnest mir auf neu beblümten Matten
> Und meinen Anblick scheust du nicht.
> Es ist als ob du lebtest in der Frühe,
> Wo uns der Tau auf Einem Feld erquickt,
> Und nach des Tages unwillkommner Mühe

---

25 'The consuming force hidden in the whole of nature is my heart's undoing'. *DjG*, IV, 139.
26 'the talent I have within me'. *HA*, VI, 534.
27 'Lord, all thy flocks and servants are perished, and I only am escaped to tell thee'. Based on Job I, 13ff. *HA*, VI, 533.
28 'That too is such a creature [...] that I like the pelican have fed with my heart's blood'. Ibid.

> Der Scheidesonne letzter Strahl entzückt;
> Zum Bleiben ich, zum Scheiden du erkoren,
> Gingst du voran — und hast nicht viel verloren.[29]

In every crucial respect, Goethe is not identical with Werther. Goethe runs from the situations that would endanger him, out into self-preservation: the anguish of heart produced is sufficient for the work of art. Werther significantly fails to do this. True, he also feels the need to create, to follow nature, not rules, to observe, to record in word and graphic image. He reflects Goethe's own thinking in many ways, but Goethe does not wish his hero to appear creative — that would be a betrayal of art. For art — everything Goethe says at the time and subsequently bears out — is a matter of energy *and* observation, genius *and* limitation, all in one. Werther's longings and urges cannot fulfil this. Hence 'zum Scheiden du erkoren'.

Empfindsamkeit[30]

How are we to read this novel? Goethe's immediate contemporaries were in no doubt. Wilhelm Heinse's response is typical of many:

> Das Herz ist einem so voll davon, und der ganze Kopf ein Gefühl von Thräne [...] Für diejenigen Damen, die das edle volle Herz des unglücklichen Werthers bey Lotten für zu jugendliche unwahrscheinliche Schüchternheit, und seinen Selbstmord mit einigen Philosophen für unmöglich halten, ist das Büchlein nicht geschrieben.[31]

---

29 'Again, you much-mourned shadow, you make bold
   To step out in the brightest light of day;
   You counter me in flowery field or fold,
   My eye meets yours, yours does not turn away.
   You live, it seems, now in the early dawn
   When dew on grass refreshes and restores,
   The parting sun's last rays adorn
   And irksome day is over, with its chores.
   I stay, you leave, so fate has deemed it fit,
   You went ahead, and have not missed a whit'. *HA*, I, 380 ('To Werther').
30 'Sensibility'.
31 'One's heart is so full of it, and one's head one whole feeling of tears. [...] For those ladies who hold poor Werther's noble full heart with Lotte to be too much youthful bashfulness and not true to life, his suicide impossible, as some philosophers do, this book was not written'. *Der junge Goethe im zeitgenössischen Urteil*, ed. by Peter Müller, Deutsche Bibliothek 2 (Berlin: Akademie, 1969), 208, 210. There were similar reactions from Gleim, Lavater, Bürger, Voss, Stolberg and many others.

It is also to the man or woman of feeling that Goethe addresses the preface of his novel, with the appeal to 'Bewunderung', 'Liebe', 'Thränen',[32] even that 'schöpfe Trost aus seinem Leiden'[33] for the weaker brethren. Interestingly enough, Goethe rejects a more overtly premonitory alternative prefatory statement in favour of the appeal to readers' sensitivities. In many ways this is surprising, for Goethe could already rely on the culture in which most of his readers were situated to engage those faculties. This culture was 'Empfindsamkeit'. The strand of sentimentality, the cult of feeling, runs right through the culture of the eighteenth century, never more prominently than when this novel was written. The inward-looking mystical tradition in German religious culture, the insistence of the movement known as Pietism that faith is not merely a question of knowledge, credal statements or articles of faith, but an experience of the heart, that self-analysis is the key to one's state of soul — all of these elements become in the course of the eighteenth century aesthetic, moral and social postulates. Writing should move the *heart*. This was essentially the notion of 'herzrührende Schreibart' ('style that moves the heart') as advocated in the 1740s by the Swiss critics Johann Jacob Bodmer and Johann Jacob Breitinger. Language and aesthetic decorum will make way for 'Empfindung', 'feeling' or rather, 'Empfindung' will create a new set of aesthetic criteria. When seeking to arouse emotion, Christian Fürchtegott Gellert's *Praktische Abhandlung von dem guten Geschmacke in Briefen/Practical Treatise on Good Taste in Letters* of 1751 informs us, 'so lasse man sein Herz mehr reden, als seinen Verstand; und seinen Witz gar nicht. Man wisse von keiner Kunst, von keiner Ordnung in seinem Briefe'.[34] Paramount are the subjugation of the rational powers of discrimination and distinction to the forces of the heart, the identification with the subject, not critical distance from it. In writing, it means effusion, outpouring; in reading, it means a passionate attempt to take the work concerned 'to heart'. The self-centred sense of joy in feeling will find expression in tears — the manifestation of virtue

---

32 'Admiration', 'love', 'tears'.
33 'Draw consolation from his sorrows'. *DjG*, IV, 105.
34 'So let one's heart speak more than one's understanding, and one's wit not at all. One should admit no artifice, no order, in one's letter'. Christian Fürchtegott Gellert, *Sämmtliche Werke*, Sammlung der besten deutschen Prosaschriftsteller, 9 vols (Carlsruhe: Schmieder, 1774), IV, 64.

and a 'fühlendes Herz'.³⁵ This phrase right at the beginning of the novel (like 'Fülle des Herzens', 'Fühlbarkeit' or 'ergießen',³⁶ themselves the secularized language of religious emotion) becomes the touchstone of behaviour, that one's 'heart is in the right place'.

'Empfindsamkeit' creates its own literature, or borrows freely from the poetry of reflective inwardness so favoured by the English. Edward Young's *Night Thoughts* (1741–45), with its lugubrious and grandiose tedium, becomes a cult book, not just for its nocturnal setting and brooding melancholy, but for its sentiments on 'Life, Death and Immortality'. It calls on the reader to withdraw into solitude, into creative introspection, to reflect amid tears and the awareness of one's inner virtue, on the universe and its creator. As the world and its design, set in motion by a benevolent deity, support all life and allow no manifestation of nature to go unexplained, so our lives and relationships do not end with earthly existence. Instead, we may look forward to reunion with our dead friends, who, as Young puts it, are 'Angels sent on Errands full of Love'.³⁷ The poetic cult of love, separation and future union is associated in Germany especially with the name of Friedrich Gottlieb Klopstock. This cult, but also Klopstock's creative use of the language of the heart and the Bible, are the reasons which underlie one of the climactic passages in the novel: Werther's and Lotte's meeting of souls in the invocation of the poet's name.

'Empfindsamkeit' is also a movement of restrained and decorous feeling. There are always warnings against overindulgence or over-identification. Goethe's contemporary Jakob Michael Reinhold Lenz, not perhaps best known for reined-in sentiment, draws attention to the 'leidenschaftlicher Leser', who reads 'auf Kosten seiner Vernunft und Moralität', instead of 'mit fester Seele'.³⁸ It is the danger of making literature into a surrogate for established modes of experience. Solitude,

---

35 'Heart full of feeling'. *DjG*, IV, 106, 119.
36 'Heart's fulness', 'given to feeling', 'outpour'.
37 Edward Young, *Night Thoughts. Night the Third* (London: Dodsley, 1742), 21.
38 'Passionate reader'; 'at the expense of his reason and morality'; 'with resolute soul'. Jakob Michael Reinhold Lenz, *Werke und Schriften*, ed. by Britte Titel and Hellmut Haug, 2 vols (Stuttgart: Goverts, 1966), I, 664. See Georg Jäger, 'Die Wertherwirkung. Ein rezeptionsästhetischer Modellfall', in *Historizität in Sprach- und Literaturwissenschaft*, ed. by Walter Müller-Seidel et al. (Munich: Fink, 1974), 389–409 (402).

1. Goethe: Die Leiden des jungen Werthers 13

which Dr Johnson calls the retreat into 'lonely wisdom',[39] must, like melancholy, involve only a temporary turning away from human society and friendship. Excess may affect the harmony between body and soul by which the medical and devotional literature of the century lays such store. This is the burden of the standard work on the subject, Johann Georg Zimmermann' s *Von der Einsamkeit/On Solitude* (1773): the man who cannot live in harmony with himself cannot live without others. The balance of the emotions, the interaction of body and soul, the avoidance of wrong stimuli, are arguments also adduced in the century's discussion of suicide. In introducing this theme into his novel, Goethe is touching on a subject that preoccupied his age and the one preceding. The European-wide debate sees suicide as the ultimate challenge to a sense of order and reason, an affront to divine and natural law, to design and providence. It opens up a world of chaos and disorder; it undermines social cohesion and moral reference. It can be 'explained' only in terms of mental aberration or confusion: Kestner's account to Goethe does precisely this in referring to those structures and norms that for Jerusalem no longer have validity. Werther quotes the standard arguments in favour. 'Das süsse Gefühl von Freyheit, und daß er diesen Kerker verlassen kann, wann er will',[40] is based on Johannes Robeck's *De morte voluntaria/On Voluntary Death* of 1736; it is essentially the case propounded by Montesquieu's *Lettres Persanes/Persian Letters* of 1721 and in its second edition of 1754, for the preservation of human dignity by putting an end to an intolerable existence.[41] Significantly, Werther's suicide has nothing ultimately to do with either of these philosophical positions: it is committed in a state of madness, beyond the reach of rational argument and for reasons so bizarrely and tragically deluded as to cancel out so much in him that was both good and dignified.

Goethe was familiar with the culture of *Empfindsamkeit* and moved freely within it. His letters from the period — emotional, disjointed,

---

39 Or, at least, the phrase is attributed to Dr Johnson. See *Solitude. Or the Effect of Occasional Retirement* [...], Originally by M. Zimmermann (London: Verner and Hood, 1800), Preface, ix.
40 'The sweet feeling of freedom, and that he may leave this prison when he chooses'. DjG, IV, 111.
41 See Roger Paulin, *Der Fall Wilhelm Jerusalem. Zum Selbstmordproblem zwischen Aufklärung und Empfindsamkeit*, Kleine Schriften zur Aufkärung 7 (Göttingen: Wallstein; Wolfenbüttel: Lessing-Akademie, 1999), 10f.

parenthetic like Werther's — take up the language of the heart or the Bible. He shares the cult of Klopstock and absorbs his language, even writing to the poet himself of 'mit welch wahrem Gefühl meine Seele an Ihnen hängt'.[42] The culture into which he places Werther is thus not alien, but intimately familiar. Goethe, too, was aware that a cult of sentiment is not proof against introspection, anguish and despair. He had sensed it in Jerusalem, and knew it in his worst moments after Wetzlar. He was to make Werther, his creation, experience that the opening up of the self, or the descent into one's own heart, the search for totality through inward identification, when unchecked and narcissistically indulged, become a 'sickness unto death' ('Krankheit zum Tode').[43]

Werther's 'Leiden'[44]

Werther is a novel, not a case history. It is not a mere clinical subject for what in Goethe's own day was known as 'Erfahrungsseelenkunde' ('clinical psychology') and what in ours has become psychoanalysis. Goethe, as he was putting the last touches to the novel, did express himself in these remarkably matter-of-fact terms:

> darin ich einen jungen Menschen darstelle, der mit einer tiefen reinen Empfindung und wahrer Penetration begabt, sich in schwärmende Träume verliert, sich durch Speculation untergräbt, bis er zuletzt durch dazutretende unglückliche Leidenschaften, besonders eine endlose Liebe zerrüttet, sich eine Kugel vor den Kopf schiesst.[45]

We should however not overlook the 'tiefe reine Empfindung und wahre Penetration'. For Goethe's dilemma (ours rather less) was to keep 'Bewunderung und Liebe'[46] in balance with the pathology, the psychopathology, of his hero. For without this pathological dimension,

---

42 'With what true feeling my heart hangs on you'. *DjG*, IV, 17.
43 *DjG*, IV, 137.
44 'Sufferings' or 'sorrows'.
45 'In which I present a young person who, endowed with a deep and pure feeling and true penetration, loses his way in extravagant dreams, is undermined by speculation, until at last, shattered by unhappy passions newly visited, not least a hopeless love, he blows his brains out'. *DjG*, IV, 22.
46 'Admiration and love'. Ibid., 105.

the work, even despite the starkness of the ending, might appear to favour suicide.

In those terms it is easy to overlook Werther's manifest virtues, just as it is not hard to expect of him things that 'normal' behaviour takes for granted. We do wrong to play down his genuine sympathy ('Mitleiden')'[47] with others, his generosity and openness of mind, affronted as it is by peevishness and niggardliness, his love of children, his quick powers of human observation, his artistic talent that is by no means uncreative. He rails, sometimes rightly, against restriction:

> O meine Freunde! warum der Strom des Genies so selten ausbricht, so selten in hohen Fluthen hereinbraust, und eure staunende Seele erschüttert. Lieben Freunde, da wohnen die gelaßnen Kerls auf beyden Seiten des Ufers, denen ihre Gartenhäuschen, Tulpenbeete, und Krautfelder zu Grunde gehen würden…[48]

Above all, we should acknowledge the nobility of his resolve at the end of Part One, to renounce and leave. Were these qualities more in evidence, it could be said that there would be no catastrophe and Part One would end in the style of Rousseau's famous novel of 1760, *La Nouvelle Héloïse*, but with an even greater and more generous sacrifice. But Werther cannot ever 'be himself', cannot fulfil himself in the terms of 'normal' social or psychological conventions: 'ich soll, ich soll nicht zu mir kommen!'[49] His ideas of fulfilment are always changing as successive attainments prove to be illusory. He will not listen to others telling him the way to himself, to effectuation and happiness. Perhaps again he cannot be blamed for aspirations that are incompatible with restriction, rules or utility. To do him justice, the excellent and impeccable advice given to him by others never seems to bear fruit, or circumstances prevent it when it appears to be within his grasp.

Other heroes of Goethe's *Sturm und Drang* period rebel against restriction: Faust, Prometheus, Götz von Berlichingen. But unique to this novel are the 'Leiden', the suffering, the sorrows 'des armen Werthers',

---

47 'Sympathy'. Ibid., 103.
48 'O my friends! Why does the stream of genius so seldom break forth, so seldom burst out in great floods and shakes your astounded soul to the core. Dear friends, on both banks live stick-in-the-muds whose summerhouses, tulip beds and cabbage patches would be ruined'. Ibid., 112.
49 'I shall never, never be myself!'. Ibid., 164.

'unser Freund', 'der arme Junge', 'Ihr könnt [...] seinem Schicksaale eure Thränen nicht versagen'.[50] All of these references are from the opening paragraph of the novel. They are, to some extent, outside of the main text, in that they represent the commentary of — presumably — the editor of the papers that have survived. Is he reliable? We have to take him on trust and accept that it is as he says: that the mass of papers, some of which never reach their addressees, represent in sequent form accurately and sympathetically the state of Werther's body and soul over a period of a year and a half. We have to take his word for instance, that Werther's 'Verdruß'[51] was a contributory cause in his final, rapid disintegration, whereas the hero's own statements reflect other and more radical preoccupations. We might wish to be told, except by implication and deduction, that Lotte and Albert survive and that somehow life goes on after the catastrophe. But the hero's words must be left largely to speak for themselves. Werther's 'sufferings' must be evident in the course of his letters; otherwise the editor's interspersed commentary would assume a weight that the economy of the novel requires it should not. What does Goethe imply by calling the novel 'Die Leiden' (pl.)? For the editor also invites the vulnerable reader to draw comfort 'aus seinem Leiden' (sing.). Does he wish to distinguish between the hero's 'anguish', his 'sorrow' and his sufferings? For the echoes of the Passion, with its sacrificial connotations, are present both in the title and the text itself. They represent the wild regions of a mind that does not scruple to exploit the ultimate Christian association, down to the hero stylizing himself into an offering for others. It is part of the whole theological pathology that assails the reader towards the end of the novel, made compelling because of its perverse logic and deliberateness. 'Leiden', singular and plural, both have religious echoes. The singular invites us to read the novel, not as something aberrant and monstrous, but more as a descent into affliction and despair. '*Das* Leiden' will engage the reader with the process of self-loss and sickness unto death. The plural — reflected in the title — highlights perhaps the acutely deluded nature of Werther's madness — and to overlook this is to miss the point of the novel at a very basic level.

---

50 'Sufferings of poor Werther'; 'our friend'; 'the poor lad'; 'you cannot keep back your tears at his fate'. *DjG*, IV, 105, 168f.
51 'Vexation'. Ibid., 150.

'Die heilige belebende Kraft, mit der ich Welt um mich schuf'[52]

By turning to the inner self, the 'heart', as the eighteenth century calls it, to create a world, and by ratifying every experience only by reference to the inner life, Werther has no objective reality beyond himself. The mystics — and Werther uses their language of flowing and fullness and penetration — also look inwards because it is only there that the union with the higher divine force takes place. Werther uses the vocabulary of this experience — notably in the letter of May 10 — without achieving little more than exaltation of spirit. The images pile up: 'mit ganzem Herzen', 'für solche Seelen geschaffen [...] wie die meine', 'näher an meinem Herzen'.[53] This is not to deny the dynamic power of that letter and its impulsion towards a state beyond words. Its free borrowings and eclecticism — from Spinoza, the Bible, neo-platonism — need not trouble us, for no image is ultimately adequate to articulate the inexpressible. Werther does not meet the divine in nature; he meets a series of disparate and impalpable impressions in his 'heart'. He uses the Platonic image of the mirror — also common in Christian mysticism — but it expresses at most the hypothetical, unattainable, the longed-for, the conditional mode of a union between man and nature that might be. The experience lasts as long as the heart or soul can sustain it, and then it fades away. For all his 'Fülle des Herzens',[54] he is always in a state of longing. The gesture of arms opened accompanies so many of his actions, but these are arms extended to seize what eludes his embrace. And so nature appears to reject him. But it is no longer nature 'out there'. It is merely his momentary sensations, overlaid and stylized by so many associations of a literary, sentimental and quasi-philosophical kind.

Thus a nature that is merely the subject of the fugitive disarray of successive fluctuations of 'Herz' will lose all structure and congruity. Its

---

52 'The sacred enlivening force with which I created a world around me'. Ibid., 161.
53 'With whole heart'; 'made for souls such as mine'; 'nearer to my heart'. Ibid., 106f.
54 'The heart's fulness/the heart brimming over'. This expression derives ultimately from Pietist religious writing. Its classic expression is Friedrich Leopold von Stolberg's dithyrambic essay, *Ueber die Fülle des Herzens* (1777). See August Langen, *Der Wortschatz des deutschen Pietismus* (Tübingen: Niemeyer, 1968), 22f.

changes will have no sense. Commenting on this, Goethe reminds his readers in *Dichtung und Wahrheit*:

> Der Wechsel von Tag und Nacht, der Jahreszeiten, der Blüten und Früchte und was uns sonst von Epoche zu Epoche entgegentritt; damit wir es genießen können und sollen, diese sind die eigentlichen Triebfedern des irdischen Lebens. Je offener wir für diese Genüsse sind, desto glücklicher fühlen wir uns; wälzt sich aber die Verschiedenheit dieser Erscheinungen vor uns auf und nieder, ohne daß wir daran teilnehmen, sind wir gegen so holde Anerbietungen unempfänglich: dann tritt das größte Übel, die schwerste Krankheit ein, man betrachtet das Leben als eine ekelhafte Last.[55]

This is encapsulated in the novel in that alarming contrast between May 10 and August 18 in Part One, from an experience of plenitude and perceived oneness to a sense of loss and imperilment and finally universal destruction: 'Mir untergräbt das Herz die verzehrende Kraft, die im All der Natur verborgen liegt':[56] an image articulated amid the same plenitude of landscape and vista that produced the May 10 and 'Klopstock!' It removes any sense of hope or enjoyment of nature. With it, Werther is turning his face away from order, design and self-preservation, all that his education and reading have taught him. Rejected by nature, he embraces the hope of taking Lotte in his arms, and, denied this, he seizes on the ultimate insane projection, 'vor dem Angesichte des Unendlichen in ewigen Umarmungen'.[57]

'Mein Herz hab ich allein'

For Werther the culture of the heart has instead become its tyranny. He speaks self-indulgently of 'mein Herzgen', 'Mein Herz hab ich allein', 'dies Herz mein einziger Stolz'.[58] Whatever else others may

---

55 'Day and night ever changing, with the seasons, the flowers and fruits and what we encounter from epoch to epoch; so that we may enjoy it — as we should — these are the sustainers of earthly life. The more open we are to such enjoyments, the happier we feel; but if we see these things as a mere succession of events and take no part in them, then the very worst happens, the gravest malady; one looks on life as an intolerable burden.' *HA*, IX, 578.
56 'My heart sinks at the consuming power hidden in nature's all'. Ibid., 139.
57 'Before the face of the Infinite in embraces without end'. *DjG*, IV, 182.
58 'My little heart'; 'my heart I have alone'; 'this heart my sole pride'. *DjG*, IV, 108, 155.

have — preferments, settled existence, limited horizons — Werther has his heart. It is part of that 'herrlich Ding', 'Freude an sich selbst'.[59] It conditions the ultimate self-indulgence that can declare of Lotte, 'wie ich mich selbst anbete, seitdem sie mich liebt',[60] an enormity of egoism were its consequences not also deeply tragic. Yet Werther's heart is capable of the noblest of sensations, and his sensitivities often become persuasively ours, the readers'. But too often his heart and its effects are the 'krankes Kind'.[61] Like those many images of sickness and malady, real or imagined, they are designed ultimately to draw attention to himself. They become part of the willing surrender of the self to dissolution and chaos. For instance: Werther loves children because he can indulge them, a blessed relief in an insistently pedagogical century. But he also projects that indulgence on to himself. As children grasp after everything ('Greifen die Kinder nicht nach allem..?'), so he may gratify his every wish ('Und thu ihm seinen Willen').[62] The theme of children, like so many themes and images of the novel, provides no fulfilment: childhood becomes self-love, limitlessness turns into constriction. All flights end where they begin; all is subject to change and decay. Thus in Part Two we see the pathology of childhood — the mad clerk who so unsettles Werther ('eine Erscheinung, die mich aus aller Fassung bringt. Heut! o Schicksaal! o Menschheit!')[63] — that is a collapsed identity resulting from an impossible infatuation (for Lotte). It raises for Werther the overhanging threat of madness, and its terrible corollary, the thought of homicide. It leads him to his ultimate delusion, that of sacrifice. In that, too, he assumes the role of the child, the son who will be cherished in the self-constituted after-life, where God the Father and Lotte's mother will comfort him — 'biß du kommst'.[64]

Thus when he is confronted at several turnings in the story with decisions or moral imperatives to which he cannot or will not accede, he follows his own logic. Hence there can be no real dialogue, one of the most noticeable features of this epistolary novel. The letters have a monologic character: we know of Wilhelm, to whom the letters (except

---

59 'That wonderful thing joy in oneself'. Ibid., 150.
60 'How I worship myself now that she loves me'. Ibid., 128.
61 'Sick child'. Ibid., 108.
62 'Do children not reach after everything?'; 'and do what it wants'. Ibid., 161.
63 'A sight that shakes me to the core. Today! O fate! O mankind!' Ibid., 164.
64 'Till you come'. Ibid., 182.

at the very end) are addressed, mainly because Werther rejects his good advice. For Wilhelm, to some extent like Albert, is a point of reference, a propositional bearing, to be countered or disregarded at will.

And so for Werther his own heart is the sole means of self-fulfilment: 'Ich kehre in mich selbst zurük, und finde eine Welt'.[65] The admission, 'Ich könte das beste glücklichste Leben führen, wenn ich nicht ein Thor wäre',[66] states that his relationship with Lotte is absurd, but... There is no hope, but then... He hates qualifications and restrictions, the 'Zwar', the 'modificiren'.[67] Reason and feeling cannot interact as long as it is the heart that determines: 'gewiß ist's, daß unser Herz allein sein Glük macht'.[68] Thus Werther has rejected the notion of clear alternatives: 'In der Welt ist's sehr selten mit dem Entweder Oder gethan'.[69] He speaks these words to Albert. Albert of course thinks in terms of moral choices, for his is a world circumscribed by order and duty, reflecting the claims of a wider body politic, representing a counter-position to Werther's. Albert thus demonstrates that an ordered society is one in which moral decisions depend on categorizing human behaviour, a procedure unacceptable to Werther.

It is against this background that we come to Werther's tragic love for Lotte. He persists in approaching the unattainable ideal. There is nothing new in this, for 'Empfindsamkeit', too, has its Petrarchan streak, the pursuit of the unachievable. She cannot be his; her hand is promised to another; her true element is family, affection, self-sacrifice, self-abnegation. He recognizes these as her true qualities, and he realizes that his own role can at most be that of a spectator. Yet he acts as if what he does not wish to see were not there; his commitment is to an inward response nurtured by the surrogate experience of literature and the cult of feeling. Lotte, however, meets him on much narrower ground. She may join him in 'Klopstock!', in sentimental hopes of reunion after death ('Wiedersehen')[70] or Ossian; she can indulge the sentiment and 'Schwärmerei' that Albert, his feet too solidly on the ground, cannot fulfil. She does not even wish all this away; she would not have it

---

65 'I turn in on myself and find there a world'. *DjG*, IV, 133.
66 'I could lead the happiest of lives were I not a fool'. Ibid., 133.
67 'Although', 'qualify' (in German the word 'zwar' must be followed by a qualifying word). Ibid., 134.
68 'One thing is certain: our heart alone brings happiness.' Ibid., 133.
69 'In the world things are hardly ever either or'. Ibid., 132.
70 'Reunion'.

otherwise. The ending of Part One, a tour de force of that culture, puts her at the centre of that most 'empfindsam' of scenes. Hence, for most of the novel, Lotte tolerates Werther. It is the very passivity of their relationship that leads to tragedy: he will not leave; she will not force him to do so. For there is — until the novel's last pages — none of the aggressive sexual jealousy one might expect, no hint of a *ménage à trois*, no attempt to possess the object of one's desire by force. Werther, to do him full credit, while seeking fulfilment with the only being who is denied him, actually does succeed at the end of Part One in renouncing her. But the tyranny of his heart demands that he return, to continue his previous behaviour after their marriage, to live in a state of infantile dependence on her every favour, imagined look or feeling ('sie fühlt, was ich dulde').[71] All three — Lotte, Albert and Werther — seek to avoid hurt, not to precipitate the crisis. When it does come, its anguish is all the greater for that 'zum erstenmal' and 'zum leztenmale',[72] with Lotte's first real admission of her feelings for Werther, their first and last embrace, and the lunacy of Werther's reaction to those words.

It is a measure of the artistry of this novel that what could be potentially absurd seizes the reader in its tragic grip. Themes take on an intensity, attitudes become obsessions, being oneself means losing oneself — all with a narrative inexorability leading towards the final implosion and collapse. It affects the characters differently. Lotte wakes up from an unreal world: it is literature (the reading of Ossian) that is the agent of her awakening. Werther indulges unreality and believes that renunciation can succeed a second time — but this time through the sacrifice of himself. As at the end of Part One, he wishes no hurt on another person: 'mache den Engel glüklich'[73] are his last words to Albert. For others, life in the here and now may continue. For him, there can be no sexual union with the beloved, and he sacrifices himself to expiate his carnal lusts. Only in the afterlife will things be ordained differently: the child will become 'Mann'[74] and enter into the sexual territory that on earth is forbidden. This time, all the wishes of his sick heart will be fulfilled. These fantasies end in the maimed body and bloody death of

---

71   'She feels what I am going through'. *DjG*, IV, 163.
72   'For the first time'; 'for the last time'. Ibid., 181.
73   'Make the angel happy'. Ibid., 184.
74   This term means both 'man' and 'husband'. Ibid., 162.

the hero and in the disintegration of the extended family of which he felt so much a part. Goethe does not spare his readers, indeed he dare not.

Society and 'Verdruß'[75]

Did society force Werther into the inward life by denying him an outlet for his talents and apportioning him only the terrain of melancholy and solitude? The novel does represent a structured society where, on the face of it, Werther has no clearly ordained place. It is based on the hierarchy of absolutist ruler, court, administration, established religion and university, the family unit representing a microcosm of the larger order. Werther has been trained at university, presumably for useful employment, not merely for private study or literature. He chooses to reject the *grand monde* of society in which his talents and character might otherwise guarantee him a career. Instead, he constitutes an anti-society, a society within society. Lotte (when time permits) may join him there. There, all is sensitivity, the barriers of society or class fall down, religion may be de-institutionalized, the imagination and nature hold sway. To do him credit, he does try accommodation with the real world, but falls foul of its rules and conventions. These are patently absurd, and we admire his stand against mere class and privilege. We know all the same that Werther is familiar with the charade into whose pretence he no longer wishes to enter. The 'Verdruß' — Werther's being asked to leave the soirée — does reflect society's inflexibility and arrogance, but it need not spell the end of his career. But does it not suit him all the same? It is employment in that very society, with its pretensions, that stands between him and the return to what he has so nobly renounced. The 'Verdruß' and its aftermath occur neatly between the letters expressing the 'Hölle'[76] of Albert's and Lotte's forthcoming union, and the 'vergebliche Wünsche'[77] of a lost possession. He will come back, he must come back: 'Und ich lache über mein eigen Herz — und thu ihm seinen Willen'.[78]

---

75 'Vexation' or 'mishap'.
76 'Hell'. Ibid., 150.
77 'Forlorn wishes'. Ibid., 156.
78 'And I laugh at my own heart — and do its bidding'. Ibid.

Fig. 2 View of the Bay of Naples. Friedrich Leopold zu Stolberg, *Reise in Deutschland der Schweiz, Italien und Sicilien in den Jahren 1791 bis 1792*, in *Gesammelte Werke der Brüder Christian und Friedrich Leopold Grafen zu Stolberg*, 20 vols (Hamburg: Perthes und Besser, 1820–25), VII, plate facing p. 340.

2. Goethe and Stolberg in Italy
The Consequences for Romantic Art[1]

The eighteenth century saw travel literature come into its own as a major literary genre. Not only did it give accounts of actual travels: it also contained useful information for the traveller, real or intended, on what to see, which places to visit, which paintings to look at (which hazards to avoid). With the emergence of the Grand Tour in Italy in the eighteenth century, travel accounts provided the necessary vade-mecum. When Johann Wolfgang Goethe and Friedrich Leopold von Stolberg went to Italy, within five years of each other in the latter part of that century, they used travelling companions and artists as guides, but also had recourse to — by then — standard travelogues, some of which they also cite by name: Johann Heinrich Bartels and Patrick Brydone (Stolberg) and Johann Hermann von Riedesel and Johann Jacob Volkmann (Goethe).

But I run ahead of my subject. We should take a moment to refresh our memories of the essential facts of Goethe's *Italienische Reise/Italian Journey*. Travelling through Italy had been his lifelong desire, and this was finally fulfilled in September 1786, when he left Carlsbad and made his way over the Brenner, through Venice, Bologna, Perugia and Rome. Afterwards, he stopped in Naples and Sicily, and then returned to Rome. He kept records throughout his travels, including notes and letters home, and in 1789, he published his first work relating to Italy, *Das Römische Carneval/The Roman Carnival*. This was to be the first of several.[2]

---

1   An earlier version of this paper was given at the University of Groningen in 1992. On the subject of Goethe and Romantic art, see the older but still essential work by Richard Benz, *Goethe und die romantische Kunst* (Munich: Piper, 1940) and the more recent *'Ein Dichter hatte uns alle geweckt'. Goethe und die literarische Romantik*, ed. by Christoph Perels (Frankfurt am Main: Freies Deutsches Hochstift, 1999).

2   These are found in Erich Schmidt, ed., *Tagebücher und Briefe Goethes aus Italien an Frau von Stein und Herder*, Schriften der Goethe-Gesellschaft 2 (Weimar:

Goethe wished to return to Italy a second time to create an exhaustive description of the country, its people and their customs. However, despite his evidently thorough preparations, the Revolutionary Wars prevented him from doing so.[3]

While working on his autobiography, *Dichtung und Wahrheit /Poetry and Truth*, begun in 1813–14, and thus in self-reflective mood, Goethe revisited his notes on his Italian journey of 1786–87. They were to appear in published form as *Italienische Reise*, in three parts; the first two volumes detailed his time up to and including Sicily and appeared in 1816–17, while the last volume (*Zweiter Römischer Aufenthalt/Second Sojourn in Rome*) came out in 1829. Goethe showed little sentimentality towards his sources, cutting up letters he had received during his travels and sticking them on to the manuscript of his autobiography. Posterity may be aghast, but why do unnecessary copying? The *Italienische Reise*, however brought about, is worth the result.[4]

The facts concerning Goethe's *Italienische Reise* and its emergence as a cult book — W. H. Auden is one of its more recent admirers and translators[5] — need not be further rehearsed here. My purpose is to record reactions from some of Goethe's younger contemporaries, the Romantics — themselves no mean travellers — and to explain their mainly aggrieved tone at reading his *Italian Journey* and what followed it. It will be necessary to quote from Goethe's original, but to contrast it with the account of Italy given by Friedrich Leopold Count Stolberg, whose four volumes of *Reise durch Deutschland, die Schweiz, Italien und Sicilien in den Jahren 1791–92/Travels through Germany, Switzerland, Italy and Sicily in the Years 1791–92* came out in 1794. (Goethe later quotes

---

   Goethe-Gesellschaft, 1886) and *Goethes Werke, herausgegeben im Auftrage der Großherzogin Sophie von Sachsen-Weimar*, 143 vols (Weimar: Böhlau, 1887–1919), Abt. iii, i and Abt. IV, 8.
3 *Goethes Werke*, XXXIV, ii.
4 See Melitta Gerhard, 'Die Redaktion der "Italienischen Reise" im Lichte von Goethes autobiographischem Gesamtwerk', *Jahrbuch des Freien Deutschen Hochstifts* (1930), 131–50; Albert Meier (ed.), *Ein unsäglich schönes Land. Goethes 'Italienische Reise' und der Mythos Siziliens/Un paese indicibilmente bello. Il 'Viaggio in Italia' di Goethe e il mito della Sicilia'* (Palermo: Sellerio, 1987); Gerhard Schulz, 'Goethes Itaienische Reise', in: *Goethe in Italy, 1786–1986. A Bi-Centennial Symposium November 14–15, 1986, University of California, Santa Barbara: Proceedings Volume*, ed. by Gerhart Hoffmeister, Amsterdamer Publikationen zur Sprache und Literatur, 76 (Amsterdam: Rodopi, 1988), 5–19.
5 Johann Wolfgang Goethe, *Italian Journey, 1786–1788*, trans. by W. H. Auden and Elizabeth Mayer (London: Collins, 1962).

2. Goethe and Stolberg in Italy: The Consequences for Romantic Art 27

from them.) Through quotation and comparison, we may gain some insight into why the Romantics reacted as they did. It will emerge that Stolberg's account in many ways prefigures much of what the Romantics were later to espouse. Our comparison makes sense in that Goethe and Stolberg were near contemporaries; more than that: they were acquaintances, having gone together to Switzerland in 1775, and were within a few years of travelling to Italy on their separate — and very different — journeys. The much later publication date of Goethe's *Italian Journey* is crucial to Romantic reactions. It was not the Goethe to whom they had once looked up and revered. When Stolberg reissued his account of Italy in 1821–23, many of his attitudes to art and culture of 1791–92 would be accepted and welcomed by an even younger generation of German painters, mainly based in Rome and known as the Nazarenes.

It is crucial, as said, to note the late year of publication of Goethe's *Italian Journey* (nearly thirty years after the event) and the similarly late reactions of the two Romantics cited, Friedrich Schlegel and Ludwig Tieck. For both of them, Goethe's later attitudes to art, as encapsulated in his *Italian Journey* are hurtful to their mature sensitivities but are representative of a Goethe whom they had clearly misunderstood. They were however the ones who had changed, not Goethe. True, the brothers August Wilhelm and Friedrich Schlegel had adulated Goethe and had made him the centre of a cult in the 1790s, and he in his turn had been gracious to them. Their periodical *Athenaeum* (1798–1800) had placed Goethe on a pedestal, elevating him to the very incarnation of modern progressive poetry, while Goethe in his turn liked the energy and verve of these young men, who also included Tieck. But this mutual relationship was one based on selection and a willingness to overlook major differences. Goethe did not care for the increasingly Christian tendencies of their art appreciation and their preference for religious art. Goethe revered Raphael, as they did, but saw him through classical Greek eyes and not only as the sublime painter of the Sistine Madonna.[6] The Romantics chose not to look too closely at the passages in Goethe's periodical *Propyläen* (1798–1800), many of which stood at variance with

---

6   Cf. Goethe, *Sämtliche Werke, Artemis-Gedenkausgabe*, ed. by Ernst Beutler, 18 vols (Munich: dtv, 1977), XIII, 846 (all subsequent references to Goethe's works are from this edition, cited as *SW*).

what they themselves professed on art in *Athenaeum* (notably in August Wilhelm Schlegel's long article *Die Gemählde/The Paintings* of 1799).[7] Goethe, in presenting Schlegel with a complimentary copy of *Propyläen*,[8] may not have drawn his special attention to Heinrich Meyer's article there on the 'subjects of art'.[9] For Meyer, Goethe's acolyte and guide in matters of art, had effectively excluded many sacred icons of Christian art from the artist's repertoire (no crucifixions, no martyrdoms). But attitudes had not yet hardened, as they would later, and the Romantics believed that a co-existence was possible. They could not yet read Goethe's ungracious words of 1805 about 'das klosterbrudrisierende, sternbaldisierende Unwesen', which were directed against the young Tieck and his now dead friend Wilhelm Heinrich Wackenroder and what Goethe perceived as the fakery of their veneration of Christian art.[10] But then again Goethe could equally not yet have read August Wilhelm Schlegel's epistle from Rome in the same year that elevated a new school of German art there, one which would continue to alienate Goethe.[11] Furthermore, the Romantics were increasingly turning to Italian masters who were never Goethe's favourites: Antonio da Correggio was a good example.

Yet in technical terms, the differences between Goethe and the Romantics were more apparent than real. In matters of subject, however, Goethe preferred the bright light of Classicism, not the penumbra — as he saw it — of religious rite and the cult of death. Both schools paid homage to the classical principles enunciated by Johann Joachim Winckelmann, but Goethe — again in 1805 — had forced the issue by publishing a Life of the great art historian, little more than a hagiography, and had

---

7   *Athenaeum. Eine Zeitschrift von August Wilhelm und Friedrich Schlegel*, 3 vols (Berlin: Vieweg, 1798; Unger 1799–1800), II, i, 39–151.

8   See Roger Paulin, 'Der kosmopolitische Büchersammler. Zu August Wilhelm Schlegels *Verzeichniß meiner Bücher im December 1811*', in *Kooperative Informationsstrukturen als Chance und Herausforderung*, ed. by Achim Bonte and Juliane Rehnolt, Thomas Bürger zum 65. Geburtstag (Berlin, Boston: De Gruyter, 2018), 317–25, ref. 322.

9   'Über die Gegenstände der bildenden Kunst' (co-authored with Goethe), in *Propyläen. Eine periodische Schrift von Goethe*, 3 vols (Tübingen: Cotta, 1798–1800), I, i, 20–54.

10 'Trumpery of Sternbald and the art-loving friar'. Benz, *Goethe und die romantische Kunst*, 119f.

11 August Wilhelm Schlegel, 'Schreiben an Goethe über einige Arbeiten in Rom lebender Künstler. Im Sommer 1805', *Sämmtliche Werke*, 12 vols (Leipzig: Weidmann, 1846–47), IX, 231–66.

stressed the pagan side of Winckelmann's art appreciation.¹² Further polarities ensued when Friedrich Schlegel converted to Catholicism in 1808, while Tieck and August Wilhelm Schlegel had at various times stood in the odour of Catholicizing proselytism.

While it is one-sided to claim that Goethe wrote his *Italienische Reise* against the grain of Romantic art appreciation — and similar claims have been made for his novel *Die Wahlverwandtschaften* — it is certainly true that his account, playing down as it does religious observances and religious art and identifying more with the 'klassischer Boden', the subsoil of classical culture, might offend some Romantic sensitivities. Tieck and August Wilhelm Schlegel had already been to Italy and could draw their own conclusions (Friedrich would go in 1819). But the publication in 1817 under Goethe's sponsorship of the article *Neudeutsche religios-patriotische Kunst* was bound to ruffle some feelings.¹³ For its main target was the school of young religious painters in Rome, the Nazarenes, who also included Friedrich Schlegel's stepsons, Johannes and Philipp Veit. Schlegel in his turn was no longer the co-editor of *Athenaeum*, once so well-disposed to Goethe, but was about to embark on the ultramontane and conservative periodical *Concordia*. His reaction has to be seen against this background:

> Goethe hat selbst bey seinen entschiedensten Anbetern mit seinem Angriff gegen die neue Kunst gar kein Glück gemacht. Endlich habe ich denn nun diese sämtlichen Kunst- und Druckhefte auch gelesen und kann nicht genug erstaunen über den über, oder beßer zu sagen unter aller Erwartung miserablen Mischmasch und Quark. In der That laßen sich doch die Deutschen alles bieten, wenn sie einmal einen Narren an einem gefressen haben. Dagegen lese ich seine erste italiänische Reise von 86 mit vielem Vergnügen. Das ist doch frisch und unbefangen beschrieben und sehr viel Schönes darin, obgleich auch schon viel Feindliches und Schlechtgesinntes daneben. Besonders sieht man aber aus mehrern äußerst naiven Bekenntnissen, wie er eigentlich damals (wie auch noch jetzt) gar nichts von der Kunst verstanden. Von den unbedeutendsten oder gemeinsten Sachen macht er einen großen Lärm und das Größte läßt er unbemerkt vorübergehn.¹⁴

---

12 'Winckelmann und sein Jahrhundert', SW, XIII, 407–50.
13 *Ueber Kunst und Alterthum*, 6 vols (Stuttgart: Cotta, 1816–27), 2. Heft (1817), 5–62, 135–62.
14 'Even Goethe's most devoted acolytes were unhappy with his attack on the new art style. At last I too have found time to read the whole lot of these art brochures and prints, and what an amazing and incredible farrago they are. The Germans will

Schlegel is here conflating the *Italian Journey*, parts of which he had clearly enjoyed, with Goethe's (and Meyer's) rejection of the up-and-coming school of painters in Rome to which he felt ideologically and personally close. Where the *Italian Journey* had veiled much under its engaging style, it was now galling to read in all clarity that the Nazarene school, based on the so-called Italian primitives, stood for credulity and dogma in its manifestations of art. It had not always been so: Goethe shared some of the Romantic enthusiasm for the Middle Ages, indeed it was he who had helped to touch off the cult of things medieval away back in the 1770s. He had admired the Boisserée collection of medieval art (now in Munich) and had cultivated its sponsors. But, Schlegel avers, he had not acknowledged the Romantics' part in opening up the appreciation — veneration — of this older art. Hence the tone of pique and affront.

Ludwig Tieck's letter of 1816 is equally querulous:

> Goethes Buch über Italien hat mich angezogen und mir äußerst wohlgetan. Nicht, daß ich seiner Meinung immer wäre, daß ich dieselben Dinge zum Teil nicht ganz anders gesehen hätte; sondern diese Erscheinung hat mich nun endlich nach vielen Jahren von dem Zauber erlöst (ich kann es nicht anders nennen), in welchem ich mich zu Goethe verhielt: [...] Ist es Ihnen nicht auch aufgefallen, wie dieses herrliche Gemüt eigentlich aus Verstimmung, Überdruß sich einseitig in das Altertum wirft und recht vorsätzlich nicht rechts und nicht links sieht? Und nun: ergreift er denn nicht auch so oft den Schein des Wirklichen statt des Wirklichen? [...] Er vergißt um so mehr, daß unsere reine Sehnsucht nach dem Untergegangenen, wo keine Gegenwart uns mehr stören kann, diese Reliquien und Fragmente verklärt und in jene reine Region der Kunst hinüberzieht. Diese ist aber auch niemals so auf Erden gewesen, daß wir unsere Sitte, Vaterland und Religion deshalb geringschätzen dürften [...] Ich hatte auch die Antike gesehen, Sankt Peter, und konnte den Straßburger Münster nur um so mehr bewundern. Nach dem auswendig gelernten Raffael verstand ich erst die Lieblichkeit

---

really swallow everything once they have taken a shine to someone. On the other hand I really am enjoying reading his first Italian journey of 86. Its style is fresh and direct and it is full of lovely things but of course a lot that are hostile and wrong-headed as well. But above all a number of extremely naive admissions make clear just how little he understood about art then and of course still does now. The most trivial and base things he makes a great fuss about and the greatest things he passes over'. Friedrich Schlegel, *Kritische Ausgabe*, ed. by Ernst Behler et al. (Paderborn: Schöningh, 1958-), XXX, 211.

und Würde altdeutscher Kunst — und dies wäre Oberflächlichkeit, Einseitigkeit etc. in mir gewesen? Ich liebe die Italiener und ihr leichtes Wesen, bin aber in Italien erst recht zum Deutschen geworden.

Und nun! Ist Goethe als Greis nicht gewissermaßen von neuem irre geworden? Und etwa durch neue Entdeckungen? Durch dasselbe, was auch in seiner Jugend da war, was er zum Teil kannte, durch Gedanken, die er zuerst ausgesprochen. Ohne Vaterland kein Dichter! Sich von diesem losreißen wollen, heißt die Musen verleugnen.[15]

The testiness of this letter is all the greater for Tieck's once having been one of Goethe's most sedulous admirers. He is suggesting that Goethe's insistence on the timeless and classical in art had alienated him from national values, that Goethe in Italy had in effect 'gone native'. He, Tieck, by contrast, had discovered his own true national identity there. But the fact is that Tieck, had by 1816 also moved on. He had of course not neglected his early Romantic beginnings: the collection of stories and plays called *Phantasus* (1812–16) was witness to that.[16] Nor had he been disloyal to the memory of his dead friends Wackenroder and Novalis. But he was devoting more and more time to Shakespeare, for whom Goethe by now had but qualified enthusiasm, and he was rediscovering Heinrich von Kleist and Jakob Michael Reinhold Lenz, in his eyes

---

15   'I was much taken with Goethe's book on Italy and I read it with great pleasure. Of course I did not always share his views, and our ideas on some things diverged utterly. But the publication of this book has finally broken the spell (I have no other word for it) in which Goethe kept me bound. [...] Have you not noticed as well how this man with his wonderful mind has gone charging into antiquity at the expense of everything else? And pique and peevishness make him deliberately overlook what is there for all to see? And now: does he not grasp at the appearance of things instead of the things themselves? [...] He forgets all the more that when we express a pure longing for past things without letting the present interfere, it transfigures these relics and fragments and draws them over into the pure sphere of art. But nowhere has this meant that we should find no value in our own custom, country or religion [...] I too had seen Roman ruins, St Peter's, but that led me to admire the Strasbourg Minster all the more. Only when I knew Raphael backwards did I begin to understand Old German art and its grace and dignity. And was I being merely being one-sided or superficial? I love the Italians and their easy ways, but it was in Italy that I first really became a German.
And now! Has Goethe taken leave of his senses again in old age? Were new things and discoveries responsible? It was the same things that were there in his youth. He knew them in part, and he was the first to articulate these thoughts. There can be no poet without his native land! Tear yourself loose from this and you deny the Muses'. Tieck to Solger, December 16, 1816. *Goethe in vertraulichen Briefen seiner Zeitgenossen*, ed. by Wilhelm Bode, 3 vols (Weimar: Aufbau, 1979), II, 667f.

16   See Chapter 8 in this volume.

wrongly neglected authors, in Goethe's, however, objects of abhorrence. There were clearly misunderstandings on both sides, a talking past each other that would culminate in Goethe's famous disqualification of Romanticism in 1829 as 'das Kranke', the 'unhealthy'.[17]

How justified were these reactions? Even allowing for the one-sidedness of Schlegel's and Tieck's contrariety, it is evident that Goethe's *Italienische Reise* brought out a body of resentment on the part of his erstwhile admirers. Was there a view of Italy which was more suited to their sensitivities? There is no evidence that they preferred Stolberg's *Reise durch Deutschland, die Schweiz, Italien und Sicilien in den Jahren 1791– 92* (published 1794),[18] for the simple reason that he was not Goethe. And yet a comparison of selected passages from Stolberg's *Reise* of 1794 and Goethe's later redaction of his notes from 1786–87, the *Italienische Reise*, show that in many ways Stolberg was closer to their way of thinking. It will at any rate enable us to think beyond the aggressive tones of Schlegel and Tieck and look at essentials.

In many ways the very titles suffice by way of comparison, for Stolberg's account is not restricted to Italy — after 300 pages he has only got as far as Geneva — although clearly the sections on Germany and Switzerland are a lead-up to the ultimate southern experience. Goethe, as he makes clear, was following an urge away from the German lands to the long-awaited fulfilment of imperative wishes and could not wait to achieve that aim. True, as already said, Goethe had planned a less rushed visit with the intention of giving a more comprehensive account of the country, its antiquities and *moeurs*, but nothing had come of this. It is not entirely surprising that the Romantics took little immediate notice of Stolberg's *Reise*: it is almost wearyingly comprehensive. True, he took with him in his baggage a set of ideological presuppositions altogether different from Goethe's, some, but not all, of which might appeal to the younger generation. But he was also still in many ways rooted in the 1770s, still unashamedly 'empfindsam', given to the cult of feeling that had once produced *Werther*. That novel still had resonances

---

17 As recorded by Eckermann on April 2, 1829. Johann Peter Eckermann, *Gespräche mit Goethe in den letzten Jahren seines Lebens*, ed. by Ludwig Geiger (Leipzig: Hesse, n.d. [1902]), 265.

18 4 vols (Königsberg, Leipzig: Nicolovius, 1794). All references to this work and to others by Stolberg are found in *Gesammelte Werke der Brüder Christian und Friedrich Leopold Grafen zu Stolberg*, 20 vols (Hamburg: Perthes u. Besser, 1820–25) (referred to subsequently as *GW* with volume number).

with the young Romantics, and his adulation of Edward Young (of the *Night Thoughts*)[19] would find an echo in Novalis's reading of that text. But no-one still shared the cult of Friedrich Gottlieb Klopstock, with whom Stolberg was exchanging reverential letters and whose relations with Goethe had notably ended in a fracas. But there was more. Whereas Goethe's Greekness was pagan, sensuous, Stolberg — also a notable translator from the Greek — sought to reconcile Plato and Christ. Stolberg's remarks on Raphael lead almost seamlessly into the Romantic cult of 'der göttliche Raphael'. What is more: Stolberg was to attack Friedrich Schiller's poem, 'Die Götter Griechenlands/The Gods of Greece', with its threnody for the old Greek pantheon; Schiller was for him seeking 'after strange gods'. Worse (depending on one's viewpoint) was to come. Stolberg's conversion to Catholicism in 1800 was to cause general éclat. It helped to define ideological positions, for a step taken by a member of the high nobility might attract those of lower social status. While remaining on good terms with Goethe, Stolberg became a Catholic apologist and saw history and art through that tinted lens. He became a kind of older, aristocratic mentor to Romantic converts like Friedrich Schlegel. This was, however, some time in the future.

For all that, Goethe and Stolberg as sojourners in Italy are looking for essentially the same things and follow the same antiquarian authorities, even if Stolberg may try our patience with endless quotations from classical authors (or from Klopstock). They look at the identical landscape, the antiquities, the art, yet with different consequences. We notice a difference in tone: Stolberg is serious to a fault, while Goethe has his lighter moments. Each has his own view of 'klassischer Boden', Goethe conveying a real sense of how people and customs form a unity with antiquity and art, not shying away from seemingly prosaic details of a botanical or geological nature (which doubtless so annoyed Friedrich Schlegel). Yet compared with Stolberg, Goethe is selective. Stolberg — who had chosen to come over the Alps whereas Goethe had come via the Brenner — does not omit any notable city or feature and proceeds systematically as if following a guidebook. Behind this is a purpose: while sorting through his notes towards the planned *Reise*, Stolberg could write to Christoph Martin Wieland on January 30, 1794

---

19   With whom he corresponded. *The Correspondence of Edward Young 1683–1765*, ed. by Henry Pettit (Oxford: Clarendon, 1971), 539.

of how his enjoyment of Italy was to be subjected to high moral uplift and an amplitude of scope:

> Elisische Schönheit der Natur, Milde u: Ergiebigkeit des Klima, Charakter des Volks. Flüchtiger Blick auf die Geschichte der Länder u: Städte, besonders in Großgriechenland u: Sicilien; Vergegenwärtigung der alten Schriftsteller, vorzügl: der Dichter u: Geschichtschreiber, durch Darstellung des Localen u: der Sitten; Wercke der alten u: der neuen Kunst, in sofern ein Dilettante der hierin Leie ist, u: nur seine Empfindung reden läßt, [davon sprechen kann,] das sind meine vorzüglichsten Gesichtspuncte. Daß während eines volljährigen Aufenthalts in Italien u: Sicilien, unter dem lebhaftesten Volk Europens, einem Volck dessen Geisteslanlage sehr ausgezeichnet ist, dessen Liebenswürdigkeit von vielen verkannt wird, manche kleine Charakterzüge mir auffallen müßten, stellen Sie sich leicht vor. Unter dem liebenswürdigen Landvolk der paradisischen Insel Ischia, u: im hohen Felsenthal am Meer bey Sorento, habe ich die glücklichsten Monate der Reise zugebracht. Ich habe zwey Eruptionen des Vesuv, eine glühende Lavakatarakte des Aetna, u: vom Gipfel des Aetna ganz Sicilien gesehen. Die meisten Reisenden gehen nur bis Neapel. Wenn sie nur die ganze Küste des Neapler Meerbusens u: dessen Inseln besuchen, u: Vietri u: Cava besuchen wolten, so sähen sie schon Paradiese, aber die wenigsten thun einmal das.[20]

There we have it. Where commentators have noted Goethe's reticences or ambivalences (on Christian iconography, on ruins) and thus a certain preferentiality of detail, Stolberg's published text by contrast is concerned to integrate all of Italy into a higher scheme of things *sub specie aeternitatis*, as this passage further illustrates:

---

20 'The Elysian beauty of nature, a mild and fruitful climate, the national character. A fleeting glance at the history of the regions and cities, esp. in Magna Graecia and Sicily. Bringing alive the ancient authors, esp. the poets and historians, by describing local customs and ways; works of ancient and modern art, if a dilettante, who can only be a layman and can only speak through his feelings, may have his say on them. These are the things that I am mainly looking for. You may well imagine that I took note of characteristics here and there, having a whole year's stay in Italy and Sicily among the liveliest people in Europe, a people with a fine spirit, whose friendliness has been misunderstood by many. I have spent the happiest months of the journey staying with the lovely country folk on the island of Ischia, a real paradise, and in the lofty crags on the coast at Sorrento. I have seen two eruptions of Vesuvius and the fiery lava flowing down the slopes of Etna. From the top of Etna I have seen the whole of Sicily. Most travellers only go as far as Naples. If only they were to visit the whole of the coast of the Bay of Naples and its islands, and Vietri and Cava, they would already see paradises. But hardly anyone does even that'. Friedrich Leopold Graf zu Stolberg, *Briefe*, ed. by Jürgen Behrens, Kieler Studien zur deutschen Literaturgescbichte 5 (Neumünster: Wachhholz, 1966), 304.

Es ist ein großer Anblick, wenn man diese Alpen hinter sich sieht. Sie trennen nicht nur Italien von Savoyen, sie trennen unsere neuere Welt von jener ehrwürdigen, älteren, von welcher wir alles, was gesittete Menschen von Barbaren unterscheidet, Künste, das Licht der Wissenschaften, ja das heilige Feuer der Religion erhalten haben. Italien war genau mit Griechenland verbunden, dessen Pflanzstädte dem untern Theile dieses Landes den Namen Groß-Griechenland gaben. Andre griechische Völker wohnten in Klein-Asien; ihre Pflanzstädte waren auf der Küste von Afrika und von Asien zerstreut, in Egypten saßen griechische Könige auf dem alten Thron der Pharaone, ehe es eine römische Provinz ward. Die Herrschaft Roms vereinigte alle Völker, die das mittelländische Meer umwohnen. Bald hoffe ich am Gestade dieses Meers zu stehen, dessen Wogen Italien und Sicilien, die Trümmer von Karthago, Griechenlands Vesten in Europa und Asien, wo jeder Strom und jedes Vorgebürge durch Fabel und Geschichte berühmt ward, seine besungenen Inseln, das mystische Egypten, und Israels geweihtes Erbe anspülen, wo die durch lange Morgenröthe ihrer Geschichte, und durch das Hahnengeschrei der Propheten angekündigte Sonne der Wahrheit und der Liebe aufging, welche bald über Alpen und Meere, vom Ganges bis zum Eisgestade strahlend, die Völker leuchtend erwärmte; zwar durch aufsteigende Erddünste oft verdunkelt wird, aber an ihrem Himmel auch am Ende der Tage nicht untergehen soll![21]

We tread here the realm of comparative mythology, with not just Italy but the whole of the Mediterranean, its cosmogony and the cultures issuing from it. One notes the all-enveloping nature of the physical and historical panorama, with an accompanying insouciance for

---

21 'A huge vista opens up when one stands facing away from the Alps. They do not merely separate Italy from Savoy; they separate two worlds, that of today from the other venerable and more ancient one. From it has come down everything that separates men of culture from barbarians, the arts, the light of science, even the sacred fire of religion. Italy was closely bound up with Greece, and its colonies in the bottom part of this country were given the name of Magna Graecia. Other Greek peoples lived in Asia Minor, while other colonies were scattered along the coast of Africa and Asia. In Egypt, before it became a Roman province, Greek kings sat on the ancient throne of the pharaohs. Under Roman rule all the peoples who lived round the Mediterreanean coast were united. Soon I hope to stand on the shore of this sea. Its billows lave Italy and Sicily, the ruins of Carthage, Greek fortresses in Europe and Asia. There, every stream and every foothill was famed by fable and history, its islands sung in song, mystic Egypt and the sacred inheritance of Israel. The sun of love and truth, heralded in the long dawn of history and the prophets' clarion call, was soon radiating over alps and seas, from the Ganges to Greenland, shedding its warming light on the peoples. Vapours ascending from the earth may obscure it, but this sun in its heaven will never set, even at the end of time'. *GW*, VI, 311.

distinctions. This is Stolberg's grand entry into Italy. Goethe, on the other side of northern Italy, for his part notes a specific topographical and meteorological feature:

> Nach Mitternacht bläst der Wind von Norden nach Süden, wer also den See hinab will, muß zu dieser Zeit fahren; denn schon einige Stunden vor Sonnenaufgang wendet sich der Luftstrom und zieht nordwärts. Jetzo nachmittag wehet er stark gegen mich und kühlt die heiße Sonne gar lieblich. Zugleich lehrt mich Volkmann, daß dieser See ehemals Benacus geheißen, und bringt einen Vers des Virgil, worin dessen gedacht wird:
>
> *Fluctibus et fremitu resonans Benace marino.*
>
> Der erste lateinische Vers, dessen Inhalt lebendig vor mir steht, und der in dem Augenblicke, da der Wind immer stärker wächst und der See höhere Wellen gegen die Anfahrt wirft, noch heute so wahr ist als vor vielen Jahrhunderten. So manches hat sich verändert, noch aber stürmt der Wind in dem See, dessen Anblick eine Zeile Virgils noch immer veredelt.[22]

While Stolberg is kept warm by his religious zeal, Goethe studies the weather. But Volkmann, his travel guide, has conveniently provided a quotation from Virgil's *Georgics*, bringing 'klassischer Boden' alive to him in a way that perhaps the reams of Stolberg's Latinity (and Greek) do not.

But what of the obtrusive evidence of earlier civilizations? Both travellers have their artist companions like Christoph Heinrich Kniep or Johann Heinrich Wilhelm Tischbein or Jakob Philipp Hackert, their experts like Karl Philipp Moritz, to keep them on the straight and narrow and record or explicate the archaeological sites and the

---

22 'After midnight the wind starts blowing from north to south. The traveller down the lake must set out at this time, as already an hour or two before sunrise the air current veers to the north. Now, in the afternoon, the wind is blowing strongly in my face and cools the sun's hot rays very nicely. At the same time Volkmann informs me that this lake was formerly called Benacus and quotes a line of Virgil alluding to it:
Fluctibus et fremitu resonans Benace marino.
The first line of Latin whose subject I have seen with my own eyes. As I write, with the wind increasing in strength and the traveller having to face higher waves on the lake, the verse is as true today as many centuries ago. Much has changed, but the wind still whips up storms on the lake, its aspect still is ennobled by a line of Virgil'. SW, XI, 31 f.

vistas. Goethe himself does drawings. Hackert illustrates the first edition of Stolberg's *Reise*, an unnamed artist the second. Thus, ruins (a necessary corollary of antiquarian tourism) could be made into accessories or aids to the picturesque, and the many illustrated editions of Goethe's *Italienische Reise* do precisely this. Their description in the text is another matter. Both authors, Goethe and Stolberg, face the question as to whether ruins are part of the natural order of things or supervenient, the result of catastrophe or natural disaster. Goethe had come to change some of his views. Long before going to Italy, Goethe had written a poem, 'Der Wandrer/The Wanderer' (1774),[23] in which an idyllic conversation takes place among classical ruins which have reverted through nature to provide the dwelling for a bucolic couple and their child. Vegetation — nature — has smoothed over the wrecks of time; a resolution is found in the style of 'peinture des ruines'. In Goethe's poem, the 'Wandrer' is on his way to the archaeological site of Cumae, which Goethe was to visit in 1786. In his account of Sicily, Goethe was to describe the temple ruins of Segesta rising up from among the late spring flowers, in one of the descriptive high points of the *Italienische Reise*, drawing attention to the landscape, not the (for him) less impressive archaeological ambience. But it was to be Stolberg who came closest to the spirit of Goethe's early poem. For Goethe, the Sicilian ruins — Segesta, Girgenti — seemed out of scale and did not conform to Vitruvian or Palladian norms of the classical orders.[24] In Girgenti, he saw disorder — heaps of masonry — and struggled to find a natural explanantion:

> Der Tempel des Herkules hingegen ließ noch Spuren vormaliger Symmetrie entdecken. Die zwei Säulenreihen, die den Tempel hüben und drüben begleiteten, lagen in gleicher Richtung wie auf einmal zusammen hingelegt, von Norden nach Süden; jene einen Hügel hinaufwärts, diese hinabwärts. Der Hügel mochte aus der zerfallenen Zelle entstanden sein. Die Säulen, wahrscheinlich durch das Gebälk zusammengehalten, stürzten auf einmal, vielleicht durch Sturmwut niedergestreckt, und sie liegen noch regelmäßig, in die Stücke, aus denen sie zusammengesetzt waren, zerfallen. Dieses merkwürdige

---
23   *SW*, I, 378–84.
24   See Wilhelm Erich Mühlmann, 'Goethe, Sizilien und wir', *Germanisch-Romanische Monatsschrift*, NF 26 (1976), 440–51, ref. 442; Ernst Osterkamp, ed., *Sizilien. Reisebilder aus drei Jahrhunderten* (Munich: Winkler, 1986), 370ff.

Vorkommen genau zu zeichnen, spitzte Kniep schon in Gedanken seine Stifte.[25]

One observes how Goethe, a convinced 'Neptunist', surrounded by the evidence of seismic or eruptive activity — as it were, in the shadow of Etna — is not willing to admit this as possible cause of the degradation. It must have been a storm: hence the regularity of the fallen columns. If this explanation does not suffice, art, in the form of Kniep the landscape artist, will come to restore order. The contrast with Stolberg could not be greater:

> Ich bin versichert, daß diese Tempel, so wie auch die von Selinus, durch ein fürchterliches Erdbeben, vielleicht durch verschiedene, in solche Steinhaufen verwandelt worden. Zerstörende Menschenhand wirft alles flach über einander; nur der Natur gewaltiger Arm vermochte diese ungeheuern Massen so durch einander zu schleudern.
>
> Siegend lächelt sie jetzt, diese immer junge Natur; unter den Trümmern der stolzen gegen sie ohnmächtigen Kunst. Mitten unter den Steinhaufen entgrünet dem Boden ein Hain von Feigen- und Mandelbäumen. Im Tempel des olympischen Zeus sah ich zum erstenmal einen Pistazienbaum. Er war schon bedeckt mit vielen noch kleinen röthlichen Nüssen, und blühete zugleich.[26]

Stolberg stands at two removes from the scene of ruination. There is nature, and for him this is always 'die göttliche Natur', a divine agency, whose 'mighty arm' has been manifested in this scene of destruction. It is

---

25 'The temple of Hercules on the other hand still betrayed traces of a symmetry it once had. The two rows of columns at right and left which accompanied the temple at each end lay in the same direction, as if they had fallen down together, from north to south, one uphill, the other downhill. The hill may have been formed out of the body of the temple as it collapsed. The columns, no doubt held together by the structure, collapsed all of a sudden, perhaps flattened by a violent storm, and they lie still in order, their ruins in the sections from which they were formed. Kniep was already mentally sharpening his pencils at the idea of recording this strange phenomenon'. *SW*, XI, 302.

26 'I am told on good authority that these temples, like those at Selinus, were reduced to such heaps of rubble by a terrible earthquake, perhaps by several. The destructive hand of man lays everything flat; only the mighty arm of nature was able to topple and jumble these huge masses.
Now she rules in triumph, nature ever young; powerless against her, proud art lies in ruins. Sprouting up among the lumps of stone is a grove of figs and almonds. In the temple of Olympian Zeus was where I saw for the first time a pistachio tree. It was already covered with a mass of reddish nuts, quite small yet, and was flowering at the same time'. *GW*, VIII, 464.

the same force that shows itself in the earthquake, the volcano (Stolberg climbed Etna) or in the plant-life which comes to restore order, where an impotent art cannot. Here we see the parallel with Goethe's early poem, with that 'entgrünet', 'sprouting up', as a nice Klopstockian touch. But we are incidentally only one year after the publication of Constantin de Volney's *Les Ruines, ou Méditations sur les Révolutions/The Ruins, or Meditations on Revolutions and Empires* (1791), where ruins are made to relate to the grand scheme of human affairs (for Stolberg, of course, ruins formed part of a larger religious framework).

In Rome this time, not in Sicily, Goethe and Stolberg see an essentially different Eternal City, in the Colosseum and the Pantheon respectively.

> Von der Schönheit, im vollen Mondschein Rom zu durchgehen, hat man, ohne es gesehen zu haben, keinen Begriff. Alles Einzelne wird von den großen Massen des Lichts und Schattens verschlungen, und nur die größten, allgemeinsten Bilder stellen sich dem Auge dar. Seit drei Tagen haben wir die hellsten und herrlichsten Nächte wohl und vollständig genossen. Einen vorzüglich schönen Anblick gewährt das Coliseo. Es wird nachts zugeschlossen, ein Eremit wohnt darin an einem Kirchelchen und Bettler nisten in den verfallenen Gewölben. Sie hatten auf flachem Boden ein Feuer angelegt, und eine stille Luft trieb den Rauch erst auf der Arena hin, daß der untere Teil der Ruinen bedeckt war und die ungeheuern Mauern oben drüber finster herausragten; wir standen am Gitter und sahen dem Phänomen zu, der Mond stand hoch und heiter. Nach und nach zog sich der Rauch durch die Wände, Lücken und Öffungen, ihn beleuchtete der Mond wie einen Nebel. Der Anblick war köstlich. So muß man das Pantheon, das Kapitol beleuchtet sehn, den Vorhof der Peterskirche und andere große Straßen und Plätze. Und so haben Sonne und Mond, eben wie der Menschengeist, hier ein ganz anderes Geschäft als anderer Orten, hier, wo ihrem Blick ungeheure und doch gebildete Massen entgegenstehn.[27]

---

27 'You have no idea how beautiful it is walking through Rome in the moonlight: one must have seen it for oneself. Every detail is swallowed by the huge masses of light and shadow, and only the greatest and most readily visible images stand out. For the last three days we have been enjoying to the full the brightest and most splendid of nights. Among the beautiful sights the Coliseum stands out. It is closed at night. A hermit has his lodging in a little chapel, and beggars find shelter in the ruined vaults. They had built a fire on the flat ground, and in the stillness of the air the smoke was driven out over the arena, so that one could not see the lower part of the ruins, and the massive walls above stood out in the darkness; we stood at the lattice and watched the spectacle, the moon standing high and serene. By and by the smoke escaped through the walls, cracks and openings, in the moon's light, like

Goethe's is an artist's description, and another of the high moments of its kind in the *Italian Journey*, but not one of the standard views of the Colosseum like those of the painters Giovanni Volpato, Luigi Vanvitelli or Richard Wilson. It is in prose and must make use of the devices which that medium can offer. The great sights of Rome, antique or Renaissance, become fused in the interplay of light and shade, as the city is bathed in moonlight. There are questions of mass and contour, but the Colosseum also offers a friendly, human aspect (it is not the former scene of martyrdoms), populated as it is by Roman vagrants, with the impalpable column of smoke from their fires having the aesthetic effect of blurring contours and bringing out 'gebildete Massen'. Light effects also dominate Stolberg's view of the Pantheon:

> Ein großes Gefühl ergreift einen, wenn man mitten in der Rotunda steht, umfangen vom Eindruck der hohen Einfalt, die von allen Seiten auf das Auge, tief auf die Empfindung wirkt. Die Reihe der Jahrhunderte, welche seit der Gründung dieses Tempels entflohen sind, schwebet mit ihren in Staub gesunknen Menschengeschlechtern vor dir vorüber. Die Erde war mit Götzenaltären bedeckt, als Agrippa dieses Denkmaal von der Macht des Augustus erhub. Es wehete die Morgenröthe der Sonne, welche den Erdkreis erhellen sollte. Dem lebendigen Gotte ist nun der Götzentempel gewidmet. Ich empfand es mit frohem Schauer, sah auf, und da strahlte über der offnen Wölbung die Bläue des unendlichen Himmels. Wolken umhüllen ihn dann und wann, aber sie weichen dem Strahl der allerleuchtenden Sonne.[28]

Stolberg carries out an immediate shift of meaning, from the stance of the beholder, to that of the worshipper. The Pantheon's former function

---

a fog. It was a wonderful sight. This is the way one must see the Pantheon and the Capitol lit up, the forecourt of St Peter's and other great streets and squares as well. And so like the spirit of man, sun and moon have tasks other than elsewhere, for here their rays strike up against huge masses, once formed into shapes'. SW, XI, 182f.

28 'The beholder is seized by a great feeling, standing in the centre of the rotunda, and is impressed by the higher simplicity around him. The eye and the soul are everywhere profoundly affected. Centuries one after the other have vanished since this temple was founded; they rise up before you, and the generations that lived then and now are returned to dust. The earth was covered with altars to idols when Agrippa set up this monument to the might of Augustus. The first rays of the sun were being shed, to lighten the whole world. Now this pagan temple is for the worship of the all-living God. I felt it. Joy ran through me as I looked up: the blue of the vast sky shone over the open vault. Now and again clouds obscure it, but the ray of the sun disperses them and spreads its light over all things'. GW, VII, 274.

2. Goethe and Stolberg in Italy: The Consequences for Romantic Art 41

as a sanctuary to the gods is seized on, but given new significance as a temple of the Christian rite, symbolized in the shaft of light shining down from the rotunda. By implication: as once Augustus exemplified in his person the universal sway of Rome, so the newly functioned temple stands for the new dawn of the Roman-Christian era. Here, the proximity of Stolberg, already in 1792, to the later, ultramontane Friedrich Schlegel, is striking.

When, however, both Goethe and Stolberg both describe a painting by Raphael, they proceed aesthetically from common ground. They are both schooled in the art appreciation that has been handed down from French theory and connoisseurship to Winckelmann: the description is not technical in the modern sense but is intended rather to bring out states of mind and moral categories.

> (Goethe) Trifft man denn gar wieder einmal auf eine Arbeit von Raffael, oder die ihm wenigstens mit einiger Wahrscheinlichkeit zugeschrieben wird, so ist man gleich vollkommen geheilt und froh. So habe ich eine heilige Agathe gefunden, ein kostbares, obgleich nicht ganz wohl erhaltenes Bild. Der Künstler hat ihr eine gesunde, sichere Jungfräulichkeit gegeben, doch ohne Kälte und Roheit. Ich habe mir die Gestalt wohl gemerkt und werde ihr im Geist meine ‚Iphigenie' vorlesen und meine Heldin nichts sagen lassen, was diese Heilige nicht aussprechen möchte.[29]

> (Stolberg) Im Pallaste Ranuzzi ist eine heilige Agatha von Rafael, welche mir lieber ist, als die viel berühmtere Cecilia. Jene hat den vollen Ausdruck erhabner Ruhe, mit weiblicher Anmuth verbunden, welche kein Maler so wie Rafael darzustellen weiß.[30]

We are at the high point of European Raphael adulation, but still in the eighteenth century before the later discipline of art history puts an end to speculative attributions. For the Raphael they both admire — like the one that the young Tieck and Wackenroder claimed to see in

---

29 'Coming back to a work by Raphael or one that is fairly likely to be ascribed to him, I feel my health and joy restored. And so I have found a St Agatha, a wonderful picture, although not in a very good state of preservation. The artist has given her a healthy and serene virginity, but without it being frigid or coarse. I have taken this figure in. I will imagine myself reading my 'Iphigenie' to her and will not allow my heroine to say anything that this saint would not wish to utter'. *SW*, XI, 116.

30 'In the Palazzo Ranuzzi there is a St Agatha by Raphael. I prefer her to the much more famous Cecilia. She has the full expression of sublime calm, and with it goes a feminine grace, that no painter is able to represent like Raphael'. *GW*, VII, 42f.

Pommersfelden in 1793 — is alas not the genuine article, something that Goethe even hints at. Both, as said, are heirs to Winckelmann's notions of classical repose, order and nobility in the work of art, and neither is concerned with technical details. Neither Goethe nor Stolberg spends time on the *vita sacra* behind the painting's subject. Nor is this surprising, given Goethe's dislike of aspects of the iconography of Christian legend. What Goethe sees in Raphael— or expects to see—are human qualities, pleasurable sensations that are good for the mind and the soul. The picture in question exudes a 'healthy chastity' (no ecstasies, no aureoles) which can immediately be related to the work by Goethe which in Italy reached its final form: *Iphigenie auf Tauris/Iphigenia in Tauris*. It has always been noted that this Euripidean adaptation — blank verse instead of trimeters — neatly fuses the moral and spiritual values and language of Platonism with those of Christianity, but secularized, non-dogmatic and of general human import: friendship, fraternal love, gentleness, mercy, kindness, truthfulness. That these were not always to the fore in Euripides is not the issue. Thus, Goethe's Iphigenia and Raphael's St Agatha may meet in common human values across the divide of religious observance. Indeed, in 1818 Goethe was to state that Raphael — for the young Tieck and the older Friedrich Schlegel the unattainable model of later Christian art — had become a Greek, that in fact every genuine artist had to become one.[31]

Stolberg's admiration for Raphael comes out at various turnings of his *Reise*. After visiting the *stanze* of Raphael in the Vatican, he is inspired to write the nearly four-page-long dithyrambic poem, 'Rafael'. It rehearses the Raphael hagiography, not least a nightly vision to the Pantheon (the site of Raphael's grave), where the Muse of Apelles (the ultimate in Greek painting) speaks the lines:

> Und dankbar weihtest der Religion
> Deiner Pinsel Zauber und Empfindung dar.[32]

It is 'der unsterbliche Rafael', the 'immortal Raphael', but a step from Wackenroder and Tieck's 'divine' Raphael of 1796 and his sanctification in Romantic art criticism. The prose passage here tells us nothing of

---

31 *SW*, XIII, 846.
32 'Devote in thanks to religion
    Yours brushes and their magic touch'. *GW*, VII, 220.

the painting itself; the pre-Romantic (Stolberg) and the Romantic (Wackenroder and Tieck) cult of Raphael is not concerned with painterly qualities: it reads from the heart. Both, as said, are heirs to Winckelmann's notions of classical repose, order and nobility in the work of art, but nevertheless they regard Raphael differently and note what they are predisposed to seeing. Stolberg falls back on the language of feeling which is never far from aesthetic discourse in the last quarter of the eighteenth century: 'erhabene Ruhe', 'weiblicher Anmuth' could be pure Winckelmann, were it not for the fact that Stolberg is describing not an antique statue but the Renaissance depiction of a Christian saint.

Had the Romantics looked at what Goethe had had to say, instead of living in the world of *Werther* or *Iphigenie*, had they looked with intent at *Propyläen* or his Winckelmann essay, they might have been less affronted by the *Italian Journey* and its reservations about many aspects of Christian art. Had they read his periodical *Ueber Kunst und Alterthum* (first volume 1816), they would have noted a lively human interest in the Christian Middle Ages that stopped short of veneration or surrender to dogma. Stolberg could never replace Goethe in their scheme of things, but his journey to Italy, published twenty years before Goethe's account, was already closer to their aspirations. These two passages, by Friedrich Schlegel and Tieck, thus shed light on the causes of the Romantics' often troubled relationship with Goethe and offer an alternative to his uncompromising Greekness.

Fig. 3 Wallenstein, from Friedrich Schiller's drama trilogy *Wallenstein*, steel engraving after a drawing by Friedrich Pecht, c. 1859. Wikimedia, https://commons.wikimedia.org/wiki/File:Wallenstein_aus_Schillers_Wallenstein.jpg, public domain.

3. Schiller

Wallenstein[1]

Critics and commentators are in general agreement that *Wallenstein* represents the pinnacle of Friedrich Schiller's achievement as a dramatist.[2] Contemporaries like Johann Wolfgang Goethe and Wilhelm von Humboldt sensed that this was a new high point in German tragedy. Goethe had followed the genesis of the play in his correspondence with Schiller and was even behind the idea of using a trilogy as the only aesthetically satisfactory means of presenting the vast panorama of history. Samuel Taylor Coleridge's and Benjamin Constant's translations are an indication of its reception beyond Germany.

Only those critics who identified one-sidedly with another tradition or with different notions of tragedy found fault with *Wallenstein*. Georg Wilhelm Friedrich Hegel around 1800 saw no religious sense behind the presence of fate in the drama, comparing it unfavourably

---

1   This chapter is largely based on my 'Schiller, *Wallenstein*', in *Landmarks in German Drama*, ed. by Peter Hutchinson (Berne: Peter Lang, 2002), 47–57. It also appeared as the introduction to Flora Kimmich's translation of Friedrich Schiller, *Wallenstein: A Dramatic Poem* (Cambridge: Open Book Publishers, 2017), https://doi.org/10.11647/OBP.0101

2   For an account of the reception of Wallenstein, with an extensive bibliography, see *Schillers 'Wallenstein'*, ed. by Fritz Heuer and Werner Keller, Wege der Forschung 420 (Darmstadt: Wissenschaftliche Buchgesellschaft, 1977). See also Friedrich Schiller, *'Wallenstein': Erläuterungen und Dokumente*, ed. by Kurt Rothmann, Reclams Universal-Bibliothek 8136 [3] (Stuttgart: Reclam, 1982). Recent studies in English include T. J. Reed, *The Classical Centre. Goethe and Weimar 1775–1832* (Oxford: Clarendon, 1980), 136–49; T. J. Reed, *Schiller*, Past Masters (Oxford and New York: Oxford University Press, 1991), 80–85; Lesley Sharpe, *Schiller and the Historical Character. Presentation and Interpretation in the Historiographical Works and in the Historical Dramas* (Oxford: Oxford University Press, 1982), 72–105; Lesley Sharpe, *Friedrich Schiller, Drama, Thought and Politics* (Cambridge: Cambridge University Press, 1991), 217–50; F. J. Lamport, '*Wallenstein* on the English Stage', *German Life and Letters*, 48 (1995), 124–47.

with Greek tragedy.³ Ludwig Tieck, in 1826, found the love scenes superfluous and not organic to the action, making comparisons with Shakespeare's very different technique in *Romeo and Juliet*.⁴ Otto Ludwig, in 1859, found Wallenstein's 'reflective' nature unheroic and untragic and — crucially — un-Shakespearean.⁵ *Wallenstein* does not reduce so easily to the classic relations between free will and necessity that inform traditional tragic practice.

These criticisms indicate nevertheless that the modern writer of tragedy is bound to be subjected to the scrutiny of the two major traditions that go before him: Greek drama and Shakespeare, in German terms 'fate' versus 'character'. Anyone who cares to look will find elements of Sophocles or Shakespeare (especially *Henry IV, Macbeth* and *Richard III*) or even Racine in *Wallenstein*. We know that the reading of Shakespearean plays during the early stages of work on the play helped Schiller to resolve, to his own satisfaction, the questions of history, fate and character. But we need to bear in mind that Schiller's historical and aesthetic sense was that of his own age and its needs. He was deeply aware of the unique and irrevocable nature of classical antiquity, the 'unrepeatability' of Sophocles. Similarly, his reading of Shakespeare recognized elements irreconcilable with his own dramatic practice. His dramatic development — from *Die Räuber/The Robbers* to *Fiesco* to *Don Carlos* — shows a move away from Shakespearean characterization to figures in the guise of the idealist. These act not so much out of passions and emotions in themselves, but come to represent a kind of philosophical postulate (freedom in the case of Karl Moor, 'Gedankenfreiheit'⁶ in the case of Marquis Posa). In that sense, *Wallenstein*, with its ambiguities, is hardly a continuation of Schiller's dramatic practice of the 1780s.

There is another major difference. Schiller, between writing *Don Carlos* and *Wallenstein*, had been active on two fronts. He had been a practising historian, and he had committed to writing abstract notions about the idea of human moral freedom in the work of art. Is *Wallenstein* therefore a demonstration in dramatic form of, say, Schiller's reception of Immanuel Kant? It has been common to test *Wallenstein* against some

---

3   G. W. F. Hegel, 'Über *Wallenstein*', in *Schillers ,Wallenstein'*, ed. by Heuer and Keller, 15f.
4   Ludwig Tieck, '*Die Piccolomini. Wallensteins Tod*', ibid., 21–40.
5   Otto Ludwig, 'Schillers *Wallenstein*', ibid., 47–52.
6   'Freedom of thought'.

aspects of Schiller's indebtedness to Kant: the categories of 'erhaben' and 'schön',[7] of 'Realist' and 'Idealist', of 'moralisch' and 'ästhetisch'. But none in practice gives secure purchase. The aim of theatre to create 'die wahre Kunstwelt des Poeten', the world of aesthetic 'Schein', of 'freies Spiel'[8] against the merely material, is only partially fulfilled in the sombre interplay of mankind and history.

We must always remember that Schiller is a dramatist to his fingertips, not a philosopher who thinks in dialogue. Yet it is right to seek a philosophical, theoretical and dramatic centre to this play, a problem around which it revolves. Goethe, so much involved in its genesis, believed he had put his finger on it in 1799: it was the 'phantastischer Geist' associated with 'das Große und Idealische', as against 'das gemeine wirkliche Leben'.[9] But how could one square those fairly abstract ideas with the material that underlies the whole action, the history of Wallenstein in his own age? Wilhelm Dilthey, looking back on the emergence of the genre in the nineteenth century, called *Wallenstein* the first German historical drama.[10] That is certainly true in the sense that Schiller is in this play closer to his historical sources than in any other (despite the invention of Max and Thekla). It is also true in that Schiller agonized over the material he had expertly marshalled in his *Geschichte des dreissigjährigen Krieges/History of the Thirty Years' War* and its sources and over the best way to present it dramatically. We might question whether his deference to Goethe's suggestion of a trilogy was the best solution, especially since Schiller was acutely aware of Goethe's shortcomings as a dramatist.

Yet Schiller never regarded history as more than the quarry from which he drew the raw material for the finished work of art. History is a means to an end, nothing more. But he possesses nevertheless the historian's sense of a great figure standing out from his own age, incorporating it, explaining its currents and impulses, part of it yet transcending it. He does not abandon the ability to document, but he has the capacity to sum up what is dramatically essential in history. 'So fiel Wallenstein, nicht weil er Rebell war, sondern er rebellierte, weil er

---

7   'Sublime'; 'beautiful'.
8   'The true artistic world of the poet'; 'seeming'; 'free play'.
9   'Phantastic spirit'; 'the great and idealistic'; 'common and everyday life'. Goethe, 'Die Piccolomini. *Wallensteins* erster Teil', ibid., 3–9 (9).
10 Wilhelm Dilthey, '*Wallenstein*', ibid., 74–103 (76).

fiel'[11] is the proposition in *Geschichte des dreissigjährigen Krieges*. It is a philosophical paradox, and an aphorism, held together in the figure of the chiasmus. It is stating that Schiller is not primarily concerned with the tradition of the rise and fall of the great, the pattern that informed Greek and Senecan and seventeenth-century German tragedy. *Wallenstein* cannot be explained solely in terms of superbia, hubris, overweening ambition, although they are part of his character. Rather he displays a sense of the inadequacy of the material world, a will to change that glimpses beyond the world of the senses to some kind of ideal state. This is the aspect of Wallenstein which Schiller found most fascinating. He is not like Macbeth, in whom we can clearly trace the steps leading up to his crime and the stages towards his downfall. The dramatic graph is different. At the time of the action, over a decade of the Thirty Years' War is past, with Wallenstein's greatest deeds of heroism and generalship, the years of the Count of Tilly and Gustavus Adolphus, the battle of Lützen, now over.

Rather it is the sense of an age that Schiller wishes to convey. Indeed, his prologue had expressed the appropriateness of the work of art to sum up the essentials of his own times:

> Nicht unwert des erhabenen Moments
> Der Zeit, in dem wir strebend uns bewegen.[12]

Historical drama, as an aesthetic exercise, may point to the great movements and commotions of its own age, in Schiller's case the aftermath of the French Revolution (the reference is to the First Consul, Bonaparte). By the same token, the work of art is not bound to the limits of its own circumstances; art by its very nature raises and transcends:

> Ja danket ihrs, daß sie das düstre Bild
> Der Wahrheit in das heitre Reich der Kunst
> Hinüberspielt, die Täuschung, die sie schafft,
> Aufrichtig selbst zerstört und ihren Schein

---

11 'Thus Wallenstein fell, not because he was a rebel, but he rebelled because he was falling'. All quotations from Schiller are taken from *Sämtliche Werke*, ed. by Gerhard Fricke, Herbert G. Göpfert and Herbert Stubenrauch, 5 vols (Munich: Hanser, 1960), here IV, 688. References in footnotes indicate part and line number.

12 '[...] Not unworthy of the exalted hour,
The time in which we strive and live'. *Prologue*, 55–56.

> Der Wahrheit nicht betrüglich unterschiebt,
> Ernst ist das Leben, heiter ist die Kunst.[13]

How can 'das düstre Bild der Wahrheit' and 'das heitre Reich der Kunst' be reconciled, and how can they be made to reflect both the historical moment and a transcendent ideal?

Schiller's use of the trilogy to some degree reflects the resolution of this. *Wallensteins Lager/Wallenstein's Camp* presents us with the great general's power base, not the man himself; *Die Piccolomini/The Piccolomini* centres on the conflict between father and son, Octavio and Max Piccolomini; *Wallensteins Tod/Wallenstein's Death* brings us the act of rebellion and the downfall. Each part of the trilogy has its own terms of reference and 'feel'. Schiller does not follow the Shakespearean pattern of alternation between high and low styles — a pattern that has consequences for nineteenth-century verse tragedy in general. *Die Piccolomini* and *Wallensteins Tod* are characterized by the interior setting of French tragedy, with its restricted numbers on stage, and use of verse (here blank verse). The *Lager* stands out formally through the use of 'Knittelverse' and their 'altteutsch' ('old German') or Faustian associations and the comic mode of the Capuchin monk's sermon. Wallenstein does not appear. For this is the army that is occupying Bohemia and draining its substance. It is characterized by venality, materialism, the forces of 'Glück' and 'Spiel'.[14]

Schiller's own commentary is 'Sein Lager nur erkläret sein Verbrechen'.[15] Here he is close to the sense of baroque drama. For there is an interpenetration of all spheres of the high tragedy by the Lager. We see this in the very first scene of *Die Piccolomini*, where the generals, not the 'Soldateska' ('soldiery') are assembled, with its military language, its use of 'Fremdwörter' ('foreign words') and above all the accentuated theatricality of its stage directions ('nachdenkend', 'mit Bedeutung', 'betroffen').[16] Buttler's 'Wir gehn nicht von hier, wie wir kamen'[17] has

---

13 '[...] Thank her that she the gloomy face
    Of truth brings over into art's serene
    Domain, the feinted, her creation,
    Breaks with her own hand, and truth
    Does not give out for its appearance.
    Serious is life, but art serene'. *Prologue,* 133–38.
14 'Fortune'; 'game'.
15 'His camp alone explains his crime'. *Prologue,* 118.
16 'Deep in thought', 'pointedly', 'taken aback'. *Piccolomini,* 40, 41, 77.
17 'We leave this place, but not the way we came'. *Piccolomini,* 81.

an ominous ring — when we know of his later role in Wallenstein's fall. We sense that Wallenstein's power base is built not on high ideals but on mercenary service and plunder. The much-vaunted charismatic power of Wallenstein to raise armies — another reason why Buttler must murder him in the night before the Swedes are due to arrive — is based also on his power to pay ('der Königlichgesinnte',[18] as the venal condottiere Isolani calls him). Wallenstein is aware of this, as he stoically notes when Isolani deserts him for the Emperor.[19] It is the world of the Lager — but reflected in its highest officers — that enters into the proceedings at the banquet in *Die Piccolomini* where Isolani and Illo brawl; that disturbs the action of *Wallensteins Tod*, in the representatives of the Pappenheim regiment; that explains the mentality of Buttler and his hired assassins, and which ultimately underlies the punchline of the play, 'Dem *Fürsten* Piccolomini'.[20]

We should not overlook that, at significant moments in the play, Wallenstein does fulfil the claims made about him in the *Lager*: he demonstrates an unsentimental and almost brutal attitude towards those in power and those close to him. We might cite here the scenes with Questenberg and Wrangel, his attitude to Thekla, and his insensitive dismissal of Max as a potential son-in-law. Instead, once his power to act is invoked — as at the end of *Wallensteins Tod* I — his personality shows a formidable and awesome aspect, confirming Max's words at the end of *Die Piccolomini*:

> Denn dieser Königliche, wenn er fällt,
> Wird eine Welt im Sturze mit sich reißen,
> Und wie ein Schiff, das mitten auf dem Weltmeer
> In Brand gerät mit einem Mal, und berstend
> Auffliegt, und alle Mannschaft, die es trug,
> Ausschüttet plötzlich zwischen Meer und Himmel,
> Wird er uns alle, die wir an sein Glück
> Befestigt sind, in seinen Fall hinabziehn.[21]

---

18 'With soul of kings'. *Piccolomini*, 66.
19 *Tod*, 1620ff.
20 'To *Prince* Piccolimini'. *Tod*, 3867.
21 '[...] For this kingly man's downfall
Will bring a world down when it collapses,
And as when a ship upon the main
Goes up in flames and bursts
Apart, and all its crew

The first two lines suggest the Shakespearean analogy with Caesar; the image of ship and fortune — but with explosive power of expression — reminds us the century that produced both the historical Wallenstein and baroque drama.

Goethe, in the first important analysis of the play, contrasted the 'gemeine Wirklichkeit' ('base reality') of power and the 'phantastischer Geist' ('fantastic mind') of an ideal that this world cannot fulfil.[22] We note in *Die Piccolomini* and in the early scenes of *Wallensteins Tod* the preoccupation with the word time, 'Zeit': that it is not yet time to act, that things will be ordained in their own time. This is not merely the hubris of the Macbeth-like ruler (for hubris involves choosing the wrong time): Wallenstein also believes in a constellation of things beyond time. Think of the opening of *Wallensteins Tod*:

> WALLENSTEIN. Glückseliger Aspekt! So stellt sich endlich
> Die große Drei verhängnisvoll zusammen,
> Und beide Segenssterne, *Jupiter*
> Und *Venus*, nehmen den verderblichen,
> Den tückschen *Mars* in ihre Mitte, zwingen
> Den alten Schadenstifter mir zu dienen.
> [...]
> SENI. Und beide große Lumina von keinem
> Malefico beleidigt! der Saturn
> Unschädlich, machtlos, *in cadente domo*.
> WALLENSTEIN. Saturnus' Reich ist aus, der die geheime
> Geburt der Dinge in dem Erdenschoß
> Und in den Tiefen des Gemüts beherrscht
> Und über allem, was das Licht scheut, waltet.
> Nicht Zeit ists mehr zu brüten und zu sinnen,
> Denn Jupiter, der glänzende, regiert
> Und zieht das dunkel zubereite Werk
> Gewaltig in das Reich des Lichts - Jetzt muß
> Gehandelt werden, schleunig, eh die Glücks-
> Gestalt mir wieder wegflieht überm Haupt,
> Denn stets in Wandlung ist der Himmelsbogen.
> (*Es geschehen Schläge an die Tür*).[23]

Flings out, up in the air,
So he will tear down in his fall
All those dependent on his fortunes'. *Piccolomini*, 2639ff.
22   Goethe, 'Die Piccolomini', 8f.
23   W. 'See! In our favour, how at last
Fate's hand unites the mighty Three,

Here Jupiter (majesty) and Venus (beauty) hold destructive Mars in check, Saturn, the earth powerless. 'The shining one', not 'all that shuns the light', is in control. This alone gives Wallenstein the assurance that he can act. How different from Macbeth who trusts the witches. And yet he cannot act as he would wish. Note the stage directions (knocks at the door); Terzky arrives, then Wrangel. In the next scene, the instruction ('Er macht heftige Schritte durchs Zimmer, dann bleibt er wieder sinnend stehen')[24] stresses the anguished necessity of acting within time. Political man does not enjoy the luxury of reflexion, of 'des Mutes freier Trieb', of 'Überfluß des Herzens',[25] let alone the ideal aesthetic freedom which Schiller sees as vested in the beautiful, 'das Schöne'. This scene, relatively abstract in its language, trusting in trope, where the images do not come tumbling out as in Shakespeare, is in many ways the turning-point of the tragedy. But is everything programmed for downfall and disaster merely because Wallenstein has decided that his options are foreclosed and he must act? Rather, it talks of things that once seemed to be ('Traum'; 'Gedanken'; 'Hoffnung'; 'Überfluß des Herzens') and that no longer are.[26] These are words connoting freedom from constraint, creations of the mind, imaginings indulged. They lifted him *from* time: now he must act *in* time. They

---

  While Jupiter and Venus, ascendant,
  Force devious Mars between them
  To make him serve me.'
  S. 'And both great Lumina not crossed
  By any Malifico! While Saturn
  Shorn of power, in cadente domo.'
  W. 'Saturn's rule is ended, he who
  Controls the secret birth of things
  In earth's womb and in the humours' depths,
  Commanding all that shuns the light.
  This is no time to brood now or to ponder,
  For jovial Jupiter commands
  And draws the processes of darkness
  Over to the realm of light.
  Now we must act, and quick, before
  My lucky star flies out beyond my ken,
  For the arc of heaven is constantly at move.'
  (*There are knocks at the door.*) *Tod*, 9–35.

24 'He strides agitatedly through the room, stands still, in contemplation'. *Tod*, 183.
25 'Courage light and free', *Tod*, 180; 'the overflow of heart', *Tod*, 174.
26 'Dream', *Tod*, 143; 'thought', *Tod*, 148; 'hope', *Tod*, 151; 'the overflow of heart', *Tod*, 174.

raised him above the demeaning effects of 'das ganz Gemeine':[27] he now must grapple with them.

This pivotal scene may tell us what the tragedy of Wallenstein is. Of course, Schiller only calls *Wallensteins Tod* 'ein Trauerspiel': the whole play is 'ein dramatisches Gedicht',[28] the more neutral term that Gothold Ephraim Lessing's *Nathan der Weise/Nathan the Wise* made current. Does that mean that the world of *Wallensteins Lager*, as it spills over into *Die Piccolomini*, is less tragic than the trilogy's dénouement? The first two parts are more closely linked with the actual stuff of political power and the jostlings for supremacy in that world. Wallenstein's great monologues, like the one in *Wallensteins Tod* I, 4, seem hardly to form part of this, showing as they do a character too complex to be confined in categories of good generalship or a warlord's fortune. He has always been complex: trusting moods, intuitions, signs, coincidences, as he chooses. Now, he is forced to act. That does not make him tragic, although there is a tragic irony underwriting all of his tactical decisions. Surely what makes the major characters in this play tragic, not just Wallenstein, but Max, Thekla or Octavio, is that they have identified something beyond the historical and political moment, to which they appeal — in vain. It is summed up in the abstract noun that occurs repeatedly in this play: 'Herz', heart. It signifies something different at each usage, and it is never uncontaminated with other, often baser, associations. It situates this play in both the lexis and self-awareness of idealism and 'Empfindsamkeit', the cult of feeling; not the grand events that spur on the action in Shakespeare, but the appeal to inner sentiments. It is one reason why Schiller, in his explicit stage directions, wishes us to experience the interplay of inner and exterior reactions. It is what always sets Schiller apart from Shakespeare, even when the sentiments, as with Karl Moor or Marquis Posa, are often stridently expressed or inadequately excogitated. Had Wallenstein been Macbeth, he would have said at Max's death: 'He should have died hereafter'. Instead, his pondering of what 'das Schöne' in a human life might mean takes him into a moral sphere quite different from Macbeth's. Had he been merely the 'Realist' of Schiller's theory, he would not have allowed his mind to rise above the pragmatics of the situation. But 'Herz' is multivalent and

---

27 'The common round', *Tod*, 207f.
28 'Tragedy'; 'a dramatic poem'.

ambiguous, like 'remembrance' in *Hamlet* or 'honest' in *Othello*. It means love, honour, probity, the integrated self; it helps to explain why loyalty can become a key issue in this historical drama, so unlike the naked struggles in Shakespeare's Histories. But examining one's heart means also consulting other interests: Octavio's appeal to Max's heart also involves imperial and dynastic loyalties; Wallenstein, similarly, but also Max's 'zwischen dir und meinem Herzen',[29] which, as we know, means as much choosing Thekla as remaining loyal to Emperor Ferdinand. 'Herz' also invites us to think, not in categories (such as 'schöne Seele', 'beautiful soul') but according to human experience. Max's desperate end cannot be read as 'schön': what is there left to live for? Wallenstein's heart goes out to Max — it is in human terms the most convincing love in the play — but it cannot be divorced from retaining the Pappenheim regiment and it rules out Max as a son-in-law. Hence we are seized and moved by Wallenstein's 'Herz' in the elegiac mode of Acts Four and Five of *Wallensteins Tod* when there can be no more manoeuvrings and temporizings — and when thugs are planning his murder. Octavio is never more tragic than when he realises at the end that 'Herz' involves losing a son in the cause he espouses.

The figure of Max distinguishes this play further from Shakespeare, a figure who represents 'das Schöne', while, as we saw, being drawn into the world of reality by family affiliation and profession. Shakespeare's technique is different: his villains, Richard or Macbeth, are so commanding that they steal the show from the powers of legitimacy (Richmond, Malcolm). Yet Schiller's play is not just a conflict between, in his terms, the 'idealist' and the 'realist'. Max's despair and death do not belong in the pure realm any more than Wallenstein's actions. But it is Wallenstein who enunciates the principle of pragmatic action, while also looking beyond it. That is the sense of his famous speech in the second act of *Wallensteins Tod*, 'Schnell fertig ist die Jugend mit dem Wort',[30] with its awareness of the contrasting spheres of 'weit' or 'rein' as opposed to 'hart', 'grob', 'böse' or 'falsch',[31] its essential call for compromise, its opposition to what Max calls 'Herz'. Through an irony, it is only after Max's death that Wallenstein can appreciate the 'dream' of humanity he sees Max as representing:

---

29 'Between you and my heart'. *Tod*, 718.
30 'How glib the tongue of youth'. *Tod*, 779ff.
31 'Wide'; 'pure'; 'hard'; 'rough'; 'bad'; 'false'.

Er machte mir das Wirkliche zum Traum.[32]

Max, as son, as the object of affection ('Kind des Hauses'),[33] brings out the inner side of the ruler, hidden from the world of the *Lager*.[34] One thinks of Thomas Mann's gloss on the line 'Daß mich der Max verlassen kann',[35] where Wallenstein's familiar, slightly colloquial word sums up his moral dilemma. He is bound by forces of affection, but he also needs Max's regiment as part of the retention of power.

Max, too, is linked with that other aspect of Wallenstein's belief in some higher awareness. Pragmatists simply write off Wallenstein's vision as chance ('Zufall'). For Wallenstein, it confirms that he may implicity rely on Max's father, Ocatvio. One is reminded of the well-known speech in *Wallensteins Tod*, II, 3 ('Und mitten in der Schlacht ward ich geführt / Im Geist').[36] Wallenstein's belief is guaranteed by an inner sense of security and wellbeing. But we note that Max, by an irony in the economy of the action, finds his death in a scene (IV, 10) which echoes Wallenstein's original dream vision.

Thus in the last scenes of the play, as Wallenstein accepts the guilt for Max's death, we sense almost a sublimity ('Erhabenheit', in Schiller's sense) entering in. It is not real, but dramatically devised. Wallenstein has not so much changed; he is not on an ascendant moral curve. But our aesthetic satisfaction demands that his end be different from Macbeth's or Richard's. Think of the moving scene V, 3, with its renunciation ('trüglich wankenden Planeten').[37] It contrasts with the tragic sense of impending catastrophe and end, and rises above the sphere of the brutal Buttler and his henchmen. The heavens are darkened; the atmosphere is lyrical; Max is the light of his life, not extinguished, but safe from the things that have held Wallenstein in their thrall, 'Schicksal', 'Planeten', 'Unglück' and 'Stunde'.[38] Yet for all that, Wallenstein has not entirely abandoned his hopes for the coming day, which for him will never dawn. It takes us back to his earlier monologue in the first act (I, 4). His ambition is

---

32 'He made real things into a dream'. *Tod*, 3446.
33 'The son of the house', *Tod*, 2160.
34 *Tod*, III, 18.
35 'That Max, *my* Max, can leave me' [my italics]. *Tod*, 2162. Thomas Mann, 'Schillers Wallenstein', ed. by Heuer and Keller, 139–56 (141).
36 'And in my mind was led into the thick of the fray'. *Tod*, 926ff.
37 'Fickle shifting planets'. *Tod*, 3428.
38 'Fate', 'planets', 'misfortune', 'hour'. *Tod*, 208ff.

not just to rule, but to fulfil a vision of change, to set new values against 'Gewohnheit', 'sich befestigt', 'das ganz Gemeine', 'das ewig Gestrige', 'alter Hausrat' and 'Erbstück'.[39] It is a vision, not of habitual recurrence, but of change. It lifts us — momentarily only — above intrigue. It deludes Wallenstein into thinking that ambition, double-dealing and the naked exercise of power may be justified if the end is worthwhile. It is this vision which constitutes the major difference between Octavio (and by extension the Emperor) and Wallenstein, between the old order and a glimpse of the new. It is related to Max's vision of peace and humanity, 'Menschlichkeit', in *Die Piccolomini* I, 4. But Wallenstein is too taken up with the present, with the ambition of a crown, a dynasty, a pax romana, to grasp the full implications of this 'Menschlichkeit'. He sees fulfilment in the other, Max, not in himself. Wallenstein still sets his face against the real future, which we know will bring his demise and the tragic denouement; for Max there is no future to fear:

> Für ihn ist keine Zukunft mehr, ihm spinnt
> Das Schicksal keine Tücke mehr, — sein Leben
> Liegt faltenlos und leuchtend ausgebreitet,
> Kein dunkler Flecken blieb darin zurück,
> Und unglückbringend pocht ihm keine Stunde.[40]

---

39 'Habit', 'holds fast', 'the common round', 'the eternal yesterday', 'old lumber', 'inheritance handed down'. *Tod*, 197, 198, 208, 213, 214.
40 'For him there is no future, and no fate
Spins malice in its toils,
His life is bright and without crease
Unfolded, no dark spot there to mar,
Fate knocks not at the door with its bad tidings'. *Tod*, 3422–26.

Fig. 4 *Laocoon and his Sons*, also known as the *Laocoon Group*. Marble, copy after an Hellenistic original from ca. 200 BC. Found in the Baths of Trajan, 1506, Wikimedia, https://commons.wikimedia.org/wiki/File:Laocoon_Pio-Clementino_Inv1059-1064-1067.jpg, public domain.

4. Laocoon, Dante, Shakespeare, August Wilhelm Schlegel and the Overcoming of Tragedy[1]

A more precise title for this chapter would be simply 'Overcoming Tragedy Around 1800. A German View'. To a scholar of German, the idea of overcoming tragedy would have immediate associations. We think of discussions about what Aristotle really meant by pity and fear, and whether perhaps he was talking more about empathy, and certainly not about terror. We note the choice of dramatic subjects that kept tragic action in the background and concentrated more on the values of the human heart. One thinks of how Johann Wolfgang Goethe adapted Euripides' Iphigenia story to this very effect; or how Friedrich Schiller constructs a whole theory of tragedy around the notions of 'sublime soul' or 'beautiful soul' and seeks to illustrate this in the 1790s in his two tragedies *Wallenstein* and *Maria Stuart*; even how Schiller in 1800 produces a version of *Macbeth* with distinctly neoclassical overtones. And, finally, we recollect how August Wilhelm Schlegel, the great translator and critic — the main subject of my remarks here — in 1797 produced a reading of *Romeo and Juliet* that played down the stark connotations of the young Shakespeare's tragedy and instead read in it values of the human heart that mitigated 'never was a story of more woe'.

Since writing my book on Shakespeare's critical reception in Germany,[2] I have come to see Schlegel's essay of 1797 in a wider context: this context

---

1 This chapter developed out of a paper, hitherto unpublished, given at the Shakespeare Institute in Stratford on Avon in 2010.
2 Roger Paulin, *The Critical Reception of Shakespeare in Germany 1682–1914. Native Literature and Foreign Genius*, Anglistische und Amerikanistische Texte und Studien 11 (Hildesheim, New York: Olms, 2003).

did not necessarily cast more light on his attitude to Shakespeare per se, but it made that reading of *Romeo and Juliet* more plausible. For within a year of his *Romeo and Juliet* essay, Schlegel had been translating parts of Dante and writing a commentary on him.[3] He had been faced with the stark awfulness of the story of Ugolino della Gherardesca in Dante's *Inferno*.[4] In grasping for words to express what was plainly there in the text but from which he instinctively recoiled, Schlegel mentioned the name of Laocoon (from Greek mythology). In the same year as his essay on *Romeo and Juliet*, Schlegel wrote a poem which states with brevity and succinctness the insights that the essay develops at greater length and with sometimes deliberate shifts of meaning. This is the background to my remarks. It is what enables images of Laocoon and Ugolino to cohabit with Shakespeare and how these can be incorporated into a wider discourse, even one where his name is not even mentioned.

Ultimately, however, my subject has to do with the reception of Shakespeare in Germany, and also with the wider issues raised by that particular debate. The primary question is: what is it that draws the Germans to Shakespeare and confers on them — or leads them to confer on themselves — a special relationship to Shakespeare, so that Schlegel in 1796 could speak of Shakespeare as 'ganz unser' ('entirely ours').[5] I am not posing these questions in the abstract, because they impinge quite directly on my subject. What is it then that accords to the Germans that special relationship to Shakespeare?

One can safely state as a general principle that all non-English reception of Shakespeare is really a debate with existing national traditions and their preoccupations, especially in the eighteenth century.[6] The French for instance spend more time on the question of Shakespeare and their own *drame classique* that on anything else. The Italians ask themselves whether some of the qualities being exhibited in Shakespeare do not relate to their own golden age (Dante) and whether

---

3   August Wilhelm Schlegel, 'Dante's Hölle', in *Die Horen eine Monatsschrift*, ed. by Friedrich Schiller (Tübingen: Cotta, 1795–97), 1. Jg. (1795), 3. Stück, 22–29, 4. Stück, 31–49, 8. Stück, 35–74.

4   '"Ugolino und Ruggieri" Fortsetzung von Dante's Hölle', ibid., Jg. 1795, 8. Stück, 35–74.

5   August Wilhelm Schlegel, 'Etwas über Hamlet bey Gelegenheit Wilhelm Meisters', *Die Horen*, 2. Jg. (1796), 4. Stück, 57–112, ref. 79.

6   See Roger Paulin, 'Ein deutsch-europäischer Shakespeare im 18. Jahrhundert?', in *Shakespeare im 18. Jahrhundert*, ed. by Roger Paulin, Das achtzehnte Jahrhundert. Supplementa 3 (Göttingen: Wallstein, 2007), 7–35.

a renaissance of their national literature is possible. The eighteenth century in Germany, when the reception of Shakespeare begins in earnest and at whose end we have that extraordinary proprietary claim, 'ganz unser', is — I am simplifying complex processes here — a time of self-definition. The question is being asked: do we have a national literature? And if we do not, how are we to go about acquiring one? Are we to follow foreign models — the French, the Greeks, the English, or elements of all three? Or are we to look to the resources of our own native tradition? The history of German literature in the eighteenth century involves all of these elements. For some writers and poets, Shakespeare is an irrelevance. For many however he is not. He is the way forward, in terms of self-definition, inspiration, attitudes to form and its models, and much else besides. They are remarking and absorbing a Shakespeare as known in the eighteenth century, Shakespeare as mediated by Voltaire, or Alexander Pope, or John Milton, or Edward Young, or Mark Akenside or Ossian. Shakespeare is made to relate to the issues that occupy each successive generation. The eighteenth century sees two important moments of self-definition in German literature, both of them conducive to the Germans finding their own voice and their own stylistic expression, one commencing in the 1740s, the other around 1770. The second of these is known as the *Sturm und Drang* ('Storm and Stress'), and it is, as the name suggests, explosive, urgent, concerned with issues of originality, nature, creative forces, the definition of the self, and the expression of all of this in poetry and prose. In this period the Germans first begin to say things about Shakespeare that are their own and not borrowed from others. It is also worth reminding ourselves in terms of European Shakespeare reception that 1770, using this as a rough date, is the time around which a major reaction takes place in European Shakespeare reception, a rejection of his alleged 'faults' and imperfections, a reaction against the 'misrepresentations of Mons. de Voltaire',[7] as Elizabeth Montagu states in 1769, and an attempt to explore the nature of his genius.

An example from Germany in this very period is the dithyrambic essay *Das Hochburger Schloss/The Ruined Castle of Hochburg* of 1777 by

---

7   Elizabeth Montagu, *An Essay on the Writings and Genius of Shakespeare Compared with the Greek and French Dramatic Poets. With Some Remarks Upon the Misrepresentations of Mons. de Voltaire* (London: Dilly, 1772), title page.

Jakob Michael Reinhold Lenz (1751–92). It is a rejection of Voltaire and Pope, of anyone who dares, who presumes, to raise a voice of criticism against Shakespeare. Who, he says, can utter reservations about King Lear? Who is not shattered to the core by this spectacle? Who can even begin to speak of it, to find words to express it? 'Doch wer darf über Laokoon reden? Und über Lear, wer darf das? — '[8] For all its impulsive force, this is a rhetorical figure, a variation on the 'words fail me' trope (called hyperoche): Shakespeare will lead us into the realms of the unsayable, the inexpressible. But why Laocoon, and, one might venture to ask, who dares bracket him with Lear?

Laocoon is, of course, the Trojan priest who was punished by the goddess Athena for warning the Trojans about the wooden horse. The goddess sent venomous snakes out of the sea to bite and strangle him and his two sons. The Laocoon, a Hellenistic group of statuary discovered in Rome in 1506, becomes in eighteenth-century Germany a cipher for all kinds of aesthetic and moral debates and a criterion of taste. Depending on one's views, it is an unsurpassed model of classical harmony in art, an exemplar of stoical suffering and moral greatness, or a martyr enduring the pain of death, offering defiance to the gods in the very act of punishment. The question of why Laocoon and his sons suffer in the way they do is not in the forefront of eighteenth-century debates. The contemplation of this group of statuary is concerned rather with drawing out of it qualities of human endeavour, inner capacities of mind and soul. Thus it is that everyone who matters in the eighteenth century has something to say about Laocoon: Johann Joachim Winckelmann, Gothold Ephraim Lessing, Johann Gottfried Herder, Schiller, Goethe, and many others, a roll-call of the great names of eighteenth-century German criticism, thought and poetry.[9] Such observations are not restricted to Germany; witness Sir Joshua Reynolds noting that the Laocoon can depict but the

---

8   'Who may venture to speak of Laocoon? Who of Lear, who dares it?' Jakob Michael Reinhold Lenz, *Das Hochburger Schloß* (1777), in *Shakespeare-Rezeption. Die Diskussion um Shakespeare in Deutschland. I: Ausgewählte Texte von 1741 bis 1788*, ed. by Hans-Jürgen Blinn (Berlin: Erich Schmidt, 1982), 148.

9   See the definitive account by Hugh Barr Nisbet, 'Laocoon in Germany. The Reception of the Group since Winckelmann', in *On the Literature and Thought of the German Classical Era* (Cambridge: Open Book Publishers, 2021), 241–90, http://doi.org/10.11647/OBP.0180

'general expression of pain'.¹⁰ And so Lenz's shorthand reference to Laocoon taps into current debates and aligns him with those who see in this statuary the depiction of tragic suffering. But Lenz goes further: he is saying that for him Laocoon represents, like Lear, the limits of the expressible, takes us out beyond analysis, outside of articulation, beyond critical debate, into spheres of the absolute. We do not concern ourselves with details, with motivations, with questions of guilt or innocence. Words do not suffice.

Let us now jump nearly twenty years, to 1795, to a figure better known in German Shakespeare reception, August Wilhelm Schlegel, the great translator and the author of the *Vorlesungen über dramatische Kunst und Literatur/Lectures on Dramatic Art and Literature* that so influenced Samuel Taylor Coleridge. Except that in 1795 he is neither of these things. Although he has produced a draft version of *A Midsummer Night's Dream*,¹¹ he is for the moment occupied with other matters, notably with Dante. Whereas references to Dante and Shakespeare in eighteenth-century English Shakespearean discourse are so rare as hardly to count, the position in Germany is different. For them, the great figures of world literature represent a continuity of poetry, in different epochs, in cyclical progression. But poetry remains whole and undivided all the same. Schlegel's brother Friedrich expressed this in 1798 in the following terms:

> Dante's prophetisches Gedicht ist das einzige System der transcendenten Poesie, immer noch das höchste seiner Art. Shakespeare's Universalität ist wie der Mittelpunkt der romantischen Kunst. Goethe's rein poetische Poesie ist die vollständigste Poesie der Poesie. Das ist der große Dreyklang der modernen Poesie [..]¹²

---

10 *The Discourses of Sir Joshua Reynolds*, ed. by John Burnet (London: James Carpenter, 1842), 114.

11 See Frank Jolles, *A. W. Schlegels Sommernachtstraum in der ersten Fassung vom Jahre 1789 nach den Handschriften herausgegeben*, Palaestra 244 (Göttingen: Vandenhoek & Ruprecht, 1967).

12 'Dante's prophetic poem is a system of transcendental poetry in one, and still the highest of its kind. Shakespeare's universality is like the midpoint of Romantic art. Goethe's pure poetic poetry is poetry of poetry at its most perfect. This is the great threefold chord of modern poetry [...]'. *Athenaeum. Eine Zeitschrift von August Wilhelm Schlegel und Friedrich Schlegel*, 3 vols (Berlin: Vieweg, 1798; Unger, 1799–1800), I, 244.

You will see from this quotation that poetry does not stand still. It is progressive and extends into the modern period as well (Goethe). The Romantics, August Wilhelm Schlegel among them, never hesitated to name Dante and Shakespeare as the highest 'archpoets', and so in a sense what he says about Dante can by analogy be applied to Shakespeare. I am going to take what he says in 1795 about Dante and apply it by analogy to his attitude to Shakespeare, especially Shakespearean tragedy, around 1800.

And so first of all to Dante. Schlegel is translating selected parts of the *Divine Comedy*, hitherto never rendered in the original verse form, and in 1795 he is translating the first part, the *Inferno*. (We should not forget that Schlegel did translations from Italian, Spanish, Portuguese and Sanskrit, as well as of Shakespeare.) The Dante essay and translation appears in Schiller's periodical *Die Horen/The Horae*, a journal concerned with bringing together all men of good will in a common purpose. Schlegel was in good company, for it is here that Schiller published his *Briefe über die ästhetische Erziehung des Menschen/Letters on the Aesthetic Education of Man* and *Über naïve und sentimentalische Dichtung/On Naïve and Sentimental Poetry*, Goethe his *Unterhaltungen deutscher Ausgewanderten/ Conversations of German Refugees* and *Römische Elegien/Roman Elegies*, and it was in this same journal that Schlegel also published his first important statements on Shakespeare. Schlegel, in translating the Ugolino episode, then commenting on it, was not plucking his example out of the air. He knew that the subject had a pre-history.[13] Precociously knowledgeable as he was, he must have been be aware that, as far back as 1741, the Swiss critic Johann Jacob Bodmer had drawn attention to this passage and had even translated a part of it.[14] (Over his later drama *Der Hunger-Thurn in Pisa*, based on the same episode in Dante, a veil is best drawn.)[15] Bodmer is also one of the founding figures of German

---

13 On the Ugolino episode and its various mutations, see the old positivist study, still useful, by Montague Jacobs, *Gerstenbergs Ugolino. Ein Vorläufer des Geniedramas*, Berliner Beiträge zur germanischen und romanischen Philologie 14 (Berlin: Ebering, 1898); and more recently, Frances Yates, 'Transformations of Dante's Ugolino', *Journal of the Warburg and Courtauld Institutes*, 14 (1951), 92–117; Yvonne-Patricia Ahlefeld, '"Der Simplicität der Griechen am nächsten kommen". Entfesselte Animalität in Heinrich Wilhelm von Gerstenbergs Ugolino', *Herder Jahrbuch*, 6 (2002), 63–82.
14 Jacobs, *Gerstenbergs Ugolino*, 16f.
15 Johann Jacob Bodmer, *Der Hunger-Thurn in Pisa. Ein Trauerspiel* (Chur und Lindau: Typographische Gesellschaft, 1769).

Shakespeare reception. The juxtaposition of these two 'archpoets' was therefore not the Romantics' invention. It was, however, not in Schlegel's interests, writing as he was in *Die Horen*, a journal at the cutting edge of criticism and philosophical reflexion, to allude to a figure so unmodern and dated. He may not have known that Schiller himself, from early on, had taken a lively interest in the most notable manifestation in Germany of Dante's Ugolino episode, Heinrich Wilhelm von Gerstenberg's tragedy *Ugolino* (1768).[16] Not only that: Gerstenberg is an important voice in the Shakespearean reception of the *Sturm und Drang*, and for him Shakespeare and Dante are commensurate figures. Do you expect smoothness in the works of genius, his *Briefe über Merkwürdigkeiten der Literatur/Letters on Curiosities of Literature* (1766–67) asks ('denn großen Genies sind Auswüchse wesentlich: erinnern Sie sich des *Dante* und *Shakespear* [sic]?').[17] Thus it is that Schlegel can find admiring words for Gerstenberg while nevertheless admitting that the subject is hardly suitable for dramatic adaptation, at least not in the form chosen.[18]

Lessing, too, had alluded to Ugolino in a passage in his *Laokoon* (1766) referring to repellent subjects in poetry.[19] It was however not he who was to review Gerstenberg's play, but Herder, in 1770.[20] Herder was generally laudatory, but with some reservations. The chief of these is that Gerstenberg, Shakespeareanizing in typically *Sturm und Drang* fashion, had overlooked the essential difference between Ugolino and Shakespeare's subjects. While horror is penetratingly present in Shakespeare, it is never the main point; it never forms, as here, the whole substance of the dramatic plot. Similar points are to be found later in Schiller, himself never averse to the spectacle of cruelty in dramatic subjects.[21]

---

16 Jacobs, *Gerstenbergs Ugolino*, 125f.
17 'For irregularities are an essential part of genius: do you remember Dante and Shakespeare?' Heinrich Wilhelm von Gerstenberg, *Briefe über Merkwürdigkeiten der Literatur*. Vollständige Neuausgabe mit einer Biographie des Dichters, hg. von Karl-Maria Guth, Sammlung Hofenberg (Berlin: Contumax, 2013), 2. Sammlung, 12. Brief, 70.
18 Schlegel, '"Ugolino und Ruggieri"', 65–67.
19 Gotthold Ephraim Lessing, *Werke*, ed. by Franz Muncker, 12 vols (Stuttgart: Göschen, 1890), VII, 360.
20 Herder's review is most accessible in Heinrich Wilhelm von Gerstenberg, *Ugolino. Eine Tragödie in fünf Aufzügen*. Mit einem Anhang und einer Auswahl aus den theoretischen und kritischen Schriften, hg. von Christoph Siegrist, Reclams Universal-Bibliothek 141 (2) (Stuttgart: Reclam, 1977), 74–86.
21 See Karl S. Guthke, 'Schiller, Shakespeare und das Theater der Grausamkeit', *Shakespeare im 18. Jahrhundert*, 181–94.

This pre-history — which can only be sketched here — is doubtless the reason why Schlegel chooses this particular passage for translation and comment. Not his very first public statement on Dante, it has nevertheless a milestone quality in that it contains the first version of the rhyme-scheme *terza rima* in German (Schlegel refers nowhere by name to the previous prose translation by Johann Nicolaus Meinhard, only disdainfully to 'mattere Umschreibungen').[22] Foretaste samples of the first blank-verse translations of *Romeo and Juliet*, *The Tempest* and *Julius Caesar*, also by Schlegel, were to be published in *Die Horen*, followed by his two great essays on Shakespeare. Echoing Herder, Schegel, too, considers what Shakespeare might have made of such as subject as Ugolino.[23] Of course such an idea was never in Shakespeare's mind. Schlegel must nevertheless come to terms with tragic horror in all its starkness, whether in Dante or in Shakespeare; whether in Dante's account of Ugolino and his sons' death by starvation or the action in *Romeo and Juliet*, where the number of corpses even exceeds Dante's. But first, Ugolino.

As a translator, Schlegel is confronted with the passage in Canto XXXIII of the *Inferno* that for him and many other readers besides represents the scene of the most appalling horror: the story of Ugolino. For what was seen as an act of treachery, Ugolino, his sons and grandsons were incarcerated and left to die of hunger. Dante, with his guide and mentor, Virgil, meets Ugolino in Hell and hears his story. Schlegel the translator makes two points: he is inadequate to express the full force of Dante's original, but must nevertheless do justice to what Dante has written.[24] For the text hints at even worse: how Ugolino was tempted to commit two desperate acts, to feed on his dead sons, and also to put an end to his own life, but did neither, as Dante puts it, 'Until hunger did what anguish could not do'.[25]

Despite this, Ugolino is punished eternally in Hell, for betraying the trust that was placed in him. But Schlegel sees deeper processes at work in Dante's depiction. He says that Dante, by using Ugolino's own words as he describes his own torture and death, appeals to our hearts,

---

22 'Fairly dull transcriptions'. Schlegel, '"Ugolino und Ruggieri"', 58. Meinhard's translation in Gerstenberg, *Ugolino*, 72–74.
23 Schlegel, '"Ugolino und Ruggieri"', 67.
24 Ibid., 58f.
25 In Schlegel's version: 'Dann that der Hunger, was dem Schmerz mislang'. Ibid., 57.

to our sympathies: 'no-one could pass by and not be affected', is how Schlegel puts it.[26] Over this whole account, says Schlegel, are written in an invisible hand the words 'To Humankind'.[27] Through the atrocities he is forced to recount, there shines Dante's own sense of humanity, his own natural innocence and his sense of natural recompense. There must, Schlegel avers, be here a belief in a divine justice higher that the events depicted. Otherwise, our hearts and souls would revolt at the sights and sounds evoked in the poetry and we would wish them veiled from our sight; the punishment would be out of all proportion to our sense of justice. In all, we sense virtues, heroism and self-sacrifice; after horror, we are filled with admiration and pity; as an equilibrium is restored in our hearts, we are healed and reconciled.[28] You will note that here Schlegel is using the well-tried vocabulary of catharsis, the pseudo-Aristotelian theory of inner purification through the spectacle of pity and fear at others' sufferings. Is Schlegel attempting to accommodate Ugolino to Schiller's notion of tragic art that is essentially concerned with inner moral values? If so, Schiller does not seem to have minded having the extreme example of Dante's translated text published in his journal. Even then, Schlegel seems to wish to mitigate: Ugolino is not Dante's invention, but history's;[29] he merely reports what he has learned through other sources (which overlooks Ugolino's punishment in Hell). This argument is somewhat specious, for Dante did after all choose his subject. Or: Dante is only recording history; he is not its inventor, suffused as he is by a natural sense of justice. But we might just as easily say that Shakespeare did not invent the child murders in *King Henry VI*, *King John* and *King Richard III*, but he chose nevertheless to display them to dramatic effect. Schlegel is seeking factors that might compensate and balance the 'Ekel und Abscheu' ('disgust and abhorrence'), what he calls 'Entschädigung'.[30] Our natural sense of pity at the deaths of children is invoked, rather than our distress at the sight of the cannibalism to which Ugolino is condemned eternally, inflicted on his earthly adversary, Ruggieri.

---

26 'Wer hier untheilnehmend vorübergienge, müßte seine Natur verläugnen oder vergessen'; 'An die Menschheit'. Ibid., 59.
27 Ibid., 57.
28 Ibid., 60.
29 Ibid., 59.
30 Ibid., 61,

Even that, says Schlegel, cannot suffice. We may be able to bear the spectacle of others' physical sufferings — as with Philoctetes (the Greek hero of the Trojan war who endured a wound for ten years) or Laocoon[31] — but there is something infinitely more terrible in the thought of Ugolino being part of a chain of sin and retribution ('I shudder even to imagine this idea', says Schlegel).[32] Was he reminded of the doctrine of eternal punishment in which his own father, a Lutheran pastor, had still believed? The real crime that Ugolino committed stands in no proportion to the sufferings he underwent. But Dante's sense of truth and justice is inerrant, almost inhumanly so. We admire, but do not wish to enter into these regions ourselves.

The brief, passing reference to Laocoon is interesting, not as an explanation of the Ugolino story but as an analogy. It would suggest that Schlegel subscribes to the view of Laocoon as eliciting our admiration and our empathy through the spectacle of his suffering and that of his sons. It is a reference that takes us out of literature proper and into the fine arts, away from the story as such and into its depiction in this group of statuary. Without referring to it by name, Schlegel turns to the subject of Lessing's *Laokoon* of 1766: the distinction between the art forms, the visual arts and poetry. Can a painting or sculpture elicit our empathy in the way that Dante's text has done? I find it interesting that Schlegel near the end of his essay refers briefly to the painting of Ugolino and his sons by Sir Joshua Reynolds.[33]

It seems to me that this painting has some affinities with Laocoon: not so much with the bodies writhing in their last agonies, but with the pyramidal structure of the Laocoon group, a feature that many eighteenth-century observers note.[34] Reynolds's Ugolino sits stoically, heedless of his imploring sons and grandsons, who alone represent an unruly element in the painting. I see similar analogies with contemporary paintings of Shakespearean scenes, notably those in the Boydell Gallery, James Northcote's or Josiah Boydell's depiction of the father and son dying on the battlefield in *3 Henry VI*, for instance, or James Barry's of Lear and Cordelia, even perhaps John Opie's of Romeo and Juliet. I

---

31 Ibid.
32 'Ich schaudre mich weiter in diese Vorstellungen zu vertiefen'. Ibid., 61f.
33 Ibid., 73.
34 See Nisbet, 'Laocoon in Germany', 251.

Fig. 5 Joshua Reynolds, *Count Ugolino and his Children in the Dungeon* (1770–73), National Trust Collection.

do not wish to pursue these iconographical links any further,[35] at least not here. At most, they all point to some reconciliation beyond tragedy, some resolution: Laocoon's nobility (as many saw it), Ugolino's stoicism (not the pangs of starvation), an artistically harmonious solution in the Shakespearean paintings through the juxtaposition and ensemble of bodies live and dead, as indeed the theory of history painting at the time demanded.

With this, we leave Laocoon, but not Ugolino. In 1799, Schlegel writes an enthusiastic review of the outline engravings of scenes from Dante done by John Flaxman, the great neoclassical illustrator and sculptor.[36] Flaxman cannot rightly omit Ugolino, nor indeed does he disappoint us. Flaxman is not Reynolds. Reynolds's Ugolino could, Schlegel says, be 'any old man starving',[37] not Dante's character. Not so Flaxman. He makes two scenes out of Dante's story, and thus shows a 'much higher

---

35 See *The Boydell Shakespeare Gallery*, ed. by Walter Pape and Frederick Burwick in collaboration with the German Shakespeare Society (Bottrop: Pomp, 1996), 261, 262, 281, 283.

36 'Ueber Zeichnungen zu Gedichten und John Flaxman's Umrisse', *Athenaeum*, II, ii, 193–246.

37 Ibid., 212.

perception'.[38] For the first sheet shows the arrest of Ugolino and his family, how they are jostled and bound by rough soldiery, the man Ugolino, unbroken and unshaken in their midst forming the central character around which everything else in the engraving is resolved. His accusers skulk in the background, aware of the enormity of what they are about to perpetrate. (He does not say it, but one thinks by analogy of the arrest of Christ.) The second sheet shows Ugolino surrounded by his dying and dead sons and grandsons. Schlegel quotes two lines of Dante, without commentary, and restricts himself to a short technical note on how Flaxman centres the figure of Ugolino.[39] Nothing more. There are no words now on the inexpressibility of horror and judgment. In fact, it seems that Schlegel in this essay is only too happy to escape from the pressing repugnances of *Inferno* to the etherealities of *Paradiso*, in other words, to avoid the pressing reality of sheer tragedy.

Fig. 6 John Flaxman, illustration of Dante, *Inferno*, Canto 33 (Rome?, 1802), showing Ugolino and his sons. Courtesy of the Master and Fellows of Trinity College, Cambridge.

---

38 'Viel höhere Ansicht', ibid.
39 Ibid.

4. *The Overcoming of Tragedy* 71

Fig. 7 John Flaxman, illustration of Dante, *Inferno*, Canto 33 (Rome?, 1802), showing Ugolino and his sons. Courtesy of the Master and Fellows of Trinity College, Cambridge.

I have spent some time on Laocoon and Ugolino because I think that they provide for us important analogies for Schlegel's attitude to Shakespeare and tragedy. He never obliges us, like Lenz, by mentioning Lear and Laocoon in one breath, or indeed Ugolino and Lear. But he does show how you can, as it were, 'face up' to what is staring you starkly in the face by seeing inner structures, by referring to higher orders of cause and effect, by seeing those words that are not there in the text: 'To Humankind'.

But first of all, some facts and some chronology. Schlegel's remarks on Ugolino were, as we saw, published in 1795. In 1796, Schlegel published his programmatic essay on translating Shakespeare, in 1797, his great essay on *Romeo and Juliet*, and in the same year, 1797, he begins issuing his translation of Shakespeare. The play that ushers in the translation, with the first volume, is *Romeo and Juliet*. Not only that: in the same year again, he publishes a seven-stanza poem in *ottava rima*, a dedication to *Romeo and Juliet*. *Hamlet*, a far greater test for the translator, has to wait until 1798.

It is worth noting which plays Schlegel did translate and which he did not, in the creative burst of translation activity between 1797 and 1802: *Romeo and Juliet, Hamlet, Julius Caesar, A Midsummer Night's Dream, The Tempest, As You Like It, Twelfth Night, The Merchant of Venice* and all of the Histories except *Henry VIII*. He then puts down his pen until 1810, to issue *Richard III*, then nothing more. There are clearly some notable absentees: no *Macbeth*, no *Lear*, no *Othello*, no 'problem plays'. In a sense, he is translating those plays that appeal to the taste of his own age, or which, like *Hamlet*, have been the subject of prolonged discussion and debate. Goethe and Schiller, however, wanted the big tragedies for performance on the Weimar stage. Schiller had to do a version of *Macbeth* himself in order to meet that need. Schlegel seemed to have other priorities. (And, incidentally, Schiller's version has a special interest, in that it is one great dramatist translating another.)

Of course, the Histories are not short of tragic themes or moments of pity and terror — those deaths of children in *King John, 3 Henry VI* or *Richard III* — but the Histories have a special agenda of their own in Schlegel's thinking, one that transcends these dark points in the dramatic narrative. Schlegel is not concerned with linking the deaths of innocents in the Histories with their equivalents in the so-called Big Tragedies. When in the *Lectures on Dramatic Art and Literature* (1808) he comes to talk about the Histories, he places them very much in a political context that has resonances for his own day.

Given that *Hamlet* is the subject of several essays in German during the 1790s and indeed is a determining factor in the first part of Goethe's novel *Wilhelm Meister* in 1795–96, it is noteworthy that Schlegel's essay of 1796 has relatively little to say about the play itself or about its central character. It is, under the disguise of its title 'Some Remarks on Hamlet Occasioned by Wilhelm Meister', really Schlegel setting out his stall as a critic, and it is a statement of Schlegel's translation principles. By emphasizing how one puts Shakespeare into German, he is in effect saying: read my text, a line-by-line version, and explore that text for yourselves. The text is to be read for itself, not to be explicated.[40] Thus the evidence points to *Romeo and Juliet*, not *Hamlet*, as being for Schlegel

---

40   See the distinction drawn in this respect between Coleridge and Shakespeare by Reginald Foulkes, 'Samuel Taylor Coleridge', in *Voltaire, Goethe, Schlegel, Coleridge*, ed. by Roger Paulin, Great Shakespeareans 3 (London, New York: continuum, 2010), 128–72 (146), https://doi.org/10.5040/9781472555557.ch-004

the paradigmatic text with which to introduce Shakespeare to a wider audience, the reading public, but also the spectators in the theatre. It had, like *Hamlet*, been part of the repertoire in adapted form since the 1760s; it is the first tragedy that Schlegel translates, and it becomes, as said, the subject of an essay and a long poem.

For Schlegel, criticism is part of the creative process; it is related, as he says in the *Hamlet* essay of 1796, to the 'divine power, ability, to create for oneself'.[41] There is criticism which is merely carping and atomizing, for example Samuel Johnson's, and there is 'real criticism'[42] that enters into these workings of the spirit. Not only that: there is 'philological criticism' and there is criticism that makes connections and links and is able to see the essentials in related phenomena, what he later calls 'vermittelnde Kritik' ('criticism that crosses borders').[43] And so, as we approach the *Romeo and Juliet* essay, we may expect to see elements of the 'set piece' work of criticism. Now, there were views on *Romeo and Juliet* circulating in the group that in this same decade was to call itself 'Romantic', that Schlegel certainly knew.[44] His own brother Friedrich had stressed the antithetical nature of the play; how these antitheses are never resolved; they remind us, amid the insouciance of youth, of the general pointlessness of life itself, the emptiness of all existence. Using other images, it is a 'thunderstorm amid the full blossoms of a spring day', a 'rose, with a thorn that goes to the very core'. Schlegel's wife Caroline, who copied out the manuscript of the play for the printer, saw in it occasional 'harshness and lack of beauty'. Ludwig Tieck had noted privately that 'melancholy' and 'Schwärmerei' (a difficult word to translate, but its connotations are enthusiasm, fanciful visionary aberrations of the mind), in other words a failure to connect with reality is at the base of the play. In fact what we note is that Schlegel took a number of these images, the ones from his brother and his wife, and incorporated them into his essay, but with a different emphasis, with the sharp edges blunted, the blossoms divested of their thorns. It is therefore interesting to note what Schlegel does not say about *Romeo and Juliet*, let alone about *Hamlet*, for that matter: that the stage is littered with corpses

---

41 Schlegel, 'Etwas über Hamlet bey Gelegenheit Wilhelm Meisters', 60.
42 Ibid., 59.
43 Schlegel, *Vorlesungen über dramatische Kunst und Litteratur, Kritische Ausgabe der Vorlesungen*, IV, i, ed. by Stefan Knödler (Paderborn: Schöningh, 2018), 282.
44 See Paulin, *The Critical Reception of Shakespeare in Germany*, 288–94.

at the end, as befits the 'tale of woe'. True, Schlegel had said in 1795 in connection with Dante, that Shakespeare would never have chosen a subject like Ugolino, with its never-ending suffering. Instead, he sought resolution, essentially Herder's point of 1773. Shakespeare nevertheless confronts us with horror, with death on the stage. But Schlegel will have none of this, sharing as he does the late eighteenth century's reluctance towards such displays (Schiller, for instance, in his version of *Macbeth*, leaves out the killing of the children, and he has Macbeth's armour and crown, but not his head, borne in triumph at the end).

Schlegel[45] takes the play away from any historical context it may have (such as being an early work of Shakespeare's) and transposes it into a realm of its own, a kind of capsule, an 'inner unity' whose secrets we are to fathom, to sound (the verb he actually uses, 'ergründen', means more than that; it is related to its stem-word 'Grund', which in German has religious and mystical connotations of depth, the fathomless love of God). Into these 'inner depths', as he calls them, the critic is called to descend, not to be content with surface analysis and 'conventional explanations'.[46] True, the play rests on a conflict, an antithesis, the feud between the two houses, but Schlegel is concerned to mitigate the effects of this dissonance: words like lyrical, tender, sacred, true, mild, determine his discourse, despite the necessary acknowledgment of reality and the sense of a fate that is intent on frustrating this tender, spring-like love. And so Schlegel has the lovers inhabiting a sphere where nothing matters but love, a place inaccessible to reason, where their actions, their language, the very mannerisms of love, their sense of being wrapped up in themselves are everything; not the pressing realities of life 'out there', not the malevolence of some higher agencies. He can exonerate the lovers, as living in a capsule of their own, speaking language that only they understand and which even in its extravagances was for them natural and appropriate. It was, one might say, a Petrarchan reading that removed the negative connotations of the word 'conceit', that made this poetic language 'right'; it was not evidence that the lovers had lost all sense of dimension and proportion. Of course, Schlegel cannot deny the tragic outcome: but the play, he emphasizes, despite everything, ends in reconciliation; it does not end abruptly, but on a note of circularity,

---

45 'Ueber Shakespeare's Romeo und Julia', *Die Horen*, 3. Jg. (1797), 6. Stück, 18–48.
46 Ibid., 24.

in that the asperities with which it began are now overcome and the 'course of things' may begin again.

Schlegel's poem of the same year, 'Zueignung des Trauerspiels Romeo und Julia'/'Dedication of the Tragedy Romeo and Juliet',[47] is less well-known. Free of the element of critical commentary, it concentrates even more than the essay on the good and positive things that *Romeo and Juliet* stand for, their loss of self in love, their heedlessness of the outside world, their triumph over adversity, the inventiveness of their love, their union of body and soul. Their language, not governed by real constraints, seeks extreme and extravagantly polar expression. Their love, though fleeting, is nevertheless fulfilled; they are to be admired, not merely pitied, because they found the joy that is given to the gods ('Götterwonne'). It is fleeting and brief, but not evanescent, in that the lovers still stand for the fulfilment of the moment; it is not all inconstancy and frailty: as lovers, they enter 'heaven's gate'.

And yet they die. Forces are marshalled against them that frustrate even the purest and most fulfilled of loves. Shakespeare, as we know, has a whole range of expressions for this: calamity, happy, misfortune, hanging in the stars, and the like. Schlegel the translator does not have this array at his disposal, and so the words in German that he chooses have a monosyllabic finality about them: 'Glück', 'Noth', balancing the 'Lieb' and 'Leiden'.[48] Despite this linguistic insistence on the lexis of fate and death, we are told that Romeo's and Juliet's love did last in the face of fate or fortune. They did know that state where, as the poem declares, 'Love drowns in bliss inside its very chalice',[49] but even that love must in the end be extinguished.

If Schlegel's choice among Shakespeare's tragedies falls on one that in his terms can demonstrate a reconciliation beyond tragedy, this is also the case when he comes in 1802–03 to speak of the tragedy of the Greeks. He is now lecturing to an audience in Berlin on the history of poetry. He must face up to the terrible realities of Greek tragedy, just as he had confronted Dante's. This he indeed does: he must explicate the mythology that informs Greek tragedy, in conflict with human striving,

---

47 August Wilhelm Schlegel, *Sämmtliche Werke*, 12 vols (Leipzig: Weidmann, 1846–47), I, 35–37.
48 'Bliss', 'oppression', 'love', 'suffering'. Ibid., 36, 38 ('Glück'), 36 ('Noth'), 35, 37 ('Lieb', 'Leiden').
49 'Ertränkt sich Lieb' im Becher eigner Wonnen', ibid., 36.

and he must allude to its darkly orgiastic beginnings. Significantly, his preference falls on Sophocles, and on the Oedipus trilogy, not so much on the *Oedipus Rex*, with its story of murder, incest, suicide and blinding, but on the *Oedipus at Colonus*, the sequel as it were, for Schlegel the resolution, the harmonization of dissonances that were so strident in the earlier part of the play. He does not see only starkness and bleakness; instead, we have the 'mildness of humanity', as the Furies lead the hero away from the horror into a blissful grove, where the tragic effect is diminished — or so he would have us believe.[50]

The same applies to Schlegel's so-called Vienna *Lectures on Dramatic Art and Literature*, 1808 (published 1809–11) where he discusses the full range of Shakespeare's plays. When Schlegel comes to treat *Romeo and Juliet* in this framework, he does little more than rehearse what he had had so say in 1797, but more succinctly: reunion beyond the grave, purity of heart, gentleness of spirit, an idealistic canvas, triumph over the forces that separate them, a 'sigh that never ends'.[51] This is romantic vocabulary (with a small r). In 1797, as we saw, there was no question of relating this play to its tragic neighbours. In his Lectures, Schlegel must now do this, and we sense that he does it only because he must. After the section on *Romeo and Juliet* comes that on *Othello*. The red skies of dawn that in *Romeo and Juliet* announce the storm of a sultry spring day, give way to the dark and sombre colours of *Othello*. Desdemona's love, while noble and innocent, cannot match Juliet's. Othello's defiance of Venice he does liken to the feud of the Montagues and Capulets, but whereas language is adequate to describe the exemplary love of Romeo and Juliet, 'no rhetoric is capable of expressing the destructive force of the catastrophe in Othello', 'which in one moment plumbs the abysses of eternity'.[52] *Hamlet* leaves Schlegel with a distinctly uneasy feeling about the character of the hero, and the fate of humans caught up in this tragic conflict is likened to an enormous sphinx, ready to tear into the abyss all those who cannot solve her riddles.[53] Both tragedies are about

---

50 August Wilhelm Schlegel, *Kritische Ausgabe der Vorlesungen*, ed. by Ernst Behler et al., 4 vols (Paderborn, etc.: Schöningh, 1989-), I [Vorlesungen über Ästhetik I 1798–1803], 745.
51 'Unendlicher Seufzer'. Schlegel, *Vorlesungen über dramatische Kunst und Litteratur*, 330.
52 Ibid., 331.
53 Ibid., 335.

4. The Overcoming of Tragedy   77

inexpressibility, about forces that consign humans to the nether regions, mysterious, uncontrollable.

What of *Macbeth*?[54] Schiller, Schlegel says, was wrong to make the witches into Greek Furies, thus mitigating what is by nature obscene and magical and inexplicable. Yet Schlegel is prepared to alleviate the starkness. He is not above comparing the workings of fate in *Macbeth* with those of the ancient dramatists. The natural heroism of Macbeth's character is not extinguished by his crimes. In the same way as Aeschylus and Sophocles wrote their tragedies to their greater glory of the Greek state of Athens, so the story of *Macbeth* has national connotations.[55] With *King Lear*, hardly finding adequate words to express his revulsion at the horrors piled one on top of the other, Schlegel nevertheless sees a moment of light in the chaos and darkness and points to Cordelia, who shares the same beauty of soul ('Seelenschönheit') as Sophocles' Antigone.[56]

Schlegel needs desperately to be able to save something of common humanity out of a world of moral and political disorder. Hence his recourse to Greek tragedy in the case of *Macbeth* and *Lear*. For *Romeo and Juliet*, however, the qualities are innate to the play itself; the characters have their own sets of values with their own validity and congruences. We may — by analogy — read moral greatness and obliviousness to fate into the writhings of Laocoon; we may see a banner with 'To Humanity' as Ugolino and his sons and grandsons starve to death. In the same way, though fate seems to ordain otherwise, we may read into *Romeo and Juliet* a reconciliation and a love that has its own validity in the face of adversity.

---

54 Ibid., 336–39.
55 Ibid., 339.
56 Ibid., 341.

Fig. 8 [Karl Gottlieb Hofmann], *Pantheon der Deutschen*, 3 parts (Chemnitz: Karl Gottlieb Hofmann, 1794–1800), part 2 (1795), frontispiece and title page.

5. Adding Stones to the Edifice

Patterns of German Biography[1]

Despite disavowals in its country of origin, there is such a thing as a great German biographical tradition. Why, then, do we not hear more of it, and what has happened meanwhile to the art of biography in the German-speaking lands? Inevitably, comparisons are made with the Anglo-Saxon tradition of biographical writing and scholarship. These are of only limited help. For German comment on Anglo-Saxon literary or scholarly traditions tends to notice only two things. One is the sense of continuity, the unbroken succession of literary modes, the straightforward acceptance of institutions that are deemed satisfactory and that 'work'. The other is a certain lack of depth or bottom, a tendency to dwell on the surface, even to pursue readability and general accessibility at the expense of high seriousness and reflection. Thus, in the art of biography, the Anglo-Saxons, it is said, get on with the business of writing, insouciant of charges of reductionism or positivism, and even deserve a measure of grudging admiration for such moving and doing.

The Germans, it is maintained, do not have such an uninhibited relationship to past traditions in any field of intellectual endeavour.

---

1   An earlier version of this chapter is found in *Mapping Lives. The Uses of Biography*, ed. by Peter France and William St Clair (London: The British Academy; Oxford: Oxford University Press, 2002), 103–14. Since I wrote this chapter, a whole new wave of biography has emerged in Germany, accompanied by a new critical assessment of theory and practice. This chapter thus reflects another important aspect of literary reception: changes in attitude and taste. See Christian Klein, *Grundlagen der Biographik. Theorie und Praxis des biographischen Schreibens* (Stuttgart: Metzler, 2002) and Christian Klein, ed., *Handbuch Biographie. Methoden, Traditionen, Theorien* (Stuttgart: Metzler, 2009) and my reviews of both of these books, *Modern Language Review* 99 (2004), 119f. and 106 (2011), 607–09.

© 2021 Roger Paulin, CC BY 4.0   https://doi.org/10.11647/OBP.0258.05

Political considerations are made partly responsible for this. While one should not lightly underestimate their effects, they are not the only factors for discontinuity. In purely formal terms, biography has never been fully accepted into the scheme of German poetics. To some extent, the answer lies in the nature of the German biographical tradition itself. It has always been seen as part of historiography, so that its development belongs rather to 'Wissenschaftsgeschichte' ('History of Science') than to belles-lettres. Thus, Thomas Carlyle belongs fairly and squarely to English literature as well as to historical writing, whereas Leopold von Ranke, the most readable of the German historian-biographers, does not.

Then there is the function of this biographical tradition. It is not just the record of great names, but a hierarchy of cultural role models, canonical literary figures and representative individuals. As a determiner of national moral values — spiritual and political — it does more than merely memorialize. It is one of the many intellectual institutions before 1871 that speak for a German nation not yet politically in being but which coalesces in cultural terms around a shared linguistic and historical heritage. 'Representatives of the nation' can thus become focal points for all kinds of aspirations not yet underwritten by actual political institutions. Gustav Schwab's much-read biography of Friedrich Schiller,[2] for example, aligns itself with a visible sign of national greatness, the first statue erected to the poet's memory, in 1840. And it is not by chance that so many German liberal aspirations before 1871 centred on public celebrations of Schiller's life and works, of which biographies are one important manifestation.[3]

It is also not fortuitous that the great age of the German biography is roughly 1830–90, spanning the period that gave us works as disparate as Johann Gustav Droysen's life of Alexander the Great (1833),[4] Herman Grimm's of Michelangelo (1860–63),[5] Ranke's of Wallenstein (1869),[6] and Erich Schmidt's of Gothold Ephraim Lessing (1884–92),[7] the years leading through reaction and revolution up to the 'Gründerzeit'

---

2 Gustav Schwab, *Schiller's Leben in drei Büchern* (Stuttgart: Liesching, 1840).
3 Thomas Nipperdey, *Deutsche Geschichte 1800–1866: Bürgerwelt und starker Staat* (Munich: Beck, 1984), 722.
4 Johann Gustav Droysen, *Geschichte Alexander des Grossen* (Berlin, Finke, 1833).
5 Herman Grimm, *Leben Michelangelo's* (Hanover: Rümpler, 1860–63).
6 Leopold von Ranke, *Geschichte Wallenstein's* (Leipzig: Duncker & Humblot, 1869).
7 Erich Schmidt, *Lessing: Geschichte seines Lebens und seiner Schriften*, 2 vols (Berlin: Weidmann 1884–92).

('founding period') of the Second Empire and its apogee. All relate in their several ways to these processes and refer to them. Droysen reflects on the nature of the 'monarchic organism',[8] Grimm on the role of great men in the events of history, Ranke similarly on the relationship of the individual to the general development of an epoch, Schmidt on the emergence of German literary culture. Each one is a kind of monumental 'Representative Man' for which Carlyle's *The Life of Friedrich Schiller* (1825) provided an early model. This would link the German biography to the high seriousness of the Victorians. But the German biographies also reflect the nineteenth century's awareness that the Life forms an entity in itself around an 'organizing centre'[9] that aggregates and co-ordinates the individual events that befall it. In that sense, nineteenthcentury biographers are heirs to the insight, enshrined in German idealist and Romantic thought, that the individual is the visible and tangible representative of the total forces — intellectual, moral, historical — of an age or culture. Thus the Life and the Works reflect one another, support each other, and in the final analysis bear the same relation to the 'Ganzes', the totality.

Seen in these terms, the German biographical tradition might appear to be the product of national liberalism, its function to annex the lives of the great for the sake of overarching cultural and political ends. Schmidt's monumental life of Lessing could serve as a prime example. It is not for the faint-hearted: it is huge, 'philological', painstaking, supremely 'wissenschaftlich', and it sets the capstone (if that is the right image for so weighty a work) on nearly a century's proclamation of Lessing as the founder of modern German literature and thought.

But had the biography, the heir to both positivism and historicism, become crushed under the weight of its erudition? Friedrich Nietzsche, speaking of a 'biographical epidemic',[10] seemed to think so. And others, who shared Nietzsche's disdain for diligent philology as an end in itself and applauded his remarks on mere progress or utilitarianism — the

---

8   Droysen, *Geschichte*, 538.
9   Wilhelm Dilthey's phrase, 'die organisierende Mitte', quoted in Ulfert Ricklefs, 'Leben und Schrift: Autobiographische und biographische Diskurse. Ihre Intertextualität in Literatur und Literaturwissenschaft', *Editio: Internationales Jahrbuch für Editionswissenschaft*, 9 (1995), 37–62 (47).
10 Friedrich Nietzsche, *Werke*, ed. by Karl Schlechta, 3 vols (Munich: Hanser, 1969), III, 366.

harnessing of art or scholarship to an 'official' culture — would have concurred. Instead, if there were to be 'Lives', they must be of the aristocrats of the mind, representing timeless poetic genius; they should be sufficient in themselves, adequate in their powers of utterance, beholden to no tradition; they should transcend mere influence and be explicable only in terms of the epoch on which they stamped their individuality — figures such as Johann Wolfgang Goethe, Ludwig van Beethoven or Richard Wagner. The German biographical tradition comes to an end as it bifurcates into accounts of unapproachable genius (e.g. Friedrich Gundolf's studies of Caesar, Shakespeare, Goethe or Stefan George) or popular (and immensely readable) accounts by the likes of Emil Ludwig or Stefan Zweig.

All along, however, the biography had had a competitor in the form of the scholarly apparatus to those historical-critical editions, or the volumes of edited correspondence, that are in many ways the greatest German contribution to scholarship. There is an unwillingness to make this corpus of material readily available to the non-specialist reader, an unease at the potential loss of scholarly standards. There are inhibitions at material being allowed to float freely in the narrative mode. A good example would be August Wilhelm Schlegel, of whom there has never been a biography: Schlegel, companion to Madame de Staël, following her from Coppet to St Petersburg and back, whose *Vorlesungen über dramatische Kunst und Literatur/Lectures on Dramatic Art and Literature* had proclaimed Romantic doctrine 'from Cadiz to Edinburgh, Stockholm and St Petersburg'.[11] Comtesse Jean de Pange, coming from another biographical tradition (and perhaps a little too close to its André Maurois wing) documented Staël and Schlegel.[12] But Germany has produced volume after volume of edited correspondence, its apparatus fairly bristling with biographical facts. Schlegel was captious, vain (Byron disliked him, a sure sign), generally unattractive as a person (so was Staël), but his Life has never been structured or documented except through the letters. This is not an isolated example.[13]

---

11 Georg Hirzel, 'Ungedruckte Briefe an Georg Andreas Reimer', *Deutsche Revue*, XVIII (Oct.-Dec. 1893), 98–114, 238–53 (249).

12 Comtesse Jean de Pange, *Auguste-Guillaume Schlegel et Madame de Staël d'après des documents inédits* (Paris: Albert, 1938).

13 When I originally wrote this article in 2002, I little knew that I was to write the first extended biography of Schlegel. See Roger Paulin, *The Life of August Wilhelm Schlegel. Cosmopolitan of Art and Poetry* (Cambridge: Open Book Publishers, 2016), https://doi.org/10.11647/OBP.0069

After 1945, commentators were in fairly broad agreement that there was no going back to what many now claimed was a nineteenth-century discipline, although many of the older biographies remained in print.[14] Friedrich Sengle's *Wieland* (1949) remained for long the only large-scale literary biography combining readability, empiricism and scholarly reassessment.[15] It has not found many successors, if any. German biographies often are anti-biographies, breaking with older, discredited conventions, amalgams of fiction and autobiography. The conventional form requires some sense of conviction. Thus, in the eyes of one critic (and historian of biography), Golo Mann's splendid *Wallenstein* (1971) takes us little further than the nineteenth century![16] This remark was not intended to be a compliment: it was not the same as a modern Anglo-Saxon biographer hearing a flattering comparison with Elizabeth Gaskell or Hallam Tennyson. It illustrates the discontinuous and problematic tradition of historical or literary biography in Germany. Indeed, the potential German biographer might instead be told that he or she is breaking taboos, is entering a terrain not accessible to theory or scholarly criticism, is challenging modern anti-narrative positions, is positing an 'individual' where Freud or Foucault have told us that there is, properly speaking, no such thing. Above all, he or she may learn that this kind of thing is best left to the Anglo-Saxons and their tradition of the Lives of the Poets.[17] While I do not rate highly the chances of a revival of German biographical writing, I am encouraged by an increasing willingness to explore what there once was. The rest of this chapter therefore focuses on one aspect of that 'German biographical tradition', one that involves the relationship between hagiography and national literary canon.

---

14 Such as Droysen, Herman Grimm or Carl Justi. I pointed this out in my review of Klein, *Handuch Biographie* in *Modern Language Review*, 106 (2011), 609.

15 Friedrich Sengle, *Wieland* (Stuttgart: Metzler, 1949).

16 Helmut Scheuer, 'Biographie: Überlegungen zu einer Gattungsbeschreibung', in *Vom Anderen und vom Selbst: Beiträge zu Fragen der Biographie und Autobiographie*, ed. by Reinhold Grimm and Jost Hermand (Königstein im Taunus: Athenäum, 1982), 9–29 (10).

17 See esp. Gerhart von Graevenitz, 'Geschichte aus dem Geist des Nekrologs: Zur Begründung der Biographie im 19. Jahrhundert', *Deutsche Vierteljahrsschrift für Literaturwissenschaft und Geistesgeschichte*, 54 (1980), 105–70 (105–10); Ernst Ribbat, 'Der Dichter und sein Monograph: Zu den Aussichten einer fragwürdigen Gattung', in *Germanistik: Forschungsstand und Perspektiven* (*Vorträge des Deutschen Germanistentages 1984*, 2. Teil. *Ältere Deutsche Literatur. Neuere Deutsche Literatur*, ed. by Georg Stötzel (Berlin, New York: De Gruyter, 1985), 589–99. Fortunately, these commentators have been proved wrong (see footnote 1).

The emergence of German literary biography — Lives of the Poets — in the late eighteenth century has to be seen in the context of a national identity that was not fully realized until three or four generations later. Its background is a tentatively emerging national canon, centred on but a few commanding figures. There was, of course, agreement on a supranational canon — Homer, Dante, Tasso, Ariosto, Shakespeare, Cervantes, Ossian — but Germany had produced nothing commensurate. The different critical schools in the German-speaking lands could not agree on indigenous models. Outstanding figures were few. The many lives of Martin Luther — some fifty between 1546 and the end of the eighteenth century — reflected the concentration of German spiritual and intellectual culture in the Protestant heartlands; while Joachim von Sandrart's memorialization of Albrecht Dürer accorded a German painter a pre-eminent status, akin to Raphael or Michelangelo.[18] Much of the biographical activity of the period was, in any case, conducted in the spirit of learned compendia or necrologies. One might have to search diligently among the dross to find nuggets of excellence.

Where individual names did provide the focus for an emergent literary canon, other traditions of biography had to be invoked. The first German poet to become part of this new canon was Friedrich Gottlieb Klopstock, the author of *Der Messias* (1749–73) and as such the most translated German author of the eighteenth and nineteenth centuries. In Klopstock converge the Homeric, the Miltonic, the Youngian, all strands of 'original composition'. But this achievement can only be fused with the Life through another strain of biography: hagiography. It is, of course, no longer veneration per se, but the structuring and schematizing of a life around considerations of edification, amplification and transfiguration. The rich seam of pietism can be tapped and merged with the inspirational theory of poetry and the aspirations of national cultural renewal. Thus, Klopstock is also the first major modern German poet to be the subject of a biography during his own lifetime.[19] And it is Klopstock more than any

---

[18] Joachim von Sandrart, 'Albrecht Dürer Mahler/Bildhauer/Kupferstecher und Baumeister von Nürnberg', in *L'Academia Todesca delle Architectura, Scultura & Pittura: Oder Deutsche Academie der Edlen Bau- Bild- und Mahlerey-Kunste*, 2 vols (Nuremberg: Miltenberger, 1675–79), I., II. Theils III. Buch, III. Capitel, 222–29.

[19] Carl Friedrich Cramer, *Klopstock: Er, und über ihn*, 5 vols (Hamburg: Schniebes, Dessau: Gelehrten Buchhandlung; Leipzig and Altona: Kaven, 1780–92).

other canonical figure who receives the accolade of 'divine',[20] analogous to the Renaissance 'alter deus' or 'divino artista' but now harnessed to the religious connotations of genius. Like the prophetic patriarch Edward Young, to whom Klopstock had once addressed an early ode, age and venerability (Klopstock lived to be seventy-nine) go hand in hand with the biblical virtues which his Life illustrates.

The 'minor canonizations' — in the form of biographical prefaces — of poets from the Klopstock circle who died young and without the fulfilment of age show a similar insistence on the association of life and works.[21] It informs much of the discussion of individual poets or artists as suitable models for a literature that is not merely national in name but which illustrates the national virtues (also sung by Klopstock) of honesty, loyalty or forthrightness of mind. Schiller's stringent review of the works of the *Sturm und Drang* ('Storm and Stress') poet Gottfried August Bürger (1791) also makes this link, placing severe obligations on the poet's individuality if he is to rise to the supreme challenge of reflecting humanity as a whole. And the Romantic imitation of Giorgio Vasari, Wilhelm Heinrich Wackenroder and Ludwig Tieck's *Herzensergiessungen eines kunstliebenden Klosterbruders/Heart's Outpourings of a Lay Brother Devoted to Art* (1796) regarded all personal aberrations or freakishness as a barrier to ultimate artistic greatness.

Klopstock's life centred on the fulfilment of *Der Messias*. After his death, the religious poet and his epic poem could merge in symbiotic form under the heading 'representative of the German nation'.[22] The same could not, however, be said for Lessing. Lessing had died in 1781, not much over fifty. In contrast to Klopstock, he had led a shifting and unstable existence, subject to exigencies and deprivations, some of his own making, often due to his generosity. Yet his life, too, could be made to suit the record of his works, an achievement which an early biographer saw fit to compare with Christopher Columbus's or James Cook's.[23]

---

20 'Von diesem Göttlichen'. See Klamer Schmidt, ed., *Klopstock und seine Freunde* (Halberstadt: Bureau für Literatur und Kunst, 1810), iv.
21 As in the biographical prefaces to the works of Nikolas Dietrich Giseke (1767) and Ludwig Heinrich Christoph Hölty (1783).
22 As the preface to his works states: Friedrich Gottlieb Klopstock, *Sämmtliche Werke*, 10 vols (Leipzig, 1854–55 [1844–45]), I, xxx.
23 Johann Friedrich Schink, 'Charakteristik Gotthold Ephraim Lessings', in *Pantheon der Deutschen*, ed. by Karl Gottlieb Hofmann, 3 vols (Chemnitz, Leipzig: Hofmann, 1794–1795), II, 1–192 (5f.).

Even so, the individual uniqueness of Lessing's life could be subsumed under the commonplaces of hagiography and the cult of genius. While Klopstock's works would, in the eyes of his contemporaries, be dominated by the supreme *Messias*, much of Lessing's oeuvre remained to be revealed. Thus the first Lessing biography is a two-volume introduction to works not published during his lifetime.[24] The works therefore suspend the arbitrariness and relative brevity of the life. In the extraordinary letter from Moses Mendelssohn to Lessing's brother, with which the first volume of the life ends, his achievement is likened to Nicolaus Copernicus, who 'discovered a new system, and died'.[25] He had achieved everything in the realm of the senses and had passed into the supersensory realm: 'Like the sons of the prophets, they looked in wonderment at the place from which he went up and was seen no more'.[26] The Jewish hagiography (II Kings 2, 11) — easily merged with its Christian counterpart — equates acceptance into the canon with Elijah's translation in the whirlwind. It is too good a quotation for Johann Friedrich Schink, Lessing's next biographer, to miss and he duly repeats it.[27] But Schink's concern as a biographer is couched in terms of a different, if ultimately also religious, image, that of the monument. Indeed, his biography forms part of a three-volume *Pantheon der Deutschen/Pantheon of the Germans*, and his stated task is to add 'a few stones to the edifice begun by German patriotism, leaving the columns themselves to posterity'.[28] Schink's biography stands free of the works themselves (it is he who is prepared to press the analogies with Columbus and Cook). But to fulfil the patterns of edification, to make the life appear more exemplary and yet more humanly accessible, he adds two plates: one shows the young Lessing's obedience to his parents, the other his integrity as a pursuer of truth, and both are as such obliquely hagiographic.

Both Klopstock and Lessing enter the canon foremost as German writers in an established German line of achievement. 'He stands as the first column of German originality',[29] states an early nineteenth-century

---

24   *Gotthold Ephraim Lessings Leben, nebst seinem noch übrigen litterarischen Nachlasse*, ed. by K. G. Lessing, 3 vols (Berlin: Voss, 1793–95).
25   Ibid., I, 451.
26   Ibid., I, 452.
27   Schink, 'Charakteristik Gotthold Ephraim Lessings', 192.
28   Ibid., 7.
29   [K. Nicolai], *Klopstock: Ein Denkmahl zur Säcularfeier seines Geburtstages am zweiten Julius 1824* (Quedlinburg: Basse, 1824), 6.

Klopstock biography, also finding the monumental image congenial. They illustrate how language and culture establish national bonds, not the scattered multiplicity of political institutions that called themselves the 'German lands'. Part of the anecdotal — and incidental — material on Klopstock's and Lessing's lives recounts how they moved as equals among kings and princes, yet spurned preferments that might inhibit their genius. (This would overlook the negative role of Frederick the Great in the establishment of German literature, or the hopes both placed in the young reforming emperor Joseph II.) It is a variation on Renaissance commonplaces, relevant to readers aware that it was culture, and not so much rulers, that held the nation together. Christoph Martin Wieland, a contemporary of Lessing and Klopstock, found less automatic entry into the German literary pantheon. For some, he might appear too cosmopolitan to deserve the accolade of 'deutscher Dichter' ('German poet'). But the nearly thousand-page biography which his editor, Johann Gottfried Gruber, appended to his edition of the works, removes such doubts by recounting Wieland's meeting with Napoleon in 1806.[30] They converse on the basis of equality, not deference; worldly authority (it is just after the battles of Jena and Auerstädt) acknowledges the power of the intellect — across national borders. Again, this somewhat implausible point is too good for others to miss. Schiller's sister-in-law Caroline von Wolzogen, in her biography of 1830, embellishes his life-story with the fantasy that Schiller, had he lived, would have encountered the 'world conqueror' with equal dignity and composure,[31] as the representative of 'Humanität' ('Humanity'). (It is also a tactical ploy to get round Schiller's marked progression from

---

30   J. G. Gruber, *C. M. Wielands Leben*, 4 vols (Leipzig: Göschen, 1827–28), IV, 420–28. This forms vols L-LIII of *Sämmtliche Werke*, 53 vols (Leipzig: Göschen, 1824–28). There is a venerable tradition for this. We learn for instance how the great scholars Selmasius, Lipsius and Heinsius were fêted by potentates and kings but remained true to their métier. Adolphus Clarmundus, [Johann Christoph Rüdiger], *VITAE CLARISSIMORUM in re literaria Virorum. Das ist Lebens-Beschreibung etlicher Hauptgelehrten Männer/so von der Literatur profeß gemacht. Worinnen Viel sonderbahre und notable Sachen/ so wohl von ihren Leben/als geführten Studiis entdecket. Allen curieusen Gemüthern zu sonderbahrem Nutzen und Vergnügen entworffen/von ADOLPHO CLARMUNDO.* (Wittenberg: Christian Gottlieb Ludwig, 1704–05).

31   [Caroline von Wolzogen], *Schillers Leben, verfaßt aus Erinnerungen der Familie, seinen eigenen Briefen und den Nachrichten seines Freundes Körner*, 2 vols (Stuttgart,Tübingen: Cotta, 1830), II, 297. Cf. Lesley Sharpe, '"Wahrheit allein sollte mich leiten": Caroline von Wolzogen's Schiller Biography', *Publications of the English Goethe Society*, 68 (1999), 70–81.

rebellious and antiauthoritarian youth to respect for crowned heads in maturity.)

The biographical commonplaces — of hagiography, of traditional panegyric, of the 'divino artista' — that accompany this early stage of German Lives of the Classical Poets, can be concentrated so as to make life and works one 'single entity', one 'symbolic form', one 'individuality'. These are phrases taken from Friedrich Schlegel's *Ueber Lessing/About Lessing* of 1801,[32] not a biography as such, but a 'Charakteristik', the attempt to reduce to their essentials the adventitious and cluttered details of personality and writings. This symbolic unity is the ideal, not the norm or the reality: 'the golden age of literature will be when prefaces are no longer needed' (one might say, biographical introductions).[33] As yet, however, the Life was deemed necessary as an accompaniment or corroboration of the Works.

Shortly after Schlegel's essay on Lessing, Goethe attempted something similar to this 'Charakteristik'. He, too, was concerned to elevate his subject, the art historian Johann Joachim Winckelmann, to canonical status. He had no less serious a purpose than had Lessing's or Klopstock's sponsors. As an account of the father of modern European Neoclassicism, it is not free of an ideological or even polemical — anti-Romantic — intention. But it records that Germany's greatest living poet saw the function of biography as a means of making a public statement. His *Skizze zu einer Schilderung Winckelmanns/Sketch towards a Description of Winckelmann* (1805) is not free-standing, but forms the introduction to a collection of Winckelmann's letters. Goethe's approach is different from Schlegel's, in that it refers less to 'das Ganze', the whole,[34] than to a series of abstract categories, superimposed on the mass of biographical detail ('ancient art', 'friendship', 'beauty', 'Rome', 'passing'). They structure a life that already conforms in some respects to hagiographic patterns (humble origins overcome through higher intervention leading to career and ultimate apotheosis). We do not read the essay to be

---

32 Friedrich Schlegel, 'Ueber Lessing', in *Charakeristiken und Kritiken*, ed. by August Wilhelm Schlegel and Friedrich Schlegel, 2 vols (Königsberg: Nicolovius, 1801), I, 170–270: 'Beziehungen aufs Ganze', 266; 'symbolische Form', 263; 'Individualität', 193.
33 Ibid., 124.
34 Cf. Hans-Martin Kruckis, '*Ein potenziertes Abbild der Menschheit': Biographischer Diskurs und Etablierung der Neugermanistik in der Goethe-Biographik bis Gundolf*, Probleme der Dichtung 24 (Heidelberg: Winter, 1995), 47.

informed of the mere facts of Winckelmann's life: there is not a single date in the text. Such account of the life as there is, and of its various stages, is determined completely by the work, and not vice versa: 'everything that he produces is extraordinary and estimable because his character was revealed in item'.[35] Goethe embellishes and harmonizes. Like Raphael, Winckelmann dies at the apogee of his career: the squalid circumstances of his life in Rome and especially of his death (he was robbed and murdered in Trieste) are passed over. Instead, we have this extraordinary final section:

> So war er denn auf der höchsten Stufe des Glücks, das er sich nur hätte wünschen dürfen, der Welt verschwunden. Ihn erwartete sein Vaterland, ihm streckten seine Freunde die Arme entgegen, alle Äußerungen der Liebe, deren er sehr bedurfte, alle Zeugnisse der öffentlichen Achtung, auf die er so viel Wert legte, warteten seiner Erscheinung, um ihn zu überhäufen. Und in diesem Sinne dürfen wir ihn wohl glücklich preisen, daß er von dem Gipfel des menschlichen Daseins zu den Seligen emporgestiegen, daß ein kurzer Schrecken, ein schneller Schmerz ihn von den Seinigen hinweggenommen. Die Gebrechen des Alters, die Abnahme der Geisteskräfte hat er nicht empfunden, die Zerstreuung der Kunstschätze, die er obgleich in in einem andern Sinne, vorausgesagt, ist nicht vor seinen Augen geschehen. Er hat als ein Mann gelebt, und ist als ein vollständiger Mann von hinnen gegangen. Nun genießt er im Andenken der Nachwelt den Vorteil, als ein ewig Tüchtiger und Kräftiger zu erscheinen, denn in der Gestalt, wie der Mensch die Erde verläßt, wandelt er unter den Schatten, und so bleibt uns Achill als ewig strebender Jüngling gegenwärtig.[36]

---

35   'Daß alles dasjenige, was er hervorbringt, hauptsächlich deswegen merkwürdig und schätzenswert ist, weil sein Charakter sich immer dabei offenbart'. Johann Wolfgang Goethe, 'Winckelmann und sein Jahrhundert', *Sämtliche Werke*, 18 vols (Zurich: Artemis, 1977), XIII, 407–50 (443).

36   'Thus, at the summit of the good fortune he could only have wished for himself, he was removed from this world. His native country was expecting him, his friends awaited him with outstretched arms, all the expressions of affection, so essential to him, all the terms of public recognition, so important for him, waited for his advent, to overwhelm him. And in this sense we may call him fortunate, that he has gone up from the summit of human existence to join the immortals, that a brief moment of terror, a quick second of pain snatched him away from the living. He did not experience the infirmities of age, the diminution of his intellectual powers; the dispersal of art treasures, that he said would happen, if perhaps in another sense, did not occur before his eyes. He lived as a man, and as a man at the height of his powers he has departed this life. Now in the memory of those he has left behind he enjoys the good fortune of appearing always forceful and worthy through and through: for in the shape that a man leaves the world, so he walks

That remarkable image of Achilles, like its biblical equivalent in the lives of Lessing, was not to be restricted to Winckelmann alone. Goethe is clearly making a legend of Winckelmann, laying down the essentials of artistic existence and their application. Winckelmann becomes a symbol, in that Goethe fuses the particular, the Life, with the ancient world and its afterlife, the general. It comes therefore as no surprise to find Goethe's Achilles passage invoked as part of much more potent cultural myth-making: Gustav Schwab's life of Schiller (1840). It belongs to the retouching of detail which is so necessary for the construction of literary monuments. The quotation is (correctly) attributed to Goethe and dated 1805, the year of its appearance and also of Schiller's death.[37] The biographer must somehow reconcile Goethe's attested close friendship with Schiller with his failure to attend Schiller's funeral. Goethe, as is well known, hated the panoply associated with death and could not bring himself to join the sparse number of mourners at Schiller's hurried burial. The resourceful Schwab makes a virtue out of necessity by stating that 'Goethe stepped forward and spoke to the nation'.[38] But Schwab is merely continuing a hagiography that had even extended to Schiller when living. He recounts the false report of Schiller's death in 1791, which had caused his Danish friends to create a secular memorial around 'Freude, schöner Götterfunken',[39] and later to rejoice at the 'resurrection of our immortal and deathless Schiller'.[40] Such veneration and legend-making moves effortlessly among the mythologies and cults and plucks at will the images needed for its purposes.

While Lessing and Klopstock found general acceptance in terms of the symbolic unity of life and works, other figures had a less easy passage into canonicity. The Romantics remembered Schiller as their most implacable opponent and found little pleasure in his sanctification by biographers and editors (especially when these included Goethe and Wilhelm von Humboldt). Hearing the threnodic note of a Schiller dying at the height of his powers, they could reflect that their own movement also had its necrology and cult of remembrance, not merely those figures

---

among the shades, and thus Achilles remains ever present for us as a young man, ever striving'. Ibid., 450.
37 'Vor die Nation aber trat Göthe und sprach'. Schwab, *Schiller's Leben*, 633f.
38 Ibid., 663.
39 'Joy, thou lovely spark immortal', ibid., 366f.
40 'von des unsterblichen und ungestorbenen Schillers Auferstehung', ibid., 368.

now being enthroned by Goethe and his Weimar acolytes. Ludwig Tieck, as the senior surviving poet of German Romanticism, wished to set the record straight — through the life-and-works approach. The opportunity was afforded by the reissue in 1815 of the works of his close friend Friedrich von Hardenberg, known as Novalis. Part of the last section of the short biography reads:

> So starb, ehe er noch das neun und zwanzigste Jahr vollendet hatte, unser Freund, an dem man eben so sehr seine ausgebreiteten Kenntnisse, sein philosophisches Genie, wie sein Dichtertalent lieben und bewundern muß. Da er seiner Zeit so vorgeeilt war, so durfte sich das Vaterland außerordentliche Dinge von ihm versprechen, wenn ihn dieser frühe Tod nicht übereilt hätte, doch haben seine unvollendeten nachgelassenen Schriften schon viel gewürkt und viele seiner großen Gedanken werden noch in Zukunft begeistern und edle Gemüther und tiefe Denker werden von den Funken seines Geistes erleuchtet und entzündet werden. [...] dem geübteren Auge aber bot er die Erscheinung der Schönheit dar. Der Umriß und der Ausdruck seines Geistes kam sehr dem Evangelisten Johannes nahe, wie wir ihn auf der herrlichen großen Tafel von A. Dürer sehn, die Nürnberg und München aufbewahrt'.⁴¹

Here artistic integrity, religious piety, national pride and genius are conflated. The reminiscence of the Dürer portrait not only invokes a Christian iconography opposed to Goethe's pagan reference to Achilles; it is a reminder of the religion of art which Tieck himself and his dead friend Wackenroder had propounded as young men, centred on Raphael and Dürer. In the same way as Goethe's vision of Winckelmann makes its subject into the exemplar of the Classicism that Goethe affirms, so Tieck fashions Novalis according to an image that stresses the Romantic poet, seer and visionary.

---

41 'Before he reached his twenty-ninth year, our friend thus died, whose extensive knowledge, philosophical genius and poetic talent one can only love and admire. He hastened ahead of his time, so that his native country ought to have expected extraordinary things from him, had this early death not overtaken him. The unfinished writings he left have been widely received and many of his great thoughts will in future still inspire, and noble minds and profound thinkers will be illumined and fired by the sparks of his intellect. [...] For the more experienced eye his aspect was one of beauty. The outline and expression of his face approached that of John the Evangelist as we see him in the wonderful great picture by A. Dürer, once to be seen in Nuremberg, now in Munich'. Ludwig Tieck, preface to the third edition of Novalis: *Schriften* (1815)', in Novalis, *Schriften. Historisch-kritische Ausgabe*, ed. by Paul Kluckhohn and Richard Samuel et al., 6 vols (Stuttgart: Kohlhammer, 1960–88), IV, 551–60 (558).

This pattern of commemoration was especially suited to writers whose brief lives denied them the canonical status of those who had had full use of their powers. Gustav Schwab's accounts of Wilhelm Müller and Wilhelm Hauff,[42] both writers who died in their twenties, conform to its general conventions. It could be turned on its head, as Tieck himself did with his biographical introduction to the works of Heinrich von Kleist.[43] Despite his admiration for Kleist's poetic talent, and his tolerant words for a writer who had taken his own life, Tieck cannot find the unity, the symbolic wholeness that Friedrich Schlegel's account of Lessing had posited. The works and the life diverge and follow patterns of their own, the one leading to the hope of future recognition, the other registering the failure of the person to fulfil the talent with which he undeniably was blessed by nature. This highly influential biographical essay is a factor in the withholding of recognition from Kleist during the nineteenth century and the denial of his place in the canon. His life and works are pulled apart; his qualities of poetic genius are countered by symbolic patterns of light and darkness. Here, Tieck is unable to employ the hagiographic patterns of explication and selective embellishment that hitherto had done service and continued to be potent forces in the establishment of a German national literary canon for the rest of the century. It is not his last word on these matters. Later in the same decade, he was wrapping these biographical devices in a fictional guise, to produce the ultimate ideal 'Life': William Shakespeare's.[44] It was intended to suit all the needs of nineteenth-century cultural ideology. Thus, not only Lessing, Klopstock or Schiller, but also the greatest English 'Representative Man' may be annexed for the purposes of national role models.

---

42 Gustav Schwab, 'Wilhelm Hauff's Leben [1827]', in Wilhelm Hauff, *Sämmtliche Werke*, ed. by Gustav Schwab, 5 vols, 5th ed. (Stuttgart: Brodhag, 1853), I, 5–20; Gustav Schwab, 'Wilhelm Müller's Leben', in Wilhelm Müller, *Vermischte Schriften*, ed. by Gustav Schwab, 5 vols (Leipzig: Brockhaus, 1830), I, xvii–lxii.

43 Heinrich von Kleist, *Hinterlassene Schriften* (Berlin: Reimer, 1821) and *Gesammelte Schriften* (Berlin: Reimer, 1826).

44 Ludwig Tieck, *Dichterleben* (1826, 1831), most accessible in Ludwig Tieck, *Schriften*, 20 vols (Berlin: Reimer, 1828–46), XVIII.

Fig. 9 Ernest Julian Stern and Heinz Herald, 'Penthesilea, Reinhardt und seine Bühne, Bilder von der Arbeit des Deutschen Theaters', 1919, Wikimedia, https://commons.wikimedia.org/wiki/File:Penthesilea_(Kleist)_-_Amazone.jpg, public domain.

6. Kleist's Metamorphoses

Some Remarks on the Use of Mythology in *Penthesilea*[1]

> Gods of the wingèd shoe!
> With them the silver hounds,
>   sniffing the trace of air!
> Haie! Haie!
>   These were the swift to harry;
> These were the keen-scented;
> These were the souls of blood.
>
> (Ezra Pound, 'The Return')[2]

It has never been exactly fashionable to talk about the sources of Heinrich von Kleist's plays. One can see why: *Amphitryon* does not make adequate sense in terms either of Plautus or Molière; *Die Hermannsschlacht/Hermann's Battle* has little essentially to do with Friedrich Gottlieb Klopstock (or Tacitus); *Prinz Friedrich von Homburg/The Prince of Homburg* very soon moves away from its already dubious historical base. We find that, even having established sources and influences, we

---

1   An earlier version of this chapter was published as 'Kleist's Metamorphoses. Some Remarks on the Use of Mythology in *Penthesilea*', *Oxford German Studies*, 14 (1983), 35–53. Kleist studies have moved on a great deal since this paper was published. Above all, the subject of metamorphosis and sacrifice has been enhanced by application of the insights of Walter Burkert, *Homo necans: Interpretationen altgriechischer Opferriten und Mythen* (Berlin: De Gruyter, 1972). Examination of Kleist's sources is, however, still not a superfluous occupation.

2   This is a much-expanded version of a paper read at Trinity College, Dublin in April, 1982. The Ezra Pound poem I include by way of acknowledgment of my debt to Mr Charles Tomlinson's Clark Lectures on the Metamorphic Tradition, given in Cambridge during the Lent Term, 1982 and published as *Poetry and Metamorphosis* (Cambridge: Cambridge University Press, 1983).

© 2021 Roger Paulin, CC BY 4.0   https://doi.org/10.11647/OBP.0258.06

are nowhere into the works, still outside their frame of reference and ignorant of the interplay of characters. Or at least one assumes this to be so. For most of the monographs on Kleist over the last two generations or so — and it is not my intention to list them — tend to discuss heroes, plot, language, feeling, fate and tragedy, without referring substantially either to Kleist the man in his times or Kleist the user of sources. Most of the discussion of his neoclassical tragedy *Penthesilea*, with some notable exceptions,[3] falls into this same category.

But even so it might not really matter. For the use of classical sources in the Classical and Romantic periods is no absolute guide to the nature of a work. Examples spring to mind. We have still a great deal to explore once we have established that Johann Wolfgang Goethe's *Iphigenie auf Tauris/Iphigenia in Tauris* is based on Euripides or that *Die Braut von Messina/The Bride of Messina* has affinities with *Oedipus Rex*. We might well recognize that these two works are more 'modern' than 'classical': that, despite the costume, neither play is 'antique'; that each has its own age's, not antiquity's, view of mythology; that there is consequently no single absolute and given 'world picture', but several; that each play is general and tends toward set formulae of expression. Having established this, however, we should be well on our way towards understanding the text: not only as a 'timeless' work but also as a product of its time;[4] as the product of a certain understanding of classical antiquity, whereby ancient myth or archetypal situation is 'metamorphosed' to suit the need of a special, later age.

---

3   For a useful discussion of the mythological sources in *Penthesilea* see Gerhard Kaiser, 'Mythos und Person in Kleists "Penthesilea"', in *Wandrer und Idylle. Goethe und die Phänomenologie der Natur in der deutschen Dichtung von Gessner bis Gottfried Keller* (Göttingen: Vandenhoek & Ruprecht, 1977), 209–39; see also Denys Dyer, 'The Imagery of Kleist's "Penthesilea"', *PEGS*, NS 31 (1960–61), 1–23; Volker Klotz, 'Tragödie der Jagd. Zu Kleists "Penthesilea", in *Kurze Kommentare zu Stücken und Gedichten*, Hessische Beiträge zur deutschen Literatur (Darmstadt: Roether, 1962), 14–21; also the relevant sections of Hilda M. Brown, *Kleist and the Tragic Ideal. A Study of Penthesilea and its Relationship to Kleist's Personal and Literary Development 1806–1808*, European University Papers I, German Language and Literature 203 (Berne, Frankfurt, Las Vegas: Lang, 1977); Albrecht Sieck, *Kleists Penthesilea. Versuch einer neuen Interpretation*, Literatur und Wirklichkeit 14 (Bonn: Bouvier, 1976).

4   Cf Friedrich Sengle, '"Die Braut von Messina"', in, *Arbeiten zur deutschen Literatur 1750–1859* (Stuttgart: Metzler, 1965), 94–117; Wolfgang Schadewaldt, 'Schillers Griechentum', in *Schiller. Reden im Gedenkjahr 1959*, ed. by Bernhard Zeller (Stuttgart: Klett, 1961), 258–70.

And yet with Kleist it seems to be different. If we try to compare *Penthesilea* with the other classicizing dramas just cited, we find irreconcilable differences, gulfs fixed, between Kleist and the traditions of Weimar. Indeed, Kleist seems to have wished it so: in a letter of February 6, 1808, Adam Müller, Kleist's collaborator in *Phöbus*, could write to Friedrich Gentz : 'Demnach ist Kleist sehr mit Ihnen zufrieden, wenn Sie von der Penthesilea sagen, dass sie nicht antik sey'.[5] *Penthesilea*, Müller avers, is not beholden to tradition; it eschews 'Ruhe' and 'Wohllaut' and 'Annehmlichkeit'[6] — the accepted bienséance of classicizing tragedy in any tradition; indeed, it deliberately does not imitate the Greeks in the manner received in *Iphigenie* or *Die Braut von Messina*. Nor even does it veer in the opposite direction; it is not Christian in the Romantic, medievalizing, sense of, say, Friedrich Schlegel's *Alarcos* or Zacharias Werner's *Attila* or Ludwig Tieck's *Genoveva*. Coming closer to the 'antik', it is not Goethe's *Pandora* or the mellifluous trimeters of Wilhelm von Schütz. Indeed, Ludwig Robert, writing in 1824 to Kleist's first editor, Tieck, remarked on the play's 'derbe Auffassung des Antiquen',[7] as if anticipating those many reactions, right up to the present day, to the supposed anti-classical, anti-*Iphigenie*, anti-*Pandora* strain of the tragedy.

It would of course depend on what one understood by 'classical'. It would also depend on the choice of subject. For *Penthesilea* is not, like *Iphigenie*, based on a single Greek original; nor is it, like *Die Braut von Messina*, a freely invented story in a framework of classical tragedy. It is known to be an adaptation of several different stories, or myths, from Greek antiquity. The dignity of the classical subject, yet the dynamic urgency towards action on or off stage, remind us, however, of Kleist's stated ambition from the outset of his career as a dramatist: his bid to conjoin Sophocles and Shakespeare, but also, with a female central character and a suitably tragic subject, to outdo Friedrich Schiller. Going back beyond the later Schiller, it would even seem to retain much of the *Sturm und Drang*'s ('Storm and Stress') active and dynamic understanding of Shakespeare, and some of that movement's energetic,

---

5   'This would make Kleist very pleased with you if you say of Penthesilea that is not antique'. Heinrich von Kleist, *Penthesilea. Dokumente und Zeugnisse*, ed. by Helmut Sembdner (Frankfurt am Main: Insel, 1967), 20. The full letter quoted in H. M. Brown, *Kleist and the Tragic Ideal*, 136–38.
6   'Calm', 'euphony', 'harmony and balance'.
7   'Crude notion of the antique'. *Penthesilea*, ed. by Sembdner, 43.

'Dionysian' attitude to classical antiquity. But all this must remain speculation until we examine the subject matter itself.

Where did Kleist find the subject in the first place? It is worth noticing first of all where he did not seek it: he did not follow the standard practice of neoclassical writers and look to Sophocles or Euripides or Seneca, not, therefore, to the lineage of Cristoph Martin Wieland's *Alceste* or Goethe's *Iphigenie* or even August Wilhelm Schlegel's *Ion*. Another possibility open to him was the extension of an existing story, and here the parallel with Goethe's epic fragment *Achilleis* springs to mind. But *Penthesilea* is, if anything, certainly not Homeric, even though it draws briefly on sources relating to the continuation of the Trojan War. Instead of a single story, Kleist seems to have taken several, disparate, mythologically seemingly unrelated elements and to have moulded them into an organic whole. The source he used — this was established generations ago — was Benjamin Hederich's *Gründliches mythologisches Lexicon/Compendious Mythological Dictionary*. I repeat this highly accessible piece of information solely because Kleist scholars only rarely draw on it.[8]

Hederich's *Lexicon* is a garrulous, ramshackle and fusty mythological compendium, an inventory of all the stories of gods and heroes that antiquity had to offer. The subtitle of the 1770 edition makes its stated function clear: 'Zu besserm Verständisse der schönen Künste und Wissenschaften nicht nur für Studierende, sondern auch viele Künstler und Liebhaber der alten Kunstwerke'.[9] Such compendia belong to the hidden stock-in-trade of so much of German Classicism. Goethe is known to have used Hederich, if not exactly to have noised the fact abroad. The continued popularity of such lexica is indicated by Goethe's former companion in Rome, Karl Philipp Moritz, producing a dictionary of mythology more in keeping with Weimar Classicism, *Götterlehre oder mythologische Dichtungen der Alten/The Gods of the Greeks and their*

---

8   The classical parallels were established in the apparatus to the first critical edition of Kleist, *Werke. Kritisch durchgesehene Gesamtausgabe*, ed. by Erich Schmidt, Georg Minde-Pouet and Reinhold Steig, 5 vols (Leipzig, Vienna: Bibliographisches Institut, 1904–05). Helmut Sembdner draws on this material in his editions of Kleist and *Penthesiliea*.

9   'For a better understanding of the fine arts and sciences not only for students but also for many artists and aficionados of the antique art works'. Benjamin Hederich, *Gründliches Mythologisches Lexicon* [...] (Leipzig: Gleditsch, 1770; repr. Darmstadt: Wissenschaftliche Buchgesellschaft, 1967).

Mythology of 1791, and interlarding its sections with suitable quotations from Goethe's poetry and from *Iphigenie*. But such a compendium on classical antiquity could only be a kind of charnel-house of dead knowledge until metamorphosed by poetry into life. Goethe makes this plain in *Faust II*, in the scene 'Laboratorium'. There, Wagner, not inspired by the essential life-giving quality of the material he has assembled in his retort, is left behind by Homunculus, not joining the great festival of mythological creatures, gods and demigods, inert and living elements, which is the 'Klassische Walpurgisnacht'.

Wagner — whose fate is to collect and collate — and the quirkily loquacious Hederich assembled much that was contradictory, superfluous or plain unsuitable. Kleist's way of dealing with them was to be the same as Goethe's: to give the disparate a symbolic unity. For if Goethe strove in the 'Klassische Walpurgisnacht' and the Helen scenes for a harmony of the Euripidean and the Baroque, the tragic and the grotesque, spirit and flesh, the Bacchic and the Winckelmannian, so Kleist in *Penthesilea* would draw — through Hederich — on Euripides and Ovid, but also on a whole host of unconnected, seemingly mutually irreconcilable material and conflate a private mythology, if one incompatible with all that Goethe's stood for.

The main points of Kleist's reading of Hederich can be summed up fairly briefly; it is their implications that are more important. We can safely assume that he found his subject in the *Lexicon*. For, even supposing that 'Amazonian' subjects were not unknown to an eighteenth century much more eclectic in its attitude to classical antiquity than is generally acknowledged,[10] it is certain that an impetuous and ambitious Kleist would not search for information which is tucked away in Hyginus and Dictys, is the subject of a sustained simile in the eleventh book of the *Aeneid*, when it is all the time conveniently related by the indefatigable Hederich. But even that obliging well of information offered different accounts from its various sources: Penthesilea, who some — indeed most — say was vanquished by Achilles, is credited in one single obscure source with having conquered and killed the hero:

> So erzählen auch wiederum andere, sie habe den Achilles erst selbst erleget , es sey aber solcher auf der Thetis, seiner Mutter, Bitten, wieder

---

10   Cf. Paul Kluckhohn, 'Penthesilea', *Germanisch-Romanische Monatsschrift* II (1914), 276–88.

lebendig geworden, und habe sodann erst die Penthesilea wieder hingerichtet.[11]

This Kleist changes. One may assume, because the myths place Achilles in the foreground; like *Das Käthchen von Heilbronn*, the play which Kleist enjoins Heinrich von Collin, in the famous letter of December 8, 1808, to see in polar relation to *Penthesilea*,[12] the man is to be but the inadequate interpreter of woman's signs and intuitions. The arrogant and heedless Graf Wetter vom Strahl is to be led to understanding by one who is as a child; the Homeric demigod is to gain intimations of a love which has no place in Homer's account.

Did Kleist's eyes then light on the next entry in Hederich, on the same page as 'PENTHESILEA': 'PENTHEVS',[13] the story of a man torn to pieces by women, recorded in Euripides' *Bacchae* and in Book Three of Ovid's *Metamorphoses*? Did he use Hederich's excellent system of cross-references, to move from PENTHEVS to the genealogical table of the descendants of Cadmus, finding that Agaue, the mother of Pentheus, was also the sister of Autinoë, the mother of the unfortunate Actaeon, another Ovidian metamorphosis of man into beast? Actaeon, whose name crosses the lips of one of the maidens bathing in Kleist's unsettling, disturbing and distinctly unpleasant attempt at a Boucher-like rococo idyll, *Der Schrecken im Bade/Fright while Bathing*,[14] and like the first Actaeon reminiscence in the original fragment of *Penthesilea*, also published in *Phöbus*? At any rate, the Amazon queen's mastiffs which 'ein grässliches Geheul anstimmen'[15] bear names taken not only from Ovid, but from Hederich's compendious list under 'ACTAEON'.[16] So, too, the monstrous account of the practices of the Amazons which Penthesilea relates to an incredulous Achilles, is, even if Kleist introduces a slightly different device for Amazonian self-mutilation, borrowed from Hederich.[17] Again — but here we enter the realm of speculation — he

---

11 'On the other hand there are sources recounting that she herself slew Achilles, but that he was restored to life at the pleading of his mother Thetis and thereupon put Penthesilea to death'. Hederich, *Gründliches Mythologisches Lexicon*, col. 1940.
12 Heinrich von Kleist, *Sämtliche Werke und Briefe*, ed. by Helmut Semdner, 2 vols (Munich: Hanser, 1961), II, 818. Henceforth cited as *SW* in references.
13 Hederich, *Gründliches Mythologisches Lexicon*, col. 1940f.
14 *SW*, I, 15–20.
15 'Which set up a frightful howling'. *SW*, I, 405.
16 Hederich, *Gründliches Mythologisches Lexicon*, col. 52f.
17 Ibid., col. 203–10.

might have established from the ingenious cross-reference system and the excellent mythological tables, that Penthesilea, through Otrere, was a descendant of the terrible Mars, but that Cadmus and his unfortunate descendants are also ultimately of the same lineage.[18]

But all this, these fragments of classical myth, even though bound by a thematic relation, would go nowhere towards constituting a work of art. Not even the overt reminiscences of Euripides or Ovid, which Erich Schmidt and others established so long ago, would do that. It is nevertheless not irrelevant to reflect on what this mass of material amounts to. It is, as commentator after commentator has remarked, not the line of 'Griechentum und Goethezeit'; of 'Götterstille und Göttertrauer', which in Walther Rehm's titles sum up the consensus of eighteenth-century Classicism.[19] It seems rather the world of antiquity, the 'Heathen World', of which Alexander Pope, in the preface to the Iliad, noted with Augustan displeasure: 'Who can be so prejudiced in their Favour as to magnify the Felicity of those Ages, when a Spirit of Revenge and Cruelty, join'd with the practice of Rapine and Robbery reign'd thro' the World'.[20] And indeed, the Homeric heroes of Kleist, Achilles excepted, are not paragons except in their lustfulness and brutality. But is the well-ordered Amazon state, its practices and its cult, anything other than monstrous and unnatural? Are we really supposed to believe in a *contrat social*, a divinely ordained hierarchy? Can the reminiscences of Jean-Jacques Rousseau be any other than a cruel parody of human equality, such as deludes the characters in *Das Erdbeben in Chili/The Earthquake in Chile,* like the noble ideas of the Abbé Raynal so dashed in *Die Verlobung in St. Domingo/The Engagement in St. Domingo* or the natural justice saved only in the nick of time, and with a conviction born of comedy, by the chance interventions in *Der zerbrochne Krug/The Broken Jug*? Nor is the Amazon state compatible with Hermann's patriotic — if equally monstrous — vision of country before right and justice, or the Brandenburg of Homburg's poetically idealized, paradisal dream. The Amazon state, of which Penthesilea is

---

18 Ibid., TAB. XIII.
19 'The Greek Spirit and the Age of Goethe'; 'The Calm of the Gods and Their Mourning'. Walther Rehm, *Griechentum und Goethezeit. Geschichte eines Glaubens* (Berne: Francke, 1951); *Götterstille und Göttertrauer. Aufsätze zur deutsch-griechischen Begegnung* (Munich: Lehnen, 1951).
20 *The Twickenham Edition of the Poems of Alexander Pope*, 10 vols (London: Methuen, 1939–69), VII, 14.

admittedly not the willing servant, stands between her and fulfilment. We should not overlook one of her last instructions, as she prepares for death: to scatter their most sacred relic, the ashes of Tanaïs.

Allusions to the Bacchic-Dionysian and Orphic revivals in German poetry do not provide a satisfactory answer to Penthesilea, either. For 'Zeus erhabner trunckner Sohn',[21] as Klopstock so eloquently addresses him, the Dionysus of the early Goethe and of Heinse, even more that of Friedrich Hölderlin, while he belongs to a world of dark urge, mystery and numinousness, is also the god of the Dionysian, dithyrambic and frenzied line, who proclaims that poetry will be born out of tension, not stasis, out of dissolution into formlessness and primeval articulation — 'spotten des Spotts mag gern frohlokkender Wahnsinn'[22] — into living form, civilization in enthusiasm. As Klopstock's opening to 'Auf meine Freunde', one of the century's great Dionysian preludes, admits, echoing Plutarch centuries before and anticipating Nietzsche a century later, Dionysus is the god of manifold change, whose worship is full of destructions and disappearances, rending limb from limb; hence he continues with the line 'Wie mit dem goldnen Köcher Latonens Sohn',[23] stressing that Apollo's simplicity, unity and purity are needed to achieve form. The Dionysian, Euripidean, allusion in *Penthesilea*, to Pentheus, and Agaue, has to do rather with the awesome bull-headed Bromius, the 'sexual animal' who punishes with death and madness those who defile his worship.[24]

Prothoe's words — 'Es ist die Welt noch, die gebrechliche, / Auf die nur fern die Götter niederschaun'[25] — suggest that the gods' interventions in human affairs are inscrutable, ineffable, if not malevolent, impervious to human goodness, feeling and love, rendering frustrate man's attempts to reach out to his fellows in nobler endeavour, in dignity and affection. Kleist's Diana seems more like the goddess described in Johann Arnold

---

21 'Zeus' mighty, drunken son'. Friedrich Gottlieb Klopstock, *Werke und Briefe. Historisch-kritische Ausgabe*, ed. by Horst Gronemeyer et al., 26 vols (Berlin, New York, De Gruyter, 1979-), I, i, 6.
22 'May jubilant madness laugh at those who deride it' (Michael Hamburger). Friedrich Hölderlin, *Große Stuttgarter Ausgabe*, ed. by Friedrich Beissner et al., 8 vols in 15 (Stuttgart: Kohlhammer, 1946–1985), II, I, 91.
23 'As with the golden quiver Latona's son'. Klopstock, *Werke und Briefe*, I, i, 6.
24 R. P. Winnington-Ingram, *Euripides and Dionysus. An Interpretation of the Bacchae* (Amsterdam: Hakkert, 1969), 9.
25 'It is the world still, the fragile,/ On which the gods look down but from afar'. *SW*, I, 2854f.

Kanne's *Mythologie der Griechen/Greek Mythology* of 1805, demanding blood sacrifice, closer to her dog-headed sister Hecate;[26] the 'queen and huntress chaste and fair' is not the one who ministers to women, but she, who, not content with tearing men apart who unwittingly stray into the sphere of her virginity, exacts a terrible punishment of maidens who break their vow to her. And Phoebus Apollo, whom Penthesilea invokes, whom she sees in the unattainable demigod Achilles, is not so much Musagetes, the god of healing and light and form, as seemingly the arrow-shooter, the god of plague and sudden death.

There is however nothing surprisingly new in Kleist's depiction of the gods in an inhumane aspect. It might indeed be hasty to see in *Penthesilea* the anti-*Iphigenie* which it so manifestly seems to be. For Goethe's so morally virtuous heroine has nevertheless to live with a Diana who demands appeasement by blood sacrifice and whose barbarous cult can be revived at any moment, and with an Apollo whose obedience requires, or seems to require, deceit. The 'Parzenlied'[27] is an integral part of the play, not a mere reminiscence of a theogony now relegated to the past. If Iphigenie triumphs, then it is through her own inner strength of moral will and integrity, not because the gods themselves dispense harmony and light and humanity.[14] Moritz's *Götterlehre* was not silent on this side of the gods: 'Denn der Mensch ist in diesen poetischen Darstellungen der höhern Wesen so etwas Untergeordnetes, dass auf ihn überhaupt, und also auch auf seine moralischen Bedürfnisse wenig Rücksicht genommen wird'.[28] And he shows percipience in interspersing into his compendium the solemn verses of Goethe's poem 'Gränzen der Menschheit/Limits of Humanity' [sic] and Iphigenie's 'Parzenlied'.[29] Nor did Goethe's later forays into Greek mythological drama exclude this aspect. *Pandora* contains in its completed form and in the planned continuation, the element of Dionysian frenzy and destructive mania. The scene 'Vor dem Palaste des Menelas' in *Faust II* is suffused with Euripidean dread and blood worship. And the same Goethe, who in

---

26 Johann Arnold Kanne, *Mythologie der Griechen*, Erster Theil (Leipzig: Breitkopf und Härtel, 1805), 105, 120.
27 'Song of the Fates'.
28 'For in these poetic representations of the higher beings man is something so subordinate that little notice if any is taken of his moral needs'. Karl Philipp Moritz, *Götterlehre oder mythologische Dichtungen der Alten*, 3rd ed. (Berlin: Unger, 1804), 4.
29 Ibid., 76ff., 263f.

1826 evinced only 'Schauder und Abscheu' at the memory of Kleist,[30] was, a year later, to publish a fragment from the very scene of Euripides' *Bacchae* that provides Kleist with his Euripidean quotation in scene 24 of *Penthesilea*.[31] Yet the answer to all this is ready at hand. It is never Goethe's final word; for him, daemonic, undirected energy never stands alone without reflection, contemplation and inner self-awareness.

Without entering in to a discussion of the ground of Goethe's notions of wholeness and harmony, we may remark that his view of classical mythology is shared by his younger contemporaries. For the Weimar-oriented mythology or theogony of Karl Philipp Moritz and the Romantic philosophy of symbol and myth had one significant feature in common: while admitting man's impotence before the divine numen, the 'Spiel der höheren Mächte' (Moritz), 'Alles, was nur geahnet wird' (Georg Friedrich Creuzer), they were in basic agreement that myth was a means of leading to the absolute, the 'Hülle der reinsten Liebe' (Joseph Görres), 'im Unendlichen das Endliche' (Creuzer);[32] as Ernst Cassirer says of Friedrich Wilhelm Joseph Schelling: 'ein Prozess, in dem Gott selbst wird, in dem er sich, als der wahre Gott, stufenweise erzeugt'.[33] It leads, as Cassirer sums up the thought underlying the Romantic preoccupation with myth, to a sense of 'unmittelbare Totalität des Daseins und Geschehens', to 'Einheit eines universellen Raumgefühls'.[34] Thus when Goethe uses, for instance, Creuzer's *Symbolik und Mythologie*

---

30 'Revulsion and abhorrence', Johann Wolfgang Goethe, *Sämtliche Werke*, 18 vols (Zurich: Artemis, 1977), XV, 294–97. Cf. Karl Kerényi, 'Die Bacchantinnen des Euripides', in *Auf Spuren des Mythos, Werke in Einzelausgaben, II* (Munich, Vienna: Langen-Müller, 1967), 277–84.

31 In the review 'Ludwig Tiecks Dramaturgische Blätter', in Goethe, *Sämtliche Werke*, XIV, 129.

32 'Play of the higher powers'; 'everything that can only be fathomed'; 'fulness of purest love'; 'the finite in the infinite'. These quotations are taken from Karl Kerényi, ed., *Die Eröffnung des Zugangs zum Mythos. Ein Lesebuch*, Wege der Forschung 20 (Darmstadt: Wissenschaftliche Buchgesellschaft, 1967), 8 (Moritz), 36 (Creuzer), 32 (Görres), 35 (Creuzer). The notions of myth as recorded by Kerényi are confirmed by Heinz Gockel, 'Mythologie als Onotologie. Zum Mythosbegriff im 19. Jahrhundert', in *Mythos und Mythologie in der Literatur des 19. Jahrhunderts*, ed. by Helmut Koopmann, Studien zur Philosophie und Literatur des neunzehnten Jahrhunderts 36 (Frankfurt am Main: Klostermann, 1979), 25–58.

33 'A process in which God becomes himself, in which he, as the true God, generates himself step by step'. Ernst Cassirer, *Philosophie der symbolischen Formen*, 3 vols (Berlin: Bruno Cassirer, 1923–29), II, 10.

34 'Direct totality of existence and events'; 'a unity in universal awareness of space'. Cassirer, *Philosophie*, 97, 80.

der alten Völker/Symbolism and Mythology of Ancient Peoples, he is sharing an underlying religious and philosophical perception of myth. Kleist — although analogies with Creuzer or Schelling are helpful and illuminating — seemingly does not. It is the same with other Romantics and their contemporaries: Friedrich Schlegel's *Über das Studium der Griechischen Poesie/On the Study of Greek Poetry* of 1795–97 or *Geschichte der Poesie der Griechen und Römer/History of the Poetry of the Greeks and Romans* of 1798 see the Bacchic, and the formal discipline, in Greek poetry, as equally valid parts of a historical process of organic development. (His brother August Wilhelm, while less an admirer of Euripides' *Bacchae*, never abjures his allegiance to Johann Joachim Winckelmann.) Even Kleist's friend Adam Müller, to whom I shall return later, shares the same underlying views of Greek tragedy as the Schlegels or Karl Wilhelm Ferdinand Solger, Tieck's friend and the translator of Sophocles.

But, one may ask, is mythology really the key to Kleist's play? Might he, like the Goethe of the recently-published *Pandora*, not simply abandon myth-making and concentrate on the psychological mysteries of his heroine? Could the mythological apparatus not be merely a means to an end? It is the perennial problem of classical adaptations, taking the elements one needs and adjusting them to one's own, later culture, often running counter to the established mythological base (as in Goethe's *Iphigenie*) or in Kleist's case actually reversing the standard Homer-based narrative. I doubt it. For Kleist's Greeks, Amazon piety is a source of bemused wonderment, even for Achilles the son of Thetis. But for the Amazons, the mythology (based, incidentally, fairly closely on Hederich) is binding, valid and imperative. Their mythology is their very existence. Their Amazon-ness is the key to their actions and to Penthesilea's as well.[35] Achilles' presupposition seems to be, as was Schelling's belief of Greek religion, that serving Mars before Troy is part of his own particular social order — different from Penthesilea's — of some intelligible sense of community, of 'Volk', of family in the accepted sense; that, in Cassirer's words again, 'der "Götterstaat" wird zum getreuen Abbild des Organismus des sozialen Lebens'.[36] For Achilles, it is natural that Penthesilea should return as his queen to Phthia, where, as a

---

35 Kaiser, 'Mythos und Person', 222f.
36 'The "gods' state" becomes a true image of the organism of social life'. Cassirer, *Philosophie*, 218.

reflection of the divine community on Olympus (where such conquests are also not unknown) the social order may be re-established. But such a human society, with dynasty, ruler and subject, as a macrocosm of the family, is for Penthesilea a consideration of secondary importance.

> ACHILLES. Und woher quillt, von wannen ein Gesetz,
> Unweiblich, du vergibst mir, unnatürlich,
> Dem übrigen Geschlecht der Menschen fremd?

> PENTHESILEA. Fern aus der Urne alles Heiligen,
> O Jüngling: von der Zeiten Gipfel nieder,
> Den unbetretnen, die der Himmel ewig
> In Wolkenduft geheimnisvoll verhüllt.
> Der ersten Mütter Wort entschied es also,
> Und dem verstummen wir, Neridensohn,
> Wie deiner ersten Väter Worten du.[37]

'Er nennt sich marserzeugt, mein Völkerstamm'[38] is for Penthesilea all she needs to know. Mars the bringer of war and discord, has, it is true, freed the Amazons from male bondage and slavery, if by deceit and massacre. It is, as it were, the stories of Judith and Holofernes or Jaël and Sisera, extended to a whole state. But Mars' service is not perfect freedom; it is 'unweiblich', 'unnatürlich', capricious, heedless of personal choice, inexorable in obedience. Small wonder that Otrere, Penthesilea's mother, in order 'Mars [...] weniger zu gefallen',[39] has tried to subvert the Amazonian rules in her daughter's favour by recommending Achilles to her as a chosen mate. Mars, the father of Otrere (here Kleist changes the mythology slightly), but also of Harmonia, the mother of Cadmus, dwells, not in Olympian splendour, but in Hades, attended by the Furies:

---

37 ACHILLES: 'Whence springs a law, and when,
    Not woman's, pray, 'gainst nature,
    Not known to mortal race elsewhere?
    PENTHESILEA: Far, from the urn of all that's sacred,
    O youth, from the pinnacles of time,
    Untrod, which heaven keeps
    Wreathed in mysterious clouds.
    Our primal mothers' word decreed it so,
    We silently obey, o Nereid's son,
    As you the words of your first fathers.' *SW*, I, 1902ff.
38 'My people trace their origins to Mars'. *SW*, I, 1825.
39 'To please Mars less'. *SW*, I, 2167ff.

> CHOR DER JUNGFRAUN mit Musik.
> Ares entweicht!
> Seht, wie sein weisses Gespann
> Fernhin dampfend zum Orkus niedereilt!
> Die Eumeniden öffnen, die scheusslichen:
> Sie schliessen die Tore wieder hinter ihm zu.[40]

The Eumenides, the black-skinned, grey-garmented maiden bitch-goddesses,[41] the 'Rasereyen', 'welche diejenigen nach Verdienste peinigten, die etwas böses begangen hatten und darüber mit den Göttern nicht wieder waren ausgesöhnet worden',[42] from Gryphius' *Papinian* to Goethe's *Iphigenie* associated with melancholy of soul, are part of Penthesilea's own consciousness. For she in her turn associates her own emotional confusion, the welling turmoil of her breast, her 'Freud' and 'Schmerz',[43] with the same Eumenides, who flee only in that moment when she senses that 'Zum Tode war ich nie so reif als jetzt'.[44]

But Diana, too, whose cult is celebrated in the orgies at Themiscyra, is a stern goddess who exacts cruel revenge on the disobedient. It is under the aegis of the austere huntress, the arrow-shooter, that love is to be consummated in a feast of animal-like procreation. When Penthesilea in her despair once involuntarily invokes the love goddess Aphrodite, the priestesses of Diana expostulate:

> DIE OBERPRIESTERIN. Die Unselige!
>
> DIE ERSTE PRIESTERIN. Verloren ist sie!
>
> DIE ZWEITE. Den Erinnyen
> Zum Raub ist ihre Seele hingegeben![45]

---

40 'Ares goes hence!
See how his white steeds
Flee panting down to Orcus!
The Eumenids, frightful sisters,
Open for him the doors and shut them'. *SW*, I, 1735ff.
41 Karl Kerényi, *The Gods of the Greeks*, Pelican Books 429 (Harmondsworth: Penguin Books, 1958), 41f.
42 'Who tormented those according to their deserts who had done something wicked and were not reconciled again to the gods'. Hederich, *Gründliches Mythologisches Lexicon*, col. 1129.
43 'Joy', 'pain'.
44 'For death was I never so ripe as now'. *SW*, I, 1682.
45 'HIGH PRIESTESS: Accursed one!
FIRST PRIESTESS: She is lost!

Aphrodite, the other love, not of mate for mate, but of partner for partner, which has no place in Themiscyra, is a name sacrilegious to the Amazons. We saw, too, how Diana's brother, Phoebus Apollo, has his part in Penthesilea's yearnings for Achilles. Yet he, too, is Ovid's 'deus arcitenens' ('bow-wielding god'), Klopstock's 'mit dem goldnen Köcher Latonens Sohn', whose arrows can bring life or death.

The mythology therefore contains a symbolic unity, which is further sustained by important patterns of imagery in the play itself. The emblem of Mars' sovereignty over the Amazons is the great bow borne by the queen; Diana and Apollo are marked by the same attribute. The Furies are deities of pursuit. All is now ready for the drama of chase and hunt.[46] The imagery of the hunt has now become sufficiently established by commentators as to form part of the standard repertoire of studies on *Penthesilea*;[25] bow and arrow, hounds and stag or lion are the dominant figures which bear the action along from the merely pictorial at the beginning to the enacted grisliness of the end. From the image of Achilles pursuing Penthesilea:

> Denn wie die Dogg entkoppelt, mit Geheul
> In das Geweih des Hirsches fällt: der Jäger,
> Erfüllt von Sorge, lockt und ruft sie ab;
> Jedoch verbissen in des Prachttiers Nacken,
> Tanzt sie durch Berge neben ihm, und Ströme,
> Fern in des Waldes Nacht hinein: so er,
> Der Rasende, seit in der Forst des Krieges
> Dies Wild sich von so seltner Art, ihm zeigte.[47]

to Penthesilea's savage revenge on the 'stag' Achilles:

> Jetzt unter ihren Hunden wütet sie,
> Mit schaumbedeckter Lipp, und nennt sie Schwestern,

THE SECOND: Her soul is given to the Furies
For spoil!'. *SW*, I, 1231ff.

46 As in the studies by Dyer, Klotz, Brown, Kaiser and Sieck, referred to above in footnote 3.

47 'And like the baying hound once off the leash
Leaps on the antlered stag; and the hunter
Alarmed, calls out to entice it back:
But it, its teeth sunk in the noble neck,
It dances at his side through stream and heights
And forest's night; so he,
The crazed one, since through the trees of war
A prize as rare as this one crossed his path'. *SW*, I, 213ff.

> Die heulenden, und der Mänade gleich,
> Mit ihrem Bogen durch die Felder tanzend,
> Hetzt sie die Meute, die mordatmende,
> Die sie umringt, das schönste Wild zu fangen,
> Das je die Erde, wie sie sagt, durchschweift.[48]

The tearing to pieces of Achilles is, in every sense, the climax of the play, the end towards which the female hunting instinct, the paradoxical affront to inviolate chastity, and the frenzy of frustrated feeling, must impel. It is, mythologically speaking, Ares, Diana, and now, Dionysus. Indeed, the climax of the action brings about a mythological process whereby humans not merely use the language of the chase, but are actually transformed, in reality or deluded frenzy, into beasts.

It is what the ancients called metamorphosis.[49] It is the passing of one form to another, an alteration of appearance, circumstances and character, in myth, for which Ovid's stories of Echo and Narcissus, Apollo and Daphne, Philemon and Baucis, or Orpheus and Eurydice, have become archetypes. But metamorphosis is also the poetic process by which we see these religious myths reshaped and remoulded to suit the changing emphases of human consciousness from the times of the Greeks down to Rainer Maria Rilke, Paul Valéry, Ezra Pound or T. S. Eliot, W. H. Auden or Hans Werner Henze. They serve differing symbolic functions for aspects of human behaviour and emotions; they flesh out abstractions; they give some utterance towards saying that which otherwise cannot be spoken. Metamorphosis may be the act of kindness by which the gods transform men or women into birds or plants: Philomela the nightingale or Phyllis the almond tree or Daphne the laurel. It is that 'Wolle die Wandlung' of Rilke's Orpheus.[50] But not all of the Ovidian metamorphoses are benevolent or beneficent: indeed, Book Three of the *Metamorphoses* records the dreadful catalogue of

---

48 'Now among her dogs she rages,
   Foam-lipped, and calls them sisters,
   Amid their howls, and Maenad-like,
   Dancing through the fields with her bow,
   Urges the pack, on murder bent,
   Encircling her, to catch the finest prey
   That ever, as she says, roamed on the earth'. *SW*, I, 2567ff.
49 On the modern use of mythological metamorphosis see Sister M. Bernetta Quinn, *The Metamorphic Tradition in Modern Poetry* (New York: Geordian Press, 1972), esp. 2–5.
50 'Wish for change'.

punishment on the children of Cadmus, the fearful vengeance of Juno and Diana and Dionysus. On this, Kleist seizes.

We do not know whether Kleist had read Kanne's *Mythologie der Griechen* — there is no evidence; yet Kanne makes an interesting remark about the nature of metamorphosis: 'die Strafe eines Gottes hatte Menschen in Thiere verwandelt und nur menschenähnlich lebten diese im Thiere fort. So entstand die Metamorphose'. Later, Kanne informs us, it was 'nicht Strafe, sondern Mitleiden der Götter'.[51] And here Philomela or Daphne spring to mind. If we follow Kanne's point further, we might say that Kleist has gone back to the primitive roots of Greek religion, beyond notions of pity or justice or compassion, to that of punishment. Actaeon was punished as part of the gods' displeasure with the house of Cadmus; but the immediate cause was his unwitting incursion into the chaste regions of Diana's bathing-place. Like Achilles, he unknowingly provoked the goddess's wrath and was transformed immediately into a stag. Penthesilea, affronted, outraged, incensed by what she reads as Achilles' deception, sees him as the stag on to which she sets her Ovidian-named hounds. But the frenzy, the Maenad-like dismembering of the object of her love, is Agaue's. For as Agaue believes that she has torn a young lion and returns in triumph bearing instead the head of her son Pentheus, so Penthesilea emerges speechless, somnambulant, in a trance:

> PENTHESILEA *nach einer Pause, mit einer Art von Verzückung.*
> Ich bin so selig, Schwester! Überselig!
> Ganz reif zum Tod o Diana, fühl ich mich !
> Zwar weiss ich nicht , was hier mit mir geschehn,
> Doch gleich des festen Glaubens könnt ich sterben,
> Dass ich mir den Peliden überwand.[52]

Agaue's frenzy was induced by Dionysus, for her failing to believe in the divinity of his mother, her sister Semele;[53] and Pentheus' death

---

51 'The punishment of a god had changed men into animals, and these lived on like men in the animal. Thus metamorphosis came about', 'not punishment, but the pity of the gods'. Kanne, op. cit., xx, xxi.
52 'PENTHESILEA *after a pause, in a kind of transport.*
I am so blissful, sister, more than bliss!
Ripe for death, Diana, is how I feel!
What came over me I do not know,
But in the sure belief I could now die
That the Pelid fell to me in single combat'. *SW*, I, 2864ff.
53 Kerényi, 'Die Bacchantinnen', 281.

was a fearful reminder that the gods requite the merest slight to their divinity, amid cruel mockery.[54] Penthesilea, in the terms of the Amazon state, and in the eyes of its priestesses, has been made to become as one of Actaeon's mastiffs or as the fawnskin-draped Bacchante Agaue, because she has disobeyed Mars and Diana. Her very attempt to worship or approach Achilles, the unattainable Phoebus, had been suffused with intimations of a bliss near to death, an awareness that the hunt could never bring her to the object of her desire. What she in human terms most ardently and naturally desires is a blasphemy and affront to a divine order, 'In Wolkenduft geheimnisvoll verhüllt'. Like another heroine visited with madness because the order of state denies her heart's fulfilment — Ophelia — Penthesilea, also in a frenzied state which reveals the true extent of her sexual longing, decks herself 'with fantastic garlands', 'fantastically dressed with straws and flowers':

> Seht, seht, ihr Fraun! - Da schreitet sie heran,
> Bekränzt mit Nesseln, die Entsetzliche,
> Dem dürren Reif des Hag'dorns eingewebt,
> An Lorbeerschmuckes Statt, und folgt der Leiche,
> Die Grässliche, den Bogen festlich schulternd,
> Als wärs der Todfeind, den sie überwunden![55]

This modern Shakespearean analogy, with a play whose scenic structure has more affinity with Shakespeare, seems in many ways more appropriate than one from religiously-based Greek tragedy. For Euripides' *Bacchae*, and the Roman *Metamorphoses*, are originally texts relating to religious cult. As Ulrich von Wilamowitz-Moellendorff remarks:

> Wir sehen bei Euripides, dass ein Vertreter des Gottes, ein Träger seines Geistes da sein muss, der die Gläubigen weiht, den Geist auf sie durch sakramentale Handlungen überträgt, sie die erforderten heiligen Handlungen, die Orgia, lehrt.[56]

---

54 Winnington-Ingram, *Euripides and Dionysus*, 10f.
55 'Look, women, look, how she prances,
   Crowned with nettles, fearful sight,
   Woven in with thornbush hoar
   In place of bays, behind the corpse,
   Gruesome view, shoulders the festive bow,
   As if her deadliest enemy she'd conquered'. *SW*, I, 2704ff.
56 'We see in Euripides that a representative of the god, a bearer of his spirit, has to be there, who inducts the faithful, transfers his spirit on to them in sacramental acts, and teaches them the required sacred acts, the orgia'. Wilamowitz-Moellendorf,

Yet we seem to be closer to Kleist in a remark made in 1808, the year of *Penthesilea*, by August Wilhelm Schlegel, talking of a 'Romantic' Hamlet: 'Das Schicksal der Menschheit steht da wie eine riesenhafte Sphinx, die jeden, der ihr furchtbares Rätsel nicht zu lösen vermag, in den Abgrund des Zweifels hinabzustürzen droht'.[57] Kleist's striving for a fusion of Greek tragedy and Shakespeare had, to borrow Schlegel's words again, little of the religious 'Besitz', the 'Boden der Gegenwart' which are the Goethezeit's secularized notions of Greek tragedy, but at most the modern 'Sehnsucht', 'Schwermut' and 'Ahnung'[58] of a postlapsarian view of man. Kleist had metamorphosed Hederich's account of ancient religious belief and practice into a 'letter that killeth'.

This would have *Penthesilea* presenting a uniformly bleak, uncompromising, cheerless and desperate aspect. And yet it might be possible, by turning to a source other than Hederich, to find a different, more positive, sense of 'metamorphosis' for this play.

My argument hitherto has been based on a simple application of known source material to the text of the play. It is possible to extend such evidence, this time more in the direction of biographical documentation, to a similar end. The merely biographical, of course, 'proves' nothing. On the other hand, a certain legitimacy seems to have established itself in studies of *Penthesilea,* whereby analogies from contemporary poetry and criticism are adduced by way of corroboration. In this way, it has been possible· to avoid the extreme position of seeing Kleist as a poet writing out of no tradition, or solely in reaction against it (as in the case of his reading of Kant), while circumnavigating another promontory: that of seeing Kleist merely as the sum of impulses or reactions from outside. The notion of 'metamorphosis', as already defined, involves both assimilation, and recreation under the stamp of an independent personality. The assumptions behind my remaining remarks are largely biographical, not textual. They state facts readily available. It would of course be simplistic to rely too much on such evidence if there did

---

Griechische Tragödien übersetzt von Ulrich von Wilamowitz-Moellendorf, xiii: Euripides, Die Bakchen (Berlin: Weidmann, 1923), 17.

57 'The fate of man stands there like an enormous sphinx, which casts everyone who fails to grasp her dreadful riddle into the abyss of doubt'. August Wilhelm Schlegel, *Vorlesungen über dramatische Kunst und Literatur, Kritische Ausgabe der Vorlesungen,* IV, i, ed. by Stefan Knödler (Paderborn: Schöningh, 2018), 335.

58 'Possession'; 'the ground of the present'; 'longing'; 'melancholy'; 'intuition'. Ibid., V, 25.

not seem to be some thematic links with the play in question and its metamorphosis from mere source material into art. The facts in question are, simply, that Kleist attended Gotthilf Heinrich Schubert's lectures in Dresden in the winter of 1807 and that Kleist, the co-editor of *Phöbus*, accepted and published material on the nature of tragedy. The question is: could he have been attracted by what he heard, and may he have assimilated ideas similar to those published?

Schubert's lectures, delivered during the period in which Kleist is assumed to have been writing *Penthesilea*, were published in 1808 as *Ansichten von der Nachtseite der Naturwissenschaft/Intimations of the Night Side of Science*. There is a general consensus that Schubert's notions of 'Ahndung'[59] and somnambulism, of higher intimations occasioned by states of magnetic sleep, mesmerism or hypnosis, are of considerable importance for our understanding of *Das Käthchen von Heilbronn*.[60] That would seem appropriate for the 'grosses historisches Ritterschauspiel'[61] and its 'romantic' connotations, some of which even a tried practitioner like Ludwig Tieck found too extreme. Schubert it is, too, who uses the analogy of the negative and positive poles (of a magnet) to distinguish between active striving for a higher existence, 'Selbstthätigkeit', on the one hand (positive) and 'wahrhafte Passivität, welche uns der höheren Einwirkung fähig macht' (negative), on the other.[62] It might be the germ of Kleist's muchquoted letter to Collin about the interrelation of *Käthchen* and *Penthesilea*: yet there is no reason why Kleist, who already uses the image of magnetic poles in his letter to Marie von Kleist, which Sembdner dates as late autumn 1807,[63] could not have lighted on the analogy independently.[64] It is not my intention to force an interesting image common both to Kleist and Schubert. I mention it for what it may be worth. There are nevertheless, on the surface at least, striking parallels

---

59   'Intuition'.
60   Cf. Ursula Thomas, 'Heinrich von Kleist and Gotthilf Heinrich Schubert', *Monatshefte*, 51 (1959), 249–61 (NB: Thomas does not discuss *Penthesilea*).
61   'Grand romantic historical spectacle'.
62   'The activity of the self'; 'true passivity that makes us receptive to higher intuitions'. Gotthilf Heinrich Schubert, *Ansichten von der Nachtseite der Naturwissenschaft* (Dresden: Arnold, 1808), 323 (all subsequent references to Schubert are taken from this text).
63   *SW*, II, 797.
64   There might, however, be some justification for redating the letter to the actual time when Schubert was giving his lectures, i.e. winter 1807.

between certain passages in the *Ansichten* and *Penthesilea*. Again, we must be circumspect, for aspects of Schubert's nature mysticism, with their roots in various hermetic traditions (Jacob Böhme) and their echoes of Novalis or Steffens or Schelling or Ritter, may well not have appealed to Kleist, grounded as he was in less heady mathematical and scientific parallelism. Yet we know that Kleist's fellow-countryman Achim von Arnim — for all their differences in outlook and temperament — who began in the empirical school of Ludwig Wilhelm Gilbert's *Annalen der Physik/Annals of Physics*, was strikingly drawn by speculative mysticism such as Heinrich Jung-Stilling's *Theorie der Geisterkunde/Theory of Spectrology* and Schubert's *Ansichten*. All the same, passage after passage in Schubert has a striking ring when read with *Penthesilea* in mind. I quote a few of the more remarkable:

> Es ist ein ewiges Naturgesetz, das so klar da liegt, dass es sich dem Geist des Menschen zuerst aufdringen müssen, dass die vergängliche Form der Dinge untergeht, wenn ein neues, höheres Streben in ihnen erwacht, und dass nicht die Zeit, nicht die Aussenwelt, sondern die Psyche selber ihre Hülle zerstört, wenn die Schwingen eines neuen, freyeren Daseyns sich in ihr entfalten. Ich habe in dem ersten Theil meiner schon angeführten Schrift, da wo ich von einem scheinbaren Streben der Dinge nach ihrer eignen Vernichtung gehandelt, in vielen Beyspielen gezeigt, dass gerade in der Gluth der seeligsten und am meisten erstrebten Augenblicke des Daseyns, dieses sich selber auflöset und zerstört. Es welkt die Blume sogleich, wenn der höchste Augenblick des Blühens vorüber ist, und das bunte Insekt sucht in der einen Stunde der Liebe zugleich die seines Todes, und empfängt in dem Tempel der Hochzeit selber sein Grab. Ja es sind bey dem Menschen gerade die seeligsten und geistigsten Augenblicke des Lebens, für dieses selber die zerstörendsten, und wir finden öfters in dem höchsten und heiligsten Streben unsres Wesens, einen seeligen Untergang.[65]

---

65 'It is an eternal law of nature, and one so evidently clear, that the human mind needs to be made conscious of it, that the transitory form of things perishes when a new, higher striving awakes in them, and that it is not time, not the eternal world, but the psyche that breaks free, when the wings of a new and freer existence unfold in it. I have shown with many examples from the first part of my already quoted publication, in the section dealing with a seeming urge of things towards their destruction, that in the very glowing heat of the most blissful moment, the object of the highest striving, this dissolves and destroys itself. The flower fades in the very highest moment of its flowering, the shiny insect seeks in the one hour of love that of its death, and receives in the nuptial temple its own grave. With humans it is the very highest blissful and spiritual moments that are for them the most destructive,

Es hat auch die Vorwelt in diesem Gesetz, welches die höchsten Momente des Lebens unmittelbar mit dem Tode verknüpft, das Geheimniss der Liebe und des Todes, die Hoffnung einer unsterblichen Fortdauer unsres Wesens, und den Trost über den Untergang der hohen alten Vergangenheit gefunden. Es wurde deshalb in den Mysterien der Egypter und zu Eleusis, auf die Geschichte der alten Zeit gedeutet, und den Eingeweiheten die Zuversicht einer seeligen Fortdauer nach dem Tode gegeben. Das Bild, unter welchem in den Mysterien der Tod erschien, stellte diesen dem Gemüth vielmehr lieblich und süss als schrecklich dar, und die Einweihung wurde deshalb als ein Mittel gegen die Furcht vor dem Tode gepriesen. Ja es ward noch den Sterbenden, und nach einem frommen Glauben selbst den Todten der Hinübertritt in ein neues Daseyn durch die heilige Weihe erleichtert.[66]

So erschienen Liebe und Tod, das seeligste Streben des Gemüths und der Untergang des Individuums vereint.[67]

So ist in allen jenen Mysterien, der Tod und die Liebe, der Untergang und die Wiedererneuerung der Dinge, zu Einem Bild vereint, dargestellt worden.[68]

So ist es ein Hauptinnhalt der meisten Mysterien und heiligen Sagen, dass der Tod aus der Liebe, Untergang des Individuellen aus dem höchsten Streben der Seele hervorgienge. Hiermit verliert der Tod seine Schrecken, und es erscheint in ihm der Moment, wo jene höheren Organe, jene höheren Kräfte, die wir während des Lebens vergeblich erstrebt haben, in uns durch die Flamme eines grossen Augenblicks erweckt werden. Alsdann wird der Psyche diese Hülle zu enge, es vergeht diese Form, damit eine neue höhere aus ihr wiederkehre.[69]

---

and often we find in the highest and most sacred strivings of our being a blissful end'. Schubert, *Ansichten*, p. 69f.

66 'From earliest times there has been a law that unites the highest moments of life as one with death, the secret of love and death, the hope of continuing life forever, and the consolation for the loss of a past both ancient and great. For this reason the mysteries of the Egyptians and of Eleusis were taken to refer to the history of ancient times, and the initiates were granted the certainty of life continuing after death. The image in which death appeared in the mysteries was pleasant and sweet rather than terrible, and the initiation was therefore praised as a means against the fear of death. Indeed the dying and those who died in pious faith were assisted in their passing into a new existence'. Ibid., 71f.

67 'Thus love and death, the most blissful striving of the mind and individual's end, seemed united'. Ibid., 73.

68 'Thus, in all these mysteries, death and love, the end and the renewal of things, was represented as one image'. Ibid., 76.

69 'Thus it is a major component of most mysteries and sacred lays that death proceeds from love, the end of the individual out of the highest strivings of the soul. Thus,

Schubert is also able to fuse his important notions of animal magnetism with the above:

> Ueberhaupt ist es diese Verwandtschaft des thierischen Magnetismus mit dem Tode, welche die vorzüglichste Aufmerksamkeit verdient. Die Natur hebt solche sonst unheilbaren Krankheiten, die nur dem Magnetismus weichen, durch den Tod, und giebt so durch eine vollkommene Umwandlung, der kranken menschlichen Natur die verlohrne innre Harmonie zurück. Der Magnetismus, welcher nicht selten ein Erstarren der Glieder wie im Tode, und andre hiermit verwanden Symptome zur ersten Wirkung hat, ist auch hierin das im Kleinen, was der Tod im Grossen und auf eine vollkommnere Weise ist.[70]

We can distil from these quotations the following points: that the self-destruction of the psyche in the blissful moment of death is the natural transition to new life, indeed that all religious mysteries and mystical beliefs are based on this awareness of 'ein neues Daseyn durch die heilige Weihe';[71] that this is indeed a 'Naturgesetz' which enables humans to find a 'Trost über das frühe Versinken des alten Glücks'.[72] We find in fact a different, more comforting, more reassuring perception of the word 'metamorphosis' than our previous examinations of this notion allowed us to entertain. For there are those, says Schubert, who in the moment of death receive the utterance denied them in life, a 'striving' so much in contradiction with the rest of their existence, 'dass wir noch fast an der Gränze des Lebens eine höhere Metamorphose ihres Wesen eintreten sehen'.[73]

If we for a moment relate these passages to *Penthesilea*, we find the following. That the heroine, caught in an inhumane system, inimical to

---

   with this, death loses its terror, and in it is revealed the moment where those higher organs, those higher forces, that we strive for in vain in life, are awakened in us through the flame of a great moment. And then their outward mortal cocoon becomes too restricted, this form passes away, to let a new and higher one return from it'. Ibid., 79.
70 'Generally it is this relationship of animal magnetism with death that deserves the utmost attention. Nature annuls maladies, otherwise incurable and only accessible through animal magnetism, through death, and thus through the complete transformation affected in human nature's malady it restores the inner harmony that was lost. Magnetism, whose first effect so often is to paralyse the limbs as in death, and other related symptoms, is thus on a small scale what death is on a large scale and in a more perfect form'. Ibid., 357.
71 'A new existence through a higher consecration'. Ibid., 72.
72 'Natural law'; 'consolation for the early loss of its former happiness'. Ibid., 80.
73 'That almost on the brink of life we see a higher metamorphosis of its being'. Schubert, *Ansichten*, 319.

the feeling which would free her for a higher existence and fulfilment of her personality, feels, in a manner unable to be articulated in words, the bliss of imminent death in those very moments when her imaginings are most obsessively engaged with Achilles. They run, sometimes linked with the image of the unattainable sun-god, through all the main strands of the action.

> Doch taub schien sie der Stimme der Vernunft.[74]
>
> Ach, meine Seel ist matt bis in den Tod![75]
>
> Da liegt er mir zu Füssen ja! Nimm mich –
> Sie will in den Fluss sinken[76]
>
> Ich will in ewge Finsternis mich bergen![77]
>
> Zum Entzücken! [...] Bin ich in Elysium?[78]
>
> Ich bin so selig, Schwester! Überselig!
> Ganz reif zum Tod o Diana, fühl ich mich![79]
>
> Ich sage vom Gesetz der Fraun mich los,
> Und folge diesem Jüngling hier[80]
>
> Denn jetzt steig ich in meinen Busen nieder[81]

The images in the play which might run counter to this passivity, those of stoic acceptance (the arch) or of heroic grandeur (the oak) are significantly not Penthesilea's own, but Prothoe's. They are a commentary on the tragic greatness of the heroine who stands and falls while 'tücksche Götter uns die Hand [führen]'.[82] Penthesilea herself must experience the constant draw of death as the consequence of her attraction to Achilles, must metamorphose herself and her

---

74 'But deaf she seemed to reason's voice'. *SW*, I, 1074.
75 'Ah, my spirit is heavy unto death'. Ibid., 1237.
76 'There he lies at my feet, Yes, take me –
    She makes to sink into the river'. Ibid., 1388.
77 'In everlasting darkness I will hide'. Ibid., 2351.
78 'O transport! Am I in Elysium?' Ibid., 284f.
79 'I am so blissful, sister, more than bliss!
    Ripe unto death, o Diana, is how I feel'. Ibid., 2864f.
80 'I free myself from the women's law
    And follow this young hero here'. Ibid., 3012f.
81 'And now descend down into my bosom'. Ibid., 3025.
82 'Fickle gods guide our hand'. Ibid., 2890.

lover into animals, pursuer and pursued, before the ecstatic vision of 'höhere Metamorphose' is granted to her. There is no clear suggestion that she enters into a higher existence with Achilles in death, only that in metamorphosis and death, she gains the sense, the feeling of fulfilment, as if their deaths were indeed a union of body and soul, a vision of the dignity of existence which divine malevolence otherwise denies her. Only in this sense of a changed state of mind, induced by a frenzied longing for love in death, can Penthesilea's 'metamorphosis' be transfigured from the bleakest, starkest of tragedies into a tragedy where vision and intimation open the inner eye to paradisal, blissful states not granted to humans in time and space but in hope and dream. In this we see also a thematic sequence which leads from Kleist's *Marionettentheater/Marionette Theatre* to *Prinz Friedrich von Homburg*. We see, too, the thematic continuity of the motif of physical unconsciousness, of fainting or psychic disturbance, which accompanies the moment of 'Ahndung', intuition, in so many of Kleist's works — independent of Schubert or any other source.

If *Penthesilea*, then, ends on a note of loss, but also of glimpsed vision, it also has affinities with the theories of tragedy published in extract by Adam Müller in *Phöbus*. One thinks especially of his chapter, 'Vom religiösen Character der griechischen Bühne',[83] in which he adumbrates those moments of tragic experience which lead, ladder-like, to a higher existence: 'Auferstehungsmoment', 'höherer Todesmoment', 'Himmelfahrtsmoment'.[84] The analogy is interesting and has been pursued before;[85] indeed the evidently Christian connotations of Müller's categories for Greek tragedy are no contradiction in times when Zacharias Werner postulates a higher fusion of Schiller and Pedro Calderón, and Müller himself invokes Goethe's classicizing elegy 'Euphrosyne'. To Kleist wrestling with Sophocles and Shakespeare, such 'Romantic' connotations of tragedy might well lend themselves. Yet we remember Müller's own words to Friedrich Gentz, which warn us against the pursuit of too close a parallel with Tieck's, the Schlegels' or Werner's practice. There is no heaven for Penthesilea, none of the

---

83 'On the Religious Character of the Greek Stage'. Adam Müller, 'Vom religiösen Character der griechischen Bühne'. *Phöbus. Ein Journal für die Kunst*, ed. by Heinrich v. Kleist und Adam H. Müller (Dresden: Gärtner, 1808), 9. u. 10 Stück, 7.
84 'Moment of resurrection', 'higher moment of death', 'moment of ascension'.
85 Cf. Brown, *Kleist and the Tragic Ideal*, 44ff.

'Unvergänglichkeit und Himmel',[86] of which Müller's *Phöbus* lecture speaks and which is the tacit understanding behind Schubert's 'Ahndung'. Rather, we might quote Müller's words:

> Welches Heilige man nicht auf würdige Weise zu entschleiern vermag, sollte man, sagt' ich in der vorigen Stunde, lieber verschleiert lassen: dieser mir selbst gegebenen Vorschrift folge ich, der ich den Verdacht des Mysticismus scheue, und würde dennoch stolz darauf sein, durch das bisher gesagte, in manchem Mitgliede dieser verehrungswürdigen Versammlung, eine Ahndung erweckt zu haben, wie nemlich die Tragödie auch bei uns zu dem erhoben werden könnte, was sie bei den Griechen war, zum religiösen Fest.[87]

Yet one other contributor to *Phöbus*, Wilhelm Nienstädt, the now-forgotten author of the essay 'Von der didaktischen Poesie',[88] did see fit to link his remarks with Schubert. Nienstädt's remarks are less heady than Müller's, more concerned with the actual dichotomies of poetry and life, more reflective of the national penchant 'Jegliches zuvor inwendig zu verarbeiten, ehe man ihm nach aussen Gestaltung giebt', conscious of the perils of 'Innerlichkeit' if poetry is to be truly 'didaktisch', that is, expressive of the 'harmonischer Staat' and not merely 'luftiges Gebilde'. Schubert, says Nienstädt, is 'wahrhaftig zeitmässig und didaktisch' and affords us insight into a future union of the subjective and the objective.[89] Further words of Nienstädt would, however, seem more apposite to *Penthesilea*:

> In einem Zeitalter daher, wo man immer tiefer und mit immer neu aufgeregter Begier dem Unendlichen nachforscht, zugleich aber auch immer klarer der eignen Freiheit, der Höhe und Tiefe des Geistes inne wird, muss auf jener Seite die Freude am Unvergänglichen auf dieser das Vorgefühl des Besitzes sich vor andern kund thun, wie davon das

---

86 'Imperishability and heaven'.
87 'Whatever sacred mystery that cannot be unveiled in seemly fashion we should rather leave veiled; as I said in the previous lecture. I follow this self-imposed ordinance, shying away from all suspicion of mysticism, but would still be proud if my previous words had kindled in some members of this worthy assembly an inkling of how tragedy in our land could be elevated to the status it enjoyed under the Greeks, a religious festival'. Müller, 'Vom religiösen Character', 9.-10. Stück, 5.
88 'On Didactic Poetry'.
89 'To go through everything inwardly before giving it an external shape'; 'inwardness'; 'harmonious state'; 'airy substance'; 'truly fit for our times and didactic'. Müller, 'Vom religiösen Character', 8. Stück, 27.

> Lyrische in unsern Poesien Zeuge ist. Was hülfe es dem Menschen auch alles jenes, wenn es nicht mit seiner unergründlichen Natur vereinbart und unter den Menschen eingebürgert würde, wie es nur die Poesie vermag?[90]

In *Penthesilea*, it is only 'Poesie', the moment of higher imagining and perception, that affords possession ('Besitz'). But that possession is never real outside the inner sphere; it is the creation of 'Poesie', a 'Begier nach dem Unendlichen',[91] but one that human social and political reality can only thwart and frustrate. The 'metamorphosis' into the mythical reality of Actaeon and Agaue is the only means of breaking — with ferocious tragic violence — out of a world ruled by capricious gods of evil intent. Yet the Schubertian metamorphosis 'an der Gränze des Lebens'[92] is no less 'Poesie'. It is the glimpse of paradise, of prelapsarian harmony and knowledge, given to fragile humanity, yet also taken away in the demands and limitations of existence:

> Ach! Wie gebrechlich ist der Mensch, ihr Götter![93]

As an ideal, however, it receives dignity by the very desire to reach out into spheres not troubled by human imperfection and frailty:

> Sie sank, weil sie zu stolz und kräftig blühte![94]

As a 'mythological' tragedy, but also as the tragedy of personal relationships, *Penthesilea* is a witness to Kleist's powers of metamorphosis. Indeed, as in his play the man becomes the sacrificial victim and the woman is transformed into the Bassarid, Kleist may have recognized that myth has less to do with the clarity of Apollo than with the darker urges of which in our own day Robert Graves speaks:

---

90 'In an age, therefore, that is so intently searching after the infinite, but at the same time is with greater clarity conscious of its own freedom and the heights and depths of the spirit, there must above all on the one hand be joy in things imperishable, on the other the expression of a possession yet to be gained, to which the lyrical part of our poetry bears witness. What would all this avail mankind if it were not joined with its unfathomable nature and was received among men, as only poetry is able?' Ibid., 26.
91 'Desire for the infinite'.
92 'On the brink of life'.
93 'O how fragile humans are, you gods!' SW, I, 3037.
94 'She sank, too proud and forceful was her flowering!' Ibid., 3040.

Poetry began in the matriarchal age, and derives its magic from the moon, not from the sun. No poet can hope to understand the nature of poetry unless he has had a vision of the Naked King crucified to the lopped oak, and watched the dancers, red-eyed from the acrid smoke of the sacrificial fires, stamping out the measure of the dance, their bodies bent uncouthly forward, with a monotonous chant of: 'Kill! kill! kill!' and 'Blood! blood! blood!'[95]

---

95 Robert Graves, *The White Goddess. A Historical Grammar of Poetic Myth* (London, Boston: Faber & Faber, 1961), 448.

Fig. 10 [Jacob and Wilhelm Grimm], *Kinder- und Hausmärchen*, 2nd ed. (Berlin: Reimer, 1819–22), vol. 1 (1819), frontispiece and title page. Courtesy of the Master and Fellows of Trinity College.

7. Goethe, the Brothers Grimm and Academic Freedom[1]

My subject is German professors. It may need a word by way of prefatory explanation. For if in the Anglo-Saxon tradition, especially in the nineteenth century, so few men and women of excellence in letters, the arts and learning in general were associated with universities, the old ones in particular, the opposite was true for Germany. In 1842, John Sterling, the friend of Julius Hare and John Stuart Mill and F. D. Maurice and the subject of a Life by Thomas Carlyle, wrote an essay, 'Characteristics

---

1   An earlier version of this chapter was published as *Goethe, the Brothers Grimm and Academic Freedom. An Inaugural Lecture Delivered before the University of Cambridge 9 May 1990* (Cambridge: Cambridge University Press, 1990). It seemed to me in 1990, not long after the Education Reform Bill was enacted, that academic freedom was a relevant subject for an inaugural lecture. It still does. See Stefan Collini, *What Are Universities For?* (London: Penguin, 2012) and by same author, *Speaking of Universities* (London, New York: Verso, 2017); Stanley Fish, *Versions of Academic Freedom: From Professionalism to Revolution*, The Rice University Campbell Lectures (Chicago: University of Chicago Press, 2014), https://doi.org/10.7208/chicago/9780226170251.001.0001. On German universities in general, see the still indispensable account in Friedrich Paulsen, *Die deutschen Universitäten und das Universitätsstudium* (Berlin: Asher, 1902), trans. as *The German Universities and University Study* by Frank Thilly and William W. Elwang, preface by M. E. Sadler (London: Longmans Green 1906). A much shortened version is found in Friedrich Paulsen, 'Überblick über die geschichtliche Entwicklung der deutschen Universitäten mit besonderer Rücksicht auf ihr Verhältnis zur Wissenschaft', in *Die Universitäten im deutschen Reich*, ed. by W. Lexis, Das Unterrichtswesen im Deutschen Reich 1 (Berlin: Asher, 1904), 1–38; now standard is Charles E. McClelland, *State, Society, and University in Germany 1700–1914* (Cambridge: Cambridge University Press, 1980). Of further general interest are Richard Graf du Moulin Eckart, *Geschichte der deutschen Universitäten* (Stuttgart: Enke, 1929); S. D. Stirk, *German Universities — Through English Eyes* (London: Gollancz, 1946); Ernst Anrich, *Die Idee der deutschen Universität und die Reform der deutschen Universitäten* (Darmstadt: Wissenschaftliche Buchgesellschaft, 1960); Hans Peter Bleuel, *Deutschlands Bekenner. Professoren zwischen Kaiserreich und Diktatur* (Berne: Scherz, 1968).

of German Genius'. After praising German 'elevation and fulness',[2] 'reflection' and 'earnestness of heart',[3] he produced a list of about thirty German notabilities in what he called the 'three great forms assumed by the genius of the Germans, — in History, Philosophy, and Poetry'.[4] Over half of the names listed were at some time university professors (he forgot Martin Luther): Cristoph Martin Wieland, Friedrich Heinrich Jacobi, Friedrich Schiller, Georg Wilhelm Friedrich Hegel, Friedrich Schleiermacher, Karl Friedrich Eichhorn, Johannes von Müller, both Schlegel brothers, F. A. Wolf, Immanuel Kant, Johann Gottlieb Fichte, Friedrich Wilhelm Joseph Schelling, Johann Heinrich Voss, Barthold Georg Niebuhr, Friedrich Carl von Savigny (both brothers, Jacob and Wilhelm Grimm, were closely associated with the Humboldt brothers, Wilhelm and Alexander).[5] Some of these are also poets, and the list of poet-academics in Germany could also be extended. We are not dealing here with a subject marginal to German culture, but one which is central. It is therefore important to clear away misapprehensions and to see aright its role in the specific area which I have chosen from among the many possibilities it offers: academic freedom.

The Times Higher Education Supplement, commenting on Lord Jenkins of Hillhead's successful amendment of May 26, 1988 to the Education Reform Bill then before the House of Lords, whereby academics were guaranteed the freedom to question established knowledge, to advance new ideas irrespective of their controversial or even unpopular nature, without the danger of losing post or privileges in the institutions in which they work, went on to say: 'Lord Jenkins's amendment does not insist on the lehrfreiheit [freedom in teaching] enjoyed by Prussian universities in the 19th century. In our evaluation of academic freedom we have fallen below Bismarck's Germany'.[6] The tone suggests acquaintance with the high moral stance of Matthew Arnold. It is nevertheless hard to know quite what the leader-writer meant, but I take the inference to be drawn to be this: that, if Otto von Bismarck's Germany, which we know to have been strident, rampageous, illiberal to Catholics and Social

---

2   John Sterling, 'Characteristics of German Genius', in *Essays and Tales, Collected and Edited, With a Memoir of his Life*, ed. by Julius Charles Hare, 2 vols (London: Parker, 1848), II, 383.
3   Ibid., 406, 409.
4   Ibid., 417.
5   Ibid., 415.
6   *The Times Higher Education Supplement* (May 27, 1988), 36.

Democrats, expansionist, pushy, could nevertheless guarantee academic freedom, should we, in more enlightened times and with the benefit of a historical perspective, settle for less than they enjoyed a hundred years ago? Such a view is not new. In 1846, perhaps with more justification, Walter C. Perry, in his book *German University Education, or the Professors and Students of Germany* (a work that, incidentally, anticipates much of what Matthew Arnold has to say) states:

> We find it difficult, at first, to understand how such a degree of liberty can consist with an arbitrary form of government like that of Prussia. Yet we know that this 'Lehrfreiheit' is no empty boast, but a solid, and, to a country without a constitution, an invaluable privilege — a privilege so dear to every German's heart, that there are probably not more than two or three of the sovereigns of Germany who would desire or venture to infringe upon it.[7]

Probably true. Perhaps we students and teachers of German in this country are partly to blame that sentiments, certainly true in 1846, can in 1988 be applied by a reputable journal with little differentiation to the years 1871–90. For the Germans themselves of Bismarck's day were acutely aware that academic freedom, which now — let us not forget — went hand in hand with a great deal of political and constitutional freedom, had not been bought without a struggle and was a prize most securely to be held on to. Indeed, if there was a period in German history in which academics positively luxuriated in privileges guaranteed by the state, it was under Bismarck. But it was also a time when academics, of the distinction of Theodor Mommsen or Rudolf Virchow, were active in liberal politics. But, then again, we are using a generalization which is slipshod and misleading. In mentioning Bismarck, let us not forget that, in matters of higher education, the Prussian writ did not run in at least half of the German universities; and important centres of culture, academic or otherwise, were to be found outside the confines of that state or its chancellor.

Whether in Protestant Berlin or in Catholic Munich, the privileges were the same: addressing the University of Munich in 1867 (not long before German unification), Ignaz von Döllinger was able to speak of

---

7   Walter C. Perry, *German University Education, or the Professors and Students of Germany. To which is Added, a Brief Account of the Public Schools of Prussia, with Observations on the Influence of Philosophy on the Studies of the German Universities*, 2nd ed. (London: Longman, Brown, Green, 1846), 11.

universities as the 'highest court of appeal in matters of the intellect', its teachers as a 'priesthood' of scholarship.[8] The historian Friedrich Meinecke, looking back in his memoir, *Die deutsche Katastrophe/The German Catastrophe*, on his own university days in Bismarckian Berlin, recalled that while these were but the silver age of classical liberalism, not the golden, they were days in which men like his academic teachers, Johann Gustav Droysen, Heinrich von Treitschke and Wilhelm Scherer, were still scholars of real distinction, while the thought of a cultural collapse such as that later produced by National Socialism seemed impossible.[9] There were, of course, academics in those days who abused their privileged status (some would say that of the historian Treitschke, even more so of that Berlin professor who called the university the spiritual life guards of the house of Hohenzollern).[10] There were voices which warned of the pernicious encroachments of the state, of particular interests, on the universities' hallowed ground[11] (Meinecke tells how the plan to set up a chair of history in a faculty of Catholic theology was seen by Mommsen as an axe laid to the tree of academic freedom).[12] These were perhaps not good days in which to be a Social Democrat and an academic, but, then again, the state could be secure in its assumption that very few academics were.[13] Eduard Spranger, writing in 1913, spoke doubtless for most in saying that those who are subject to direct state intervention usually owe it to their ill-chosen and tactless behaviour ('reichlich ungeschickte Formen').[14] The assumption that universities should be guaranteed maximum freedom to pursue

---

8   Dr. Joh. Jos. Ign. von Döllinger, *Die Universitäten sonst und jetzt*, 2nd ed. (Munich: Manz, 1867), 50, 52.
9   Friedrich Meinecke, *Die deutsche Katastrophe*, in *Werke*, ed. by Friedrich-Meinecke-Institut der Freien Universität Berlin, Hans Herzfeld et al., 8 vols (Stuttgart: Köhler, 1958–69), VIII, 333f. Also *Erlebtes 1862–1901*, loc. cit., 50–5.
10 The words, quoted in various different forms, were uttered by Emil Du Bois-Reymond in his rectorial address on August 3, 1870: 'Nun wohl, die Berliner Universität, dem Palaste des Königs gegenüber einquartiert, ist durch ihre Stiftungsurkunde das geistige Leibregiment des Hauses Hohenzollern'. Emil Du Bois-Reymond, *Reden*, ed. by Estelle Du Bois, 2 vols, 2nd ed. (Leipzig; Veit, 1912), I, 418.
11 For one among many see Ernst Bernheim, *Die gefährdete Stellung unserer deutschen Universitäten*, Festreden der Universität Greifswald 8 (Greifswald: Abel, 1899), esp. 13 and 21.
12 Meinecke, *Die deutsche Katastrophe*, 139.
13 A reference to the notorious 'Lex Arons'. See F. Paulsen, *The German Universities*, 252; and McClelland, *State, Society, and University in Germany*, 267f.
14 Eduard Spranger, *Wandlungen im Wesen der Universität seit 100 Jahren* (Leipzig: Wiegandt, 1913), 13.

research and to teach — within widely extended limits — was one which still informed two of Max Weber's most important essays, 'Der Sinn der "Wertfreiheit" der soziologischen und ökonomischen Wissenschaften/ The Meaning of Ethical Neutrality in Sociology and Economics' (1917) and 'Wissenschaft als Beruf/Science as a Vocation' (1919). It was not always so, and it was not always to remain so. For the rest of my time, I wish to examine, not how academic freedom actually was won and certainly not how professors basked in it, but how university and state collided in their separate interests and how this typifies the intellectual climate of Germany in what Meinecke called its 'golden age'.

What is academic freedom? What did the Germans mean by it? How was it defined? Why was it so important? The very phrase has a German ring to it, for it was a peculiarly German concern. Let us begin with the definition used by an acute observer of the German university system, Matthew Arnold: 'Lehrfreiheit and Lernfreiheit, liberty of the teacher and liberty for the learner; and Wissenschaft, scientific knowledge systematically pursued and prized in and for itself, are the fundamental ideas of that system'.[15] That was by and large the reality which Arnold was able to observe in Bismarckian Germany. Writing earlier in the century, before 1848, however, Perry, in the already-cited book on German university education, gave the whole matter a rather different slant:

> It is this important feature in their constitution which has gained for the universities the honourable designation of the 'last bulwark of German freedom'. It is this which ensures to the highly-gifted minds of Germany, the means and opportunity for the full and free development of their powers, and a fitting sphere of usefulness and honour. It is this which secures a ready entrance for newly-discovered truths of science into the minds of the rising generation, at the very time when they are most free from prejudice, and filled with the most disinterested love of truth and knowledge. If in an evil hour — and there are many who are capable of advising such a measure — the sovereigns of Germany should be induced to circumscribe or destroy the liberty of teaching of their

---

15 Matthew Arnold, 'Superior or University Instruction in Prussia', in *Schools and Universities on the Continent*, ed. by R. H. Super, The Complete Prose Works (Ann Arbor: University of Michigan Press, 1979), IV, 263.

professors, the glory of their universities will quickly pass away, and the progress of science itself will receive a powerful check.[16]

Perhaps even more tellingly, Perry goes on to quote Jacob Grimm's dictum that academic freedom was 'freedom from restraint which is enjoyed at the university, and there alone',[17] thus a permitted liberty which it was in the interest of the state to promote and foster.

Depending on how you approached them, German universities in the eighteenth and nineteenth centuries had a double function: to train suitable candidates for the civil service and state administration, and to promote scholarship. In the eighteenth century, these two aims rarely met on common ground.[18] The University of Halle, the first Prussian university institution effectively to deserve that name, may serve as a convenient illustration. Its statutes of 1694 had been based on the notion of 'libertas philosophandi',[19] the freedom to teach and do research. Yet time and time again, the university and its professors were to be reminded by the state, often in trenchant personal memoranda from the king himself, that what was required was orthodoxy, in matters of religion and philosophy; it wanted utilitarian courses completed in a minimum of time, and it wanted results — hence the infamous order from King Frederick William I to the rationalist philosopher Christian Wolff in 1723, to leave Halle and all Prussian territories within forty-eight hours on pain of death;[20] but, even under his great-nephew Frederick William II in 1794, instructions to two theologians to stop teaching the new theology if they wished to avoid dismissal.[21] Or the instruction to the professors of 1731 that 'die Professores fleissig, sowohl publice als privatim über nützliche Materien lesen, auch die Collegia in jeder Fakultaet dergestalt mit einander concertiren sollen, damit die Studiosi so geschwind als es möglich, ein jeder in der Scientz

---

16 Perry, *German University Education*, 11.
17 Ibid., 16.
18 See Notker Hammerstein, 'Zur Geschichte der Deutschen Universität im Zeitalter der Aufklärung', in *Universität und Gelehrtenstand 1400–1800, Büdinger Vorträge 1966*, ed. by Hellmuth Rössler and Günther Franz, Deutsche Führungsschichten der Neuzeit 4 (Limburg/Lahn: Starke, 1970), 5–82; Gertrud Schubart-Fikentscher, *Studienreform. Fragen von Leibniz bis Goethe, Sitzungsberichte der Sächsischen Akad. d. Wiss. zu Leipzig*, Phil.-hist. Klasse 116.4 (Berlin: Akademie, 1973).
19 Paulsen, *The German Universities*, 46.
20 Wilhelm Schrader, *Geschichte der Friedrichs-Universität zu Halle*, 2 vols (Berlin: Dümmler, 1894), II, 459.
21 Ibid., 480.

worzu er Lust hat, seinen cursum bequemlich absolviren könne';[22] or Wilhelm von Humboldt's predecessor as minister responsible for education, Julius Eberhard von Massow, decreeing as late as 1804 that the notion of independent research being superior to teaching the young was not even worthy of further discussion.[23] In the thirty universities that the German-speaking lands had around 1800, the general tone was hardly different: at most it depended on the ruler or his appointed servants. Christian Thomasius, incidentally the first German professor to lecture in his native language, and also the first rector of the University of Halle, might show concern for general education, seeing the universities as *seminaria reipublicae*, 'Pflanz-Garten des Friedens'.[24] But these were far removed from notions of 'Bildung' or 'self-cultivation', as defined by my predecessor W. H. Bruford.[25] Johann Gottfried Herder's 'friedliche Provinz',[26] that he imagined as he sketched a grand scheme of education on his way from Riga to Nantes in 1769, remained for most of his lifetime remote from reality. In real life, academic existence was dismal, repetitious, straitened, apart perhaps from the kingdom of Hanover's show-case University of Göttingen; its only real advantage perhaps being that it offered to those of poor and humble background — Kant, the classicist Christian Gottlob Heyne, Fichte among them — the chance to rise through the state's pedagogical province into a social status and respect that the less gifted of their estate could not achieve, to escape the rigidity of the social hierarchy.[27] And yet, as the century proceeded, some of these universities, Halle in terms of freedom of pedagogical activity, Göttingen in terms of the freedom of political thought and Jena in terms of speculative philosophy, became places

---

22 'The professors, to read diligently both privately and in public on useful subjects, coordinating courses in each faculty in such a way that the students, each one in his chosen discipline, may finish their courses as swiftly as possible'. Ibid., 464.

23 Ibid., 494.

24 'Seedbeds of peace', Gertrud Schubart-Fikentscher, *Studienreform*, 13.

25 See W. H. Bruford, *The German Tradition of Self-Cultivation: 'Bildung' from Humboldt to Thomas Mann* (Cambridge: Cambridge University Press, 1975).

26 'Peaceful province'. Johann Gottfried Herder, *Journal meiner Reise im Jahre 1769, Sämtliche Werke*, ed. by Bernhard Suphan, 33 vols (Berlin 1877–1913), IV, 37f.

27 See Anthony J. La Vopa, *Grace, Talent, and Merit. Poor Students, Clerical Careers, and Professional Ideology in Eighteenth-Century Germany* (Cambridge: Cambridge University Press, 1988).

where alternatives to the state-ordained and state-dominated system, the mere maidservant of absolutism, were posited. The new critical philosophy of Kant, the French Revolution, the speculative systems of Romantic idealist philosophy, and not least the collapse of the old political order in the German states, notably after 1806: all of these factors contributed to the formulation of new ideas of university and state and their interrelation.

The key word was 'Wissenschaft', a word difficult to translate accurately into English, only satisfactorily rendered as 'science' in the older and no longer current sense of the unity of all knowledge. Kant, in 1798, in his *Der Streit der Fakultäten/The Contest of Faculties*, had claimed that it was the role of philosophy to establish truth for all branches of knowledge, speculative or practical, thus positing an overarching principle of truth as opposed to one of mere utilitarianism.[28] In statements all made in the first decade of the nineteenth century, Fichte, Schelling, Schleiermacher, Henrik Steffens, and Wilhelm von Humboldt, later Hegel, all proceeded from the central notion of the unity of all knowledge, its universal totality, its organic wholeness.[29] Thus, for Fichte, science was a process of continuous intellectual productivity; for Schelling, it was an organism, whole in itself, in which even the smallest part of the organization reflects that whole.[30] In Schleiermacher's formulation,[31] it was the concern of a university to waken in the young the idea of 'Wissenschaft'; to enable this idea to take hold in each specialized area of study, so that it would be as second nature to relate everything to 'Wissenschaft'; not to examine each area on its own, but in its relation to and in connection with the 'großer Zusammenhang', the

---

28　Spranger, *Wandlungen im Wesen der Universität*, 10f.
29　For the following see McClelland, *State, Society, and University in Germany*, 77ff.; Spranger, *Wandlungen im Wesen der Universität*, 9–15; Spranger, *Wilhelm von Humboldt und die Reform des Bildungswesens*, 2nd ed. (Tübingen: Niemeyer, 1960), 201–08.
30　F. W. J. Schelling, *Vorlesungen über die Methode des akademischen Studiums. Auf der Grundlage des Texts der Ausgabe von Otto Weiss*, ed. by Walter E. Ehrhardt, Philosophische Bibliothek 275 (Hamburg: Meiner, 1974), 111.
31　Quoted from *Idee und Wirklichkeit einer Universität. Dokumente zur Geschichte der Friedrich-Wilhelms-Universität zu Berlin. In Zusammenarbeit mit Wolfgang Müller-Lauter u. Michael Theunissen*, ed. by Wilhelm Weischedel, Gedenkschrift der Freien Universität Berlin zur 50. Wiederkehr des Gründungsjahres der Friedrich-Wilhelms-Universität zu Berlin (Berlin: De Gruyter, 1960), 125 (referred to subsequently as Weischedel, *Idee und Wirklichkeit*).

wider and general contexts and issues; bearing in mind at all times the unity and totality ('Einheit und Allheit') of perception, which will lead to independent research, discovery, and presentation.[32] How was such an ideal to be realised? How was such 'Wissenschaft' to thrive, when, in Schelling's words, it was part of 'Urwissen', primal knowledge itself and drawn from the absolute realm of infinity,[33] where 'Wissenschaft' ceases to be itself the moment it is relegated to being a mere means to an end and not an end in itself? There were basically two answers, neither of them radically different in their ultimate implications. Either the state must be excluded altogether from the affairs of 'Wissenschaft', that is, the university in its proper calling (Schleiermacher's, Humboldt's and Fichte's view); or, in Schelling's and Steffens' view, the state must become the bearer and agent of all the very highest ideas, and thus function as the guarantor of independent and disinterested scientific endeavour.[34] Schelling and Steffens were doubtless naive; but they had none of the shameful self-confidence with which Martin Heidegger in 1934, over a century later, helped to preside over the complete sell-out of the Humboldtian idea and tradition to the National Socialist state.

All of these notions were in the air, and formed part of the founding declarations of the great University of Berlin which came into being in 1810, the first German university consciously and deliberately set up in a capital city at the centre of state control, but to be independent of it. There were also very practical ideological reasons for not wishing to be meshed with the state: the French, as occupying powers in Prussia and elsewhere in Germany, had closed the University of Halle and were planning to abolish others and set up a number of separate specialist schools in the kingdom of Westphalia. The recent political shake-up had seen a number of universities, once ancient and venerable, disappear in reorganization or conquest: Erfurt, Mainz, Wittenberg, Helmstedt, to mention but four. Berlin would provide — and this is also Wilhelm von Humboldt's vision — a place where the state and true humanity would kiss each other, where 'Bildung' and statecraft would lie down together in an organism that was humane and liberal. The state would leave the

---

32   Weischedel, *Idee und Wirklichkeit*, 123.
33   Schelling, *Vorlesungen über die Methode des akademischen Studiums*, 12f.
34   Spranger, *Wilhelm von Humboldt und die Reform des Bildungswesens*, 203–94; Spranger, *Wandlungen im Wesen der Universität*, 14.

sciences ('Wissenschaften') to themselves, where they would work out the unifying principle behind all knowledge. All must be subject to one ideal, derived from one principle; these two in their turn to be subsumed under one overall idea.[35] The air this university would breathe would be, in Fichte's word, academic freedom, this itself vested in divine and natural law.[36] Small wonder that, when Hegel delivered his inaugural lecture in Berlin 1818, he could proudly claim that the closed entity of the universe has no power that can resist the force of philosophical perception.[37] For it was to be the philosophers who were to believe above all in this system that the state university seemed to guarantee and underwrite. It might not occur to them, as it did to the great physician Virchow in his rectorial address in 1893, looking back over the century, that while Wilhelm von Humboldt's University of Berlin in 1810 may have been the finest expression of the philosophical age, the return in 1827 to Berlin of his brother, Alexander von Humboldt, ushered in the 'naturwissenschaftliches Zeitalter', the age of science and its inevitable specialization.[38]

Whereas the Prussian state universities, and subsequently all within the German confederation, were to accept the principle of freedom of teaching and learning, academic freedom in a very general sense, this did not mean that the state was handing over the authority for its institutions of higher learning to a state-free republic of letters and sciences. For, as an irony, Prussia introduced state examinations for candidates for its administrative service in 1810, the very year of the foundation of the University of Berlin, the 'Staatsexamen' that has become an accepted part of the universities' function ever since.[39] Indeed, the price to be paid for freedom within the university system, a liberty, which, as the English commentators noted, was not enjoyed by most of their fellows, was in fact an arrangement with the state; the state, for very practical reasons but also out of concern for prestige, not wishing to lose its reputation for fostering learning and scholarship. This meant, in effect, a deal between the state and the university teacher. We see for instance August Wilhelm

---

35   Weischedel, *Idee und Wirklichkeit*, 193–06.
36   Ibid., 231.
37   Ibid., 314.
38   Ibid., 417.
39   Spranger, *Wandlungen im Wesen der Universität*, 15.

Schlegel, professing Sanskrit at the new Prussian University of Bonn, engaged in epistolary tussles with the Prussian authorities over his status, and privileges and salary,[40] while stating grandly elsewhere that historical criticism must, if it is to prosper, enjoy total autonomy, not be subservient to any authority outside itself, it alone to decide on the veracity of its own problems (Weber's 'Wertfreiheit').[41] The state did, indeed, put up with behaviour on a personal level that hardly sat well with Fichte's or Schelling's ideals. Schleiermacher and Hegel were at daggers drawn; Fichte was as prickly a colleague as one could imagine; Wilhelm von Humboldt echoed other university administrators in likening academics to a bunch of actors[42] (an ominous foreshadowing of King Ernest Augustus of Hanover's analogy with harlots and dancing-girls, on the occasion of the dismissal of the Göttingen Seven). The state could, and did, tolerate the prima donna (Hegel, for instance) where its own interests were not in question. Yet, where strong academic personalities, in the name of freedom — an extension of academic freedom — came into direct conflict with the state, the reaction was different. Already the Carlsbad Decrees of 1819 saw in Prussia dismissals and suspensions and a general clampdown.

The two examples to which I now turn and which form the actual title of my lecture on academic freedom and the long and difficult way towards its eventual achievement, are those of Johann Wolfgang Goethe and the brothers Grimm, one the university administrator, the others professors, in their separate ways caught up in their concern for academic standards inside a constitutionally guaranteed system, both illustrating, again in different ways, the gulf fixed between Humboldtian ideals and Realpolitik. I can only touch on the main points as I see them, but in my view they are significant ones for the subject under discussion. For here

---

40   This is documented in *Briefe von und an August Wiilhelm Schlegel*, ed. by Josef Körner, 2 vols (Zurich, Leipzig, Vienna: Amalthea, 1930), I, 362, 373.

41   August Wilhelm Schlegel, 'Abriß von den Europäischen Verhältnissen der deutschen Literatur', in *Sämmtliche Werke*, ed. by Eduard Böcking, 12 vols (Leipzig: Weidmann, 1846–47), VIII, 207–19. See generally Christian Renger, *Die Gründung und Einrichtung der Universität Bonn und die Berufungspolitik des Kultusministers Altenstein*, Academica Bonnensia 7 (Bonn: Röhrscheid, 1982).

42   Weischedel, *Idee und Wirklichkeit*, xxii. Goethe's colleague, the minister C. G. von Voigt, referred to the Jena professors as 'eine dem Theatermenschen ähnliche Faction'. Quoted in Schubart-Fikentscher, *Studienreform*, 27.

we see Goethe the universal poetic genius submitting to the restrictions of state polity.

The subject of Goethe and the university, like Goethe and the law, Goethe and justice, Goethe and revolution, is not one easily addressed or easily answered. On the one hand, one can say that Goethe saw universities rather as a means to an end than as an end in themselves. His own university career in law had been a practical training for legal practice and stood him in good stead as an administrator and eventually a minister of state in the small duchy of Saxe-Weimar, where he was later to assume responsibility for the affairs of the scientific collections and institutes of learning, notably the University of Jena. Goethe's own forays into the world of learning and scientific endeavour were not those of the academic expert, but rather of the privatier — in the eighteenth-century sense — the individualist who has no need to concern himself with the merely academic side of a debate or a merely academic audience. On the one hand, in administration, Goethe was an eighteenth-century cameralist; on the other, he was concerned that there should be interdependence between the estates and organic progression towards improvement of the common weal. But universities raised particular problems of statecraft, especially in the post-revolutionary ferment. On the one hand, Goethe regarded the University of Jena as a 'geistiger Freihafen',[43] a haven of the intellect, where ideas that elsewhere might seem seditious could be expressed; but the other side involved the real concern that things might get out of hand, the students might become even more riotous as they picked up the ideas current in Paris; there might be the need to restrain the ruling Duke Carl August — a Prussian general to boot — from sending in the troops against the students and provoking the very violence from which Goethe by nature recoiled.

There had been the recent calamitous and damaging incident in 1799 of the dismissal by the duke of none other than Fichte[44] from his post

---

43 Hans Tümmler, 'Goethes Anteil an der Entlassung Fichtes von seinem Jenaer Lehramt 1799', in *Goethe in Staat und Politik. Gesammelte Aufsätze*, Kölner Historische Abhandlungen 9 (Cologne, Graz: Böhlau, 1964), 132–66 (155).

44 On the Fichte affair, see Waldtraut Beyer, 'Der Atheismusstreit um Fichte', in *Debatten und Kontroversen. Literarische Auseinandersetzungen in Deutschland am Ende des 18. Jahrhunderts*, ed. by Hans-Dieter Dahnke and Bernd Leistner, 2 vols (Berlin, Weimar: Aufbau, 1989), II, 154–45; Friedrich Sengle, *Das Genie und sein Fürst. Die Gesschichte der Lebensgemeinschaft Goethes mit dem Herzog Karl August* (Stuttgart, Weimar: Metzler, 1993), 168–75.

as professor extraordinary at Jena, originally on a charge of atheism, but in fact for *maledictio principis*, insulting the ruling prince through unhelpfully intemperate outbursts that impugned the honour of all who disagreed with him. But then, the presence in Jena of an unruly and unpredictable intellectual was probably more than a small state and its university administration could cope with. It might detract from the university's reputation. Its existence was precarious enough, with only the petty states of Weimar, Gotha, Meiningen, and Coburg to finance it. Universities like Wittenberg and Helmstedt were being closed; might Jena go the same way? Yet Fichte had been imprudence itself in his behaviour in Jena and had quarrelled with most of his colleagues; his very presence invited student unrest. Goethe's role in all this is not unequivocal: he was prepared to use his power base in Weimar when it suited him and no amount of 'Goethepietät' can get round that. The damage done by Fichte in Jena was in fact nothing compared with that caused by him once out of Jena; it moved a number of able men to leave Jena (Schelling, for instance) and was contributory to the break-up of the Romantic circle in Jena; the student numbers sank. For this we cannot blame Goethe; instead, we must acknowledge that his position of confidence and trust with Duke Carl August involved him in severe tests of loyalty where even-handedness was not a possible option. Yet Goethe shared his master's fear of disorder and revolutionary stirring: he passed over the prospect of obtaining Schelling for Jena in 1816, fearing not only a re-run of the Fichte affair but revolution itself (whatever that might mean).[45] Ironically, Schelling went on to have many ribbons pinned to his coat and to accept a Bavarian patent of nobility — the other, and less attractive, aspect of academic freedom.

The case of the Jena professor Lorenz Oken[46] may, however, have been the immediate cause of Goethe's unwillingness to have Schelling around to compound his troubles. Here are the main points. Oken, like

---

45 Hans Tümmler, 'Der Minister Goethe und die Jenaer Universitätsreform', in *Das klassische Weimar und das große Zeitgeschehen. Historische Studien*, Mitteldeutsche Forschungen 78 (Cologne, Vienna: Böhlau, 1975) 12–40 (22).

46 On the Oken affair, see esp. Max Pfannenstiel and Rudolph Zaunick, 'Lorenz Oken und J. W. von Goethe', *Sudhoffs Archiv f. Geschichte der Medizin u. der Naturwissenschaften*, 33 (1941), 113–73; Hans Tümmler, 'Goethe, Voigt und die Weimarische Pressefreiheit 1815–1819', in *Goethe in Staat und Politik*, 240–69; Hermann Bräuning-Oktavio, *Oken und Goethe im Lichte neuer Quellen* (Weimar: Arion, 1959), Sengle, *Das Genie und sein Fürst*, 368ff.

Fichte, from humble background and with the same forthrightness of expression and lack of deference that had been Fichte's undoing, had come to Jena in 1807 as a 'prof. extr. Med'. His inaugural lecture as a professor of zoology, in 1809, *Ueber den Werth der Naturgeschichte, besonders fur die Bildung der Deutschen/On the Merit of Natural History Especially for the Education of the Germans*,[47] owed much to the spirit of Fichte and Schelling in its emphasis on the dependence of all specialized science on a philosophy of nature which is itself the ground and guarantor of all moral, political, and legal systems. Echoing Schelling, that philosophy is now returning to its roots in nature philosophy, he states the need for 'ein Ganzes'[51] ('a whole') as the basis of all scientific endeavour, involving not just the systems of nature itself, the animal and plant world, but its relationship to man and the state. His peroration pleads in a direct address to the students that they have not come to university for 'Versorgung', i.e., to provide for later professional needs, but for 'universale Bildung' ('education on a universal scale').[48] Thus the professor of zoology is making here the unchallenged claim for academic 'Lehrfreiheit' as the basis of all his subsequent lecture courses (Humboldt avant la lettre). Goethe would not be in basic disagreement with any of this, only he had a different emphasis, seeing in the closely observed phenomenon, the limited sphere of activity, not just in the grand system, evidence of the same universal type or archetype that is Oken's concern. He may not however, have been best pleased that Oken nowhere made reference to his discovery of the intermaxillary bone, where we have conclusive proof that Oken knew of Goethe's work in comparative anatomy and never mentioned it.[49] That was, to say the least, undiplomatic and was not to help him when he issued a direct challenge to state authority.

For what happens when academic freedom, as defined in the very general terms of Fichte and Schleiermacher, becomes a weapon for political freedom? Notions of academic freedom that surrounded the

---

47 *Ueber den Werth der Naturgeschichte, besonders für die Bildung der Deutschen. Von Oken, bei der Eröffnung seiner Vorlesungen über Zoologie* (Jena: Frommannn, 1809). The only copy of this rare work in this country appears to be in Julius Hare's collection in Trinity College. See Chapter 17 in this volume.
48 Ibid., 18.
49 Bräuning-Oktavio, *Oken und Goethe*, 35.

foundation of the University of Berlin were not out of place in the atmosphere of Prussian reform and the calls before 1815 for a nation that would throw off the French yoke. After 1815, however, more care might be needed. True, the petty state of Saxe-Weimar had put on a liberal face by adopting a constitution, admittedly of a very limited sort, yet allowing for freedom of the press. Goethe, his political instincts normally conservative, was not pleased, fearing opposition, not harmony, between the estates. His attitude to Oken remained ambivalent: while admitting (later, and privately) that Oken's work might be mentioned in the same breath as Alexander von Humboldt's,[50] he found Oken's overbearing behaviour (and failure to show deference to him, Goethe, the scientist) unbearable. His worst fears about press freedom were confirmed when in 1816 Oken began publishing his periodical *Isis* (our hermetic tradition again).[51] For *Isis* was not only a platform for Oken's scientific ideas — for which it remains important in the history of zoology; it used (abused, in Goethe's view) its press privilege to offer affront and insult to other states in the post-1815 settlement. One is indeed surprised that Oken got away for so long with what he did and that the authorities (that included Goethe) chose to ignore him for as long as they did.[52] A compromise was mooted: banning the printer in Jena, but not the publisher. But then the Wartburg student festival in the summer of 1817, warmly supported by Oken and *Isis*, although not in any revolutionary sense, had been on Duke Carl August of Weimar's territory. More powerful neighbours like Austria and Prussia took note: Goethe had had what may have been a *mauvais quart d'heure* with Metternich in Carlsbad on the subject.

An insult offered to a Russian official in February of 1819 brought things further to a head; if that was not enough, the former Jena student Karl Sand chose that moment to murder the poet, courtier and Russian police spy August von Kotzebue in Mannheim. It only needed §78 of the Carlsbad Decrees for Oken's dismissal to become inevitable; for here academic freedom was hedged around with words concerning 'misuse

---

50 Ibid., 74.
51 *Isis oder Encyclopedische Zeitung von Oken* (Jena: Expedition der Isis, Leipzig: Brockhaus, 1817–48), esp. I, xi, xii, 64–87.
52 For most of this see Bräuning-Oktavio, *Oken und Goethe*, 75–95.

of position in influencing the minds of the young',[53] which was open to very large and commodious interpretation. The Berlin theological professor de Wette, who had written a letter to the mother of Carl Sand, lost his post — despite energetic protests from his colleagues.[54] The Jena professors — to their credit — did the same in respect of Oken (whose dismissal had none of the grim immediacy surrounding Christian Wolff's from Halle nearly a hundred years earlier). Goethe's position in this is, again, equivocal. It is all very well to say that Goethe opposed the institution for which Oken stood, not the man himself.[55] That is only applying sophistry to a thoroughly disagreeable and unedifying incident. If we do wish to see it in perspective, it might be worth saying instead that Oken's pattern follows closely that of Fichte's: the anti-courtly, anti-authoritarian strain of the university generation around 1790 (with the explorer and revolutionary Georg Forster as a kind of academic mentor) or the rhetoric of the Freikorps and Burschenschaften found their limits in severe test cases where the state saw its function as restoring order. And Goethe was for order, in the form of a paternal and patriarchal enlightened absolutism. Yet that was hardly compatible with the inhibiting spirit of the Carlsbad Decrees.

Oken's tragedy had been his failure to recognize that 'Bildung zur ernsten Humanitaet' and 'Liebe zum Ganzen' (phrases from his inaugural lecture)[56] were not proof against the interests of the state, if the state saw these threatened by a freedom of utterance underwritten by 'libertas philosophandi'. Cynics might say that Oken should have done like so many academics of his generation and enjoyed the rich pickings offered by a regenerated university system that was prepared to tolerate more from its academic citizenry than from the rest of its subjects. But even those in positions of some prestige — Schleiermacher, for instance — knew that vigilance was necessary if academic freedom

---

53 Ibid., 78.
54 Weischedel, *Idee und Wirklichkeit*, 275–84.
55 Hans Tümmler speaks of 'spezifisch Goethesche Humanität'. 'Goethe, Voigt und die Weimarische Pressefreiheit 1815–1819', *Goethe in Staat und Politik*, 256. A very fair assessment of Goethe's difficult position in Friedrich Sengle, 'Zum Problem der Goethewertung: ein Versuch', in *Neues zu Goethe. Essays und Vorträge* (Stuttgart: Metzler, 1989), 235–54 (252f.).
56 'Education promoting serious humanity'; 'love of the whole'. Oken, *Ueber den Werth der Naturgeschichte*, 11.

was to be little more than the heady rhetoric of a founding generation.[57] Wilhelm von Humboldt, it should be noted, had withdrawn completely from the *vita activa* into the private *vita contemplativa* of comparative linguistics, where the real needs and concerns of the university no longer intrude. And, in fairness to Goethe, it must be recorded that he too refused to continue in university politics after the Oken affair.

My second example, the case of Jacob and Wilhelm Grimm, the best known of the so-called Göttingen Seven, is linked with Humboldt and his reforms in an important way. On a perhaps superficial level it marks the Grimm brothers' emergence out of the world of purely private scholarship into that of the university and its peculiar responsibilities. For the Grimms were, until their translation to Göttingen in 1830, librarians and archivists, not immune to the conflicts between state and scholarship (they had to work for King Jerome in Kassel) but shielded from some of its effects. In securing them, the University of Göttingen was enhancing its reputation as a centre of pure scholarship — in the national language and literature, something that the Romantic movement had brought about. In another sense, it was aligning itself with the main thrust of the Humboldtian ideal in scholarship. Jacob Grimm's autobiographical sketch of 1831 makes that clear. The reminiscence of student days in Marburg leads over to the awareness that, since then, the state has extended its influence over university affairs — through those very Staatsexamina that were part of the price paid for the Humboldt reform.[58] Uniformity, pressure of examinations, coverage of material, all these are factors which impede the flight of the intellect (Grimm's image). If the state can never allow the student fully to pursue his course of study without some consideration of the end in view, he hopes that professors at least may be free from prescription in the material on which they lecture. For Grimm's account of himself makes it clear that it was not the study of the law in itself (his original course), but the incidental study of history and literature that made him what he was later to become. In a way more concrete than Fichte or Schelling or Schleiermacher could formulate it, the Grimm brothers, in their various philological, lexicographical, literary and antiquarian

---

57 Weischedel, *Idee und Wirklichkeit*, 293–98.
58 Jacob Grimm, 'Selbstbiographie', in *Kleinere Schriften*, 8 vols (Berlin: Dümmler, 1879–1884, Gütersloh: Bertelsmann, 1890), I, 7f.

studies, proceed from an original unity. They may not use words like 'Allheit', but they do believe in the essential oneness of all cultural manifestations that are informed by language, a common language that is the key to national past, national present, national personality, national progress, national virtue. It will involve the shift of meaning in the word 'Vaterland' from being the place in which one was born and grew up, to the territory in which all are united in a political 'Allheit' through language. (That is the stated ideal.) This will involve the most careful scrutiny of the past, the present, and the future — as both brothers formulated it in letters to their friend, the Romantic poet Achim von Arnim.[59] The scrutiny of that national continuum requires of the scholar and liberal intellectual a vigilance towards the state and its constitutional guarantees.[60] If, therefore, a constitution granted by King William IV of Great Britain and Hanover is peremptorily suspended by his brother and successor, the brutish Ernest Augustus (the least attractive of Queen Victoria's assortment of uncles), the intellectual must raise his voice. Jacob Grimm makes the point that if beneficiaries of a freedom unique to universities do not speak out, who then will?

The case of the Göttingen Seven, dismissed by King Ernest Augustus and told to leave Hanoverian territory, becomes the test against which all subsequent questions of university and state in Germany are measured (even more than 1848–49). It is very interesting to find the standard books on the German universities, written about the turn of the century, looking back at Göttingen and registering how far we have come since then[61] (perhaps not without the satisfying thought that Göttingen was now Prussian). Yet, in referring to 'German' universities, I am committing an all-too-common solecism: commentators at the time and since have not been slow in pointing out that the Göttingen Seven need only cross the border into Hesse-Cassel and enter into the service of other states in the confederation[62] where the ruler did not refer to his professors as

---

59 As set out in *Achim von Arnim und die ihm nahe standen*, ed. by Reinhold Steig and Herman Grimm, 3 vols (Stuttgart: Cotta, 1894–1913), III, 5–44.
60 Set out in Jacob Grimm, 'Ueber meine Entlassung', *Kleinere Schriften*, I, 25–56.
61 Such as Paulsen, *The German Universities*, 260.
62 Ibid., 77.

'Huren und Tänzerinnen'.[63] (And the only time, incidentally, when it was true to speak of 'German' universities under central state control, was under National Socialism.)

And yet it would be wrong to leave the Grimm brothers and academic freedom on that note. Wilhelm Grimm is incidentally one of the many professors at the Frankfurt parliament of 1848–49. Their courage, liberalism and quiet dignity finds its best expression in a place where perhaps we would least expect it and in a work that has been read throughout the world more than Goethe or Schiller or Thomas Mann or Kafka: the famous *Kinder- und Hausmärchen*, Grimms' *Fairy Tales*. No English reader of the tales then and now would read the preface to the 1840 edition, for these prefaces were never translated, and few modern readers of the German edition will find those words reprinted, except in a scholarly context.[64] Students of the nineteenth century will find, to my mind, no book more symbolical in iconography, layout and text than this one of 1840, in expressing at once the 'elevation and fulness' that so appealed to John Sterling, their appeal to 'Gemüth', where the soul, emotions, and the finer sensitivities meet, and the sobriety conditional on experiencing political tyranny. For we proceed from a frontispiece (Brother and Sister) with its child, deer, flower-bearing angel, witch and owl (the underlying message of the stories) to a title page decorated with the life-giving symbols of insects, to the second preface to Bettina von Arnim, whose children had been the first recipients of the collection.[65] Wilhelm Grimm had sent her the revised edition in 1837, still affirming the tradition of scholarship in Göttingen as professed by the great classicist Heyne; shortly after he and his family were forced out of Göttingen, it was she who had received them and given them succour. Now in the spring of 1840 nature comes to foster

---

63 'Whores and dancing-girls'. *Briefe von Alexander von Humboldt an Varnhagen von Ense aus den Jahren 1827 bis 1858* (Leipzig: Brockhaus, 1860), 11.

64 See David Blamires, *Telling Tales. The Impact of Germany on English Children's Books 1780–1918* (Cambridge: Open Book Publishers, 2009), 147–80, https://doi.org/10.11647/obp.0004

65 Wilhelm Grimm, dedication to *Kinder- und Hausmärchen* (Göttingen: Dieterich, 1840), quoted here from *Kleinere Schriften*, ed. by Gustav Hinrichs, 4 vols (Berlin: Dümmler, 1881–83, Gütersloh: Bertelsmann, 1887), I, 318f. The standard edition of the *Kinder- und Hausmärchen*, 3 vols (Göttingen: Dieterich, 1837, 1855) omits this controversial section.

love and temper hatred, a reminder of how, in the spring of 1813, when the first volume appeared, the Russians had been garrisoned in Kassel and the hope of liberation was as spring ('war das Gefühl der Befreiung der Frühlingshauch'). Yes, Romantic language from one of the great representatives of the Romantic movement. Yet a reminder that the movement and its great achievement in university reform — perhaps its greatest lasting achievement — was caught up in the real issues of politics and was forced to come to terms with the exigencies of a system that represented but few of the ideals that ushered in the University of Berlin. The fairy-tales — and their preface — are part of that Romantic cultural 'Allheit', the most accessible part no doubt; but they stand symbolically beyond that for academic integrity in the face of crude deployment of power and for a proper sense of the role of the university in the life and affairs of the nation.

> Mit diesen Worten sendete ich Ihnen das Buch vor drei Jahren aus Göttingen, heute sende ich es Ihnen wieder aus meinem Geburtslande, wie das erste Mal. Ich konnte in Göttingen aus meinem Arbeitszimmer nur ein Paar über die Dächer hinausragende Linden sehen, die Heyne hinter seinem Hause gepflanzt hatte, und die mit dem Ruhm der Universität aufgewachsen waren: ihre Blätter waren gelb und wollten abfallen, als ich am 3. Oktober 1838 meine Wohnung verliess; ich glaube nicht dass ich sie je wieder im Frühlingsschmuck erblicke. Ich musste noch einige Wochen dort verweilen und brachte sie in dem Hause eines Freundes zu, im Umgange mit denen, welche mir lieb geworden und lieb geblieben waren. Als ich abreiste, wurde mein Wagen von einem Zug aufgehalten: es war die Universität, die einer Leiche folgte. Ich langte in der Dunkelheit hier an und trat in dasselbe Haus, das ich vor acht Jahren in bitterer Kälte verlassen hatte: wie war ich überrascht, als ich Sie, liebe Bettine, fand neben den Meinigen sitzend, Beistand und Hülfe meiner kranken Frau leistend. Seit jener verhängnisvollen Zeit, die unser ruhiges Leben zerstörte, haben Sie mit warmer Treue an unserem Geschick Theil genommen, und ich empfinde diese Theilnahme ebenso wohlthätig als die Wärme des blauen Himmels, der jetzt in mein Zimmer herein blickt, wo ich die Sonne wieder am Morgen aufsteigen und ihre Bahn über die Berge vollenden sehe, unter welchen der Fluss glänzend herzieht; die Düfte der Orangen und Linden dringen aus dem Park herauf, und ich fühle mich in Liebe und Hass jugendlich erfrischt. Kann ich eine bessere Zeit wünschen, um mit diesen Märchen mich wieder zu beschäftigen? Hatte ich doch auch im Jahre 1813 an dem zweiten Band geschrieben, als wir Geschwister von der Einquartierung bedrängt waren und russische Soldaten neben in dem Zimmer lärmten, aber damals war das Gefühl der

Befreiung der Frühlingshauch, der die Brust erweiterte und jede Sorge verzehrte.⁶⁶

Cassel am 17. September 1840

---

66 'With these words I sent you the book three years ago from Göttingen; today I send it to you again from the place where I was born, like the first time. In Göttingen I could see from my study lime trees rising high above the roofs, planted by Heyne at the rear of his house, that had grown up with the university's renown: the leaves were yellow and about to drop when I left my dwelling on 3 October 1838: I do not believe I shall ever catch sight of them again in full spring leaf. I was detained there some weeks, which I spent in a friend's house, in the company of those whose affections I shared. When I took my leave, my carriage was held up by a procession: it was the university joining a funeral cortege. I reached here in the dark and entered the same house that I had left eight years ago in the bitter cold: how surprised I was when I found you, dear Bettina, sitting beside my loved ones and giving aid and succour to my ill wife. Since that fateful time that destroyed my peaceful existence you have been warm and loyal in sharing our lot, and the feeling that imparts is like the beneficent warmth of the blue sky that now casts its light into my room, where I see again the sun, from its rise in the morning until it completes its course over the mountains, the river flashing by at their feet: the scent of oranges and limes makes its way up to me from the park and I feel that I am youthfully invigorated in love as in hate. Can I wish for a better time to take up these fairy-tales again? For it was in the year 1813 that I was working on the second volume, when my brothers and sisters and I could scarcely move for troops billeted in our house, Russian soldiers making noise in the next room; but in those days the feeling of liberation was the spring air that made us breathe freely and made off with every care'.

ROMANTICISM

Fig. 11 Adrian Ludwig Richter, *Genoveva* (1820–84), The Metropolitan Museum of Art, public domain.

8. Fairy Stories for Very Sophisticated Children
Ludwig Tieck's *Phantasus*[1]

No movement spoke more of children, their simplicity and innocence, or the symbolic significance of children and youth, than did the German Romantics. Yet by the same token, never was such childlike simple-heartedness expressed with greater sophistication or invested with more subliminal meaning. Romantic iconography, as perhaps the most accessible of the movement's art forms, bears this out. Philipp Otto Runge's best-known paintings of children, *The Hülsenbeck Children*, *Rest on the Flight to Egypt* and the final version of *Morning*, place the newborn or the young into a cyclical process of transience and renewal. The symbolic flowers that accompany the images of children are guarantors of the mystical pervasiveness of divine love, seen, at several neo-platonic removes from its ideal source and centre, in the lasting values of marriage and family life. Runge contributed two Low German stories to the most famous of all German collections for children, the Grimms' *Kinder- und Hausmärchen/Grimms' Fairy Tales*. This is not the place to discuss those two tales, *Von den Fischer un siine Fru/The Fisherman and His Wife* and *Van den Machandel-Boom/The Juniper Tree*, or the context in which they stand. Yet no-one today, despite the dedication of the *Kinder- und Hausmärchen* to the real child of real friends (Bettina von Arnim and her son Johannes

---

[1] An earlier version of this chapter was published in *Bulletin of the John Rylands University Library of Manchester*, 76 (1994), 59–68. On these aspects of Runge see Werner Hofmann, 'Antiker und christlicher Mythos — Natursymbolik — Kinder — Familie und Freunde' in the catalogue *Runge in seiner Zeit* (Hamburg, Kunsthalle and Munich: Prestel, 1977), 278–79, 288–9.

© 2021 Roger Paulin, CC BY 4.0   https://doi.org/10.11647/OBP.0258.08

Freimund) and the later intermarriage of the two families, regards the collection as naive.

True, the artist member of the Grimm family, Ludwig Emil, did in the frontispiece and vignettes do his best to foster a kind of naivety through a deliberately stylized lack of sophistication. But neither the early editions, nor the revised one of 1840, could be read without their prefaces, with their scholarly credo, and in the case of the later revision, their unrepentant affirmation of academic freedom.[2] Ludwig Emil Grimm had also done the frontispiece for an earlier Romantic collection for children: *Kinderlieder/Nursery Rhymes* (1808), the third part of the famous *Des Knaben Wunderhorn/The Boy's Magic Horn* compiled by Achim von Arnim and Clemens Brentano. Ludwig Emil was at that stage still in his teens and not yet fully in charge of his individual style. Yet students of the Romantic engraving will not fail to notice the connection with those done in 1806 by the Riepenhausen brothers for Ludwig Tieck's *Genoveva*[3] and the use of the sweetish faux-naif in the service of piety and simplicity of heart. The *Kinderlieder* themselves were not free of this kind of concession to the religious connotations of folk custom. They were, however, also a record of the local variants of children's rhymes and of verse enactments by and for children. They had a basis in the wider context of popular oral and written culture that German Romanticism also sought both to compile and foster. Some of these verses came later to be interpolated into a work by another member of this extended clan: Brentano. His *Gockel Hinkel Gackeleia* of 1838, a re-telling of Italian fairytales, with plates provided by Ludwig Emil Grimm and others, is part of Brentano's late religious and poetic symbolism, where poetry is the ladder that leads through the sufferings of this world into eternity. And Brentano was, as an earlier essay of his shows, aware even at this level of the complementary functions of icon and extrapolated significance.[4]

Tieck, although Runge's vignettes for his *Minnelieder aus dem Schwäbischen Zeitalter/Love Songs from the Swabian Era* (1803) associate him

---

2 See Chapter 7 in this volume.
3 Franz and Johannes Riepenhausen, *Leben und Tod der heiligen Genoveva* (Frankfurt am Main: Varrentrapp und Wenner, 1806).
4 Clemens Brentano, 'Erklärung der Sinnbilder auf dem Umschlage dieser Zeitschrift', in *Werke*, ed. by Wolfgang Frühwald, Bernhard Gajek and Friedhelm Kemp, 4 vols (Munich: Hanser, 1963–68), II, 1046–54, esp. 1046.

with this thematic complex, was less concerned with the multivalence of symbolic or mythological iconography. Having introduced Runge to Jacob Böhme and the hermetic tradition in which he stands, Tieck withdrew from what seemed too disjunct a view of the world, one too sharply divided into the symbols of light and darkness. Tieck could not embrace Runge's child-like and implicit faith through which alone these seeming disharmonies might be resolved. But he had stated (or had had a character state) in his most-read and most influential book for the younger generation, *Franz Sternbalds Wanderungen/Franz Sternbald's Journeyings* (1798):

> Alle Kunst ist allegorisch. [...] Was kann der Mensch darstellen, einzig und für sich bestehend, abgesondert und ewig geschieden von der übrigen Welt, wie wir die Gegenstände vor uns sehn? Die Kunst soll es auch nicht: wir fügen zusammen, wir suchen dem einzelnen einen allgemeinen Sinn aufzuheften, und so entsteht die Allegorie. Das Wort bezeichnet nichts anders als die wahrhafte Poesie, die das Hohe und Edle sucht und es nur auf diesem Wege finden kann.[5]

Brentano echoed this fourteen years later in stressing 'Die tiefere Bedeutung, das freie Gleichgewicht und die zierliche Zusammenstellung'[6] of symbolic icons, free of conventional associations, yet concrete, not ethereal. This is central Romantic doctrine, akin to that 'Hindeutung auf das Höhere, Unendliche'[7] of Friedrich Schlegel's *Gespräch uber die Poesie/Conversation on Poetry* in *Athenaeum* (1800) or Novalis's aphoristic definition of 'Romantisieren'. True allegorical art will be co-extensive with true Romantic art in that it is the things and objects accessible to the finite mind and senses that will supply the link to a higher perception and will point to the absolute. It is Caspar David Friedrich's

---

5   'All art is allegorical. [...] What can man depict, sufficiently in itself, separate and forever remote from the rest of the world, as we see the objects before us? Art also should not attempt it: we put together, we seek to attach a general meaning to the individual, and thus allegory comes into being. The word denotes nothing less than true poetry that seeks the high and noble and can only find it by this route'. Ludwig Tieck, *Franz Sternbalds Wanderungen*, ed. by Alfred Anger, Reclams Universal-Bibliothek 8715–21 (Stuttgart: Reclam, 1966), 257f.

6   'Deeper significance, free balance and graceful accentuation'. Brentano, 'Erklärung der Sinnbilder', 1046.

7   '"Pointing to the higher, never-ending". Friedrich Schlegel, 'Gespräch über die Poesie', in *Athenaeum. Eine Zeitschrift von August Wilhelm und Friedrich Schlegel*, 3 vols (Berlin: Vieweg, 1798; Unger, 1799–1800), III, i, 121.

later quasi-mystical insight, in respect of this higher function of art: 'Der Maler soll nicht bloß malen, was er vor sich sieht, sondern auch, was er in sich sieht'.[8]

Tieck returned to these notions of allegory in a seemingly unexpected place, the discussion of 'Märchen' ('Fairytales') in the first part of his *Phantasus* (1812).[9] A brief description of this work, published in Berlin in three parts between 1812 and 1816, may be appropriate. Its subtitle, 'Eine Sammlung von Mährchen, Erzählungen, Schauspielen und Novellen, herausgegeben von Ludwig Tieck' ('a collection of fairytales, tales, plays and novellas, edited by Ludwig Tieck'), is not without the agreeable irony of that fictional editorship. For the author of all the works is none other than Tieck himself. The device was not new: in 1798, *Franz Sternbalds Wanderungen* also bore 'herausgegeben von Ludwig Tieck' on its title page (a ploy borrowed from Johann Wolfgang Goethe's *Wilhelm Meister*). But in those days, the imparting of the sacred truths of art demanded self-effacement, like the common venture with Wilhelm Heinrich Wackenroder of 1796, *Herzensergiessungen eines kunstliebenden Klosterbruders/Heart's Outpourings of an Art-Loving Friar*, innocent of all authorial attribution. Now, in 1812–16, the irony was one of distance from works, once associated with his name over a period of some fifteen to twenty years, that he was now 'editing' with commentary, and subjecting to the scrutiny of a sophisticated country-house gathering. That society, full of literary associations to its very fingertips, is in its turn ironically aware of playing a literary game first invented by Giovanni Boccaccio (sharing their creator's prejudice for the pre-1789 Goethe, the assembled persons overlook Goethe's recent revival of the form for Germany, or Christoph Martin Wieland's).[10]

It is fair to say that the re-publication of his various earlier works in *Phantasus* (itself reprinted in 1828) gave them a cohesion that they had lacked before; augmented by three more in a slightly different vein, they establish the essential corpus of the Romantic tale of wonder or terror

---

8   'The painter is not merely to paint what he sees in front of him, but also what he sees in himself'. *Caspar David Friedrich in Briefen und Bekenntnissen*, ed. by Sigrid Hinz (Berlin: Henschel, 1984), 129.

9   All references to *Phantasus* are taken from Ludwig Tieck, *Schriften in zwölf Bänden*, ed. by Manfred Frank et al., 6 vols (Frankfurt am Main: Deutscher Klassiker Verlag, 1985-) VI.

10 Goethe's *Unterhaltungen deutscher Ausgewanderten/Conversations of German Émigrés* of 1795 and Wieland's *Hexameron von Rosenhain* of 1800.

before it becomes associated with E. T. A. Hoffmann or Arnim, not to speak of less fastidious devotees of the mode. Five of them are the ones chosen by Thomas Carlyle in 1827[11] to signal the, for him, most significant developments in modern German short prose fiction: *Der blonde Eckbert/ Fair-Haired Eckbert*, *Der getreue Eckart/Faithful Eckart*, *Der Runenberg/The Rune Mountain*, *Die Elfen/The Elves* and *Der Pokal/The Goblet* (without, however, the uncanniest of all, *Liebeszauber/Love's Magic*). But included in *Phantasus* would be other, discrete works, some of which specifically bore the subtitle 'Märchen', such as the dramatic adaptations of Charles Perrault, *Rothkäppchen/Red Riding Hood*, *Der Blaubart/Bluebeard*, *Der gestiefelte Kater/Puss in Boots* and *Däumchen/Hop o' My Thumb*.[12] The long (and somewhat tedious) chapbook adaptation, *Fortunat*, is also subtitled 'Ein Märchen'. This placed it in a category with *Die schöne Magelone/ Fair Magelone*, the other 'Volksbuch' reworking, given here pride of place over a number of earlier ones now excluded.[13] The tone of the collection thus appears to be dominated by a wide and commodious definition of fairytale. The 125 pages of introductory conversation in volume one that precede the reading and discussion of the stories, is not essentially restricted to matters of genre or tone. And it is here that Tieck comes the closest in his middle years to defining what 'Märchen' means and what it takes in or excludes.

A number of these works, prose or drama, had appeared first in 1796 in a collection called *Volksmährchen/Folktales*.[14] That they manifestly were folktales only in respect of the traditions of other nations, or that they

---

11   [Thomas Carlyle], *German Romance: Specimens of its Chief Authors*, 4 vols (Edinburgh and London: Tait, 1827).

12   *Der Blaubart* is a dramatic adaptation of *Bluebeard*, in prose. Originally published in 1796, it was Tieck's attempt at producing a 'fantastic' subject for the stage, along the lines of Gozzi. It was never a stage success, being too literary and too self-consciously aware of that literary quality. *Der gestiefelte Kater*, first published in 1797, is similarly a drama in prose. It is both a satire on the contemporary theatre and its bad taste, and a 'play within a play' with audience participation. Many critics have taken it to illustrate the principles of Romantic irony, particularly on account of its deliberate breaking of dramatic illusion. *Rothkäppchen* appeared in 1800. This time in verse, this little play introduces more direct satire on conventional piety and popular philosophy, with the wolf as 'sansculotte' into the bargain. *Däumchen* was first published in *Phantasus* in 1812. Here there is much more literary satire, including some unlikely mixtures, such as the classical trimeter and the Arthurian court.

13   These are *Die Geschichte von den Heymons Kindern*, *Denkwürdige Geschichtschronik der Schildbürger*, and *Sehr wunderbare Historie von der Melusina*.

14   *Popular Fairy Tales*, ed. by Peter Leberecht, 3 vols (Berlin: Carl August Nicolai, 1797).

teased and tweaked the reader with fictitious places of publication such as 'Bergamo' or 'Istambul', need not concern or surprise us unduly.[15] Johann Carl August Musäus, whose tone of ironic archness is a source of particular irritation to the Tieck of *Phantasus*, had called his collection of 1782–86 *Volksmärchen der Deutschen/German Folktales*, and this they too by no means all were. The early Tieck was scrupulous enough to recall that all adaptations — whether from German sources or others — were in a sense 'popular'. Only, the ironic, bantering, witty aside-taking of the reader occasionally suggested the sophistication of the *Cabinet des fées* or even the French rococo, and the introduction of stock figures from the *commedia dell'arte* was doubtless rooted in Tieck's precocious reading of Carlo Gozzi as a schoolboy. The circle of young literary men and women in Berlin and Jena, who saw themselves as creating a new awareness of poetry, poetic tradition, and the poetic process, and who were to call themselves 'Romantic', saw Tieck's 'Märchen' as a demonstration of what they, too, were striving for. August Wilhelm Schlegel's review of *Ritter Blaubart/Sir Bluebeard* (as it was then known) and *Der gestiefelte Kater* in the Jena *Allgemeine Literatur-Zeitung* in 1797[16] can with justification be seen as one of the important first links forged between Tieck and the Jena circle. The continuation of the *Volksmährchen* that came out in 1799–1800, now bore the name of *Romantische Dichtungen/Poetic Works in a Romantic Vein*. And it would be fair to say that, for Tieck at least, 'Romantic' was indeed synonymous with three elements of his early works summed up in these titles: 'Volksdichtung', but its adaptation in a succession of sophisticated self-mirrorings (as in his Romantic legend drama *Genoveva*);[17] 'Märchen', but in the widest sense, giving fullest rein to the creative imagination; and as the movement's name of 'Romantic' implied, the receptive and eclectic drawing on a wide range of poetic traditions from the Middle Ages to the present.

---

15   The title pages read: *Der gestiefelte Kater. Kindermärchen in drei Akten, mit Zwischenspielen, einem Prologe und Epiloge von Peter Leberecht. Aus dem Italienischen. Erste unverbesserte Auflage. Bergamo 1797. In Commission bei Onario Senzacolpa. Die sieben Weiber des Blaubart. Eine wahre Familiengeschichte herausgegeben von Gottlieb Färber. Istambul, bey Heraklius Murusi Hofbuchhändler der hohen Pforte; im Jahr der Hedschrah 1212.*

16   August Wilhelm Schlegel, *Sämmtliche Werke*, ed. by Eduard Böcking, 12 vols (Leipzig: Weidmann, 1846–47), XI, 136–50.

17   *Leben und Tod der heiligen Genoveva. Ein Trauerspiel*. In: *Romantische Dichtungen von Ludwig Tieck*, 2 vols (Jena: Frommann, 1799–1800), II, 1–272.

In that sense, 'Märchen', as he was to define it in the exchange of opinions in *Phantasus*, was part of Tieck's wider programme of literary renewal and reception. The dedication of *Phantasus* to August Wilhelm Schlegel, with its reminder of their once close association, reinforces the connection. The themes, the old and new loves, but also the prejudices that are rehearsed in the framework discussion in *Phantasus*, are a catalogue of his literary interests over more than a generation, often of his unrepentant advocacy, against all the evidence, of the influences he considered to be formative on his youthful poetic development. They need not concern us here, except in the sense that the discussion of 'Märchen' is positioned amid a shifting swirl of images, all stations in a pilgrimage (Tieck uses the words 'andächtige Wallfahrt')[18] to the scenes of old acquaintances and affections. The discussions are 'framed', but Tieck initiates inside each frame processes that inform of unfulfilled states, longing, reflections that constantly change perspective and dimension. Of that longing, 'Sehnsucht', a discussion partner speaks in these telling words:

> [...] ja, es gibt eine ewige Jugend, eine Sehnsucht, die ewig währt, weil sie ewig nicht erfüllt wird; weder getäuscht noch hintergangen, sondern nur nicht erfüllt, damit sie nicht sterbe, denn sie sehnt sich im innersten Herzen nach sich selbst, sie spiegelt in unendlich wechselnden Gestalten das Bild der nimmer vergänglichen Liebe, das Nahe im Fernen, die himmlische Ferne im Allernächsten.[19]

Thus the polyvalency of poetry is but part of this self-reflection, this reaching out in order to turn in on oneself, this self-discovery in all objects 'out there'. In the same way, no landscape stands still, but shifts and undulates in the movement of the eye, always withholding new perspectives yet to be discovered, as music is lost even as the melodic line takes shape. And these two means of sensory perception join forces with the spoken word to produce, not merely a symposium of opinions and readings, but a synaesthesia.

---

18   'Devout pilgrimage'. *Phantasus*, 15.
19   '[...] yes, there is an eternal youth, a longing that lasts forever, because it forever cannot be fulfilled; neither deceived nor betrayed, but only not fulfilled, so as not to die, for it longs in its innermost heart for itself, it mirrors in an endlessly changing array of figures the image of a love that never passes away, the near in the distant, heavenly distance in that which is the very closest'. *Phantasus*, 33.

By the same token, there is no contradiction in a work seemingly so devoted to the celebration of German traditions, for the whole to be 'framed', at the beginning and end of the discussion, between Italy and Spain. In the evocation of Lago Maggiore at the beginning (called 'romantisch'), the Italian landscape seen through German eyes (as Goethe at that very moment was preparing to recall), we are reminded of how the Nazarenes, the school of German Romantic painters, enter into the sensuousness of Italy through a meticulousness that owes much to Dürer; and the ending in a 'spanische Glosse', a contrived technical strophic device, can nevertheless conjoin music, love and longing as one aesthetic experience. They remind us that 'romantisch' may also mean the lands of romance, 'das alte romantische Land'[20] of the opening to Wieland's Ariostian verse epic *Oberon* of 1780. And without that 'romance' component, Tieck's collection would lack its love story, *Magelone*; even its dramatized tale of human folly, *Fortunat*, draws on so many themes of common provenance in other literatures. The lowering, threatening and terrifying, as exemplified in the German forest landscape (*Der blonde Eckbert*, *Der Runenberg*) or enacted in the narrow lanes of a German town (*Liebeszauber*) are complemented by the wit, elegance and very sophisticated playfulness of Ludovico Ariosto or Perrault. This, too, is quintessentially Romantic. For the Schlegel brothers, the publication of Old French or Provençal texts was not subordinated to a preoccupation with things Germanic. And for Tieck, the ultimate in poetic incarnation, William Shakespeare, is unthinkable without the widest associations with the literature of the European Renaissance.

In a similar way, the landscapes invoked in the framework discussion serve a variety of functions. They are in one sense 'real', in that beholders stand in front of them and feel drawn to them. They are, however, extended as 'mythische Gegenden'[21] that summon up the widest and most varied sets of associations, human, artistic, musical. They become symbols of other poetic processes; the romantic landscape becomes the Romantic poem; its sinuosities and undulations, its relationship of near and far suggest the Romantic narrative and its constant reference beyond itself to unfulfilled desires and longings. But ruins, waterfalls, formal parks and English gardens all have associations with the widest

---

20 'The old romantic land'.
21 'Mythical regions'. *Phantasus*, 18.

manifestations of art forms, even when our aesthetic sense may be offended by eccentric invention or excrescence. Thus Ariosto's 'zarter, blumenartiger Witz'[22] suggests the arabesque, Pedro Calderón the formal garden of French provenance, and Shakespeare, not surprisingly, the English park. Tieck does not exclude even the grotesque, the Bomarzo-style monstrosity, from the range of landscape evocation.

All this has significant implications both for Tieck's definition of 'Märchen' and for his practice as a narrator. Wieland, in his *Hexameron* of 1800, for instance, had seen little distinction between short fiction narratives ('Erzählung') and 'Märchen'. The first section of *Phantasus* (that is, after the introduction) and the one that contains the prose narratives in the collection, is preceded by two attempts to qualify 'Märchen', one real and the other allegorical. The group of literary friends and acquaintances wishes, before it hears fairy stories read aloud, to decide among itself what this art form is. But is it merely a phenomenon restricted to aesthetic or poetological criteria? Evidently not; for, a few pages earlier, it having been decided that their story-telling should begin with a 'Märchen', it had been variously described as relating to deeper processes of experience. 'Mit Märchen […] fängt das Leben an',[23] one of the company volunteers; they are the means by which the child's play and imagination take shape and form. But the spectacle of the sinking sun elicits the response: 'Auch ein Märchen'.[24] The onset of night, the stealing in of shadows, awaken the sense of longing for what is about to be lost forever from our sight. In its main discussion, the company proceeds from concrete examples: the ones some do not like (Hamilton's in the *Cabinet des fées* or Musäus), the ones others do (Goethe, Novalis). If the witty rococo-style tale suffers all kinds of interruptions and interpolations, the real 'Märchen' calls for consistency of composition, and instead of that knowing cleverness, an innocence that is neither too obtrusive nor too mannered. This is where Goethe and Novalis reap praise, evidence, should any be needed, of Tieck's manifestly literary preferences. The mention of Ariosto (literature again) elicits a double response: some find him lacking in shape and order, too fragmented, others defend his lightness of touch, his deft moves from one theme

---

22　'Gentle, flower-like wit'. *Phantasus*, 108.
23　'Life begins with fairytales'. *Phantasus*, 98.
24　'A fairytale too'. Ibid.

or adventure to another. As neither nature nor architecture can abide an excess of unheightened expanse, but require this to be broken and relieved, so Ariosto fulfils this decorative, arabesque-like function to perfection (here follows a disquisition on garden style).

The remaining general discussion is brief but crucial. If the 'Märchen' could hitherto be informed by the processes of the imagination and longing, its other side now comes to the fore. The 'Märchen' also comes about where our premonitions and intimations, our existential angst, take over and populate a landscape, symbolic or real, with the projections of our inner anxieties. The unnerving and ultimately terrifying aspect of such tales is that commonplace or banal objects are invested by the imagination with a significance beyond themselves. It is here that the word 'allegorisch'[25] occurs and the link is forged with central tenets of Romantic poetic theory. It is the awareness that no product of the imagination, no form of poetic expression of whatever kind, has substance without that higher referentiality.

Tieck is not Novalis (or Friedrich Schlegel). He is concerned less with the philosophical connotations of allegory than with its actual manifestation. How better to do this than in the allegorical poem, *Phantasus*, that follows. If the winged boy Phantasus has affinities with Puck or Ariel, it is also he who leads away from brooding introspection, book-learning and speculation, into a symbolic landscape. The plants and metals there, or the sunrise over all of nature, suggest Philipp Otto Runge's world of higher significance, the glimpse of an 'Ideenparadies' in the symbolic progression from earth to heaven, from darkness to light. But Tieck's imagination never becomes ethereal: we are still in the world of 'Märchen'. Its allegorical denizens have names: 'Schreck', 'liebe Albernheit', 'Scherz' and 'Liebe'.[26] Only 'Liebe' shares affinities with Runge's cosmic vision, as that force that is felt by all things, animate and inanimate alike. But here Tieck abruptly switches mythologies. True to the awareness that the universal may be hidden in the objects around us, *Phantasus* brings about the ultimate allegorical transference of meaning. The landscape of mountain, grotto and forest reveals itself as a huge head or face:[27] it is the god Pan himself, 'von allem der Erhalter', the

---

25 'Allegorical'. *Phantasus*, 113.
26 'Fright', 'sweet silliness', 'pleasantry', 'love'.
27 Cf. modern examples of the anthropomorphic landscape in: Ferdinand Hodler, *Landschaften*, ed. by Oskar Bätschmann et al., Schweizerisches Institut für

source and upholder of all things. Perhaps Tieck wishes less to strain the limits of allegory as to remind us — in a reminiscence of allusions that stretch from Hieronymus Bosch and François Rabelais or both Tassos to his contemporary Joseph Görres[28] — that well-being and terror are never far from each other. In August Wilhelm Schlegel's review of 1797, that realm had been characterized by the co-existence of these two, 'Behagen' and 'Entsetzen'.[29] But we must not overlook Tieck's particular emphasis. Pan produces horror, it is true, 'Graun' and 'Schauder' (strong words)[30] but also 'Schreck'. Earlier in the poem it is 'Schreck' and 'liebe Albernheit', fright and agreeable silliness, who aid and abet each other in games of terror whose outcome is predictable but deliciously chilling all the same. And no-one is fonder of sheer 'Albernheit' than, by his own admission,[31] Tieck himself. His *Hop o' My Thumb* adaptation, *Däumchen*, for all its parodistic asides, is ample proof, if any were needed.

It is true that the stories now read in the society tend towards the uncanny and the horrific. *Der blonde Eckbert* adds the fantastic for good measure, but fetches it back into our present consciousness in order to blur distinctions between imagination and reality, moral responsibility and malign contingency. *Liebeszauber* suggests that by looking in on any window in any back alley we may be confronted with visions of terror and obscenity, unmotivated and consuming, that may re-emerge as destructive, if avenging forces. It is thus significant that, of all the stories, *Die schöne Magelone* is provided with a preface. The garden or landscape symbols there are invoked anew in order to summon up, not terror, but the wondrous world of a past in which this exemplary love-story is situated. The aesthetic justification of renewal or modernization of an old story (with the attendant perils of the falsely archaic) must lie in the revocation of the near-paradisal state of lost innocence where

---

Kunstwissenschaft (Zurich: Verlagshaus Zürich, 1987), 42f.; Max Klinger, *Wege zum Gesamtkunstwwerk* (Mainz: Philipp von Zabern, 1984), 221.

28 Gustav René Hocke, *Die Welt als Labyrinth. Manier und Manie in der europäischen Kunst. Von 1520 bis 1650 und in der Gegenwart*, rowohlts deutsche enzyklopädie 50–51, 2 vols (Hamburg: Rowohlt, 1957), I , 86f.; Elisabeth Stopp, 'Die Kunstform der Tollheit: zu Clemens Brentanos und Joseph Görres' "BOGS der Uhrmacher"', in *Clemens Brentano. Beiträge des Kolloquiums im Freien Deutschen Hochstift 1978*, ed. by Detlev Lüders (Tübingen: Niemeyer, 1980), 358–76, esp. 375.

29 'Contentment' and 'revulsion'. August Wilhelm Schlegel, *Sämmtliche Werke*, XI, 136.

30 'Spine-tingling horror' and 'awfulness'.

31 Roger Paulin, *Ludwig Tieck: A Literary Biography* (Oxford: Clarendon Press, 1985), 62, 358.

once all things stood in harmony with each other, the world summoned up by Novalis in the Atlantis story in his novel *Heinrich von Ofterdingen*. To tell of that innocence, unaffected by time or transience, must also be the function of the 'Märchen'. It is the substance of some of Tieck's most-quoted lines, from his adaptation of another 'Volksbuch', *Kaiser Octavianus* (1804):

> Mondbeglänzte Zaubernacht,
> Die den Sinn gefangen hält,
> Wundervolle Märchenwelt,
> Steig' auf in der alten Pracht![32]

These lines become a kind of poetic credo when chosen in 1828 to lead the procession of products of that imagination in volume one of Tieck's own definitive edition of his works (*Schriften*) begun in that year. Titles like *Romantische Dichtungen* are no longer necessary: the symbolic evocation of the past and its wondrous harmony and unity, the celebration of the love and chivalry recorded in romance (of whatever provenance), also constitute 'Märchen' and are by definition 'romantisch'. But we dare not overlook that that world of 'Märchen' has to co-exist with the panicked terror produced when the harmonious landscape that we see before us suddenly turns into one of the monsters in the Bomarzo garden.

---

32 'Moonbeam-lit magic night,
    That holds the mind in thrall,
    Wondrous magic world,
    Rise up in glory as of old!'
    Kaiser Octavianus. Ein Lustspiel in zwei Theilen von Ludwig Tieck (Jena: Frommann, 1804), 35.

Fig. 12 Friedrich Gundolf, photograph by Jacob Hilsdorf (1911), University Library Heidelberg, Wikimedia, https://commons.wikimedia.org/wiki/File:Friedrich_Gundolf_(HeidICON_33461).jpg, CC BY-SA 4.0.

9. Gundolf's Romanticism[1]

Romantik und Kritizismus (Schriftstellertum). Schlegel. Wackenroder. In der ganzen Romantik ist der *Geist*, die Ironie die Hauptsache. Sie ist tief literarisch. Tieck. Wackenroder, ein Standard Werk der Romantik, ganz analytisch-schriftstellerisch. Und naiv. Ebenso Lucinde. Die Romantiker im Ganzen keine starken Plastiker: philosophisch. Ihre Naivetät (sic) ist Raffinement. 'Welch ein Wissen vom Dichterischen, von Sprache und Bildung...' (Gundolf).[2]

This jotting by Thomas Mann, written sometime after 1907, after the appearance of Friedrich Gundolf's *Romantiker-Briefe/Romantics' Letters*, may serve by way of introduction to our subject. It demonstrates how pervasive and influential an approach to Romanticism such as Gundolf's could be, one that was free of mere scholarly or academic detail or pedantry, which was presented with an analytical sweep, a self-confidence in judgement, a contentiousness reinforced at every turn by intriguing and tantalizing formulation, and above all a control of language; the whole revealing its author to be one who had, in a masterly and masterful fashion, read widely and in detail but had also drunk deep at the well of historical and philosophical speculation that owed much to Jacob Burckhardt or even Friedrich Nietzsche. Mann's

---

1   An earlier version of this chapter was published as 'Gundolf's Romanticism', in *Deutsche Romantik und das 20. Jahrhundert. Londoner Symposion 1985*, ed. by Hanne Castein and Alexander Stillmark, Stuttgarter Arbeiten zur Germanistik 177 (Stuttgart: Heinz, 1986), 25–40. On this subject, but with a different accentuation, see Peter Küpper, 'Gundolf und die Romantik', *Euphorion* 75 (1981), 194–203.

2   '*Romanticism* and criticism (writings authored by them). Schlegel. Wackenroder. In all of Romanticism spirit, irony is predominant. It is deeply literary. Tieck. Wackenroder, a standard work of Romanticism, analytical and literary to the core. And naïve. Lucinde the same. The Romantics in general have no strong sense of form. Philosophical. Their naivete is over-cultivation. "What knowledge of matters poetic, of language and culture..." (Gundolf)'. Thomas Mann, quoted in T. J. Reed, *Thomas Mann. The Uses of Tradition* (Oxford: Clarendon Press, 1974), 129.

(and others') knowledge of German Romanticism may have come from reading of single writers (notably Novalis and E. T. A. Hoffmann) or through the mediation of Richard Wagner; but one is also tempted to say that the synthetic and highly individual approach to the whole movement used by Gundolf not only in 1907, but time and time again in other writings, had an influence on the intellectually and culturally aware reader that may have been incalculable.

If we turn from the incalculable to the certain, the following seems to emerge. It is customary to see Gundolf's views on Romanticism as an emanation of the Stefan George circle, the critical prose *obbligato* to the severe poetic tones of the master to whom Gundolf — publicly and privately — so selflessly and abjectly deferred. Seen thus, Gundolf's two works on Romanticism, the *Romantiker-Briefe* of 1907, and *Romantiker/ Romantics* of 1930–31, but notably also *Shakespeare und der deutsche Geist/Shakespeare and the German Spirit* (1911), seem to reflect the preferences and prejudices of an exclusive circle. I believe this view to be in some need of revision: for the very simple, primary and obvious reason that the actual scholarly activity of the George circle or its associates cannot be subsumed under such general categories. One has only to mention the names of Norbert von Hellingrath, and his work on Friedrich Hölderlin, Karl Wolfskehl and his energetic activity on the literature of the Middle Ages and the Baroque, and Gundolf himself, with his highly disparate oeuvre, to remind oneself that the circle encompassed a wide range of intellectual and scholarly endeavour: editions, essays, translations, anthologies, critical studies.

Yet the especial closeness of Gundolf to George, his role as the beloved disciple, the boundless love and respect of one for the other, seems to admit of a distinction in the case of Gundolf. Romanticism, seen from this perspective, might seem to represent rather more the crumbs from off the table where the feast of great names from history's temple of fame is served: Caesar, Dante, William Shakespeare, Johann Wolfgang Goethe, Nietzsche and George himself, confirming George's own view of the nineteenth century as an age of spiritual and intellectual decline, as he writes on June 11, 1910 to Gundolf, with the following adaptation of Nietzsche:

> Wie kommt es dass das gesamtergebnis kein GOETHE sondern ein CHAOS ist, ein nihilistisches Seufzen, ein nicht-wissen wo-aus-wo-ein ein

instinkt von ermüdung der in praxi immer dazu treibt zum achtzehnten
JAHRHUNDERT ZURÜCKZUGREIFEN?³

This would leave us with only the 'great figures' of earlier history, or those few of the nineteenth century who have upheld standards against the rush of so-called progress and materialism, those names from across the ages that George invokes in the opening pages of *Der siebente Ring / The Seventh Ring*: Dante, Goethe, Nietzsche, Arnold Böcklin. To these names from the previous century Gundolf would hasten to add Burckhardt, Leopold von Ranke, Theodor Mommsen, Herman Grimm (the biographer of Michelangelo), even Conrad Ferdinand Meyer, for having kept their heads high amidst 'unsäglich öden stoffseligen doktrinären und bildungswütig-seichten Zeitalter der Presse, der Technik, des naturwissenschaftlichen Forschtriumphes und eines missverstandenen Bismarck'.⁴ The return to Goethe in particular is a means of confirming a new and more exclusive awareness of culture and the poetic office; the return to the age which Goethe dominated, to which in Gundolf's eyes he gave its quintessential poetic expression, receives — but essentially through the reference to Goethe — its most adequate justification.

In these terms, two strands emerge in Gundolf's writings, both affirmations, but one distinctly subordinated to the other. This seems to me to be at the very heart of Gundolf's approach to literature — and by extension to Romanticism. Karl Wolfskehl, on receiving proofs of the Friedrich Schlegel section to Gundolf's introduction to the *Romantiker-Briefe*, put his finger on the problem in this highly perceptive statement:

> Dass das Aufregende, Saaten Streuende, wetternde, pflügende, das Vorbotenhafte, Mehr, wichtiger, menschlicher sei als die Zeiten oder Wesen der Erfüllung sag ich nicht, ich sage nur es sei eine

---

3   'How is it that the end result is not a GOETHE but CHAOS, a nihilistic sighing, not knowing one way or the other, an instinct of lassitude that in practice impels us back to EMBRACE THE EIGHTEENTH CENTURY?' Friedrich Gundolf, *Briefwechsel*, ed. by Robert Boehringer and Georg Peter Landmann (Munich, Düsseldorf: Küpper, 1962), 202.

4   'An age that was unbelievably tedious, materially-oriented, doctrinaire and embracing culture but shallowly, an age of the press, technology, triumphant scientific progress and a Bismarck they failed to appreciate'. Letter to Wolfskehl, September 29, 1905. Karl and Hanna Wolfskehl, *Briefwechsel mit Friedrich Gundolf 1899–1931*, ed. by Karlheinz Kluncker, 2 vols, Publications of the Institute of Germanic Studies, University of London (Amsterdam: Castrum Peregrini, 1977), II, 30.

> Geschmacksfrage, wie Nietzsche am besten und — Peinlichsten zeigt, ob einem Heraklit lieber ist oder Platon.[5]

Heraclitus or Plato? Gundolf sees it in less philosophical terms, but the implications are the same. In almost every major work of Gundolf's or in almost every statement about a, for him, major figure, we will find these two opposite positions stated and their polarity defended:

> Fur Platon waren die Ideen, für Jesus das Himmelreich, für Hölderlin Hellas gelebte Gegenwart, für die Romantiker waren sie die Ferne, das Andre, das Noch-nicht oder Nicht-mehr.
>
> (*Caesar*)[6]

> Die Romantik hat sich nicht in großen Menschen erfüllt und nicht in Werken ihr eigentümliches Leben zusammendrängen und festhalten können. Nur dichterische und gedankliche Bruchstücke geben uns Kunde von ihr als einer — weit über ihre Ergebnisse hinaus — eindringlichen und umfassenden Bewegung, wie angespülte Trümmer vom Sturm.[7]

> Schon nach dieser Weltverfassung konnten die Romantiker nicht das Individuum suchen wollen, an Ausbildung der Persönlichkeit dachten sie nur, sofern dadurch ihr Spiel und die Fülle ihrer Gesichte gesteigert wurde. Sie sind darin die Widerrenaissance und stellen das Goethesche Ideal in Frage. Sie fühlten sich als Fragmente, als Wellen einer großen Vibration.
>
> (*Romantiker-Briefe*)[8]

---

5   'I won't say that excitement, dissemination, lightning flashes, tilling, pointing the way — are more, more significant, more human than times of fulfilment and their agents. I merely say: it is a matter of taste, as Nietzsche best shows — and most notoriously so — whether Heraclitus is more to one's taste than Plato'. Ibid., II, 48.

6   'For Plato it was ideas, for Jesus the kingdom of heaven, for Hölderlin Hellas, the very present times they lived in, for the Romantics it was the distant, the other, the as yet fulfilled or not yet fulfilled'. Gundolf, *Caesar. Geschichte seines Ruhms* [1924], reprinted in *Caesar. Geschichte seines Ruhms* (Darmstadt: Wissenschaftliche Buchgesellschaft, 1968), 251.

7   'Romanticism did not find fulfilment in great names and was not able to concentrate and give form to the essential features of its life. Only fragments of poetry and thought bear witness to it — and far beyond what it actually produced — as an encompassing and penetrating movement — like jetsam after a storm'. Gundolf, *Beiträge zur Literatur- und Geistesgeschichte*, ed. by Victor A. Schmitz und Fritz Martini, Veröffentlichungen der Deutschen Akademie für Sprache und Dichtung Darmstadt 54 (Heidelberg: Lambert Schneider, 1980), 85 (referred to subsequently as *Beiträge*).

8   'Given their way of seeing the world, the Romantics could not and would not seek the individual; they were only concerned with the development of personality, and

Allerdings hat in der eigentlichen Dichtung das klassischplastische Prinzip seinen endgültigen Ausdruck nur in dem einen Goethe gefunden. Die Romantik hat sich in der Dichtung nicht bis zu eigenen Formen verdichten können, ist Tendenz geblieben.

(*Shakespeare und der deutsche Geist*)[9]

Sein Hellas hat also nichts mit Ruinen-sentimentalität, auch nicht — wie man seit Haym meist annimmt — mit romantischer Sehnsucht zu tun, die aus der Leere kommt und durch Traum ersetzt, was die Wirklichkeit versagt.

(*Hölderlins Archipelagus*)[10]

Es ist ein wesentliches Zeichen der klassischen Naturen daß bei ihnen Instinkt, Genie und Denken in derselben Richtung arbeiten. Ihr Denken ist nur die bewußte, hell gewordene Verlängerung des dunklen Lebensstroms der aus ihrer Mitte bricht, nur der genaue und gewissenhafte Vollzieher dessen was der Grundtrieb ihres Lebens ihm befiehlt, ihr Denken hat nicht, wie bei den Romantikern, Mystikern, Musikern eine eigene gesetzgebende oder gesetzstürzende Gewalt, sondern nur eine exekutive. Bei solchen Naturen sind die Äußerungen des formenden Bewußtseins nur der getreue Index dessen was in der dunklen Mitte und Tiefe vorgeht, die Helle ihrer Glut, der Logos ihres Eros. Denn Logos und Eros sind dann nicht notwendige Gegensätze, es sind nur verschiedene Helligkeitsgrade desselben Zustandes. Für diese klassische Geistesart, welche im Altertum uns immer wieder als Norm bezaubert, ist in der neuen Welt Goethe das größte, sicher das deutlichste Beispiel.

(*Goethe*)[11]

---

that only to enhance their play and their multiform visions. In that respect they are the Counter-Renaissance and they call the Goethean ideal into question. They had a sense of being fragments, waves of a great vibration'. Ibid., 88.

9 'Of course in real poetry a classical principle of form found its final and ultimate expression in Goethe. Romanticism was unable to achieve concentrated form and has never gained established status'. Gundolf, *Shakespeare und der deutsche Geist* (Berlin: Bondi, 1920 [1911]), 322.

10 'His Hellas has nothing to do with a sentimental cult of ruins, or — as Haym would have us believe — with Romantic longing, that comes out of the void and supplants through dream what reality does not supply'. Gundolf, *Dem lebendigen Geist*, ed. by Dorothea Berger und Marga Frank, Veröffentlichungen der Deutschen Akademie für Sprache und Dichtung Darmstadt 27 (Heidelberg, Darmstadt: Lambert Schneider, 1962), 30.

11 'It is an essential characteristic of classical natures that instinct, genius and thought all work in one and the same direction. Their thinking is but the extension, made

> Die Romantik lebte in einer Zwischenschicht zwischen den ewigen Kräften und den Zeitzuständen, in der „Bildung": sie wucherte auf den von Goethe, Herder, Kant begründeten Ordnungen üppig weiter, ohne mit ihren Wurzeln in den Grund selbst hinunterzureichen. (...) Der Historismus, der nur Vergangenes sieht, das Epigonentum, das nur Vergangenes treibt, sind ihre Erben, ohne ihre Höhe und ihr Feuer, mehr und mehr dem toten Stoff verfallend und den leeren Formen.
>
> (*George*)[12]

It is not by coincidence that the most extreme polarization and the most severe rejection of Romanticism come in the context of Shakespeare, Goethe and George. But we will find in Gundolf's discussion of Romanticism proper words or phrases like the following, which characterize his position very clearly: 'Bewegung', 'Spiel', 'Vorliebe für alles Schwanke, Schwebende, Nacht, Geheimnis und Dämmerung', 'grenzenlos', 'expansiv'.[13] In his very percipient — and remarkably fair — review of *Shakespeare und der deutsche Geist*, Oskar Walzel, no mean synthesist himself, takes Gundolf to task for not examining seriously enough the actual philosophical ideas of the Romantics, for overlooking its very marked sense of programme and system, for seeing only the ironical and protean side of the movement, and for rejecting almost the entire nineteenth century that followed.[14] Gundolf's view

---

clear and conscious, of the dark life-stream gushing forth from their inward parts, but the exact and conscientious executor of their basic urge and its demands. Their thinking, not as with the Romantics, or as with mystics or musicians, has power to make rules or overthrow them, only of putting into action. With natures like these the utterances that give conscious form are but an accurate indication of processes in their dark centre and depths, the bright flame of their blaze, the logos of their eros. For logos and eros are then not necessarily opposites; they are only different degrees of brightness of the same state. For this classical frame of mind, which fascinates us ever again, as a norm in classical antiquity, Goethe in the new era is the greatest and surely the most obvious example'. Gundolf, *Goethe* (Berlin: Bondi, 1930 [1916]), 12f.

12 'Romanticism lived in a median realm between the eternal forces and the events of its day, in 'culture': a rank growth on the foundations laid by Goethe, Herder and Kant, but not taking root as they did. Historicism, which only sees the past, epigonism, which only furthers the past, are their inheritance, without their status and their fire, ever more given over to dead material and its empty forms'. Gundolf, *George* (Berlin: Bondi, 1930), 5.

13 'Movement'; 'play'; 'prefer everything that is wavering, floating, night, mystery and twilight'; 'expansive'; 'without borders'. *Beiträge*, 87, 88, 95.

14 Oskar Walzel, 'Review of *Shakespeare und der deutsche Geist*', *Jahrbuch der deutschen Shakespeare-Gesellschaft* 48 (1912), 259–74.

of Romanticism is less a rejection of what Walzel stood for than a disdainful declaration that the patient philology of Erich Schmidt, Jakob Minor, Carl Schüddekopf or Reinhold Steig was at most an inadequate means to a dubious end: but it comes perilously close to the notion of 'romantische Schule' which we may trace back to Karl Rosenkranz and to Heinrich Heine, and then to those very different figures, Rudolf Haym, Wilhelm Dilthey and Ricarda Huch; Haym, with his rejection of the Romantics as unstable, lacking moral fibre, inchoate, formless; Dilthey, fairer, but distinguishing perhaps too little between individual figures of the movement and submerging personalities into some higher entity; Huch with her vitalism. This Gundolf does too. For him Romanticism is 'ein Individuum':[15] 'Wir haben das Recht, die ganze Romantik wie eine Person anzusehen'.[16]

There is more to this than the mere prejudice it seems to be and certainly is. We see this from Gundolf's essay 'Jacob Burckhardt und seine "Weltgeschichtlichen Betrachtungen"' in the *Preußische Jahrbücher* of 1907, the same year as his *Romantiker-Briefe*.[17] In numerous other statements in various places, Gundolf makes it very clear that he sees himself by calling and inclination as the successor to the great tradition of 'der einzige Ranke',[18] the historiography of the nineteenth century (as opposed to mere 'historicism'): 'Grundsätzlich erstrebe ich nichts anderes als Scherer oder Ranke, Erkenntnis dessen was geschehen ist'.[19] The Burckhardt essay makes a few aspects of his method clearer. He admires in the great historian the 'Bedürfnis nach philosophischer Durchdringung des Materials bei bewußter Ablehnung philosophischer Methode und Spekulation',[20] he admires Burckhardt's 'irae et studia',[21] his willingness to abandon mere objectivity for the sake of a compelling truth that is dear to his heart, his rejection of 'alles Systematische'.[22] But

---

15   'An individual'. *Beiträge*, 100.
16   'We have the right to see Romanticism in its entirety as one individual'. *Beiträge*, 88.
17   'Jacob Burckhardt and his "Reflections on History"'. *Beiträge*, 58–71.
18   'The inimitable Ranke'. Gundolf, *Briefe. Neue Folge*, ed. by Lothar Helbing and Claus Victor Bock (Amsterdam: Castrum Peregrini, 1965), 80.
19   'Basically, I am striving for nothing different from Scherer or Ranke: awareness of that which has once been'. Ibid., 221.
20   'The need to penetrate the material philosophically while rejecting philosophical method and speculation'. *Beiträge*, 59.
21   Ibid., 60.
22   'Everything systematic'. Ibid., 60.

Burckhardt also incorporates an 'Aristokratismus',[23] a disdain for mere progress or utilitarianism, not as extreme as Nietzsche's immoralism, not as mystically one-sided as Carlyle's cult of the hero. What especially attracts Gundolf in Burckhardt is the 'Verdichtung des Weltgeschichtlichen in den Heroen',[24] the view — allied to Hegel's — that 'große Männer' are 'Vollzieher eines über ihr Individuum hinausreichenden Willens',[25] are (here closer to Nietzsche, if not to the 'Übermensch' or 'Jenseits von Gut und Böse') 'das Entscheidende, Reifende, und allseitig Erziehende'.[26]

It would seem to me that this essay explains much of what we find in Gundolf's studies of Caesar, Goethe, Shakespeare and George: there are, on the one hand, figures representing timeless poetic genius, sufficient in themselves, adequate in their powers of utterance, beholden to no tradition, or transcending mere influence, not explicable only in terms of their own age but instead giving their personality to a whole epoch. Hence the classic formulation on Shakespeare of 1928: 'Wir fassen nicht Shakespeares Werk aus seinem Zeitalter, sondern sein Zeitalter durch sein Werk'.[27] On the other hand we have movers and initiators, explorers of the intellect and of the poetic imagination, those for whom the pursuit of new vistas of the mind is an end in itself. These were not of the first rank, but without them our century would be impoverished. This is Gundolf's more conciliatory view of Romanticism. In German terms, therefore, without Friedrich Schlegel, Novalis, Tieck, especially without August Wilhelm Schlegel's Shakespeare, the realm of the intellect and the imagination, the scope of poetic expression would be diminished. In European terms, without Byron, Heine, Victor Hugo, Alphonse de Lamartine or Adam Mickiewicz, there might not be a Mommsen or Burckhardt or even a Nietzsche; for they, too, are part of that process directed against 'historistische Lähmung',[28] the reaction against which reaches its zenith in Nietzsche's 'seelenkünderische Wissenschaft'.[29]

---

23 Ibid., 64.
24 'The concentration of world history in heroes'. Ibid., 62.
25 'Great men' are 'the executors of a will that extends beyond them as individuals'. Ibid., 67.
26 'What is decisive, brings fruition, gives universal instruction'. Ibid., 68.
27 'We do not grasp Shakespeare's works by way of his age; we grasp his age through his works.' Gundolf, *Shakespeare. Sein Wesen und Werk*, 2 vols (Berlin: Bondi, 1928), I, 11.
28 'Historical paralysis'. Gundolf, *Caesar im neunzehnten Jahrhundert*, in *Caesar*, 252.
29 'A science that proclaims the soul'. Ibid.

And so if we examine in more detail Gundolf's statements on German Romanticism, we are left with the impression that he saw a gulf fixed between the 'great' unapproachable names and the eminently approachable Romantics. Whereas the 'great' names are meaningless in mere human or biographical terms, the Romantics must be seen in just that very light, as products of their own age, if they are to be appreciated at all. In his *Romantiker-Briefe* and *Shakespeare und der deutsche Geist*, Gundolf suggests that there is a 'romantische Schule' in the older, less complimentary sense, an entity that is more communal than individual, where single figures reflect a corporate ethos or spirit, where the same characteristics, kaleidoscopically changing, recur in constant variations and refractions. His two-volume *Romantiker* of 1930–31 seem much more concerned with the individual figures (notably Ludwig Tieck) and are less stringent in their chronological definition of Romanticism (hence they include Franz Grillparzer, Annette von Droste-Hülshoff and Eduard Mörike) and more concerned to hold on to what the early to mid-nineteenth century was able to achieve before positivism, historicism or materialism swept all standards away. Goethe, of course, remains extra-territorial; similarly, Hölderlin's 'positiver hellenischer Glaube'[30] cannot be subsumed under mere groupings; while Heinrich von Kleist's fierce individualism excludes him from the start,[31] and Gundolf is inclined to keep Jean Paul separate.[32] Gundolf does not of course alter a jot of his anti-Romantic stance in the third edition of *George* in 1930,[33] but in the different context of *Romantiker* in 1930–31 he is more willing to see Romanticism as the interrelation of various notable personalities, not a mere amorphous and inchoate state of non-fulfilment. This does not mean to say that *Romantiker* is free of prejudice or even outrageous near-travesty (especially the essay on Friedrich Schlegel), but it speaks with a greater — if sometimes misguided and partial — authority than *Romantiker-Briefe* of 1907.

For Gundolf the disciple of George cannot entirely deny in himself the scholarly training received at the hands of Erich Schmidt and Gustav Roethe (if later repudiated); he cannot abjure a love of the obscure

---

30 'Positive Hellenic faith'. Gundolf, *Dem lebendigen Geist*, 36.
31 *Beiträge*, 85.
32 Ibid., 37.
33 Gundolf, *George*, 5, 10.

reference, the recondite print, the antiquarian edition. He may cover his tracks very well by disdaining the footnote or even the index, but the intimate acquaintance with texts, the 'homework', if one so will, is there. The best example is *Shakespeare und der deutsche Geist*, a book whose conclusion and climax in August Wilhelm Schlegel's translation nobody has to date effectively challenged and the patterns of which are reflected in nearly all the anthologies of material relative to Shakespeare in Germany.[34] But we note also Gundolf's historical sense if we compare him with Wilhelm Dilthey, Ludwig Klages or Herbert Cysarz. All this is to some extent nurtured within the George circle itself: there is George's own philological austerity and lack of self-indulgence guiding Gundolf on Shakespeare; there is Wolfskehl's less orderly spirit suggesting all kinds of excursions and anabases into the world of the curious and the erudite. One feels therefore that the 'public' contexts, the prefaces, the articles, the occasional addresses, display a greater openness of spirit.

Gundolf claimed in a letter that he was 'mehr menschensichtig als problemgriffig'.[35] If we apply this statement to his view of Romanticism, we are bound to say that he is more successful in discussing figures who have, in his eyes at least, some human interest or some lasting achievement. In response to Wolfskehl's criticism of his treatment of Friedrich Schlegel, Gundolf replies 'dass es meine Aufgabe war, Menschen zu zeichnen und nicht Gährungen'.[36] Indeed his aspect of Friedrich Schlegel is too much one of a man blown about by doctrines, responding feverishly to the times and exploring restlessly every path of the intellect — but little more. August Wilhelm Schlegel, on the other hand, although not emerging as a person, receives Gundolf's accolade of approval for having produced Shakespeare in 'unauflösliche Gestalt'.[37] True, the Shakespeare translation is not an 'Urerlebnis ',[38] but the mere 'Anwendung der durch Goethes sprachgewordenes Erleben geschaffenen Sprachmöglichkeiten auf Shakespeares Werk'.[39]

---

34 Such as *Shakespeare-Rezeption. Die Diskussion um Shakespeare in Deutschland. 1. Ausgewählte Texte von 1741 bis 1788.*, ed. by Hansjürgen Blinn (Berlin: Erich Schmidt, 1982).
35 'Better at seeing people than solving problems'. Gundolf, *Briefe*, 220.
36 'It was my task to depict people and not ferments'. Wolfskehl-Gundolf, *Briefwechsel*, II, 46.
37 'A figure, one and indivisible'. Gundolf, *Shakespeare und der deutsche Geist*, 349.
38 'Fundamentally new experience'. Ibid., 353.
39 'Using the resources of the language released by Goethe's experience and become word, and applying them to Shakespeare's works'. Ibid.

There is however one particular aspect of Gundolf's reception of the Romantics which shows him to be not so much — or not only — the recorder of their subordinate status compared with the 'great figures', but in a deeper way the continuer of their work and their attitudes. One is perhaps not surprised that Gundolf fails to honour August Wilhelm Schlegel's other side, his critical achievement in the Berlin and Vienna lectures, leaving only the translator of Shakespeare. His view of Tieck, too, although he scrupulously discusses nearly all the many facets of that writer's long and many-sided career, is more concerned with showing Tieck's importance than his intrinsic quality;[40] that is, his significance as the great initiator of so much in subsequent fiction, drama and poetry, the butterfly drinking from every flower, bewitched by every tradition. It is true that so much of Tieck did, as it were, slip into the mainstream of German literary and intellectual culture without its originator being recognizable in the end product: the European and American tale of terror, the 'Gesamtkunstwerk' of Wagnerian provenance, the vision of the Renaissance later seen by Burckhardt or Conrad Ferdinand Meyer, the discursive, conversational mode of fiction perfected by Theodor Fontane, the celebration of the 'great' figures of national poetry, Dante, Shakespeare, Miguel de Cervantes, Luís de Camões, Goethe. Some of these Gundolf found congenial, many distinctly not. Thus it may be that Gundolf, himself in thrall to that 'Verdichtung des Weltgeschichtlichen in den Heroen',[41] while recognizing Hegel's or Carlyle's, Burckhardt's or Nietzsche's role in isolating and celebrating greatness, chose to overlook that the Romantics themselves began this process — in other terms and for other purposes — with their establishment of a canon of Romantic poetry enshrined in names like Dante, Shakespeare or Cervantes (the trinity of the Schlegels' *Athenaeum*), with Goethe only, never Schiller, as the modern embodiment of the rebirth of the universal poetic spirit. Indeed this opening up of the national literature to the Middle Ages and the Renaissance — the Romantic — may rightly be seen as the real lasting achievement of the Schlegel brothers. It explains why so much of their endeavour is directed towards the figures of Goethe and

---

40 First published as 'Ludwig Tieck' in *Jahrbuch des Freien Deutschen Hochstifts* (1929), 99–195, subsequently in *Romantiker. Neue Folge* (Berlin-Wilmersdorf: Heinrich Keller, 1929), 5–139. Cf. E. C. Stopp, 'Wandlungen des Tieckbildes', *DVjs.* 17 (1939), 252–76.
41 'Concentration of world history in heroes'.

Shakespeare, why, in Tieck's case, these two became a preoccupation and an obsession.

Bardolatry one can certainly hold against Tieck;[42] Goetheolatry, certainly in later life, rather less so. Gundolf places both on the altar of his idolatry. What is more, he adduces one in defence of the other. For it is the Goethe of *Shakespeare und kein Ende!* that Gundolf invokes in both of his works on Shakespeare, in order to justify the somewhat shaky thesis that first Herder and then Goethe had established Shakespeare as something indivisible from 'deutscher Geist'. Shakespeare is thus not essentially of the stage, is 'wahrer Sinn' as opposed to mere 'Handlung'.[43] This enables Gundolf to play down the theatrical, rhetorical tradition represented by Schiller[44] and later by Grillparzer whom he condemns on account of his very theatricality.[45] It affords a convenient side-swipe against the 'Synthetiker' Hugo von Hofmannsthal.[46] This view of Shakespeare would not necessarily separate him from Schlegel, whose notion of the stage has less to do with theatre than with national character expressed in dramatic form. It would however go against everything that Tieck stood for. In several other significant ways, Gundolf stood in agreement or coincidence with much of what is representative of both Schlegel and Tieck as Shakespeare scholars and critics.[47] First: his purely literary knowledge of English (plus a dislike of the nation itself)[48] which made him choose the Romantic-Classical, 'Goethean' Schlegel translation as the model for his own version of the Shakespeare text[49] and to disregard or disdain any subsequent attempts to render Shakespeare into German. Second: the open disregard for source material and philological apparatus (although statements in letters make it quite clear that he

---

42 See Roger Paulin, *Ludwig Tieck: A Literary Biography* (Oxford: Clarendon, 1985), 239–59.
43 'True sense'; 'action'. Cf. Eudo C. Mason, 'Gundolf und Shakespeare', *Shakespeare Jahrbuch*, 98 (1962), 110–77, esp. 123f. On Gundolf and Shakespeare cf. further Rudolf Sühnel, 'Gundolfs Shakespeare. Rezeption-Übertragung-Deutung', *Euphorion*, 75 (1981), 245–74.
44 Gundolf, *Shakespeare und der deutsche Geist*, 187f.
45 *Beiträge*, 349.
46 Ibid., 134.
47 The main points set out by Mason, 'Gundolf und Shakespeare', without parallels being drawn.
48 George-Gundolf, *Briefwechsel*, 259.
49 Cf. *Shakespeare in deutscher Sprache. Neue Ausgabe in sechs Bänden,* ed. and trans. by Friedrich Gundolf (Berlin: Bondi, 1922), I, 5, 7.

did use them),⁵⁰ notably those of English provenance. Like Schlegel's *Vorlesungen über dramatische Kunst und Literatur/Lectures on Dramatic Art and Literature* of 1809–11, Gundolf's two-volume *Shakespeare. Sein Wesen und Werk/Shakespeare. His Life and Work* of 1928 rises up seemingly from the pure source of the Bard himself, innocent of the footnote or the merely learned aside. Indeed, one might say that this discreet covering of tracks is one of the sources of fascination for the reader of any of Gundolf's works and a compelling source of authority. (It is, in fairness, worth remembering that nineteenth century commentators⁵¹ also do this, the much-despised Georg Gottfried Gervinus and the more respected Otto Ludwig.)⁵² Third: Gundolf's interest in character rather than in dramatic action is central to Schlegel's approach to Shakespeare, but also indicates how closely he, like Samuel Taylor Coleridge at the same time, sees the plays in terms of dominating, often eponymous, figures.

There are indications that Gundolf occasionally repeats or continues the particular emphases of his Romantic predecessors. Take Lady Macbeth, one of Tieck's more daring, even outrageous, attempts to break with traditional characterization in Shakespeare, and in this case, with Schiller's, which was to postulate a more female, femininely tender, Lady Macbeth. For Gundolf, too, she is 'kein selbstisches Mannweib', but 'die schmiegsam kluge und starke Gefährtin' with 'geselliges Weibstum', 'Hausfrau und Schaffnerin', 'höfliche, umsichtige, ja bezaubernde Wirtin', 'die Berechnende' as opposed to 'der Besessene' who is her husband.⁵³ Take Falstaff. Like Schlegel, Gundolf, while fascinated by the breath-taking effrontery of this character and the sheer impudence of his wit, does not overlook that he is underneath it all 'alt und dabey lüstern und liederlich' (Schlegel),⁵⁴ 'ein saftiger Lump' (Gundolf).⁵⁵ Or, turning this time away from character to action, take *A Midsummer Night's Dream*.

---

50 Cf. George-Gundolf, *Briefwechsel*, 184, 191, 275.
51 Gundolf, *Shakespeare und der deutsche Geist*, 353.
52 Wolsfkehl-Gundolf, *Briefwechsel*, I, 86.
53 'No self-possessed virago'; 'accommodating, wise and strong companion'; 'welcoming female presence'; 'housewife and housekeeper'; 'polite, gracious and charming host'; 'calculating'; 'possessed'. Gundolf, *Shakespeare. Sein Wesen und Werk*, II, 296. Paulin, *Ludwig Tieck*, 252f.
54 'Old and loose and lascivious'. August Wilhelm Schlegel, *Vorlesungen über dramatische Kunst und Littteratur, Kritische Ausgabe der Vorlesungen*, IV, i, ed. by Stefan Knödler (Paderborn, etc.: Schöningh, 2018), 352.
55 'An out and out rascal'. Gundolf, *Shakespeare. Sein Wesen und Werk*, I, 296.

Both Schlegel and Gundolf draw especial attention to the different levels of action — the wedding of Theseus, the quarrel between Oberon and Titania, the two pairs of lovers, and the 'rude mechanicals' and how they form part of one indivisible whole: 'so leicht und glücklich verflochten, daß sie durchaus zu einander zu gehören scheinen, um ein Ganzes zu bilden' (Schlegel),[56] 'ein rhythmisch ausgewogenes Zusammen, Gegeneinander und Durcheinander' (Gundolf).[57] I draw particular attention to these three examples, which are not randomly chosen: they are those on which Eudo Mason dwells in his article 'Gundolf und Shakespeare' as instances of Gundolf's perception and sensitivity as a Shakespeare critic.[58] For me, they show in addition a remarkable case of the persistence of Romantic approaches to Shakespeare — so very different from the technical and analytical approach of, say, Otto Ludwig, to whom Gundolf was nearer in time if not in spirit.

Even then our analogies are not exhausted. This time, Gundolf seems nearer to Tieck than to Schlegel. Take his tripartite division of Shakespeare's life,[59] a central part of Tieck's fragmentary *Buch über Shakespeare/Book about Shakespeare*[60] and incidentally also integral to Coleridge's chronology of Shakespeare. Like both Tieck and Coleridge, Gundolf is once or twice only (to his credit) tempted to postulate a chronology of Shakespeare's works different from the usual standard, in order to accommodate a seeming inconsistency or contradiction. Thus, for instance, he dates *Henry V* before *Henry IV*.[61] But Gundolf comes closest to Tieck in his assertion of Shakespeare's uniqueness, as the one figure bestriding all like a colossus.[62] Tieck, who knew his Elizabethans and Jacobeans much better than Gundolf did, was of course concerned to relate every aspect of English drama between 1580 and 1615 to Shakespeare, to prove that no development came about without the Bard. It led him, on the one hand, to ludicrous extensions of

---

56 'Lightly and felicitously woven together that they seem to belong together and form a whole'. Schlegel, *Vorlesungen über dramatische Kunst und Littteratur*, 325.
57 'A rhythmical balance of coherence, antagonism and confusion'. Gundolf, *Shakespeare. Sein Wesen und Werk*, I, 210. The same point is made by Gundolf in the discussion of most of the Comedies.
58 Mason, 'Gundolf und Shakespeare', 116f., 118f.
59 Cf. ibid., 125.
60 Cf. Paulin, *Ludwig Tieck*, 246f.
61 Gundolf, *Shakespeare. Sein Wesen und Werk*, I, 373.
62 As, for instance, in his assertion that *Titus Andronicus* contains all of Marlowe's achievement. Ibid., I, 27.

the Shakespeare canon, a craziness of which we cannot accuse Gundolf.[63] It led him also, and here we see Gundolf coming nearer to Tieck, to diminish and disparage the achievements of other Elizabethans, notably Marlowe. Both Tieck and Gundolf, in different contexts, are concerned to prove that the nobility, the magnanimity, the spiritual greatness, the heroic wilfulness, manifested in the plays are all part of Shakespeare's own character. Tieck does this in fictive guise, in a contrast between Shakespeare's assumed character and that of his contemporaries;[64] for Gundolf, such a contrast is a postulate worthy of the 'Allgeist'[65] that is Shakespeare. Shakespeare, too, while absorbing elements of the Middle Ages or of 'Renaissance-individualismus'[66] displays these, significantly enough, only in the early stages of his career, as the author of *Henry VI* or *Love's Labour's Lost*, but not in the mature works where he is beholden to no 'influence' or 'school'. Christopher Marlowe, by contrast, is 'der eigentliche elisabethanische Renaissance-dramatiker'.[67] In this, Tieck would heartily concur.

One final coincidence of ideas binds Tieck and Gundolf. Both are connoisseurs of the German drama of the sixteenth and seventeenth centuries (Tieck its first real editor).[68] Both, although separated by a span of a hundred years, are unable to appreciate the peculiar style of drama that the Jesuits, the Dutch, the German Silesians and, to some extent, Pierre Corneille brought about. Here the contrast with Shakespeare serves to do little more than cloud the issue, as in Gundolf's short monograph on Andreas Gryphius.[69] For Tieck, this might be pardonable, for Gundolf, less so. It was to be Walter Benjamin who first demonstrated convincingly that there is little to be gained by confronting the 'great names' of Aeschylus or Calderón or Shakespeare with Martin Opitz, Andreas Gryphius or Daniel Casper von Lohenstein. Similarly, we are bound to say that it was a pupil of Gundolf's Heidelberg colleague Max von Waldberg, the young Richard Alewyn,[70] who was to establish

---

63 Cf. Paulin, *Ludwig Tieck*, 245f.
64 Ibid.
65 'Universal spirit'. Cf. Mason, 'Gundolf und Shakespeare', 138.
66 Gundolf, *Shakespeare. Sein Wesen und Werk*, I, 79.
67 'The quintessential Elizabethan Renaissance dramatist'. Ibid.
68 Cf. Tieck's *Deutsches Theater* (1817).
69 Gundolf, *Andreas Gryphius* (Heidelberg: Winter, 1927), 20.
70 Richard Alewyn, 'Vorbarocker Klassizismus und griechische Tragödie. Analyse der "Antigone"-Übersetzung des Martin Opitz', *Neue Heidelberger Jahrbücher* (1926), 3–63.

that tradition and study of formal devices were of greater assistance in the understanding of seventeenth-century literary texts than some amorphous notion of 'Geist'.

I have said much of Gundolf's limitations as a writer on German Romanticism. His writings nevertheless remain to this day eminently readable and stimulating and are part of the 'Geistesgeschichte' of the first decades of the twentieth century. Perhaps the time has come, nearly fifty-five years after Gundolf' s death, to view them less in terms of strict philology or academic literary criticism, but as creative insights, the product very of their own age, written not in an anxious awe of the letter or the page but with imagination and sometimes uncanny intuitive vision, conjuring up, not through factual accumulation or adherence to doctrine, some of the essential spirit of a movement: in short, as literature.

NINETEENTH CENTURY

Fig. 13 Wilhelm Müller, engraving by Johann Friedrich Schröter (c. 1830), Wikimedia, https://commons.wikimedia.org/wiki/File:Wilhelm_M%C3%BCller_by_Schr%C3%B6ter.jpg, public domain.

10. Some Remarks on the New Edition of the Works of Wilhelm Müller[1]

To coincide with the two-hundredth anniversary of Wilhelm Müller's birth in 1794, the first collected edition of his works since 1830 has been produced.[2] This must be regarded as a literary event that will give pleasure alike to friends and lovers of 'Die schöne Müllerin' ('The Fair Maid of the Mill') or 'Die Winterreise' ('The Winter Journey') and to scholars of Romanticism and Biedermeier. Not everyone may be aware that there is an 'Internationale Wilhelm Müller-Gesellschaft'; its support was an important factor in the production of this much-needed edition. The catalogue of an exhibition mounted in his birthplace, Dessau, marks the same event with useful documentation and fascinating pictorial material.[3] The word 'minor' punctuates the whole literature on Müller,

---

1 This chapter was originally published in *Modern Language Review*, 92 (1997), 363–78.
2 *Wilhelm Müller: Werke, Tagebücher, Briefe*, ed. by Maria-Verena Leistner, intr. by Bernd Leistner, 5 vols (Berlin: Mathias Gatza, 1994). This edition is referred to in footnotes by volume and page number. Vol. I: *Gedichte I*; Vol. II: *Gedichte II*; Vol. III: *Reisebeschreibungen. Novellen*; Vol. IV: *Schriften zur Literatur*; Vol. V: *Tagebücher. Briefe*. There is a separate index volume. I have attempted to establish some holdings in the British Isles of works by Müller now considered rare. The holding institutions are identified in footnotes by abbreviations: London, British Library [BL]; London, Senate House Library [L]; Cambridge University Library [CUL], Trinity College Library, Cambridge [CTrin]; Oxford, Bodleian Library [OB]; Oxford, Taylorian Institution [OT]; John Rylands University Library of Manchester [JRULM]; Scotland, National Library of Scotland [Nat]; St Andrews University Library [StA]; Glasgow University Library [Glas]; and Edinburgh University Library [Edin].
3 *Wilhelm Müller. Eine Lebensreise. Zum 200. Geburtstag des Dichters*, ed. by Norbert Michels, Kataloge der anhaltischen Gemäldegalerie Dessau (Weimar: Böhlau, 1994). Cited henceforth as *Cat*.

but surely it is on this occasion not inappropriate to speak of a 'minor' literary sensation.

Wilhelm Müller is one of those figures in the history of German literature who stand in the shadow of others mightier than themselves. First there is Franz Schubert. It is now surely impossible to unravel the composer of 'Die schöne Müllerin' and 'Die Winterreise' from their author, so much have they assumed an existence of their own. Then there is Heinrich Heine. To many, perhaps to most, Müller appears as Heine's forerunner. The famous and much-quoted letter of July 1826, a little over a year before Müller's tragically early death, for all its deferentiality (and its pleasure at being well reviewed by the other),[4] places Müller in most readers' minds in a relationship where personal genius lies finally with the essentially greater figure, with Müller the spur for the superior achievement:

> Ich bin groß genug, Ihnen offen zu bekennen, daß mein kleines Intermezzo-Metrum nicht blos zufällige Ähnlichkeit mit Ihrem gewöhnlichen Metrum hat, sondern daß es wahrscheinlich seinen geheimsten Tonfall Ihren Liedern verdankt, indem es die lieben Müller'schen Lieder waren, die ich zu eben der Zeit kennen lernte, als ich das Intermezzo schrieb. Ich habe sehr früh schon das deutsche Volkslied auf mich einwirken lassen, späterhin, als ich in Bonn studirte, hat mir August Schlegel viel metrische Geheimnisse aufgeschlossen, aber ich glaube erst in Ihren Liedern den reinen Klang und die wahre Einfachheit, wonach ich immer strebte, gefunden zu haben. Wie rein, wie klar sind Ihre Lieder und sämmtlich sind es Volkslieder. In meinen Gedichten hingegen ist nur die Form einigermaßen volksthümlich, der Inhalt gehört der conventionnellen Gesellschaft. Ja, ich bin groß genug, es sogar bestimmt zu wiederholen, und Sie werden es mal öffentlich ausgesprochen finden, daß mir durch die Lectüre Ihrer 77 Gedichte zuerst klar geworden, wie man aus den alten, vorhandenen Volksliedformen neue Formen bilden kann, die ebenfalls volksthümlich sind, ohne daß man nöthig hat, die alten Sprachholperigkeiten und Unbeholfenheiten nachzuahmen. Im zweiten Theile Ihrer Gedichte fand ich die Form noch reiner, noch durchsichtig klarer — doch, was spreche ich viel von Formwesen, es drängt mich mehr, Ihnen zu sagen, daß ich keinen Liederdichter außer Goethe so sehr liebe wie Sie.[5]

---

4 'Über H. Heine' (1823), in Wilhelm Müller, *Vermischte Schriften. Herausgegeben mit einer Biographie Müller's begleitet von Gustav Schwab*, 5 vols (Leipzig: Brockhaus, 1830), V, 440. Cited henceforth as *VSchr.* [BL, L, OT, Edin].

5 'I can freely admit to you that my little Intermezzo does not have a mere chance similarity to your accustomed metre, but that it most likely owes the inner secret of

There is a double irony here (a word purposely chosen). The *Sieben und siebzig Gedichte aus den hinterlassenen Papieren eines reisenden Waldhornisten / Seventy-Seven Poems from the Literary Remains of a Travelling Horn Player* (the seventy-seven poems referred to), with their dedication to Ludwig Tieck, are, like all of Müller's collections, a miscellany: naturally and preeminently, 'Die schöne Müllerin', but also 'Wanderlieder', 'Reiselieder', 'Ländliche Lieder',[6] sonnets, poems to nature, to wine, to love, to friendship. The second part of the collection, which Heine in his letter claims so much to have enjoyed, contains 'Johannes und Esther', poems with another conventional theme, unfulfilled love, but in a context that gives the Petrarchan patterns a particular twist: boy (Christian) loves girl (Jew). It is the subject (or rather, one of them) of Müller's later Novelle *Debora* and none the better for appearing in that collection of modish narrative clichés. Heine is prepared to be accommodating. For Müller, with consummate grace and ease, has assembled the most accessible lyrical forms and themes of the almanacs and florilegia both of the late eighteenth century and of Romanticism. With the exception of some sonnets, which Müller, like Heine, can turn as well as the next poet, these are by and large in 'Volksliedstrophen', but there are sections that will recall the anacreontic poetry so popular in Germany since Hagedorn and rarely exceeded in quality since his day. The esoteric, 'difficult', un-folk-like Romance stanzaic forms are absent from Müller's collection, but not, as his reviews make clear, from the efforts of so many early Biedermeier poetasters. Another irony lies in the reflection that

---

its modulation to your songs, in that it was the sweet Müller songs that I became acquainted with when I wrote the Intermezzo. I have from very early on absorbed the German folksong; later, when I was a student in Bonn August Schlegel opened up a number of metrical secrets to me, but I believe it was in your songs first that I believed I had found the pure sound and the true simplicity that I had always sought after. How pure, how clear your songs are, every one of them a folksong. In my songs, by contrast, only the form is approximately folk-like, while the content belongs to conventional society. Yes, I freely repeat it again, and you will duly find it stated in public, that reading your 77 poems brought home to me how one can create new forms from the old folksongs that we have, that are just as folk-like, but without the need to imitate the old jingles and bad rhymes. In the second part of your poems I found the form even purer, of even brighter clarity — but what is all this talk of formal matters, I feel the urge to tell you that I love no song-writer, Goethe excepted, more than you'. Heinrich Heine, *Säkularausgabe. Werke. Briefwechsel. Lebenszeugnisse*, ed. by the Nationale Forschungs- und Gedenkstätten der klassischen deutschen Literatur in Weimar and the Centre National de la Recherche Scientifique in Paris, 27 vols (Berlin: Akademie; Paris: Éditions du CNRS, 1970–84), XX, 250.

6   'Songs of the Wayfarer'; 'Songs of Travel'; 'Country Songs'.

Müller himself said words similar to Heine's about both Ludwig Uhland and Justinus Kerner, not privately but in print, in the important article in Brockhaus's periodical *Hermes*, 'Über die neueste lyrische Poesie der Deutschen' ('On the Latest Lyrical Poetry of the Germans', 1827).[7] Heine is thus enunciating not so much a statement of personal discipleship as a set of criteria to which nearly all the great lyrical poets of the nineteenth century subscribed. Theodor Storm, whose two anthologies of 1859 and 1870 draw generously on both these poets, articulates in his credally formulated introductions the principles that Müller and Heine had expressed before him. Yet all of them know and admit that it was Gottfried August Bürger and Goethe who first showed them the simplicity of poetic language producing the 'Natursprache', the 'Urmutter aller Poesie',[8] that can appeal directly to the heart. It will be rhymed, readily set to music, not rhetorical (Klopstock's and Schiller's failing), not archaicizing, arch, or faux-naif (the lesser Romantics' weakness).

Goethe, whom Heine placed on a rather higher altar of his idolatry, seems to have had an off day when Müller visited him in Weimar in 1827, committing unflattering comments to Kanzler von Müller ('eine unangenehme Personnage, sagte er, süffisant, überdies Brillen tragend, was mir das Unleidlichste ist').[9] Heine linked Goethe and Müller as lyric poets, but both the *Italienische Reise/Italian Journey* and Müller's highly readable *Rom, Römer und Römerinnen/Rome, Roman Men and Roman Women* of 1820, largely forgotten today, are formative texts for his own Italian memoirs and point forward to Heine's own inimitable style. The sentence from Heine's *Reise von München nach Genua/Journey from Munich to Genua*, 'ach, er [Müller] war ein deutscher Dichter!'[10] thus places him in a double relationship, as a lyrical poet in the folk mode, but also as a master of the witty and interesting travelogue.

Müller, born in 1794, was six years younger than Byron, for whose fame and reputation in Germany he did so much, and three years older than Heine, whose eloquent admissions of debt I have just quoted. These are years of brief spans of talent (like Wilhelm Hauff, 1802–27)

---

7   *Wilhelm Müller*, IV, 297–342.
8   'The language of nature'; 'the earth-mother of all poetry'. Ibid., 299.
9   'An unattractive person, he said, full of himself, and in addition wearing spectacles, something I absolutely cannot bear'. Goethe, *Gedenkausgabe der Werke, Briefe und Gespräche*, ed. by Ernst Beutler, 27 vols (Zurich: Artemis, 1948–71), XIII, 514–15.
10 'Oh, he was a German poet!'. Heine, *Säkularausgabe*, VI, 55.

or genius (like Franz Schubert, 1797–1828). Whatever else Müller may have in common with Byron and Heine, arguably the two greatest masters of poetic form of their century, he shares the problem of their true place in literary history and of their subsequent reputations. But am I not setting my sights just a little too high in linking Müller with these manifestly superior names? It is a matter of degree. To deal with the last aspect first: it is understandable that Müller's reputation, while freeing itself in the course of the century from the mild hagiography of Gustav Schwab's introductory 'Wilhelm Müller's Leben' of 1830,[11] had nothing to fear from the kind of personal revelation that was to prove injurious to Byron and to some extent Heine. But in associating the three poets I am making a slightly different point. All three belong, for differing reasons, fairly and squarely in the century that gave them birth, and yet (allowing for Müller's lesser stature) they are associated with revolutionary movements that are part of the political tissue of the nineteenth: Greek, and to some extent Italian, national determination, or the future constitution of the German nation. Müller had taken part in the Wars of Liberation in 1813–15, and there is no doubt that this experience and his subsequent association with figures like (and as unlikely as) 'Turnvater' Jahn or Kalckreuth senior and junior, or Friedrich de la Motte Fouqué, were at least factors in his admiration for the hero of Missolonghi. The young Müller shared briefly some of the inanities of patriotic professors and firebrand students, but he did also cherish liberal ideals, especially after the clampdown of Karlsbad. His short career as a writer had to contend with censorship, known, it is true, for its severity but also its capriciousness. Generally, Müller politically played safe and sailed less close to the wind than Heine was (later) to do. The example of Béranger across the border was not encouraging, but it did not prevent Müller from writing a generous and warm-hearted defence of the man and poet, at that time in prison for his views.[12] His several reviews and articles on Byron, quoting copious extracts from the man himself, sentimental, witty, but also outrageous and subversive ('Lord Byron ist vielleicht das größte und fruchtbarste, aber auch das gefährlichste Dichtergenie unsers Zeitalters'),[13] send

---

11 *VSchr*, I, xvii-lxiii.
12 *Wilhelm Müller*, IV, 151–55.
13 'Lord Byron is perhaps the greatest and most fertile, but also the most dangerous genius of our age'. *VSchr*, V, 156.

out an encoded message to his liberal-minded and educated readers arguably more effective than all the young poets who were emulating *Cain* or *Manfred*. It is a message different from Goethe's: what the older man found fascinating was daemonic poetic genius, not a heroic death in the Morea. If Müller never created an Euphorion (or Heine's William Ratcliff), he does deserve some credit as the man who for a short period of years kept the name of Byron fairly and squarely before the literary reading public.

There is, in a literary age so given to eclecticism, no contradiction between the folk mode and that of the 'conventionnelle Gesellschaft'.[14] And, as both Byron and Heine demonstrate, the mastery of form is no barrier to the expression of deep feeling. At his level of achievement, Müller's poetry reflects both these willingly borne constraints. It also, I feel, shares in the fortunes of both Byron's and Heine's receptions. The *oeuvre* of both these great poets survives during the latter part of the nineteenth century essentially on a reduced and narrowed base. Byron cannot easily provide a ready model for generations that produce Alfred Tennyson, Matthew Arnold, Dante Gabriel Rossetti or Algernon Charles Swinburne; Heine, so formative for Storm, has less to say to Gottfried Keller and nothing at all to Conrad Ferdinand Meyer, let alone Hugo von Hofmannsthal or Stefan George. But both have passed on enough into the life-stream of their respective national poetic traditions to ensure that they are known and read, and can be revived when times are more receptive to their particular styles. Müller at his level, is altogether more vulnerable. He survives as part of the 'Hausschatz der deutschen Lyrik',[15] and as the sung text of two of Schubert's song cycles. His complete poetry is never out of print during the nineteenth century: Gustav Schwab's edition of 1837[16] is succeeded by, among others, Max Müller's reissue of his father's poems in 1868 and a nearly 400-page Reclam volume in 1898.[17] But the five-volume *Vermischte Schriften* edited by the same Gustav Schwab in 1830, which are the essential monument

---

14 'Conventional society'.
15 'Treasury of German Poetry for the Home'.
16 *Gedichte von Wilhelm Müller. Herausgegeben und mit einer Biographie Müller's begleitet von Gustav Schwab*, 2 vols (Leipzig: Brockhaus, 1837). [BL, L, CTrin]
17 *Gedichte von Wilhelm Müller. Mit Einleitung und Anmerkungen herausgegeben von Max Müller*, 2 parts, Bibliothek der Deutschen Nationalliteratur des achtzehnten und neunzehnten Jahrhunderts (Leipzig: Brockhaus, 1868) (henceforth cited as *Gedichte* (1868)); *Gedichte von Wilhelm Müller. Gesamt-Ausgabe. Mit einer biographischen*

to the full range of Müller's achievement, have had to wait until 1994 for the nearest approach to a reprint. The reception of Heine's works, by contrast, with the exception of the shameful interlude of 1933–45, is clearly and deservedly different.

My association of Byron and Heine with Müller is not intended to crank his reputation up to a level with theirs. Nor do the nearly twenty-five pages of entries in the standard bibliography, the 1905 edition of Karl Goedeke's *Grundriß*,[18] necessarily justify a major rehabilitation of all aspects of his *oeuvre*, although they make for interesting and salutary reading. Friedrich Sengle, for whom Müller was a significant (but not central) figure in his Biedermeier constellation, dealt with him in a few deft and masterly strokes and stressed the centrality of 'Lieder-Müller'.[19] The editors of the new edition also place the major (but not sole) emphasis on the song-writer and the range of his lyrical activity. My own view is that much of Müller, not just the lyrical poetry but even the less-read and less-readable output, can serve to place a period and its major figures in focus. For that reason, I now dwell a little on his short life and his circumstances.

Schwab, the dutiful chronicler of Schiller's and Hauff's lives, produced a short biography of Wilhelm Müller for the *Vermischte Schriften*, which appeared in 1830. Schwab made Müller's personal acquaintance in the last year of his life, and this note tinges his assessment of the other poet's work and character:

> Wenn mich schon seine Lieder dem liebenswerthen Dichtergeiste recht nahe gebracht hatten, so versprach die Woche, die ich ihm ausschließend widmen durfte, mir ein langes, inniges Verhältniß mit Müller dem Menschen. Seine Gedichte ließen harmloses Wohlwollen gegen jedermann, schnelle Begeisterung für Schönes und Gutes, Talent für Geselligkeit und geistreiche Unterhaltung zum voraus ahnen. Im nähern Umgang aber entwickelte sich bei ihm auch ein Ernst der Gesinnung, ein biederer Sinn, eine sittliche Zuverlässigkeit, die, wenn man sie einmal

---

    Einleitung und einem Vorwort herausgegeben von Curt Müller (Leipzig: Reclam, 1898) (henceforth cited as *Gedichte* (1898)).

18 Karl Goedeke, *Grundriß zur Geschichte der deutschen Dichtung [...]*, cont. by Edmund Goetze, Vol. VIII, i: *Vom Weltfrieden bis zur französischen Revolution 1830* (Dresden: Ehlermann, 1905), 255–87, 707–09.

19 Friedrich Sengle, *Biedermeierzeit. Deutsche Dichtung im Spannungsfeld zwischen Restauration und Revolution 1815–1848*, 3 vols (Stuttgart: Metzler, 1971–80), II, 517–18.

erkannt hatte, auch den leichtesten Producten seiner heitern Muse ein besonders reizendes Ansehen verliehen, wie Lusthütten, die auf Felsen gebaut sind.[20]

His famous son, Max Müller, in the preface to his edition for the 'Bibliothek der Deutschen Nationalliteratur' in 1868, could also write from the heart, and his words 'ich habe ihn ja kaum gekannt'[21] have a certain poignancy. But he was, or was to be, in possession of family papers that showed his father in a more human light, notably his early diaries. Max Müller, as befits the times, and, it is fair to say, his own convictions, writes more of his father's political views and his contention with the censor than does Schwab. He is by the same token now aware that not all of his father's *oeuvre* is secure. Both of these biographical sketches stress the harmony between Müller's poetic persona and his actual character, and that is in keeping with nineteenth-century literary biography in general. Schwab's comments are, however, telling. For there was no immediate reason why Müller, a North German, should appeal to the Swabian school of poets, to Schwab himself in particular, but also to Ludwig Uhland and Justinus Kerner. But Schwab, later mercilessly harried by Heine along with his fellow-countrymen, is making the point that the happy coexistence of simple lyricism, 'Talent for Geselligkeit',[22] and what Heine called 'conventionnelle Gesellschaft', was not regionally limited and that it appealed to a broad national reading public. Indeed, Heine's style was not very much different from that favoured in Stuttgart except for its being more witty, less conventional, and, crucially, more talented. One could, after all, read Heine without approving of him. Prince Metternich read Heine's love poetry attentively while also allowing his minions to wield the blue pencil on the political writings; he may have also enjoyed Müller's 'biederer Sinn' ('honest sense') while

---

20 'If his Lieder brought this agreeable poetic personality very close to me, the week that I was to devote exclusively to him promised me a long and intimate relationship with Müller the man. His poems gave intimation of innocence, benevolence towards everyone, a quick enthusiasm for the beautiful and good, a talent for conviviality and witty conversation. But on closer acquaintance one was also made aware of a serious-mindedness, an inner worth, a sureness in moral matters, which, once one was made aware of them, gave even his lightest products a particularly charming aspect, like summer-houses built on rocks'. *VSchr*, I, lvi-lvii.
21 'I hardly knew him'. *Gedichte* (1868), xi.
22 'Talent for conviviality'.

noting his more carefully phrased subversiveness. In terms of the history of style and taste, Müller represents what he himself, talking of the ultimate model Goethe, called 'Vieltönigkeit'.[23] It is the principle of versatility and even eclecticism that can be found in nearly all the poets, great and small, in the Biedermeier period, that dominates their major publication outlet, the literary almanac, and that provides the most important factor of continuity with the century that first allowed *poésies fugitives,* 'Volkslied' ('folksong'), and sentimentality to coexist: the eighteenth. Thus Müller, who so admires in Schmidt von Lübeck the 'echt deutscher Liedersänger von reiner, voller und herzlich bewegter Stimme'[24] and in Kerner 'jenes rückhaltslose Erschließen des innersten Herzens',[25] is equally at home in the poetry of wine and mild eroticism, of friendship and 'deutscher Sang', but he can also display an intolerance of revealed religion's embrace of political reaction. None of these positions is incompatible with the other. They were not all handed down to the poet; some, indeed, would need the impulse of his own times for their acquisition and mastering.

Müller lived and died in Dessau, the capital and residence of Anhalt-Dessau, one of the more liberal, if patriarchal, states of the post-1815 'Bund'. If Dessau later gave him a professional base and enabled him to carry out a wide range of literary activities for publishers in several different centres, it was Berlin that proved in the first instance formative. Müller's father was a master tailor, who, after a period of financial uncertainty, and a second marriage, could be called fairly well-off. It seemed reasonable and proper that his son should proceed to the liberal and enlightened 'Hauptschule' in the town, and Müller's excellent knowledge of both classical and modern languages was certainly acquired there. When later giving an account of Byron's miserable schooldays and love-hate relationship with the ancient classics, Müller might well reflect that however much Germany lacked in Byronic panache and effrontery, it certainly produced well-educated writers. Anhalt not having a university of its own, the choice for higher study fell on Berlin. Again, the contrast between Humboldt's University of Berlin and Byron's Trinity College,

---

23 'Singing in many tones'. *Wilhelm Müller*, IV, 417.
24 'True German song-writer of pure, full voice, moved from the heart'. Ibid., 426
25 'This opening of the inner heart without any restraint'. Ibid., 476.

as yet innocent of William Whewell, Julius Hare or Connop Thirlwall, cannot be stressed too much, except, of course, for the poets it brought forth. Yet for a young man of a scholarly turn of mind, it might be bliss to be alive in Berlin in 1813, in the university of Friedrich August Wolf, of Karl Wilhelm Ferdinand Solger, of August Böckh, Johann Wilhelm Süvern, Friedrich Rühs (the list could be extended). Müller's father could finance Wilhelm's studies, but was immediately confronted (his reaction is not recorded) with a less studious side of his son's character. Müller, at the age of eighteen, responded to the King of Prussia's call to arms after Napoleon's defeat in Russia. This was easily enough done, until one considered that Anhalt-Dessau, despite the 'Alter Dessauer'[26] and his role in Frederick II's greatness, was not a Prussian fief. Clearly, local dynastic differences were not holding back the patriotic fervour of the young. From 1813 to 1815, Müller was a soldier, rising to the rank of lieutenant. This puts him in the company of those other soldier poets and painters (Joseph von Eichendorff, Max von Schenkendorf, Theodor Körner, Friedrich Rückert, Fouqué, Ferdinand Olivier, Philipp Veit, and others) whose formative experience was the Wars of Liberation. Yet Müller never wrote anything approaching 'Der gute Kamerad' or even 'Lützows wilde Jagd';[27] we have no images of him in uniform, as in Georg Friedrich Kersting's well-known painting of Körner and comrades.[28] It may therefore come as a surprise to find the singer of 'Die Winterreise' as a young man expressing animadversions like these:

> Aus Franzenschädeln trinken wir
> Dort unsern deutschen Trank
> Und feiern Wilhelms Siegeszier
> Mit altem Bardensang.[29]

---

26 Prince Leopold of Anhalt-Dessau ('the Dessauer') was a general in Prussian service under Frederick William I and Frederick the Great.
27 'The Good Comrade', 'Lützow's Mad Wild Chase', two of the best-known patriotic poems from the Wars of Liberation, by Uhland and Körner respectively.
28 Illustrated in *The Romantic Spirit in German Art 1790–1990*, ed. by Keith Hartley et al., Exhibition Catalogue (Edinburgh: National Galleries of Scotland; London: South Bank Centre; Munich: Oktagon, 1994–95), 248.
29 'From Frenchmen's skulls we quaff
   There our German wine
   And mark Wilhelm's victory bays
   With bard-song as of yore!'. *Wilhelm Müller*, I, 4.

These calamitous verses are from Müller's first collection of poetry, *Bundesblüthen* (1816).[30] It is significant that neither Schwab nor any subsequent nineteenth-century editor, even in an age fairly flowing with patriotic gore, chose to include this early stuff. The later *Lieder der Griechen/Songs of the Greeks*, where the skulls might be Turkish and the wine Chian, would be sufficient reminder of Müller the political bard. This side of his *oeuvre* cannot be overlooked, and, as already stated, it is part, but part only, of his admiration for Byron and political freedom. For all that, it did mean that he had actually wielded the 'Schwert' while also stringing the 'Leyer',[31] and that his warrior pose was marginally more convincing than had been Johann Wilhelm Ludwig Gleim's enfeebled calls to arms under Frederick (or even the minor Romantics' under Frederick William III).

Müller saw action at Grossgörschen and Kulm in 1813, then postings at headquarters in Prague and Brussels. In Brussels there was a shadowy love-affair with 'Therese', and there have been those who have wished to identify her as the Jew of 'Johannes und Maria' and later of *Debora*. Returning to Berlin in the autumn of 1815, he was to experience another variant of the Petrarchan cycle; meeting the young artist and bemedalled war veteran Wilhelm Hensel and entering his house circle, Müller fell in love with his sister Luise. That might be too gross an expression for this relationship; the two lovers met in a common religious inwardness: their virginal devotion was to be sustained by the suppression of the flesh and its earthly lust ('böse Erdenlust').[32] Luise's spirituality and ethereality were later to try the sexual patience of Clemens Brentano, ever ready to sublimate his baser desires in otherworldly devotion. If Müller's diary fragments from the period reveal less self-maceration, they are documents of a young man urgently eager to be pure, patriotic and poetic. The relationship with Luise came to nothing. Yet Müller, like Heine, both knew the Petrarchan literary mode and experienced its real-life counterpart. Brooding melancholy, but also the forceful overcoming of introspection, are as much part of the tissue of his poetic cycles as they are of Heine's *Buch der Lieder/Book of Songs*. But whereas

---

30 *Bundesblüthen*, compiled by Georg Graf von Blankensee, Wilhelm Hensel, Friedrich Graf von Kalckreuth, Wilhelm Müller, Wilhelm von Studnitz (Berlin: Maurer, 1816). [BL].
31 A reference to Körner's collection *Leyer und Schwert/Lyre and Sword* (1814).
32 'Wicked earthly lust'. *Wilhelm Müller*, V, 55.

Heine compensates by challenging accepted norms, Müller more often than not has recourse to conviviality and friendship as the cure for *Weltschmerz*.³³ It was with friends, including Hensel and the young count Friedrich Kalckreuth, that the collection *Bundesblüthen* of 1816 came about. It displeased the Prussian censor, not for its exquisite badness, but for its possible seditiousness.³⁴ With these particular friends it could be said that Müller had fallen socially and professionally on his feet. His rather bland portrait drawing joins the gallery of Biedermeier notables (Heine, the Mendelssohns, Brentano, Rahel Varnhagen) in Hensel's portfolio.³⁵ Kalckreuth is the son of the Prussian field marshal. Friedrich de la Motte Fouqué, a mere baron and a major, receives a letter containing this sentence: 'Und so war es auch gestern abend, als er den freundlichen Händedruck des Mannes fühlte, dem er nächst Gott und seinen Eltern das Meiste und Beste verdankt, ich meine nicht die vergänglichen Wohltaten des Lebens, sondern die immergrüne Saat des Guten und Schönen in ihm, so jung sie auch noch sein mag, mit einem Worte, ein deutsches Herz und einen deutschen Geschmack'.³⁶ Müller later had cause to be ashamed of such sentiments, and of his association with the 'Gesellschaft für deutsche Sprache', the Germanophile society that harboured the xenophobia, illiberalism and anti-Semitism of Berlin notables like Jahn, Böckh, or Rühs. Yet his first non-poetic publication, if one will, his first scholarly effort, was a product of these circles: *Blumenlese aus den Minnesingern / Florilegium from the Minnesingers* (1816).³⁷ Was this just an interest in Petrarchism, this time German-style, or a harbinger of something deeper? Müller reprints Johann Jacob Bodmer's Middle High German based on the Manesse text, adding his own modern version *en face* (it is not encouraging to find the Kürenberger's famous poem

---

33 'Melancholy', 'mal du siècle'.
34 *Wilhelm Müller*, I, 279.
35 *Wilhelm Hensel 1794–1861. Portraitist und Maler. Werke und Dokumente. Ausstellung zum 200. Geburtstag, veranstaltet vom Mendelssohn-Archiv der Staatsbibliothek zu Berlin-Preußischer Kulturbesitz 15. Dezember 1994 bis 29. Januar 1995* (Wiesbaden: Reichert, 1994), 23.
36 'And thus it was yesterday evening, too, when he felt the friendly hand-clasp of the man to whom next to God and his parents, he owed the most and best, I do not mean the fleeting benefits of life, but the evergreen seed of the good and beautiful in him, however young it may be, in a word, a German heart and German taste'. *Wilhelm Müller*, V, 109–10.
37 *Blumenlese aus den Minnesingern*, ed. by Wilhelm Müller (Berlin: Maurer, 1816). [BL, OT, StA].

masquerading as 'Fräuleins Klage').[38] Other eighteenth-century revivals of Minnesang, Gleim's or Bürger's, had been more interested in the psychological stance of speaker and addressee than in textual niceties. The Romantics, Ludwig Tieck and Friedrich Heinrich von der Hagen, modernizing and making accessible texts they saw as appealing to the spirit of their times, were at the same time continuing the previous century's antiquarianism. Tieck, following Friedrich Schlegel, had postulated a continuity of 'Eine Poesie'[39] throughout the undulations and anfractuosities of the historical process. Müller's preface reflects his deference to the great Friedrich August Wolf and his 'Liedertheorie' of Homer, already turning the heads of sober classical scholars like Niebuhr. The mode of transmission from the heroic age or even the 'schwäbisches Zeitalter',[40] of epic or lyrical texts in older Germanic dialects might, in Müller's eyes, best be compared with that of the songs of Homer as they passed through many hands and became remoter from the texts that the rhapsodists had once sung. As a philologist (and Müller can lay claim to this title) he sides less with academic scholars like Georg Friedrich Benecke or the Grimms or Karl Lachmann. There is a wider reading public in mind; the style is clear and elegant; his models are Johann Heinrich Voss, August Wilhelm Schlegel and Goethe.[41] 'Wissenschaftliche Prosa'[42] of this kind was still highly regarded by teachers of aesthetics and 'Beredsamkeit' ('eloquence'), and it has the advantage of accessibility and readability: it is the tradition that became great in the hands of Ranke and Mommsen, Alexander von Humboldt and (later) the Grimm brothers.

Of further significance during Müller's period in Berlin was the circle around August von Stägemann and his wife Elisabeth. Stägemann was a man of affairs, close to the chancellor Karl August von Hardenberg, but, on less secure ground, also a poet of sorts. His wife's salon brought together Berlin notabilities: here Müller met Friedrich Förster, whose *Die Sängerfahrt/The Minstrel's Journey* is one of the key texts of Berlin late Romanticism, and most likely Achim von Arnim, with whom he was to collaborate in translating Christopher Marlowe. The Stägemann

---

38 'Young Lady's Complaint'.
39 'One sole poetry'.
40 'Era of the Swabian emperors'.
41 *Wilhelm Müller*, IV, 75.
42 'Scholarly prose'.

house was musical, convivial and literary: it contained the elements that were to launch Müller on a career in letters. We may assume that his contributions to almanacs and literary magazines (such as Friedrich Wilhelm Gubitz's much-read periodical *Der Gesellschafter,* in which both Arnim and Brentano published) were in some measure due to the contacts the concourse in the Stägemanns' house afforded. Some of these early efforts contain the first versions of the works that were to bring Müller fame: *Der Gesellschafter* for 1818, for instance, contained twelve 'Müller-Lieder', some written for a lyrical dramolet in the Stägemann house and now taking on lineaments of their own.

Before Müller emerged as a literary persona, he had to undergo yet another formative influence: Italy. It was to have been Greece, but unromantic circumstances deemed otherwise. Had it been Greece, it is conceivable that he might have followed an academic career, for Friedrich August Wolf was involved in the matter. He had been approached by Baron Albert von Sack, a gentleman of means and leisure who wished to spend two years travelling in Greece and the Near East and sought a suitably qualified young travelling companion. Wolf and Böckh recommended Müller, who in his turn had good reason to turn away from the cloying religious and patriotic atmosphere of the last two years. This was in August, 1817; the journey was to lead from Vienna to Constantinople. In Vienna, Müller met for the first time Greeks exiled through the political circumstances of their native country; it was the germ of the later *Lieder der Griechen.* In Vienna, too, the news reached the travellers that an outbreak of plague had made the Ottoman lands unsafe. Baron Sack, not lacking resource, decided to do the Italian leg of the journey, originally planned for the return stage. Thus it was that Müller made the journey to Rome; his other travelling companion was the Nazarene artist Julius Schnorr von Carolsfeld, for whose society he later had cause to be grateful. Once arrived in Rome, Müller parted company with Sack amid recriminations, and he was glad of contacts among the Nazarenes: Schnorr[43] and Philipp Fohr did portrait drawings of him (Schnorr's the kind of superbly severe head-and-shoulders likeness in which the brotherhood excelled), and the art historian and patron Carl Friedrich von Rumohr, ever interested in young men, lent him money. It may be hard to imagine Müller among the company in

---

43 *Cat.*, 120.

the Caffè Greco depicted by Fohr before his tragic death in the Tiber:[44] there was already too much 'altdeutsche Tracht',[45] too much intense seriousness, too much religiosity. But like the Nazarenes, Müller sought relief from the Roman heat in the Albano mountains, not idealizing the local inhabitants as backdrop studies for religious paintings, as their scenes of Olevano tend to do, but trying to understand their mentality. Although Müller befriended August Sigismund Ruhl,[46] one of the few Nazarenes who actually broke his bond with the brotherhood, he seems to have found the company of Per Daniel Amadeus Atterbom, the Swedish Romantic, more congenial. Each is commemorated: Ruhl is the dedicatee of the sonnet collection 'Die Monate/The Months' in the *Sieben und siebzig Gedichte,* while Atterbom is more aptly remembered in the preface to Book II of *Rom, Römer und Römerinnen/Rome, Roman Men and Roman Women.* That text, which appeared in 1820,[47] revealed that the Italian experience was a search for both his personal and his national identity, while claiming to offer some insights into the mentality of a people much written about by the Germans but equally often misjudged by them. Müller did not echo Tieck's testy words of 1816 to his friend Solger: 'Ich liebe die Italiener und ihr leichtes Wesen, bin aber in Italien erst recht zum Deutschen geworden'.[48] That was an ungenerous reaction to Goethe's *Italienische Reise,* a text that had not scrupled to treat Romantic sensibilities with some little severity. Müller, for his part, did not omit some unflattering asides on the subject of the Nazarenes, but that was all part of the business of casting off native prejudices and inborn preconceptions. The servants of revealed religion do not emerge well from Müller's account, except where they display scholarship and learning, but by the same token Northern Protestant 'Verinnerlichung'[49] emerges as the main barrier to understanding the Italian character and

---

44 Illustrated in *Deutsche Romantik. Handzeichnungen,* ed. by Marianne Bernhard, 2 vols (Munich: Rogner & Bernhard, 1974), I, 306–07.
45 'Old German costume'.
46 *Deutsche Romantik. Handzeichnungen,* I, 1476.
47 *Rom, Römer und Römerinnen. Eine Sammlung vertrauter Briefe aus Rom und Albano mit einigen späteren Zusätzen und Belegen von Wilhelm Müller,* 2 vols (Berlin: Duncker & Humblot, 1820). [BL, CTrin, OB, OT].
48 'I love the Italians and their easy ways, but Italy first made a German of me'. *Goethe in vertraulichen Briefen seiner Zeitgenossen,* ed. by Wilhelm Bode, 3 vols (Berlin and Weimar: Aufbau,1979), II, 667–68. See Chapter Two of this volume.
49 'Inwardness'.

its notions of right and wrong. Müller does see religion in Italy, but it is enshrined in observances that are already present in the mythology and customs of Roman antiquity. This mythological interest could be called Romantic, but it also casts a wry and dispassionate eye over things considered sacred and 'naive' by the Nazarenes. Above all, Müller seeks to discard received moral and cultural ideas, to understand a national character while gaining comprehension of himself. In practical terms that means learning the language and its dialects, not blenching at its sexual mores or its robust folk-song, playing the *flâneur*, listening and keeping one's eyes open. These are also features that the best Roman sections of Goethe's *Italienische Reise* contain. *Rom, Römer und Römerinnen* keeps the figure of the exploring author firmly before the reader; he may not be the famous 'pittore' hiding his identity, but he is a young man bent on finding his psychological feet in a foreign land.

One senses that Müller returned from Italy late in 1818 having cast off his priggishness and many of his inhibitions. He did, however, face a crucial decision. What could one do after Berlin and Rome? A matter-of-fact solution was reached: to return home to Dessau. Had Müller abandoned the *monde* that had seemed to beckon, or the hopes of academic preferment? Perhaps not without some sense of resignation, he seems, like so many of his contemporaries, to have concluded that home is best. If Dessau was not Berlin or Leipzig or Dresden, in a pre-railway age it was not far from these cultural centres either. Literary magazines and almanacs could be published even in Altona or Karlsruhe or Bunzlau and still reach the reading public on which they depended. Yet Müller as a teaching assistant at the Latin school that had replaced his own old institution does seem a depressing climb-down, a Carl Spitzweg painting without the humour or the whimsy. He found an outlet in the duties of a librarian, for Dessau was to receive a public library, and, after struggles with his superiors, he was eventually to be entrusted with its charge. But that was not until 1823. He had first to establish himself socially and economically. The irony is that he had only a few more years to live, and the tragedy is that he seems almost to have worked himself to death.

The return from Italy coincided with publications reflecting the first flush of his lyrical energy, but also *Die Sängerfahrt* and *Doktor Faustus*.[50]

---

50 *Die Sängerfahrt. Eine Neujahrsgabe für Freunde der Dichtkunst und Mahlerey* [...] *Gesammelt von Friedrich Förster* [...] (Berlin: Maurer, 1818), ed. by Siegfried Sudhof

The former, so significant for its stories by Brentano and Arnim, hardly does Müller credit. For the latter, Müller was certainly better versed in English than Arnim and certainly more knowledgeable. Not even Arnim's preface would touch off any great wave of interest in Marlowe's work in Germany, an uphill task against the 'Shakespearomanie' in which neither poet, to their credit, chose to join. But Arnim was generous and entrusted one of his longer and better poems to Müller's short-lived periodical *Askania*.[51]

For the remainder of his short life, Müller pitched himself into a frenetic series of activities. This, at least, is how they seem to the observer at today's distance. It does, however, emerge that Müller was tidy, well organized, wrote easily, and could readily draw on the vast fund of literary knowledge in several languages that he had acquired in Berlin and Italy. In 1821 he married Adelheid Basedow, the granddaughter of the famous educationalist of the Philanthropin: Wilhelm Hensel obliged this time with a double portrait, anodyne like the first and lacking the forceful character of Schnorr's. Like most of Hensel's portrait drawings, it bore an autograph: 'Werde glücklich wie der durch ein Weib wie die!',[52] the Biedermeier marriage ideal in a nutshell.

Müller was professionally a librarian. In the terms of his day that also meant being an antiquarian, a side that emerges in his editions of seventeenth-century German poetry. He remained a classical scholar, but of the more popularizing kind: *Homerische Vorschule/Homer's Forebears* is the result. He was well and truly harnessed into what might seem the ephemeral world of reviewing and contributions to reference works. He kept several almanacs stocked with his occasional verse, including Amadeus Wendt's *Taschenbuch zum geselligen Vergnügen/Almanac for Social Enjoyment*, even his own *Askania*, the mayfly that did not outlive the year 1820, and out of these emerged the collections for some of which he is remembered today. He joined in gregariousness and conviviality of all kinds: so much of his verse seems to have been written for occasions where time stood still and the song and the wine flowed. But there

---

(Heidelberg: Lambert Schneider, n.d. [1969]); *Doktor Faustus. Tragödie von Christoph Marlowe*, trans. by Wilhelm Müller, preface by Achim von Arnim (Berlin: Maurer, 1818). [BL, L, CUL].

51 'Elegie auf den Tod eines Geistlichen/Elegy on the Death of a Clergyman'. *Askania. Zeitschrift für Leben, Litteratur und Kunst*, 1 (1820), 364–69. [BL].

52 'Be happy like him with a wife like her!' *Cat.*, 119.

was also a shrewdness underlying this flurry of activity. He chose his publishers with care: Friedrich Arnold, and later Heinrich, Brockhaus in Leipzig, had every cause to be satisfied with their young author in Dessau, and they paid well for work always punctually delivered. Friedrich Arnold Brockhaus, as an astute publisher, kept a variety of different enterprises going: *Literarisches Conversations-Blatt/Literary Conversations*, *Hermes oder kritisches Jahrbuch der Literatur/Hermes, or Critical Yearbook of Literature*, the almanac *Urania*, the famous *Conversations-Lexicon*. Müller contributed to them all, but he also kept his options open, playing off the cautious Brockhaus against the mighty Johann Friedrich Cotta and his *Morgenblatt für die gebildeten Stände/Morning Paper for Educated Classes*, yet not entrusting his *Waldhornist* collections to either and having them printed locally in Dessau. As his literary reputation increased, he could bargain for better royalties, not quite yet in the league of popular writers like Heinrich Clauren or Carl Franz van der Velde or Tieck, but the mild tussle with Brockhaus over *Debora* shows Müller standing his ground in monetary matters.[53]

Müller was well received in literary circles, notably those in Dresden, and especially those around Ludwig Tieck. The dedications of the *Waldhornist* volumes to Tieck and Carl Maria von Weber respectively are not mere conventional deferentiality. Weber (also working himself to death) was a reminder of the important links between poetry and music; that the naked text of so much seemingly trivial verse of the period is calling out for the decent covering of a musical setting. For a younger writer, Tieck was a model in both a positive and negative sense. His poetry, by then at last available in collected form,[54] would provide the base line for so many of the young generation, the vocabulary, the attitudes, the clichés. His Novellen, the product of a pen that Müller rightly calls 'flüchtig',[55] might convince the younger and less experienced that they too could extract a fairly good story from a set of stock situations. Perhaps Wilhelm Hauff could; Müller certainly could not. Tieck was a warning example of how not to dissipate one's time and talents in conflicting and multifarious projects. Yet Müller did not share Tieck's consuming passion for the theatre and for Shakespeare.

---

53 *Wilhelm Müller*, V, 413–14.
54 *Gedichte von L. Tieck*, 3 parts (Dresden: Hilscher, 1821–23).
55 'Fugitive'. *Wilhelm Müller*, IV, 411.

His corpus of reviews at their best recall more of the later Goethe's range of interests, in their catholicity, their sense of 'Weltliteratur/World literature', their admiration of the folk traditions of southern Europe, their (differently accentuated) fascination with Byron. If the actual meeting with Goethe went badly, at least Müller's reception in Dresden compensated, where he stayed in the grandeur of the Kalckreuths' Villa Grassi. There he joined the lesser lights of that city, Malsburg, Förster, Loeben, as they revolved around the star attraction of Tieck, or paid brief homage to Weber.

How many of the writings of this almost manic spurt of activity actually deserve to survive? With this question I also approach the problems of the selection principles faced by past and present editors. Leaving aside the poetry proper for the moment, it emerges that nearly all of his writings actually impact on questions of poetic tradition, taste, or convention, on the relationship of the written to the spoken word. *Rom, Römer und Römerinnen*, already alluded to for its function in Müller's development, has important sections on Italian folksong, which it quotes liberally, noting the ability of unlettered Italian street singers to improvise, but also their extraordinary feats of memory (a point also observed by Goethe).[56] Hearing an Italian recite from memory canto after canto of Tasso is a living reminder of the 'Geist der alten natürlichen Poesie',[57] the oral tradition that exists outside written documentation or inscription, and adapts to the times in which the stories are being recounted, which is inevitably accompanied by dance and music. The quotation comes from Müller's *Homerische Vorschule. Eine Einleitung in das Studium der Ilias und Odyssee/Homer's Forebears. An Introduction into the Study of the Iliad and the Odyssey*,[58] easily written off as Friedrich August Wolf made accessible for the aesthetic tea-table (it is his only scholarly work to go into a second edition), yet for Müller proof that natural sung language is a reflection of the essence of those who sing, the 'Stimme der Völker'.[59] His praise of the Volkslied and of those who practise it well (Goethe, Uhland, Kerner) links him with Herder's

---

56 Goethe, *Gedenkausgabe*, XIV, 410.
57 'Spirit of ancient natural poetry'.
58 *Homerische Vorschule. Eine Einleitung in das Studium der Ilias und Odyssee* (Leipzig: Brockhaus, 1824). [BL, OB, Glas]. I use the second edition, ed. by Detlev Carl Wilh. Baumgarten-Crusius (Leipzig: Brockhaus, 1836), 22. [BL, CUL, OB, OT, JRULM].
59 'Voice of the nations'.

concerns half a century or so earlier, but, as already noted, it postulates a national poetry for the Germans that will be from the heart, natural, and free of artifice. It speaks the language of Goethe's famous review of *Des Knaben Wunderhorn*, and it is fair to say that Müller, by precept and example, is a major factor in the process that eventually denies legitimacy to mere formalism and rhetoric in lyrical poetry. These concerns inform his best literary criticism, in a negative sense his unease at what formal poets like Platen or Rückert were producing, his ill-concealed contempt for so much of the poetic almanacs (and his ironic self-deprecation at being so dependent on them); more positively, his praise of the best Swabian poetry, but a word of commendation for the 'durch heitre Ironie gemilderte Schwermut'[60] of lesser lights such as Schmidt von Lübeck. When Müller produced his major anthology *Bibliothek deutscher Dichter des siebzehnten Jahrhunderts/Library of German Poets of the Seventeenth Century*[61] he was not pursuing mere antiquarianism (although collating the texts also involves that) but seeking to reacquaint the Germans with a tradition of their own poetry on which they had all but turned their backs. Modern Baroque scholars should pay some deference to Müller as one who tried, but ultimately failed, to secure some of the best older lyrical poetry for the nation. If he preferred Paul Fleming and Simon Dach to Martin Opitz and Andreas Gryphius, this is consistent with his general criteria, where 'bürgerliche Biederkeit und Unumwundenheit'[62] (referring to Dach) rank higher than formal correctness or *vanitas*. In rehabilitating Johann Christian Günther as the only genuine poet in a half-century of aridity, he had Goethe's judgement on his side.

These criteria extend without qualification to foreign literatures. The translator must know how to employ them in his task of 'Eindringen und Untergehen'[63] in an alien tongue. I draw attention to the word Müller uses for particularly successful translations in these terms, namely 'Ueberdichtungen', a word not known to the *Deutsches*

---

60 'Melancholy tempered with a light touch of irony'. *Wilhelm Müller*, IV, 424.
61 *Bibliothek deutscher Dichter des siebzehnten Jahrhunderts. Herausgegeben von Wilhelm Müller*, 14 vols (Leipzig: Brockhaus, 1822–38) (vols XI–XIV, 1828–38, bear the subtitle 'Begonnen von Wilhelm Müller. Fortgesetzt von Karl Förster'). [BL, CTrin (i–vii only), OT].
62 'Good old-fashioned forthrightness'. *Wilhelm Müller*, IV, 106.
63 'Penetrating and submerging'. '*Gries* und *Streckfuß* Uebersetzungen von *Tasso's* befreitem Jerusalem', *Hermes oder kritisches Jahrbuch der Literatur*, 18, 2. Stuck (1823), 261–300 (280). [BL, CUL, CTrin, OB, JRULM, Nat, StA].

Wörterbuch/German Dictionary and not readily translatable,[64] yet one that expresses concerns peculiarly close to nineteenth-century German poetic endeavour. Müller himself is no great translator:

> War das der Blick, der tausend Schiffe trieb
> In's Meer, der Trojas hohe Zinnen stürzte?[65]

This is hardly the Marlowe we know and love. His major corpus of translated work, *Neugriechische Volkslieder/Modern Greek Folksongs*, is itself a reworking of Claude Charles Fauriel's French version.[66] When discussing Pierre-Jean de Béranger or Byron or Thomas Moore or modern Greek poetry, Müller blends his remarks with factors that are more or less overtly political. The texts of *Neugriechische Volkslieder* pre-date the main struggle for independence and are in some ways closer to older ballad traditions or even the Serbian folksongs that so appealed to Goethe. They gain through their formulaic quality a tone that is alien to Müller's own *Lieder der Griechen*, where moral outrage (and even rant) are never too far from the surface. In reviewing Moore's poetry for *Hermes* in 1823 Müller made a crucial distinction between verse that was merely 'demagogisch' and patriotic poetry that could produce 'unmittelbare Begeisterung durch die Zeit'.[67] While admitting that Moore did not always observe this rule, Müller might well have reflected that his *Lieder der Griechen* were closer to the former than to the latter. It is hard to be fair to political poetry at the best of times. To cite an analogy: Heine at his best would satisfy the nobler of Müller's two categories; Ferdinand Freiligrath or Georg Herwegh would fall into the lesser. It is easy to write off German 'Griechenlieder/Songs of the Greeks' (Müller's are but one example among many) or 'Polenlieder/Songs of the Poles' as being vicarious or surrogate, as not addressing directly the need for freedom at home and, with questionable honesty, embracing the needs of those conveniently remote in space and culture. His interest in Byron

---

64 'Transpoeticization', perhaps. Ibid., 281.
65 'Was this the face that launched a thousand ships
   And burnt the topless towers of Ilium?' *Doktor Faustus*, 131.
66 *Neugriechische Volkslieder*, ed. by C. Fauriel, trans. by Wilhelm Müller, 2 parts (Leipzig: Voss, 1825). [BL, CUL, CTrin, OB, Edin].
67 'Demagogic'; 'with the times providing direct enthusiasm'. 'Ueber die Gedichte des Thomas Moore', *Hermes oder kritisches Jahrbuch der Literatur*, 20, 4. Stuck (1823), 184–211 (207–08).

and Moore and Walter Scott and so much other foreign literature might by the same token be a mere attempt to counteract the political stuffiness and limitation which he was powerless to change. Neither of these views is really fair. I therefore quote in full his poem 'Die verpestete Freiheit/ Freedom under the Plague', not for its poetic qualities, although its contained rage is not without effect, but for what it actually says:

> Was schreit das Pharisäervolk so ängstlich durch die Länder,
> Die Häupter dick mit Staub bestreut, zerrissen die Gewänder?
> Sie schreien: Sperrt die Häfen zu, umzieht mit Quarantänen
> Die Grenzen und die Ufer schnell vor Schiffen und vor Kähnen!
> Die Pest ist unter ihrer Schar. Da seht die Strafgerichte,
> Damit des Herrn gerechte Hand Empörer macht zunichte!
> Die Freiheit selber, wie es heißt, ist von der Pest befallen,
> Und flüchtet sich nach Westen nun mit ihren Jüngern allen.
> O seht euch vor, daß in das Land die Freiheit euch nicht schleiche,
> Und der gesunden Völker Herz mit ihrem Hauch erreiche!
> Sie kleidet sich zu dieser Zeit in vielerlei Gestalten:
> Bald Weib, bald Mann, bald nur ein Kind, bald hat sie greise Falten.
> Drum lasset keinen Flüchtling ein, der kommt vom Griechenlande,
> Daß nicht die Freiheit ihre Pest bring in die guten Lande![68]

This is Müller accepting the limits imposed by censorship and political constraint, but also registering a point that still (alas) has relevance in the Europe of 1995 (or 2021).

Inevitably, the two collections, *Sieben und siebzig Gedichte aus den hinterlassenen Papieren eines reisenden Waldhornisten* of 1821 (dedicated to Tieck and containing 'Die schöne Müllerin') and *Gedichte aus den hinterlassenen Papieren eines reisenden Waldhornisten* of 1824 (dedicated to

---

68 'Why do the Pharisees rage so excitedly through the lands,
Their heads strewn with dust, garments torn to bands?
They cry: Close down the ports and put a quarantine
On all our borders, ship and barquentine!
The plague has broken out. See the court that sits,
For the Lord's just hand to smite his enemies in bits!
For freedom, so we hear, the plague has got,
And is fleeing westwards bringing all her lot.
Beware that freedom does not slip into the land
And taint the people's hearts with pestilential hand!
She puts on many guises in our day:
Man, woman, child, even heads grey.
Keep out all refugees arriving from Greek isles,
Or freedom brings its plague and with it all its wiles!'. *Wilhelm Müller*, II, 285.

Carl Maria von Weber and containing the full text of 'Die Winterreise') must command more attention than any other aspect of his oeuvre, for these encapsulate quintessentially the 'Lieder-Müller' whose survival is assured. It will, however, not do simply to isolate the Schubert texts and forget the rest, for that would overlook the complexity of the relationship between melodic and poetic line. It is also not merely a question of noting where the major differences lie between Müller's and Schubert's respective order and phrasing (especially with reference to 'Die Winterreise'). Müller set both these lyrical cycles of 'Rollenlieder' in collections (sometimes containing further, different sets of 'Rollenlieder') and he seems to be inviting the reader of the Waldhornisten poems, as it were, to forget Schubert and look at the overall context. The phrase 'durch heitre Ironie gemilderte Schwermut',[69] quoted above in respect of Schmidt von Lübeck, can serve as a cautionary superscription to both of these collections. In giving them the titles he does, Müller is making a statement about the mixed nature of his poetry, or rather, the unforced coexistence of various components in forming a harmonious whole. Thus, while 'Die schöne Müllerin' and 'Die Winterreise' are undoubtedly texts of *Weltschmerz* ('melancholy'), there is enough in the collections that frame them to counteract any sense of utter existential loss. 'Die schöne Müllerin' even contains those two poems, 'Der Dichter, als Prolog/The Poet as Prologue' and 'Der Dichter, als Epilog/The Poet as Epilogue', ironizing through a deliberate 'Stimmungsbrechung'[70] the lapse from fulfilment into despair that the encapsulated poems express. But the titles of these poetic collections' titles keep a similar set of contradictory components in balance: the 'Waldhornist' immediately has associations with Tieck's Romantic novel *Franz Sternbald* and its constant horn serenades amid forest glades, 'reisend' as befits a novel that never reaches its destination, with 'hinterlassene Papiere' suggesting perhaps that he, too, has gone the way of the young miller. We must, however, accept the fiction that the 'Waldhornist' in his turn is also the author of all the poems, 'Reiselieder/Songs of Travel' or 'Ländliche Lieder/Songs of the Country' or 'Tafellieder/Drinking Songs', that contain the therapy against the despair of the 'Winterreise'. Schubert, never otherwise noted for the sureness of his literary taste, found 'Die schöne Müllerin' in

---

69 *Wilhelm Müller*, IV, 424.
70 'Break in tone'.

the 1821 collection and promptly excluded the prologue and epilogue poems. This changes Müller's text and leads the way for the domination of words by music. 'Die Winterreise' is more complex, in that Schubert first composed the twelve poems that had come out in *Urania* (1823), with an order slightly different from the 1824 edition, then added the remaining poems, but in a sequence that was not Müller's but his own. Thus, while the *Weltschmerz* of 'Die schone Müllerin' comes out fully only in the musical setting, the text of 'Die Winterreise' is altogether more pointed in its message. Winter already has bleak connotations. We are clearly not in the late eighteenth-century rococo winter landscape of, say, Günther von Goeckingk's 'Als der erste Schnee fiel/When the First Snow Fell',[71] with Nantchen wrapped up in her muff, but in a world of doors that close, houses that remain shut, nature that is inimical, trackless, without destination, where wandering is a symbol of the human state. Schubert, even without altering the text, intensifies the *Weltschmerz* ('melancholy') and makes it the dominant tone; the poet, in his turn, invites us to read back or read on and find a more cheerful collection to raise our spirits, perhaps those 'Tafellieder' that appealed to two other composers, not alas of Schubert's stature.

Müller's remaining lyrical collection, *Lyrische Reisen und epigrammatische Spaziergänge/Lyrical Journeys and Epigrammatic Strolls* (1827), is presumably to be read in a similar fashion: 'Lieder aus dem Meerbusen von Salerno/Songs from the Gulf of Salerno', 'Lieder aus Franzensbad bei Eger/Songs from Franzensbad Near Eger', 'Frühlingskranz aus dem Plauenschen Grunde bei Dresden/Spring Nosegay from the Plauenscher Grund near Dresden', 'Muscheln von der Insel Rügen/Shells from the Island of Rügen' (echoes of Heine here), 'Berenice. Ein erotischer Spaziergang/Berenice. An Erotic Promenade'. He did not live to unite other remaining disparate items. Fatigued, with eye and heart trouble, seeking convalescence on Rügen or in Franzensbad, even granted a temporary Tusculum in Dessau by his reigning prince, he worked on to the end. The visit to Stuttgart and Tübingen, to Schwab, Uhland and Kerner, was his last personal triumph. A heart attack brought his life to an end on September 30, 1827, just short of his thirty-third birthday. It was left to Gustav Schwab to commemorate his newly found friend in the five-volume *Vermischte*

---

71 A well-known anthology poem (1778).

Schriften of 1830, and the two-volume *Gedichte* of 1837 that reprinted the first two parts of the earlier edition.

An editor of Müller's works will be both constrained and encouraged by the printing history of his disparate *oeuvre*, whereas a commemorative volume will seek to do justice to all significant aspects of the man and writer. The *Vermischte Schriften* contain the poetry, the Novellen and the major critical essays (including those on the Tasso and Dante translations, on Uhland and Kerner, on almanac literature, on Rückert and on Willibald Alexis's *Walladamor*), the crucial account of Byron's life and works, and a miscellany of almanac and magazine contributions. They exclude much that was still in print in 1830, such as the collections and editions. The first two volumes provided a basis for the various editions of the poems, enabling these to remain within reach of the reading public. The poetry in both the 1830 and 1837 editions, even in Max Müller's 1868 edition, was grouped round thematic clusters, not in strict chronological progression. The diaries and letters were edited by Philip Allen and James Hatfield in 1903,[25] publishing the early Berlin diary and such correspondence as was available at the time. Hatfield in his turn did a critical edition of the poems in 1906,[72] and Heinrich Lohre's 'Lebensbild' of 1927 added important letters to Brockhaus.[73] Much of the material in the later volumes of the *Vermischte Schriften* has never been reprinted, but *Debora,* for reasons best known to the compilers, made its way into Paul Heyse's and Hermann Kurz's *Deutscher Novellenschatz*.[74] *Rom, Römer und Römerinnen* has until now never been republished in its entirety. *Doktor Faustus* was reprinted in 1911,[75] and the recent reprint of *Die Sängeifahrt/The Minstrels' Journey* picked up the few, hardly significant, contributions Müller made to that collection. Neither of these works is, however, truly central to Müller. Much else is in the rare book category and difficult of access: the Müller scholar still needs a

---

72 *Diary and Letters of Wilhelm Müller,* ed. by Philip Schuyler Allen and James Taft Hatfield (Chicago: Chicago University Press, 1903).

73 *Gedichte von Wilhelm Müller. Vollständige kritische Ausgabe,* ed. by James Taft Hatfield, Deutsche Literaturdenkmale des 18. und 19. Jahrhunderts 137 (Berlin: Behr, 1906); *Wilhelm Müller als Kritiker und Erzähler. Ein Lebensbild mit Briefen an F. A. Brockhaus und anderen Schriftstücken,* ed. by Heinrich Lohre, Aus dem Archiv F. A. Brockhaus, Zeugnisse zur Geschichte geistigen Schaffens 2 (Leipzig: Brockhaus, 1927).

74 *Deutscher Novellenschatz,* ed. by Paul Heyse and Hermann Kurz, 24 vols (Munich, Leipzig: Oldenbourg 1871–74), XVIII, 1–148.

75 Ed. by Bertha Badt, Pandora 11 (Munich: Georg Müller, 1911).

'hands-on' approach to texts; reprinted prefaces alone do not give the feel, texture or scope of many of the large-scale works.

Müller is not an author for whom a historical-critical approach is appropriate. Thus this multi-volume and splendidly produced edition by Maria-Verena Leistner is inevitably a selection, a generous and judicious one for all that. The poetry and the diaries and travel accounts are virtually complete; the letters are well chosen. I could have done without the Novellen, but that is a personal judgement and not a scholarly criterion. My own selection of the critical writing might well have been different from the editor's, but only in detail (I should have preferred the Tasso and Moore pieces to one or two published here). I should single out for special mention the prefaces to the Minnesinger and Opitz selections (republished for the first time), the large and important article on Byron, and the review of Uhland and Kerner. I regret that the decision was made, however understandable, to exclude the contributions to encyclopaedias: the printing history of these publications is a bibliographer's nightmare, and not even Goedeke ventured into this veritable minefield. Encyclopaedias are, however, the single most important mode of dissemination of useful knowledge in the period, Müller almost coinciding with the inception of Brockhaus's or Ersch-Gruber's enterprises. They also represent a factor of continuity amid the changes of critical theory and literary canon.[76] The scholarly apparatus of this edition consists of a fifty-eight-page introduction to Volume I, by Bernd Leistner, short introductions to each work or set of works, and notes. Volume V contains a select bibliography of primary and secondary literature, an important orientation for non-specialist and specialist alike. The editorial principles set out in the same volume are matter-of-fact and without fuss. While accepting that most of Müller's work does not exist in manuscript, and that he made alterations to his own works during his lifetime, the principle of manuscript or first printing is adhered to, with variants available in the notes. The spelling has been modernized in accordance with good sense and practice. The notes themselves, especially those of a bibliographical nature, are useful, and clearly much research into sources has gone into

---

[76] Walther Killy, 'Große deutsche Lexika und ihre Lexikographen 1711–1835. Hederich, Hübner, Walch, Pierer', in *Große deutsche Lexika. Aufklärung und neunzehntes Jahrhundert* (Munich: K. G. Saur, 1992), 1–35.

them. Unlike those of the 'Bibliothek deutscher Klassiker', for instance, they are more cryptic than expansive. Thus in some cases just a few more chosen sentences of introduction would have been useful, as on Byron, or the Greek wars of independence, or even on, say, the *Bibliothek deutscher Dichter des siebzehnten Jahrhunderts/Library of German Poets of the Seventeenth Century*. True, Leistner's highly useful introductory essay to Volume I does this in a few, sometimes very few, well-weighed words. The decision not to document except in passing Müller's contributions to encyclopaedias means that references to these are not as clear as they might be. These are very small criticisms to raise of an edition of this scope and significance.

The commemorative volume, *Wilhelm Müller. Eine Lebensreise/ Wilhelm Müller's Life's Journey* contains contributions by both Bernd and Maria-Verena Leistner, but also by a dozen other experts.[77] These range from essays of more local interest to articles dealing with major aspects of Müller's *oeuvre* and thinking. These roughly 100 pages form a corpus of knowledge (I have drawn on it extensively for this article) that will, I hope, help to bring Müller back into a wider general consciousness, and, who knows, attract visitors to his birthplace. There are superb illustrations based on the exhibition that gave rise to the volume.

---

77 The contributions are: Bernd Leistner, 'Wilhelm Müller. Leben und Werk', 11–31; Ulla Jablonski, 'Wilhelm Müller in Dessau. Wirtschaft und Gesellschaft der kleinen Residenzstadt um 1800', 33–39; Annette Gerlach, 'Wilhelm Müller als Bibliothekar', 41–45; Maria-Verena Leistner, 'Wilhelm Müller als Literaturkritiker', 47–55; Roswitha Schieb, '"Die schöne Müllerin" und "Die Winterreise". Möglichkeiten und Grenzen romantischen Sprechens', 57–69; Andreas Klenner, 'Kein Sänger der Weltflucht. Wilhelm Müller als kritischer Beobachter seiner Zeit', 71–75; Barbara Czerannowski, '"Ohne die Freiheit, was wärest du, Hellas? Ohne dich, Hellas, was wäre die Welt?". Wilhelm Müller und der Philhellenismus', 77–83; Hildegard Eilert, '"Ich denke doch, wir müssen die Römer mit ihrer eigenen Nase beurteilen". Wilhelm Müllers Kritik des deutschen Italien-Bildes in "Rom, Römer und Römerinnen"', 85–95; Hans-Udo Kreuels, '"Die Winterreise" des Wilhelm Müller (und des Franz Schubert). Versuch einer behutsamen, gegenseitigen Distanzierung', 97–102.

Fig. 14. Anna Jameson, *Characteristics of Women, Moral, Poetical, and Historical. With Fifty Vignette Etchings,* second edition (London: Saunders & Otley, 1833), volume 1, p. 1. The Master and Fellows of Trinity College, Cambridge.

11. Heine and Shakespeare[1]

William Shakespeare is a major figure of bearing, reference and identification in Heinrich Heine's oeuvre and also the subject of a whole work, *Shakespeares Mädchen und Frauen/Shakespeare's Girls and Women* (1838).[2] The experts cannot agree whether it is a minor piece with major overtones, or perhaps a larger complex that remains fragmentary (a Shakespeare project) or even a kind of extension of his 'Deutschland-Schriften'[3] which start around 1832. Certainly it has elements of all these, but above all it is an occasional piece, eclectic, pluralistic, open-ended,

---

1   An earlier version of this chapter was published as: 'Heine and Shakespeare', in *Heine und die Weltliteratur*, ed. by T. J. Reed and Alexander Stillmark (Oxford, London: Legenda, 2000), 51–63.
2   For *Shakespeares Mädchen und Frauen*, see particularly the apparatus to Heinrich Heine, *Gesamtausgabe der Werke*, ed. by Manfred Windfuhr et al., 16 vols in 23 (Hamburg: Hoffmann & Campe, 1973–1997), X (referred to henceforth as *DA*); Heinrich Heine, *Sämtliche Schriften*, ed. by Klaus Briegleb, 6 vols in 7 (Munich: Hanser, 1968–76), VII (referred to henceforth as *SS*); Heinrich Heine, *Shakespeares Mädchen und Frauen*, ed. by Volkmar Hansen (Frankfurt am Main: Insel, 1978); Walter Wadepuhl, 'Shakespeares Mädchen und Frauen. Heine und Shakespeare', in *Heine-Studien* (Weimar: Arion, 1956), 114–34; Siegbert Prawer, *Heine's Shakespeare. A Study in Contexts. Inaugural Lecture delivered before the University of Oxford on 5 May 1970* (Oxford: Clarendon Press, 1970); Karl Josef Höltgen, 'Über *Shakespeares Mädchen und Frauen*. Heine, Shakespeare und England', in *Internationaler Heine-Kongreß. Düsseldorf 1972. Referate und Diskussionen*, ed. by Manfred Windfuhr (Hamburg: Hoffmann & Campe, 1973), 464–88; Walter Wadepuhl, *Heinrich Heine. Sein Leben und seine Werke* (Cologne, Vienna: Böhlau, 1974), 225–39. On the general background see Werner Habicht, 'Shakespeare in Nineteenth-Century Germany. The Making of a Myth', in *Nineteenth-Century Germany*, ed. by Modris Ecksteins and Hildegard Hammerschmidt-Hummel (Tübingen: Narr, 1983), 141–57; Werner Habicht, *Shakespeare and the German Imagination*, International Shakespeare-Association Occasional Paper 5 (Herford: International Shakespeare-Association, 1994); Roger Paulin, '"Shakspeare's allmähliches Bekanntwerden in Deutschland". Aspekte der Institutionalisierung Shakespeares 1840–1875', in *Bildung und Konfession. Politik, Religion und literarische Identitätsbildung 1850–1918*, ed. by Martin Huber and Gerhard Lauer, Studien und Texte zur Sozialgeschichte der Literatur 59 (Tübingen: Niemeyer, 1996), 9–20.
3   'Writings on Germany'.

like so much of Heine's own creation and his view of creation itself. It is also, as opposed to allusions, his last major statement on Shakespeare.

Under the disarming subtitle of *Erläuterungen/Explanatory Notes* and with Heine adopting the role of the guide to a kind of stately home, throwing open the various rooms, he manages to address subjects well known from the major works of the 1830s: the role of the poet as diviner or seer, standing above 'mere' history; the question of national literature and national appropriation; the monarchy of states and letters as against the *république*, and much besides. I do not wish to discuss all, or for that matter any, of these in any systematic way. Rather, I hope to enter into the spirit of improvisation that breathes through these pages.

It is a pity that *Shakespeares Mädchen und Frauen* does not have a section on *The Winter's Tale*. We know of course that Heine was aware of the connotations of 'Wintermärchen' when he chose that subtitle for his imaginary journey through Germany. As a nineteenth-century German Shakespeare edition defines it, a 'Wintermärchen' is '[e]ine schauerliche oder rührende Geschichte'.[4] It is also a world encompassing antiquity and Renaissance, improbabilities and coincidences, oracles and bears, disguises and revelations. Above all, it is mythical and ends happily. It is not unlike his general view of Shakespeare, and, with the notable exception of that happy ending, it is not dissimilar to his view of Germany.

Our symposium has the overall theme 'Heine and World Literature'.[5] That notion of 'world literature' is by common agreement, if not necessarily a Goethean creation, certainly a coining of Johann Wolfgang Goethe's, and is a reflection of the opening up, from the 1790s on, of perspectives across national, cultural, and linguistic borders, the 'Kosmopolitismus des Blicks'[6] of which Jean Paul had spoken, the throwing open of windows in which the Romantics had had such a part. On a more modest scale it was fostered by Heine's much-revered Wilhelm Müller. To all this, Heine is heir, but also to its controversies and polemics. One notes with what care Goethe chooses a paradigm

---

4 'A ghastly or touching story'. *William Shakespeare's dramatische Werke*, trans. by Friedrich Bodenstedt et al., 38 vols (Leipzig: Brockhaus, 1867–71), XXX, iv.
5 See footnote 1.
6 'Cosmpolitanism of outlook'. Horst Günther, 'Klassik und Weltliteratur', in *Literarische Klassik*, ed. by Hans-Joachim Simm, suhrkamp taschenbuch 2084 (Frankfurt am Main: Suhrkamp, 1988), 87–100 (92).

for the process by which a foreign literary culture may transfer back to its country of origin an insight and a penetration not yet available at home. It is, of course, Thomas Carlyle's *Life of Schiller*. The example is right and proper and well chosen. One does note, however, that Shakespeare (except in the very broadest sense) is less prominent in this Goethean construct of 'Weltliteratur'. The English Romantics almost to a man — and one of them, Samuel Taylor Coleridge, coming mightily close to plagiarism — were saying that it was now the Germans who were leading the field in Shakespeare studies. Would that not also constitute a prime example of those cosmopolitan border-crossings and fructifications? But Goethe had chosen the model of Carlyle and Friedrich Schiller because in addition it demonstrated that, while Schiller's reputation in Germany was slumping in the 1820s, it had entered into the blood-stream of world literature, and that was what mattered. Who was responsible for that collapse in German esteem? The Romantics, of course. It is thus no coincidence that Goethe in 1828–29 published his correspondence with Schiller, in the lifetime (just) of both Schlegel brothers, whose critical machinations (as Goethe might perceive it) had seen to it that Goethe's reputation increased while Schiller's decreased.

By giving such prominence to literary politics and controversy I am perhaps distorting the many coincidences and areas of agreement between these literary generations. Is this one of the bad habits one picks up as a literary biographer? It is however observable that Shakespeare — our subject, not Goethe or Schiller — is a divisive and unruly force in the German republic of letters. One notes that three of the most devastating annihilations of reputation and character in German literary criticism occur in the context of Shakespeare or to figures once involved in his reception: Gothold Ephraim Lessing's of Johann Christoph Gottsched, Schiller's of Gottfried August Bürger, and Heine's of August Wilhelm Schlegel. The task was done with such thoroughness that these names are all but expunged from the annals of literature, the victims referred to in hushed embarrassment, like a mad aunt or uncle in an otherwise respectable family. Take August Wilhelm Schlegel: there has been no proper critical edition of his works since 1846, no satisfactory critical edition to date of the world-famous *Vorlesungen uber dramatische Kunst und Literatur/Lectures on Dramatic Art and Literature* (even the Düsseldorf Heine edition has recourse to an unsatisfactory edition),[7] no biographer, no scholarly reprint of the original Shakespeare translation of 1796–1810. His reputation has been subject to the continuing 'destruction' in the nineteenth century of the older Romantics (note the speaking title of Rudolf Haym's *Die romantische Schule/The Romantic School* [1870]) in favour of the more accessible talents of Clemens Brentano, Arnim or Eichendorff. He is not even mentioned in Friedrich Gundolf's *Romantiker* of 1929. Did Heine's infamous attack on Schlegel in *Die romantische Schule* bring this about? Of course not: teleological reductionism makes for bad criticism and bad literary history. Schlegel's reputation lived on in France and England. He was, besides, in later life singularly unattractive, and himself no mean controversialist. There is another answer. Siegbert Prawer, in his inaugural lecture of 1970, draws attention to the visceral image that Heine employs in *Die romantische Schule*, of Indigenous peoples of North America killing their elders when they become old and decrepit.[8] Like James Frazer's potent image of the priests of Nemi, it reminds us, too, that the stiletto knife in the back is Heine's ultimate sanction.[9]

Leaving such severities, it is much more profitable to see Heine and Schlegel and Heine and Shakespeare in another and better perspective. As with so many internecine inter-generational relationships, there is more in common between Heine and Schlegel than what separates them. Surely Schlegel is an important model for the elegant style Heine so cultivates and which is one of the few qualities in the older man singled out for praise in *Die romantische Schule*.[10] More importantly, Schlegel's critical method and historical perspective is close to Heine's. Schlegel followed only to a limited extent Johann Gottfried Herder's notion of organic development, change and decay, or revolution, in German culture. He is far happier setting up constructs, pairs of opposites (Classical and Romantic being the best-known) only loosely based on some kind of historical continuity and owing more to inner artistic or aesthetic qualities. The Heinean notions of 'Romantische Schule', set up

---

7   August Wilhelm Schlegel, *Vorlesungen über dramatische Kunst und Literatur*, ed. by Giovanno Vittorio Amoretti (Bonn and Leipzig: Schroeder, 1923). See *DA*, X, 377.
8   Prawer (note 1), 7.
9   Note of 2021: this was the case when I wrote this in 1997. Fortunately the situation has now much changed for the better, although it has taken 150 years to do so. See below, footnote 38.
10 *SS*, V, 417.

against its cosmopolitan or Protestant or classical counter-equivalents, or even the notion of a 'Kunstperiode',[11] are not alien to general Romantic thinking, Schlegel's or others'. The Romantics' term 'universal' could have embracing connotations similar to Heine's 'cosmopolitan'. Heine in *Die romantische Schule* notes that Schlegel's Shakespeare translation is hardly in keeping with his usual (perceived) Christian, Catholic, anti-cosmopolitan, mystical and Calderonian orientation.[12] Of course, August Wilhelm's embrace of Catholicism (as opposed to Friedrich's) had been short-lived. More importantly, his Shakespeare translation is the work of a philologist, not an apologist, and the polarization of Schlegel and Voss in *Die romantische Schule* is a critical device to tear apart two figures who basically converge on the same object from different corners, making 'classical' literature (in the fullest sense, antiquity and Renaissance) available to the educated German reader. Schlegel is also the only classical philologist of his day to face Johann Heinrich Voss on equal terms.

On the other hand, Heine may not have known how much Schlegel hated the English — as opposed to Shakespeare, of course. By and large, the German Romantics are not great anglophiles. Schlegel the Hanoverian cannot comprehend that 'die frostigen, stupiden Seelen auf dieser brutalen Insel'[13] could have produced such genius. Hence his lack of interest in the 'Life and Times' of Shakespeare. The greatest disappointment in Ludwig Tieck's life was his trip to England in 1817. Heine could find in William Hazlitt the insight that the older English Shakespeare critics, Samuel Johnson especially, had failed to appreciate Shakespeare's genius: but it was already there in Schlegel, and English readers duly noted and deferred to it. Heine, despite his fine poetic ear, is not a philologist or translator. We cannot take too seriously his plan for an illustrated prose translation in 1839. He is unfair to Schlegel the translator, but his unfairness is that of a younger generation that regarded rendering of Shakespeare into German as a process in being and not one already concluded. Not only do the various different sources

---

11   'The epoch of art'. Heine's 'Ende der Kunstperiode' can be applied historically to the long and daunting shadow of the Goethean achievement, to Shakespeare's similarly.
12   Ibid., 4n and 375.
13   'The frigid stupid souls on that brutal island'. *Ludwig Tieck und die Brüder Schlegel*, ed. by Edgar Lohner (Munich: Winkler, 1972), 23.

for his quotations in *Shakespeares Mädchen und Frauen* bear witness to that fact[14] (as well as to his hasty improvisation). His generation by and large did not regard the positions reached by Schlegel or Tieck as fixed or final. Georg Herwegh and Ferdinand Freiligrath are examples, as is also the young Theodor Fontane, and it was only the adoption by the Deutsche Shakespeare-Gesellschaft (founded in 1864) of the so-called 'Schlegel-Tieck' that conferred on this translation the classic status it still, rightly or wrongly, enjoys. In the final analysis, Schlegel and Heine are not so much divided over Shakespeare as over more concrete, personal factors: Schlegel had revived his noble title and had accepted preferment in the Prussian state. That was where Romanticism got you. Heine, despite being disrespectful and malicious to the old 'Hofrat' Tieck, is much more appreciative of his Shakespearean studies and his general contribution to 'Capriccio' and 'Scherz',[15] certainly more than he deserved. He may not have known that it was Schlegel who put Tieck on to the idea of translating Cervantes while he got on with Calderón. Now, while Heine rightly sensed that he had knifed Schlegel the old priest in the sacred grove, he was aware that Schlegel's colleague, Tieck, was still at large. One reason for his urgency in throwing together *Shakespeares Mädchen und Frauen* is the fear that Julius Campe might turn to Tieck![16] In the event, Heine need not have feared. It is nonetheless right to see *Shakespeares Mädchen und Frauen* in the wider context of German Shakespeare reception: of all those translations, of course, but also illustrated editions, biographies, life and works, analyses of plays, a huge activity predicated on the awareness that Shakespeare is German property and inheritance, a classic. In the words of Franz Horn, a figure much maligned by Heine, 'wir wollen streben, daß Shakspeare ganz der unsrige werde'.[17]

Shakespeares Mädchen und Frauen is, of course, different from Schlegel's *Vorlesungen über dramatische Kunst und Literatur* of 1808 in that its concern, by and large (and when it does not allow itself to be side-tracked) is with character, not with plot structure, especially with character as it is realized both in its textual and dramatic development.

---

14 *DA*, X, 356.
15 *SS*, V, 421–31.
16 Heine, *Shakespeares Mädchen*, ed. Hansen, 221.
17 'We wish to do our utmost to make Shakespeare our own'. Franz Horn, *Shakespeare's Schauspiele*, 3 vols (Leipzig: Brockhaus, 1823–31), I, 444.

In this respect, Goethe was of little assistance as an alternative to Schlegel. For *Shakespeare und kein Ende!/Shakespeare and No End* (last part 1826) had postulated a Shakespeare above concerns of character and stage, a kind of 'Urphänomen' of creativity, a measure of the creative process itself. Schlegel's lectures had held out the hope that a historical drama could now be within the Germans' grasp, were poets but to use the historical past in respectful imitation of Shakespeare. Goethe (but this time more in private) had warned that Shakespeare was a great inhibitor of talent (a warning too little heeded in the nineteenth century).[18] Christian Dietrich Grabbe's *Über die Shakespearo-Manie/On Shakespeare Mania* of 1828 had set up danger signs for the would-be Shakespeareanizing dramatist and the pitfalls he might face. The stridency of Grabbe's tone, his presumption in drawing attention to Shakespeare's 'faults' (about which little had been heard since Herder banished them from the critical agenda), his pointing to other, safer models, are indications that, for him, Shakespeare might well cause a loss of national literary identity. Heine, too, has his word in season for Shakespearean imitators, but they again are not his major concern. Above all, the consistency, not to say stridency, of Grabbe's essay is not his approach. He found much more common ground in Tieck's *Dramaturgische Blätter/Essays on Drama* (1826), a loose concatenation of drama reviews that, as it were incidentally, also turned to deeper issues of character and interpretation (often controversially), allowing digressions and anabases and asides. The seeming outrageousness of Tieck's reading of *Hamlet* and *Macbeth* was an indication that he perceived a need to break with what were by then 'standard' interpretations. So as not to show too much deference to the old Romantic for whom he had a soft spot, Heine pushes one of Tieck's less favoured authors, Hazlitt, into the foreground. It is Hazlitt in translation, of course, which made him sound more German. Thus Heine found Hazlitt's attack on Johnson to his liking.[19] It reminded him, perhaps, of his own dealings with August Wilhelm Schlegel, without of course the personal, scandalous and wounding aspects. The English

---

18   Goethe to Eckermann, December 25, 1825. Johann Wolfgang Goethe, *Gedenkausgabe der Werke, Briefe und Gespräche*, ed. by Ernst Beutler, 27 vols (Zurich, Munich: Artemis, 1948–54), XXIV, 167.

19   'On Characters of Shakespeare's Plays' (1817). *The Complete Works of William Hazlitt*, ed. by P. P. Howe, 21 vols (London, Toronto: Dent, 1930–34), IV, 174–78.

Romantics' sense of literary continuity means that, while they may not like the Augustan age or Johnson the critic, they are nevertheless aware of the 'debt of the past' and sense acutely the 'anxiety of influence'. Hazlitt (and to some extent Anna Jameson) escape the anathema Heine visited on the English. His account of French Shakespearean reception is however rather sketchier and more skewed. With few exceptions, he says, the French have read Shakespeare through a trivialized Romantic vision, have failed to distinguish atmosphere and stage-property from substance, have elevated plurality of style to an absolute without an understanding of Shakespeare's subtleties, especially in his comedies. They are, as imitators, more like Christopher Marlowe or Thomas Heywood.[20] Had Heine been reading Tieck's Novelle *Dichterleben/The Life of the Poet*, where the so-called minor Elizabethans have an uncanny resemblance to the younger generation of poets of his own day. Only François Guizot, the historian and critic, receives Heine's favour, as one who is able to see Shakespeare in a wider span of English history, something his contemporaries, Victor Hugo, Alfred de Vigny and Alfred de Musset, with their uncreative frenzies,[21] fail to do. Heine's point is interesting. Doubtless it was the Shakespeareanizing Hugo, not so much Shakespeare himself, who influenced the young Georg Büchner (the translator of *Lucrèce Borgia* and *Marie Tudor*).

Guizot's remarks on the several approaches to comedy by Aristotle, Molière and Shakespeare raise the discussion on to the level of the nature of the comic muse herself, in place and historical time. We are close here to Heine's passing insight on Molière's greatness from the first book of *Zur Geschichte der Religion und Philosophie in Deutschland/ On the History of Philosophy and Religion in Germany*: 'Darum ist eben Moliere so groß, weil er, gleich Aristophanes und Cervantes, nicht bloß temporelle Zufälligkeiten, sondern das Ewig Lächerliche, die Urschwächen der Menschheit, persifliert'.[22] It is the cosmic trope of a world theatre, the comedy of human history, in which these poets share. It is also the other distinction that Heine draws, between 'Weltgeschichte', with its disharmonies and clangour, and 'Geschichte

---

20 *SS*, VII, 283.
21 Ibid., 281–90.
22 'Molière is so great for that reason, because, like Aristophanes and Cervantes, he pokes fun not just at the casual matters of everyday life but at the ever-ridiculous, the inborn foibles of humanity'. Ibid., V, 535.

der Menschheit',[23] where in Heine's image one can hear above the din of human affairs the sweet eternal melodies of mankind. Heine's canonically 'great poets' inhabit these regions — and Shakespeare is almost always to the fore because of the primacy of drama (here we see Schlegel's influence as well as Hegel's). Does it matter that Heine's 'core canon' is essentially the Romantics', itself formulated embryonically by the *Sturm und Drang* ('Storm and Stress') generation? Certainly, the Schlegel brothers in their *Athenaeum* incarnation would not have dissented from the triumvirate (the 'Dichtertriumvirat')[24] later set up by Heine, of Goethe, Miguel de Cervantes and Shakespeare. It remained essentially Tieck's trinitarian position in his poetic doctrine. Where Tieck spoke of 'Erzpoeten',[25] Heine refers to 'Urpoeten'[26] (his list is Aristophanes, Goethe and Shakespeare). These transcending figures are of course wreathed in myth (the 'Kunstperiode' is one such), are heroic, supernal, 'Napoleonic', if you will. They represent universals, just as their names were associated in Romantic discourse with the notion of 'Universalpoesie'. They stand, not for thought, not for political engagement, not even for 'esprit', but for 'poetry' or 'art'. That, in the final analysis, is the criterion of their canonicity. I used before the term 'inhibitor of talent', and indeed all of Heine's 'Urpoeten' are that. The image of the poet-genius standing above quotidian human concerns is of course not new (think of the opening of Herder's Shakespeare essay). As there, it is also a metaphor of creativity. 'Shakespeare gesellt sich zum Weltgeist',[27] says Goethe in *Shakespeare und kein Ende!*, through him we gain insight into the living processes of which we are part. Heine, too, speaks of Shakespeare and the 'Weltgeist'. In the Jessica section of *Shakespeares Mädchen und Frauen*, we read that Shakespeare, in writing *The Merchant of Venice*, may have wished to write comedy, he may have even wished to present us with 'einen gedrillten Werwolf'[28] in Shylock:

---

23 'Human history', 'history of mankind'. Ibid., 69.
24 'Triumvirate of poets'. Ibid., III, 260.
25 'Archpoets'. *Ludwig Tieck und die Brüder Schlegel*, ed. Lohner, 25.
26 'Real poets'. SS, III, 287.
27 'Shakespeare allies himself with the world spirit'. Goethe, *Gedenkausgabe der Werke*, XIV, 758.
28 'A tamed werewolf'. SS, VII, 251.

> Aber der Genius des Dichters, der Weltgeist, der in ihm waltet, steht immer höher als sein Privatwille, und so geschah es, daß er in Shylock, trotz der grellen Fratzenhaftigkeit, die Justifikation einer unglücklichen Sekte aussprach, welche von der Vorsehung, aus geheimnisvollen Gründen, mit dem Haß des niedern und vornehmen Pöbels belastet worden, und diesen Haß nicht immer mit Liebe vergelten wollte.
>
> Aber was sag' ich? Der Genius des Shakespeare erhebt sich noch über den Kleinhader zweier Glaubensparteien, und sein Drama zeigt uns eigentlich weder Juden noch Christen, sondern Unterdrücker und Unterdrückte [...].[29]

Of course a little care is needed here, for this is not a subject about which Heine could be objective. It may be an astute rhetorical ploy to introduce that 'Weltgeist' and then smuggle under its accommodating wings a private reading of The Merchant of Venice. But so often, for so many different purposes, Heine is inviting us to see a problem from a universal, cosmic, mythical angle. It is essentially the device used to exculpate Jessica, the convert. Is she not, like Desdemona or Imogen, a 'Tochter Evas',[30] wilful, disobedient, unheeding — like the mother of us all? And so Shakespeares Mädchen und Frauen ends with the grand cosmic conceit, indeed a plurality of worlds, with the sun (Miranda), the moon (Juliet), and the comet (Cleopatra), the three stages of civilization, from 'unbefleckte[r] Boden', 'schauerliche Reinheit', to the 'Sinnenglut' of the Renaissance, and 'erkrankte Zivilisation' and 'Zerstörungslust'.[31]

It follows that Heine is not really interested in the Shakespearean ideologies current in his time, such as the 'Life' and the 'Man', nor in what can be called 'Shakespeare-Philologie'. Thus his learned reference to William Prynne's Histriomastix is simply part of his anti-English agenda, the Puritan, Cromwellian, stolid, pragmatic streak of Albion that he so detests.[32] A poet in touch with the 'Weltgeist' will be above

---

29 'But the poet's genius, the world spirit that operates in him, always ranks higher than his private will, and so it came about that he enunciated in Shylock, despite having made a crude caricature of him, the justification of an unfortunate sect, that providence, for reasons best known to itself, has saddled with the hate of the rabble, high and low, and that did not always wish to pay back this hate with love.
But what am I saying? Shakespeare's genius rises above the petty squabbles of the two sectarian factions, and his drama shows us in real fact neither Jew nor Christian, but oppressors and oppressed'. SS, VII, 251.
30 'Daughter of Eve'. Ibid., 257.
31 'Unsullied ground'; 'fearsome purity'; 'sensual fire'; 'civilization in decay'; 'destructive passion'. Ibid., 292–93.
32 Ibid., 175.

anecdotes, even above rigid genre distinctions (Heine subdivides the plays more than most critics). Above all, the critic may look behind any historical context of the plays or any possible intention on the part of the poet (as with *The Merchant of Venice*), and see things that are new, startling, perhaps even seditious.

Which brings me finally to *Shakespeares Mädchen und Frauen* itself. Certainly it must rank as one of the most 'occasional' of Heine's major works, in the sense that it came about in an improvised and hand-to-mouth fashion. As the only major work devoted to a single non-German author, it makes no pretensions to 'mere' objectivity; its strength is in details, not in encompassing arguments. It quite openly accommodates current ideologies inside its framework; indeed it welcomes them. Thus in a sense the whole work is responding to Karl Gutzkow's promptings that there should be a Young German position in the wider debate on Shakespeare[33] (the same Gutzkow, incidentally, who in 1864 will give the official tercentenary address in Weimar!). I have indicated unexpected fraternalities between *Shakespeares Mädchen und Frauen* and other Shakespeare studies. It likes to confront, outrageously if necessary. Who, for instance, had ever begun a study of Shakespeare's characters with *Troilus and Cressida*? (Anna Jameson does not even refer to this play.) Its loves and hates are plain for all to see, although it is a pity that Heine is so uncomplimentary about the French in their second great wave of Shakespeare reception, but that of course had been initiated by Schlegel's companion, Madame de Staël. Perhaps there is more than a hint of rivalry. At least there is no sign yet of those later proprietary claims by German nineteenth-century Shakespearean scholarship which deny the French houseroom altogether. Naturally, it owes much to Anna Jameson (in translation),[34] and it defers not a little to the unfortunate Franz Horn, whose gentle soul had expired the year before. In 1831, Horn wrote this:

> In Shakespeare's Werken finden wir die vollständigste Galerie der Frauen, die, wenn wir sie Jahre lang und mit Genauigkeit und Liebe betrachtet haben, uns endlich überzeugen muß, daß nie ein Dichter gelebt, der dem weiblichen Geschlechte so reine Huldigung dargebracht hat wie er. Es

---

33 Heine, *Shakespeares Mädchen*, ed. Hansen, 221.
34 Anna Jameson, *Characteristics of Woman. Moral, Political, and Historical*, 2 vols (London: Saunders and Ottley, 1832).

giebt in seinen Werken keinen männlichen Charakter, in welchem der Verein des Guten und Schönen, des Freien und Nothwendigen, der Tiefe und Klarheit, der Anmuth und Würde zu einer ganz vollendeten Einheit gebracht worden wäre [...].³⁵

This 'Galerie der Frauen' Heine supplies in 1838, in the form of the series of English lithographs which accompany his text. And the less said about them the better, except that they are very much of their time.

Many of the most memorable passages in *Shakespeares Mädchen und Frauen* are only tenuously about Shakespeare himself: the assassination of the English character, the mouse dialogue, the lament for the Jewish people which goes far beyond Jessica (or even Shylock) and extends in a great parabola before ending on that 'Jessika, mein Kind'.³⁶ Let me take that wonderful mouse vision as an example.³⁷ Note that these mice are the device employed to introduce the Histories, the plays that Schlegel calls a 'historisches Heldengedicht',³⁸ and to which he gives an attention never hitherto granted them. Heine does not even subdivide the plays into Histories as such, grouping instead their heroines chronologically. That is of course not the same as writing about history itself. Historical drama is however another matter. 'Ein alter Mauserich',³⁹ with long experience of human affairs, is Heine's witness. It is essentially a catalogue of 'eine nur maskierte Wiederkehr derselben Naturen und Ereignisse';⁴⁰ 'man amüsiert sich mit weiser Gelassenheit'.⁴¹ The historical drama as such (not least Ernst von Raupach's 'Hohenstaufenbandwürmer',⁴² in Friedrich Hebbel's dismissive phrase) tells us about theories of history

---

35 'In Shakespeare's works we find the most complete gallery of women, which, when we have closely and lovingly studied them for years, must in the end convince us that never has a poet lived who has paid such pure homage to the female sex as he did. There is no male character in his works in whom the good and the beautiful, freedom and necessity, depth and clarity, grace and dignity combine in perfect unity'. Horn, *Shakespeare's Schauspiele*, V, 98.
36 'Jessica, my child'. *SS*, VII, 266.
37 Ibid., pp. 215–17.
38 'Historical epic poem'. August Wilhelm Schlegel, *Vorlesungen über dramatische Kunst und Litteratur, Kritische Ausgabe der Vorlesungen*, IV, I, ed. by Stefan Knödler (Paderborn, etc.: Schöningh, 2018), 346.
39 'An old father mouse'.
40 'A recurrence of the same natures and events, only masked'. *SS*, VII, 215.
41 'One takes a wise, amused view of it'. Ibid., 211.
42 'Hohenstaufen tapeworms'. Friedrich Hebbel, preface to *Maria Magdalene. Werke*, ed. by Gerhard Fricke, Werner Keller and Karl Pörnbacher, 5 vols (Munich: Hanser, 1963–67), I, 325.

(hence the account of the 'Souffleur' with Hegelian overtones), but not about man's 'progress' as such. And Heine is using his mice to tell us that it is not the business of historical drama to do so. By following Anna Jameson's device of selecting *Shakespeares Mädchen und Frauen* — female characters — he is automatically downgrading the Histories; for the heroines are only there 'weil die darzustellende Historie ihre Einmischung erforderte',[43] not because they are part of the integral portrayal of historical events. But the opportunity afforded by historical examples or incidents is quite another matter. Shakespeare knows more than we do. With due respect to Friedrich Schlegel, he becomes 'ein in die Vergangenheit schauender Prophet';[44] he does not depict history itself but fills 'die Lakunen der Historie'.[45] Our attention is seized by his historical figures because they bear out our own experience with kings and rulers in our own times. Knowing Heine as we do, we must expect some unflattering parallels. We have one in the sustained comparison of Bolingbroke in *Richard II* and Louis Philippe: 'ein schlauer Held, ein kriechender Riese, ein Titan der Verstellung, entsetzlich, ja empörend ruhig, die Tatze in einem samtnen Handschuh, und damit die öffentliche Meinung streichelnd [...]'[46] Although this is supposed to relate to the section on Lady Gray from *Henry VI*, we leap from *Richard II* to *2 Henry IV*, to the usurper king's last words to his son, 'die Shakspeare schon längst für ihn [i.e. Louis Philippe] aufgeschrieben'.[47] Thus, too, the Joan of Arc section (*1 Henry VI*) insists on the multiform injustices of the English towards the French, from the Maid of Orleans — to Napoleon.

Heine had of course been reading some history, the 'geniales Buch' of Jules Michelet.[48] Heine is not interested in Michelet's basic thesis that English literary culture is anti-Christian. He does not utilize Michelet's rather cheap point that the Shakespearean legends depict the Bard beginning as a butcher. But he cannot resist Michelet's sustained account of English commercialism, mercantilism and hard-headedness, the

---

43 'Because history, as it was to be presented, required them to be involved'. *SS*, VII, 218.
44 'A prophet able to look back into the past'. Ibid., 230.
45 'The gaps in history'. Ibid., 229.
46 'A cunning hero, a creeping giant, a Titan at deception, calm to a terrible, even outrageous degree, his claws in a velvet glove, stroking public opinion with it.' Ibid., 231.
47 'That Shakespeare had long since written down for him'. Ibid.
48 'Brilliant book'. *SS*, VII, 226.

technical superiority by which their foot-soldiery at Crécy destroyed the 'fine fleur' of French chivalry. Immediately Heine sees the opportunity for another image: the battle between prose and poetry. We almost believe that he is going to fall for the French 'Ritteromantik'[49] that Hugo and Alexandre Dumas *père* so eloquently represent. But his return to 'objectivity' is half-hearted: 'Die Triumphe der Engländer sind immer eine Schande der Menschheit, seit den Tagen von Crécy und Poitiers, bis auf Waterloo. Klio ist immer ein Weib, trotz ihrer parteilosen Kälte, ist sie empfindlich für Ritterlichkeit und Heldensinn; und ich bin überzeugt, nur mit knirschendem Herzen verzeichnet sie in ihre Denktafeln die Siege der Engländer'.[50]

I believe it is also essentially from Michelet that Heine introduces into Shakespeare discussion the notion of 'Renaissance'.[51] At least I am not sure of its use before him. By introducing it into his account of Portia (also at the end, in his description of Juliet)[52] he places the Christian-Jewish contrast into even sharper relief, between 'Glück' and 'Mißgeschick',[53] between the 'Nachblüte des griechischen Geistes'[54] and the claustrophobic restrictions of Judaism. I need not tell this company that this is a conflict unresolved in Heine himself. For nineteenth-century Shakespeare studies at large, the notion of Renaissance is a means towards situating his work historically and culturally inside a framework that involves France, Italy and England. And that in itself shows how *Shakespeares Mädchen und Frauen* succeeds — if that is the right expression — in remaining outside institutionalized German Shakespeare reception.

---

49 'Chivalric Romanticism'.
50 'The triumphs of the English are always a scandal to humanity, from the days of Crécy and Poitiers to those of Waterloo. Clio is always female, and despite her cold even-handedness, she has a soft spot for chivalry and heroics, and I am convinced that she only lists the victories of the English in her annals through gritted teeth'. *SS*, VII, 229.
51 Ibid., VI, 262.
52 Ibid., VII, 292.
53 'Fortune' and 'calamity'. Ibid., 262.
54 'Late flowering of the Greek spirit'.

Fig. 15 Engraving by Carl Jäger, *Erinnerung an die Schillerfeier 1859*, "erfunden und radirt von C. Jaeger."; erschienen *im Nürnberger Künstlervereins-Album; C. H. Zeh'sche Buch & Kunsthandlung in Nürnberg*. Wikimedia, https://de.wikipedia.org/wiki/Datei:Karl_J%C3%A4ger_Erinnerung_an_die_Schillerfeier_1859_800x1296pixel.jpg, public domain.

12. The 'Schillerfeier' of 1859 and the 'Shakespearefest' of 1864

With Some Remarks on Theodor Fontane's Contributions[1]

Occasional poetry has a double focus. It may involve the immediate (or seemingly immediate) reaction to events (victories, celebrations). It may stand back from those events, in reflection or reconsideration of the implications of adventitious happening, and try to wrap mere contingency in some explanatory religious or ethical or philosophical envelope. The event may, on the other hand, bring to the surface untried forms and formulations, now 'occasioned'. The centenary of Friedrich Schiller's birth in 1859 was,[2] like our millennium, an event plotted and prepared for, and it reflected that directional quality. It was also an occasion that touched off spontaneous reactions. The story of Schiller as a subject in German poetry does not of course start in 1859, nor does it end there.[3] Conrad Ferdinand Meyer's later poem and anthology piece 'Schillers Bestattung/Schiller's Burial' (1882) can afford to be sparse and economical in detail because it comes towards the end of a biographical (hagiographical) and historicizing century that had both documented Schiller and rhetoricized his achievement. It sets aside the merely

---

1   An earlier version of this chapter was published with the same title in *History and Literature. Essays in Honor of Karl S. Guthke*, ed. by William Collins Donahue and Scott Denham (Tübingen: Stauffenburg, 2000), 351–65.
2   Cf. above all Rainer Noltenius, *Dichterfeiern in Deutschland. Rezeptionsgeschichte als Sozialgeschichte am Beispiel der Schiller- und Freiligrath-Feiern* (Munich: Fink, 1984), esp. 71–181; Noltenius, 'Die Nation und Schiller', in *Dichter und ihre Nation*, ed. by Helmut Scheuer (Frankfurt am Main: Suhrkamp, 1993), 151–75.
3   Cf. Hans Mayer, 'Schillers Nachruhm', *Sinn und Form*, 11 (1959), 701–14.

© 2021 Roger Paulin, CC BY 4.0   https://doi.org/10.11647/OBP.0258.12

circumstantial and gives us the punchline, 'Der Menschheit Genius war's'.[4] Like Karl Gutzkow's earlier remark on the same subject — 'Es war der Genius des deutschen Volks'[5] — it ends the anecdotal speculation begun, say, by Gustav Schwab's biography of 1840, and now states a myth. At the other end of the scale, Johann Wolfgang Goethe's poem 'Epilog zu Schillers "Glocke"/Epilogue to Schiller's "Bell"' of 1805 is also an occasional poem (his attempt at a more elaborate apotheosis of Schiller in 1805 collapsed).[6] Unlike the Romantics, who saw the vacant throne left by Schiller rather than his actual achievement, Goethe used his authority to foreclose such counterclaims and to reinstate Schiller in the national canon where he felt him to belong:

> Denn er war unser! Mag das stolze Wort
> Den lauten Schmerz gewaltig übertönen!
> Er mochte sich bei uns im sichern Port,
> Nach wildem Sturm, zum Daurenden gewöhnen.
> Indessen schritt sein Geist gewaltig fort
> Ins Ewige des Wahren, Guten, Schönen,
> Und hinter ihm, in wesenlosem Scheine,
> Lag, was uns alle bändigt, das Gemeine.[7]

Those words, 'Denn er war unser!' might be a stumbling-block to some in 1805, but in 1859 few would dare to contradict their self-evident validity. The irony was that, at face value, they were equally applicable

---

4   'It was mankind's genius'. Where possible, quotations relating to the reception of Schiller are taken from *Schiller — Zeitgenosse aller Epochen. Dokumente zur Wirkungsgeschichte Schillers in Deutschland*, ed. by Norbert Oellers, 2 vols, I: 1782–1859. II: 1860–1966, Wirkung der Literatur. Deutsche Autoren im Urteil ihrer Kritiker, 1–2, ed. by Karl Robert Mandelkow (Frankfurt am Main: Athenäum, 1970), II, 476 (henceforth cited as *Schiller*).
5   'It was the genius of the German people'. Karl Gutzkow, *Vom Baum der Erkenntnis*, Werke, ed. by Reinhold Gensel, 12 vols (Berlin, Leipzig, Vienna, Stuttgart: Bong, n.d. [1910]), XII, 119, also 282f.
6   Goethe, 'Schillers Todtenfeyer', *Goethes Werke, herausgegeben im Auftrage der Großherzogin Sophie von Sachsen-Weimar*, 143 vols (Weimar: Böhlau, 1887–1919), XVI, 561-69.
7   'For he was ours! And may the mighty word
    Sound louder than our cries of pain!
    He felt at ease with us in our safe port,
    The storm now past, to settle was his gain.
    His spirit now in giant strides set forth
    Towards eternal truth and goodness, beauty's fame,
    Behind him lay, reduced to dimmest light,
    What binds us all, the base and common plight'. *Schiller*, I, 484.

to Shakespeare in 1864, indeed after Franz Dingelstedt's proprietary statement of 1858, 'Unser Shakspeare',[8] the present tense would seem more appropriate.

* * *

This is, rightly speaking, a large subject, and one whose wider implications I do not wish to explore. The commemoration of Schiller's hundredth birthday in 1859,[9] however strong it might have been on ideology, hardly produced much poetry of the quality of Goethe's in 1805. The event proper commands more attention. It has national, nation-wide and international significance — celebrated in 440 German and fifty foreign towns — 'zu Melbourne in Australien wie zu Valparaiso am Stillen Ozean' in Jacob Burckhardt' s embracing phrase[10] — and as such it has been documented in almost exhaustive detail. Quite the same cannot be said of the Shakespeare festivities in Germany in 1864. On a much more modest scale and with another emphasis, it too is an important event for German 'Bildungsbürgertum' (educated middle class). Whereas the national occasion could command names to conjure with — Jacob Grimm, Paul Heyse, Ferdinand Freiligrath, Friedrich Theodor Vischer, the young and still unknown Wilhelm Raabe, and just across the border Jacob Burckhardt and Gottfried Keller, to mention but a few — the international happening was by its very nature more restricted. There were a few who lent their voices to both events, notable Shakespearean scholars or translators featuring prominently in 1859: Hermann Marggraff, Friedrich von Bodenstedt, Franz Dingelstedt, Rudolph Genée (and in exile, Freiligrath and Georg Herwegh). Karl Gutzkow, forgetting his earlier animus against Schiller, is represented at

---

8   Franz Dingelstedt, *Studien und Copien nach Shakspeare* (Pesth: Hartleben, 1858), 5.
9   An indication of the extent of the celebrations may be gained from two contemporary publications: Adolph Büchting, *Verzeichniß der zur hundertjährigen Geburtsfeier Friedrich von Schiller's erschienenen Bücher, Kunstblätter, Kunstwerke, Musikalien, Denkmünzen etc.* [...] (Nordhausen: Büchting, 1860) and Karl Tropus, *Schiller-Denkmal*, 2 vols (Berlin: Riegel, 1860) (henceforth cited as *Schiller-Denkmal*). In addition, the names are listed in Karl Goedeke, *Grundriß zur Geschichte der deutschen Dichtung*, continued by Edmund Goetze et al., 10 vols (Dresden: Ehlermann, 1893), V, i, 128–32.
10 'In Melbourne in Australia as in Valparaiso on the Pacific Ocean'. *Schiller*, I, 415.

both events.[11] Friedrich Hebbel, ambivalent as ever on the subject of the relative merits of the two great poets, restricted his views on Schiller to a smaller circle, having refused Dingelstedt's suggestion that he might complete Schiller's unfinished *Demetrius*.[12] In 1864, he was already dead. Otto Ludwig, his trenchant distinction between Shakespeare and Schiller not yet available to the reading public, took no part. Franz Grillparzer's scepticism towards the event kept him from delivering the speech he had written.[13] Both occasions produced institutions, the 'Schillerstiftung', and the 'Deutsche Shakespeare-Gesellschaft', respectively, and it is fair to say that the 'official' and 'institutional' set the tone for both 1859 and 1864. Then there was Theodor Fontane, addressing the 'Tunnel' society in 1859 with the poem 'Zum Schillerfest des "Tunnel"/For the "Tunnel"'s Schiller Festival' and in 1864 delivering the extended speech known as 'Zum Shakespeare-Fest'. In the scheme of things in both years, and among the many names of the great and the good, Fontane's could as yet mean little to most of his contemporaries. 1859 was not another stepping-stone to higher preferment and enhanced reputation, as it was, say, for his old associate Heyse.[14]

Inside Fontane studies, it is not a subject that has commanded much interest. This need not matter unduly, for surely his later theatrical criticism is the major area in his oeuvre where Schiller and Shakespeare meet. That critical corpus serves a double function. The following remark from 1873 is not untypical: 'Meine Empfindung verwirft Uriel Acosta und ist umgekehrt nicht nur durch alles Shakespearsche hingerissen, sondern sogar auch durch die Räuber'.[15] Schiller and Shakespeare serve to remind his readers that there is a canon superior to contemporaries like Paul Lindau, Rudolf Gottschall, Ernst von Wildenbruch (or — the example cited — Karl Gutzkow). At the same time, however, Fontane is

---

11 Gutzkow, 'Ein Schillerfestspruch vom 9. November 1859', in *Vom Baum der Erkenntnis*, X, 95–100; same author, *Eine Shakspearefeier an der Ilm* (Leipzig: Brockhaus, 1864).

12 Ludger Lütkehaus, 'Hebbels Schiller-Feier — unsere Hebbel-Feier. Dichterfeste zwischen Jubiläum und „Jubilitis"', *Hebbel-Jahrbuch* (1989), 231–42.

13 *Schiller*, I, 428f., 583f.

14 Heyse's contributions can be found in Paul Heyse, *Lyrische Dichtungen*, 4 vols (Stuttgart and Berlin: Cotta, 1911), II, 319–25.

15 'My feeling rejects *Uriel Acosta* [a play by Gutzkow], but by the same token is not just enraptured by all of Shakespeare, but also by the Robbers'. Theodor Fontane, *Werke, Schriften und Briefe*, ed. by Walter Keitel and Helmuth Nürnberger, 20 vols (Munich: Hanser, 1964–84). Henceforth cited as *SW*, followed by section, volume and page number; here IV (*Briefe*), i, 431f.

making important distinctions and registering preferences, inside both Schiller's and Shakespeare's oeuvre as they appear in Berlin productions. My concern here is not to open up a far-ranging discussion of Fontane's attitudes to Schiller and Shakespeare — 'ein zu weites Feld' — but to set him in a more general context where he also has his place.

Before turning specifically to Fontane, it may do to sketch in a little of the background to the two events in which he shared. Neither occasion — if we except the unforeseen and unforeseeable political development of the Schleswig-Holstein crisis in 1864 — seemed to do little more than confirm tendencies and developments already culminant. Who needed the fortuitous cycle of birthdates to remind one of reputations already securely and firmly established? Certainly the animadversions expressed about Shakespeare in 1864 had been common currency for the best part of half a century and hardly needed the rhetorical reiterations and insistences of German professors and 'Oberlehrer'. No one was in doubt as to Shakespeare's supernal and universal genius: history's arsenal of commensurate names would include Homer, or Michelangelo, Columbus or Raphael.[16] There was general agreement, too, on the Germanic brotherhood that embraced Shakespeare, with the added piquancy that the German part of that confraternity had turned the tables on the English and was now, by general admission, taking the lead in Shakespearean appreciation and scholarship. Direct comparisons between Shakespeare and Schiller (or Goethe) on the other hand, were a problem (only really solved by Friedrich Gundolf's ideologically charged *Shakespeare und der deutsche Geist/Shakespeare and the German Spirit* of 1911).[17] They were best avoided. One could distinguish the national (Schiller) from the universal (Shakespeare), and accord to each its validity. Or one could invoke the powerful ideological mythologies and self-assured teleological reductionisms that associated the renewal of German literature proper with the 'Geistesheld' Lessing, the true forerunner of Weimar greatness, and his crucial sponsoring of Shakespeare against the French. This did

---

16 Cf. A. L. Lua, *William Shakespeare. Eine Festrede, gehalten bei der volksthtümlichen Feier des dreihundertjährigen Geburtstags des Dichters im Saale des alten Weinbergs zu Schidlitz* (Danzig: Constantin Ziemssen, 1864), 11. Heinrich Kuenzel, *William Shakespeare. Zum Gedächtniss seines dreihundertjährigen Geburtstages am 23. April 1864* (Darmstadt: Victor Gross, 1864), 3.

17 Friedrich Gundolf, *Shakespeare und der deutsche Geist* (Berlin: Bondi, 1911).

not involve reading the small print of Lessing's seventeenth *Literaturbrief* of 1759, an approach not seemly to the broad-brush technique of nineteenth-century German literary historiography.[18]

These positions were not without their differentiations, paradoxes, and inconsistencies. There was what appeared like a tacit agreement between the older Romantics, August Wilhelm Schlegel and Ludwig Tieck, and Georg Wilhelm Friedrich Hegel, to raise Shakespeare above any indigenous dramatic production, notably Schiller's. Instead, the aim was to make Shakespeare the exemplar of principles, features and ideas that knew no national or temporal constraints. In reality however, useful though it may be to compare the older Romantics and Hegel in their respective attitudes to Shakespeare and Schiller, there are major divergences. Schlegel saw Aeschylus, Sophocles and Shakespeare as supernal representatives of the tragic, equally valid, yet separated through time, culture, and religion, the 'Classical' as against the 'Romantic'. Hegel by contrast, perceived in Shakespeare's major figures affinities with the ultimate creations of classical Greek tragedy; only Shakespeare's modern, 'innerlich' position was for him the last strand of Romantic art before its dissolution into subjectivity.[19] Where they converged was in the Romantic disapproval of Schiller and their cult of Shakespeare, and in Hegel's interest in Shakespeare as the representative of the post-classical, Romantic drama, and his growing disenchantment with Schiller the dramatist and thinker.[20] Be that as it may, sets of prejudices — the Romantics' animus against Schiller, or their Bardolatry — were hardly good either for dramatic production or for a proper understanding of one's own indigenous traditions. The first major reaction against this comes, not by chance, from Christian Dietrich Grabbe, a dramatist beholden to both Shakespearean and Schillerian practice, but concerned also to find a 'national' style: in his

---

18 Cf. my article '"Shakspeare's allmähliches Bekanntwerden in Deutschland". Aspekte der Institutionalisierung Shakespeares 1840–1875', in *Bildung und Konfession. Politik, Religion und Identitätsbildung 1850–1918*, ed. by Martin Huber and Gerhard Lauer, Studien und Texte zur Sozialgeschichte der Literatur 59 (Tübingen: Niemeyer, 1996), 9–20.

19 Cf. Emil Wolff, 'Hegel und Shakespeare', in *Vom Geist der Dichtung. Gedächtnisschrift für Robert Petsch*, ed. by Fritz Martini (Hamburg: Hoffmann und Campe, 1949), 120–79.

20 Cf. Annemarie Gethmann-Siefert, *Die Funktion der Kunst in der Geschichte*, Hegel-Studien Beiheft 25 (Bonn: Bouvier, 1984), esp. 353–59.

Über die Shakespearo-Manie/On Shakespeare-Mania of 1827. The attempts by the first major nineteenth-century literary historians — August Koberstein, Georg Gottfried Gervinus, Julian Schmidt, Hermann Hettner, August Friedrich Vilmar — to accord Schiller his rightful place in 'Nationalliteratur' and to counteract both Romantic and Young German strictures, were also not without their problems.[21] For often these same historians, like Koberstein, Gervinus and Schmidt, were also votaries of Shakespeare, who if pressed would make unflattering contrasts between the merits of Shakespeare's Elizabethan age, and current literary and cultural conditions in Germany. The Shakespeare cult could conveniently join forces with neo-Hegelian aesthetics, more often than not lacking Hegel's differentiated analysis — Hermann Ulrici, Heinrich Theodor Rötscher, Friedrich Theodor Vischer — and inclined to see in Shakespeare's world the workings of a 'Grundidee' or a 'Weltgesetz'.[22]

That is, in Gustav Freytag's later phrase, the 'ideal nexus' of the discussion of Schiller and Shakespeare, the debate reserved for the aestheticians, the theoreticians, and the professoriate. But what of its 'pragmatic' coefficient, the popular reception, the reactions of the general educated reader? In the 1840s, it is Shakespeare's Hamlet who appears, in Ferdinand Freiligrath's terms at least ('Deutschland ist Hamlet'), to be a symbol more appropriate to Germany's political condition than, say, Schiller's Marquis Posa. But even Freiligrath's famous reference should not be exaggerated beyond its immediate significance. Above all, one should not overlook the place of Schiller in the articulation of national political aspirations. Whatever doubts literary historians or aestheticians might express, Schiller was assuming a commanding status, backed by a popular movement of considerable momentum. Some of this energy was directed towards the fostering of local patriotic pride: the celebrations of the Stuttgart 'Liederkranz' in 1825 and 1826, for

---

21 Cf. Eva D. Becker, 'Klassiker in der deutschen Literaturgeschichtsschreibung zwischen 1780 und 1860' (1968), in *Literarisches Leben. Umschreibungen der deutschen Literaturgeschichte*, Saarbrücker Beiträge zur Literaturwissenschaft 45 (St. Ingbert: Röhrig, 1994), 7–26; Jürgen Fohrmann, '"Wir besprechen uns in bequemen Stunden..." Zum Goethe-Schiller-Verhältnis und seiner Rezeption im 19. Jahrhundert', in *Klassik im Vergleich. Normativität und Historizität europäischer Klassiken, DFG Symposion 1990*, ed. by Wilhelm Vosskamp (Stuttgart, Weimar: Metzler, 1993), 571–93, esp. 580ff.

22 'Basic idea', 'world law'.

instance, or the unveiling in Stuttgart of Thorwaldsen's statue of Schiller in 1839 (before the monuments to Goethe in Frankfurt and to Lessing in Braunschweig), or Andreas Streicher's, Gustav Schwab's and Hermann Kurz's biographies. The 'Schiller-Vereine' of the 1840s, in Leipzig, in Breslau (Hoffmann von Fallersleben), and in Stuttgart, were actual centres of 'Vormärz' opposition and liberal aspiration. In some sense, therefore, the particular national, political and cultural significance of the Schiller year of 1859, without which the occasion could not have burgeoned into what it did, lay very much in galvanizing forces already present, active, and vociferous.[23]

Could the same be said about Shakespeare? At such a popular level, clearly not. The claim that Shakespeare was 'ours' did not need Dingelstedt's muchquoted declaration of 1858, for it had been current at least since Tieck and Schlegel. Everything seemed to speak for the validity of the statement made in 1864 by a Marburg professor: 'Jetzt steht der brittische Shakespeare im deutschen Gewande in der Bibliothek eines jeden gebildeten deutschen Hausvaters',[24] and there would be not just the 'Schlegel-Tieck' translation, but many different versions to choose from. Bibliographical evidence alone indicates a wide range of reception, from 'Familien-Shakespeare' or popular biography, translations of Shakespeareana from the English or the French, or illustrated works, to studies of characters or scholarly enquiries into matters of text or dating. Again, the year 1864 merely crystallizes momentarily a whole process; yet it, too, has its unmistakable time reference.

The 'Schillerfeier' of 1859, and its correlatives, the 'Schillerstiftung' and the 'Schillerpreis' — on this all modern scholars are agreed — was an eminently political occasion.[25] It united all liberal and national

---

23 Cf. Noltenius, *Dichterfeiern* and 'Die Nation'; Lucie Prinz, *Schillerbilder. Die Schiller-Verehrung am Beispiel der Festreden des Stuttgarter Liederkranzes (1825–1992)* (Marburg: diagonal-Verlag, 1994); Paul Raabe, 'Lorbeerkranz und Denkmal. Wandlungen der Dichterhuldigung in Deutschland', in *Festschrift für Klaus Ziegler*, ed. by Eckehard Catholy and Winfried Hellmann (Tübingen: Niemeyer, 1968), 411–26; Jörg Garner, 'Goethe-Denkmä!er — Schiller-Denkmäler', in *Denkmäler im 19. Jahrhundert. Deutung und Kritik*, ed. by Hans-Ernst Mittig and Volker Pagemann, Studien zur Kunst des 19. Jahrhunderts 20 (Munich: Prestel, 1972), 141–62.

24 'Now the British Shakespeare in German guise is to be found in the library of every educated German husband and father'. L. O. Lemcke, *Shakspeare in seinem Verhälltnisse zu Deutschland. Ein Vortrag gehalten im Rathhaussaale zu Marburg am 16. Febr. 1864* (Leipzig: Vogel, 1864), 26.

25 On the 'Schillerfeier': Noltenius, *Dichterfeiern* and 'Die Nation'; Karl Obermann, 'Die deutsche Einheitsbewegung und die Schillerfeiern 1859', *Zeitschrift für*

forces across a wide spectrum of the population and across the divides of educational attainment. It was perhaps short on landowners and peasants, on Catholic clergy, officers or the nobility, as those least affected by the atmosphere of liberalism that characterizes the late 1850s and the early 1860s. That such a popular demonstration did not attend the truly muted celebrations of Goethe's anniversary in 1849 is a tribute to the change in course since that year of reaction. Yet we should not forget Gottfried Kinkel, Freiligrath and Georg Herwegh, who added their voices to the general jubilation, while still exiles from the year of revolutions. It was a reflection of Schiller's status as 'Nationaldichter', despite the monumental symbol of Ernst Rietschel's statue in Weimar, on which both poets, Goethe and Schiller, clasp the same laurels. On the intellectual level, Rudolf Haym's article in the recently-founded *Preussische Jahrbücher* sums up the best national, liberal and cultural expectations of the event:

> Wie kein zweiter Dichter lebt dieser unsterblich in dem Herzen seines Volkes. Die Welt hat das unvergleichliche Schauspiel gesehn, daß die getheilten Stämme, ja die zerrissenen und über den Erdball zerstreuten Glieder unsres Volkes in der Verehrung dieses Dichters sich ähnlich einmüthig begegnen, wie einst die Griechen in dem Preise und dem Verständniß des Homer. Es war diese Novemberfeier, wie es in einer der Festreden heißt, die uns vorliegen, ein ‚rechtes Siegesfest des Geistes', ein Beweis von der Dauer, ja von der unvergänglichen Lebendigkeit geistiger Wirkungen. Sie war vor Allem ein Nationalfest. Ein Bekenntniß legte die deutsche Nation ab, daß sie, wie zerrissen auch äußerlich, innerlich unzerreißbar ist, und daß die Symbole ihrer Einheit ihr über Alles theuer sind. Mehr aber als das. Man darf sagen, daß eine Unsterblichkeit und ein Ruhm wie dieser noch niemals ausgetheilt worden ist. Denn mit der Größe des Dichters haben wir auch das gefeiert, was ihm zur letzten Vollendung noch mangelte. Indem wir mit dem Dichter den Menschen feierten, ist er uns als ein Symbol aller der moralischen Güter

---

Geschichtswissenschaft, 3 (1955), 705–34; Thomas Nipperdey, *Deutsche Geschichte 1800–1866. Bürgerwelt und starker Staat*, 2nd ed (Munich: Beck, 1984), 722; George L. Mosse, *The Nationalization of the Masses. Political Symbolism and Mass Movements in Germany from the Napoleonic Wars through the Third Reich* (New York: Howard Fertig, 1975), 87–89. On the 'Schillerstiftung': Wolfgang Sowa, *Der Staat und das Drama. Der preußische Schillerpreis 1859–1918. Eine Untersuchung zum literarischen Leben im Königreich Preußen und im deutschen Kaiserreich*, Regensburger Beiträge zur deutschen Sprach- und Literaturwissenschaft, Reihe B. Untersuchungen 36 (Frankfurt am Main, Berne, New York, Paris: Lang, 1988).

erschienen, die uns noch vorenthalten sind, und zu denen wir daher in einer Stimmung emporblicken, welche die Grundstimmung sämmtlicher Schillerschen Dichtungen ist.[26]

Yet one senses that this nobility of tone — Jacob Grimm reaches similar heights, like Burckhardt, who understandably omits any reference to the German nation — was reserved for the discriminating audience or reader. When Dr. Oskar Jäger (later head of the Königl. Friedrich Wilhelm Gymnasium in Cologne and a pillar of Wilhelmian rectitude) addresses the festive gathering in Prussian Wetzlar, he also stresses to his young charges the 'Einmütigkeit' occasioned by the event, but casts an eye back to Schiller's place (as he saw it) in the political developments around 1813, his 'nationale Gesinnung', his role as 'Seher'. Stepping outside of the assembly hall and into the open, he declares his hand: 'Ja, meine Herren, jetzt, wo unter den Auspizien eines hochherzigen Regenten Preußen die Fahne dieser maßvollen und männlichen Freiheit den deutschen Stämmen voranträgt'[27] (the rest is predictable). Again, one senses that the authorities, elsewhere nervous about the occasion getting out of hand and provoking civil disorder, would warm to the appropriateness of these sentiments. Perhaps it is worth recalling that the 'Schillerfeier', for all its laudable and almost universally expressed notions of 'bürgerliche Freiheit',[28] did not infect all its participants

---

26 'Like no other poet he lives immortal in the hearts of his people. The world has seen the unforgettable spectacle of the divided tribes, our people torn apart in great numbers, scattered throughout the globe, meeting together in the veneration of this poet, just as once the Greeks did in their praise and appreciation of Homer. This November celebration, as one of the festive speeches we have read called it, was a 'true victory festival of the mind', a testimony to the lasting power and imperishable liveliness of the workings of the spirit. It was above all a national festival. The German people admitted that, however outwardly torn, it is inwardly indestructible, and that the symbols of its unity are more dear to it than anything else. But more than that. One can say that immortality and fame like this has never before been bestowed. For with the poet's greatness we have celebrated what he was still lacking in ultimate perfection. By celebrating the man with the poet, he has appeared as a symbol of all the moral qualities that we are still lacking and towards which we cast our eyes, filled with the same sensation that the whole of Schiller's poetry engenders in us'. Rudolf Haym, 'Schiller an seinem hundertjährigen Jubiläum', *Gesammelte Aufsätze* (Berlin: Weidmann , 1903), 49–120 (118f).

27 'Accord'; 'national feeling'; 'seer'; 'Yes, gentlemen, now that, under the auspices of a magnanimous regent, Prussia bears the banner of this measured and manly freedom to the German lands'. Oskar Jäger, *Zu Schillers Gedächtnis* (Wetzlar: n.p., 1859); Jäger, *Pro Domo. Reden und Aufsätze* (Berlin: Seehagen, 1894), 3–10 (3, 7, 9).

28 'Civic freedom'.

with high solemnity: Gottfried Keller's, Paul Heyse's and Friedrich Hebbel's private reactions are revealing.[29] It also had elements that were less spontaneous. On November 9, 1859, by royal decree of the regent of Prussia, was issued the declaration of the 'Schillerpreis' and the 'Schillerstiftung'.[30] If the popular demonstrations reflected political liberalization (however short-lived) and liberal notions of 'Volk' and culture, the 'Schillerpreis' was a more overt attempt at annexing for cultural politics the name of the greatest German dramatist, to harness the theatre, the temple of art, the 'sittliche Idee des Staates' (Rudolf Gottschall's words).[31] The great and good on the jury — Leopold von Ranke, Theodor Mommsen, Johann Gustav Droysen, Georg Gottfried Gervinus, Gustav Freytag, later Hermann Hettner, Julian Schmidt, Heinrich von Treitschke and Wilhelm Scherer — and their association with this attempt to raise literary standards in the drama, had little effect on the generally mediocre level of those honoured (only Hebbel and Otto Ludwig stand out, both now spent forces).

As the 'Schillerfeier' merged into the 'Shakespearefest', the irony was that these years, while reflecting the high status of dramatic art, its classical authority and the canonicity of its major representatives (with Shakespeare in first place of esteem), were generally ones of epigonal formalism and imitation, accompanied by a dearth of real talent.[32] Grillparzer was silent; Hebbel and Ludwig, as mentioned, were cut off through the supervention of circumstances. As Helmut Schanze has shown, 1859 is symbolic in seeing the publication of two major works which dispense with conventional dramatic theory: the third edition of Arthur Schopenhauer's *Die Welt als Wille und Vorstellung/The World as Will and Representation*, and the posthumous *Philosophie der Kunst/Philosophy of Art* of F. W. J. Schelling.[33] These exceptions apart, the problems

---

29 Cf. Lütkehaus, 'Hebbels Schiller-Feier'; Gottfried Keller, *Gesammelte Briefe*, ed. by Carl Helbing, 4 vols (Berne: Benteli, 1950–54), I, 441; II, 91; III, i, 11; *Der Briefwechsel zwischen Emanuel Geibel und Paul Heyse*, ed. by Erich Petzel (Munich: Lehmann, 1922), 122f.
30 Cf. Sowa, *Der Staat*, 30–125 (42).
31 'The moral idea of the state'. Ibid., 42.
32 Helmut Schanze, 'Die Anschauung vom hohen Rang des Dramas in der zweiten Hälfte des 19. Jahrhunderts und seine tatsächliche Schwäche', in *Beiträge zur Theorie der Künste im 19. Jahrhundert*, vol. I, ed. by Helmut Koopmann and J. Adolf Schmoll gen. Eisenwerth, Studien zur Philosophie und Literatur des neunzehnten Jahrhunderts 12.1 (Frankfurt am Main: Klostermann, 1971), 85–96.
33 Schanze, 'Die Anschauung', 87–9; Schanze, *Drama im bürgerlichen Realismus (1850–1890). Theorie und Praxis*, Studien zur Philosophie und Literatur des neunzehnten

attendant on celebrations of this kind were that they elevated poets to paradigms or absolutes, and placed them on pedestals beyond the reach of the young and not-so-young alike. They imposed patterns — the historical drama springs most readily to mind — that had once been appropriate in their own time, in both Shakespeare's and Schiller's, indeed eminently worthy of emulation, but that were not endlessly transferrable to Hohenstaufens, or Habsburgs — or Hohenzollerns. These awarenesses form part of the current general discussion of dramatic technique, which, while not coinciding exactly with these celebrations, certainly provided its broad theoretical background. What is more, they bring together the names of Shakespeare and Schiller as role models for a German tragedy of the future.[34]

For all that its rhetorical gesturings and orotundity seemed to indicate a rehearsal of 1859, the 'Shakespearefest' of 1864 nevertheless had accentuations of its own. Even those who saw the links between the occasions were aware of this. Dr. Paul Möbius, who addressed the festive assembly in Leipzig, makes this point:

> Selbst das wichtigste und großartigste von allen, die Schillerfeier von 1859, durch welche erst der Grund für die nachfolgenden geebnet wurde, so verschiedenartig noch während der Festtage selbst ihre eigentliche Bedeutung aufgefaßt wurde, galt zuletzt doch nichts Anderem, als was nachher ein Schützenfest zu Frankfurt, ein Turnfest zu Leipzig und endlich in ebendemselben Jahre die erhabene Gedenkfeier unseres Vaterlandes von französischer Knechtschaft noch zu klarerem Ausdrucke bringen sollte.
>
> Es war die herzerhebende Freude, in dem Dichter einen Mittelpunkt für alle Stämme und Parteien der Nation gefunden zu haben, einen Mittelpunkt, der Bürgschaft zu geben schien, daß der Geist, der schon vorhanden, sich zuletzt doch noch eine Form verschaffen werde, die auch den rauhesten Stürmen der Wirklichkeit Widerstand zu leisten vermöge.
>
> Und heute feiern wir abermals das Geburtsfest eines Dichters und abermals ist es nicht unsere Stadt, nicht unser Land allein, das an dieser Feier Theil nimmt. Schon längst drang die Kunde zu uns, daß auch diesmal, ähnlich wie 1859, an den Orten der verschiedensten Länder, ja

---

Jahrhunderts 21 (Frankfurt am Main: Klostermann, 1973), 26–30.

34 For an indication of the extent of these discussions, see the bibliography in *Realismus und Gründerzeit. Manifeste und Dokumente zur deutschen Literatur 1848–1880*, vol. I, ed. by Max Bücher, Werner Hahl, Georg Jäger and Reinhard Wittmann (Stuttgart: Metzler, 1976), 452–56.

Welttheile, wo Deutsche zu Deutschen sich gefunden, sie zu festlichem Beginnen zusammentreten und das Andenken des großen Shakespeare feiern wollen.[35]

Of note is that insight that a poet has become the 'Mittelpunkt für alle Stämme und Parteien der Nation'.[36] Certainly in 1859 Schiller the poet was the focus for whatever was associated with the idea of a nation. But could Shakespeare fulfil such a function in 1864? Clearly not in the same way. For Möbius, in common with most speakers, goes on to stress the special nature of the Shakespeare celebrations. Here, also, two different strands are apparent. Clearly this cannot be a national occasion except in a very general sense; rather, other phrases from Möbius like 'Blick auf das Ewige' or 'Weltbürgertum'[37] indicate the overarching, universal appeal of the Shakespearean achievement, one that, if pressed, speakers might declare to be superior to Goethe's or Schiller's, indeed the greatest of all time. But, whether in verse pageants, declamations, speeches or whatever — all along the lines of 1859 — particular German concerns obtrude. The main note is 'er ist unser';[38] we have annexed him and Germany is his 'zweite Heimath,'[39] the scene of a new

---

35 'Even the greatest and most signal of all, the Schiller celebrations of 1859, which laid the ground for the ones that followed, despite the differences in their actual significance, that became manifest as they unfolded, was in reality aimed at nothing which would not be expressed at rifle-club festivals in Frankfurt or a gymnastics display in Leipzig, and in the same year as the mighty commemoration of our fatherland's liberation from French vassalage.
It warmed the heart to find the poet providing a focal point, an earnest, for all the regions and parties of the nation, for our hopes, that the spirit, already present, will find a form that will be able to withstand even the roughest storms of reality.
And today we celebrate again the birthday of a poet, and again it is not our city, not our country alone, that joins in this festival. We have long since received the news that this time, like as in 1859, in places in the most disparate countries, or continents, where German meets German, they come together to celebrate and to mark the memory of the great Shakespeare'. Paul Möbius, *Shakespeare als Dichter der Naturwahrheit. Festrede bei der Shakespearefeier zu Leipzig am 23. April 1864 gehalten* (Leipzig: Voigt & Günther, 1864), 5f.
36 'Focal point for all regions and parties of the nation'.
37 'A view into the eternal'; 'citizenship of the world'. Möbius, *Die deutsche Shakespearefeier. Eine Rechtfertigung derselben nach einem im kaufmännischen Vereine zu Leipzig gehaltenen Vortrage* (Leipzig: Julius Werner, 1864), 5; Möbius, *Shakespeare als Dichter*, 15.
38 'He is ours'. J. J. Rietmann, *Shakspeare und seine Bedeutung. Festrede gesprochen an der Shakespearefeier in St. Gallen* (St. Gallen: Huber, 1864), 13.
39 'Second homeland'. August Schwartzkopff, *Shakespeare, in seiner Bedeutung für die Kirche unserer Tage dargestellt* [...], 2nd ed. (Halle: Richard Mühlmann, 1864), 3.

'Bellalliance'[40] (note the terminology). This, in its turn, has a double emphasis. Following Julian Schmidt's insight of a few years earlier, it is Shakespeare the 'Protestant',[41] the representative of a literary culture for so long denied in Germany who is ultimately responsible for the 'Wiedergeburt des zweiten goldenen Zeitalters'[42] across the water, who is the 'Vater und Meister'[43] of modern German poetry. But this annexation has meant that the Germans —Coleridge, after all, had said it — are now the true guardians of the sacred flame of the Shakespearean heritage ('am Hausaltare deutscher Nation').[44] In this Germanic brotherhood, 'Fleisch vom eignen Fleisch', 'Blut vom eignen Blut',[45] it is Shakespeare who represents the deepest and most lasting bond. For it was 'deutsches Talent, deutscher Geschmack, deutscher Scharfsinn und deutscher Fleiß'[46] that had been largely responsible for the current revival of things Shakespearean, the restoration of the Shakespearean text, or philosophical and historical insights into the plays themselves. And it is true that the translations into English of major German Shakespeare scholars like Hermann Ulrici, Georg Gotfried Gervinus, later Karl Elze, or the seeming over-representation of Germans in the notes to the great Variorum edition started in 1874, might well bear this out. The main product of the German Shakespeare celebrations of 1864 is of course the foundation of the 'Deutsche Shakespeare-Gesellschaft'.[47] This is not the place to discuss the significance of that society. Suffice it to say, however, that the statement of intent prepared in 1863 by Wilhelm Oechelhäuser, later its president, stresses the wider, national, propaedeutic function of the society and its forthcoming celebration:

> Es wird vielmehr in dieser Beziehung die wesentliche Aufgabe des beginnenden vierten Jahrhunderts nach Shakespeare's Geburt bleiben,

---

40 A reference to the battle of Waterloo. Kuenzel, *William Shakespeare*, 44.
41 Lua, *William Shakespeare*, 11.
42 'Rebirth of a second golden age'. Kuenzel, *William Shakespeare*, 2.
43 'Father and master'. F.A.Th. Kreyssig, *Ueber die sittliche und volksthümliche Berechtigung des Shakespeare-Cultus. Festrede, bei der Shakespeare-Feier in Elbing am 23. April 1864 gehalten* (Elbing: Neumann Hartmann, 1864), 9.
44 'At the tutelary altar of the German nation'. Ibid.
45 'Flesh of our flesh'; 'blood of our blood'. Möbius, *Die deutsche Shakespearefeier*, 12.
46 'German talent, German taste, German intelligence, and German industry'. Kreyssig, *Ueber die sittliche*, 8.
47 Cf. Robert Fricker, 'Hundert Jahre Shakespeare-Jahrbuch', *Shakespeare Jahrbuch (West)*, 100 (1964), 33–67; Martin Lehnert, 'Hundert Jahre Deutsche Shakespeare-Gesellschaft', *Shakespeare Jahrbuch*, 100–01 (1964–65), 9–54.

seine Werke und deren klare Erkenntniss noch viel weiter zu verbreiten, damit sie noch weit tiefer in das Volk, soweit dessen Bildungsgrad es überhaupt dazu befähigt, eindringen mögen. Für die gesunde Fortentwicklung, nicht bloss unserer dramatischen Literatur, sondern des ganzen sittlichen und intellectuellen Lebens der Nation, ist das Wachsen der Erkenntniss dieses grossen Apostels der Humanität und echten Lebensweisheit ein wahres Bedürfniss.[48]

There is an irony that this takes place against a background where the first cloud to overshadow Anglo-German political relations had appeared on the horizon: the Schleswig-Holstein affair. Several anniversary speakers are at pains to remind their audiences that the England with whom they are culturally bonded is not that of Palmerston, Russell and the free press.[49] The 'Shakespeare-Gesellschaft' is, of course, too fastidious to bring politics of this nature into its founding statements (a scruple which it abandons but briefly in 1870–71). It is also worth reflecting that the great period of early Victorian reception of things German — Fontane still experiences its high point while in London — was now moving into a less uncritical phase. And there is in German historiography and historical thinking the awareness that, whereas Shakespeare might represent the highest modern human achievement in poetry, he does not possess the 'innere geistige Reife' of the classical German tradition or its association with philosophy and scholarship and its rooting in antiquity.[50] Nor does the open-handed acceptance of the Shakespearean Weltanschauung and its political and intellectual implications involve an identity with his present-day countrymen or their institutions.

Which brings me back to Theodor Fontane. Any reader of his works and letters will need no reminder of the respect and love that both Schiller

---

48 'In this regard the essential task of the fourth century after Shakespeare's birth, now upon us, will remain the further dissemination of his works and the clear message, towards a deeper understanding among the people, inasmuch as its education permits. For our dramatic literature, but also the whole moral and intellectual life of its nation, to develop and prosper an enhanced awareness of this great apostle of humanity and of a genuine understanding of life, is what we truly need'. Wilhelm Oechelhaueser [sic], 'Die deutsche Shakespeare-Gesellschaft', *Shakespeareana* (Berlin: Springer, 1894), 1–22 (3f.).

49 Möbius, *Shakespeare als Dichter*, 7; Möbius, *Die deutsche Shakespearefeier*, 3–5; Kreyssig, *Ueber die sittliche*, 6f.; Lemcke, *Shakespeare* 12; Kuenzel, *William Shakespeare*, 28f. Cf. Paul M. Kennedy, *The Rise of the Anglo-German Antagonism 1860–1914* (London: Allen & Unwin, 1980), 13.

50 'Inner spiritual maturity'. Conrad Hermann, *Philosophie der Geschichte* (Leipzig: Fleischer, 1870), 590.

and Shakespeare enjoy in his esteem. It is not unqualified or uncritical, especially in Schiller's case. The words in a letter to Maximilian Ludwig of 1878 — 'Daß ich im Uebrigen meinen Schiller aufrichtiger liebe und bewundere, als es das nachplappernde Phrasenvolk, das Salon und Schule unsicher macht, beim besten Willen imstande ist, brauche ich Ihnen nicht erst zu versichern'[51] — come after fairly uncharitable remarks on Die Räuber/The Robbers. Even at the very beginning of his poetic career, brought up as he was on a forced diet of Schillerian ballads, he had made fun of the Schiller cult. His occasional poem 'Zum Schillerfest des "Tunnel"' is a toast or 'Trinkspruch', an occasional poem, which gains its dignity from the 'occasion':

> Es sprach Apoll: "Ich bin der Lieder müde
> Zu Ehren all der Damons und Damöte,
> Ich mag nicht mehr, was unwahr und was prüde".
>
> Und siehe da, anbrach die Morgenröte
> Der deutschen Kunst, vom Berge stieg zu Tale
> Die hehre Doppelsonne Klopstock-Goethe.
>
> Geboren war die Welt der Ideale;
> Hell schien das Licht; nur für die nächt'gen Zeiten
> Gebrach uns noch das Feuer der Fanale;
>
> Gebrach uns noch das Feuer, das von Weiten
> Zu Waffen ruft, von hohem Bergeskamme,
> Wenn's gilt für Sitte, Land und Thron zu streiten;
>
> Gebrach uns noch die hohe, heil'ge Flamme,
> Die unsren Sinn von Kleinheit, Selbstsucht reinigt
> Und uns zusammenschweißt zu einem Stamme;
>
> Und Schiller kam und Deutschland war geeinigt.[52]

---

51 'That I incidentally am a far greater lover and admirer of Schiller than all the cliché-mongers who are at large in salons and schools are capable of, however hard they try, I hardly need to assure you'. SW, IV, ii, 567.

52 'Apollo spoke: "I'm tired of songs
That honour all the swains and their swainesses
And all that to untruth and prudes belongs".
Lo and behold, the dawn undid her tresses
On German art, from mount to dale
The double sun of Klopstock–Goethe presses.
And born was now the world of true ideals;
Bright shone the light; but for the hours of night

The occasion is all-important. This is not Zurich, where Gottfried Keller produces stanza after stanza of high-sounding verse to impress elevated seriousness on his fellow-citizens. This is the more intimate atmosphere of the 'Tunnel' society, among fellow-poets, as it were; without the whole declamatory apparatus that lesser and greater talents were inflicting on captive audiences. Indeed one states in less hushed and reverential terms what speaker after speaker was saying (or was going to say, for the 'Schillerfeier' of the 'Tunnel' took place on the 8th, not on the 9th of November, the actual birthday).[53] Clearly this is not a poem which sustains too great a degree of formal analysis. It is clearly tongue-in-cheek: the disjunction between the rhetorical flights it perpetrates and the rhyme framework (*terza rima*) it employs, gives it away. 'Damöte'/'Morgenröte' might seem bad enough, but 'Und siehe da, anbrach die Morgenröte' is certainly no better. One notes with interest, however, a coincidence between Fontane's two opening stanzas and a section of Jacob Grimm's speech, with its progression from 'poesielose Orgons- und Damonstücke'[54] to the heights and achievements of Klopstock and Goethe. But Grimm in his turn was rehearsing the perceptions — the clichés — attendant on nineteenth-century awareness of 'Nationalliteratur'. The insight that the 'Schillerfeier' restores 'was uns gebrach'[55] and is a force for the spiritual unanimity that must precede actual political union, is the real point of Fontane's poem, one in 1859 reiterated endlessly at various levels of sophistication. It is not even the only poem produced by the 'Tunnel' for the occasion. Fontane's friend and fellow-poet Scherenberg delivered himself of several execrable stanzas,[56] overladen with rhetoric and inventive conceits, against which Fontane's seems restrained and apposite. For all that has been noted about its tone, it is enshrined in Adolph Büchting's *Verzeichniß/Directory* of 1860, an important source of

---

>   We needed fire to follow on its heels.
>   We needed fire to call out from the night
>   To arms, from highest mountain top,
>   For home and hearth and throne to fight;
>   We needed sacred lofty flame — no sop –
>   To clear our minds in pettiness benighted
>   And weld us in one undivided knot.
>   And Schiller came: and Germany was united'. SW, VI, 470f.

53 Ibid., I, 470.
54 'Orgons and Damons and their unpoetic stuff'. *Schiller*, I, 444.
55 'What we were lacking'.
56 *Schiller-Denkmal*, I, 199–221.

information about the 1859 celebrations,[57] and its text graces Tropus's *Schiller-Denkmal* of the same year.[58]

Fontane's Shakespeare piece was, however, not published in his lifetime and has not been the subject of any significant critical interest.[59] We need not take too seriously his diary entry that it was 'aufs Papier hingeschmissen wohl oder übel'.[60] He had made notes, which suggests a degree of reflexion. In essence, however, he needed no preparation. Shakespeare was already long since enshrined in his scheme of things, through a knowledge of the text, and experience of live performance at home and in London.[61] Fontane is part of the generation that includes Freiligrath, Herwegh and Bodenstedt; like the first two, he is aware of the political charge of the Shakespearean text (as in that early poem, 'Shakespeare an einen deutschen Fürsten/Shakespeare to a German Prince');[62] like all three of them, he does not regard the so-called 'Schlegel-Tieck' version as definitive. There had been the rash experiment of a *Hamlet* translation (a version of *A Midsummer Night's Dream* is lost), the theatre criticism from London, with its emphasis on authenticity and closeness to human experience. He had noted the way in which Shakespeare was still a 'Dichter des Volks' in England,[63] part of an almost unbroken tradition of theatrical performance and role creation — in contrast with Germany, where Schiller had that function, whereas Shakespeare is 'etwas Apartes'.[64] It is worth mentioning that his two other English-language role models, Walter Scott and Charles Dickens, are in a sense part of a wider texture of Shakespeare reception, through the intertextual allusions which form part of the tissue of their

---

57   Büchting, *Verzeichniß*, 74. The title in *Schiller-Denkmal* reads 'Toast auf Schiller von Th. Fontane, gesprochen im literarischen Sonntags-Verein (Tunnel) am 8. November'.
58   *Schiller-Denkmal*, I, 121.
59   The full text is published, as 'Rede zum Shakespeare-Fest', in *SW, Aufsätze*, I, 195–204.
60   'Dashed off as it comes'. *SW, Aufsätze*, I, 798.
61   See Helmuth Nürnberger, *Der junge Fontane. Politik. Poesie. Geschichte 1840 bis 1860* (Hamburg: Wegner, 1967), 100–04; Peter Michelsen, 'Theodor Fontane als Kritiker englischer Shakespeare-Aufführungen', *Shakespeare-Jahrbuch (West)* (1967), 96–122; Andrea Deffner, 'Die "Hamlet"-Übersetzung Theodor Fontanes' (unpublished doctoral thesis, University of Heidelberg, 1991).
62   *SW*, I, 758f.
63   'Poet of the people'. *SW, Aufsätze*, I, 110.
64   'Something very special'. Ibid., 107.

work. Both Shakespeare and Scott come together to influence those early historical fragments, *Wolsey*, and especially the drama *Carl Stuart*. Fontane is aware of the discussion of Shakespeare in his formative years as a writer (Wagner's *Das Drama der Zukunft* [sic], for instance)[65] without necessarily subscribing to its proprietary claims. Above all — and this is crucial for his Shakespeare speech and marks it out from all others in 1864 known to me at least — he had been to the sacred place of pilgrimage, Stratford, the 'Pilgerstätte', the 'Wallfahrtsort'.[66] Again, that gave his remarks the stamp of authenticity that a more literary approach could not.

That is not to say that Fontane's speech does not have a specifically German emphasis or an accentuation that is peculiarly his own. With others as well, he distinguishes Schiller the 'Lieblingsdichter'[67] of 1859 from the superior genius of Shakespeare. The Germanophile proprietary claim 'Shakespeare ist unser'[68] is qualified by the later reference to '[die] ganz[e] gebildet[e] Welt'[69] (another important difference from Schiller), the universal commonalty of Shakespearean connoisseurship and appreciation that knows no national boundaries. Fontane is steering a middle course between crude German partisanship (there is no mention of Schleswig-Holstein, for instance, a subject about which he has decided views) and an uncritical Anglophile stance. For all his fascination with English historical fact and fiction, he is not willing, as Gervinus or Julian Schmidt had been, to berate his fellow-countrymen for their failure to achieve a symbiosis of political and literary culture like that from which Shakespeare once emerged. At most the Histories could serve that function. The great tragedies — *Hamlet*, *King Lear*, *Othello*, *Romeo and Juliet* — are however free of these associations: their presentation of the human heart is the key to their appeal in all ages and nations. This point, it need hardly be said, had been common currency in German Shakespeare appreciation since Herder and was one of the first indications of an independence from English-language criticism. Quoting the words 'Wunderkind' or 'Naturkind',[70] Fontane evokes

---

65   Ibid., 99.
66   Ibid., 202.
67   'Favourite poet'. Ibid., 195.
68   'Shakespeare is ours'. Ibid.
69   'The whole of the educated world'. Ibid., 196.
70   'Wondrous child'; 'nature's child'. Ibid., 197.

the oldest strands of Shakespearean reception and not the nineteenth century's sophistication, and frees notions like 'nature's child' or 'negative capability' from any anchorage in space and time and sites such genius anywhere — if need be, in Germany.

Fontane's seemingly magisterial dismissal of the old biographical, anecdotal approach to Shakespeare — another of the nineteenth century's obsessions — is however subject to gradations. Instead, he turns to topography: London and Stratford. Here, too, there are clear affinities with his own preoccupations, which find their expression not only in *Ein Sommer in London/A Summer in London, Aus England/ From England* and *Jenseit des Tweed/Beyond the Tweed*, but also in his first major literary achievement, *Wanderungen durch die Mark Brandenburg/ Walks through the March of Brandenburg*. London (and to some extent Manchester) emerges in Fontane's account not so much as the living site of past history, but as the repository of evidence and documentation of that past. London, the huge seething city, then as we now know at the apogee of its world-wide influence, lacks in Fontane's eyes the quality of a past time-frame, of history caught in arrest, of living historical associations. This he finds in Waltham Abbey, in Oxford, in Chester, almost everywhere in Scotland (he turns aside from a visit to Glasgow) — and not least in Stratford. England, a country so obsessed with the changes conditional on world trade and naval and military might, has swept away so much of the old — in London more radically than elsewhere — and has thrown up edifices of the new. Thus Shakespeare's London (Fontane accepts the effects of the Great Fire) exists only in images and documents or inscriptions. Its icon is not some haunt on the South Bank, but the bust in Poets' Corner (and Fontane cannot resist the reference to Shakespeare's near-neighbour in that place, Handel, a near-topos of German Shakespearean studies). Warwickshire, and more especially Stratford itself, is an enclave amid change and progress (witness its proximity to the cradle of the Industrial Revolution). Its cultural roots go even deeper than Shakespeare, back to the old folk ballads of a pre-industrial, pre-enclosure era. Thus Stratford — and Fontane knows all the other literary associations of Warwickshire — is all the more precious for having living traces of 'das alte heitre Land'.[71] But we are, as it were, with the writer all the time; he accompanies us

---

71 'The old happy land'. Ibid., 201.

to this place of pilgrimage ('Pilgerstätte', 'Wallfahrtsort'); we stoop to enter the humble birthplace, we add our fingers to the thousands who have touched its walls. We are made aware — Washington Irving, who becomes a kind of spiritual ancestor of the *Wanderungen*,[72] made the same point much earlier — that this may be against all reason and factual foundation, but we enter willingly and consciously into these pious delusions. And our human sense and our experience of life is invoked when Fontane examines the inscription on Shakespeare's tomb and declares: 'Es sind Worte, die nichts andres ausdrücken wollen, als die tiefe Sehnsucht nach Ruhe'.[73] The vignettes, the linking of history and personal musing, the blending of the concretely factual with wider spheres of human experience, that 'wir' that involves us vicariously in the experience — all these point forward to the Fontane of *Wanderungen durch die Mark Brandenburg*, on which he was then working . And — to revert to our overall theme — among the many speeches delivered on the occasion of Shakespeare's tercentenary, it is unique for these very qualities. But let us not forget that the technique being unfolded in the Shakespeare piece and in the *Wanderungen* is also the basis of his later mature novel style: the importance of 'place', but above all its symbolism and human associations, the awareness that the particular and the local also involve, if not the universal, but certainly insights conditional on the widest range of human experience and (if we could but see it) human wisdom.

---

72 Ibid., 202.
73 'They are words that express nothing more than the deep longing for peace'. Ibid., 204.

Fig. 16 Theaterplatz in Dresden. Photo by author, CC BY-SA 4.0.

13. Under the Horse's Tail

The Poets, Statuary and the Literary Canon in Nineteenth-Century Germany[1]

My real subject in this chapter is 'lieux de mémoire', 'Erinnerungsorte', 'loci memoriae' or 'places of memory'. I shall be looking at three examples in a German context and will be examining them as they affect the national memory and its myths, but also the way the nation viewed its national poets and the emergent canon that served to galvanize national cultural aspirations. If we look at the 'Urtext' of this cult of memory, Pierre Nora's *Les Lieux de mémoire* (1984–92)[2] and especially its German equivalent, Étienne François' and Hagen Schulze's *Deutsche Erinnerungsorte* (2000),[3] we notice that the concept of these national monuments, places or spaces, common to both works, is very commodious. It can be a place, like the Minster in Strasbourg or the Brandenburg Gate in Berlin or the city of Dresden. It can also be a person, like Arminius or Frederick the Great or Otto von Bismarck. Or it can be an event like the year 1968. These figures all mark out a space in the national memory and consciousness. Seen in these terms, therefore, figures in the literary canon like Johann Wolfgang Goethe and Friedrich Schiller, the one with *Faust*, the other with *Wilhelm Tell*, also constitute such places.

And yet we must be aware of the separateness of places of memory in France and Germany as presented by Nora and François and Schulze respectively. There can be no Rheims or Panthéon for Germany (no

---

1   This is the much expanded and revised version of a paper first written in 2002, but hitherto unpublished.
2   Pierre Nora et al., *Les Lieux de mémoire*, 7 vols (Paris: Gallimard, 1984–1992).
3   *Deutsche Erinnerungsorte*, ed. by Étienne François and Hagen Schulze (Munich: Beck, 2003 [2001]).

Westminster Abbey); Victor Hugo, Jules Michelet, François Guizot and Augustin Thierry may have created the nineteenth-century view of France that in many ways is still current, but Germany has no Hugo, and the greatest of its nineteenth-century historians, such as Leopold von Ranke or Theodor Mommsen, are focused elsewhere. The Teutoburger Wald, Potsdam, the Wartburg, the Walhalla are all expressions of a nineteenth-century desire for nationhood, but none of them is in a capital city like Paris. The monuments in royal capitals like Munich or Berlin, though attempts at creating a historical panorama or progression, are nevertheless above all tokens of Bavarian or Prussian achievements and are unthinkable in any other context. This is not to diminish the significance of such representations of the national history, but a comparison with France is not in the first instance workable or desirable.[4]

François' and Schulze's volumes do recapture much of what the nineteenth century would have regarded as the central symbolism and iconography of its aspirations before and after 1848 or 1871, whereas places of memory in the twentieth century cannot be disassociated from the memorialization of a less positive past, 'Mahnmale', warning monuments, not just 'Erinnerungsorte'.[5] Thus the city of Dresden, which these volumes mark,[6] is at once the 'Elbflorenz', the pearl of German cities, the cultural jewel with its matchless art collections, but also the city ravaged and laid waste on February 13, 1945, the city, too, described in Victor Klemperer's diaries that was still overseeing the deportation of its Jews almost up to the eve of that terrible night. I will stay with Dresden because it is a convenient example with which to lead into my subject. Today, one may be grateful for every corner of Dresden that has survived the fire from heaven in 1945 and has been subsequently restored. We should not however forget that the city and its famous skyline, already immortalized in the eighteenth century by Canaletto and Bernardo Bellotto, is a cultural artefact made up of various styles,

---

4   A point which emerges in François and Schulze's introduction, 'Einleitung', in *Deutsche Erinnerungsorte*, I, 9–24.
5   As in the articles by Peter Reichel, 'Auschwitz' and by Klaus Neumann, 'Mahnmale' in *Deutsche Erinnerungsorte*, III, 600–21 and 622–57. Cf. also Aleida Assmann, *Erinnerungsräume. Formen und Wandlungen des kulturellen Gedächtnisses* (Munich: Beck, 1999), 328–39.
6   Olaf B. Rader, 'Dresden', in *Deutsche Erinnerungsorte*, I, 451–70.

eclectically framed together over nearly two centuries (and let us not forget that the same Bellotto records its bombardment in 1759–60 during the Seven Years' War, an act of vandalism at the hands of Frederick the Great, about whom more later).

Whereas it is appropriate and legitimate in identifying 'Erinnerungsorte' to refer to historical cultural manifestations in the widest of terms, as in the article 'Dresden' in François and Schulze, the cultural or literary or art historian may wish to examine aspects of these places with an emphasis different from mine. (I qualify only as a literary historian.) Thus when my wife and I stood in 2002 on what was once called the Schlossplatz and has become the Theaterplatz, armed with a camera and some memories of our first visit to Dresden in 1974, we remarked that we were standing on a many-layered 'lieu de mémoire', not least because two of the constituent buildings, the royal palace and the opera house, still ruins in 1974, had been rebuilt since the 1980s, so that the symbolism of the royal capital of Saxony that the city once was, had been restored for a purpose very different from that intended in the nineteenth century. For if we take in all sides of this square — as we are intended to do — we move from the royal palace, mainly Renaissance and much restored in 1890–1902,[7] to the baroque Hofkirche (now Dom), to Gottfried Semper's picture gallery (behind which one can see that baroque extravaganza the Zwinger), to the opera house (after Semper's design: the original building was destroyed by fire) to the centre, the equestrian statue of King John of Saxony (König Johann), by Johannes Schilling and erected in 1889 (see Fig. 16).[8]

Clearly this is a congeries of buildings demonstrating royal power and its cultural attachments in the widest sense. The king, who reigned from 1854 to 1873, dominates the scene from his vantage point above a

---

7 Fritz Löffler, *Das alte Dresden. Geschichte seiner Bauten* (Dresden: Sachsenverlag, 1958), 353.
8 On King John of Saxony see especially *König Johann von Sachsen. Zwischen zwei Welten*, ed. by der Sächsischen Schlossverwaltung und dem Staatlichen Schlossbetrieb Weesenstein (Halle: Janos Stekovics, 2001) and *Zwischen Tradition und Modernität. König Johann von Sachsen 1801–1873*, ed. by Winifried Müller and Martina Schattkowsky, Schriften zur sächsischen Geschichte und Volkskunde 8 (Leipzig: Leipziger Universitätsverlag, 2004). Reference will be made to the individual essays in these volumes. On the statue itself, see Simone Mergen, 'Die Enthüllung des König-Johann-Denkmals in Dresden anlässlich der Wettin-Feier 1889. Jubiläum und Denkmal im monarchischen Kult des 19. Jahrhunderts', in *König Johann von Sachsen*, 425–48.

high and elaborate plinth, the whole competing with the great squares of Europe (see Fig. 17). Looking at the king, with his accoutrements, the traditional royal mantle and sceptre over a modern uniform, with stirrups, we might be tempted to see here the symbol of military power. But this is not, say, King Ludwig I of Bavaria on the Odeonsplatz in Munich with raised sword and defiant gesture. It is an essentially unmartial king, who tried to preserve Saxony's independence, but backed the wrong side in 1866 and was only spared the fate of Hanover through Bismarck's generosity. He is a king who went without great enthusiasm into the 'Reich' of 1871 (he was not present at Versailles and does not figure on the definitive version of Anton von Werner's famous monumental painting of the proclamation of the German Empire). Yet a monument to a king will hardly commemorate what he did not do. What sort of monument is this?

Fig. 17 Equestrian statue of King John of Saxony, Dresden Theaterplatz, by Johannes Schilling (1889). Photo by author, CC BY 4.0.

In his seminal article in the *Historische Zeitschrift* in 1968,[9] Thomas Nipperdey identifies five different kinds of monuments which express and symbolize German ideas and aspirations in the nineteenth century. 1) The national and monarchic or dynastic (such as Frederick the Great's statue in Berlin, about which more later, or Kaiser William's (now lost); 2) the memorial church; 3) the monument to the national culture (such as the Walhalla near Regensburg); 4) the national monument of a democratically constituted nation (the Befreiungshalle at Kelheim or Hermann dominating the Teutoburg Forest); or 5) the monument of a nation now politically coalesced (the many commemorating Bismarck).

The monument to King John has manifestly elements of several of these. Erected by his son, the martial and highly popular King Albert, it is the dynastic homage to the royal house of Wettin (as indicated by the crown on the rear of the plinth), but also to the constitutional monarch (although instinctively conservative), the 'father of his people', who presides over the arts of war and peace, the 'Landesvater'. For if we read the frieze on the plinth from right to left, we see in order of sequence soldiers in the uniforms of the Franco-Prussian War, the industrial arts and crafts and agriculture, then the fine arts. There are links here with nineteenth-century kings of the stamp of King Frederick William IV of Prussia or King Ludwig I of Bavaria, both of whom were indeed King John's brothers-in-law, one with artistic leanings and the other a poet in his own right, but both very different all the same. Albert, Prince Consort, in this country, has perhaps more affinities. For the figures on the plinth are not merely borrowed from traditional iconography; they reflect the king's lively interest in all of his kingdom's activities, technical, administrative and cultural (see Fig. 18).

But what of the back of the plinth, directly under the horse's tail? It is clearly not a place of dishonour, but rather of distinction, for there one will remark the royal crown of Saxony and, below it, a relief portrait of Dante (see Fig. 19). It is a reminder that the king is also Philalethes, who as Prince John of Saxony produced a metrical (iambic) translation of the *Divine Comedy* between 1830 and 1849 and who as king issued a revised edition in 1866. Dante on the plinth does not come as a surprise when we know that the great Italian poet had already formed part of

---

9   Thomas Nipperdey, 'Nationalidee und Nationaldenkmal in Deutschland im 19. Jahrhundert', *Historische Zeitschrift*, 206 (1968), 529–85.

Fig. 18 Equestrian statue of King John of Saxony, detail of plinth. Photo by author, CC BY 4.0.

Fig. 19 Equestrian statue of King John of Saxony, rear of plinth. Photo by author, CC BY 4.0.

the king's official iconography during his lifetime, a Dante bust already featuring on several of his official portraits or representations[10]

He is also noted for assembling around him an 'Accademia Dantesca' that included the poet and translator Ludwig Tieck, the translator Wolf von Baudissin, and the physician and painter Carl Gustav Carus, who between them had the oversight of the royal translation and offered their several poetic or scientific skills and insights. This is not the place to discuss the merits of this translation, as compared, say, with his contemporaries August Kopisch or Karl Ludwig Friedrich Kannegiesser or Karl Streckfuss, nor the role of the 'Accademia'.[11] What is important in this context is that Philalethes' Dante is one those projects in the nineteenth century which linked foreign and native cultures, thereby representing a symbiosis between German 'Bildung' and alien poetry. It descends lineally from the German reception of the Greeks, then of Shakespeare, Cervantes and others, including Dante. Its origins lie in the idea that a cultivated nation, while not yet politically united and without a capital city, may nevertheless make its mark in cultural terms. As Georg Forster formulated it in 1791:

> Geographical position, political constitution and various other factors have given the Germans the eclectic character by which they can explore without prejudice and for its own sake the beautiful, the good and the perfect which is scattered in fragments and adaptations all over the earth's surface, collecting and collating it until such time as the edifice of human knowledge stands complete before us.[12]

---

10 See *König Johann von Sachsen. Zwischen zwei Welten*, frontis., plates 29, 299.
11 See Sebastian Neumeister, 'Philalethes: König Johann als Dante-Übersetzer' in *Zwischen Tradition*, 203–16; but also Elisabeth Stopp, 'Ludwig Tieck: Unveröffentlichte Aufzeichnungen zu Purgatorio VI–XXIII anläßlich der deutschen Übersetzung von Philalethes, ediert und erläutert', *Deutsches Dante Jahrbuch*, 60 (1985) , 7–72 and 'Ludwig Tieck and Dante', *Deutsches Dante Jahrbuch*, 60 (1985), 73–95.
12 Georg Forster, *Sämtliche Schriften, Tagebücher, Briefe*, ed. by Deutsche Akademie der Wissenschaften zu Berlin, 18 vols (Berlin: Akademie, 1963-), IV, 285. The original reads: 'Gleichwohl hat uns geographische Lage, politische Verfassung und so manches mitwirkende Verhältniß den eklektischen Charakter verliehen, womit wir das Schöne, Gute und Vollkommene, was hie und dort in Bruchstücken und Modifikationen auf der ganzen Erdoberfläche zerstreut ist, uneingennüzig um sein selbst willen erforschen, sammlen und so lange ordnen sollen, bis etwa der Bau des menschlichen Wissens volendet da steht, —oder unsre Rolle gespielt ist und künftige Menschenalter die Steine, die wir zusammentrugen, zu einem neuen Gebäude brauchen'.

The translator and critic August Wilhelm Schlegel,[13] lecturing on European literature in Berlin in 1801, stated that the Germans, while yet essentially without a nationality of their own, do possess depth and universality, a different way of expressing the German cultural embrace of the Other. Or in 1818–19, in a very different cultural and political climate, the literary historian Ludwig Wachler, though fixated on the idea of the renewal of the national fibre through Teutonic virtues, nevertheless praises openness to other nations' attainments (Dante, Calderón, Shakespeare) as an essentially German quality.[14] Something similar is still being echoed by Georg Gottfried Gervinus in his *Neue Geschichte der poetischen Literatur der Deutschen / New History of the Poetic Literature of the Germans* (1842) and his call there to incorporate into the national literary culture those aspects that are common to Europe as a whole (such as the reception of Shakespeare).[15] Like the so-called 'Schlegel-Tieck' translation of Shakespeare, like A. W. Schlegel's Sanskrit editions — but exceeding both in the extent of it annotations — Philalethes' *Göttliche Comödie* sees itself as both scholarly and poetic.[16]

In that sense, the Theaterplatz in Dresden is a 'lieu de mémoire', not just a memorial to national or dynastic values. It is, more discreetly (the small plaque of Dante) a monument to those aspects of the national character which expressed themselves in the belief that the Germans had an innate empathy with certain figures of foreign national culture and might be seen to understand them as well if not better than their own compatriots. The example of Shakespeare springs to mind. This place of memory might be Saxony's response to another monument

---

13 August Wilhelm Schlegel, *Kritische Ausgabe der Vorlesungen*, ed. by Ernst Behler, Frank Jolles et al., 6 vols (Paderborn etc.: Schöningh, 1989-), I, 195 ('sie [die Deutschen] allein verbinden Tiefe und Universalität, und ihre Nationalität besteht darin, sich derselben willig entäußern zu können').

14 Ludwig Wachler, *Vorlesungen über die Geschichte der deutschen Nationalliteratur*, 2 vols (Frankfurt am Main: Hermann, 1818–19), I, 17 ('dankbare Gerechtigkeit gegen Gutes, Wahres, Schönes, von wannen es komme, als Gründung teutscher Eigentümlichkeit zu gelten').

15 See Jürgen Fohrmann, *Das Projekt der deutschen Literaturgeschichte. Entstehen und Scheitern einer nationalen Literaturgeschichte zwischen Humanismus und Deutschem Kaiserreich* (Stuttgart: Metzler, 1989), 38f.

16 'Ein Dichter wie *Dante*, der voll historischer, theologischer, astronomischer u.s.w. Beziehungen ist, bleibt ohne Noten ungeniessbar'. *Dante Alighieri's Göttliche Comödie. Metrisch übertragen und mit kritischen und historischen Erläuterungen versehen von Philalethes*, 2. unveränderter Abdruck der berichtigten Ausgabe von 1865–66, 3 vols in 2 (Leipzig: Teubner, 1871), I, i, vii (preface of 1833).

(about which more later) that makes quite a different cultural statement, Berlin's statue of Frederick the Great. For that statue, like the one to Frederick William III in Cologne, is, as we shall see, flanked by significant ancillary figures, whereas King John stands above, but also represents symbolically, the 'general people' who populate his plinth. It might also be a restrained message to William II, the newly ascended young Kaiser, ridden by the same cultural meddlesomeness as his great-uncle Frederick William IV but who, unlike him, was about to embark on two decades of royally and imperially sponsored vulgarity.

But to make the Theaterplatz a 'place of memory' in the full sense, we must of course not overlook that it has on one side one of the great world-class collections of Italian, Spanish and French art, forming one flank of the square, a reminder that the appellation 'Florence on the Elbe' was open to the widest and most positive of interpretations. Moving however to Semper's opera house, also in its turn a monument to European, not exclusively national, culture, and coming round to its right entrance, we see two over-life-size seated statues. They are Goethe and Schiller, looking across to the king and poet-translator on his pedestal, both classically attired and surmounting symbolic reliefs with the connotations of genius and inspiration. They are here for what they are, but also because as young men both underwent crucial experiences in this city. Given their supernal status in the nineteenth century, one might almost say that they were necessary to round off the iconography and symbolism of this public square as a cultural and political space and entity.

Leaving Dresden, we move to Prussia, the royal house of Hohenzollern and the residence of Sanssouci in Potsdam. There is no need even to begin to justify ranking this among the potential 'lieux de mémoire' of Germany, any more than one would need to produce arguments for Versailles in France, so commanding is the case for inclusion (François and Schulze however think differently). Of course, on the surface, we may have to look hard and possibly in vain for any connection here with a specifically German culture, so much do Frederick the Great's palaces and park bear the stamp of French taste and artistic execution. Yet let us not forget that two Prussian kings, not just Frederick, were active in setting the mark of their very different personalities on this cultural landscape: Frederick the Great of course, but also his great-great-nephew, Frederick William IV, the so-called 'Romantic on the Throne'. In fact Frederick William was, out of piety for his famous ancestor, responsible for restoring the palace of Sanssouci to its original French rococo state. On the other hand, as crown prince and then as king, he interspersed throughout the park of Sanssouci buildings that stand in marked contrast to Frederick's. They are either Italianate (like the Neue Orangerie) or Romanesque, like the Friedenskirche, where he and his wife are buried, with its very un-Hohenzollern sentiments on the 'Prince of Peace', or they are classical Roman, like the Charlottenhof, to which I now turn.[17]

Built for his wife Elisabeth, the Charlottenhof emerged between 1826 and 1851 under the guidance of the architects Karl Friedrich Schinkel, Ludwig Persius and Peter Joseph Lenné (quite a trio in their own right). It seems to have been transplanted from the Roman countryside, with its Doric-columned front, its vestibule, and its park with copies of Greek statues, and its herms. The herms, designed in 1851 by Gustav Bläser, certainly look very classical in form until we look closer and remark that their sculpted heads are in fact modern. For as we enter one of the alleys of the grove to the rear of the house, we encounter Goethe and Schiller, and on the other side Cristoph Martin Wieland and Johann Gottfried Herder. At the other end, complementing them, are Dante, Boccaccio, Ariosto and Tasso.

Clearly the king did not wish the park of Sanssouci to echo only to the now departed sounds of French. To that end he had used his famous ancestor's Neues Palais and its rococo theatre, where in Frederick's day nothing in German would have been performed, for the first German production of *A Midsummer Night's Dream*. It was that epoch-making event in 1843, with Ludwig Tieck directing and Felix Mendelssohn Bartholdy providing the incidental music. Eclectic to a fault, he had also had Sophocles' *Antigone* and Jean Racine's *Athalie* performed, with the same producer and composer. But nothing concrete remains to commemorate that event in German musical and theatrical history except the music itself.

But what of the herms, but a short walk distant from the Neues Palais? Was the king thinking of the garden at Belriguardo in Goethe's

---

17 On the Charlottenhof, see Florian Müller-Klug, 'Schloss und Park Charlottenhof — Ein Arkadien', *Clio Berlin* (December 2, 2014), https://clioberlin.de/blog-architektur/76-schloss-und-park-charlottenhof-ein-arkadien.html

Fig. 20 Herms of poets at Charlottenhof, Potsdam. Photo by author, CC BY 4.0.

Torquato Tasso, with the herms there of Virgil and Ariosto? Whatever, these figures ensure that the park of Sanssouci has its own corner that makes a statement about the national literary canon.

At a time (1851) when public monuments to Germany's heroes of culture were springing up, to Albrecht Dürer in Nuremberg (1829), to Johannes Gutenberg in Mainz (1834), to Schiller in Stuttgart (1839), to Ludwig van Beethoven in Bonn (1846), the king sets up his own idea of who is significant in German — and Italian — letters. The Italians need not surprise us: Frederick William's additions to the park of Sanssouci are themselves a blend of the German and the Italianate. But the Romantic on the Throne, who shared his love of Dante with his royal cousin and brother-in-law in Dresden and who followed closely the progress of Philalethes' translation,[18] would know that it was the German Romantics who had done so much for the mythology of the great 'archpoets', Dante especially. But Wieland and Goethe, too, form part of the statuary of the Charlottenhof, the one (Wieland) also associated with the Ariostian epic in German guise, the other (Goethe) with the

---

18   Cf. Hubert Ermisch, 'König Johann und König Friedrich Wilhelm IV.', *Neues Archiv f. Sächsische Geschichte und Altertumskunde*, 32 (1921), 89–135 (95).

troubled life of Tasso. (And both had revived the Boccaccian novella in their respective collections.) The Italians were there too in Schiller's *Über naïve und sentimentalische Dichtung/On Naïve and Sentimental Poetry* (where Schiller even tried his hand at translating a passage of Ariosto) and in Herder's grand schemes of western poetry and its canon. In a sense, by inviting the frail and elderly Ludwig Tieck to be a kind of court poet in Potsdam, Frederick William was honouring not only the Shakespearean scholar but also the former member of his royal cousin Philalethes' 'Accademia Dantesca'.

The king's taste in German literature still accorded with the general classical ranking granted to Goethe and Schiller, whose status was beyond doubt, but also to Wieland and Herder. True, a liberal historian (and liberal politician) like Georg Gottfried Gervinus, might withhold some recognition from Weimar Classicism and its court culture,[19] for him a triumph in poetic terms only, but not the galvanizing force of a cultural nation. Seen thus, all four German poets in the Charlottenhof garden — Goethe, Schiller, Herder, Wieland — could be seen to represent a Weimar under princely patronage. It is a conservative canon: there is no Gothold Ephraim Lessing, but Berlin would make up that deficiency (as the statue of Lessing in Brunswick already had). But German poets had received no recognition from Frederick the Great, and so here, in this very Frederician 'lieu de mémoire', they are receiving some belated remembrance.

Lessing, as said, had not been forgotten, but his initial commemoration in Prussia was to be almost incidental, in a much more public space than Sanssouci: on Unter den Linden, the most important thoroughfare in Berlin, but as a supporting figure on one of its most prominent features, the statue of Frederick the Great by Christian Daniel Rauch, unveiled on March 31, 1851, the same year as the herms of Sanssouci (see Fig. 21). (Lessing did not receive his own memorial in Berlin until 1890, the one still standing in the Tiergarten.)

Frederick, it hardly need be said, is an 'Erinnerungsort' in his own right.[20] The statue has a storied past. Suffice it to say that plans for such a commemoration went back as far as the last years of the great king's

---

19 G. G. Gervinus, *Neuere Geschichte der poetischen National-Literatur der Deutschen. Vierter Theil* (Leipzig: Engelmann, 1843), 5f.
20 Frank-Lothar Kroll, 'Friedrich der Große', in *Deutsche Erinnerungsorte*, III, 620–35.

Fig. 21 Equestrian statue of Frederick the Great by Christian Daniel Rauch (1851), Unter den Linden, Berlin. Photo by author, CC BY 4.0.

reign.[21] Some, if executed, would have involved huge mausolea or Trajan-style columns. Looking at Rauch's statue today, we find it hard to visualize it as a part of the huge 'lieu de mémoire' that its precinct once was and was to become, extending from the royal palace as far as the Tiergarten park. Thus, in 1918, at the end of the Hohenzollerns' reign, it would have presented the beholder with a whole forest of statuary, from Andreas Schlüter's equestrian Great Elector in front of the palace, Alexander Calandrelli's equestrian statue of Frederick William IV in front of the National Gallery, Reinhold Begas's enormous monument to Kaiser William I on the other side, various allegorical nudities on the Schlossbrücke, Prussian generals flanking Karl Friedrich Schinkel's Neue Wache, then Christian Daniel Rauch's Frederick himself, with Begas's Bismarck in front of the Reichstag building, then Kaiser William II's supreme folly and triumphal avenue, the Siegesallee in the Tiergarten, with its three dozen Hohenzollern rulers in marble, a riot of dynastic self-display and ostentation. What is left? In the mean time, the palace

---

21 On the history of the monuments to Frederick the Great see Friedrich Mielke and Jutta von Simson, *Das Berliner Denkmal für Friedrich II., den Großen* (Frankfurt, Berlin, Vienna: Propyläen, 1975).

has been blown up (the Humboldt Forum is now emerging in its place), the Great Elector is in Charlottenburg, William I has gone (only the lions from his monument survive, but elsewhere). Frederick William IV is still there, but the generals languish in the Prinzessinnengarten, Bismarck is on the Grosser Stern, and the Siegesallee, or what is left of it, is in a private museum in Spandau.[22] Unlike Paris, where in the nineteenth and twentieth centuries statues came and went,[23] Berlin ultimately had World War Two and its aftermath to thank for the radical reordering of its monuments. (Frederick was even banished to a corner of Sanssouci between 1950 and 1980.) That leaves Frederick isolated in a way that he never was for a good part of the nineteenth century and well into the twentieth. His nearest neighbours now are the brothers Humboldt, whose statues sit in front of the former palace of the king's brother Prince Heinrich, today the Humboldt University. These are all good reasons for not passing him by and for looking very hard at the rider, the horse and what is under the tail.

The statue is the one chosen by Thomas Nipperdey to exemplify his category of 'national monarchical or dynastic monuments'.[24] In that sense it is very different from Frederick William IV's private neoclassical villa in Sanssouci. But if one looks at all aspects of the statue it emerges as a hybrid. The king, though over-life-size, does not completely dominate the area, for he is flanked on the plinth by numerous other figures, also larger than life, who have been brought into the king's ambit. Some words of explanation are needed.

For the foundation stone to be laid on June 1, 1840, the centenary of Frederick the Great's accession to the throne, numerous elements had to be in place. There had to be agreement on the form and costume of the statue — and royal assent to it. It was not be antique; it was to reflect not just Frederick's military achievements but all aspects — administrative and cultural — of his reign. These were to be represented by supplementary figures on the plinth. It was also to be the apotheosis

---

22 On this see Oliver Moody, 'Germany Offers Statue Topplers a Lesson in How to Master the Past', *The Times* (June 26, 2020), https://www.thetimes.co.uk/article/germany-offers-statue-topplers-a-lesson-in-how-to-master-the-past-9j6brshls and generally Richard J. Evans, 'The History Wars', *New Statesman* (June 19, 2020), https://www.newstatesman.com/international/2020/06/history-wars

23 June Hargrove, 'Les statues de Paris', in Nora, *Les Lieux*, La Nation II, 245–83.

24 Nipperdey, 'Nationalidee', 534–40.

of an enlightened reign: Alexander von Humboldt's speech to the Prussian Academy of Sciences (founded by the king in 1740) stressed the 'wise man on the throne' who had reconciled the conflicting needs of rule and freedom.[25] The works of Frederick the Great (all in French) were also issued between 1846 and 1857 by a distinguished committee of the Prussian Academy,[26] a further token of the king's contribution to eighteenth-century European culture. A happy coincidence saw C. F. Köppen's *Friedrich der Große und seine Widersacher. Eine Jubelschrift / Frederick the Great and his Adversaries. A Festive Volume* appear in 1840, with its emphasis on the king's enlightened values. Eduard Duller's *Die Geschichte des deutschen Volkes / The History of the German People* in the same year, with illustrations by Ludwig Richter[27] and above all Franz Kugler's *Geschichte Friedrichs des Großen / History of Frederick the Great*, illustrated by the young Adolph Menzel (also 1840 and successively reprinted) were able to present Frederick as a figure of national identification.[28] That these values were to be subject to severe constraints during the years 1848–49 and challenged by the sentiments uttered at the unveiling in 1851, does not affect the figures on the plinth, which are our main concern here.

If the period roughly 1840 to 1870 sees, as one author has put it, 'literary history in bronze and stone'[29] through the erection of monuments to the emerging nation's greatest poets, do those incorporated on royal statues in Dresden, Berlin or, as we shall see, Cologne, differ in status from more general forms of poetic memorialization? Would they not seem to be a continuation of earlier patterns, like the poetic 'Grabmal' (Gellert's in Leipzig is the best-known example), the bust in a discreet corner of a royal park, the plaque, the shrine-like grave (such as Klopstock's in Ottensen)? Whereas the free-standing civic statue is an unmistakable and

---

25 Richard Nürnberger, 'Rauch's Friedrich-Denkmal historisch-politisch gesehen', *Jahrbuch Preußischer Kulturbesitz*, 8 (1979), 115–24 (120–21).
26 *Oeuvres de Frédéric le Grand*, 30 vols (Berlin: Decker, 1846–47).
27 Nürnberger, 'Rauch's Friedrich-Denkmal', 117.
28 Dorothea Entrup, *Adolph Menzels Illustrationen zu Franz Kuglers 'Geschichte Friedrichs des Grossen'. Ein Beitrag zur stilistischen und historischen Bewertung der Kunst des jungen Menzel* (Weimar: VDG, 1990), 272.
29 Rolf Selbmann, *Dichterdenkmäler in Deutschland. Literaturgeschichte in Erz und Stein* (Stuttgart: Metzler, 1988). See also Günter Hess, 'Panorama und Denkmal. Erinnerung als Denkform zwischen Vormärz und Grunderzeit, in *Literatur in der sozialen Bewegung. Aufsätze und Forschungsberichte zum 19. Jahrhundert*, ed. by Alberto Martino (Tübingen: Niemeyer, 1977), 130–206, esp. 150–53.

visual tribute to national and local pride (Schiller in Stuttgart, Goethe in Frankfurt, Jean Paul in Bayreuth), the poetic memorialization on a royal statue is always secondary and ancillary. Only informed beholders will be aware of the significance of Dante on King John of Saxony's plinth, whereas Goethe and Schiller stand free in their own right. Even King Ludwig's Walhalla (inaugurated in 1842) is first and foremost a public architectural monument with a symbolic setting between East and West. The interior contains a (later) full-size seated figure of the king himself, whereas the 'worthies', who include a number of poets, are reduced in size under the huge vault and its allegorical representations.[30]

It was only in the first years of the post-1815 Restoration that monuments to non-royal personages were permitted in the German lands. Significantly, the first was to a military hero, Blücher (1818) and then not in Prussia.[31] The first in Prussia was the Luther statue in Wittenberg (1821), but then again both person and place transcended any mere local significance and took on the lineaments of a national monument.[32] Frederick William III's opposition to a Beethoven statue in Bonn, completed under his son Frederick William IV, is well documented.[33] It is noticeable that the first statues to figures in German national culture are in Free Imperial Cities or their equivalent (Dürer in Nuremberg, Gutenberg in Mainz, Goethe in Frankfurt) or in minor residences (Lessing in Brunswick, Schiller in Stuttgart, Johann Peter Hebel in Karlsruhe).[34] In Prussia, by contrast, statues to Immanuel Kant in Königsberg, to Lessing, Goethe and Schiller in Berlin, came relatively later, and in the case of Berlin never in competition with the main royal and dynastic 'lieu de mémoire'. The inclusion of such figures (Lessing,

---

30 The selection of poets' busts, done mainly some time before the completion of the Walhalla, is eclectic but reflects literary taste around 1815: Goethe and Schiller, Wieland and Klopstock, Herder and Johannes von Müller, Bürger and Heinse (there is no Lessing). It is almost Madame de Staël's pantheon. Cf. Nipperdey, 'Nationalidee', 556–8 ('betont monarchiches Denkmal').

31 Ibid., 557.

32 Ibid.

33 See Horst Hallensleben, 'Das Bonner Beethoven-Denkmal als frühes bürgerliches Standbild'; Susan Schaal, 'Das Beethoven-Denkmal von Ernst Julius Hähnel in Bonn', in *Monument für Beethoven. Zur Geschichte des Beethoven-Denkmals (1845) und der frühen Beethoven-Rezeption in Bonn*, ed. by Ingrid Bodsch, Katalog zur Ausstellung des Stadtmuseums Bonn und des Beethoven-Hauses (Bonn: Stadtmuseum, 1995), 28–37, 39–133.

34 Hess, 'Panorama und Denkmal', 152.

Kant) as ancillaries or incidentals on Rauch's statue of Frederick the Great is therefore of some significance. From the point of view of art history, it is somewhat of a hybrid, while from a purely cultural viewpoint it is an attempt to summarize in bronze a whole epoch, not its supreme hero alone.

We need to bear in mind that eleven years passed between the laying of the foundation stone of Frederick's statue in 1840 and its unveiling in 1851. The liberal hopes that had been expressed in 1840 had been subjected to the ultimate test of 1848, and the aspirations once placed in Frederick William IV as a liberal and cultured monarch had been severely tried. The speeches at the unveiling were thus not free of references to the recent 'fateful year' and what it had boded and to the need to reflect on the Prussian virtues for which Frederick had stood: order, discipline, hard work, the military qualities that had accompanied his victories.[35] Although the emphasis in 1851 was not entirely or exclusively on his military prowess, it nevertheless set the tone and helped to initiate more strident identifications with Frederick the Great later in the century.

But we have not examined the statue itself. It shows the king in old age in the historical costume of the eighteenth century, with tricorne and marshal's baton,[36] his achievements behind him, not as he may have placed himself at the head of his army as it marched eastwards along the Frankfurter Strasse towards Küstrin, Kunersdorf or Prague. Below, flanking the plinth, are his generals, one architect of his victories on each corner, accompanied by allegorical representations of fame, peace and the like. At the rear (see Fig. 22), which interests us, are the equestrian statues of the generals Seydlitz and Zieten. Immediately below the tail of Frederick's horse are two allegorical figures representing the arts and sciences, between them an image of fame, below them peace and plenty (the branch and the cornucopia). Grouped around the base of the rear plinth, between the generals, are Ernst Wilhelm von Schlabrendorff, the defender of Silesia, Carl Wilhelm Finck von Finckenstein, Frederick's

---

35 Nürnberger, 'Rauch's Friedrich-Denkmal', 121f.
36 Mielke and Simson, *Das Berliner*, 17; Alfred Kuhn, *Die neuere Plastik von Achtzehnhundert bis zur Gegenwart* (Munich: Delphin, 1922), 30; Walter von Zur Westen, *Zur Enthüllung des Rauchschen Friedrichsdenkmals in Berlin. Fest- und Erinnerungsblätter aus dem Anlaß der 75. Wiederkehr des Enthüllungstages* (Berlin, n.p. 1926), 10.

cabinet minister, Johann Heinrich von Carmer, the jurist and one of the framers of the 'Landrecht', Carl Heinrich Graun, Frederick's court composer, then Lessing and Kant. Beneath these, there is a plaque listing names that include Samuel von Cocceji, Georg Wenzeslas von Knobelsdorff, Christian Wolff, Karl Wilhelm Ramler, Johann Wilhelm Ludwig Gleim, Christian Garve, Ewald von Kleist, Christian Fürchtegott Gellert, Pierre Louis Maupertuis, Antoine Pesne, Charles-Étienne Jordan and Johann Joachim Winckelmann.

Fig. 22 Equestrian statue of Frederick the Great, detail of plinth. Photo by author. CC BY 4.0.

A strategy similar to that on the later statue of King John of Saxony is being observed; the rear of the plinth is clearly reserved for non-military deeds or achievements. We are expected to read along the pedestal from front to rear in a symbolic order. As we saw on the Dresden statue, we read (German terminology) from 'Wehrstand' to 'Nährstand' to 'Lehrstand', defence, agriculture, learning, and we end our survey at the rear. Frederick rarely had anything good to say about poets or 'Scribenten' in general, especially those writing in German. But the sculptor, acting according to later royal wishes, has placed administration (Jordan), law (Cocceji), music (Graun), poetry and thought in equality of position, with Lessing and Kant as embodied representatives. I find it therefore surprising to read in an otherwise very informed study of nineteenth-century monuments to poets and thinkers (1988) the view expressed that Kant's position 'under the horse's tail' represented the reaction of 1851, a historical panorama in which the liberal aspirations of the educated middle classes were trampled underfoot.[37] I think the observable facts speak for themselves, remarkable enough as they are. For the decision to include Kant and Lessing was part of a general design approved in the 1830s by the king and the crown prince.[38]

If these figures or names are intended to represent the Enlightenment for which Frederick the Great also stood, they are well chosen. Graun illustrates the king's love of music and deserves his prominence for that reason, a kind of 'Flötenkonzert' in bronze. Kant's admiration of Frederick is well known and documented (and regretted by some), although the king never received him or even set eyes upon him, which is another matter. But Lessing is quite a different proposition: a non-Prussian, but associated with Berlin nevertheless, no friend of Frederick's however. Indeed, liberal commentators on Lessing in the 1840s and 1850s make the point that Frederick was actually ill-disposed towards Lessing.

Yet the royal committee in the 1830s had caught the spirit of things. For Lessing emerges in the literary historiography of the nineteenth century, from the 1820s onwards, as the great pioneer and liberator, a second Luther, indeed a figure more positively evaluated than Goethe and Schiller.[39] And in 1851 we are chronologically not far from the re-writing of German national literary history from roughly 1860 on, with say Hermann Hettner, that equates Lessing's role in the realm of the mind with that of Frederick in the sphere of war and politics. It prepares the way for the reinterpretation of history in the biography by Erich Schmidt (1884–92) in which Lessing becomes a loyal Prussian and Wilhelmian and where Bismarckian ideologies can be satisfied. And so the 'sacra conversazione' on the rear of the statue, between

---

37 Selbmann, *Dichterdenkmäler*, 60.
38 Christian Eggers, *Christian Daniel Rauch*, 5 vols (Berlin: Duncker, 1873–91), IV, 71–103.
39 See Eva D. Becker, 'Klassiker in der deutschen Literaturgeschichtsschreibung zwischen 1780 und 1860' (1968), in *Literarisches Leben. Umschreibungen der deutschen Literaturgeschichte*, Saarbrücker Beiträge zur Literaturwissenschaft 45 (St. Ingbert: Röhrig, 1994), 7–26 (21–23).

Lessing and Kant (which cannot be real) is symbolic of a coalescence of intellectual forces as the nineteenth century perceived them. Kant seems to be making a point to Lessing, who listens intently. But the statue is not dealing in philosophical nuances: Kant is addressing Lessing, one assumes, as the author of *Die Erziehung des Menschengeschlechts/The Education of the Human Race*, less as the author of *Emilia Galotti* or *Nathan der Weise*.

What of the 'supplementary list' appended below the 'big six'? Here we encounter some of the names mentioned and illustrated in Kugler's and Menzel's popularizing account of 1840, men who surrounded Frederick with taste and wit and learning: Knobelsdorff, the architect of Sanssouci, Pesne, the court painter, Maupertuis, mathematician and first president of the Prussian Academy of Sciences, Jordan, Frederick's secretary and confidant (this would have pleased Berlin's Huguenot community, whose church on the Gendarmenmarkt Frederick built). Indeed two of Menzel's best-known images, of the circle at Sanssouci, and of Pesne decorating the interior at Rheinsberg, are associated with this list.[40] Ewald von Kleist's is another name in that work, as far as I can see the only German writer whom Kugler and Menzel mention or illustrate, not for his poetry, but for his ultimate death at the battle of Kunersdorf. Christian Wolff, the rationalist philosopher banned by Frederick's father but called back by the son, needs no introduction, except that Kant, the author of the First Critique might find his presence dubious, and Lessing also might have his doubts. Christian Garve, the practical moralist, is a Silesian, which commends him to Frederick the annexer of that province, but he is also the translator of Cicero's *De officiis* for the king. The poets Gleim and Ramler both sang of Frederick's deeds, indeed Ramler is a kind of unofficial German court poet, while of course never actually being received at Frederick's court. Both Ramler and Gleim still hold their own in histories of literature around 1850, so that their inclusion here is not anachronistic or a retrospective canonization merely for their association with Frederick. Gellert is still remembered in 1850 for his fables, but also for his legendary meeting with Frederick that had entered into the royal folklore. Like Lessing, he is also a Saxon, here

---

40 See generally Jost Hermand, *Adolph Menzel das Flötenkonzert in Sanssouci. Ein realistisch geträumtes Preußenbild* (Frankfurt am Main: Fischer Taschenbuch-Verlag, 1985).

enrolled among the honorary Prussians. Winckelmann was from Stendal and thus Frederick's subject, but he turned his face against anything Prussian[41] and never came back to his homeland. He is doubtless here for the sake of completeness, not of historical accuracy, for it was the court in Dresden, not in Berlin, that enabled him on his way to Rome. His is the only 'big name' among these *poetae minores* on the plaque, and one might question the commodiousness and legitimacy of this account of Frederician culture which does not stop at cultural annexation.

The omissions are also patent. Where is Anna Louisa Karsch, who so praised Frederick? But women, it seems, must not feature in this account of a misogynist king. (She had also slipped in general esteem.) Where is Moses Mendelssohn, the Berliner by choice and famed well beyond its confines? But Jews, especially ones whom Frederick refused to receive, must not form part of this narrative either. Where is Voltaire, so memorably portrayed by Menzel in conversation with the king at Sanssouci? But Voltaire, unlike Frederick's loyal Frenchmen, had become slippery and perfidious. Not least, his enlightened scepticism could be associated with the French Revolution and thus with recent events in Berlin, of unhappy memory. Generally, it could be said that Frederick William IV, through his capricious and unpredictable behaviour in 1848, had forfeited the legacy of enlightened liberalism that people were still willing to associate with Frederick in 1840. Nevertheless, the canon of German writers, conceived largely in the 1830s and visible only to diligent beholders willing to devote a thorough scrutiny to the plinth, was one which had not lost its validity in the debates concerning the king's physical representation. It could be said that the martial monument and the notion of a national or patriotic literature maintained a balance that would be sustained for a good part of the nineteenth century.[42]

The less well-known equestrian figure of Frederick William III on the Heumarkt in Cologne, sends a slightly different message. The work of Gustav Bläser and others, with its foundation stone laid in 1865 and unveiled in 1878, a generation after Rauch, it has elements of the Berlin statue, the monarch represented by horse and rider but with mantle and sceptre, and supplemented by supporting figures on the plinth. It might

---

41   His inclusion was at the insistence of Baron Bunsen in 1845. Eggers, *Christian Daniel Rauch*, IV, 118f.
42   Hess, 'Panorama und Denkmal', 150–52.

Fig. 23 Equestrian statue of Frederick William III, Cologne. Wikimedia, https://commons.wikimedia.org/wiki/File:Reiterstandbild_Friedrich_Wilhelm_III_K%C3%B6ln_Heumarkt.jpg, CC BY-SA 4.0.

appear at first glance to symbolize the superimposition of Prussian (and Protestant) rule on a less than willing Rhineland in 1815 under the aegis of Frederick William III, and some features seem to bear this out. Yet it was erected as a result of a local initiative, not through a directive from Berlin.[43] The emphasis was to be on the Wars of Liberation and

---

43   See Michael Puls, 'Zur Genese des Reiterdenkmals für Friedrich Wilhelm III. in Köln bis 1878. Ein Thema in plastischen Variationen zwischen Rauch und Begas', in *Köln: Das Reiterdenkmal für König Friedrich Wilhelm III. auf dem Heumarkt*, ed. by Rolf Beines, Walter Geis and Ulrich Krings (Cologne: Bachem, 2004), 74–199 (76).

the Restoration of 1815,⁴⁴ years which had also seen the foundation of the University of Bonn (under Frederick William's son, Bonn also received its Beethoven monument). The flanking figures are mainly generals or administrators (Blücher, Gerhard von Scharnhorst, Freiherr vom Stein, Prince Hardenberg, for example), with the brothers Wilhelm and Alexander von Humboldt, Ernst Moritz Arndt and Barthold Georg Niebuhr representing science and culture. Some (Alexander von Humboldt, Niebuhr, Arndt) have Rhineland connections, but all are Protestants. It is on the relief panels placed behind the main supporting figures that we remark the useful arts, industries and trades of the Rhineland provinces. Individual figures are picked out in friezes representing these areas. Here at least there are some Catholics, such as the brothers Sulpiz and Melchior Boisserée or Ferdinand Franz Wallraf (under 'Baukunst') or even Beethoven himself. But there are also poets and writers. What narrative do they provide about the poetic canon in 1865 or 1878? One, August Wilhelm Schlegel, might once have been part of such a canon, but no more;⁴⁵ in fact, after Heinrich Heine's attack of 1835 and Rudolf Haym's disparagement of 1871 he was at the nadir of his esteem. And so he is here as a founding professor at the University of Bonn, under 'Wissenschaften' and next to the Berlin luminaries Schleiermacher or Hegel, which might have irked him. There was some amnesia at work in the choice of the main supporting figures, but this was not the place for nuances: Wilhelm von Humboldt had been dismissed by the king; Alexander, his brother, was more oriented to France than to Berlin; at least Arndt, whom the king had suspended from office, maintained his reputation as a poet and patriot throughout the century and was part of its canon. Seven minute figures representing 'Freiheitskriege' might seem to be out of touch with the times in 1878.⁴⁶ But one, Fichte, was never absent from the general consciousness, if only for his *Reden an die deutsche Nation / Addresses to the German Nation* of 1808. Three other figures, all poets, had outlived any exclusive association with the Wars of Liberation: Max von Schenkendorf's works were reprinted in 1871, Theodor Körner's frequently during the nineteenth century (twice during the 1870s), while Friedrich Rückert, who had died as recently

---

44   Ibid., 89f.
45   Becker, 'Klassiker', 24.
46   Puls, 'Zur Genese', 150.

as 1866, was now known better for his oriental poetry. As in Berlin, it is only the enterprising beholder, climbing on to the plinth, who can garner this information on the history of literature .

The Rauch statue in Berlin had an unfortunate sequel in the 'Siegesallee' that Kaiser William II created as a triumphal account of the house of Hohenzollern.[47] If Rauch's figures still contained some reverence for the notion of a Prussian enlightenment tinged with French ideas, the Siegesalleee was an unadorned display of monarchical principles and the divine right of kings. The statues of rulers, which are unmemorable, need not concern us here, but the supporting figures may do. For each ruler is flanked by the bust (at suitable distance) of two prominent representatives of his respective reign. There is no place for poets in this scheme of things, but there are some notable redistributions. Schwerin, Frederick's field marshal, stays with his king but is joined — astonishingly — by the Thuringian Johann Sebastian Bach, doubtless on account of his one visit to Sanssouci and his Musical Offering. But Bach, near the end of his life when he came to Sanssouci, is a rather anachronistic choice. Frederick William II is joined, as is appropriate, by Johann Heinrich von Carmer, who saw the Allgemeines Landrecht to its completion. But he is made to share the company of Kant. The inclusion of Kant is truly bizarre, for the edicts of Frederick William's minister Johann Christoph von Wöllner had almost put an end to Kant's publishing and teaching career and represented a reaction against everything that Kant had stood for. It did not worry William II, and this late Wilhelmian statuary has in the fullest and most literal sense stood under the horse's tail of history, in a place of dishonour and now of oblivion.

---

47   See Uta Lehnert, *Der Kaiser und die Siegesallee. Réclame Royale* (Berlin: Reimer, 1998).

POETRY

Fig. 24 Friedrich Gottlieb Klopstock, c. 1760. Wikimedia, https://commons.wikimedia.org/wiki/File:Friedrich_Gottlieb_Klopstock-01.jpg, public domain.

14. Friedrich Gottlieb Klopstock
'Der Zürchersee'[1]

Schön ist, Mutter Natur, deiner Erfindung Pracht
Auf die Fluren verstreut, schöner ein froh Gesicht,
Das den großen Gedanken
Deiner Schöpfung noch Einmal denkt.

Von des schimmernden Sees Traubengestaden her,
Oder, flohest du schon wieder zum Himmel auf,
Kom in röthendem Strale
Auf dem Flügel der Abendluft,

Kom, und lehre mein Lied jugendlich heiter seyn,
Süße Freude, wie du! gleich dem beseelteren
Schnellen Jauchzen des Jünglings,
Sanft, der fühlenden Fanny gleich.

Schon lag hinter uns weit Uto, an dessen Fuß
Zürch in ruhigem Tal freye Bewohner nährt;
Schon war manches Gebirge
Voll von Reben vorbeygeflohn.

Jetzt entwölkte sich fern silberner Alpen Höh,
Und der Jünglinge Herz schlug schon empfindender,
Schon verrieth es beredter
Sich der schönen Begleiterin.

"Hallers Doris", die sang, selber des Liedes werth,
Hirzels Daphne, den Kleist innig wie Gleimen liebt;

---

[1] For a translation of this poem see Appendix One at the end of this chapter. An earlier version of this chapter appeared in *Landmarks in German Poetry*, ed. by Peter Hutchinson, British and Irish Studies in German Language and Literature 20 (Berne, etc.: Peter Lang, 2000), 41–56.

© 2021 Roger Paulin, CC BY 4.0 https://doi.org/10.11647/OBP.0258.14

Und wir Jünglinge sangen,
Und empfanden, wie Hagedorn.

Jetzo nahm uns die Au in die beschattenden
Kühlen Arme des Walds, welcher die Insel krönt;
Da, da kamest du, Freude!
Volles Maßes auf uns herab!

Göttin Freude, du selbst! dich, wir empfanden dich!
Ja, du warest es selbst, Schwester der Menschlichkeit,
Deiner Unschuld Gespielin,
Die sich über uns ganz ergoß!

Süß ist, fröhlicher Lenz, deiner Begeistrung Hauch,
Wenn die Flur dich gebiert, wenn sich dein Odem sanft
In der Jünglinge Herzen,
Und die Herzen der Mädchen gießt.

Ach du machst das Gefühl siegend, es steigt durch dich
Jede blühende Brust schöner und bebender,
Lauter redet der Liebe
Nun entzauberter Mund durch dich!

Lieblich winket der Wein, wenn er Empfindungen,
Beßre sanftere Lust, wenn er Gedanken winkt,
Im sokratischen Becher
Von der thauenden Ros' umkränzt;

Wenn er dringt bis ins Herz, und zu Entschließungen,
Die der Säufer verkennt, jeden Gedanken weckt,
Wenn er lehret verachten,
Was nicht würdig des Weisen ist.

Reizvoll klinget des Ruhms lockender Silberton
In das schlagende Herz, und die Unsterblichkeit
Ist ein großer Gedanke,
Ist des Schweisses der Edeln werth!

Durch der Lieder Gewalt, bey der Urenkelin
Sohn und Tochter noch seyn; mit der Entzückung Ton
Oft beym Namen genennet,
Oft gerufen vom Grabe her,

Dann ihr sanfteres Herz bilden, und, Liebe, dich,
Fromme Tugend, dich auch gießen, ins sanfte Herz,
Ist, beym Himmel! nicht wenig!

Ist des Schweisses der Edlen werth!

Aber süßer ist noch, schöner und reizender,
In dem Arme des Freunds wissen ein Freund zu seyn!
So das Leben genießen,
Nicht unwürdig der Ewigkeit!

Treuer Zärtlichkeit voll, in den Umschattungen,
In den Lüften des Walds, und mit gesenktem Blick
Auf die silberne Welle,
That ich schweigend den frommen Wunsch:

Wäret ihr auch bey uns, die ihr mich ferne liebt,
In des Vaterlands Schooß einsam von mir verstreut,
Die in seligen Stunden
Meine suchende Seele fand;

O so bauten wir hier Hütten der Freundschaft uns!
Ewig wohnten wir hier, ewig! Der Schattenwald
Wandelt' uns sich in Tempe,
Jenes Thal in Elysium![2]

The eighteenth century which produced Friedrich Gottlieb Klopstock is two things. It is an age of contentment with its existing poetic achievements, with its mastery of rules and *bienséances*, its crafting of a language consonant with these aims. But it is also an age unruly in itself, filled with an inner unease and with the hope that the masters of German poetry might find better ways of exploring the deeper urges of the human soul and might be more adequate to the task of saying what the heart wishes to utter. One remedy might be to look at great outside models and their forms, Greek and Roman, for instance, and this poem bears some of that influence. Or one might look at one's own native tradition of German poetry, the great formers and moulders of the German language. It comes as no surprise that Klopstock counts as one of the revivers of what we might call the Germanic inheritance, not in any strictly historical sense, but in his general awareness of standing in a line of descent which first peaks with Martin Luther and continues with Martin Opitz and Albrecht von Haller. When in 1750 he went to Zurich and this poem came about, it was at the invitation of Johann Jacob Bodmer. Bodmer counts as the first major renewer and editor of Middle High German poetry in the eighteenth century. We associate him, not always happily, with the movement towards a new expressiveness in the German language. In this, his true, if rather wayward, disciple is Klopstock. Klopstock dedicates an ode to him ('An Bodmer'), written in the same year as 'Der Zürchersee/Lake Zurich'. It has to do with moral and poetic models — and with friendship. Of all these factors, it is the sense of a new mastery of poetic language that is carried over into the poem with which we are concerned here.

Nowhere else in Europe was poetry like this being written around 1750. But it is not enough to say that Klopstock is better than William Collins or Thomas Gray or Jean-Baptiste Rousseau or Albrecht von Haller. As a landmark the poem remains difficult and slightly intractable. It is 'difficult' in the sense that today so much of it requires explanation and explication. Its subject is friendship. This is not necessarily something alien to modern experience, at least it shouldn't be. But modern poems tend to deal more with friends than with the notion or concept of friendship itself. Thus in 1977 the East German poet Volker Braun, actually quoting Klopstock's poem, wrote

>   Aber am schönsten ist
>   *Von des schimmernden Sees Traubengestaden her*
>   in der Zeit Wirre
>   Die die Freunde verstreut roh
>   Vom Herzen mir, eins zu sein
>   Mit seinem Land, und
>   Gedacht
>   Mit Freunden voll das Schiff [...]³

These are lines very different in tone from Klopstock's, despite ranging poetry and friendship with national language and nation ('eins zu sein / Mit seinem Land'). For Braun's is a political poem about friends, 'all in the same boat', but some are now tipped out of it by the course which others steer. Klopstock's poem provides for Braun the intertext and the contexture for reflexions on nation and state that Klopstock,

---

3   'But sweeter by far
     From the vineyard shores of the shimmering lake
     In the tumult of times
     That rudely scattered the friends
     From my heart, to be one with one's land and
                         Thought
     Full with friends the ship'
     Volker Braun, 'Der Müggelsee', first published in *Die sanfte Revolution*, ed. by Stefan Heym and Werner Heiduczek (Leipzig, Weimar: Kiepenheuer, 1990), 42.

at least in 1750, kept out of his poetic considerations: It might seem different when Friedrich Hölderlin, in 1789 and again in 1790, copied out stanzas thirteen and fourteen of Klopstock's poem for his friends Johann Christoph Benjamin Rümelin and Clemens Christian Camerer:

> Reizvoll klinget des Ruhms lockender Silberton
> In das schlagende Herz, und die Unsterblichkeit
> Ist ein großer Gedanke,
> Ist des Schweisses der Edlen werth!
>
> Durch der Lieder Gewalt, bey der Urenkelin
> Sohn und Tochter noch seyn; mit der Entzückung Ton
> Oft beym Namen genennet,
> Oft gerufen vom Grabe her [...]⁴

Yet the young Hölderlin, despite the importance for him of the addressees of poems as a friendly and reassuring presence, extracts from Klopstock not the notion of friendship, but the sound of poetic fame. This is what he wants to share with his friends. And when in another early poem, 'Mein Vorsaz/My Purpose', he talks of striving after 'Klopstoksgröße',⁵ he is already aligning himself with the grand tradition of Pindar and Horace that he sees represented in German by the older man's poetry. And yet, as I hope to demonstrate, Hölderlin, like Goethe before him, engraved 'Der Zürchersee' in his memory and retrieved from it something that Klopstock would have regarded as incidental: the extraordinary landscape description.

For us today that landscape description has landmark quality. A line like 'Von des schimmernden Sees Traubengestaden her'⁶ has rhythm and musicality, but also inner dynamism ('Von [...] her') and inventiveness ('Traubengestaden'): not just the lake shore covered with vineyards, but the much more concrete lake shore seemingly hanging with bunches of grapes. When Hölderlin later writes his most famous first stanza, for 'Hälfte des Lebens', we note how much he has learned from Klopstock with that merging of fruit and shore in one process ('Mit gelben Birnen hänget [...] Das Land in den See').⁷ And it is fair to say that no poet in

---

7 'Half-Way Through Life
  With yellow pears hangs,
  And full of wild roses,
  The land into the lake'.

German before 1750 and few since, have managed such a good line as Klopstock's here, certainly Goethe and Hölderlin, but there our short list ends. But as I said, for Klopstock the landscape is incidental, the background, at most the scene of other things much closer to his heart. How do we know? The opening of the poem will tell us:

> Schön ist, Mutter Natur, deiner Erfindung Pracht
> Auf die Fluren verstreut, schöner ein froh Gesicht,
> Das den großen Gedanken
> Deiner Schöpfung noch Einmal denkt.[8]

We can see from this prelude to 'Der Zürchersee' how alien a landmark it is, certainly to post-Goethean or post-Wordsworthian sensitivities. But a poem written 250 years ago, especially one as complex as this, is unlikely to reveal its qualities without some understanding of the period in which it was written and of the poet who wrote it.[9] We must be very careful not to misread this opening. Mother Nature, far from being the commonplace it is now (although the idea of all-provident maternal nature existed long since as a trope in religious and semi-religious discourse),[10] was regarded by Klopstock's conservative contemporaries as too bold and thus inappropriate. Far from suggesting with that verb 'denkt' ('ponder') that we should turn away from nature to rational activity, Klopstock is actually using it more or less in the same sense as 'empfinden' ('feeling').[11] Thus the first stanza recognizes nature in its fulness, but also claims for the human mind the faculty of recreating through the processes of inward contemplation and feeling what is 'out there'. That still leaves us, however, with that irksome word 'Gedanken'

---

8 'Mother Nature, how sweet when your works you unfold
On the meadows about, sweeter, a gladsome face
Pondering o'er the great thought
Of your handiwork yet again.'

9 Three studies can be recommended, two older and one more recent: Friedrich Beissner, *Klopstocks Ode 'Der Zürcherseee': Ein Vortrag* (Münster, Cologne: Böhlau, 1952); Emil Staiger, 'Klopstock: "Der Zürchersee"', in *Die Kunst der Interpretation: Studien zur deutschen Literaturgeschichte* (Zurich: Artemis, 1955), 50–74; Gerhard Sauder, 'Die "Freude der Freundschaft": Klopstocks Ode "Der Zürchersee"', in *Gedichte und Interpretationen*, II, ed. by Karl Richter (Stuttgart: Reclam, 1984), 228–39.

10 Cf. Friedrich Gottlieb Klopstock, *Ausgewählte Werke*, ed. by Karl August Schleiden (Munich: Hanser, 1962), 1228.

11 'Feeling'. See Gerhard Kaiser, *Klopstock: Religion und Dichtung*, Studien zur Religion, Geschichte und Geisteswissenschaft 1 (Gütersloh: Mohn, 1963), 94ff.

('thought'). Time and again, Klopstock makes it clear that for him, the religious poet that he sees himself to be, it is the creator, not creation, that has prominence in the scheme of the universe. The opening of the ode 'Dem Unendlichen/To the Eternal One' (1764) is even more uncompromising that our poem's:

> Wie erhebt sich das Herz, wenn es dich,
> Unendlicher, denkt! wie sinkt es,
> Wenns auf sich herunterschaut! [...][12]

Klopstock is here formulating an idea which we associate with the word sublime (in German 'das Erhabene'), the contemplation of the grand and elevated to produce an effect, as he says, 'Wie erhebt sich das Herz' ('How the heart leaps'). With 'Der Zürchersee' we are just seven years before Edmund Burke separated the categories of the sublime and beautiful. We find them both prefigured in a letter of Klopstock's closely connected in time and place with 'Der Zürchersee'. On his way to Zurich in 1750 he is visiting that 'must' for all eighteenth-century travellers, the falls on the Rhine at Schaffhausen:

Dem Rheinfalle gegenüber
auf einem schattigen Hügel.

Welch ein großer Gedanke der Schöpfung ist dieser Wasserfall! — Ich kann itzt davon weiter nichts sagen, ich muß diesen großen Gedanken sehen und hören. — Sei gegrüßt, Strom! der du zwischen Hügeln herunter stäubst und donnerst und du, der den Strom hoch dahin führt, sei dreimal, o Schöpfer! in deiner Herrlichkeit angebetet!

Hier im Angesichte des großen Rheinfalls, in dem Getöse seines mächtigen Brausens, auf einer holdseligen Höhe im Grase gestreckt, hier grüß ich Euch, nahe und ferne Freunde, und vor allem dich, du werthes Land, das mein Fuß jetzt betreten soll! Seyd mir tausendmal gegrüßet! —O! daß ich Alle, die ich liebe, hieher versammlen könnte, mit ihnen eines solchen Werkes der Natur recht zu genießen! Hier möcht' ich mein Leben zubringen und an dieser Stelle sterben, so schön ist sie. — Weiter kann ich davon nichts ausdrücken. Hier kann man keinen andern

---

12 'To the Eternal One
    How the heart leaps when you,
    Eternal One, are its thought, and how
    It sinks when it contemplates you!'. *HKA*, I, i, 224.

Gedanken und keinen Wunsch hegen, als seine Freunde um sich zu haben und beständig hier zu bleiben.

Und ich sage im Namen aller dieser Freunde: Amen! Hallelujah! ——

Klopstock.[13]

This remarkable passage makes it clear that 'Der Zürchersee' is expressing notions of nature, creation and friendship that are close to Klopstock's heart. We notice words like 'schön' and 'holdselig' ('beautiful', 'beauteous') but also 'Getöse seines mächtigen Brausens' ('resounding noise of its uproar', the sublime). We note how a nature depiction similar in its boldness to 'Der Zürchersee' ('der du zwischen Hügeln herunter stäubst und donnerst'/'that beween the hills sprays and thunders') is placed in the wider context of the One who created it; how nature becomes the expression of the soul of God himself. Equally significant is the human relationship most appropriate for the enjoyment of the spectacle and its implications: friendship. In this religious context, where poetry seeks — however inadequately — to tell the wonders of creation, it is friends who form the only appropriate companionship. The theme of friendship as such comes as no surprise, perhaps only its intensity and exclusiveness. For Aristotle, Cicero, Montaigne, even Voltaire and so many others, friendship is the ideal human relation; it crosses the dividing lines of classical *humanitas* to embrace the virtues common to both ancient and Christian moral thinking. In the eighteenth century, where feeling, the practice of virtue, and social intercourse are perceived as one human activity, giving rise to the direct expression of emotions, the classical greatness of soul traditionally associated with

---

13 'Opposite the Rhine falls, on a shady hill. What a great thought of creation is this waterfall — I can say no more about it here, I have to see and hear this great thought — Greetings, stream! that between the hills sprays and thunders, and thou, who draws the stream through, be threefold adored, Creator, in thy glory.
Here, in front of the great Rhine falls, in the resounding noise of its uproar, lying on the grass on a beauteous height, here I greet you, friends, near and far, and above all you, worthy country, whose soil I am about to tread! A thousand greetings! O that I could gather here all those whom I Iove, to enjoy with them such a work of nature! Here I would gladly spend my life and die in this place of such beauty — Words cannot express further. Here one can have no other thought and can express no other wish: than to have one's friends about one and remain here forever! And I say in the name of all of these friends
Amen! Halleluia
Klopstock'. *HKA*, Abt. Briefe, I, 125f.

friendship is ratified by the Christian experience of 'where two or three are gathered together'.¹⁴ Klopstock need not have looked farther than the literary practice of his own time to remark the pervasiveness of friendship as a theme. Yet, when a slightly older contemporary, Samuel Gotthold Lange, begins a poem 'Die Freunde' (1745) with 'Ich will, ich will die Freunde besingen',¹⁵ we feel that he is cranking up a piece of cumbersome mechanism. Klopstock, on the other hand, is prepared to invest friendship with the supreme attributes of the high style of poetry: his long ode in classical alcaic stanzas, 'Auf meine Freunde/To My Friends' (1747), invokes in its opening stanzas Apollo, Dionysus and Pindar before apostrophizing his friends collectively and singly. His friends become part of the poetic act that is unfolding in verses like:

> Wie Hebe, kühn und jugendlich ungestüm,
> Wie mit dem goldnen Köcher Latonens Sohn,
> Unsterblich, sing ich meine Freunde
> Feyrend in mächtigen Dithyramben.
>
> Wilst du zu Strophen werden, o Lied oder
> Ununterwürfig, Pindars Gesängen gleich,
> Gleich Zeus erhabnem trunknem Sohne,
> Frey aus der schaffenden Sel enttaumeln?¹⁶

I have mentioned all of this extra-textual material to assist us on our way into the first stanza of the poem. Before looking more closely at the text stanza by stanza, we ought to consider the circumstances that led to its being written in the first place. In 1750, on a journey to Switzerland (as quoted above), Klopstock sojourned in Zurich. Zurich, the home of Johann Jacob Bodmer and Johann Jacob Breitinger, is the centre of the new poetry and the new aesthetics that are causing rifts and dissensions

---

14 Matthew, 18:20.
15 'The Friends'; 'The friends, the friends, I will sing'. Samuel Gotthold Lange, *Horatzische Oden. Nebst Georg Friedrich Meiers Vorrede vom Werthe der Reime* (Halle: Hemmerde, 1747) 142.
16 'To My Friends
   Like Hebe, bold, youthful, impetuous,
   As with his golden quiver Latona's son,
   Immortal, I sing of my friends,
   In paeans of mighty dithyrambs.
   Would you become verse, o song, or
   Unyielding, like to Pindar's strain,
   Like Zeus' great drunken son,
   Come tumbling straight from the soul, creating?' *HKA*, I, i, 6.

in the world of German letters. Zurich is on the side of imagination and feeling ('hertzrührende Schreibart'). Breitinger's *Critische Dichtkunst/ Critical Poetics* (1740) sums up 'die bewegliche und hertzrührende Schreibart'[17] as follows:

> Die Eigenschaft dieser Sprache bestehet demnach darinnen, daß sie in der Anordnung ihres Vortrags, in der Verbindung und Zusammensetzung der Wörter und Redensarten, und in der Einrichtung der Rede-Sätze sich an kein grammatisches Gesetze, oder logicalische Ordnung, die ein gesezteres Gemüthe erfordern, bindet; sondern der Rede eine solche Art der Verbindung, der Zusammenordnung giebt, wie es die raschen Vorstellungen einer durch die Wuth der Leidenschaften auf einem gewissen Grad erhizten Phantasie erheischen [...].[18]

Breitinger is not advocating chaos and disorder in poetic discourse, but a form of order and combination not subject to mechanisms, able to free itself from the bonds of logical order at the behest of non-rational intimations. Klopstock, almost on cue, arrives in Zurich as the author of the opening cantos of a religious epic, *Der Messias/The Messiah*, which is a declaration in favour of the poetry of emotion, of expression, of imagination, of bold formal experiment. Klopstock is taken by friends on a boating excursion on the Lake of Zurich, done in his honour. He leaves a long factual account in a letter to his cousin; Johann Kaspar Hirzel, mentioned in the poem, wrote similarly to Ewald von Kleist, also immortalized.[19] We learn who the company was and where they went. Klopstock flirted with the sister of one of the society. But the bare bones of Klopstock's account do not prepare us in any way for the poem that arises from the occasion. I use that phrase in preference to 'occasional poem'. For the poem that proceeds from a certain time and

---

17 'Style that moves the heart'.
18 'Thus the quality of this language may be so defined: in the order of its diction, in the combination and ordering of words and styles, of the way the phrases are so arranged so as not to be bound by any grammatical law or logical order such as a more moderate soul requires, but gives speech such a way of combining and ordering as are demanded by the rage of passion and a certain degree of heated imagination'. Johann Jacob Breitinger, *Critische Dichtkunst*, ed. by Wolfgang Bender, Deutsche Neudrucke. Reihe Texte des 18. Jh., 2 vols (Stuttgart: Metzler, 1966), II, 354.
19 The letter of Klopstock to his cousin Johann Christoph Schmidt, in *HKA*, Briefe I, 130f; the letter of Johann Kaspar Hirzel to Ewald von Kleist (both mentioned in the poem) in F. G. Klopstock, *Oden. Eine Auswahl*, ed. by Karl Ludwig Schneider, Reclams Universal-Bibliothek 13.91102 (Stuttgart: Reclam, 1966), 138–42.

place transcends the occasion and arcs over into central concerns of the poet, not subject to the bonds and constraints of time or place.

The incidentals of experience are transformed by the shaping hand of metrical form. The dignity of classical verse removes these events from the purely adventitious sphere and translates them into that of rhetoric, the high style. It is classical rhetoric in the service of 'den großen Gedanken', the great thought. It involves an ultimately religious contemplation of nature, but also the active will to extract from it a precept and an example for Christian ethics, what older religious language called 'conversation'. That is why the poem will not permit 'Mutter Natur' more than a secondary place in its scheme of things. Klopstock chooses as his verse the fourth asclepiad ode stanza, known to generations of schoolchildren through Horace's 'O fons Bandusiae, splendidior vitro'. He takes the metrical pattern of the classical original and makes its quantities correspond to the strong and weak beats of German poetry. That is, his language follows the normal accentuation of German, so that 'Schön ist, Mutter Natur, deiner Erfindung Pracht' can be read as a line of verse, but also as quite naturally cadenced German. These ode stanzas (alcaic, asclepiad, sapphic) appeal because they can express both the order and the imaginative enthusiasm that Breitinger spoke of. Their introduction into German by Klopstock is the major breakthrough in eighteenth-century German poetry before Goethe. The asclepiad stanza is largely dactylic (-xx), so that there is movement implicit in the verse form. This isn't stately verse like the alcaic ('Wie Hebe kühn und jugendlich ungestüm', the opening of 'Auf meine Freunde'); it is characterized by movement inside each line, with a marked masculine ending to verses one, two and four.[20] Those strong beats are important, for they start and end each line. Klopstock puts his connecting words at the beginning of the stanza: 'Komm', 'Schön', 'Jetzt', 'Jetzo'. He often ends his stanza with a dynamically stressed word: 'Abendluft', 'vorbeigeflohn', 'auf uns herab', 'ganz ergoß' etc. And so we hear those unusual words — new — his compounds ('Traubengestaden', 'entwölkte', 'vorbeigeflohn') or his intensifying comparatives ('beseelteren', 'empfindender', 'beredter', 'bebender', 'sanfter'), which English cannot render, inside the structure of the verse.

---

20 It goes without saying that my English version cannot reproduce these features of the original.

That is why the line 'Von des schimmernden Sees Traubengestaden her' is so remarkable, in terms of vocabulary, verbal experiment and poetic musicality. Klopstock isn't all tortuous syntax or interruption, as some of the older standard wisdom on the subject would have it.[21] It is true that his poetry exemplifies what he calls 'Darstellung': 'Unvermutetes, scheinbare Unordnung, schnelles Abbrechen des Gedankens, erregte Erwartung, alles dieses setzt die Seele in eine Bewegung, die sie für die Eindrücke empfänglicher macht'.[22] Stanza two, with its difficult inversions ('Oder, flohest du schon wieder vom Himmel auf') might illustrate the point, as might stanza six with its double objective 'Hallers Doris, die sang [...] Hirzels Daphne, den Kleist innig wie Gleimen liebt'. But anyone with a musical ear will, I hope, hear the harmony and grace of 'Jetzt entwölkte sich fern silbener Alpen Höh' or 'Jetzo nahm uns die Au in die beschattenden/Kühlen Arme des Walds'. Through this kind of verse — this needs to be said — German poetry is liberated from the grip of those 'vers communs', rhymed iambic pentameter, that dominate the high style or the didactic mode before the 1740s, or from shapeless madrigal verses, such as Barthold Heinrich Brockes's, with their varying line length. The releasing of poetic energy with Klopstock is unstoppable. He does not directly influence all subsequent developments in eighteenth-century German poetry. But he produces a willingness to respond to a whole variety of forms and influences that produce the extraordinary 'mix' of the next fifty years or so of German poetic expression. That is the essential link forward from 'Der Zürchersee' to Goethe, Schiller and Hölderlin.

To return to our poem. Perhaps it is not by chance that Klopstock often ends his rhetorical sections by introducing more cadenced nature passages. Thus, stanza one with its double apostrophe to Mother Nature and to a human apperception of nature, breaks off and leads over to 'Von des schimmernden Sees Traubengestaden her'. This in turn produces the unruly and inverted stanzas two and three that apostrophize joy. For the lake shore is only important as the place where joy, here

---

21 Such as the highly influential Eric Blackall, *The Emergence of German as a Literary Language* (Cambridge: Cambridge University Press, 1959), 347.
22 'Representation'. 'Unexpected seeming disorder, thought abruptly breaking off, feverish expectancy, all this sets the soul in movement and this makes it more receptive to impressions'. Friedrich Gottlieb Klopstock, *Ausgewählte Werke*, ed. by Karl August Schleiden (Munich: Hanser, 1962), 1034.

personified, descends in the evening zephyr, to produce 'Jauchzen', her more ecstatic manifestation, but also gentler feelings ('sanft'). It is as if joy were coming down in that very moment to assist the writing of the poem, suggesting that its artistry is really improvised on the spur of the moment. Klopstock does not want his poem to be impersonal, so he names the young woman who is susceptible to such tender feeling. In the first printing of the poem he wrote 'Sch ... inn', meaning his cousin Fanny Schmidt. As in that other poem 'An Gott' ('To God'), so excoriated by Lessing, Klopstock is not above introducing the object of his personal hopes and devotion in the context of his poetic metier. It shows our poet to be very human after all. (Fanny Schmidt rejected him.)

Klopstock then changes tense to the imperfect, to introduce five stanzas dealing with the boat excursion, his companions, and their feelings. The abruptness of this transition is at first bewildering: 'Schon lag'. We are taken into the real event, in medias res, to be told, not what they saw, but what was already 'hinter uns', 'vorbeigeflohn'. It leads over to that remarkable line 'Jetzt entwölkte sich fern silberner Alpen Höh', running slap against a sublime manifestation of nature, in a dramatic confrontation. Stanza after stanza of Albrecht von Haller's 'Die Alpen', one of the century's great didactic poems, never came up with a line like this. But it is not nature, it is human company that quickens the pulse ('empfindender') and gives more eloquent utterance ('beredter'). Note that a technical and syntactical device, much favoured by Klopstock, the anastrophic genitive, enables him to stress — and link — 'Höh' and 'Herz'. Feeling and words now combine in that strangely tortuous next stanza six. Once we have teased out its syntax, we might be tempted to dismiss it as one of the poem's weak spots. But look at its positioning in the very centre of those five stanzas that describe the journey on the lake. It is this invocation of names that leads over to the renewed apostrophizing of joy, 'Freude' or 'Göttin Freude' in stanzas seven and eight. Eighteenth-century poetry is not inhibited about naming names, and so many of Klopstock's poems address real persons. Hölderlin, too, takes comfort in the presence of the friends to whom he dedicates his poems: 'sagst du', 'Aber Freund', to Heinse in 'Brod und Wein', 'mein Sinklair' to Isaak von Sinclair in 'Der Rhein'.[23] Klopstock's stanza links

---

23 'My Sinclair', 'you say', 'But, my friend', 'Bread and Wine', 'my Sinclair', 'The Rhine'.

friends (Hirzel and his wife) and friends who also are poets. Hirzel's wife, here given the stylized Arcadian name of Daphne, sang Haller's ode to Doris; Hirzel, of whom Kleist is as fond as he is of Gleim. Ewald von Kleist, Gleim and Hagedorn are poet-friends; the respected older Swiss poet Haller is a congenial spirit. For Klopstock, poetry and friendship belong together; the creative act is also a corporate act. Poetry gives the legitimation to the expression of such feeling.

That stanza six, with its two-fold stressed 'Und' now urges over to stanzas seven and eight, 'Jetzo', 'da', 'auf uns herab', 'Dich'. The communal experience in nature ('in die beschattenden / Kühlen Arme des Walds') brings the renewed presence of joy, descending in personified guise, the sister of its guileless companion, humanity. Eighteenth-century German poets, from Hagedorn to Schiller, have a weakness for addresses to joy, 'An die Freude', or to other allegorical virtues.[24] But this poem, as we see, is not a mere ode to joy like Hagedorn's. Its descent to Schiller's poem is also not direct. Were it not for those verbs of action 'kamest [...] herab' and 'ergoß' (stanza 8), we might nevertheless say that the poem has moved rapidly away from real persons in real places to abstractions. The next seven stanzas (9–15) in fact make no direct reference to the excursion, subsumed as they are under that general experience of joy. Instead, they mark a process of intensification, from the visual ('fröhlicher Lenz'), to taste ('winket der Wein'), to sound ('klinget des Ruhms lockender Silberton'). That process is plotted by nature, but a very non-specific nature ('Lenz', 'Flur', 'Odem') couched in conventional language. And nature makes feeling triumphant; it removes the inhibitions between 'der Jünglinge Herzen' and 'die Herzen der Mädchen'. Wine gladdens the heart of men, but the gladness it imparts is enhanced by moderation (the 'sokratischer Becher'). It is the teacher who tells us what is worthy of 'der Weise'. This is not an easy word to translate: it has associations with wisdom, but also with moderation and abstinence and the stoical satisfaction with one's lot. It is also the subject of a poem by Friedrich von Hagedorn, whom Klopstock has already addressed. The scale has even higher stages. For fame, immortality that outlives its own generation, transferred through the act of poetry, nurturing the virtues of love and

---

24 See H. B. Nisbet, 'Schiller's "Ode to Joy": A Reappraisal', in *On the Literature and Thought of the German Classical Era* (Cambridge: Open Book Publishers, 2021), 215–40, https://doi.org/10.11647/OBP.0180

goodness ('fromm'), is worthy of the highest effort of the noble soul. The young Hölderlin clearly found this sentiment appropriate for his friends' commonplace books. These seven stanzas, with their invocation of nature, wine, and fame, are also related to the earlier address to the poet-friends. Kleist, Gleim and Hagedorn represent the strand of eighteenth-century poetry that celebrates the gentle virtues, the happy life without excess; Albrecht von Haller sings the high moral qualities of the human soul. All of them value friendship. Thus, the sections are thematically linked.

Our poem could end here. It has catalogued joy, feeling, wise moderation, and fame, in an ascending scale. Part of that process of impulsion upwards has been sustained by the use of absolute comparatives: 'schöner', 'bebender', 'Lauter', 'sanfter'. It cannot seemingly mount higher. It can. 'Gedanken', 'Entschließungen', 'Ruhm and 'Tugend' cede the place of honour to 'life' and 'eternity' 'in the arm of a friend' (stanza 15). Klopstock has described a huge arc from the 'froh Gesicht' of stanza one, has taken in the virtues of human company and conviviality, in order to state in this fifteenth stanza what humankind's highest aspiration is. But the stanza remains unspecific. Klopstock therefore appends three further stanzas to spell out the implications of friendship. He remembers the occasion that gave rise to the poem, and conflates the various earlier elements of nature description, 'schimmernder See', 'silberner Alpen Höh' and 'beschattenden / Kühlen Arme des Walds' to produce 'Umschattungen' and 'silberne Welle', a poetic shorthand for those earlier lines. Note that now the gaze is not directed upwards towards the snowclad peaks, but downwards ('mit gesenktem Blick'), inwards, in silence. Like the letter I quoted earlier, the ending of the poem can imagine nothing better than the epiphany of friends. Perhaps theophany is the right word. For the final stanza does nothing less than equate the tabernacles of the Mount of Transfiguration in Matthew xvii ('Lord, it is good to be here', 'one for Moses and one for Elias'), with the gathering of friends. But Klopstock, by another fine poetic reminiscence from earlier in the poem, takes us from the unspecific Mount of Tabor (the place of the biblical transfiguration) to the here and now. He remembers again the 'beschattenden / Kühlen Arme des Walds', and the 'Umschattungen' two stanzas up, and produces 'Schattenwald'. The wooded place in which we are standing, with its nature evocation, would become the classical Vale of Tempe, the valley over there might be the Elysian fields. Klopstock has no qualms about merging Christian and classical mythology: it is an old Renaissance tradition. It goes hand in hand with the adapting of classical forms to the expressive needs of modern poetry. In this final stanza, Klopstock has fulfilled the promise of stanza one. The delights of Mother Nature are not forgotten, only they are translated on to a higher sphere, hypostasized into mythological association. The great embracing of friends would take place here, amid the 'Schattenwald' and 'jenes Tal'. But thinking 'den großen Gedanken deiner Schöpfung' makes them into Tabor and Tempe, the highest places of inspiration in the classical and Christian traditions.

Klopstock's poem has dynamics that my stanza-by-stanza analysis has not brought out. It plots abstract and unqualified notions in ascending order: 'Mutter Natur', 'froh Gesicht', 'süße Freude', 'Empfindungen', 'Entschließungen', 'Unsterblichkeit', 'Elysium'. But these would be unpoetic, at most didactic, were they not accompanied by a progression in verbal action: 'denkt', 'lehre', 'sang', 'empfanden', 'ergoß', 'steigt', 'winkt', 'dringt', 'klinget', 'bilden', 'gießen', 'genießen'. They represent a movement away from learning or apprehending to feeling and fulfilling. Several of those verbs are compounds: 'flohest [...] auf', 'kamest herab'. We saw how, in the first part especially, the poem was impelled along by strongly stressed words like 'Schon', 'Jetzto', 'Dann', 'Aber'. But the essential dynamics of the poem for the modern reader are surely 'Von des schimmernden Sees Traubengestaden her', 'Jetzt entwölkte sich fern silberner Alpen Höh', 'Jetzo nahm uns die Au in die beschatteten / Kühlen Arme des Walds' and 'in den Umschattungen, / In den Lüften des Walds'. When the young Goethe in 1775 retraced Klopstock's footsteps and embarked with friends on a boat on the same lake, there was not a shadow of doubt that all involved knew they were re-enacting 'Der Zürchersee'.[25] It was perhaps inevitable that Goethe, taking out his notebook and jotting down three stanzas now known as 'aufm Zürchersee', was reminded of what I call the essential dynamics of the earlier poem. Klopstock, as *Werther* testifies, is one of the important influences on Goethe for a brief time. In an extraordinary homage to Klopstock later in 1775, Goethe quotes the phrase 'Gedanken

---

25 See Roger Paulin,'Von "Der Züchersee" zu "aufm Zürchersee"', *Jahrbuch des Freien Deutschen Hochstifts* 1987, 23–49.

der Schöpfung'.[26] Goethe's is a poem very different from Klopstock's. Goethe, ever feline and wayward in friendship, is not interested in 'Hütten der Freundschaft', even if his companions may be. He is not concerned with the catalogue of virtues in Klopstock's poem, even though he will come to ponder some of them in his reflective poetry of the early 1780s. In his little poem on the lake, Mother Nature is a nourisher so exuberant that the poet gets his images mixed up ('Ich saug' an meiner Nabelschnur / Nun Nahrung aus der Welt').[27] But he takes, not in Klopstock's order, the things in nature that had helped to bear 'Der Zürchersee' along: 'Und Berge Wolkenangetan / Entgegnen unserm Lauf', 'Auf der Welle blinken / Tausend schwebende Sterne' and 'Im See bespiegelt / Sich die reifende Frucht'.[28] All of these images are bolder and more concrete than Klopstock's, especially their evocation of the light dancing on the waves. They are part of a process in the poem where the young Goethe establishes the adequacy of his poetic powers to overcome a crisis in his creative and emotional life. But generations of commentators on this poem, agonizing over the meaning of 'reifende Frucht', might have started (where they finish is another matter) with Klopstock's 'Traubengestade' or 'Gebirge, / Voll von Reben'. It is surely a tribute to Goethe's powers of observation and his sense of artistic perspective that he first looks up (to the mountain peaks), looks down (to the light on the waves) and then around him (at the shores covered with vineyards, the ripening stage of the cycle of nature). Klopstock's poem, perhaps against its stated intention, had helped him to see these processes. Hölderlin, over twenty-five years later, remembers just two of the landscape features of 'Der Zürchersee'. Its message has long since been overtaken by mythological visions alien to Klopstock. But in 'Der Rhein' (1801), we read 'Unter den silbernen Gipfeln' and 'Im Schatten des Walds', in 'Patmos' (1803) 'der schattige Wald' and 'der silberne

---

26 'Thought of creation'. Ibid., 37.
27 'I suck on my navel cord
    Nurture from the world'.
28 'And mountains decked with clouds
    Rise up to meet our path.'
    'On the wave-tops sparkle
    A thousand dancing stars'
    'In the lake is mirrored
    The ripening fruit'.

Schnee',[29] proof of the dynamic power of Klopstock's ode to penetrate poems about myth and history and the fulfilment of all things.

Appendix One

Translation of Klopstock, 'Der Zürchersee/The Lake of Zurich'

>Mother nature, how sweet when your gifts you unfold
>On the meadows about, sweeter, a gladsome face
>Pondering o'er the great thought
>Of your handiwork yet again.
>
>From the vineyard shores of the shimmering lake,
>Or, if once again you to the heavens flew,
>Come in the reddening ray
>On the wings of the evening air,
>
>Come and teach my song to be youthfully glad,
>Sweet joy, like you, like the youth's jubilation,
>Quick, and filling the soul,
>Gentle, as Fanny is, the tender.
>
>Far beyond us lay mount Uto, at whose feet
>Zurich lies in her vale, nurturing freemen in peace;
>Now many a vine-clad slope
>Had flashed past as we rowed our way.
>
>The clouds now broke to reveal the heights of silvery alps.
>The young men's hearts beat in their feelings' rush,
>Words came easier
>To their fair companion's mouth.
>
>'Haller's Doris", sang she, worthy herself of the song,
>Hirzel's Daphne: Kleist loves him as he does Gleim,
>And we young men sang
>Full of feeling like Hagedorn.
>
>Now the Au took us into the leafy shading
>Arms of the wood, that the island surmounts;
>Then, then, you descended,

---

29 'Beneath the silvery peaks', 'in the forest shade', 'the shading forest', 'the silver snow'. Hölderlin, *Große Stuttgarter Ausgabe*, II, i, 142, 147, 165f.

Joy, and our cups ran over.

Joy divine, your very self, you, yes we felt you.
Yes, it was verily you, humanity's sister,
Companion, pure in heart,
Who outpoured yourself on us.

Sweet is, springtide joy, your breath and inspiring
When the lea bears you forth, and your gentle breath
Pours into the hearts of youth
 And into the maidens' hearts as well.

O feeling triumphs through you, the breath rises,
Flourishes sweeter and beats,
Louder is the voice of love
When you loosen the magic spell.

Gently beckons wine when through it feelings,
Better desires and gentle beckon us in our thoughts,
In the Socratic beaker
Wreathed about with the dewy rose;

When it pierces the heart and resolutions are made,
To the drunkard unknown, awakens every thought,
So that we learn to abhor
What to the wise unworthy is.

Fame sounds silvery-voiced, charming, enticing
In the beating heart, and life without end is
Worthy to ponder,
Worth the sweat of the noble brow.

Passed down through song's power to generations to come,
Its charms from daughter to son, son and daughter to be,
Often named by your name,
Often called from without the grave,

Then to shape their gentle heart and pour love
And good virtue, to pour into their gentle heart,
Is, by heaven, no trifle,
Worth the sweat of the noble brow!

But sweeter by far is yet, fairer and comelier,
In the arms of a friend, knowing that friend is yours,
Sharing life in this way,
Never-ending, and worthy too.

Tender affections full, in the shadowy glades,
In the breeze of the woods, with downward look of the eye
On the silvery wave,
Silent, I made the loving wish:

Were you but all here, you who love me abroad,
Scattered here and there in the land of our birth,
Whom in hours of bliss
My soul sought out and duly found:

O then here we would build tabernacles of friendship:
Ever live here, ever. The forest's shade
To Tempe changed,
And that vale to Elysium!

Fig. 25 Johann Joseph Sprick, *Portrait of Annette von Droste-Hülshoff*, 1838. Wikimedia, https://commons.wikimedia.org/wiki/File:Droste-H%C3%BClshoff_2.jpg, public domain.

15. Annette von Droste-Hülshoff[1]

How typical are German women writers of the age in which they lived? There is Bettina von Arnim, who did not find her way to a public career as a writer until quite late, when the Romantic movement as such might be deemed to be over. With Annette von Droste-Hülshoff, chronologically at least, we find an exact fit between her times and the movement that she may be seen to represent: Biedermeier, taken roughly to refer to German literature between 1815 and 1848, between Restoration and Revolution. Her dates are 1797 to 1848. Thus she dies, perhaps symbolically, in that year of revolutions, the first ripples of which she was to feel on the Swiss shores of Lake Constance. 1848 is a difficult year for many of her contemporaries to surmount. Some, like August von Platen and Nikolaus Lenau and Eduard Mörike, are already silent; for Jeremias Gotthelf, it produces a brief burst of reaction, then death; Franz Grillparzer ceases writing altogether. These, and others, like Heinrich Heine, Georg Büchner or Friedrich Hebbel, are her contemporaries, and

---

1   An earlier version of this chapter was published in *Landmarks in German Women's Writing*, ed. by Hilary Brown, British and Irish Studies in German Language and Literature 39 (Oxford etc.: Peter Lang, 2007), 77–90.
No account of the vast secondary literature on Droste can be attempted here. Cf. the Droste bibliography by Aloys Haverbusch in Annette von Droste-Hülshoff, *Historisch-kritische Ausgabe: Werke. Briefwechsel*, ed. by Winfried Woesler, 14 vols in 28 parts (Tübingen: Niemeyer, 1971–2000), XIV, i, ii (referred to subsequently referred to *HKA* with volume number). Overviews which relate Droste to the epoch in which she lived are: Günter Häntzschel, 'Annette von Droste Hülshoff', in *Zur Literatur der Restaurationsepoche 1815–1848: Forschungsreferate und Aufsätze*, ed. by Jost Hermand and Manfred Windfuhr (Stuttgart: Metzler, 1970), 151–201; Friedrich Sengle, *Biedermeierzeit: Deutsche Literatur im Spannungsfeld zwischen Restauration und Revolution 1815–1848*, 3 vols (Stuttgart: Metzler, 1971–1980), III, 592–639. See also Josefine Nettesheim, *Die geistige Welt der Dichterin Annette Droste zu Hülshoff* (Münster: Regensberg, 1967) and Günter Häntzschel, *Tradition und Originalität: Allegorische Darstellung im Werk Annette von Droste-Hülshoffs* (Stuttgart: Kohlhammer, 1968).

the test of her eminence is that her poetry and prose stands out even in that company.

Let me rehearse some of the clichés that literary history applies to the term Biedermeier: order, political reaction, regionalism, domesticity, reverence for ordered nature, a Christian outlook, but also irony, disquiet, despondency, melancholy, for which the German words *Weltschmerz* ('melancholy') and *Zerrissenheit* ('conflict') stand. It is associated with young talents swept away before full maturity (Büchner is but one), writers who display brief bursts of activity followed by silence (Lenau, Mörike), or who are troubled by physical and mental illness (Mörike, Lenau, Grillparzer, Adalbert Stifter).

In much of this we will recognise Annette von Droste-Hülshoff, except of course in one crucial feature: the names I have mentioned are all male. She is a woman writer.[2] That does not of course, mean that we cannot align her with her male contemporaries. I wish to do this before pointing out the differences. She is aristocratic, like Lenau or Platen, and like them proud of it (it is a cachet in this period of political restoration). She is associated with rural Westphalia in the way that Mörike is with Swabia, Gotthelf with the canton of Berne, Stifter with Upper Austria, and like them, she transcends it. She is conservative, but she keeps her ear to the ground and knows what is going on, even though she may not always approve. She is physically infirm, with heart palpitations, migraines, attacks of breathlessness. Yet, in the few brief respites from this, she achieves literary recognition, and then fame, with the publication of her works by Cotta in 1844. She seems characteristically rooted in the landscape, customs and dialect of her native Westphalia. But it is journeys away from home, sojourns at Lake Constance, that provide her with the necessary creativity. She is not alone in being

---

2   Among the many recent studies by women scholars and writers see Doris Maurer, *Annette von Droste-Hülshoff: Ein Leben zwischen Auflehnung und Gehorsam: Biographie* (Bonn: Keil, 1982); Elke Friederiksen and Monika Shafi, 'Annette von Droste-Hülshoff (1797–1840): Konfliktstrukturen im Frühwerk', in *Out of Line / Ausgefallen: The Paradox of Marginality in the Writings of Nineteenth-Century German Women*, ed. by Ruth-Ellen Boetcher Joeres and Marianne Burkhard (Amsterdam: Rodopi, 1989), 115–36; *Ein Gitter aus Musik und Sprache: Feministische Analysen zu Annette von Droste-Hülshoff*, ed. by Ortrun Niethammer and Claudia Belemann (Paderborn: Schöningh, 1993). The distinguished modern poet Sarah Kirsch has produced a selection: *Annette von Droste-Hülshoff ausgewählt von Sarah Kirsch* (Cologne: Kiepenheuer & Witsch, 1986).

denied the object of her affections: the family puts a stop to hopes of marriage, and her love for Levin Schücking, a commoner and seventeen years her junior, is accompanied by the pain of renunciation (see the poem 'Lebt wohl/Farewell'). Still, the relative lack of movement that her life trajectory offers, her preoccupation with country matters that seem traditional and stable, enable her a deeper reflective and dreamlike power than that afforded by the tempo of more hurried lives.

Yet compared with, say, Mörike, a veritable church mouse in an obscure village in Swabia, she is well-connected. She has links with the aristocratic Münster circle; Dülmen, where Bettina's brother Clemens Brentano was writing down the visions of the stigmatized nun, Anna Katharina Emmerick, is close by. She corresponds with a high Catholic dignitary. She meets people from the world of letters and learning, like Adele Schopenhauer, the Grimm brothers, Ferdinand Freiligrath, Ludwig Uhland. The Schumanns in Bonn commission an opera text (it is to be on the subject of the Anabaptists in Münster, also a Westphalian theme). Her brother-in-law is Freiherr von Lassberg, the medievalist. She is, as said, published by Cotta, who has the rights to both Goethe's and Schiller's works. She knows foreign literature and she keeps abreast with debates on science.[3]

And still there is the crucial and differentiating factor. Whereas many of the men are professional writers or scholars (or both) or have another profession to fall back on, she is barred, prohibited indeed by her social status and her gender. Her position as the unmarried daughter of a widowed Freifrau (baroness) is one of obedience and deference. She is called upon to serve, to wait, to minister. She must experience constant interruptions through the calls of domesticity. Her writing is regarded as a source of suspicion or even downright scandal. She is painfully aware of the role that her particular society apportions her. She lives in an age where women often renounce their talents so as not to threaten a male-dominated culture: Bettina only 'goes public' after Achim's death in 1831; Ludwig Tieck's talented translator daughter Dorothea hides behind her father's name; Fanny Mendelssohn's compositions must

---

3 On the latter see Ritchie Robertson, 'Faith and Fossils: Annette von Droste Hülshoff's Poem "Die Mergelgrube"', in *Das schwierige neunzehnte Jahrhundert: Germanistische Tagung zum 65. Geburtstag von Eda Sagarra im August 1998*, ed. by Jürgen Barkhoff et al. (Tübingen: Niemeyer, 2000), 345–54.

not overshadow those of her brother Felix or Clara Wieck's those of her husband Robert Schumann.

She knows that women writers are typecast in their choice of subject-matter: religion, love, nature. She reflects all of this, but transcends it. She is a religious writer, but she also writes a novel, a comedy (both unfinished) and ballads. As a pious Catholic, she takes advice from the prince-bishop of Breslau, Melchior Diepenbrock, himself a minor devotional writer. Her religious poetry, however, reflects self-doubt, crises of faith, despair at the loss of grace. She expressly excludes her largest collection of poetry, *Das geistliche Jahr/The Spiritual Year*, poems on the church calendar, from the edition of 1844. But her religion is also a solace amid threatening nature or a disturbing physical state (think of poems like 'Durchwachte Nacht/Sleepless Night', 'Im Moose/In the Moss', 'Mondesaufgang/Moonrise', 'Der Knabe im Moor/The Boy in the Moor'). Or it can provide a moral framework for a theme like that of retribution ('Die Vergeltung/Retribution', 'Der Spiritus familiaris des Rosstäuschers/The Horse Dealer's Familiar Spirit'), most famously visible in *Die Judenbuch/The Jews' Tree*, where the issues are at once clear but also obscure and mystifying. For this is a poet who by her own admission has second sight, who can see beyond appearances, who has visions, often disturbing, that give intimations but intimations only, of events long since inaccessible to memory or record (as in 'Des Arztes Vermächtnis/The Physician's Testament').

How does she see herself as a poet in relation to the task that she defines as the poet's? There is nothing gratuitous, nothing lightly undertaken in her devotion to poetry. We see this in the poems, 'Der Dichter — Dichters Glück', which form a pair:

'Der Dichter — Dichters Glück/The Poet — Poet's Good Fortune'[4]

I

Die ihr beym fetten Mahle lacht
Euch eure Blumen zieht in Scherben,
Und was an Gold Euch zugedacht
Euch wohlbehaglich laßt vererben
Ihr starrt dem Dichter ins Gesicht,

---

4 A translation of the complete poem may be found in Appendix Two at the end of this chapter.

Verwundert, daß er Rosen bricht
Von Disteln, aus dem Quell der Augen
Korall und Perle weiß zu saugen

Daß er den Blitz hernieder langt
Um seine Lampe zu entzünden
Im Wettertoben wenn Euch bangt,
Den rechten Odem weiß zu finden
Ihr starrt ihn an mit halbem Neid,
Den Geistescrösus seiner Zeit
Und wißt es nicht, mit welchen Qualen
 Er seine Schätze muß bezahlen!

Wißt nicht, daß ihn, Verdammten gleich,
Nur rinnend Feuer kann ernähren,
Nur der durchstürmten Wolke Reich
Den Lebensodem kann gewähren
Daß, wo das Haupt ihr sinnend hängt
Sich blutig ihm die Thräne drängt
Nur in des schärfsten Dornes Spalten
Sich seine Blume kann entfalten

Meint ihr das Wetter zünde nicht?
Meint ihr der Sturm erschüttre nicht?
Meint ihr die Thräne brenne nicht?
Meint ihr die Dornen stechen nicht?
Ja, eine Lamp' hat er entfacht,
Die nur das Mark ihm sieden macht!
Ja Perlen fischt er und Juvele
Die kosten nichts als seine Seele!

II

Locke nicht, du Strahl aus der Höh
Denn noch lebt des Prometheus Geyer
Stille still, du buhlender See
Denn noch wachen die Ungeheuer
Neben deines Hortes kristallnem Schrein,
Senk die Hand mein fürstlicher Zecher
Dort drunten bleicht das morsche Gebein
Deß der getaucht nach dem Becher

Und du flatternder Lodenstrauß,
Du der Distel mystische Rose
Strecke nicht deine Fäden aus

> Mich umschlingend so lind und lose
> Flüstern oft hör ich dein Würmlein klein
> Das dir heilend im Schooß mag weilen
> Ach soll ich denn die Rose seyn
> Die zernagte, um Andre zu heilen?[5]

This is, let us admit it from the start, hard poetry. I think it is hard because Droste wants to tell us that the métier of the poet (that is, the office, if you like), is hard, involves sacrifices and deprivations. I am reminded of Grillparzer's poem, 'Abschied von Gastein/Leaving Gastein', where we have a similar set of images, including that of the pearl. One senses that this is a poem which is not making concessions to atmosphere or to nuance, but that it is coming at us with a series of seemingly unrelated images, none of which is part of one symbolic whole but is amplifying and illustrating the central idea of the poem: a fairly traditional use of image or symbol. We notice the use of a regular rhyme pattern: 'Der Dichter' in fact uses the traditional stanza known as *ottava rima*, much favoured by Goethe's generation and since. 'Dichters Glück' also has an eight-lined stanza, but the metre has changed from iambic to trochaic, with anapaests for variation ('du Strahl aus der Höh'). In a fairly recent volume of feminist studies on Droste, a contributor has spoken of the 'metrischer Käfig' ('metrical cage') in which Droste's poetry is enclosed, a symbol of the constraints under which her poetry was conceived and written, indicative of the enclosure in which she found herself, socially, emotionally, in her spiritual life.[6] The same article also quotes Droste's letter in which she says, 'es kümmert mich wenig, daß manche der Lieder weniger wohlklingend sind als die früheren, diese ist eine Gelegenheit wo ich der Form nicht den geringsten nützlichen Gedanken aufopfern darf'.[7] It is an interesting observation, as the author goes on to show that a few poems only, including the famous 'Im Grase' (see below), escape from that cage or confinement. Historically, the statement is problematic, as a very large part of Biedermeier lyrical poetry, indeed

---

5   *HKA*, II, i, 69f.
6   Bruna Bianchi, 'Verhinderte Überschreitung: Phänomenologie der "Grenze" in der Lyrik der Annette von Droste-Hülshoff', in *Ein Gitter aus Musik und Sprache*, 17–34 (19).
7   'I am not at all worried that some of the songs sound less well than the earlier ones. It enables me to care less about form and to follow up even the smallest thought that I can make use of'. *HKA*, IX, i, 86.

nineteenth-century lyrical poetry in general, is rhyme-bound and rhetorical, less concerned with 'Wohlklang' (the musical qualities of the lyrical form) than with what is being said, the message.

Thus in technical rhetorical terms the poem opens with an apostrophe and continues with a set of sustained phrases. It then (stanza 4) introduces a rhetorical question with a fourfold anaphora, which neatly takes up the themes of the first two stanzas and gives them renewed emphasis. Image and meaning correspond exactly, provided, that is, that you recognize the image — not always an easy feat. The second part repeats the structure of the first, but in a shorter space and with greater economy and density of words, with exclamation, apostrophe and rhetorical question. Droste is here working within an accepted framework of devices and meanings. She is not trying to mystify or to create an atmosphere; she is trying to instruct, to spell out, to make clear, unmistakably clear, what poetry is for her. In that sense, it is related to that collection of her poetry that is for today's readers least accessible, *Das geistliche Jahr*, with its allegorical approach, the absolute identification of image and meaning, the submission of the personal and the general.

In those terms, these two poems are stating that poetry does not have the function of exhausting its possibilities in the pursuit of beauty; it cannot lose sight of its basic moral function, which of course can be compatible with beauty. She says (stanza 1) that those who succeed in the material world, or are not in touch with nature ('eure Blumen zieht in Scherben'[8]) are amazed at what the poet is able to extract from the most unpromising or uncompromising of materials: roses from thistles, pearls and coral from tears. The poet seems to be the one whose gifts are richest of all: 'Geistescrösus seiner Zeit', a real Croesus of the spirit. And yet they are won at a cost. The next stanza refers to the thunderbolt of Zeus, the perilous element in which the poet has to live and the sufferings that are necessary to the work of art. All this is reality (hence that fourfold anaphora reinforcing the message), but it is a reality which leads to mortal peril ('kostet nichts als seine Seele'). 'Dichters Glück' expands on the enticements of poetic art ('Locke nicht'). The images which refer to the experience of poetry are total and all-consuming: Prometheus, Goethe's 'Der

---

8   'Grow flowers in clay pots'.

Fischer/The Fisher', Schiller's 'Der Taucher/The Diver', all changed into symbols of sacrifice for art's sake. Then the poem suddenly becomes mysterious and difficult of meaning, yet richly evocative: 'du flatternder Lodenstrauß / Du der Distel mystische Rose'.[9] It is a closely observed and highly poetic image of the thistle or teasel. Yet the word 'mystisch' gives it away, with its religious associations. Then comes 'Strecke nicht deine Fäden aus / Mich umschlingend so lind und lose'.[10] The 'mystical rose' of the thistle contains a grub or worm inside its crown, which is healing, 'heilend'. A poem which has up to now operated mainly in a conventional level, with accessible images, now confronts us with an image that few today would understand. Droste's interest in botany and in its application for healing purposes, in galvanism and homeopathy, in folk cures — this, too, is part of Heimat and 'regionalism' — comes out in this image. She is referring here to a cure known in Westphalian folk medicine: a fly that lays its eggs in the head of the thistle and whose larvae are used for various medicinal purposes. It has been a long-hallowed tradition in religious poetry and iconography to associate certain plants with spiritual qualities.[11] It is still part of the world of the stigmatized nun at Dülmen, Anna Katharina Emmerick, so venerated by Clemens Brentano. It makes the link between the scientific and the mystical sides of nature. With that essentially religious association, Droste brings herself into the poem; it becomes linked with her experience. There is almost an air of resignation as she takes upon herself the function of the thistle made by poetry into a rose. She is to be consumed inwardly so that her works may be the means of salvation ('heilend') to others. Is that 'worm' her infirmity, her self-sacrifice? She leaves us to work that out for ourselves. Note the transition from 'dem Dichter ins Gesicht' ('staring at him') of the first stanza of 'Der Dichter' to the personal in this last stanza of 'Dichters Glück'. It is announced by a change of metre in the last two verses of the poem, to introduce the personal amid all the rhetoric and metaphorical apparatus.

If the recondite associations of the nature reference in 'Dichters Glück' may seem mystifying, they nevertheless serve as a reminder

---

9 'And you, fluttering teasel head, / You mystical thistle rose'.
10 'Do not stretch out your thread / To encircle me so close'.
11 Cf. Nettesheim, *Die geistige Welt*, 32f.; Häntzschel, *Tradition und Originalität*, 16f.

that this is a poet of minute observation and an almost encyclopaedic display of knowledge about the realm of nature. It is not nature randomly observed, but grasped in a sense of order and hierarchy, almost in sequence. It is a reflection of Droste's reading of one of the nineteenth century's most popular works on nature, Friedrich Justin Bertuch's *Naturgeschichte/Natural History*.[12] But she is familiar also with the writings of the nature philosopher Lorenz Oken. She knows about the various nineteenth-century theories of the creation and origins of the earth. Hence her vocabulary betrays more than just a passing acquaintance with the scientific pursuits of her century, something she shares with Goethe: 'Den Fäden gleich, die, grünlicher Asbest, / Schaun so behaglich aus dem Wassernest'[13] or 'Gleich Bildern von Daguerre, die Deck entlang'[14] describing the terrors of lying awake at night, with the physiological detail of 'wie mir das Blut im Hirne zuckt'. Even in *Das geistliche Jahr* we find words like 'Phosphorpflanze',[15] 'elektrisch Feuer',[16] 'EMBRIO',[17] 'galvansche Kette'.[18] The collection called *Heidebilder/Heath Scenes* has sections where she describes every plant or stone or notes the light reflected on the wing-cases of a beetle; indeed, there are poems which rehearse the names of rocks in their geological formations, marl, gneiss, flint, mica, felspar. And yet this nature observation is never an end in itself and is often integrated into a more conventional set of images and topoi (sea, wild animals, house and home) that bespeak both danger and security.

Often these nature reveries produce meditations, dreams or visions. In one or two of the 'geological' poems, she sees the process of death and petrification that has produced the formations[19] — and finds herself in the realm of forlornness and death:

---

12 Cf. the final stanza of 'Die Mergelgrube'. On this, see Nettesheim, *Die geistige Welt*, 15–36.
13 'Like the threads, asbestos-green, / Gaze up from the comfort of their watery nest'. 'Die Linde/The Linden Tree', *HKA*, I, i, 44.
14 'Like images by Daguerre across the ceiling'. 'Durchwachte Nacht/Sleepless Night', ibid., 352.
15 'Phosphorus plant', *HKA*, IV, i, 81.
16 'Electric fire', ibid., 92.
17 'EMBRIO', ibid., 138.
18 'Galvanic series', ibid., 145.
19 Translations of these stanzas are to be found in Appendix Two at the end of this chapter.

'Die Mergelgrube'

Und müde, müde sank ich an den Rand
Der staub'gen Gruft; da rieselte der Grand
Auf Haar und Kleider mir, ich ward so grau
Wie eine Leich' im Katakomben-Bau,
Und mir zu Füßen hört ich leises Knirren,
Ein Rütteln, ein Gebröckel und ein Schwirren.
Es war der Totenkäfer, der im Sarg
So eben eine frische Leiche barg;[20]

'Der Hünenstein'

Ich wußte gleich, es war ein Hünengrab,
Und fester drückt' ich meine Stirn hinab,
Wollüstig saugend an des Grauens Süße,
Bis es mit eis'gen Krallen mich gepackt,
Bis wie ein Gletscher-Bronn des Blutes Takt
Aufquoll und hämmert' unterm Mantelvließe.

Die Decke über mir, gesunken, schief,
An der so blaß gehärmt das Mondlicht schlief,
Wie eine Wittwe an des Gatten Grabe;
Vom Hirtenfeuer Kohlenscheite sahn
So leichenbrandig durch den Thimian,
Daß ich sie abwärts schnellte mit dem Stabe.[21]

Note the images of physical frailty, the disquietingly strong beat of her pulse, the realms of terror into which she has entered ('leichenbrandig/ like funeral pyres').

In some of the longer 'set-piece' nature poems, like 'Mondesaufgang' or 'Durchwachte Nacht', the images of darkness and light take on their traditional allegorical significance as the realms of sin and salvation, where the moonlight or the rays of the early morning sun dispel the terrors and dangers of the night. Her almost exact English contemporary John Keble (the author of *The Christian Year* [1827]) writes there of the 'Sun of my soul' and 'It is not night if Thou be near'.[22]

But Droste's nature poems are not all visions or dreams or insomniac broodings. We see her drawing nature into her feelings of love, affection,

---

20 *HKA*, I, i, 51.
21 Ibid., 44.
22 John Keble, *The Christian Year: Thoughts in Verse for the Sundays and Holydays throughout the Year* (London: Review of Reviews Office, 1895), 3.

charity or friendship, the other abiding themes of her poetry. We should not sentimentalize them, as these themes are also bound up with isolation, renunciation or limitation. They are in many ways the only consolation left. The following final stanzas from 'Spätes Erwachen/ Late Awakening' (1843–44) should be read together with the poignant 'Lebt wohl/Farewell':[23]

> Wie ist das anders nun geworden,
> Seit ich in's Auge dir geblickt,
> Wie ist nun jeder Welle Borden
> Ein Menschenbildniß eingedrückt!
>
> Wie fühl' ich allen warmen Händen
> Nun ihre leisen Pulse nach,
> Und jedem Blick sein scheues Wenden
> Und jeder schweren Brust ihr Ach.
>
> Und alle Pfade möcht' ich fragen:
> Wo zieht ihr hin, wo ist das Haus,
> In dem lebend'ge Herzen schlagen,
> Lebend'ger Odem schwillt hinaus?
>
> Entzünden möcht' ich alle Kerzen
> Und rufen jedem milden Seyn:
> Auf ist mein Paradies im Herzen,
> Zieht alle, alle nun hinein![24]

With this, we lead over to Droste's best-known and possibly best poem, 'Im Grase/In the Grass'.[25]

> Süße Ruh', süßer Taumel im Gras,
> Von des Krautes Arom umhaucht,
> Tiefe Flut, tief tief trunkne Flut,
> Wenn die Wolk' am Azure verraucht,
> Wenn aufs müde, schwimmende Haupt
> Süßes Lachen gaukelt herab,
> Liebe Stimme säuselt und träuft
> Wie die Lindenblüth' auf ein Grab.
>
> Wenn im Busen die Todten dann
> Jede Leiche sich streckt und regt,

---

23   A translation of this poem is to be found in Appendix Two at the end of this chapter.
24   *HKA*, I, i, 323.
25   A translation of this poem is to be found in Appendix Two at the end of this chapter.

> Leise, leise den Odem zieht,
> Die geschloss'ne Wimper bewegt,
> Todte Lieb, todte Lust, todte Zeit,
> All die Schätze, im Schutt verwühlt,
> Sich berühren mit schüchternem Klang
> Gleich den Glöckchen, vom Winde umspielt.
>
> Stunden, flücht'ger ihr als der Kuß
> Eines Strahls auf den trauernden See,
> Als des zieh'nden Vogels Lied,
> Das mir niederperlt aus der Höh',
> Als des schillernden Käfers Blitz
> Wenn den Sonnenpfad er durcheilt,
> Als der flüücht'ge Druck einer Hand,
> Die zum letzten Male verweilt.
>
> Dennoch, Himmel, immer mir nur
> Dieses Eine nur: für das Lied
> Jedes freien Vogels im Blau
> Eine Seele, die mit ihm zieht,
> Nur für jeden kärglichen Strahl
> Meinen farbig schillernden Saum,
> Jeder warmen Hand meinen Druck
> Und für jedes Glück meinen Traum.[26]

Some of the quotations or references from other poems will confirm that many of the individual images of this poem are already pre-formulated. Unlike the ones already cited, this poem is only partially rhymed. For the commentator quoted earlier, it represents some breaking out of the metrical 'cage' and a greater freedom and musicality.[27] There are partial rhymes like 'See' / 'Höh', 'verwühlt' / 'umspielt'. The rhyme scheme does allow for some unrhymed endings, and the stress words — 'süß', 'Flut', 'Azure', 'müde', 'säuselt' (first stanza) — are not necessarily the rhyme words. The metre is not clearly definable, but I cannot see that it is basically anapaestic (as opposed to having some feet in this metre) nor do I feel the dancing rhythm, that the same commentator senses. In fact, it displays great subtlety in its stresses and defies exact metrical description. For instance: already the trochaic second half of the line consciously has the two strong stresses of 'Von des Krautes

---

26 *HKA*, I, i, 328.
27 Bianchi, 'Verhinderte Überschreitung', 30.

Arom umhaucht'[28] and not the anapaestic 'Arome umhaucht', as many editions print it. What we can say is that it has so called 'masculine' endings for every verse, and thus a stressed ending for every stanza, 'Grab', 'umspielt', 'verweilt', 'Traum'.

Droste's opening is a synaesthesia, a merging and blurring of sense associations. The speaker is lying in the grass, on the ground, in profound repose, producing a 'Taumel'. 'Taumel' is a vertigo, a faint, a loss of control when one is standing. Here, it is in lying, as the scents of the grass crowd in and become the very air one is breathing: 'umhaucht'. Note in the midst of this vertiginous surrender to the tang of grass how appropriate the word 'Arom' is instead of 'Duft', preparing us for the less usual 'Azur'. The merging into the scents of the grass becomes a flood, 'Flut', as the speaker, from her prone position, sees the clouds dissipated above her. Note how the long and soporific sounds of 'süß' and 'tief' have contributed to this effect in their two and threefold repetition. The element of time is kept in the centre of the stanza, 'Wenn [...] wenn'. It is hard to say whether this is a 'when' clause or an 'as' clause, whether there is a definite temporal progression of sensations, one coming after the other, or whether past and present become blurred with the blurring of vision, 'schwimmendes Haupt'. But 'süß' leads through 'tief' to 'müde'; and in that loss of mental control, akin to fainting, 'süß' is repeated. We do not have the sense of being buried in the grass and looking up into the sky, but the sensation of sounds 'herabgaukeln', spirited down by some sleight of hand, dropping mysteriously. A dear voice, 'säuselt', like a sighing or trembling of the wind; also 'träuft', which reminds us of water drops, or even honey. 'Träuft' is the first simile in the stanza: like the blossoms of the lime tree dropping on to a grave. The lime tree is of course the sentimental tree par excellence in German poetry, associated also with death and graveyards: 'Lang sah ich, Meta, schon dein Grab / Und seine Linde wehn', writes Klopstock in 'Das Wiedersehn/The Reunion'.[29] And a grave, to have a lime planted over it and in flower, would not be fresh, but old.

This seems to be borne out by the threefold repetition in the next stanza of 'Todte Lieb, todte Lust, todte Zeit'.[30] But the speaker is now, as it were, in the grave, surrounded by the dead — in her mind ('im Busen'). As in the first stanza, repetition of associative words — 'Leise, leise', 'todt', 'todt', 'todt' brings out the awareness of the dead, each one coming to life in her mind's eye, each one drawing breath, opening its eyes, a kind of general resurrection of that which is nevertheless irrevocably dead, is part of the debris and detritus of the past — until that last image of sound, another synaesthesia, brings in sense reactions that are feeling and haunting and lyrically associative.

Here, as I see it, the poem divides into a second half. The sense of loss and transitoriness in a state of 'Taumel' and semi-dream, is balanced by very precise, if fugitive, nature images. This is what those departed hours were like, that are apostrophized at the beginning of the stanza: 'Stunden, flücht'ger ihr'.[31] They are a set of sustained but unrelated images, merging only in the fact that they represent a variety of sense impressions: the flash of light on the dark water, sensuously expressed by a kiss, 'Kuß'; the song of the bird, with 'niederperlen', which suggests dew dropping (akin to 'säuselt' and 'träuft'); the sparkling wing-cases of the beetle in a beam of sunlight; the clasp of a hand for the last time, 'zum letzten Male', underlining the fleeting nature of the other images and reminding us of the brevity of human contacts.

Stanza four is difficult. On the one hand, it is terse and laconic, on the other insistent and repetitive ('immer mir nur / Dieses Eine nur').[32] It is an address to heaven that looks away from the fleeting and fugitive, a prayer that for every transitory impression or experience the poet may be granted an accompanying gift as an enrichment. For birdsong there is a soul. Does that mean that she will invest each song with a soul, with something that will give it life? Or does she think of a soul each time she hears a bird sing? For every meagre ray of light she will give, as it says, the full iridescence of her shot-silk hem. What can that mean? How are we to read 'Saum'? For feminist commentators, it means 'Grenze', 'edge', denoting the limitations of her art, thus far and thus far only.[33] Yet 'Saum' also means 'hem', familiar to German Bible readers from Isaiah 6:1 (AV, 'train'). Is it, pars pro toto, her art? Is it God's garment? Is it herself and all she can offer? The text offers no clear answer, nor do I believe that it should. But I am reminded of the analogy of two other women poets of the nineteenth century who employ a similar image. Christina Rossetti in 'A Birthday' speaks of a 'rainbow shell', 'peacocks with a hundred eyes', drawing on nature to describe her

---

31   'Hours, you more fleeting'.
32   'Grant only this, / But only this'.
33   Bianchi, 'Verhinderte Überschreitung', 32.

art.[34] Emily Dickinson, describing crocuses, is bolder, with 'Rainbow', 'World Cashmere', 'Peacock's purple Train', but she outlines a similar process where nature and human artifice are merged.[35] Nature becomes more accessible to our affections as we personify it. Our affections are enhanced by reference to the beauties of the natural world. Droste's poem still defies precise analysis, although the 'World Cashmere' may well be part of it.

For every warm hand, hers pressed into it: an affirmation of every human response to friendship or affection. And — she is a poet — her dream, her vision to accompany every happiness. Droste is shifting the emphasis away from 'flüchtig' to an affirmation of human activity for good and right and virtue, finding a blessing in every kind of human doing, discovering true humanity in the face of the very shortness and insecurity and limitation of our existence. The poem makes no direct appeal to our senses or our intellect. It is full of associations, snatches of meaning and mergers of images. And yet it is a reflective poem, where symbols are taken and presented to us without explanation, indirectly, for us to ponder the relation between nature and human experience.

Appendix Two

Translation of Droste, 'Der Dichter — Dichters Glück/The Poet — Poet's Fortune'

I

You who banquet at your ease
And grow flowers in pots of clay,
And enjoy your gold's increase
Inherited along the way;
Into the poet's face you look,
And wonder at the rose he took
From thistles, from the eye's deep well
Can suck pearls and red of coral.

---

34 *The Complete Poems of Christina Rossetti: A Variorum Edition*, ed. by R.W. Crump, 2 vols (Baton Rouge, London: Louisiana State University Press, 1979, 1986), I, 37.
35 *The Complete Poems of Emily Dickinson*, ed. by Thomas H. Johnson (London: Faber & Faber, 1970), 33.

Lightning seizes with his hand
To set his lamp aflame;
While you are cowering from the storm
He finds the breath he needs, to draw.
You stare at him, half full of spite,
A Croesus, but one of the mind,
Unheeding of the pain it brings
For the treasures that he sings.

You know not: he is like the damned,
Living fire in his hand,
Lives in tempest and storm-cloud,
Breathes only in that sphere,
And where you hang your pensive heads
From blood he presses tears,
Where thorns press, nowhere else,
Is where his flower appears.

Does the bolt not kindle?
Does the storm not shake?
Does the tear not burn?
Do the thorns not prick?
Yes, he has lit a lamp
That sears his blood.
He fishes for pearls and jewels
At no cost - but his life.

II

Beckon not, bolt from on high,
Prometheus' vulture lives still.
Peace, peace, luring lake,
The monsters keep yet their watch
Over your crystal casket's hoard.
Carousing king, drink no more up,
Below are the blanching bones
Of the man who dived for the cup.

And you, fluttering teasle head,
You mystic thistle rose,
Do not stretch out your thread
To encircle me so close.
The worm whispers in my ear.
Hidden inward, healing,
I the cankered rose once fair
Health to others bringing?

Translation of Droste, 'Die Mergelgrube/The Marl Pit'

Weary, weary, kneeling on the edge
In sand, a shower of gravel covered me,
Hair and clothes, I was a mass of grey,
A corpse entombed in stone, perhaps,
And at my feet I heard a rustling sound,
A shaking, yielding, the buzz of wings:
The death beetle in the coffin's waste
Had found a fresh corpse on which to feast.

Translation of Droste, 'Der Hünenstein/The Barrow Grave'

I knew at once it was a barrow-hill.
And pressing down my forehead harder still,
Sweet horror mixed with lust seized hold of me,
Till icy claws held me tenaciously,
Till, like a glacier stream my beating pulse,
Swelled and hammered under my coat's sheet.

The ceiling over me, sunk and out of true
With moonlight casting down its ghastly hue,
 A widow at the grave, her husband dead:
The herdsman's fire of coals seemed to shine
Like flickering funeral pyres amid the thyme;
I took a stick and pushed them to one side.

Translation of Droste, 'Spätes Erwachen/Late Awakening'

What change came over me since then,
When I first gazed into your eye,
For every wave within my ken
Bears on it your face stamped like a die.

And how I feel those hands that stay
Their warmth, their pulse's easy strain,
The shy regards once turned away
And every breast racked in pain.

And all the paths this question set:
Where goes the way and whence the dwelling
Where living hearts are beating yet
And living breath the breast is swelling?

Light up the lamps on every side
And call to every weary heart:
My paradise is open wide,
All come in: never let us part!

Translation of Droste, 'Im Grase/In the Grass'

Sweet repose, sweet faint in the grass,
The herb's aroma my breath.
Deep flood, deep, deep drunken flood
When the cloud in the azure dissolves,
When on my weary swimming head
Sweet laughter comes dancing down,
Dear voice purls down from on high
Like the linden flower on a grave.

When in my bosom then the dead,
Each body stretches and strains,
Gently, gently draws in breath,
The eyelid flickers, once closed,
Dead love, dead desire, dead time,
The stony ground reveals its store,
Shy at first, mingle their sounds
Like the tinkling of bells in the wind.

Hours! you, more fleeting than the kiss
Of a ray on the doleful lake,
Than the song of the passing bird,
A pearly sound from the height,
Than the beetle's lightning flash
As it catches the path of the sun,
Than the fleeting grasp of a hand
Held firm that one last time.

Yet still: heaven, grant only this,
But only this: for the song
Of each bird in the vault
A soul that shares its way.
For a ray, however dim,
The shot-silk hues of my hem,
For each warm hand my clasp,
And for every fortune my dream.

Fig. 26 Leonid Pasternak, Portrait of Rainer Maria Rilke, date unknown. Wikimedia Commons, https://commons.wikimedia.org/wiki/File:Leonid_Pasternak_-_Portrait_painting_of_Rainer_Maria_Rilke.jpg, public domain.

16. Rilke: Duino Elegy Ten[1]

In memoriam Leslie Seiffert, 1934–90

It is a natural reaction to see in Elegy Ten a kind of summation of the ideas and images of the whole cycle. The themes that we have been tracing do of course recur: angels, flowers, lovers, mythologies. And themes and motifs that dominate Rainer Maria Rilke's whole poetic oeuvre find a voice, the image of the night sky, for instance.[2] But the sombre grandeur of this elegy comes from the theme of death that dominates it from beginning to end, coming as it does on the heels of that affirmation of the here and now, the only existence we have, that was first introduced in Elegies Six and Seven and then reinforced in the sixfold 'ein Mal' of Elegy Nine. Not only is Elegy Ten the longest; it introduces in its well over one hundred lines several seemingly disjunct sequences that only move towards a thematic resolution when we are fifty verses into the text. In its lament for the dead, but in the fierce prophetic indignation at the loss of touch with the culture of pain and bereftness and death, it has echoes of Elegy Five. As in Elegy Five, what makes Elegy Ten both difficult and at the same time moving, is this juxtaposition of disparate moods, encapsulated in a mythology that takes us from 'Klagen' to 'Leid-Stadt' to 'Ur-Leid' ('laments' to 'Grief

---

[1] Originally published in *Rilke's Duino Elegies. Cambridge Readings*, ed. by Roger Paulin and Peter Hutchinson (London: Duckworth; Riverside, CA: Ariadne, 1996), 171–91. All quotations from Rilke are taken from Rainer Maria Rilke, *Sämtliche Werke*, ed. by the Rilke Archive, Ruth Sieber-Rilke and Ernst Zinn, 5 vols (Frankfurt am Main: Insel, 1955–66), henceforth abbreviated as *SW*, with volume and page number; and Ulrich Fülleborn and Manfred Engel, *Materialien zu Rilkes Duineser Elegien*, 3 vols (Frankfurt am Main: Suhrkamp, 1980–82), henceforth abbreviated as *DE*, with volume and page number.

[2] See Rainer Maria Rilke, *Gedichte an die Nacht*, ed. by Anthony Stephens, Bibliothek Suhrkamp 519 (Frankfurt am Main: Suhrkamp, 1983).

© 2021 Roger Paulin, CC BY 4.0   https://doi.org/10.11647/OBP.0258.16

City' to 'primal suffering'). The tone ranges from Hölderlinian sonority to the occasional foreshadowing of *The Waste Land*. An analogy from the fine arts also springs to mind. In 1912, the year of the cycle's conception (and of the first fifteen verses of our elegy), an exhibition was held in Cologne by the Sonderbund,[3] of the most significant works of the modern art movements. The examples ranged from Pierre-Auguste Renoir and Claude Monet and Max Liebermann to Pablo Picasso and Georges Braque to Robert Delaunay and Gino Severini. Cheek by jowl, one saw traditions and positions confront and challenge each other. (Seeing the repeat exhibition in 1962 was one of my lasting formative experiences.) The analogy does not work entirely. At most it reminds us that while Rilke stands at the threshold of the most radical formal experiment the twentieth century has known, he also looks back to and is firmly rooted in traditions that inform and shape the nineteenth century (Rilke's angels, for instance,[4] also link him with that period). But he does bring home to us the essential and timeless link between poetry and myth, that is, saying in human terms the expressible about the ultimately inexpressible mysteries of life and death, and of the timeless role of the poet set aside to recount human response to those mysteries. In our poem, we have two magic plants, one at the beginning and one at the end. For where would the poetry of proclamation and of lament, such as this is, be without its priests and their arcana?

As I said, one might expect of this elegy some kind of summation, some statement of achievement, some climactic message or some conspectual view. This would be a fair expectation after what may have appeared to have been a cyclical motion through nine different phases and modes of experience, now to become ten. There are numerous hints in letters from the period in which the Elegies were taking shape, that the search for meaning in 'das Hiersein',[5] 'das Hiesige',[6] essential for the *Neue Gedichte/New Poems* and *Malte Laurids Brigge/The Notebooks of Malte Laurids Brigge*, had not been abandoned. As he writes in 1915 to Princess

---

[3] Cf. the catalogue *Europäische Kunst 1912. Zum 50. Jahrstag der Ausstellung des Sonderbundes westdeutscher Kunstfreunde und Künstler in Köln* (Cologne: Wallraf-Richartz Museum, 1962).

[4] Cf. *Engel. Texte aus der Weltliteratur*, ed. by Anne Marie Fröhlich, Manesse Bibliothek der Weltliteratur (Zurich: Manesse, 1991).

[5] 'Being here'. *DE*, I, 131.

[6] 'The here and now'. Ibid., 162.

16. Rilke: Duino Elegy Ten: In memoriam Leslie Seiffert, 1934–90

Marie von Thurn und Taxis, it is in the human that we find consolation. And to this end:

> es müßte nur unser Auge eine Spur schauender, unser Ohr empfangender sein, der Geschmack einer Frucht müßte uns vollständiger eingehen, wir müßten mehr Geruch aushalten, und im Berühren und Angerührtsein geistesgegenwärtiger und weniger vergeßllch sein-: um sofort aus unseren Erfahrungen Tröstungen aufzunehmen, die überzeugender, überwiegender, wahrer wären als alles Leid, das uns erschüttern kann.[7]

> only our eyes would need to be a shade more seeing, our ear more receptive, we ought to take in more fully the taste of a fruit, we ought to be more aware of our sense of smell, and in touching and being touched more sharp-witted and less forgetful: to gain from our experiences consolations straightway, that would be more convincing, all-encompassing and true than all the suffering that can shake and undermine us.

Yet the breaking off of the Elegies in 1912 and their resumption after not quite ten years, in 1921–22, tells us that this process of lyrical perception and apprehension is beset from the outset with doubts and velleities. The 'ineffable', the 'unspeakable', the 'un-sayable' in the realm of the angels, is overcome only gradually in the resigned contentment with relationships in the here and now, and in the resumption of poetic confidence that accompanies it.

Instead of looking for some kind of grand climax in Elegy Ten, we might reverse the process and note instead that the cycle is referential within itself in ways that make us read back and forward. We are always finding premonitions and preformulations of images and motifs that achieve their definitive utterance in one or more of the Elegies. Thus, the audience of the dead in Numbers Four and Five, 'die unendlich Toten', as our elegy (1. 105) will call them, beyond recall but ever-present around us, are a more accurate point of reference in Number Ten than the invocation at its opening of the angels. At most, that address will serve as a reminder that Elegy Ten owes its first fifteen verses to the initial burst of inspiration in Duino in 1912. And yet the elegy will take up, already in its second verse, what must be the central theme of grand poetry — and *stilus altus* this poetry is, make no mistake — that of singing: 'aufsingen' and 'zustimmen' (l.

---

7   Ibid., 129.

2). We have already had 'ansingen' in Elegy One. Now, 'aufsingen' and 'zustimmen' are what we do and what the angels do respectively. So, already in the first draft of 1912, as it were, Rilke had expressed the idea that, while we cannot have a dialogue with the absolute and the ineffable, we can have a kind of antiphonal song: we singing of our experience, they of theirs, not in an equal contest, of course, but in an awareness that we see what is visible, they all that is invisible. This notion, expressed in a late letter, we can apply by extension to the central image and theme of Elegy Ten: life and death. They represent two spheres of equal validity, the one merely the side of the other turned away from us for the moment, the one for the time being not cast in light ('des Lebens abgekehrte Hälfte').[8] And in the unity of life and death, in this awareness, the angels have their dwelling.

But how can we sing all of this? When Rilke had completed the Elegies, his immediate reaction was in the language of religious, even hieratic utterance: 'Aber nun ists. Ist. Ist. Amen',[9] 'sehr, sehr sehr herrlich. Wunder. Gnade'.[10] This biblical and almost liturgical language is both helpful and misleading. For we must not forget that the composition of the Elegies coincides with one of the greatest literary events of the early twentieth century: the first issue of the complete works of Friedrich Hölderlin, by Norbert von Hellingrath in 1912–14.[11] This suddenly made certain kinds of poetic diction problematic. It sat in judgment on the nineteenth, a century which had so often been satisfied with the epigonal and the nearly good. I believe that Rilke is momentarily caught up in this event. There are clear echoes of *Brod und Wein/Bread and Wine* in Elegy One (and elsewhere). The very adaptation of the elegiac couplet is part of this. So too the *kenosis*, the emptying of oneself in the service of speaking and being spoken through; but also the more than occasional and distinctly unnerving changes of tone from the gnomic to the rhetorically expansive that we know in Hellingrath's term, as applied to Hölderlin, as 'harte Fügung' ('stone on stone without mortar'). But Hölderlin and his models, Pindar, the Psalmist and the

---

8   *DE*, I, 283.
9   'But now it is come about. Amen'. Ibid., 236.
10 'Very, very, very wondrous. A sign. Grace'. Ibid., 237.
11 Friedrich Hölderlin, *Sämtliche Werke. Historisch-kritische Ausgabe*, ed. by Norbert von Hellingrath, Friedrich Seebass and Ludwig von Pigenot, 6 vols (Munich: G. Müller, 1913–23).

prophets, are inimitable: where Rilke in other poetry between 1912–14 does in fact slip into the Hölderlinan mode, the result is not good. For in the years 1912–22 there can be can no creating of a private mythology or religion, such as Hölderlin's was. True, the early twentieth century is littered with the wrecks of such attempts, but few read Alfred Mombert or Theodor Däubler or Rudolf Borchardt today. And so 'sehr, sehr sehr herrlich, Wunder. Gnade' is an expression also of the poet's humility at having succeeded in sustaining — even against the awesome presence of a Hölderlin — his own style and his own utterance.

As if to remind us that we are in the last statement of a cycle of elegies, Rilke in Number Ten unfolds the lexis of the elegiac: Harm, Schmerz, Leid, Klage, Ur-Leid, Zorn, Tränen, Wehmut, Trauer. The two key words of the poem seem to be 'Leid' and 'Klage': one the experienced feeling, the *dolor*, the pain and suffering at the ultimate loss in death; the other, again crucial for the poet, its utterance, its sound and articulation, the *planctus*, the lament. I would go so far as to say: the 'lamentation' for this elegy is also a 'Klagelied', Martin Luther's word for Jeremiah's complaint (and it is the same word that in German poetics was once used for the later term 'Elegie'). But while this elegy reproduces the cadences of the elegiac couplet, there is no anxious attempt (as in Seven) at metrical correctness, only the framework, structure or tone of elegiac utterance. Yet if this Elegy is one thing, it is certainly not a mere disquisition on the passing of all things. Its tone is not that of *Weltschmerz* ('melancholy'): we have left that ontological 'Katzenjammer' behind in the nineteenth century where it belongs. No, here Rilke attempts to see beyond loss and transience in order to perceive some sense, in a way to turn the tables on death (John Donne's 'for thou are not so', if you like, but not quite) and to integrate death into a scheme whose totality we mortals of course never grasp (the angels do) and whose two sides we cannot experience simultaneously.

Although it is fair to say that the theme of death is omnipresent in Rilke's oeuvre, it is also worthy of note that his thinking on the subject was intensified during the years of composition of the Elegies. It was his concern, as he expressed it in a letter of 1915, to see death as that which is experienced (that is, it happens to us all) and yet which in its reality cannot be experienced. We are always conscious of it, yet never really admit it, as 'das gefährliche Glas unseres Glücks, aus dem wir jeden

Augenblick können vergossen werden'.¹² For all that, as a later letter stresses, death is not a contrary principle. Its inner essence is in reality more conscious of life, 'lebenswissender',¹³ than our most vital moments of life. We must make it our task therefore to win death's confidence, to learn daily of it, through seizing, as Rilke says, the fruit of the here and now and biting into it.¹⁴ Indeed a letter of 1923 will state categorically that death is the ultimate affirmer ('Ja-Sager'), it alone says, 'Yes' to eternity: 'Er, der Tod (ich beschwöre Sie, es zu glauben!) ist der eigentliche Ja-Sager. Er sagt nur: Ja. Vor der Ewigkeit'.¹⁵ In Elegy Ten, Rilke the poet is placing himself in a new relationship to death, as life fades, and a newer, paradoxically brighter, existence seems to beckon (although that, too, is ultimately 'unsäglich'). In terms of his thanatology, however, he is also aligning himself with a strand that goes well back into the nineteenth century, say, to Ludwig Feuerbach, stating that my death is the fulfilment of all that I have lived for, all my human relationships are completed in it — for there is nothing beyond.¹⁶ More significantly, perhaps, Rilke associates himself with the Leo Tolstoy of *The Death of Ivan Ilyich*.¹⁷ There we read of a life of squalid untruth, of unreality, finding a final purpose as the man recognizes death to be no more than the voice that declares his life to have been untrue or unfulfilled. That voice ceases, is silent, is at an end, as physical life comes to an end. More tellingly, we think of Sigmund Freud's injunction of 1916, 'man muß an ihn [den Tod] glauben',¹⁸ or of Ludwig Wittgenstein's 'Bejahung des Todes',¹⁹ that 'affirmation of death' through which we both acknowledge and also overcome its pervasive influence on life.

---

12 'The perilous glass of our happiness from which we can be poured at any moment', *DE*, I, 135.
13 Ibid., 162.
14 'Die ergriffene und aufgebissene Frucht des Hiesigen', *DE*, I, 204.
15 Ibid., 284.
16 Ludwig Feuerbach, 'Todesgedanken', in *Sämmtliche Werke*, ed. by Wilhelm Bolin and Friedrich Jodl, 10 vols (Stuttgart: Frommann, 1903–11), I, 20. '[Der Tod] ist nur die Erscheinung des Actes des inneren Ablösens, Trennens und Scheidens, die Bewahrheitung Deiner Liebe, die Verkündigung, die Du während Deines ganzen Lebens im Stillen bethätigt hast, dass Du ohne und ausser dem geliebten Gegenstand Nichts bist'.
17 *DE*, I, 137.
18 'One has to believe in it'. Sigmund Freud, 'Unser Verhältnis zum Tode', in *Zeitgemäßes über Krieg und Tod, Studienausgabe*, ed. by Alexander Mitscherlich et al., 11 vols (Frankfurt am Main: Fischer, 1969–79), X, 344
19 Brian McGuinness, *Wittgenstein: A Life. Young Ludwig, 1889–1921* (London: Duckworth, 1988), 158.

16. Rilke: Duino Elegy Ten: In memoriam Leslie Seiffert, 1934–90

But these, necessarily sketchy, preliminaries will not take us further than the threshold of the poem. There needs to be one more preliminary, if the poem is not to withhold from us another dimension that is crucial for its understanding: the poem as myth. It is, as I stressed before, not a twentieth-century attempt at yet another private mythology, along the lines that Hölderlin had so wonderfully and tragically plotted a century before. Nor is it the renewal of myth in the way we see W. B. Yeats or T. S. Eliot or Ezra Pound doing, as say in the theme of poetic metamorphosis that Charles Tomlinson chose for the theme of his Clark Lectures some years ago.[20] Instead, Rilke is giving a mythopoeic dimension to the world of the heart, of human feeling (the angels escape the realm of human sensation and emotion) and then in the whole range of experiences of the human heart that are subsumed under the key words of the poem, 'Klage' and 'Leid'. It is not a world of cogent mythological equivalents, nor is it some kind of allegory where equivalents and correspondences slot neatly into place.[21] For all that, we enter into a world that has its own terms of reference, its own structures and hierarchies, its own beginning and its own end.

> DASS ich dereinst, an dem Ausgang der grimmigen Einsicht,
> Jubel und Ruhm aufsinge zustimmenden Engeln.
> Daß von den klar geschlagenen Hämmern des Herzens
> keiner versage an weichen, zweifelnden oder
> 5 reißenden Saiten. Daß mich mein strömendes Antlitz
> glänzender mache; daß das unscheinbare Weinen
> blühe. O wie werdet ihr dann, Nächte, mir lieb sein,
> gehärmte. Daß ich euch knieender nicht, untröstliche
>   Schwestern,
> hinnahm, nicht in euer gelöstes
> 10 Haar mich gelöster ergab. Wir, Vergeuder der Schmerzen.
> Wie wir sie absehn voraus, in die traurige Dauer,
> ob sie nicht enden vielleicht. Sie aber sind ja
> unser winterwähriges Laub, unser dunkeles Sinngrün,
> eine der Zeiten des heimlichen Jahres— , nicht nur
> 15 Zeit— , sind Stelle, Siedelung, Lager, Boden, Wohnort.

---

20 Charles Tomlinson, *Poetry and Metamorphosis* (Cambridge: Cambridge University Press, 1983).
21 *DE*, II, 251.

MAY the time come when, at the end of my terrible vision,
I raise up my song of praise and delight to the voice of the angels.
And may the clear blows from the heart's hammers
not strike dully on strings that are soft, doubting
5   or brittle. And may my tear-streaming cheeks
shine all the more brightly; and the weeping in secret
bloom. Oh how dear you will be to me then, you nights
of sorrow. Would I had knelt even lower, to accept you, disconsolate sisters,
given more of myself in touching
10 your hair that was untied in mourning. We, who are wastrels of sorrows.
We see them approach, into the endless sadness,
hoping perhaps they will end. But they are
our leaves through the winter, our dark green of remembrance,
one of the times of the inward year— not merely
15 time —, are our place, settlement, encampment, ground, habitation.

The poem opens with a fivefold repetition (ll. 1–6) of the word 'daß', suggesting in its optative 'may' or 'o that' the rhetorical structure of supplication or prayer or even of affirmation. We note, however, that they are all unfulfilled statements, the first four referring to future achievement, the fifth looking back to what was not done, and in its turn leading over to the *sententia* 'Wir, Vergeuder der Schmerzen' (l. 10), then the long and sustained poetic metaphor on the nature of those sorrows of which we are so prodigal. This by now familiar structure of 'if we were to', 'if we but could' forms a kind of prooemion or prologue that is echoed and perhaps answered by the final colophon of the poem ('But if they could [...] then this' ll. 107ff.), followed by the metaphor and the rounding-off statement of general application. Set in between these 'unfulfilled' sections are the sustained narrative, the mythopoeic passages that trace the transition from life to death, from the 'Leid-Stadt' to the 'Klage-Land' to the 'Berge des Ur-Leids'.

In this series of invocations or petitions, the poet begins with the awareness that perhaps only the moment of death, some day ('dereinst'), at the moment of full recognition (when he emerges from the 'grimmige Einsicht'), will be the fitting moment to sing the angels ('aufsingen'), receiving not only their nodding approval ('zustimmenden' — a double meaning in the German) but the harmony and concinnity, where poetic and angelic voice are part of the same process, 'auf-' *and* 'zu-', as one reaches out in song and the other picks up the theme of the other voice. Indeed, this image of singing is carried over to that of the hammers of the piano on the strings and becomes one of performance: may they all be tuned and taut. Song or melody leads over to weeping and the first indication that the act of singing or invoking is also a poetic act of charity. For the coming alive and affirmation of the nights of lamentation is a new awareness: human acts, as Elegy Seven reminded us, are not only worthy when they produce tower or pylon, but also the qualities of 'Innerlichkeit', mercy and pity. Thus, the grief-stricken nights (l. 8) of weeping become the first of those elegiac mythical creations: the sisters whom I did not (past tense now) recognize for what they were (did not kneel before, whose hair untied for the rite of mourning I did not touch), unaware as I was that 'Schmerz' is not only inextricably bound up with existence, but actually has substance, more substance perhaps than a life that is limited only by 'Glück'. That knowledge and consciousness is then transferred into a supremely beautiful poetic line: 'Sie aber sind ja / Unser winterwähriges Laub, unser dunkeles Sinngrün' (ll. 12–13). Here the metre and rhythm of a near-hexameter is utilized to bring out both the possessives 'unser' but also the images of evergreen growth — with a hidden touch in that 'Sinngrün' that needs a brief gloss. For one might read 'Sinngrün' as a bold compound metaphor, playing on 'Sinn' as sense, or even on the verb 'sinnen', contemplation or reflection. That association would be legitimate. Yet 'Sinngrün' or 'Singrün' (from 'sin-', long past, long ago) is the plant that in German is also called 'Wintergrün' or 'Immergrün', that grows on the graves of the dead — and in English is the humble periwinkle, vinca minor. It is also one of the magic plants that remind us of the primitive links between divination and poetry.[22] Not only that: grief and sorrow are part of the 'inner year' of human experience, that is 'heimlich' (l. 14), both familiar (related to 'homely') and secret or hidden. And from the botanical, Rilke switches images

---

22 *Handwörterbuch des deutschen Aberglaubens*, ed. by E. Hoffmann-Kray and Hanns Bächtold-Stäuble, 10 vols (Berlin and Leipzig: De Gruyter, 1927–42), IV, 673–76; Robert Graves, *The White Goddess. A Historical Grammar of Poetic Myth* (London: Faber, 1981), 323.

to ones (six in all) of human habitation, the 'Wohnort' (l. 15), the 'Sitz im Leben', where we dwell, keeping the double association that we have in English for the word 'dwell', for both the physical necessities of existence and for the inner life. Both 'Sinngrün' and 'Wohnort' are, metrically speaking, spondees, a feature of this elegy, with their equal stress on both syllables. In this they are quite different from the distichs of German classical verse, where the Greek or Latin spondee is normally rendered by a trochee. Thus, many of the key words of the poem, the most elegiac of the cycle, have a stately accentuation in both sense and sound ('Leid-Stadt', 'Leidland', 'Ur-Leid').

Freilich, wehe, wie fremd sind die Gassen der Leid-Stadt,
wo in der falschen, aus Übertönung gemachten
Stille, stark, aus der Gußform des Leeren der Ausguß
prahlt: der vergoldete Turm, das platzende Denkmal.
20 O, wie spurlos zerträte ein Engel ihnen der Trostmarkt,
den die Kirche begrenzt, ihre fertig gekaufte:
reinlich und zu und enttäuscht wie ein Postamt am Sonntag.
Draußen aber kräuseln sich immer die Ränder von Jahrmarkt.
Schaukeln der Freiheit! Taucher und Gaukler des Eifers!
25 Und des behübschten Glücks figürliche Schießstatt,
wo es zappelt von Ziel und sich blechern benimmt,
wenn ein Geschickterer trifft. Von Beifall zu Zufall
taumelt er weiter; denn Buden jeglicher Neugier
werben, trommeln und plärrn. Für Erwachsene aber
ist noch besonders zu sehn, wie das Geld sich vermehrt,
   anatomisch,
30 alles, das Ganze, der Vorgang —, das unterrichtet und macht
   fruchtbar ....

Alas, though, how alien the streets of Grief City,
where in the counterfeit silence, made of a surfeit of noise,
blatantly struts the form that is cast in the mould
of emptiness: the tinselly din, the statue burst open.
20 O, how an angel would trample to nothing their Cure-All Fair,
with the church hard by, the one bought to order:
tidy and shut and forlorn like the Post on a Sunday.
But outside curl around still the amusement park's edges.
Swings of Freedom! Acrobats of Enthusiasm!
25 And prettified happiness' shooting gallery, befigured,
targets all jostling, each jangling the other,

>   when a good marksman scores. From claps to chance-taking
>   on his way he lurches; for sideshows are there for the curious.
>   their barkers hailing and drumming. Adults Only!
> 30 Special attraction! The reproduction of money (anatomical details),
>   not just for amusement: money's organs of gender;
>   the whole lot, nothing left out—, what they get up to — a lesson and.
>   brings you results ....

The poem now breaks off abruptly from the fifteen verses that came to Rilke in 1912. He had drafted quite a different continuation in 1913,[23] with a sustained nature image following on from 'winterwähriges Laubwerk' (the 1913 variant of 'Sinngrün'). In 1922, however, nature was first to be alienated before being given a function in the wider scheme of the poem. That disjunction comes also in the marked and sudden incongruity of 'alas, though', the fairly colloquial 'Freilich' (l. 16) and the high-style 'wehe', the elegiac word that runs through the whole cycle. From nature's cycle, and a secure place of dwelling, we move to the 'Leid-Stadt', where there is no dwelling-place, and a long, sustained catalogue of all that is cheap and counterfeit and vulgar. This city of grief, this Pandaemonium, has two aspects. First, there is a section where the very strident awfulness produces a paradoxical kind of silence, a failure to say ('aus Übertönung gemachte Stille', l. 17f.), where words like 'Lärm', 'prahlt' and 'vergoldet' set the tone. Note 'der vergoldete Lärm', like 'sich blechern benimmt' lower down, with their bold transference of senses, as if the poet in his outrage cannot find the connecting links of meaning. Is it a real city, like one of those 'Plätze in Paris' from Elegy Five where Madame Lamort holds sway? Certainly the drumming and general commotion is the same. Or is it, as some commentators have suggested (Hans-Georg Gadamer, Romano Guardini), actually the city graveyard, the necropolis, with its false pomp, a living proof of how outwardness has triumphed over inwardness, of how even the church — in Rilke's fierce joke ('wie ein Postamt am Sonntag') — forms one of the sides of the 'Trostmarkt' (l. 20) and is thus taken over by commerce and brokerage. The angels — the last time, incidentally, that we encounter them in the cycle and here in a kind of apocalyptic or

---

23   DE, I, 90f., SW, III, 64ff.

eschatological role — not knowing any distinction between the inner and the outer life, would crush this under foot, without trace, recalling Expressionist images like Ludwig Meidner's imploding cities or Georg Heym's visions of destruction. But already we hear the sounds of 'roll up, all the fun of the fair!' In Elegy Nine, human achievement was measured in terms of the craftsman's art. Here, everything is dominated by frauds, mountebanks and hucksters. Rilke's Vanity Fair takes us from sideshows of 'Freedom!' to 'Enthusiasm!' to 'Happiness!' The images become jangled and kaleidoscopically jumbled as the things to be won in the shooting-galleries, and the shooters themselves, change sides, as it were (the jumping for joy of the marksman is transferred to the targets and prizes themselves). But, 'you haven't seen anything yet'. Adults Only, anatomical waxwork displays that lay bare, with the lovelessness of the sexologist's manual, the sex act of money, money — that makes this world go round. If, as I suggested, this prophetic wrath reminds us of the Expressionists' visions of destruction, their clean sweep through material values, it is also where Rilke comes closest to *The Waste Land*. Yet we should not forget that all along, he has not abandoned his approximation to classical elegiac verse, and in l. 34 that tone begins to reassert itself.

....Oh aber gleich darüber hinaus,
35   hinter der letzten Planke, beklebt mit Plakaten des "Todlos",
jenes bitteren Biers, das den Trinkenden süß scheint,
wenn sie immer dazu frische Zerstreuungen kaun...,
gleich im Rücken der Planke, gleich dahinter, ists *wirklich*.
Kinder spielen, und Liebende halten einander, — abseits,
40   ernst, im ärmlichen Gras, und Hunde haben Natur.
Weiter noch zieht es den Jüngling; vielleicht, daß er eine junge
Klage liebt..... Hinter ihr her kommt er in Wiesen. Sie sagt:
Weit. Wir wohnen dort draußen.....
Wo? Und der Jüngling
45   folgt. Ihn rührt ihre Haltung. Die Schulter, der Hals —,
           vielleicht
ist sie von herrlicher Herkunft. Aber er läßt sie, kehrt um,
wendet sich, winkt... Was solls? Sie ist eine Klage.

....O but further beyond,
35   past the last billboards, stuck over with posters for 'Deathless',
that bitter beer that seems sweet to the drinkers

16. Rilke: Duino Elegy Ten: In memoriam Leslie Seiffert, 1934–90   325

> only as long as they chew fresh distractions to go with it....
> Past the boards, just beyond, there, things are real.
> Children are playing, lovers embracing, — away from the
> others,
> 40 pensive, on a few blades of grass, and dogs — do as dogs do.
> The boy is drawn further on; perhaps he's in love with a young
> Lament. And he follows after her over the meadows. She says:
> Far. We live away out there.
> Where? And the boy
> 45 follows, touched by her walk, her shoulder, her neck , perhaps
> she's of noble descent. But he leaves her, turns round,
> about once again, waves ... What's the point? She's a Lament.

But ('Oh, aber'), outside, beyond the last paling fence, there is the first vestige of reality ('*wirklich*', Rilke's italics). Note the fences plastered with advertisements for that 'unreal' ale 'Todlos' (l. 35), for the denial of death is, in the terms of this Elegy, a denial of any meaningful existence. But how real, despite the underlining of 'wirklich', is this bleak space outside the city? At most we could say that here there is some freedom — for children, lovers and dogs — some demonstration of feeling, but it isn't much. But it is also a final glance, almost over our shoulders, at three of the important strands and symbolic figures in the landscape of the whole cycle: children, imperilled in their innocence by death; lovers, who so seldom achieve a true meeting of souls; and animals, who do not share our sense of death.

Although there is no break in the poetry, in that Rilke does not introduce a space such as he will do later on, the poetry now enters a new sphere. It leaves for good that world where all is counterfeit or half-fulfilled. But before we enter into the new realm, we the readers should not forget with what poetic virtuosity Rilke has castigated that false and tinselly world, keeping a kind of prophetic anger sustained in the long near-distichs and displaying his full powers of virtuosity in the images of city and funfair. This is one side of the lament that this poem entails, the lamentation over the great city.

But now we have '*den* Jüngling' (my italics), unprepared, presumably one of the young people or lovers, for whom the few blades of grass provided a place for their feelings. As in the great set-piece dream sequences in Romantic novels (and as in dreams themselves), the transition into another sphere of consciousness is imperceptible. It would seem that the realm of 'Klage' is but an extension of the so-called 'real' world. We must forget the reminiscences of Homer or Virgil or Dante — or even of Rilke's two great poems 'Orpheus. Eurydice. Hermes' and 'Alkestis'. For here there is no descent into the shades, no passing through waters. And yet for all that we seem to be in some kind of transitional realm between the city of suffering and the finality of death. Here live 'Klagen', the expression and manifestation of pain both suffered and articulated. But in this space, their country, there is paradoxically more light and beauty than in the city that has been left behind. The boy, who follows the 'Klage', is presumably still alive, not yet ready to reflect on the ultimate futility of existence in the 'Leid-Stadt', and certainly not yet ready to engage in a dialogue. He turns back ('Was solls').

> Nur die jungen Toten, im ersten Zustand
> zeitlosen Gleichmuts, dem der Entwöhnung,
> 50 folgen ihr liebend. Mädchen
> wartet sie ab und befreundet sie. Zeigt ihnen leise,
> was sie an sich hat. Perlen des Leids und die feinen
> Schleier der Duldung. — Mit Jünglingen geht sie
> schweigend.

> Only the young dead, unheeding,
> untouched by time, taking slow leave of life,
> 50 follow her, loving. The girls
> she waits for and offers them friendship. Shows them gently
> what she is wearing. Pearls of Sorrow and the fine-woven
> veils of Forbearance. — With boys she walks
> in silence alongside them.

Only the young dead have this capacity, as they start their journey towards the land of silence. We have to ask ourselves a question at the outset of this journey. Leaving aside any notion of allegory: is 'Klage', the articulation of grief, its poetic expression even, that which accompanies the dead until they are, in the real sense, fully dead? For at the end of the journey there can be no sound, all is 'tonlos' (l. 106). The passage from life to death is made clear by the words 'ersten Zustand' and 'Entwöhnung' (l. 47f.): the Lament instructs and takes under her wing the young dead and shows them things that life knew little of, 'Duldung und Leid' (l. 49f.) as garments of beauty. We note in passing that it is the young maidens among the dead who are initiated into these secrets, an extension of those 'Früheentrückten' ('who have died too soon') of Elegy One who no longer need us, the living. But it is in fact the boy who is led by an older Lament into the land of the dead. She tells him — and us — of the landscape and history, the reality of expressed suffering, in a sequence of poetry that, appropriately, is remarkable for its expansion of line and its sonority and dignity.

> 55 Aber dort, wo sie wohnen, im Tal, der Älteren eine, der Klagen,
> nimmt sich des Jünglinges an, wenn er fragt:— Wir waren,
> sagt sie, ein Großes Geschlecht, einmal, wir Klagen. Die Väter
> trieben den Bergbau dort in dem großen Gebirg; bei Menschen
> findest du manchmal ein Stück geschliffenes Ur-Leid
> 60 oder, aus altem Vulkan, schlackig versteinerten Zorn.
> Ja, das stammte von dort. Einst waren wir reich. —

> 55 But there, where they live, in the valley, one of the older Laments
> answers kindly the boy as he asks: —We were,
> she says, a Mighty Nation, once, we Laments. Our fathers
> dug out the mines there in the high range of mountains; men
> sometimes will show you an ancient fragment of Suffering, polished,
> 60 or, out of a crater, Wrath, molten, rock-hardened.
> Yes, we took it from there. Once we were rich. —

This world of the Laments we must sketch briefly. It is a real and also a mythical landscape. It reflects a hierarchical order in the affairs of men and in nature, where all the elements shown and explained to the boy are extensions of the rites surrounding the dead. These are the Laments that were once part of the rites of passage and departure. Rilke describes them in his *Requiem. Für eine Freundin/Requiem for a Lady Friend* (1908) as 'Klagefrauen', whose duty is 'Klagen nachholen',[24] serving the function we know in all cultures, from the Celts to the Polynesians, to keen the dirges in the elaborate and circumstantial channelling of grief into an accessible ritual. This, as the older 'Klage' explains, was what once ruled

---

24 'Lamenting women'; 'catching up the laments'. SW, I, 653.

this country: 'Wir waren, / sagt sie, ein Großes Geschlecht, einmal, wir Klagen'. Where once there was delving and digging of the passions, the bringing up out of the depths of 'Ur-Leid' and 'Zorn' — those familiar with German Romanticism will recognize the potent symbols of mining as self-discovery[25] — we have archaeology. Now, there are just a few pyroclastic fragments, and silence (the loss of that 'aufsingen' in lament).

> Und sie leitet ihn leicht durch die weite Landschaft der Klagen,
> zeigt ihm die Säulen der Tempel oder die Trümmer
> jener Burgen, von wo Klage-Fürsten das Land
> 65 einstens weise beherrscht. Zeigt ihm die hohen
> Tränenbäume und Felder blühender Wehmut,
> (Lebendige kennen sie nur als sanftes Blattwerk);
> zeigt ihm die Tiere der Trauer, weidend, — und manchmal
> schreckt ein Vogel und zieht, flach ihnen fliegend durchs Aufschaun,
> 70 weithin das schriftliche Bild seines vereinsamten Schreis. —
> Abends führt sie ihn hin zu den Gräbern der Alten
> aus dem Klage-Geschlecht, den Sibyllen und Warn-Herrn.
> Naht aber Nacht, so wandeln sie leiser, und bald
> mondets empor, das über Alles
> 75 wachende Grab-Mal. Brüderlich jenem am Nil,
> der erhabene Sphinx — : der verschwiegenen Kammer Antlitz.
> Und sie staunen dem krönlichen Haupt, das für immer,
> schweigend, der Menschen Gesicht
> 80 auf die Waage der Sterne gelegt.

> And with ease she guides him through the Laments' wide expanses,
> shows him the columns of temples or the ruins of
> fortresses, where the Laments' princes
> 65 once held wise sway. Shows him the tall

---

25 Theodore Ziolkowski, *German Romanticism and Its Institutions* (Princeton: Princeton University Press, 1990), 18–63. Since I first wrote this article, my friend and colleague Patrick Boyde (who discussed Elegy Four in the volume from which this essay is taken) has drawn my attention to Rilke's enthusiastic reading of the *Gilgamesh* epic during the crucial years before the completion of the Elegies. The phrase 'geschliffendes Urleid' reminds us of the journey from life to an understanding of death, which is common to both works, 'Urleid' summoning up the universal grief that they also share.

>   tear-trees and fields of Doleful in blossom
>   (known to the living only when it's still in first leaf);
>   shows him the creatures of sadness, grazing — sometimes
>   a bird starts, and unfolds, flying low as they gaze upwards,
> 70   the pattern of letters made by her cry in the loneness .
>   At evening she leads him to the tombs of the patriarchs
>   of the race of Laments, the sybils and sages.
>   At nightfall their footstep is softer, and shortly,
>   bright as the moonlight, looms up
> 75   the tomb standing watch over all,
>   brother to that on the Nile, the lofty Sphinx:
>   face of the chamber hidden in silence.
>   And they take in with wonder the regal-crowned head, that
>   forever,
>   not speaking, laid the face of man
> 80   on the scales of the stars.

But the landscape also informs of a once wise order and rule — 'einstens' (l. 65) — now represented by a kind of Baalbek or Palmyra. The land itself, is, however, still fertile with plants and herds, unlike the counterfeit and sterile 'Trostmarkt' and 'Leid-Stadt' that now seems so far behind. Note that 'Wehmut' — I have rendered it as Doleful — thrives here and flowers; here the evergreen, the symbol and emblem of mourning, actually bursts into flower. We hear, too, from l. 62 onwards, how the verse sustains this account by assonating the many 'ei-' sounds: 'Und sie l*ei*tet ihn l*ei*cht durch die w*ei*te Landschaft der Klagen', '*ei*nstens w*ei*se beherrscht', 'Z*ei*gt ihm die hohen'.

Two words stand out in the account that follows: 'Aufschaun' (l. 69) and 'Schaun' (l. 82). They, and the word 'zeigen' (ll. 62, 64) that recurs in the poem's colophon (l. 107), indicate a strand of seeing and showing and signifying and indicating that is part of the elegiac process, part of the 'aufsingen'. But it is also the sign of a set of extraordinary poetic images that signify not just the poetic way of seeing, but the enhanced vision that is granted to the dead and which (in the final image of the poem), were they able, they would grant to us. Thus the bird (l. 68f.) that suddenly starts up before our eyes transfers the sound of its cry to a set of written characters; the optical and the aural are no longer in separate compartments of perception. So, too, with the image of the sphinx (l. 76f.) and the owl.

We have one or two details to clear up before we attempt that image. It is night (note that wonderful 'mondets empor', l. 73); we are led down to the figures of the doubly dead, who are dead in the realm of death and exist only as monuments — to the dead. It isn't Egypt, but clearly we are in a valley of tombs where a culture similar to Egypt's once held sway,[26] and we remember that no other culture gives death a greater significance in its cosmogony. From now on, only the moon and the stars shine down on the land of the dead. The bold verb 'mondets empor' expresses the effect of seeing the most majestic death monument of all, in the moonlight: the sphinx — 'erhaben', 'krönlich', the lord of all in this land, where 'Klage' has its supreme place in the hierarchy of emotions. The sphinx contains a burial chamber which is hidden and inaccessible but which through 'Schaun' can be seen on the face of the sphinx, and that face, expressing human features, has taken on such a significance that it has, in Rilke's image (l. 77f), been placed on the balances of the stars (a double meaning, 'Waage' denoting a pair of scales and also Libra), has become like Orion or Castor and Pollux, a named constellation. And the scales of the stars might be taken to signify the equipoise and harmony between life and death that is achieved in this sphere between the two states.

>   Nicht erfaßt es sein Blick, im Frühtod
>   schwindelnd. Aber ihr Schaun,
>   hinter dem Pschent-Rand hervor, scheucht es die Eule. Und
>   sie,
>   streifend im langsamen Abstrich die Wange entlang,
>   85 jene der reifesten Rundung,
>   zeichnet weich in das neue
>   Totengehör, über ein doppelt
>   aufgeschlagenes Blatt, den unbeschreiblichen Umriß.

>   His gaze cannot grasp it, so early dead,
>   unsteady. But their beholding,
>   over the top of the diadem, scares out the owl. It,
>   slow in its flying, barely touching the cheek,
>   85 where it rounds at its fullest,
>   softly it draws into the new

---

26 DE, I, 322.

> dead's hearing, on both halves of the paper,
> folded in two, the outline that hand cannot trace.

The boy, newly dead, cannot take in the awesomeness of this monument. But 'ihr Schaun' (her looking, or their looking — it could be both, l. 82) brings out from behind the 'Pschent' — a grandly exotic word for the crown of Upper and Lower Egypt — an owl. Rilke in 1911, lying in the moonlight in front of the sphinx, had seen just this.[27] The newly dead — and by implication we who mourn the young dead — need some idea of the dimension of this state, through 'Schaun'. The owl flies along the cheek of the sphinx, the finest contour ('die reifeste Rundung') into which the human face has been formed; it traces in the ear of the dead that contour, records it acoustically 'über ein doppelt aufgeschlagenes Blatt' (l. 87). As if taking a sheet of paper and folding it double to indicate the two sides, the owl, non-articulate, but tracing with its wing, and the ear, receiving the written character with the new 'Totengehör' (l. 87), make clear that our senses in death extend beyond any earthly physical capacity.

>   Und höher, die Sterne. Neue. Die Sterne des Leidlands.
> 90 Langsam nennt sie die Klage: — Hier,
> siehe: den **Reiter**, den **Stab**, und das vollere Sternbild
> nennen sie: **Fruchtkranz**. Dann, weiter, dem Pol zu:
> **Wiege**; **Weg**; Das **Brennende Buch**; **Puppe**; **Fenster**.
> Aber im südlichen Himmel, rein wie im Innern
> 95 einer gesegneten Hand, das klar erglänzende "**M**",
> das die Mütter bedeutet...... —
>
> Doch der Tote muß fort, und schweigend bringt ihn die älltere
> Klage bis an die Talschlucht,
> wo es schimmert im Mondschein:
> 100 die Quelle der Freude. In Ehrfurcht
> nennt sie sie, sagt: — Bei den Menschen
> ist sie ein tragender Strom. —

>   And higher, the stars. New ones. The stars of the Land of
>   Suffering.
> 90 The Lament names them slowly: — Here,

---

27 *DE*, I, 97.

>   behold: the **Rider**, the **Staff**, and the cluster of stars
>   they call **Garland of Fruits**. Then further on, nearer the Pole:
>   **Cradle; Path; The Burning Book; Puppet,· Window.**
>   But in the southern skies, pure like the palm of a
> 95   hand that is blessed, '**M**' burning clearly and brightly,
>   standing for Mothers...... —
>
>   But the dead boy must depart, and in silence the older
>   Lament brings him as far as the gorge of the valley,
>   where there gleams in the moonlight
> 100   the spring of joy. In hushed tone
>   she names it and says: — Among men
>   it is a mighty river. —

And so the Lament now shows the boy the constellations in the heavens. They are all to be taken as symbols of different processes of transition ('Wiege', 'Weg', 'Stab', 'Reiter') or of fruition and achievement ('Fruchtkranz'), of vision beyond oneself ('Fenster'), of hope and renewal ('Puppe', both in the sense of Elegy Four and in the meaning of chrysalis). Horses and riders in the stars fascinated him in other contexts ('Heißt kein Stembild "Reiter?"', 'Is there no star called Rider?' ask the *Sonette an Orpheus* I, xi, and a late poem of 1924 likens falling stars to horses).[28] The burning book might seem to be the poetic icon, in the German one letter away from the burning bush ('not consumed'), giving light and being incandescent in itself. Rilke is, of course, playing on existing names of constellations, like 'Puppis', or stars, like 'Vega' ('Wega' in German), adding a few of his own, equally concrete and exotic. They culminate in that '*M*', lighting up the whole of the southern sky (Job's 'chambers of the south', 9:9; the 'W' of Cassiopeia upside down), a good luck sign in palmistry, but reminding us that mothers, in the terms of these elegies (especially Elegy Six), are also destined to lose what they have borne. Speech now has no further function — 'schweigend' l. 96 — as the Lament brings the boy through the last stages of his journey towards silence. She has imparted her wisdom to him — and in a sense the poet, through the poetic act, is imparting it to those who mourn the young dead. The mourning learn that the dead have the 'sense' of their dying explained to them in the wisdom of the 'Klagekulturen' that are

---

28 *SW*, I, 737

unfolded before them (not, we note, through a theogony that makes of death a mystery or a terror). The 'Quelle der Freude' (l. 99) suggests perhaps that there is an inner link between grief and joy; it is that which may spring up again in those who are left behind 'bei den Menschen' (l. 100) in mourning.

> Stehn am Fuß des Gebirgs.
> Und da umarmt sie ihn, weinend.
> 105 Einsam steigt er dahin, in die Berge des Ur-Leids.
> Und nicht einmal sein Schritt klingt aus dem tonlosen Los.
>   *

> They halt at the foot of the mountains.
> And there she embraces him, weeping.
> 105 Alone he makes his way up into the mountains of
>   Once-Suffering.
> Not even the ring of his steps is heard, his lot is silence.
>   *

The poetry becomes more laconic and poignant as the language of lament gives way to silence: 'stehn am Fuß des Gebirgs' (l. 103), 'da umarmt sie ihn' (l. 104), 'Einsam steigt er dahin' (l. 105). We learn nothing of the nature of the 'Ur-Leid' (l. 105); only he will experience that in the loneliness of death. He is no longer accessible to lament or even language. When laments are silent, when the 'Klage' is no longer with the young dead, he is dead in the sense that he belongs to those whose loss we can now bear, or to those who we know are in the land of silence and forgetfulness ('das tonlose Los', l. 105).

> Aber erweckten sie uns, die unendlich Toten, ein Gleichnis,
> siehe, sie zeigten vielleicht auf die Kätzchen der leeren
> Hasel, die hängenden, oder
> 110 meinten den Regen, der fällt auf dunkles Erdreich im
>   Frühjahr. —
>
> Und wir, die an **steigendes** Glück
> denken, empfänden die Rührung,
> die uns beinah bestürzt,
> wenn ein Glückliches **fällt**.

> But were they to waken for us, the endlessly dead, a symbol,
> behold, they would point to the catkins on the bare
> hazel, hanging downwards, or
> 110 have us believe in the rain that falls on the dark soil in
> springtime. —
>
> And we, who think of happiness
> **rising**, our hearts would be moved
> more than perhaps we could bear,
> when a happy thing **falls**.

There Rilke will not leave us, in total silence, with no words, no sound. We come back to that 'would that', 'would but' of the elegy's opening that told us what, but for our inadequacy, would be the true purpose and function of the poetic act. They, 'die unendlich Toten' (l. 107), are beyond articulation, but were they able, they would give us this likeness. It is a double image, one of the hanging catkins on the hazel bush, and of the spring rain on the ground ('Erdreich', l. 110, suggesting perhaps already dug for cultivation). Rilke was not always secure in his botany, despite the many flower and plant images in his poetry, not least in this cycle. The conceit of the fig tree in Elegy Six is not encouraging. In fact, Rilke originally wanted the willow catkin to express the image of hanging and falling,[29] but, as anyone knows, it does not hang down. The alteration is significant, not just for getting the facts right, but for assuring the integrity of the text, for the 'Ding' must be congruent if it is also to be charged with meaning. Botany aside, and Rilke's intention with the image aside, we note that he has chanced on an image that may go beyond his original first association: the hanging catkins of the male flower. But then it is unlikely that he 'chanced' on anything. These flowers are in themselves not fertile, they cannot produce fruit on their own, but they are the promise of it. Similarly, the rain is not the fertility itself, but it brings about the process of fruition and plenitude. Was he thinking of the hazel's other associations, as one of the first of the bushes of the hedgerows to show blossom? It is a magic plant,[30] revered in many religions, but notably the Germanic, and for that reason it is the twig used for the water-diviner's rod. The German for that rod is

---

29 *DE*, I, 269.
30 *Handwörterbuch des deutschen Aberglaubens*, III, 1527–42.

'Wünschelrute', itself the title of one of the shortest, but most telling poems in the language, informing of the power of poetry to open up the secrets of the things around us, 'die Dinge'. It is Eichendorff's little poem:

> Schläft ein Lied in allen Dingen,
> Die da träumen fort und fort,
> Und die Welt hebt an zu singen,
> Triffst du nur das Zauberwort.[31]

> There sleeps a song in all the things
> Dreaming on and on,
> And the world begins its singing
> If you touch the magic word.

The catkin and the rain, which fall, are the symbols of this final colophon of verses. But does not hope *spring* eternal in the human breast; does not our heart *leap* up when we behold; and is this poem not prefaced with the poet's action upwards in that verb 'aufsingen'? No, we experience 'Rührung' (l. 113), implying being touched by the emotions — to our surprise ('Bestürzung', l. 114) — when hopes of happiness are dashed, when, in the terms of the poem, a young life is unfulfilled; but we come by the same token to the realisation that the so-called unfulfilled life may have its own happiness. That is perhaps one aspect. The other is the awareness that the sadness produced by falling is overcome in the hope of life that emerges from it. Rilke himself claimed that this should not be taken to imply a cyclical movement, some kind of mere biological organic process;[32] instead, the gesture of falling in itself brings happiness. We might, however, feel justified in setting his view aside. There is the evidence of another poem; from the year 1922, with the same imagery, where rain and earth, respectively, represent the processes of death and mourning.[33] And the Elegies urge us to a resolution by the very fact of

---

31   Joseph von Eichendorff, *Neue Gesamtausgabe der Werke und Schriften*, ed. by Gerhard Baumann and Siegfried Grosse, 4 vols (Stuttgart: Cotta, 1957), I, 112.
32   According to Katharina Kippenberg, *Rainer Maria Rilke, Duineser Elegien. Die Sonette an Orpheus*, Manesse Bibliothek der Weltliteratur (Zurich: Manesse, 1951), 172. Thus, Rilke would seem to stand in marked contrast to the thinking of Wilhelm Fliess, with whose views on life and death he was familiar (*DE*, I, 137f.). Cf. 'Der Tod schafft nach einer bewundernswürdigen Ordnung Raum für das erwachende Leben'. Wilhelm Fliess, *Vom Leben und vom Tod. Biologische Vorträge* (Jena: Diederichs, 1924), 93.
33   *DE*, I, 218.

their being a cycle, but not to any easy or mundane conclusion, neatly tied up and of an easy consistency for all readers. Instead, there is the awareness that poetry mediates, but in an interreaction of language and symbol that is never direct. We search therefore for indications of resolution, perhaps in terms of that 'Quelle der Freude' (l. 100) that the Lament mentions in awe ('in Ehrfurcht'). But it can be no coincidence that both the poem and the whole cycle end on the word *'fällt'* (Rilke's italics). The elegiac verse can also be read in a way that is different from the printed image, where the lines tail off into a colophon (and a colophon was originally the printer's signature; here it is the poet's). Run the third-last and the fourth-last lines together and the last two, and you will find a couplet that bears some resemblance to the elegiac distich (it's actually closer to two pentameters). Any correctly turned distich will end on a strong beat — it has to — but only the great elegy will end on a strong beat and a word that sums up the whole of what has gone before. Hölderlin's 'Brod und Wein', that some might see as the very greatest elegy in the language, does it with the final word 'schläft'. Rilke's, certainly one of the greatest, achieves it with the word 'fällt'.

BOOKS

Fig. 27 Bust of Julius Hare by Thomas Woolner (1861). The Wren Library, Trinity College, Cambridge. Photo by James Kirwan. Courtesy of the Master and Fellows of Trinity College.

17. Julius Hare's German Books in Trinity College Library, Cambridge[1]

I begin this chapter with a personal reminiscence. In the spring of 1973, Trinity College, Cambridge, anxious to find a lecturer in German, took the (for Trinity, at least) unusual step of advertising for suitable candidates and interviewing them, myself included. With time on my hands before the interview, I decided to examine the German holdings in the College library. Somewhat awed by my surroundings, I proceeded to scrutinize the catalogue entries. Beginning with Johann Wolfgang Goethe, I noted the *Ausgabe letzter Hand*, not a bad start, but became increasingly surprised to find items like *Kunst und Altertum* and various biographical works or collections of letters, such as Johann Peter Eckermann, Friedrich Wilhelm Riemer or even Bettina von Arnim's preposterous *Goethes Briefwechsel mit einem Kinde/Goethe's Correspondence with a Child* — all in

---

1   This chapter was originally published in *Transactions of the Cambridge Bibliographical Society* 9 (1987), 174–93. Since I wrote this essay, the situation in Cambridge regarding rare German holdings mainly from the Romantic period has changed considerably. The Renouf Collection in Newnham College has been catalogued and made available for scholars. Largely consisting of material relevant to Clemens Brentano and his family, and far less extensive than Hare's collection, it nevertheless has important overlaps with Hare and also some significant extensions. In addition, the Crewe Collection of rare books and manuscripts, in Trinity College since 2016, contains a small but important number of German items. Whereas in my original version of 1987 I checked titles against the British Library Catalogue and the National Union Catalog, I have now been able to update information on Hare's collection from COPAC (which has since been replaced by Jisc Library Hub Discover) and WorldCat. I have, however, on occasions noted that neither online source has complete coverage of Hare's titles. My information on comparative holdings in the UK and elsewhere does not include electronic resources and is restricted to actual original printed copies (not reprints).

first edition. Encouraged by this unexpected find, I proceeded to look up Ludwig Tieck, on whose biography I was then working. Again, a massive entry, with about one third of his works — in first edition. No collection in Britain outside the British Library seemed likely to possess such holdings. I tried other German Romantics — the Schlegel brothers, Clemens Brentano, Achim von Arnim, E. T. A. Hoffmann — with similar results. I was informed that most of the books formed part of the 'Hare collection'. There was no time for more details; my interview was imminent. Whether the hope some day of being allowed to use the said Hare collection gave me utterance during the proceedings that followed, I cannot say. I was appointed, I did use the books extensively, and have recorded my debt elsewhere.[2] It is only now, however, that I come to substantiate it in a more systematic form.

The name of Julius Charles Hare (1795–1855) is not unknown to students of English intellectual history of the 1820s, to classical scholars, to historians of the early Victorian church, and to readers of his nephew Augustus J. C. Hare's highly interesting and respectful *Memorials of a Quiet Life* and his distinctly iconoclastic *The Story of My Life*. N. Merrill Distad's biography of Hare, *Guessing at Truth* (1979),[3] adapts the title of Hare's best-known work, written together with his brother Augustus, *Guesses at Truth* (1827). There is a singular appropriateness in this use of title; for *Guesses at Truth*, a miscellany of essays and aphorisms, Coleridgean in sweep yet acknowledging a 'self-controul'[4] that, Hare claimed, the older man lacked, is a work which displays the very considerable range of intellectual competence on which Hare could draw.

In one of his many disrespectful asides concerning his stern and forbidding uncle, Julius, Augustus J. C. Hare claimed that Hare had paid homage to 'five popes':[5] William Wordsworth, Barthold Georg Niebuhr, Karl Josias von Bunsen, Frederick Maurice and Henry Edward Manning. If this were true, the list displayed a considerable eclecticism, indeed it might be difficult to reconcile these five several pontifical claims. The task is less problematic than it may seem: Maurice, Hare's brother-in-law, represents the claims of the Broad Church to which Hare adhered, he never concealing the pain which the Tractarian movement and, most acutely, Manning's defection caused him; Wordsworth (one could also say Samuel Taylor Coleridge) stands for the high moral and intellectual

---

2 Roger Paulin, *Ludwig Tieck: A Literary Biography* (Oxford: Clarendon, 1985), viii.

claims of the English Romantics, best displayed in Wordsworth's reflective poetry; with Bunsen and Niebuhr, we come closer to our real object of concern: Germany.

The circle around Baron Bunsen in Rome and London represented a world of political conservatism, religious tolerance, and theological liberalism both for the young Hare and for the later archdeacon of Lewes. It is fair to say that Bunsen, who combined scholarship and piety with all the advantages of the *grand monde,* mediated to Hare in person what a much greater and more influential figure could only pass on through the printed word: Friedrich Schleiermacher. Schleiermacher had been the particular province of Hare's friend and Trinity contemporary, Connop Thirlwall, his first translator into English. With Thirlwall, Hare had translated Niebuhr's *History of Rome.* That translation, its first two volumes appearing in 1828–32, was a token of Hare's commitment to the new German school of classical scholarship, indeed it has been claimed that Hare's German leanings may well have been the reason for his having been passed over for the Regius Chair of Greek in Cambridge in 1825.[6]

Hare's love of Germany and its literature and culture was fostered at an early age. He had been with his parents when they spent some time in Weimar at Duke Carl August's court in 1804–05; it was the year of Friedrich Schiller's death; they had met Goethe.[7] If Julius Hare, on his return to England, had needed encouragement in the study of languages and philology, he had only to reflect that his mother's sister had been married to none other than Sir William Jones. Yet the Germans had a place second to none in Hare's intellectual affections. Coleridge and Thomas Carlyle made similar claims; but their own creative powers meant that they drew on things German as and when it suited. Hare, on the other hand, was indebted to German 'Wissenschaft' as a scholarly principle. It is interesting to note him writing in 1820 of the brothers August Wilhelm and Friedrich Schlegel as having raised the art of criticism 'to the dignity of a scientific art'.[8] We perceive Hare's difficulties with the German word 'wissenschaftlich', which his friend and contemporary William Whewell was also to render as 'scientific'. Behind

---

7 According to Augustus J. C. Hare, *Memorials of a Quiet Life*, 3 vols (London: Smith Elder, 1884), I, 191.
8 *Olliers Literary Miscellany*, 4.

it all is, however, the sense that German scholarly and critical method had carried the day. Yet underlying this insight is the awareness that the Germans have never merely 'guessed at truth', but have proceeded from philosophical universals; they have, in Hare's own words, 'made nearer approaches to speculative truth than any other nation'.[9]

John Sterling, Hare's close friend, briefly his curate at Hurstmonceux, expressed better than most this sense of the Germans' genius as it appeared to their British disciples. In the essay, *Characteristics of German Genius* of 1842, Sterling saw them in terms of 'elevation and fulness',[10] as the nation that most approached the Greeks in their 'universal importance'.[11] Their very plurality, the absence of a capital city that arbitrated over fashion and taste, the stimulus of their universities as compared with Oxford and Cambridge, their *'reflection'*,[12] *'Earnestness of heart'*[13] as a Protestant culture — all these could be cited in their favour. This is, one might say, Carlyle without the fulsomeness. But the *Edinburgh Review* in 1836 had not shrunk from a comparison of modern German literature with the age of Shakespeare.[14] Sterling and his Cambridge friends are, however, concerned to extend the claims of German universality beyond the confines of mere belles-lettres, to encompass the 'three great forms assumed by the genius of the Germans, — in History, Philosophy, and Poetry'.[15] The list of German notabilities produced by Sterling, while registering the additional point that all were born Protestant, deserves attention:

Leibnitz	Hegel
Frederick II	Schleiermacher
Lessing	Eichhorn
Winkelmann	Johannes Müller
Klopfstock	Jean Paul Richter
Herder	2 Stolbergs

---

9   Letter to Edmund Venables, September 6, 1844, quoted in Hare, *Memorials of a Quiet Life*, III, 250.
10 John Sterling, 'Characteristics of German Genius', in *Essays and Tales*, ed. by Julius Charles Hare, 2 vols (London: Parker, 1848), II, 383.
11 Ibid., 384.
12 Ibid., 406.
13 Ibid., 409.
14 *The Edinburgh Review* (Oct. 1836), xcii, 334.
15 Sterling, 'Characteristics of German Genius', 417.

17. Julius Hare's German Books in Trinity College Library, Cambridge

Hamann	2 Schlegels
Wieland	2 Humboldts
F. H. Jacobi	Novalis
Goethe	Tieck
Schiller	F. A. Wolf
Kant	Voss
Fichte	Niebuhr
Schelling	Savigny.

Add the dramatist Zacharias Werner, a convert to Catholicism, and discount one or two other conversions (and correct 'Leibniz', 'Winckelmann' and 'Klopstock') and you have a very impressive list indeed of poets, philosophers, historians and philologists. It is, interestingly enough, a list that continues the direction given nearly two generations earlier by Madame de Staël in *De l'Allemagne/On Germany*.

We need to understand this sense of German achievement — as seen through English eyes — if we are to appreciate Julius Hare, the book collector. For in translating not only Niebuhr's *History of Rome* but also a work each by Tieck and Friedrich de la Motte Fouqué, Hare was showing at the outset of his scholarly and literary career that German poetry and scholarship went hand in hand as evidence of that 'reflection' and universality. Goethe, whom Hare in 1832 on hearing of his death called the 'mightiest spirit that this earth has seen, since Shakespeare left it',[16] would illustrate in one person that range of genius. The German Romantics, the brothers Schlegel or Tieck in their turn concentrated one's line of vision on a higher fraternity of supernal genius that transcends national and chronological barriers, those 'archpoets' that embody the highest of human endeavour. It was fitting therefore that Augustus J. C. Hare should commemorate his uncle by quoting a letter containing the wide sweep of 'Homer, Dante, Shakespeare, Raphael, Phidias'.[17] For Hare's books do in fact take in the range of classical antiquity, the Romance languages (especially Italian), German and English literature, the fine arts, and all kinds of antiquarian and historical scholarship.

---

16 Augustus J. C. Hare, *Memorials of a Quiet Life*, I, 429.
17 Ibid., II, 186.

How did Hare come by his books? Already in 1825, Henry Crabb Robinson, diarist and gossip, noted in the course of a visit to Cambridge and Hare:

> I had great pleasure in looking over his library of German books — the best collection of modern German books I have ever seen in England.[18]

If Hare's rooms in Trinity were ample enough for his collection, then his archidiaconal quarters at Hurstmonceux seem to have been hardly adequate for the ever-increasing number of volumes. His nephew, remembering the house more for chastisements and 'endless sermons',[19] did concede that the library at Hurstmonceux was a place to be held in one's memory:

> Inside it was lined with books from top to bottom: not only the living rooms, but the passages and every available space in the bedrooms were walled with bookcases from floor to ceiling, containing more than 14,000 works. Most of these were German, but there were many very beautiful books upon art in all languages..[20]

A. P. Stanley's memoir of Hare is more deferential, culminating, perhaps not merely by chance, in an image of organic growth that would have pleased Coleridge, emanating from the intellectual and spiritual world of Johann Gottfried Herder and the German Romantics. We note too the Baconian image of the tree of knowledge:

> It was not merely a house with a good library — the whole house was a library. The vast nucleus which he brought with him from Cambridge grew year by year, till not only study, and drawing-room, and dining room, but passage, and antechamber, and bedrooms were overrun with the ever-advancing and crowded bookshelves. At the time of his death it had reached the number of more than 12,000 volumes; and it must be further remembered that these volumes were of no ordinary kind. Of all libraries which it has been our lot to traverse, we never saw any equal to this in the combined excellence of quantity and quality; none in

---

18   *Henry Crabb Robinson und seine deutschen Freunde. Brücke zwischen England und Deutschland im Zeitalter der Romantik*, ed. by Hertha Marquardt and Kurt Schreinert, Palaestra, 237, 249 (Göttingen: Vandenhoek & Ruprecht, 1964, 1967), II, 102. On Hare's dealings with the London bookseller John Henry Bohte, see Graham Jefcoate, *An Ocean of Literature: John Henry Bohte and the Anglo-German Book Trade in the Early Nineteenth Century* (Hildesheim, Zurich, New York: Olms, 2020), esp. 129f.
19   Augustus J. C. Hare, *The Story of My Life*, I, 109.
20   Ibid., 80f.

which there were so few worthless, so many valuable works. Its original basis was classical and philological; but of later years the historical, philosophical, and theological elements outgrew all the rest. The peculiarity which distinguished the collection probably from any other, private or public, in the kingdom, was the preponderance of German literature. No work, no pamphlet of any note in the teeming catalogues of German booksellers escaped his notice; and with his knowledge of the subjects and of the probable elucidation which they would receive from this or that quarter, they formed themselves in natural and harmonious groups round what already existed, so as to give to the library both the appearance and reality, not of a mere accumulation of parts, but of an organic and self-multiplying whole. And what perhaps was yet more remarkable was the manner in which the centre of this whole was himself. Without a catalogue, without assistance, he knew where every book was to be found, for what it was valuable, what relation it bore to the rest. The library was like a magnificent tree which he had himself planted, of which he had nurtured the growth, which spread its branches far and wide over his dwelling, and in the shade of which he delighted, even if he was prevented for the moment from gathering its fruits or pruning its luxuriant foliage.[21]

Hare may have incorporated into his own collection, the libraries of German books handed down from his father and brother. He clearly had no intention, however, of merely guarding an inheritance. As collections of German books go, Hare's was larger than Alexander von Humboldt's and began to approach Tieck's or Johann Joachim Eschenburg's. As with so many German collectors, it is likely that Hare's attitude to his books was not one of mere connoisseurship but was tempered with more practical considerations. His nephew claimed that the books were intended as a 'provision',[22] that is, an investment, for his wife Esther; his collection of pictures similarly. We may be grateful that Esther Hare saw fit to present the best part of the library to Trinity, while remarking that her generosity may well have exceeded her sense of the prudential. For the Hares and Maurices were, in nineteenth-century terms, not wealthy families.

The books themselves are in most cases individually bound in leather, often with tooled decoration. Very few of the German books have original bindings, reflecting the habit of the time to have volumes,

---

21 A. P. Stanley, 'Archdeacon Hare', *The Quarterly Review* 97 (June-Sept. 1855), 1–128 (8f.).
22 Augustus J. C. Hare, *The Story of My Life*, I, 484.

often issued in paper, made up to individual specifications. The Hare collection, as originally housed in free-standing cases in the main concourse of the Wren Library, must have presented a fine array of Victorian bindings. Today, confined to a bookstore, its external merits are less easily discerned. It remains a consolation, however, that users of the Wren Library approaching it from its side access, after passing between the busts of Thirlwall, Whewell and Alfred Tennyson and before coming to the uncharacteristically décolleté James Frazer, may pay their respects before Thomas Woolner's prominently displayed enigmatic bust of Hare.

The books, although in many cases hardly, if ever, used since their incorporation into Trinity's collection, were not intended by Hare as mere scholarly decoration. Pencil marginalia, especially in periodicals, give ample evidence of extensive and discriminating use. These marginalia, on the other hand, are restricted largely to lists of contributors to periodicals, and cross-references, always in pencil. Many of these I have found useful — and always accurate. Hare the scholar-bibliophile did not deface his books: we understand perhaps his refusal to lend volumes to Coleridge,[23] who 'used' his books differently. Yet Coleridge's range of German reading — from Martin Luther to Schleiermacher, in all kinds of disciplines and speculative indisciplines — is very similar to Hare's. *Guesses at Truth*, while in no sense really comparable with *Biographia literaria*, does make abundantly clear that Hare's appreciation of German literature and scholarship went hand in hand with the particular emphases of his own collection. 'The very first novel I have happened to take up since writing the above, Arnim's *Dolores*...', 'Thus too Solger, writing about his dialogues to Tieck...', 'Niebuhr applied this...', 'ingeniously remarkt by Francis Horn...',[24] are phrases culled from just a few pages of the work, giving some small indication of Hare's acquaintance with German belles-lettres and critical scholarship.

All of Hare's contemporaries acknowledged that German was the main foundation of his collection. There is however rich material for the student of Italian (the sixteenth-century editions of Giordano Bruno, for

---

23 Cf. *Collected Letters of Samuel Taylor Coleridge*, ed. by Earl Leslie Griggs, 6 vols (Oxford: Oxford University Press, 1956–71), IV, 1019.
24 [A. W. and J. C. Hare], *Guesses at Truth by Two Brothers* (London, New York: Macmillan, 1880), 55, 59, 61, 72.

instance, that he was unwilling to lend to Coleridge);²⁵ and the historian of the early Victorian church will find the tract material of the period very fully represented. Despite confining ourselves to German, we are not withholding the real substance.

A foretaste of what Hare's books contain may be gained merely by taking one single made-up volume of 'PAMPHLETS', containing twelve miscellaneous German items. Number 1, Eduard Eversmann's *Reise von Orenburg nach Buchara* (Berlin, 1823),²⁶ a work of Central Asian ethnography, with appended Afghan word-list, is listed in five other libraries in COPAC. Following it, as Number 2, is the German Romantic magazine *Zeitung für Einsiedler* (including *Tröst Einsamkeit*) (Heidelberg, 1808), Achim von Arnim's contribution to the curious, the bizarre and the national, in German poetry. It is the finest copy I have ever seen, with engravings of original freshness, far outstripping the reprint which many libraries hold. Numbers 3 to 6 are lectures by the Jena speculative scientist, Lorenz Oken, all given there between 1808 and 1809. The British Library's copy of the polemically anti-Newtonian *Erste Ideen zur Theorie des Lichts* [...] (Jena, 1808) has annotations by Coleridge. Of the other three, Hare's copy of *Ueber das Universum als Fortsetzung des Sinnensystems* (Jena, 1808) is the sole entry in COPAC. There are copies in Paris and Harvard, but seemingly nowhere in Germany. *Grundzeichnung des natürlichen Systems der Erze* (Jena, 1809) is COPAC's but not WorldCat's only copy. *Ueber den Werth der Naturgeschichte* (also Jena 1809) is not even listed in COPAC, while Weimar has Goethe's copy. Number 7, Adam Müller's *Von der Idee des Staates und ihren Verhältnissen zu den populären Staatstheorien*, a lecture on political economy (Dresden, 1808), is the separately issued first part of his *Die Elemente der Staatskunst* (of which the only other copy in COPAC is in the British Library) and is the sole entry in COPAC. Number 8, Joseph Görres's *Teutschlands künftige Verfassung* (n.p., 1814) is the reprint of an article in his *Rheinischer Merkur*, and as such not listed in COPAC. It may well be unique. Neither 7 nor 8 is listed in WorldCat. Number 9, Bernhard Joseph Docen's *Ueber die Ursachen der Fortdauer der lateinischen Sprache* (Munich, 1815), an academy lecture, has three hits in COPAC. Two further Munich academy lectures,

---

25   *Collected Letters of Samuel Taylor Coleridge*, IV, 1019.
26   NB: Many of the German titles in this chapter are too esoteric to satisfyingly translate into English, and therefore no translation has been supplied.

numbers 10 and 11, by Friedrich Thiersch, *Ueber die Epochen der bildenden Kunst unter den Griechen* (Munich, 1816, 1819, 1829) are represented in COPAC in part by the London Library and the Cambridge Faculty of Classics, omitting to say that Hare's is the full set (Harvard University seems to have the only other). The twelfth item, a work of archaeology and comparative mythology, Peter von Köppen's *Die dreygestaltete Hekate und ihre Rolle in den Mysterien* (Vienna, 1823), is in Birmingham and Cambridge, but COPAC does not list Trinity's copy.

The sheer range of these 'PAMPHLETS', not merely their occasional rarity, gives an accurate impression of Hare's sweep of interest: religion, archaeology, science, classical philology, as well as all manifestations of literature. One volume may thus serve as an introduction to the whole collection. Pride of place must nevertheless go to Hare's collection of Luther, a made-up set of first printings of all the German-language pamphlets and sermons from 1518 to 1545, described in detail by Adams. This collection immediately places Trinity in the forefront among Cambridge Luther holdings, well supplemented, among others, by the Aldis Wright bequests. Luther is central to Hare's own position on German theology and thought, a position easily accommodated to the more modern thinking of Schleiermacher and one to be defended against the radical views of a David Friedrich Strauss. Backed up as they are by an eighteenth-century set of Luther's works (*Sämtliche Schriften/ Complete Works*, Halle 1739–50) from the centre of German pietism, the Luther holdings, we must assume, are a scholar-theologian's working collection.

There are among Hare's German books no other items from this early period in original editions, Hare clearly seeing no merit in the accumulation of early theological works as such. His theological collection does in the main take in what are the salient developments in German religious thought as seen through the eyes of Coleridge's generation. There is, after Luther, a leap in time to the first complete set of Jacob Böhme's works (Amsterdam, 1682), doubtless the 'Behmen' that he also refused to lend to less-than-reliable Coleridge[27] (we note, in passing, the Spinoza *Tractatus Theologico-Politicus* of 1674, which has eight hits in COPAC but which does not list Hare's copy). The eighteenth

---

27   Ibid.

century is represented by the father of German pietism, Jakob Spener, and the chiliast Johann Albrecht Bengel. It is only when we come to the late eighteenth century and the first half of the nineteenth that we see Hare's declared interest in German theology taking in the broadest of spectrums. The Romantic trinity of Luther, Böhme and Schleiermacher gives way to a seeming heterodoxy of nineteenth-century theological opinion: the evangelical devotional sermons of Claus Harms or the sternly Protestant conservatism of Ernst Wilhelm Hengstenberg on the one hand, and the up-to-date biblical criticism of Johann August Ernesti, Ferdinand Christian Baur, Wilhelm Martin Leberecht de Wette, Hermann Olshausen, Heinrich Wilhelm Josias Thiersch and August Tholuck, on the other. In the centre stands the commanding figure of Schleiermacher, represented by the first complete edition (*Sämmtliche Werke/Collected Works*, Berlin, 1838–64) and various separate items, also a number of contemporary studies or pamphlets on him. Of special interest is the first edition of the *Vertraute Briefe über Fr. Schlegels Lucinde* (Lübeck, 1800, five hits in COPAC excluding Hare), illustrating a side of Schleiermacher that might not necessarily appeal to the severely decorous Hare. He, however, not only possessed this work of Schleiermacher's, but also the cause of it, Friedrich Schlegel's novel *Lucinde* (1799), a work of some erotic daring (and some tedium) that sets out the German Romantics' views on the equality of the sexes in matters both of the body and the spirit (COPAC lists British Library and Hare; the first edition is generally rare). Schleiermacher's defence of this novel, coming from the chaplain of the Berlin Charité hospital, was to say the least controversial. It illustrates the largeness and the broadness of the Romantic sense of religion, a force which pervades all areas of life and culture.

It is therefore not surprising that Hare's library is strong on what might generally be called 'religion' or philosophy of religion. That would extend from Friedrich Wilhelm Joseph Schelling, David Friedrich Strauss, to comparative religion and mythology proper. Strauss's *Das Leben Jesu* is there in its first edition (Tübingen, 1835), as are various other of Strauss's works and studies on him; an indication that Hare, while not endorsing the position of George Henry Lewes and George Eliot, was fully aware of the appeal of this kind of critical theology. For the same reason, we find at least one early work by Ludwig Feuerbach

(*Geschichte der neuern Philosophie*, Ansbach, 1837). It is typical of Hare's thoroughness that, where significant or controversial figures were involved, he assembled memoirs, pamphlets and ephemera, as say in connection with Strauss's *Leben Jesu* or after Georg Wilhelm Friedrich Hegel's and Goethe's deaths. I have it on good authority that the pamphlet collection on Hegel is extraordinary. Hegelians might also note the presence of an almost complete set of the rare *Jahrbücher für Theologie und christliche Philosophie* (Frankfurt am Main, 1834–36) which is important for the reception of Hegel.

Similarly, Schelling, the most influential Romantic philosopher, is present in a wide range of works. We note the first edition of his *System der Naturphilosophie* (Jena, 1799), and early editions of *Philosophie und Religion/Philosophy and Religion* (Tübingen, 1804) and *Weltseele* (third edition, Hamburg, 1809). We recollect that Coleridge annotated his copy of *Philosophie und Religion*. The various stages of Schelling's career, from Jena to the secretaryship of the Bavarian Academy of Sciences to the chair at the University of Berlin, from philosophical avant-garde to academic establishment, are recorded faithfully in Hare's collection of over forty-five volumes. Similar espousals of orthodoxy, Catholic or Protestant, after beginnings in less established spheres, were to be found in other representatives of German religious life of the period. The issue in 1820–25 of the *Gesammelte Werke* of the brothers Friedrich Leopold and Christian von Stolberg, in the fine edition by Friedrich Perthes in Hamburg, marked the progress of these two noblemen from the Storm and Stress (and association with Goethe) to a dynamic Neoclassicism and to an eventual, and spectacular, conversion to Rome in 1800. Friedrich Stolberg's name is inseparable from the welter of Romantic conversions to Catholicism after that date. Hare's set of the Perthes Stolberg is the finest I have seen; but we should not overlook his *Geschichte der Religion Jesu Christi* (Vienna, 1817–25), an example of Stolberg's later apologetic work.

The Romantic sense of an 'Allseele', a divine force inspiring all the manifestations of nature and leading even beyond the world of observed phenomena into the secret and dark and mystical, is well documented in Hare's books. One of the first volumes one meets on his shelves is Johann Wilhelm Ritter's *Fragmente aus dem Nachlasse eines jungen Physikers* (Heidelberg, 1810: the British Library has the only other copy in COPAC), a good example of such scientific speculation; one finds too the 'classic' of this persuasion, Gotthilf Heinrich Schubert's *Ansichten von der Nachtseite der Naturwissenschaft* (Dresden, 1808; three hits in COPAC, which omits Hare), based on the lectures on animal magnetism that so influenced Heinrich von Kleist and appealed to Coleridge. Another author read by Coleridge, Heinrich Jung-Stilling, who moved from his epoch-making pietistic autobiography via spectrology to more conventional Protestant piety, is well represented in a number of later works. A set of Lorenz Oken's *Lehrbuch der Naturgeschichte* (Leipzig, 1815–16), with its mixture of religious and scientific teleology, is there as might be expected; I have already mentioned the other, rare, items by him.

In this context, too, one should mention the large and representative collection of the works of Henrich Steffens, a Norwegian who wrote in German, beginning in Schelling's nature philosophy and moving through a wide spectrum of writing in the period after 1815. Coleridge clearly thought Steffens relatively significant, for the British Library holds three copies of works by him with marginalia; one of these is *Die gegenwärtige Zeit* (Berlin, 1817), also in Hare's collection and possibly another item not subject to loan — and annotation! Hare contains three rarer items: *Drei Vorlesungen über Herrn D. Gall's Organenlehre* (Halle, 1805) is the only copy listed in COPAC (not in WorldCat), as is *Widerlegung* der *gegen ihn von Schulz erhobenen öffentlichen Anklage* (Breslau, 1823; rare outside the UK), whereas *Johann Christian Reil* (Halle, 1815) is shared with the Royal College of Physicians and Surgeons of Glasgow. Several of his fictional works are held in first, single editions. Hare's collection complements the holdings in Cambridge University Library and together they must represent the most comprehensive collection of Steffens's works in the country. His highly informative autobiography, *Was ich erlebte* (Breslau, 1840–44), is a fitting accompaniment to the scientific or apologetic works in Hare's collection.

Joseph Görres (later 'von') is a similar case from the opposite corner of Germany. Görres' radical Rhenish conservatism emerges in works like *Teutschland und die Revolution* (Coblentz, 1819), held here, as in Cambridge University Library's Acton collection, in the first edition. His progress from speculation to orthodoxy is recorded, for instance, by the early *Aphorismen über Organonomie* (Coblentz, 1803; two hits in COPAC besides Hare) and the late *Die christliche Mystik* (Regensburg,

1836), while his *Rheinischer Merkur* (Coblentz, 1813–14), from which the rare pamphlet *Teutschlands künftige Verfassung* is reprinted, represents a response to the political needs of the times.

Of special interest is Görres' important early work, *Die teutschen Volksbücher* (Heidelberg, 1807), which, together with Arnim and Brentano's *Des Knaben Wunderhorn* (present in the second edition 1808–19), initiates the wave of scholarly and poetic interest by the German Romantics in the folk culture of the past. Another of Görres's most important works is to be found in a nest of Romantic studies on comparative mythology. As if anticipating Frazer by a century, Hare assembled the key works on this subject, one which was to fascinate equally the nineteenth century and the twentieth. Görres's *Mythengeschichte der asiatischen Welt* (Heidelberg, 1810) owes in its turn much to the efforts of the Heidelberg classicist Friedrich Creuzer, whose *Symbolik* (here in the second, enlarged edition, Leipzig, 1819–23) lays the foundation of the subject. We must however not forget the lesser-known Johann Arnold Kanne, important for his *Mythologie der Griechen* (Leipzig, 1805; COPAC has four hits), *System der indischen Mythe* (Leipzig, 1813; otherwise held by the British Library and Trinity College Dublin) and *Erste Urkunden der Geschichte, oder Allgemeine Mythologie* (Bayreuth, 1815; British Library, London Library, National Library of Scotland besides Hare). No less than ten works by Kanne or associated with him held in Hare are listed in COPAC as sole copies or do not even figure at all, and are generally rare. These are mainly polemical reviews, but two of them are extremely rare novels, *Gianetta* (Bayreuth, 1809; Hare's copy not listed in WorldCat, where there are eight hits, including Rice University) and *Romane aus der Christenwelt aller Zeiten* (Nuremberg, 1817; WorldCat has eight German holdings, plus University of Pisa and Rice University). We see interest in mythology spreading out in all directions among the Romantics: Friedrich and August Wilhelm Schlegel espouse the study of Sanskrit after their sojourns in Napoleonic Paris. In Hare's collection, Friedrich's *Ueber die Sprache und Weisheit der Indier* (Heidelberg, 1808) is supplemented by August Wilhelm's edition of the *Râmâyana* (London, 1823), their friend Tieck having perhaps first given scope to the subject in Romantic circles by allowing the orientalist Friedrich Majer to publish in his short-lived periodical, *Poetisches Journal* (Jena, 1800, held otherwise by British Library, University College London and Birmingham

University). Jacob Grimm's *Deutsche Mythologie* of 1835 turns its interest northwards and takes its place among the comprehensive set of the Grimms' works brought together by Hare. These titles are however only samples from a total range of books on mythology which extends from Karl Philipp Moritz's *Götterlehre* (edition Berlin, 1804) to Sir George Grey's *Poems, Traditions, and Chaunts of the Maories* (Wellington, 1853) (see below).

From mythology and its occasionally heady speculations we move to history proper, one of John Sterling's 'three great forms assumed by the genius of the Germans'. A fine complete set of the works of the Swiss historian Johannes von Müller (Tübingen, 1810) and the first collected edition of the patriot and antiquarian Justus Möser (Berlin, 1798) set the tone. The collection of Niebuhr, as might be expected, is hardly inferior to the British Library's. Where Friedrich von Raumer and Leopold von Ranke are concerned, it would be hard for Hare to compete with the superb assemblage of Cambridge University Library's Acton Collection; Hare does however hold Ranke's *Ueber die Verschwörung gegen Venedig* (Berlin, 1831), not in the British Library, but in the Acton Collection (Cambridge) and Oxford Taylorian; while Raumer's Adam Smithian *Das Brittische Besteuerungs-System* (Berlin 1810) is in the British Library, London Library and, not surprisingly, the London School of Economics. Johann Gustav Droysen, Friedrich Christoph Dahlmann, Friedrich Christoph Schlosser and other German historians are well represented. It is appropriate that a collection rich in Hegel, both by him and about him, should include, as in a rhyming couplet, Friedrich Schlegel, one of Hegel's most outspoken opponents, with his *Philosophie der Geschichte* (Vienna, 1829).

To examine Hare's books is above all things to become acquainted with German literature and poetry from 1800 to 1850. The German scholar has much to learn from a leisurely shelf-inspection, for they have here the stuff of German literary culture in a way that few institutions, even those richer and larger, may display it. It will do only to point to the main strengths and rarities. The rest can be summarized more or less as follows. Hare did not collect eighteenth-century literature systematically or in early editions. Klopstock, Herder, Johann Heinrich Voss, Johann Joachim Winckelmann even Moritz August von Thümmel, are represented in standard collected editions mainly from the early nineteenth century. For Gotthold Ephraim Lessing, however, we have the important biography and remains issued by his brother, K. G. Lessing (Berlin, 1793–95). Even Goethe is not well represented in original editions, but then there are his periodicals, *Propyläen* (Tübingen, 1798–1800, otherwise only in the British Library) and *Kunst und Alterthum* (1818–27; also in the British Library). As if to make up for this narrowing of interest to Goethe's aesthetic and scientific writings (there is, as well, *Zur Morphologie* of 1817, also in the British Library), Hare assembled well over twenty-five significant items of Goetheana from the period 1832–37, including, as already mentioned, Bettina von Arnim, Carl Friedrich Zelter and Eckermann, but also the earlier Friedrich Karl Julius Schütz on *Goethe und Pustkuchen* (Halle 1823; also in Cambridge University Library but not in the British Library) and significant works on Goethe reception, like Karl Gutzkow's *Über Goethe im Wendepunkte zweier Jahrhunderte* (Berlin, 1836), Heinrich Döring's life of Goethe (Weimar, 1833), and the much rarer Karl Reck, *Goethe und seine Widersacher* (Weimar, 1837, British Library and Oxford Taylorian) that so annoyed the surviving Romantics.

The trio, Jean Paul, Friedrich Hölderlin and Kleist, not properly assigned to Romanticism, is under the circumstances very fairly represented. The forlorn *Gedichte* (Stuttgart, 1843) are evidence of a Hölderlin yet to be discovered by his fellow-countrymen. Tieck's edition of Kleist's *Gesammelte Schriften* (Berlin, 1826), pays tribute to 'unhappy genius' in the muted generosity of its foreword; while two further editorial undertakings of Tieck's, *Gesammelte Schriften, Von J. M. R. Lenz* (Berlin, 1828) and *Mahler Müllers Werke* (Heidelberg, 1811) commemorate other, in Tieck's eyes, imperfect talents. The edition of Novalis produced by Friedrich Schlegel and Tieck, here represented by the fourth edition (Berlin, 1826) and containing the influential and hagiographical biography prepared by Tieck for the 1815 edition, brings us by chance to a great curiosity. In 1926, the great scholar-editor Josef Körner announced the discovery in the Austrian National Library in Vienna of a surviving slip of paper produced in 1827 at Friedrich Schlegel's behest, disclaiming responsibility for the publication of Novalis's still controversial *Die Christenheit oder Europa*.[28] Unbeknown to scholarship,

---

28 Documentation on this in Novalis, *Schriften. Die Werke Friedrich von Hardenbergs*, ed. by Paul Kluckhohn and Richard Samuel et al., 6 vols in 7 (Stuttgart: Kohlhammer,

Julius Hare had had the foresight to have this disclaimer tipped into his own copy of Novalis's works. By collecting August Wilhelm Schlegel's and Tieck's *Musen-Almanach für das Jahr 1802* (Tübingen, 1802), Hare had already secured the first printing of Novalis's *Geistliche Lieder*.

Jean Paul, as befits the most-read German novelist of his time and one much admired in the English-speaking world (while defying proper translation), has twenty-two works. Only the British Library and the Brotherton collection in Leeds have comparable holdings; indeed, a leading Jean Paul scholar has told me that Trinity's set of first editions is one of the finest in any public collection. The first edition of his Gothic novel *Titan* (Berlin, 1800–03) is not rare, but only Leeds has another copy of the *Clavis Fichteana*, originally conceived as an appendix to it (Erfurt, 1800). There are a further nine first editions of Jean Paul. The political pamphlet *Dämmerung für Deutschland* (Tübingen, 1809) is COPAC's sole listing in this form. A curiosity is Hoffmann's *Fantasiestücke* (Bamberg, 1819; also in the British Library and the National Library of Scotland), with its preface by Jean Paul, duly catalogued in Trinity for generations under the older author. Thus too, the first edition of Hoffmann's *Die Elixiere des Teufels* (Berlin, 1815; otherwise, British Library only) used to masquerade under 'Medardus', the self-effacing author having put the story's hero on to the title page. *Die Serapionsbrüder* (Berlin, 1819), *Kater Murr* (Berlin, 1820) and *Meister Floh* (Frankfurt, 1822) are in Hare's shelf-list at least acknowledged as being Hoffmann's, and all three are first editions.

The Hoffmann holdings demonstrate that it is with the German Romantics proper that Hare's German books enter into their own.[29] The discerning eye of the collector is everywhere evident. Beginning with periodicals, one of the Romantics' key fields of disseminatory endeavour, while regretting the surprising absence of the Schlegel brothers' *Athenaeum*, we make do with Friedrich Schlegel's *Europa* (Frankfurt, 1803) and *Concordia* (Vienna, 1823, Acton Collection and British Library); Tieck's *Poetisches Journal* was already noted above, but not the extremely

---

1960–2006), III, 502.

29 A check against the catalogue of an exhibition of a hundred 'very rare' first editions of German Romantic books established that Hare has a quarter of the titles listed. Cf. *Deutsche Romantiker. Kostbare Bücher in Erstausgaben. Sammlung aus dem Antiquariat Gunnar A. Koldewey, Düsseldorf* (Wolfenbüttel: Herzog August Bibliothek, 1979).

rare *Kynosarges* of his brother-in-law, August Ferdinand Bernhardi (Berlin, 1802), not otherwise in COPAC and seemingly nowhere else in printed form. Adam Müller's and Heinrich von Kleist's beautiful *Phöbus* (Dresden, 1808; COPAC also lists Cambridge University Library, the British Library and Manchester) is complete but for Ferdinand Hartmann's cover engraving of the sun god over the spires of Dresden, doubtless lost in binding. Scholarly periodicals from the years after 1815, some still with Romantic associations, include the *Jahrbücher für Phiiosophie und Pädagogik* (Leipzig, 1826–30), *Hermes* (Leipzig, 1819–31), *Jahrbücher der Literatur* (Vienna, 1818–31), *Jahrbücher fur wissenschaftliche Kritik* (Stuttgart, 1827–37) and Friedrich Carl von Savigny's *Zeitschrift für geschichtliche Rechtswissenschaft* (Berlin, 1815–45).

It is Tieck, to whom Novalis wrote that he 'partakes of every thing I do', who seems almost omnipresent in this collection. The Tieck scholar based in either Cambridge or London will find over ninety percent of this enormous oeuvre spread between Trinity, the University Library and the British Library. While the British Library, the fortunate recipient of Tieck's own association copies, may thank Antonio Panizzi for its particular collection, Cambridge is largely in Hare's debt. The only major item not in the British Library is Tieck's almanac *Novellenkranz* (Berlin, 1831–32, 1834), whereas the British Library has an almost complete set of *Urania*, of which Hare has the run 1831–35, but few institutions can have finer copies of his other works. The very early Tieck is largely unrepresented, perhaps already unobtainable. We begin with that first outpouring of aesthetic enthusiasm, Wilhelm Heinrich Wackenroder's and Tieck's *Herzensergiessungen eines kunstliebenden Klosterbruders* (Berlin, 1797); and the second (and revised) edition of its sequel, *Phantasien über die Kunst* (Berlin, 1814). The rare early novel *William Lovell* is there in its second, much-revised, edition of 1813–14, the only copy in COPAC and one of nine in WorldCat, possibly more, but with none in the USA. His most influential novel, owing much to his dead friend Wackenroder, *Franz Sternbalds Wanderungen* (Berlin, 1798) is present in the original version, the one to be found under the pillow of every Nazarene artist in Rome and hence also the one excoriated by Goethe. The magnificent *Minnelieder aus dem Schwäbischen Zeitalter*, with engravings by Philipp Otto Runge (Berlin, 1803; COPAC lists British Library, London Library

Glasgow and Oxford Taylorian), still has a freshness that no reprint can match.

This is the place to explore other areas so much akin to Tieck's *Minnelieder*. Hare and his generation could quite freely speak of 'the Germans' as a cultural entity, but without a national core or focus; indeed, Hare lived through the first failed attempt to achieve a German nation, in 1848. Defeats at Napoleon's hands had earlier galvanized a sense of national identity; the rediscovery of the literary heritage of the Middle Ages could also perform that task in educated and intellectual circles. Thus, August Wilhelm Schlegel, writing in 1812, deemed the *Nibelungenlied/The Song of the Nibelungs* to be a school of national awareness for the nation's youth. Tieck had had his part in that process; the first honour goes however to Friedrich Heinrich von der Hagen. Hagen's modernized version of the medieval epic, first published in 1807, is not in Hare's collection, but a number of similar works by him or by scholarantiquarians of similar persuasion are. Appropriately, we find Eschenburg's *Denkmäler altdeutscher Dichtkunst* (Bremen, 1799) representing an older generation that included Lessing and Herder. From the Romantic generation we have, among others, such titles as Johann Gustav Büsching's *Das Lied der Nibelungen* (Altenburg, 1815) and Karl Rosenkranz's later study of it (Halle, 1829), Ludwig Uhland's *Walther von der Vogelweide* (Stuttgart 1820) and Büsching's edition of Hans Sachs (Nuremberg, 1816–24), Hagen's, Büsching's and Docen's *Museum für Altdeutsche Literatur und Kunst* (Berlin 1809), Hagen's *Der Helden Buch* (Berlin, 1811) and Tieck's *Frauendienst* (Tübingen, 1812), all relatively rare. The Romantic interest in the sixteenth and seventeenth centuries is represented by Tieck's *Deutsches Theater* (Berlin, 1817), rare enough in this edition, and Wilhelm Müller's much less known *Bibliothek deutscher Dichter des siebzehnten Jahrhunderts* (Leipzig, 1822–31; British Library and an incomplete copy at Oxford Taylorian).

Jacob and Wilhelm Grimm did not approve of the modernized and, for them, amateurized editions produced by the likes of Hagen or Büsching. It is almost to be expected that Hare, himself a classical philologist of note, should collect up to twenty-three of the Grimms' works. They include however a beautifully crisp copy of the *Kinder-und Hausmärchen* of 1819 (not listed in COPAC at all), those famous fairy-tales standing out as exceptions among the stringent scholarship of so many of the Grimms' titles, so close as they are to a large section of grammatical and philological works by names ranging from Karl Lachmann to Wilhelm von Humboldt to Franz Bopp. It does not come altogether as a surprise to read of Hare in 1838 proposing to bring Jacob Grimm over to Cambridge[30] after he had been dismissed from Göttingen by Queen Victoria's brutish and philistine uncle, King Ernest Augustus of Hanover. In the event, Frederick William IV of Prussia pre-empted any such considerations in 1840.

Neither August Wilhelm nor Friedrich Schlegel would have been content to regard himself merely as scholar or philologist, although their Sanskrit studies have already been alluded to. Neither would on the other hand have considered himself out of place in the company of classical scholars like Karl August Böttiger, Thiersch, Gustav Parthey, Friedrich Gottlieb Welcker, Karl Otfried Müller or Creuzer (all present in Hare). Thus it is interesting to find August Wilhelm's first published work, of precocious latinity, *De geographia Homerica* (Hanover 1788; quite rare, but Trinity College, Cambridge, has two copies), as the beginning of an offering of twenty titles extending from *Charakteristiken und Kritiken* (with his brother Friedrich, Königsberg, 1801; held otherwise by the British Library, Birmingham University and the Warburg Institute) to the highly important translations of Calderón (Berlin, 1809; British Library, Oxford Taylorian and the Warburg Institute) and of Shakespeare, here admittedly in the edition revised by Tieck (Berlin, 1825–33), which caused Schlegel such heartache. With Tieck's *Alt-Englisches Theater* (Berlin, 1811) and *Shakspeare's Vorschule* (Leipzig, 1823–29), German Romantic studies in Shakespeare are well represented.

Friedrich Schlegel's complete works issued in Vienna (1822–25) are in Trinity College, Cambridge, but not in Hare. The sixteen items of Hare's holdings range from late works such as *Philosophie des Lebens* (Vienna, 1828) to relative curiosities from his earlier period like the editions from the Old French, *Geschichte der Jungfrau von Orleans* (Berlin, 1802; otherwise only in the British Library and the National Library of Scotland) and *Geschichte der Margaretha von Valois* (Leipzig, 1803; only copy in COPAC). The Schlegel brothers' protege(e)s are also present: Friedrich's wife Dorothea, with a rare copy of her novel *Florentin* (Lübeck, 1801; also British Library), Tieck's sister Sophie von Knorring,

---

30 Augustus J. C. Hare, *Memorials of a Quiet Life*, III, 232.

with her extremely rare *Flore und Blanscheflur*, prefaced by August Wilhelm (Berlin 1822; COPAC only lists the British Library's copy), and his great hope, Wilhelm von Schütz, whose works are also rare and only held by the British Library, *Lacrimas* (Berlin, 1803), *Niobe* (Berlin, 1807) and *Der Graf und die Gräfin von Gleichen* (Berlin, 1807); *Der Garten der Liebe* (Berlin, 1811) seems only to be in Berlin, Weimar, Göttingen and Erfurt (WorldCat), while *Dramatische Wälder* (Leipzig, 1821, not the British Library) is more widespread. A curiosity is his much later Catholic apologetic periodical *Anticelsus* (Mainz and Speyer, 1842–45, also in the British Library).

The vast oeuvre of Brentano is present in but six samples; they include his edition of *Der Goldfaden* (Heidelberg 1809) and his *Die Gründung Prags* (Pest, 1815; COPAC, British Library and London Library). Associated with Brentano and published under his direction, are the works of the stigmatized (and now beatified) nun, Anna Katharina Emmerick. A leading Brentano scholar has told me that Trinity College, Cambridge's holdings, three volumes bound as one by Hare, are unique in bringing together Emmerick's *Das bittere Leiden unsers Herrn Jesu Christi* (Sulzbach, 1833) and its continuation, *Das letzte Abendmahl unsers Herrn Jesu Christi* (Sulzbach, 1834), along with the apologetic riposte to Steffens's attack on Emmerick, Johann Heinrich Pabst's *Ein Wort über die Ekstase* (Cologne, 1834). The last two are the only copies in COPAC, whereas the Pabst is otherwise only held by the Diocesan Library in Cologne.

Brentano's close friend and collaborator, Achim von Arnim, is altogether better represented with ten titles, including first editions of standard works like *Gräfin Dolores* (Berlin, 1810; COPAC, British Library and London Library), *Halle und Jerusalem* (Heidelberg, 1811; British Library, London Library and National Library of Scotland; COPAC has not registered Newnham College's copy), *Der Wintergarten* (Berlin, 1809; COPAC, British Library and Manchester Central Library), *Isabella von Aegypten* (Berlin 1812, British Library, London Library, Leeds and Belfast) and *Landhausleben* (Leipzig, 1826, otherwise in London Library only). A rarity is the first version of the unfinished novel, *Die Kronenwächter*, published as *Berthold's erstes und zweites Leben* (Berlin, 1817; otherwise British Library and Manchester Central Library), and a curiosity is the drama, *Der gestürzte Emporkömmling* (Ulm, 1824), attributed by Kayser's

Bücher-Lexicon to Arnim, but in reality by an unidentified, anonymous author.[31] It is the only copy in COPAC, and WorldCat lists only Berlin (Staatsbibliothek) and Stuttgart (Württembergische Landesbibliothek).

Madame de Staël, in *De l'Allemagne/On Germany*, had drawn special attention to the Romantic dramatist Zacharias Werner. It is fair to say that Werner's reputation in the first decades of the nineteenth century shone as brightly as Hoffmann's or Brentano's, certainly Kleist's. Hare's collection seems to reflect that esteem, with the result that Trinity has most likely the finest collection of first or early editions of Werner in the country, including three items not in the British Library, *Wanda* (Tübingen, 1810; other copies in Cambridge University Library, Oxford Taylorian, London Library, Glasgow and Bristol), *Cunegunde* (Leipzig, 1815; copies in Cambridge University Library, London Library and Bristol) and *Nachgelassene Predigten* (Vienna, 1836; other copy in Bristol).

Some modern scholars of Romanticism might — wrongly — regard large holdings of Zacharias Werner as a doubtful asset. Three minor Romantics are however probably more extensively represented than any of their contemporaries: Ernst Moritz Arndt, Fouqué and the Dane (and honorary German) Adam Oehlenschläger. There are personal reasons perhaps for this concentration. According to Crabb Robinson, Arndt was a friend of Hare's; more likely, he met Arndt in Bonn during his visit to August Wilhelm Schlegel in 1832. Ever a controversial figure, Arndt is covered here at all stages of his career in no fewer than twenty-five works, a good half of these dating from the time of the Wars of Liberation (notably *Lieder für Teutsche*, n.p., 1813; the British Library also holds this). Eight titles by Arndt are unique to COPAC, and two, *E. M. Arndt's Urtheil über Friedrich den Grossen* (Berlin, 1818) and *Prinz Victor von Neuwied* (Deutschland [=Frankfurt], 1821), have only three and six hits respectively in WorldCat, none outside Germany and not including Hare.

Hare's own copy of *Olliers Literary Miscellany* (London, 1820; the British Library has the only other set) gives us in part the answer to Fouqué and Oehlenschläger. For there we have Hare's own translation of Fouqué's *The Siege of Ancona. A Romantic Idyll*, and a major article on

---

31 Cf. *Arnim-Bibliographie*, ed. by Otto Mallon (Berlin 1925, reprint Hildesheim: Olms, 1965), 79.

Oehlenschläger.³² Tieck, who was dismissive of Oehlenschläger's drama *Correggio* (Stuttgart, 1816), is in this collection eclipsed in terms of numbers of works by the Danish writer — a total of over thirty, in both languages. Even Hare's stated admiration for Fouqué's *Der Zauberring* and *Sintram* can hardly account for the astounding forty-three items by this author, without any doubt the largest set of early editions in the country and possibly anywhere. They range from the earliest, published under the pseudonym of Pellegrin (*Zwei Schauspiele*, Berlin, 1805), to the late novel, *Abfall und Buße* (Berlin, 1844). COPAC lists a total of twenty items that are only in Hare. Alexander von Blomberg's *Hinterlassene poetische Schriften* (Berlin, 1820), for which Fouqué's facile pen produced the prologue, the 287-page drama *Konrad in Deutschland*, leaving Blomberg with a few slender pages of literary remains, is the sole entry in COPAC, with a mere handful in WorldCat. Fouqué is gradually staging a comeback; anyone working on him in this country would be well advised to consult this collection.

Hare did not confine himself to literary works of a Romantic persuasion but purchased a fair variety of those popularly read in the period 1815–40. A miscellany of titles will indicate this: the assiduous Bavarian courtier and indifferent dramatist Eduard von Schenk (*Schauspiele*, Stuttgart, 1829–35; British Library, University College Library and National Trust) and the collected works of his royal master, King Ludwig I of Bavaria (*Gedichte*, Munich, 1829). Another royal item is the Dante translation by Prince (later King) John of Saxony (under the pseudonym Philalethes) (Dresden and Leipzig, 1839–40; British Library, University College Library and Manchester), in the rare and handsome first edition, the draft of which had been scrutinized by Tieck, Carl Gustav Carus and Wolf von Baudissin. Literary figures once household names but subject to ephemeral fame are the prose writer Carl Wilhelm Salice Contessa (*Schriften*, Berlin 1826; otherwise, Queen's College, Oxford, and University College London) and the dramatists Ernst von Raupach (*Dramatische Werke*, Hamburg, 1829) and Ernst von Houwald (*Die Seeräuber*, Leipzig, 1831, sole hit in COPAC) who between them initiated a craze for, respectively, historical dramas on medieval themes and fate dramas. The founding father of the popular fate drama, Adolph Müllner (*Vermischte Schriften*, Stuttgart, 1824; sole hit in

---

32 *Olliers Literary Miscellany*, 54–61 (Fouqué) and 90–153 (Oehlenschläger).

COPAC) joins this company of what are now rarities. Hare was however also aware of other talents, this time in the field of prose. A scarce copy of Carl Friedrich von Rumohr's *Novellen* (Munich, 1833; sole hit in COPAC), setting a significant fashion for the Italianate in prose fiction, and a collection of early prose by Willibald Alexis, also now hard to find, are evidence of this. The ever-popular Wilhelm Müller is represented not only by his agreeable verse, but by the exotic *Rom, Römer und Römerinnen* (Berlin, 1820; British Library, Oxford Taylorian and Leeds University Library). We find on Hare's shelves also examples from this period of the plain curious. Rumohr, well displayed as an art historian and prose writer, features also as a gastronome in his *Geist der Kochkunst* (Stuttgart, 1832, under the pseudonym J. König; the only other COPAC copy is in Aberdeen University Library); whereas Gottfried Immanuel Wenzel's *Entdeckungen über die Sprache der Thiere* (Vienna, 1800; sole print copy in COPAC) examines the contribution to musicology of dogs and cats. It would, however, be wrong to seize at random on bizarre or seemingly nugatory items in Hare's collection. For they are indeed in the minority. Next to theology, philosophy and belles-lettres, the critical and aesthetic literature of the period is the most significant item, bearing out Hare's observation that the Germans had made this discipline into a 'science'. Thus we find a good sample of names like Karl Rosenkranz, Franz Horn, Robert Prutz, Karl August Varnhagen von Ense (notably his *Denkwürdigkeiten und Vermischte Schriften,* Mannheim, 1837), Tieck's friend Karl Wilhelm Ferdinand Solger (also much admired by Coleridge), Adam Müller, Wolfgang Menzel and Arnold Ruge.

It may therefore be appropriate to end this — necessarily sketchy — introduction to Hare's German collection by presenting the text of a letter tipped in to one of his books. A copy of Sir George Grey's *Poems, Traditions, and Chaunts of the Maories* (Wellington, 1853) bears a dedication to 'The Venerable Archdeacon Hare with Sir George Greys regards Septr. 1854'. Apart from his services as colonial governor and administrator, notably in South Australia and New Zealand, Grey is chiefly remembered as one of the first scholars of Polynesian mythology, the preface to his own work of the same name (1854–55) being still a standard text for the nineteenth century's understanding of 'primitive' cultures. The names of Bopp and Bunsen in Grey's letter make clear the extent to which English-language endeavour in the field of grammar and comparative religion was interwoven with the kind of German scholarship whose eloquent advocate Julius Hare remained all his active life. The letter reads:

> Windmill Hill
> Septr 22nd 1854
>
> My dear Sir
>   I feel very much obliged to you for your kind present of Bopps [sic] comparative grammar which I shall value highly as coming from you; it will be very useful to me, as I made a present of my copy of it, the English translation, to the Chief Justice of New Zealand when I left that Colony. The fifth part of the Grammar has been published, and I can peruse it this evening in London.
>   I take the liberty of begging your acceptance of the copy of a work, upon the traditional poetry of the New Zealanders which I have recently published — It will be at least a curiosity in your library, which some of your friends may like to have access ·to, and I think that the preface will interest you — will take out a copy of Bunsens [sic] work which you mention in your note.
>
> Believe me
> Truly yours
> G Grey.

Postscript 2020

Revisiting my article of 1987, I realise that Julius Hare was probably the main serious collector in Britain of books on German literature, thought and history between the years 1820 and 1840. The only really comparable collection, that in the British Library, was assembled mainly after 1840 under Antonio Panizzi. Other holdings, such as those in the Brotherton Library in Leeds, the John Rylands Library (now University Library) in Manchester, the Acton collection in Cambridge University Library, the Fiedler collection in the Taylorian Institution in Oxford, or the Priebsch collection, formerly in the old Institute of Germanic Studies and now in the Senate House Library, University of London, are of much more recent provenance. Hare's achievement lies not only in the breadth of his book collecting, but also in its enduring rarity.

Bibliography

Primary Literature

Arnim, Ludwig Achim von, *Achim von Arnim und die ihm nahe standen*, ed. by Reinhold Steig and Herman Grimm, 3 vols (Stuttgart: Cotta, 1894–1913).

—— *Arnim-Bibliographie*, ed. by Otto Mallon (Berlin: Späth, 1925, repr. Hildesheim: Olms, 1965).

Arnold, Matthew, 'Superior or University Instruction in Prussia', in *Schools and Universities on the Continent*, ed. by R. H. Super, The Complete Prose Works (Ann Arbor: University of Michigan Press, 1979).

Askania. Zeitschrift für Leben, Litteratur und Kunst, ed. by Wilhelm Müller (Dessau: Ackermann, 1820).

Athenaeurn, ed. by August Wilhelm and Friedrich Schlegel, 3 vols (Berlin: Vieweg, 1798, Unger,1799–1800).

Bodmer, Johann Jacob, *Der Hunger-Thurn in Pisa. Ein Trauerspiel* (Chur und Lindau: Typographische Gesellschaft, 1769).

Braun, Volker, 'Der Müggelsee', in *Die sanfte Revolution*, ed. by Stefan Heym and Werner Heiduczek (Leipzig, Weimar: Kiepenheuer, 1990).

Breitinger, Johann Jacob, *Critische Dichtkunst*, ed. by Wolfgang Bender, Deutsche Neudrucke. Reihe Texte des 18. Jh., 2 vols (Stuttgart: Metzler, 1966).

Brentano, Clemens, *Werke*, ed. by Wolfgang Frühwald, Bernhard Gajek and Friedhelm Kemp, 4 vols (Munich: Hanser, 1963–68).

Carlyle, Thomas, *German Romance: Specimens of its Chief Authors*, 4 vols (Edinburgh and London: Tait, 1827).

Coleridge, Samuel Taylor, *Collected Letters of Samuel Taylor Coleridge*, ed. by Earl Leslie Griggs, 6 vols (Oxford: Oxford University Press, 1956–71).

Cramer, Carl Friedrich, *Klopstock: Er, und über ihn*, 5 vols (Hamburg: Schniebes; Dessau: Gelehrten Buchhandlung; Leipzig and Altona: Kaven, 1780–92).

Dante Alighieri, *Dante Alighieri's Göttliche Comödie*, ed. by Philalethes, 3 vols in 2 (Leipzig: Teubner, 1871).

Dickinson, Emily, *The Complete Poems of Emily Dickinson*, ed. by Thomas H. Johnson (London: Faber & Faber, 1970).

Dingelstedt, Franz, *Studien und Copien nach Shakspeare* (Pesth: Hartleben, 1858).

Droste-Hülshoff, Annette von, *Historisch-kritische Ausgabe: Werke. Briefwechsel*, ed. by Winfried Woesler, 14 vols in 28 parts (Tübingen: Niemeyer, 1971–2000).

Droysen, Johann Gustav, *Geschichte Alexander des Grossen* (Berlin, Finke, 1833).

Eckermann, Johann Peter, *Gespräche mit Goethe in den letzten Jahren seines Lebens*, ed. by Ludwig Geiger (Leipzig: Hesse, n.d. [1902]).

Eichendorff, Joseph von, *Neue Gesamtausgabe der Werke und Schriften*, ed. by Gerhard Baumann and Siegfried Grosse, 4 vols. (Stuttgart: Cotta, 1957).

Engel. Texte aus der Weltliteratur, ed. by Anne Marie Fröhlich, Manesse Bibliothek der Weltliteratur (Zurich: Manesse, 1991).

Fontane, Theodor, *Werke, Schriften und Briefe*, ed. by Walter Keitel and Helmuth Nürnberger, 20 vols (Munich: Hanser, 1964–1984).

Forster, Georg, *Sämtliche Schriften, Tagebücher, Briefe*, ed. by Deutsche Akademie der Wissenschaften zu Berlin, 18 vols (Berlin: Akademie, 1963– in progress).

Freud, Sigmund, 'Unser Verhältnis zum Tode', in *Zeitgemäßes über Krieg und Tod, Studienausgabe*, ed. by Alexander Mitscherlich et al., 11 vols (Frankfurt am Main: Fischer, 1969–79), IX, 49–60.

Friedrich, Caspar David, *Caspar David Friedrich in Briefen und Bekenntnissen*, ed. by Sigrid Hinz (Berlin: Henschel, 1984).

Geibel, Emanuel, *Der Briefwechsel zwischen Emanuel Geibel und Paul Heyse*, ed. by Erich Petzel (Munich: Lehmann, 1922).

Gellert, Christian Fürchtegott, *Sämmtliche Werke, Sammlung der besten deutschen Prosaschriftsteller*, 9 parts (Carlsruhe: Schmieder, 1774).

George, Stefan, *Stefan George. Friedrich Gundolf, Briefwechsel*, ed. by Robert Boehringer and Georg Peter Landmann (Munich, Düsseldorf: Küpper, 1962).

Gerstenberg, Heinrich Wilhelm von, *Ugolino. Eine Tragödie in fünf Aufzügen. Mit einem Anhang und einer Auswahl aus den theoretischen und kritischen Schriften*, ed. by Christoph Siegrist, Reclams Universal-Bibliothek 141.2 (Stuttgart: Reclam, 1977).

—— *Briefe über Merkwürdigkeiten der Literatur. Vollständige Neuausgabe mit einer Biographie des Dichters*, ed. by Karl-Maria Guth, Sammlung Hofenberg (Berlin: Contumax, 2013).

Gervinus, Georg Gottfried, *Neuere Geschichte der poetischen National-Literatur der Deutschen. Vierter Theil* (Leipzig: Engelmann, 1843).

Goethe, Johann Wolfgang,*, Ueber Kunst und Alterthum*, 6 vols (Stuttgart: Cotta, 1816–27).

—— *Tagebücher und Briefe Goethes aus Italien an Frau von Stein und Herder*, ed. by Erich Schmidt, Schriften der Goethe-Gesellschaft 2 (Weimar: Goethe-Gesellschaft, 1886).

—— *Werke, herausgegeben im Auftrage der Großherzogin Sophie von Sachsen-Weimar*, 143 vols (Weimar: Böhlau, 1887–1919).

—— *Werke. Hamburger Ausgabe*, ed. by Erich Trunz et al., 12 vols (Hamburg: Wegner, 1948–60).

—— *Italian Journey, 1786–1788* (translation by W. H. Auden and Elizabeth Mayer) (London: Collins, 1962).

—— *Der junge Goethe. Neu bearbeitete Ausgabe in fünf Bänden*, ed. by Hanna Fischer-Lamberg, 5 vols (Berlin: De Gruyter, 1963–74).

—— *Der junge Goethe im zeitgenössischen Urteil*, ed. by Peter Müller, Deutsche Bibliothek 2 (Berlin: Akademie, 1969).

—— *Sämtliche Werke*, 18 vols (Zurich: Artemis, 1977).

—— *Goethe in vertraulichen Briefen seiner Zeitgenossen*, ed. by Wilhelm Bode, 3 vols (Berlin: Aufbau, 1979).

—— *Die Leiden des jungen Werther. Ein unklassischer Klassiker. Neu herausgegeben und mit Dokumenten und Materialien, Wertheriana und Wertheriaden*, ed. by Hans Christoph Buch, Wagenbach Taschenbücher 898 (Berlin: Wagenbach, 1982).

—— *Sämtliche Werke, Briefe, Tagebücher und Gespräche*, ed. by Dieter Borchmeyer and et al., 40 vols (Frankfurt am Main: Deutscher Klasiker Verlag, 1985–98).

—— *"Ein Dichter hatte uns alle geweckt". Goethe und die literarische Romantik*, ed. by Christoph Perels (Frankfurt am Main: Freies Deutsches Hochstift, 1999).

Grimm, Herman, *Leben Michelangelo's* (Hanover: Rümpler, 1860–63).

Grimm, Jacob, *Kleinere Schriften*, 8 vols (Berlin: Dümmler, 1879–84; Gütersloh: Bertelsmann, 1890).

Grimm, Wilhelm, *Kleinere Schriften*, ed. by Gustav Hinrichs, 4 vols (Berlin: Dümmler, 1881–83, Gütersloh: Bertelsmann, 1887).

Grimm, Jacob, and Wilhelm Grimm, *Kinder- und Hausmärchen*, 3 vols (Göttingen: Dieterich, 1837, 1855).

Gruber, J. G., *C. M. Wielands Leben*, 4 vols (Leipzig, 1827–28).

Gutzkow, Karl, *Eine Shakspearefeier an der Ilm* (Leipzig: Brockhaus, 1864).

—— *Vom Baum der Erkenntnis, Werke*, ed. by Reinhold Gensel, 12 parts (Berlin, Leipzig, Vienna, Stuttgart: Bong, n.d. [1910]), XII.

Hare, Augustus J. C., *Memorials of a Quiet Life*, 3 vols (London: Smith Elder, 1884).

—— *The Story of My Life*, 6 vols (London: George Allen, 1896).

Hare, Julius, 'A. W. Schlegel on Shakespeare's Romeo and Juliet; with Remarks upon the Character of German Criticism', *Olliers Literary Miscellany in Prose and Verse*, 1 (1820), 1–39.

Hare, A. W., and J. C. Hare, *Guesses at Truth by Two Brothers* (London, New York: Macmillan, 1880).

Hazlitt, William, 'On Characters of Shakespeare's Plays', in *The Complete Works of William Hazlitt*, ed. by P. P. Howe, 21 vols (London, Toronto: Dent, 1930–34), IV, 174–78.

Hebbel, Friedrich, *Werke*, ed. by Gerhard Fricke, Werner Keller and Karl Pörnbacher, 5 vols (Munich: Hanser, 1963–67).

Hederich, Benjamin, *Gründliches Mythologisches Lexicon* [...] (Leipzig: Gleditsch, 1770; repr. Darmstadt: Wissenschaftliche Buchgesellschaft, 1967).

Heine, Heinrich, *Säkularausgabe. Werke. Briefwechsel. Lebenszeugnisse*, ed. by the Nationale Forschungs- und Gedenkstätten der klassischen deutschen Literatur in Weimar and the Centre National de la Recherche Scientifique in Paris, 27 vols (Berlin: Akademie; Paris: Éditions du CNRS, 1970–84).

—— *Gesamtausgabe der Werke*, ed. by Manfred Windfuhr et al., 16 vols in 23 (Hamburg: Hoffmann & Campe, 1973–97).

—— *Sämtliche Schriften*, ed. by Klaus Briegleb, 6 vols in 7 (Munich: Hanser, 1968–76).

—— *Shakespeares Mädchen und Frauen*, ed. by Volkmar Hansen (Frankfurt am Main: Insel, 1978).

Herder, Johann Gottfried, *Sämtliche Werke*, ed. by Bernhard Suphan, 33 vols (Berlin 1877–1913).

Heyse, Paul, *Lyrische Dichtungen*, 4 vols (Stuttgart and Berlin: Cotta, 1911).

Heyse, Paul, and Kurz, Hermann, eds., *Deutscher Novellenschatz*, 24 vols (Munich, Leipzig: Oldenbourg 1871–74).

Hölderlin, Friedrich, *Sämtliche Werke. Große Stuttgarter Ausgabe*, ed. by Friedrich Beissner et al. (Stuttgart: Kohlhammer, 1946–85).

Die Horen eine Monatsschrift, ed. by Frierich Schiller (Tübingen: Cotta, 1795–97).

Horn, Franz, *Shakespeare's Schauspiele*, 3 parts (Leipzig: Brockhaus, 1823–31).

Humboldt, Alexander von, *Briefe von Alexander von Humboldt an Varnhagen von Ense aus den Jahren 1827 bis 1858* (Leipzig: Brockhaus, 1860).

Jäger, Oskar, *Zu Schillers Gedächtnis* (Wetzlar: n.p., 1859).

—— *Pro Domo. Reden und Aufsätze* (Berlin: Seehagen, 1894).

Jameson, Anna. *Characteristics of Woman. Moral, Political, and Historical*, 2 vols (London: Saunders and Ottley, 1832).

Kanne, Johann Arnold, *Mythologie der Griechen*, part 1 (Leipzig: Breitkopf und Härtel, 1805).

Keble, John, *The Christian Year: Thoughts in Verse for the Sundays and Holydays Throughout the Year* (London: 'Review of Reviews' Office, n.d. [1895]).

Keller, Gottfried, *Gesammelte Briefe*, ed. by Carl Helbing, 4 vols (Berne: Benteli, 1950–54).

Kleist, Heinrich von, *Hinterlassene Schriften* (Berlin: Reimer, 1821).

—— *Gesammelte Schriften* (Berlin: Reimer, 1826).

—— *Werke. Kritisch durchgesehene Gesamtausgabe*, ed. by Erich Schmidt, Georg Minde-Pouet and Reinhold Steig, 5 vols (Leipzig, Vienna: Bibliographisches Institut, 1904–05).

—— *Sämtliche Werke und Briefe*, ed. by Helmut Semdner, 2 vols (Munich: Hanser, 1961).

—— *Penthesilea. Dokumente und Zeugnisse*, ed. by Helmut Sembdner (Frankfurt am Main: Insel, 1967).

Klopstock, Friedrich Gottlieb, *Sämmtliche Werke*, 10 vols (Leipzig, 1854–55).

—— *Ausgewählte Werke*, ed. by Karl August Schleiden (Darmstadt: Wissenschaftliche Buchgesellschaft, 1961).

—— *Oden. Eine Auswahl*, ed. by Karl Ludwig Schneider, Reclams Universal-Bibliothek 13.91102 (Stuttgart: Reclam, 1966).

—— *Historisch-kritische Ausgabe*, ed. by Horst Gronemeyer et al., 26 vols (Berlin, New York: De Gruyter, 1979–).

Kreyssig, F. A. Th., *Ueber die sittliche und volksthümliche Berechtigung des Shakespeare-Cultus. Festrede, bei der Shakespeare-Feier in Elbing am 23. April 1864 gehalten* (Elbing: Neumann Hartmann, 1864).

Kuenzel, Heinrich, *William Shakespeare. Zum Gedächtniss seines dreihundertjährigen Geburtstages am 23. April 1864* (Darmstadt: Victor Gross, 1864).

Lange, Samuel Gotthold, *Horatzische Oden. Nebst Georg Friedrich Meiers Vorrede vom Werthe der Reime* (Halle: Hemmerde, 1747).

Lemcke, L. G., *Shakspeare in seinem Verhälltnisse zu Deutschland. Ein Vortrag gehalten im Rathhaussaale zu Marburg am 16. Febr. 1864* (Leipzig: Vogel, 1864).

Lenz, Jakob Michael Reinhold, *Werke und Schriften*, ed. by Britte Titel and Hellmut Haug, 2 vols (Stuttgart: Goverts, 1966).

Lessing, Gotthold Ephraim, *Gotthold Ephraim Lessings Leben, nebst seinem noch übrigen litterarischen Nachlasse*, ed. by K. G. Lessing, 3 vols (Berlin: Voss, 1793–95).

—— *Werke*, ed. by Franz Muncker, 12 vols (Stuttgart: Göschen, 1890).

Lua, A. L., *William Shakespeare. Eine Festrede, gehalten bei der volksthtümlichen Feier des dreihundertjährigen Geburtstags des Dichters im Saale des alten Weinbergs zu Schidlitz* (Danzig: Constantin Ziemssen, 1864).

Marlowe, Christopher, *Doktor Faustus. Tragödie von Christoph Marlowe*, trans. by Wilhelm Müller (Berlin: Maurer, 1818).

—— *Doktor Faustus*, ed. by Bertha Badt, Pandora 11 (Munich: Georg Müller, 1911).

Möbius, Paul, *Shakespeare als Dichter der Naturwahrheit. Festrede bei der Shakespearefeier zu Leipzig am 23. April 1864 gehalten* (Leipzig: Voigt & Günther, 1864).

—— *Die deutsche Shakespearefeier. Eine Rechtfertigung derselben nach einem im kaufmännischen Vereine zu Leipzig gehaltenen Vortrage* (Leipzig: Julius Werner, 1864).

Montagu, Elizabeth, *An Essay on the Writings and Genius of Shakespeare Compared With the Greek and French Dramatic Poets. With Some Remarks upon the Misrepresentations of Mons. de Voltaire* (London: Dilly, 1772).

Moritz, Karl Philipp, *Götterlehre oder mythologische Dichtungen der Alten*, 3. Auflage (Berlin: Unger, 1804).

Müller, Wilhelm, *Blumenlese aus den Minnesingern*, ed. by Wilhelm Müller (Berlin: Maurer, 1816).

—— *Bibliothek deutscher Dichter des siebzehnten Jahrhunderts*, ed. by Wilhelm Müller, 14 vols (Leipzig: Brockhaus, 1822–38).

—— 'Gries und Streckfuß Uebersetzungen von Tasso's befreitem Jerusalem', *Hermes oder kritisches Jahrbuch der Literatur*, 18, 2 (1823), 261–300.

—— 'Ueber die Gedichte des Thomas Moore', *Hermes oder kritisches Jahrbuch der Literatur*, 20, 4 (1823), 184–211.

—— *Homerische Vorschule. Eine Einleitung in das Studium der Ilias u. der Odyssee* (Leipzig: Brockhaus, 1824).

—— *Neugriechische Volkslieder*, ed. by C. Fauriel, trans. by Wilhelm Müller, 2 parts (Leipzig: Voss, 1825).

—— *Vermischte Schriften*, ed. by Gustav Schwab, 5 vols (Leipzig: Brockhaus, 1830).

—— *Gedichte von Wilhelm Müller*, ed. by Gustav Schwab, 2 vols (Leipzig: Brockhaus, 1837).

—— *Gedichte von Wilhelm Müller*, ed. by Max Müller, 2 parts, Bibliothek der Deutschen Nationalliteratur des achtzehnten und neunzehnten Jahrhunderts (Leipzig: Brockhaus, 1868).

—— *Gedichte von Wilhelm Müller*, ed. by Curt Müller (Leipzig: Reclam, 1898).

—— *Diary and Letters of Wilhelm Müller*, ed. by Philip Schuyler Allen and James Taft Hatfield (Chicago: Chicago University Press, 1903).

—— *Gedichte von Wilhelm Müller*, ed. by James Taft Hatfield, Deutsche Literaturdenkmale des 18. und 19. Jahrhunderts 137 (Berlin: Behr, 1906).

—— *Wilhelm Müller als Kritiker und Erzähler. Ein Lebensbild mit Briefen an F. A. Brockhaus und anderen Schriftstücken*, ed. by Heinrich Lohre, Aus dem Archiv F. A. Brockhaus, Zeugnisse zur Geschichte geistigen Schaffens 2 (Leipzig: Brockhaus, 1927).

—— *Werke, Tagebücher, Briefe*, ed. by Maria-Verena Leistner, 5 vols (Berlin: Mathias Gatza, 1994).

—— *Wilhelm Müller. Eine Lebensreise. Zum 200. Geburtstag des Dichters*, ed. by Norbert Michels, Kataloge der anhaltischen Gemäldegalerie Dessau (Weimar: Böhlau, 1994).

Nicolai, K., *Klopstock: Ein Denkmahl zur Säcularfeier seines Geburtstages am zweiten Julius 1824* (Quedlinburg: Basse, 1824).

Nietzsche, Friedrich, *Werke*, ed. by Karl Schlechta, 3 vols (Munich: Hanser, 1969).

Novalis, *Schriften. Die Werke Friedrich von Hardenbergs. Historisch-kritische Ausgabe*, ed. by Paul Kluckhohn and Richard Samuel et al., 6 vols (Stuttgart: Kohlhammer, 1960–88).

Oken, Lorenz, *Ueber den Werth der Naturgeschichte, besonders für die Bildung der Deutschen. Von Oken, bei der Eröffnung seiner Vorlesungen über Zoologie* (Jena: Frommannn, 1809).

—— *Isis oder Encyclopedische Zeitung von Oken* (Jena: Expedition der Isis, Leipzig: Brockhaus, 1817–48).

Phöbus. Ein Journal für die Kunst, ed. by Heinrich v. Kleist and Adam H. Müller (Dresden: Gärtner, 1808).

Pope, Alexander, *The Twickenham Edition of the Poems of Alexander Pope*, 10 vols in 11 (London: Methuen, 1939–69).

Propyläen. Eine periodische Schrift von Goethe, 3 vols (Tübingen: Cotta, 1798–1800).

Ranke, Leopold von, *Geschichte Wallenstein's* (Leipzig,: Duncker & Humblot, 1869).

Reynolds, Joshua, *The Discourses of Sir Joshua Reynolds*, ed. by John Burnet (London: James Carpenter, 1842).

Riepenhausen, Franz, and Johannes Riepenhausen, *Leben und Tod der heiligen Genoveva* (Frankfurt am Main: Varrentrapp und Wenner, 1806).

Rilke, Rainer Maria, *Rainer Maria Rilke, Duineser Elegien. Die Sonette an Orpheus*, ed. by Katharina Kippenberg, Manesse Bibliothek der Weltliteratur (Zurich: Manesse, 1951).

—— *Sämtliche Werke*, ed. by Rilke-Archiv, Ruth Sieber-Rilke and Ernst Zinn, 5 vols (Frankfurt am Main: Insel, 1955–66).

—— *Gedichte an die Nacht*, ed. by Anthony Stephens, Bibliothek Suhrkamp, 519 (Frankfurt am Main: Suhrkamp, 1983).

—— Fülleborn, Ulrich, and Manfred Engel, *Materialien zu Rilkes Duineser Elegien*, 3 vols (Frankfurt am Main: Suhrkamp, 1980–82).

Rossetti, Christina, *The Complete Poems of Christina Rossetti: A Variorum Edition*, ed. by R. W. Crump, 2 vols (Baton Rouge, London: Lousiana State University Press, 1979; 1986).

Rüdiger, Johann Christoph, *VITAE CLARISSIMORUM in re literaria Virorum. Das ist Lebens-Beschreibung etlicher Hauptgelehrten Männer/so von der Literatur profeß gemacht. Worinnen Viel sonderbahre und notable Sachen/so wohl von ihren Leben/als geführten Studiis entdecket. Allen curieusen Gemüthern zu sonderbahrem Nutzen und Vergnügen entworffen/von ADOLPHO CLARMUNDO* (Wittenberg: Christian Gottlieb Ludwig, 1704–05).

Sandrart, Joachim von, 'Albrecht Dürer Mahler/Bildhauer/Kupferstecher und Baumeister von Nürnberg', in *L'Academia Todesca delle Architectura, Scultura & Pittura: Oder Deutsche Academie der Edlen Bau- Bild- und Mahlerey-Kunste*, 2 vols (Nuremberg: Miltenberger, 1675–79), I., II. Theils III. Buch, III. Capitel, 222–29.

Schelling, Friedrich Wilhelm Joseph, *Vorlesungen über die Methode des akademischen Studiums*. Auf der Grundlage des Texts der Ausgabe von Otto Weiss ed. Walter E. Ehrhardt, Philosophische Bibliothek, 275 (Hamburg: Meiner, 1974).

Schiller, Friedrich, *Sämtliche Werke*, ed. by Gerhard Fricke, Herbert G. Göpfert and Herbert Stubenrauch, 5 vols (Munich: Hanser, 1960).

—— *Schiller - Zeitgenosse aller Epochen. Dokumente zur Wirkungsgeschichte Schillers in Deutschland*, ed. by Norbert Oellers, 2 vols, I: 1782–1859. II: 1860–1966, Wirkung der Literatur. Deutsche Autoren im Urteil ihrer Kritiker, 1–2, ed. by Karl Robert Mandelkow (Frankfurt am Main: Athenäum, 1970).

—— *Schillers ‚Wallenstein'*, ed. by Fritz Heuer and Werner Keller, Wege der Forschung 420 (Darmstadt: Wissenschaftliche Buchgesellschaft, 1977).

—— *Friedrich Schiller: ‚Wallenstein': Erläuterungen und Dokumente*, ed. by Kurt Rothmann, Reclams Universal-Bibliothek 8136.3 (Stuttgart: Reclam, 1982).

Schlegel, August Wilhelm, *Sämmtliche Werke*, ed. by Eduard Böcking, 12 vols (Leipzig: Weidmann, 1846–47).

—— *Kritische Ausgabe der Vorlesungen*, ed. by Ernst Behler et al., 4 vols (Paderborn, etc.: Schöningh, 1989-).

—— *Briefe von und an August Wiilhelm Schlegel*, ed. by Josef Körner, 2 vols (Zurich, Leipzig, Vienna: Amalthea, 1930).

Schlegel, Friedrich, *Kritische Ausgabe*, ed. by Ernst Behler et al., 35 vols (Paderborn etc.: Schöningh, 1958– in progress).

Schlegel, August Wilhelm, and Friedrich Schlegel, *Charakeristiken und Kritiken*, 2 vols (Königsberg: Nicolovius, 1801).

Schink, Johann Friedrich, 'Charakteristik Gotthold Ephraim Lessings', in *Pantheon der Deutschen*, ed. by Karl Gottlieb Hofmann, 3 vols (Chemnitz, Leipzig: Hofmann, 1794–95), II, 1–192.

Schmidt, Klamer, ed., *Klopstock und seine Freunde* (Halberstadt: Bureau für Literatur und Kunst, 1810).

Schubert, Gotthilf Heinrich, *Ansichten von der Nachtseite der Naturwissenschaft* (Dresden: Arnold, 1808).

Schwab, Gustav, *Schiller's Leben in drei Büchern* (Stuttgart: Liesching, 1840).

—— 'Wilhelm Müller's Leben', in *Wilhelm Müller, Vermischte Schriften*, ed. by Gustav Schwab, 5 vols (Leipzig: Brockhaus, 1830), I, xvii-lxii.

—— 'Wilhelm Hauff's Leben', in *Wilhelm Hauff, Sämmtliche Werke*, ed. by Gustav Schwab, 5 vols, 5th ed. (Stuttgart: Brodhag, 1853), I, 5–20.

Shakespeare, William, *William Shakespeare's dramatische Werke*, trans. by Friedrich Bodenstedt et al., 38 vols (Leipzig: Brockhaus, 1867–71).

—— *Shakespeare in deutscher Sprache. Neue Ausgabe in sechs Bänden*, ed. and trans. by Friedrich Gundolf (Berlin: Bondi, 1922).

—— *Shakespeare-Rezeption. Die Diskussion um Shakespeare in Deutschand. 1. Ausgewählte Texte von 1741 bis 1788*, ed. by Hansjürgen Blinn (Berlin: Erich Schmidt, 1982).

Stanley, A. P., 'Archdeacon Hare', *The Quarterly Review*, 97 (June-Sept. 1855), 1–128.

Sterling, John, 'Characteristics of German Genius', in *Essays and Tales, by John Sterling, Collected and Edited, With a Memoir of His Life*, ed. by Julius Charles Hare, 2 vols (London: Parker, 1848).

Stolberg, Friedrich Leopold von, *Gesammelte Werke der Brüder Christian und Friedrich Leopold Grafen zu Stolberg*, 20 vols (Hamburg: Perthes u. Besser, 1820–25).

—— *Briefe*, ed. by Jürgen Behrens, Kieler Studien zur deutschen Literaturgeschichte 5 (Neumünster: Wachhholz, 1966).

Tieck, Ludwig, *Der gestiefelte Kater. Kindermärchen in drei Akten, mit Zwischenspielen, einem Prologe und Epiloge von Peter Leberecht. Aus dem Italienischen* (Berlin: Carl August Nicolai, 1797).

—— *Die sieben Weiber des Blaubart. Eine wahre Familiengeschichte herausgegeben von Gottlieb Färber. Istambul, bey Heraklius Murusi Hofbuchhändler der hohen Pforte; im Jahr der Hedschrah 1212* (Berlin: Carl August Nicolai, 1797).

—— *Volksmährchen*, ed. by Peter Leberecht, 3 vols (Berlin: Carl August Nicolai, 1797).

—— *Leben und Tod der heiligen Genoveva. Ein Trauerspiel*. In: *Romantische Dichtungen von Ludwig Tieck*, 2 vols (Jena: Frommann, 1799–1800), II, 1–272.

—— *Kaiser Octavianus. Ein Lustspiel in zwei Theilen von Ludwig Tieck* (Jena: Frommann, 1804).

—— *Gedichte von L. Tieck*, 3 parts (Dresden: Hilscher, 1821–23).

—— *Schriften*, 20 vols (Berlin: Reimer, 1828–46).

—— *Franz Sternbalds Wanderungen*, ed. by Alfred Anger, Reclams Universal-Bibliothek, 8715–21 (Stuttgart: Reclam, 1966).

—— *Ludwig Tieck und die Brüder Schlegel*, ed. by Edgar Lohner (Munich: Winkler, 1972).

—— *Schriften in zwölf Bänden*, ed. by Manfred Frank et al., 6 vols (Frankfurt am Main: Deutscher Klassiker Verlag, 1985-).

Wachler, Ludwig, *Vorlesungen über die Geschichte der deutschen Nationalliteratur*, 2 vols (Frankfurt am Main: Hermann, 1818–19).

Wolfskehl, Karl, and Hanna Wolfskehl, *Briefwechsel mit Friedrich Gundolf 1899–1931*, ed. by Karlheinz Kluncker, 2 vols, Publications of the Institute of Germanic Studies, University of London (Amsterdam: Castrum Peregrini, 1977).

Wolzogen, Caroline von, *Schillers Leben, verfaßt aus Erinnerungen der Familie, seinen eigenen Briefen und den Nachrichten seines Freundes Körner*, 2 vols (Stuttgart, Tübingen: Cotta, 1830).

Young, Edward, *Night Thoughts. Night the Third* (London: Dodsley, 1742).

—— *The Correspondence of Edward Young 1683–1765*, ed. by Henry Pettit (Oxford: Clarendon, 1971).

Zimmermann, Johann Georg, *Solitude. Or The Effect of Occasional Retirement* […], *Originally by M. Zimmermann* (London: Verner and Hood, 1800).

Secondary Literature

Ahlefeld, Yvonne-Patricia, '"Der Simplicität der Griechen am nächsten kommen". Entfesselte Animalität in Heinrich Wilhelm von Gerstenbergs Ugolino', *Herder Jahrbuch*, 6 (2002), 63–82.

Alewyn, Richard, 'Vorbarocker Klassizismus und griechische Tragödie. Analyse der "Antigone"-Übersetzung des Martin Opitz', *Neue Heidelberger Jahrbücher* (1926), 3–63.

Anrich, Ernst, *Die Idee der deutschen Universität und die Reform der deutschen Universitäten* (Darmstadt: Wissensschaftliche Buchgesellschaft, 1960).

Assmann, Aleida, *Erinnerungsräume. Formen und Wandlungen des kulturellen Gedächtnisses* (Munich: Beck, 1999).

Becker, Eva D., 'Klassiker in der deutschen Literaturgeschichtsschreibung zwischen 1780 und 1860', in *Literarisches Leben. Umschreibungen der deutschen Literaturgeschichte*, Saarbrücker Beiträge zur Literaturwissenschaft 45 (St. Ingbert: Röhrig, 1994), 7–26.

Beissner, Friedrich, *Klopstocks Ode 'Der Zürcherseee': Ein Vortrag* (Münster, Cologne: Böhlau, 1952).

Benz, Richard, *Goethe und die romantische Kunst* (Munich: Piper, 1940).

Berlin, University of, *Idee und Wirklichkeit einer Universität. Dokumente zur Geschichte der Friedrich-Wilhelms-Universität zu Berlin. In Zusammenarbeit mit Wolfgang Muller-Lauter u. Michael Theunissen*, ed. by Wilhelm Weischedel, Gedenkschrift der Freien Universität Berlin zur 150. Wiederkehr des Gründungsjahres der Friedrich-Wilhelms-Universität zu Berlin (Berlin: De Gruyter, 1960).

Bleuel, Hans Peter, *Deutschlands Bekenner. Professoren zwischen Kaiserreich und Diktatur* (Berne: Scherz, 1968).

Beyer, Waldtraut, 'Der Atheismusstreit um Fichte', in *Debatten und Kontroversen. Literarische Auseinandersetzungen in Deutschland am Ende des 18. Jahrhunderts*, ed. by Hans-Dieter Dahnke and Bernd Leistner, 2 vols (Berlin, Weimar: Aufbau, 1989).

Blamires, David, *Telling Tales. The Impact of Germany on English Children's Books 1780–1918* (Cambridge: Open Book Publishers, 2009), https://doi.org/10.11647/obp.0004

Bräuning-Oktavio, Hermann, *Oken und Goethe im Lichte neuer Quellen* (Weimar: Arion, 1959).

Brink, C. O., *English Classical Scholarship. Historical Reflections on Bentley, Porson, and Housman* (Cambridge: James Clarke; Oxford: Oxford University Press, 1986).

Brown, Hilda M., *Kleist and the Tragic Ideal. A Study of Penthesilea and its Relationship to Kleist's Personal and Literary Development 1806–1808*, European University Papers 1.203 (Berne, Frankfurt, Las Vegas: Lang, 1977).

Bruford, W. H., *The German Tradition of Self-Cultivation: 'Bildung' from Humboldt to Thomas Mann* (Cambridge: Cambridge University Press, 1975).

Büchting, Adolph, *Verzeichniß der zur hundertjährigen Geburtsfeier Friedrich von Schiller's erschienenen Bücher, Kunstblätter, Kunstwerke, Musikalien, Denkmünzen etc.* (Nordhausen: Büchting, 1860).

Burkert, Walter, *Homo necans: Interpretationen altgriechischer Opferriten und Mythen* (Berlin: De Gruyter, 1972).

Cassirer, Ernst, *Philosophie der symbolischen Formen*, 3 vols (Berlin: Bruno Cassirer, 1923–29).

Collini, Stefan, *What Are Universities For?* (London: Penguin, 2012).

—— *Speaking of Universities* (London, New York: Verso, 2017).

Deffner, Andrea, 'Die "Hamlet"-Ubersetzung Theodor Fontanes' (unpublished doctoral thesis, University of Heidelberg, 1991).

Deutsche Erinnerungsorte, ed. by Étienne François and Hagen Schulze, 3 vols (Munich: Beck, 2003).

Deutsche Romantiker. Kostbare Bücher in Erstausgaben. Sammlung aus dem Antiquariat Gunnar A. Koldewey, Düsseldorf (Wolfenbüttel: Herzog August Bibliothek, 1979).

Distad, N. Merrill, *Guessing at Truth. The Life of Julius Charles Hare (1795–1855)* (Shepherdstown: Patmos, 1979).

Döllinger, Ignaz von, *Dr. Joh. Jos. Ign. von Döllinger, Die Universitäten sonst und jetzt*, 2nd ed. (Munich: Manz, 1867).

du Moulin Eckart, Richard Graf, *Geschichte der deutschen Universitäten* (Stuttgart: Enke, 1929).

Dyer, Denis, 'The Imagery of Kleist's "Penthesilea"', *PEGS*, NS 31 (1960–61), 1–23.

Eggers, Christian, *Christian Daniel Rauch*, 5 vols (Berlin: Duncker, 1873–91).

Entrup, Dorothea, *Adolph Menzels Illustrationen zu Franz Kuglers 'Geschichte Friedrichs des Grossen'. Ein Beitrag zur stilistischen und historischen Bewertung der Kunst des jungen Menzel* (Weimar: VDG, 1990).

Ermisch, Hubert, 'König Johann und König Friedrich Wilhelm IV.', *Neues Archiv f. Sächsische Geschichte und Altertumskunde*, 32 (1921), 89–135.

Evans, R. J., 'The History Wars', *New Statesman* (June 19, 2020), https://www.newstatesman.com/international/2020/06/history-wars

Fish, Stanley, *Versions of Academic Freedom: From Professionalism to Revolution*, The Rice University Campbell Lectures (Chicago: University of Chicago Press, 2014), https://doi.org/10.7208/chicago/9780226170251.001.0001

Fliess, Wilhelm, *Vom Leben und vom Tod. Biologische Vorträge* (Jena: Diederichs, 1924).

Fohrmann, Jürgen, *Das Projekt der deutschen Literaturgeschichte. Entstehen und Scheitern einer nationalen Literaturgeschichte zwischen Humanismus und Deutschem Kaiserreich* (Stuttgart: Metzler, 1989).

—— '"Wir besprechen uns in bequemen Stunden. . ." Zum Goethe-Schiller-Verhältnis und seiner Rezeption im 19. Jahrhundert', in *Klassik im Vergleich. Normativität und Historizität europäischer Klassiken, DFG Symposion 1990*, ed. by Wilhelm Vosskamp (Stuttgart, Weimar: Metzler, 1993), 571–93.

Foulkes, Reginald, 'Samuel Taylor Coleridge', in *Voltaire, Goethe, Schlegel, Coleridge*, ed. by Roger Paulin, Great Shakespeareans 3 (London, New York: continuum, 2010), 128–72, https://doi.org/10.5040/9781472555557.ch-004

Fricker, Robert, 'Hundert Jahre Shakespeare-Jahrbuch', *Shakespeare Jahrbuch (West)*, 100 (1964), 33–67.

Friederiksen, Elke, and Monika Shafi, 'Annette von Droste-Hülshoff (1797–1840): Konfliktstrukturen im Frühwerk', in *Out of Line/ Ausgefallen: The Paradox of Marginality in the Writings of Nineteenth-Century German Women*, ed. by Ruth-Ellen Boetcher Joeres and Marianne Burkhard (Amsterdam: Rodopi, 1989), 115–36.

Garner, Jörg, 'Goethe-Denkmä!er — Schiller-Denkmäler', in *Denkmäler im 19. Jahrhundert. Deutung und Kritik*, ed. by Hans-Ernst Mittig and Volker Pagemann, Studien zur Kunst des 19. Jahrhunderts 20 (Munich: Prestel, 1972), 141–62.

Gerhard, Melitta, 'Die Redaktion der "Italienischen Reise" im Lichte von Goethes autobiographischem Gesamtwerk', *Jahrbuch des Freien Deutschen Hochstifts* (1930), 131–50.

Gethmann-Siefert, Annemarie, *Die Funktion der Kunst in der Geschichte*, Hegel-Studien, Beiheft 25 (Bonn: Bouvier, 1984).

Gockel, Heinz, 'Mythologie als Onotologie. Zum Mythosbegriff im 19. Jahrhundert', in *Mythos und Mythologie in der Literatur des 19. Jahrhunderts*, ed. by Helmut Koopmann, Studien zur Philosophie und Literatur des neunzehnten Jahrhunderts 36 (Frankfurt am Main: Klostermann, 1979), 25–58.

Goedeke, Karl, *Grundriß zur Geschichte der deutschen Dichtung* [...] cont. by Edmund Goetze, Vol. VIII, i: *Vom Weltfrieden bis zur französischen Revolution 1830* (Dresden: Ehlermann, 1905).

Graevenitz, Gerhart von, 'Geschichte aus dem Geist des Nekrologs: Zur Begründung der Biographie im 19. Jahrhundert', *Deutsche Vierteljahrsschrift für Literaturwissenschaft und Geistesgeschichte*, 54 (1980), 105–70.

Graves, Robert, *The White Goddess. A Historical Grammar of Poetic Myth* (London: Faber, 1981).

Günther, Horst, 'Klassik und Weltliteratur', in *Literarische Klassik*, ed. by Hans-Joachim Simm, suhrkamp taschenbuch 2084 (Frankfurt am Main: Suhrkamp, 1988), 87–100.

Gundolf, Friedrich, *Shakespeare und der deutsche Geist* (Berlin: Bondi, 1920 [1911]).

—— *Goethe* (Berlin: Bondi, 1930 [1916]).

—— *Andreas Gryphius* (Heidelberg: Winter, 1927).

—— *Shakespeare. Sein Wesen und Werk*, 2 vols (Berlin: Bondi, 1928).

—— *Romantiker. Neue Folge* (Berlin-Wilmersdorf: Heinrich Keller, 1929).

—— *Dem lebendigen Geist*, ed. by Dorothea Berger und Marga Frank, Veröffentlichungen der Deutschen Akademie für Sprache und Dichtung Darmstadt 27 (Heidelberg, Darmstadt: Lambert Schneider, 1962).

—— *Briefe. Neue Folge*, ed. by Lothar Helbing and Claus Victor Bock (Amsterdam: Castrum Peregrini, 1965).

—— *Caesar. Geschichte seines Ruhms* (Darmstadt: Wissenschaftliche Buchgesellschafft, 1968).

—— *Beiträge zur Literatur- und Geistesgeschichte*, ed. by Victor A. Schmitz und Fritz Martini, Veröffentlichungen der Deutschen Akademie für Sprache und Dichtung Darmstadt 54 (Heidelberg: Lambert Schneider, 1980).

Guthke, Karl S., 'Schiller, Shakespeare und das Theater der Grausamkeit', in *Shakespeare im 18. Jahrhundert*, ed. by Roger Paulin, Das achtzehnte Jahrhundert. Supplementa 3 (Göttingen: Wallstein, 2007), 181–94.

Häntzschel, Günter, *Tradition und Originalität: Allegorische Darstellung im Werk Annette von Droste-Hülshoffs* (Stuttgart: Kohlhammer, 1968).

—— 'Annette von Droste Hülshoff', in *Zur Literatur der Restaurationsepoche 1815–1848: Forschungsreferate und Aufsätze*, ed. by Jost Hermand and Manfred Windfuhr (Stuttgart: Metzler, 1970), 151–201.

Habicht, Werner, 'Shakespeare in Nineteenth-Century Germany. The Making of a Myth', in *Nineteenth-Century Germany*, ed. by Modris Ecksteins and Hildegard Hammerschmidt-Hummel (Tübingen: Narr, 1983), 141–57.

—— *Shakespeare and the German Imagination*, International Shakespeare-Association Occasional Paper 5 (Herford: International Shakespeare-Association, 1994).

Hallensleben, Horst, 'Das Bonner Beethoven-Denkmal als frühes bürgerliches Standbild', in *Monument für Beethoven. Zur Geschichte des Beethoven-Denkmals (1845) und der frühen Beethoven-Rezeption in Bonn*, ed. by Ingrid Bodsch, Katalog zur Ausstellung des Stadtmuseums Bonn und des Beethoven-Hauses (Bonn: Stadtmuseum, 1995), 28–37.

Hammerstein, Notker, 'Zur Geschichte der Deutschen Universität im Zeitalter der Aufklärung', in *Universität und Gelehrtenstand 1400–1800, Büdinger Vorträge 1966*, ed. by Hellmuth Rössler and Günther Franz, Deutsche Führungsschichten der Neuzeit, 4 (Limburg/Lahn: Starke, 1970), 5–82.

Handbuch Biographie. Methoden, Traditionen, Theorien, ed. by Christian Klein (Stuttgart: Metzler, 2009).

Handwörterbuch des deutschen Aberglaubens, ed. by E. Hoffmann-Kray and Hanns Bächtold-Stäuble, 10 vols (Berlin and Leipzig: De Gruyter, 1927–42).

Rudolf Haym, 'Schiller an seinem hundertjährigen Jubiläum', in *Gesammelte Aufsätze* (Berlin: Weidmann, 1903), 49–120.

Hensel, Wilhelm, *Wilhelm Hensel 1794–1861. Portraitist und Maler. Werke und Dokumente. Ausstellung zum 200. Geburtstag, veranstaltet vom Mendelssohn-Archiv der Staatsbibliothek zu Berlin-Preußischer Kulturbesitz 15. Dezember 1994 bis 29. Januar 1995* (Wiesbaden: Reichert, 1994).

Hermand, Jost, *Adolph Menzel das Flötenkonzert in Sanssouci. Ein realistisch geträumtes* Preußenbild (Frankfurt am Main: Fischer Taschenbuch-Verlag, 1985).

Hermann, Conrad, *Philosophie der Geschichte* (Leipzig: Fleischer, 1870).

Hess, Günter, 'Panorama und Denkmal. Erinnerung als Denkform zwischen Vormärz und Gründerzeit', in *Literatur in der sozialen Bewegung. Aufsätze und Forschungsberichte zum 19. Jahrhundert*, ed. by Alberto Martino et al. (Tübingen: Niemeyer, 1977), 130–206.

Hirzel, Georg, 'Ungedruckte Briefe an Georg Andreas Reimer', *Deutsche Revue*, 18 (Oct.–Dec. 1893), 98–114, 238–53.

Hocke, Gustav René, *Die Welt als Labyrinth. Manier und Manie in der europäischen Kunst. Von 1520 bis 1650 und in der Gegenwart*, rowohlts deutsche enzyklopädie 50–51, 2 vols (Hamburg: Rowohlt, 1957).

Hodler, Ferdinand, *Landschaften*, ed. by Oskar Bätschmann et al., Schweizerisches Institut für Kunstwissenschaft (Zurich: Verlagshaus Zürich, 1987).

Höltgen, Karl Josef, 'Über *Shakespeares Mädchen und Frauen*. Heine, Shakespeare und England', in *Internationaler Heine-Kongreß. Düsseldorf 1972. Referate und Diskussionen*, ed. by Manfred Windfuhr (Hamburg: Hoffmann & Campe, 1973), 464–88.

Hofmann, Werner, 'Antiker und christlicher Mythos-Natursymbolik-Kinder-Familie und Freunde', in *Runge in seiner Zeit* (Hamburg, Kunsthalle and Munich: Prestel, 1977), 278–79, 288–89.

Jacobs, Montague, *Gerstenbergs Ugolino. Ein Vorläufer des Geniedramas*, Berliner Beiträge zur germanischen und romanischen Philologie 14 (Berlin: Ebering, 1898).

Jäger, Georg, 'Die Wertherwirkung. Ein rezeptionsästhetischer Modellfall', in *Historizität in Sprach- und Literaturwissenschaft*, ed. by Walter Müller-Seidel et al. (Munich: Fink, 1974), 389–409.

Jefcoate, Graham, *An Ocean of Literature: John Henry Bohte and the Anglo-German Book Trade in the Early Nineteenth Century* (Hildesheim, Zurich, New York: Olms, 2020).

John, king of Saxony, *König Johann von Sachsen. Zwischen zwei Welten*, ed. by der Sächsischen Schlossverwaltung und dem Staatlichen Schlossbetrieb Weesenstein (Halle: Janos Stekovics, 2001).

—— *Zwischen Tradition und Modernität. König Johann von Sachsen 1801–1873*, ed. by Winifried Müller and Martina Schattkowsky, Schriften zur sächsischen Geschichte und Volkskunde 8 (Leipzig: Leipziger Universitätsverlag, 2004).

Jolles, Frank, *A. W. Schlegels Sommernachtstraum in der ersten Fassung vom Jahre 1789 nach den Handschriften herausgegeben*, Palaestra 244 (Göttingen: Vandenhoek & Ruprecht, 1967).

Kaiser, Gerhard, *Klopstock: Religion und Dichtung*, Studien zur Religion, Geschichte und Geisteswissenschaft, 1 (Gütersloh: Mohn, 1963).

—— 'Mythos und Person in Kleists "Penthesilea"', in *Wandrer und Idylle. Goethe und die Phänomenologie der Natur in der deutschen Dichtung von Gessner bis Gottfried Keller* (Göttingen: Vandenhoek & Ruprecht, 1977), 209–39.

Kennedy, Paul M., *The Rise of the Anglo-German Antagonism 1860–1914* (London: Allen & Unwin, 1980).

Kerényi, Karl, *The Gods of the Greeks*, Pelican Books A429 (Harmondsworth: Penguin Books, 1958).

—— 'Die Bacchantinnen des Euripides', in *Auf Spuren des Mythos, Werke in Einzelausgaben, II* (Munich, Vienna: Langen-Müller, 1967), 277–84.

—— ed., *Die Eröffnung des Zugangs zum Mythos. Ein Lesebuch,* Wege der Forschung 20 (Darmstadt: Wissenschaftliche Buchgesellschaft, 1967).

Killy, Walther, 'Große deutsche Lexika und ihre Lexikographen 1711–1835. Hederich, Hübner, Walch, Pierer', in *Große deutsche Lexika. Aufklärung und neunzehntes Jahrhundert* (Munich: K. G. Saur, 1992), 1–35.

Klein, Christian, *Grundlagen der Biographik. Theorie und Praxis des biographischen Schreibens* (Stuttgart: Metzler, 2002).

Klinger, Max, *Wege zum Gesamtkunstwwerk* (Mainz: Philipp von Zabern, 1984).

Klotz, Volker, 'Tragödie der Jagd. Zu Kleists "Penthesilea"', in *Kurze Kommentare zu Stücken und Gedichten,* Hessische Beiträge zur deutschen Literatur (Darmstadt: Roether, 1962), 14–21.

Kluckhohn, Paul, 'Penthesilea', *Germanisch-Romanische Monatsschrift*, 11 (1914), 276–88.

Kruckis, Hans-Martin, *'Ein potenziertes Abbild der Menschheit': Biographischer Diskurs und Etablierung der Neugermanistik in der Goethe-Biographik bis Gundolf*, Probleme der Dichtung, 24 (Heidelberg: Winter, 1995).

Küpper, Peter, 'Gundolf und die Romantik', *Euphorion*, 75 (1981), 194–203.

Kuhn, Alfred, *Die neuere Plastik von Achtzehnhundert bis zur Gegenwart* (Munich: Delphin, 1922).

Lamport, F. J., 'Wallenstein on the English Stage', *German Life and Letters*, 48 (1995), 124–47.

Langen, August, *Der Wortschatz des deutschen Pietismus* (Tübingen: Niemeyer, 1968).

La Vopa, Anthony J., *Grace, Talent, and Merit. Poor Students, Clerical Careers, and Professional Ideology in Eighteenth-Century Germany* (Cambridge: Cambridge University Press, 1988).

Lehnert, Martin, 'Hundert Jahre Deutsche Shakespeare-Gesellschaft', *Shakespeare Jahrbuch*, 100–01 (1964–65), 9–54.

Lehnert, Uta, *Der Kaiser und die Siegesallee. Réclame Royale* (Berlin: Reimer, 1998).

Lieux de mémoire, ed. by Nora, Pierre et al., 7 vols (Paris: Gallimard, 1984–1992).

Löffler, Fritz, *Das alte Dresden. Geschichte seiner Bauten* (Dresden: Sachsenverlag, 1958).

Lütkehaus, Ludger, 'Hebbels Schiller-Feier — unsere Hebbel-Feier. Dichterfeste zwischen Jubiläum und "Jubilitis"', *Hebbel-Jahrbuch* (1989), 231–42.

McClelland, Charles E., *State, Society, and University in Germany 1700–1914* (Cambridge: Cambridge University Press, 1980).

McFarland, G. F., 'The Early Literary Career of Julius Charles Hare', *Bulletin of the John Rylands Library of Manchester*, 46 (1963–64), 42–83.

McGuinness, Brian, *Wittgenstein: A Life. Young Ludwig, 1889–1921* (London: Duckworth, 1988).

Mason, Eudo C., 'Gundolfs Shakespeare', *Shakespeare Jahrbuch*, 98 (1962), 110–77.

Maurer, Doris, *Annette von Droste-Hülshoff: Ein Leben zwischen Auflehnung und Gehorsam: Biographie* (Bonn: Keil, 1982).

Mayer, Hans, 'Schillers Nachruhm', *Sinn und Form*, 11 (1959), 701–14.

Meier, Albert, ed., *Ein unsäglich schönes Land. Goethes 'Italienische Reise' und der Mythos Siziliens / Un paese indicibilimente bello. Il 'Viaggio in Italia' di Goethe e il mito della Sicilia* (Palermo: Sellerio, 1987).

Michelsen, Peter, 'Theodor Fontane als Kritiker englischer Shakespeare-Aufführungen', *Shakespeare Jahrbuch (West)* (1967), 96–122.

Mielke, Friedrich, and Jutta von Simson, *Das Berliner Denkmal für Friedrich II., den Großen* (Frankfurt, Berlin, Vienna: Propyläen, 1975).

Moody, Oliver, 'Germany Offers Statue Topplers a Lesson in How to Master the Past', *The Times* (June 26, 2020), https://www.thetimes.co.uk/article/germany-offers-statue-topplers-a-lesson-in-how-to-master-the-past-9j6brshls

Mosse, George L., *The Nationalization of the Masses. Political Symbolism and Mass Movements in Germany from the Napoleonic Wars Through the Third Reich* (New York: Howard Fertig, 1975).

Mühlmann, Wilhelm Erich, 'Goethe, Sizilien und wir', *Germanisch-Romanische Monatsschrift*, NF 26 (1976), 440–51.

Müller-Klug, Florian, 'Schloss und Park Charlottenhof — Ein Arkadien', Clio Berlin (December 2, 2014), https://clioberlin.de/blog-architektur/76-schloss-und-park-charlottenhof-ein-arkadien.html

Nettesheim, Josefine, *Die geistige Welt der Dichterin Annette Droste zu Hülshoff* (Münster: Regensberg, 1967).

Niethammer, Ortrun, and Claudia Belemann, *Ein Gitter aus Musik und Sprache: Feministische Analysen zu Annette von Droste-Hülshoff* (Paderborn: Schöningh, 1993).

Nipperdey, Thomas, 'Nationalidee und Nationaldenkmal in Deutschland im 19. Jahrhundert', *Historische Zeitschrift*, 206 (1968), 529–85.

—— *Deutsche Geschichte 1800–1866: Bürgerwelt und starker Staat* (Munich: Beck, 1984).

Nisbet, H. B., *On the Literature and Thought of the Classical Era: Collected Essays* (Cambridge: Open Book Publishers, 2021), https://doi.org/10.11647/OBP.0180

Noltenius, Rainer, *Dichterfeiern in Deutschland. Rezeptionsgeschichte als Sozialgeschichte am Beispiel der Schiller- und Freiligrath-Feiern* (Munich: Fink, 1984).

—— 'Die Nation und Schiller', *Dichter und ihre Nation*, ed. by Helmut Scheuer (Frankfurt am Main: Suhrkamp, 1993), 151–75.

Nürnberger, Helmuth, *Der junge Fontane. Politik. Poesie. Geschichte 1840 bis 1860* (Hamburg: Wegner, 1967), 100–04.

Nürnberger, Richard, 'Rauch's Friedrich-Denkmal historisch-politisch gesehen', *Jahrbuch Preußischer Kulturbesitz*, 8 (1979), 115–24.

Obermann Peter Karl, 'Die deutsche Einheitsbewegung und die Schillerfeiern 1859', *Zeitschrift für Geschichtswissenschaft*, 3 (1955), 705–34.

Oechelhaueser, Wilhelm, 'Die deutsche Shakespeare-Gesellschaft', in *Shakespeareana* (Berlin: Springer, 1894), 1–22.

Osterkamp, Ernst, ed., *Sizilien. Reisebilder aus drei Jahrhunderten* (Munich: Winkler, 1986).

Pape, Walter, and Frederick Burwick, in collaboration with the German Shakespeare Society, eds., *The Boydell Shakespeare Gallery* (Bottrop: Pomp, 1996).

Paulin, Roger, 'Kleist's Metamophoses. Some Remarks on the Use of Mythology in *Penthesilea*', *Oxford German Studies*, 14 (1983), 35–53.

—— *Ludwig Tieck: A Literary Biography* (Oxford: Clarendon Press, 1985).

—— 'Gundolf's Romanticism', in *Deutsche Romantik und das 20. Jahrhundert. Londoner Symposion 1985*, ed. by Hanne Castein and Alexander Stillmark, Stuttgarter Arbeiten zur Germanistik 177 (Stuttgart: Heinz, 1986), 25–40.

—— 'Julius Hare's German Books in Trinity College Library, Cambridge', *Transactions of the Cambridge Bibliographical Society*, 9 (1987), 174–93.

—— *Goethe, the Brothers Grimm and Academic Freedom. An Inaugural Lecture Delivered Before the University of Cambridge 9 May 1990* (Cambridge: Cambridge University Press, 1990).

—— 'Fairy Tales for Very Sophisticated Children: Ludwig Tieck's *Phantasus*', *Bulletin of the John Rylands University Library of Manchester*, 76 (1994), 59–68.

—— 'Rilke: Duino Elegy Ten', in *Rilke's Duino Elegies. Cambridge Readings*, ed. by Roger Paulin and Peter Hutchinson (London: Duckworth; Riverside, CA: Ariadne, 1996), 171–91.

—— '"Shakspeare's allmähliches Bekanntwerden in Deutschland". Aspekte der Institutionalisierung Shakespeares 1840–1875', in *Bildung und Konfession. Politik, Religion und literarische Identitätsbildung 1850–1918*, ed. by Martin Huber and Gerhard Lauer, Studien und Texte zur Sozialgeschichte der Literatur 59 (Tübingen: Niemeyer, 1996), 9–20.

—— 'Some Remarks on the New Edition of the Works of Wilhelm Müller', *Modern Language Review*, 92 (1997), 363–78.

—— *Der Fall Wilhelm Jerusalem. Zum Selbstmordproblem zwischen Aufklärung und Empfindsamkeit*, Kleine Schriften zur Aufkärung 7 (Göttingen: Wallstein, Wolfenbüttel: Lessing-Akademie, 1999).

—— 'The "Schillerfeier" of 1859 and the "Shakespearefest" of 1864 with Some Remarks on Theodor Fontane's Contributions', in *History and Literature. Essays in Honor of Karl S. Guthke*, ed. by William Collins Donahue and Scott Denham (Tübingen: Stauffenburg, 2000), 351–65.

—— 'Heine and Shakespeare', in *Heine und die Weltliteratur*, ed. by T. J. Reed and Alexander Stillmark (Oxford, London: Legenda, 2000), 51–63.

—— 'Friedrich Gottlieb Klopstock: "Der Zürchersee"', in *Landmarks in German Poetry*, ed. by Peter Hutchinson, British and Irish Studies in German Language and Literature 20 (Berne, etc.: Peter Lang, 2000), 41–56.

—— 'Adding Stones to the Edifice: Patterns of German Biography', in *Mapping Lives. The Uses of Biography*, ed. by Peter France and William St Clair (London: The British Academy; Oxford: Oxford University Press, 2002), 103–14.

—— 'Schiller: Wallenstein', in *Landmarks in German Drama*, ed. by Peter Hutchinson, British and Irish Studies in German Language and Literature 27 (Oxford, etc: Peter Lang, 2002), 47–57.

—— 'Annette von Droste-Hülshoff', in *Landmarks in German Women's Writing*, ed. by Hilary Brown, British and Irish Studies in German Language and Literature 39 (Oxford etc.: Peter Lang, 2007), 77–90.

—— 'Ein deutsch-europäischer Shakespeare im 18. Jahrhundert?', in *Shakespeare im 18. Jahrhundert*, ed. by Roger Paulin, Das achtzehnte Jahrhundert. Supplementa 3 (Göttingen: Wallstein, 2007), 7–35.

—— *The Life of August Wilhelm Schlegel. Cosmopolitan of Art and Poetry* (Cambridge: Open Book Publishers, 2016), https://doi.org/10.11647/obp.0069

—— 'Der kosmopolitische Büchersammler. Zu August Wilhelm Schlegels *Verzeichniß meiner Bücher im December 1811*', in *Kooperative Informationsstrukturen als Chance und Herausforderung*, ed. by Achim Bonte and Juliane Rehnolt, Thomas Bürger zum 65. Geburtstag (Berlin, Boston: De Gruyter, 2018), 317–25.

Paulsen, Friedrich, *Die deutschen Universitäten und das Universitätsstudium* (Berlin: Asher, 1902).

—— 'Überblick über die geschichtliche Entwicklung der deutschen Universitäten mit besonderer Rücksicht auf ihr Verhältnis zur Wissenschaft', in *Die Universitäten im deutschen Reich*, ed. by W. Lexis, Das Unterrichtswesen im Deutschen Reich 1 (Berlin: Asher, 1904), 1–38.

—— *The German Universities and University Study*, trans. by Frank Thilly and William W. Elwang, preface by M. E. Sadler (London: Longmans Green, 1906).

Perry, Walter C., *German University Education, or the Professors and Students of Germany. To which is Added, a Brief Account of the Public Schools of Prussia, with Observations on the Influence of Philosophy on the Studies of the German Universities*, 2nd ed. (London: Longman, Brown, Green, 1846).

Prawer, Siegbert, *Heine's Shakespeare. A Study in Contexts. Inaugural Lecture delivered before the University of Oxford on 5 May 1970* (Oxford: Clarendon Press, 1970).

Prinz, Lucie, *Schillerbilder. Die Schiller-Verehrung am Beispiel der Festreden des Stuttgarter Liederkranzes (1825–1992)* (Marburg: diagonal-Verlag, 1994).

Puls, Michael, 'Zur Genese des Reiterdenkmals für Friedrich Wilhelm III. in Köln bis 1878. Ein Thema in plastischen Variationen zwischen Rauch und Begas', in *Köln: Das Reiterdenkmal für König Friedrich Wilhelm III. auf dem Heumarkt*, ed. by Rolf Beines, Walter Geis and Ulrich Krings (Cologne: Bachem, 2004), 74–199.

Quinn, Sister Bernetta M., *The Metamorphic Tradition in Modern Poetry* (New York: Geordian Press, 1972).

Raabe, Paul, 'Lorbeerkranz und Denkmal. Wandlungen der Dichterhuldigung in Deutschland', in *Festschrift für Klaus Ziegler*, ed. by Eckehard Catholy and Winfried Hellmann (Tübingen: Niemeyer, 1968), 411–26.

Realismus und Gründerzeit. Manifeste und Dokumente zur deutschen Literatur 1848–1880, ed. by Max Bücher, Werner Hahl, Georg Jäger and Reinhard Wittmann, vol. 1 (Stuttgart: Metzler, 1976).

Reed, T. J., *Thomas Mann. The Uses of Tradition* (Oxford: Clarendon Press, 1974).

—— *The Classical Centre. Goethe and Weimar 1775–1832* (Oxford: Clarendon Press, 1980).

Rehm, Walther, *Griechentum und Goethezeit. Geschichte eines Glaubens* (Berne: Francke, 1951).

—— *Götterstille und Göttertrauer. Aufsätze zur deutsch-griechischen Begegnung* (Munich: Lehnen, 1951).

Renger, Christian, *Die Gründung und Einrichtung der Universität Bonn und die Berufungspolitik des Kultusministers Altenstein*, Academica Bonnensia 7 (Bonn: Röhrscheid, 1982).

Ribbat, Ernst, 'Der Dichter und sein Monograph: Zu den Aussichten einer fragwürdigen Gattung', in *Germanistik: Forschungsstand und Perspektive. Vorträge des Deutschen Germanistentages 1984, 2. Teil. Ältere Deutsche Literatur. Neuere Deutsche Literatur*, ed. by Georg Stötzel (Berlin, New York: De Gruyter, 1985), 589–99.

Robinson, Henry Crabb, *Henry Crabb Robinson und seine deutschen Freunde. Brücke zwischen England und Deutschland im Zeitalter der Romantik*, ed. by Hertha Marquardt and Kurt Schreinert, Palaestra 237, 249 (Göttingen: Vandenhoek & Ruprecht, 1964, 1967).

Ricklefs, Ulfert, 'Leben und Schrift: Autobiographische und biographische Diskurse. Ihre Intertextualität in Literatur und Literaturwissenschaft', *Editio: Internationales Jahrbuch für Editionswissenschaft*, 9 (1995), 37–62.

Sauder, Gerhard, 'Die "Freude der Freundschaft": Klopstocks Ode "Der Zürchersee"', in *Gedichte und Interpretationen, II*, ed. by Karl Richter (Stuttgart: Reclam, 1984), 228–39.

Schaal, Susan, 'Das Beethoven-Denkmal von Ernst Julius Hähnel in Bonn', in *Monument für Beethoven. Zur Geschichte des Beethoven-Denkmals (1845) und der frühen Beethoven-Rezeption in Bonn*, ed. by Ingrid Bodsch, Katalog zur Ausstellung des Stadtmuseums Bonn und des Beethoven-Hauses (Bonn: Stadtmuseum, 1995), 39–133.

Schadewaldt, Wolfgang, 'Schillers Griechentum', in *Schiller. Reden im Gedenkjahr 1959*, ed. by Bernhard Zeller (Stuttgart: Klett, 1961), 258–70.

Schanze, Helmut, 'Die Anschauung vom hohen Rang des Dramas in der zweiten Hälfte des 19. Jahrhunderts und seine tatsächliche Schwäche', in *Beiträge zur Theorie der Künste im 19. Jahrhundert, 1*, ed. by Helmut Koopmann and J. Adolf Schmoll gen. Eisenwerth, Studien zur Philosophie und Literatur des neunzehnten Jahrhunderts 12.1 (Frankfurt am Main: Klostermann, 1971), 85–96.

—— *Drama im bürgerlichen Realismus (1850–1890). Theorie und Praxis*, Studien zur Philosophie und Literatur des neunzehnten Jahrhunderts 21 (Frankfurt am Main: Klostermann, 1973).

Scheuer, Helmut, 'Biographie: Überlegungen zu einer Gattungsbeschreibung', in *Vom Anderen und vom Selbst: Beiträge zu Fragen der Biographie und Autobiographie*, ed. by Reinhold Grimm and Jost Hermand (Königstein im Taunus: Athenäum, 1982), 9–29.

Schmidt, Erich, *Lessing: Geschichte seines Lebens und seiner Schriften*, 2 vols (Berlin: Weidmann 1884–92).

Schrader, Wilhelm, *Geschichte der Friedrichs-Universität zu Halle*, 2 vols (Berlin: Dümmler, 1894).

Schubart-Fikentscher, Gertrud, *Studienreform. Fragen von Leibniz bis Goethe, Sitzungsberichte der Sächsischen Akad. d. Wiss. zu Leipzig*, Phil.-hist. Klasse 116.4 (Berlin: Akademie, 1973).

Schulz, Gerhard, 'Goethes Itaienische Reise', in *Goethe in Italy, 1786–1986. A Bi-Centennial Symposium November 14–15, 1986, University of California, Santa Barbara: Proceedings Volume*, ed. by Gerhart Hoffmeister, Amsterdamer Publikationen zur Sprache und Literatur 76 (Amsterdam: Rodopi, 1988), 5–19.

Selbmann, Rolf, *Dichterdenkmäler in Deutschland. Literaturgeschichte in Erz und Stein* (Stuttgart: Metzler, 1988).

Sengle, Friedrich, *Wieland* (Stuttgart: Metzler, 1949).

—— '"Die Braut von Messina"', in *Arbeiten zur deutschen Literatur 1750–1859* (Stuttgart: Metzler, 1965), 94–117.

—— *Biedermeierzeit: Deutsche Literatur im Spannungsfeld zwischen Restauration und Revolution 1815–1848*, 3 vols (Stuttgart: Metzler, 1971–80).

—— 'Zum Problem der Goethewertung: ein Versuch', in *Neues zu Goethe. Essays und Vorträge* (Stuttgart: Metzler, 1989).

—— *Das Genie und sein Fürst. Die Geschichte der Lebensgemeinschaft Goethes mit dem Herzog Karl August* (Stuttgart, Weimar: Metzler, 1993).

Sharpe, Lesley, *Schiller and the Historical Character. Presentation and Interpretation in the Historiographical Works and in the Historical Dramas* (Oxford: Oxford University Press, 1982).

—— *Friedrich Schiller, Drama, Thought and Politics* (Cambridge: Cambridge University Press, 1991).

—— '"Wahrheit allein sollte mich leiten": Caroline von Wolzogen's Schiller Biography', *Publications of the English Goethe Society*, 68 (1999), 70–81.

Sieck, Albrecht, *Kleists Penthesilea. Versuch einer neuen Interpretation*, Literatur und Wirklichkeit 14 (Bonn: Bouvier, 1976).

Sowa, Wolfgang, *Der Staat und das Drama. Der preußische Schillerpreis 1859–1918. Eine Untersuchung zum literarischen Leben im Königreich Preußen und im deutschen Kaiserreich*, Regensburger Beiträge zur deutschen Sprach- und

Literaturwissenschaft, Reihe B. Untersuchungen 36 (Frankfurt am Main, Berne, New York, Paris: Lang, 1988).

Spranger, Eduard, *Wandlungen im Wesen der Universität seit 100 Jahren* (Leipzig: Wiegandt, 1913).

—— *Wilhelm von Humboldt und die Reform des Bildungswesens*, 2nd ed. (Tübingen: Niemeyer, 1960).

Staiger, Emil, 'Klopstock "Der Zürchersee"', in *Die Kunst der Interpretation: Studien zur deutschen Literaturgeschichte* (Zurich: Artemis, 1955), 50–74.

Stark, Susanne, *Behind Inverted Commas. Translation and Anglo-German Relations in the Nineteenth Century*, Topics in Translation 15 (Clevedon, Philadelphia, Toronto, Sydney: Multilingual Matters, 1999).

Stirk, S. D., *German Universities — Through English Eyes* (London: Gollancz, 1946).

Stopp, Elisabeth, 'Wandlungen des Tieckbildes', *Deutsche Vierteljahrsschrift für Literaturwissenschaft und Geistesgeschichte*, 17 (1939), 252–76.

—— 'Die Kunstform der Tollheit: zu Clemens Brentanos und Joseph Görres' "BOGS der Uhrmacher"', in *Clemens Brentano. Beiträge des Kolloquiums im Freien Deutschen Hochstift 1978*, ed. by Detlev Lüders (Tübingen: Niemeyer, 1980), 358–76.

—— 'Ludwig Tieck: Unveröffentlichte Aufzeichnungen zu Purgatorio VI–XXIII anläßlich der deutschen Übersetzung von Philalethes, ediert und erläutert', *Deutsches Dante Jahrbuch*, 60 (1985), 7–72.

—— 'Ludwig Tieck and Dante', *Deutsches Dante Jahrbuch*, 60 (1985), 73–95.

Sühnel, Rudolf, 'Gundolfs Shakespeare. Rezeption-Übertragung-Deutung', *Euphorion*, 75 (1981), 245–74.

Thomas, Ursula, 'Heinrich von Kleist and Gotthilf Heinrich Schubert', *Monatshefte*, 51 (1959), 249–61.

Tomlinson, Charles, *Poetry and Metamorphosis* (Cambridge: Cambridge University Press, 1983).

Tropus, Karl, *Schiller-Denkmal*, 2 vols (Berlin: Riegel, 1860).

Tümmler, Hans, 'Goethes Anteil an der Entlassung Fichtes von seinem Jenaer Lehramt 1799', in *Goethe in Staat und Politik. Gesammelte Aufsätze*, Kölner Historische Abhandlungen 9 (Cologne, Graz: Böhlau, 1964), 132–66.

—— 'Der Minister Goethe und die Jenaer Universitätsreform', in *Das klassische Weimar und das große Zeitgeschehen. Historische Studien*, Mitteldeutsche Forschungen 78 (Cologne, Vienna: Böhlau, 1975).

Wadepuhl, Walter, 'Shakespeares Mädchen und Frauen. Heine und Shakespeare', in *Heine-Studien* (Weimar: Arion, 1956), 114–34.

—— *Heinrich Heine. Sein Leben und seine Werke* (Cologne, Vienna: Böhlau, 1974).

Walzel, Oskar, 'Review of Friedrich Gundolf, *Shakespeare und der deutsche Geist*', *Jahrbuch der deutschen Shakespeare-Gesellschaft*, 48 (1912), 259–74.

Wilamowitz-Moellendorf, Ulrich von, *Griechische Tragödien übersetzt von Ulrich von Wilamowitz-Moellendorf, xiii: Euripides, Die Bakchen* (Berlin: Weidmann, 1923).

Winnington-Ingram, R. P., *Euripides and Dionysus. An Interpretation of the Bacchae* (Amsterdam: Hakkert, 1969).

Wolff, Emil, 'Hegel und Shakespeare', in *Vom Geist der Dichtung. Gedächtnisschrift für Robert Petsch*, ed. by Fritz Martini (Hamburg: Hoffmann und Campe, 1949), 120–79.

Yates, Frances, 'Transformations of Dante's Ugolino', *Journal of the Warburg and Courtauld Institutes*, 14 (1951), 92–117.

Ziolkowski, Theodore, *German Romanticism and Its Institutions* (Princeton: Princeton University Press, 1990).

Zur Westen, Walter von, *Zur Enthüllung des Rauchschen Friedrichsdenkmals in Berlin. Fest- und Erinnerungsblätter aus dem Anlaß der 75. Wiederkehr des Enthüllungstages* (Berlin: n.p., 1926).

List of Illustrations

Fig. 1   James Hervey, *Meditations and Contemplations* (London: J.   x
          Goodwin, 1812).
Fig. 2   View of the Bay of Naples. Friedrich Leopold zu Stolberg,   24
          *Reise in Deutschland der Schweiz, Italien und Sicilien in den Jahren
          1791 bis 1792*, in *Gesammelte Werke der Brüder Christian und
          Friedrich Leopold Grafen zu Stolberg*, 20 vols (Hamburg: Perthes
          und Besser, 1820–25), VII, plate facing p. 340.
Fig. 3   Wallenstein, from Friedrich Schiller's drama trilogy *Wallenstein*, steel   44
          engraving after a drawing by Friedrich Pecht, c. 1859. Wikimedia,
          https://commons.wikimedia.org/wiki/File:Wallenstein_aus_
          Schillers_Wallenstein.jpg, public domain.
Fig. 4   *Laocoon and his Sons*, also known as the *Laocoon Group*. Marble,   58
          copy after an Hellenistic original from ca. 200 BC. Found in
          the Baths of Trajan, 1506, Wikimedia, https://commons.
          wikimedia.org/wiki/File:Laocoon_Pio-Clementino_Inv1059-
          1064-1067.jpg, public domain.
Fig. 5   Joshua Reynolds, *Count Ugolino and his Children in the Dungeon*   69
          (1770–73), National Trust Collection.
Fig. 6   John Flaxman, illustration of Dante, *Inferno*, Canto 33 (Rome?,   70
          1802), showing Ugolino and his sons. Courtesy of the Master
          and Fellows of Trinity College, Cambridge.
Fig. 7   John Flaxman, illustration of Dante, *Inferno*, Canto 33 (Rome?,   71
          1802), showing Ugolino and his sons. Courtesy of the Master
          and Fellows of Trinity College, Cambridge.
Fig. 8   [Karl Gottlieb Hofmann], *Pantheon der Deutschen*, 3 parts   78
          (Chemnitz: Karl Gottlieb Hofmann, 1794–1800), part 2 (1795),
          frontispiece and title page.
Fig. 9   Ernest Julian Stern and Heinz Herald, 'Penthesilea, Reinhardt   94
          und seine Bühne, Bilder von der Arbeit des Deutschen
          Theaters', 1919, Wikimedia, https://commons.wikimedia.
          org/wiki/File:Penthesilea_(Kleist)_-_Amazone.jpg,   public
          domain.

Fig. 10	[Jacob and Wilhelm Grimm], *Kinder- und Haus-Märchen*, 2nd ed. (Berlin: Reimer, 1819–22), vol. 1 (1819), frontispiece and title page. Courtesy of the Master and Fellows of Trinity College.	122
Fig. 11	Adrian Ludwig Richter, *Genoveva* (1820–84), The Metropolitan Museum of Art, public domain.	146
Fig. 12	Friedrich Gundolf, photograph by Jacob Hilsdorf (1911), University Library Heidelberg, Wikimedia, https://commons.wikimedia.org/wiki/File:Friedrich_Gundolf_(HeidICON_33461).jpg, CC BY-SA 4.0.	160
Fig. 13	Wilhelm Müller, engraving by Johann Friedrich Schröter (c. 1830), Wikimedia, https://commons.wikimedia.org/wiki/File:Wilhelm_M%C3%BCller_by_Schr%C3%B6ter.jpg, public domain.	178
Fig. 14.	Anna Jameson, *Characteristics of Women, Moral, Poetical, and Historical. With Fifty Vignette Etchings*, second edition (London: Saunders & Otley, 1833), volume 1, p. 1. The Master and Fellows of Trinity College, Cambridge.	206
Fig. 15	Engraving by Carl Jäger, *Erinnerung an die Schillerfeier 1859*, "erfunden und radirt von C. Jaeger."; erschienen *im Nürnberger Künstlervereins-Album; C. H. Zeh'sche Buch & Kunsthandlung in Nürnberg*. Wikimedia, https://de.wikipedia.org/wiki/Datei:Karl_J%C3%A4ger_Erinnerung_an_die_Schillerfeier_1859_800x1296pixel.jpg, public domain.	222
Fig. 16	Theaterplatz in Dresden. Photo by author, CC BY-SA 4.0.	244
Fig. 17	Equestrian statue of King John of Saxony, Dresden Theaterplatz, by Johannes Schilling (1889). Photo by the Author, CC BY 4.0.	248
Fig. 18	Equestrian statue of King John of Saxony, detail of plinth. Photo by author, CC BY 4.0.	250
Fig. 19	Equestrian statue of King John of Saxony, rear of plinth. Photo by author, CC BY 4.0.	250
Fig. 20	Herms of poets at Charlottenhof, Potsdam. Photo by author, CC BY 4.0.	255
Fig. 21	Equestrian statue of King Frederick the Great of Prussia, by Christian Daniel Rauch (1851), Unter den Linden, Berlin. Photo by author, CC BY 4.0.	257
Fig. 22	Equestrian statue of Frederick the Great, detail of plinth. Photo by author, CC BY 4.0.	262

Fig. 23   Equestrian statue of Frederick William III, Cologne. Wikimedia, 266
https://commons.wikimedia.org/wiki/File:Reiterstandbild_
Friedrich_Wilhelm_III_K%C3%B6ln_Heumarkt.jpg, CC
BY-SA 3.0.

Fig. 24   Friedrich Gottlieb Klopstock, c. 1760. Wikimedia, https:// 270
commons.wikimedia.org/wiki/File:Friedrich_Gottlieb_
Klopstock-01.jpg, public domain.

Fig. 25   Johann Joseph Sprick, *Portrait of Annette von Droste-Hülshoff*, 292
1838. Wikimedia, https://commons.wikimedia.org/wiki/
File:Droste-H%C3%BClshoff_2.jpg, public domain.

Fig. 26   Leonid Pasternak, Portrait of Rainer Maria Rilke, date 312
unknown. Wikimedia Commons, https://commons.
wikimedia.org/wiki/File:Leonid_Pasternak_-_Portrait_
painting_of_Rainer_Maria_Rilke.jpg, public domain.

Fig. 27   Bust of Julius Hare by Thomas Woolner (1861). The Wren 338
Library, Trinity College, Cambridge. Photo by James Kirwan.
Courtesy of the Master and Fellows of Trinity College.

Index

academic freedom 123–128, 132–133, 135–138, 141, 148
Achilles 90–91, 99–101, 103, 105–106, 108–111, 117–118
Acton, Lord 363
Adams, H. M. 348
Aeschylus 77, 175, 228
Akenside, Mark 61
Albert, King of Saxony 249
Albert, Prince Consort 249
Alewyn, Richard 175
Alexander the Great 80
Alexis, Willibald 203, 362
Allen, Philip Schuyler 203
Allgemeine Literatur-Zeitung 152
Ariosto, Ludovico 84, 154–156, 254–256
Aristophanes 214–215
Aristotle 59, 214, 278
Arminius 245. See also Hermannsdenkmal (monument)
Arndt, Ernst Moritz 267, 360
 E. M. Arndt's Urtheil über Friedrich den Grossen 360
 Prinz Victor von Neuwied 360
Arnim, Achim von 114, 140, 148, 151, 191, 195, 295, 340, 346–347, 359–360
 Berthold's erstes und zweites Leben 359
 Der Wintergarten 359
 Des Knaben Wunderhorn 148, 198, 352
 Gräfin Dolores 359
 Halle und Jerusalem 359
 Isabella von Aegypten 359
 Landhausleben 359
Arnim, Bettina von 141, 147, 293, 295, 339, 354
 Goethes Briefwechsel mit einem Kinde 339, 354

Arnim, Johannes Freimund von 147–148
Arnold, Matthew 124–125, 127, 184
Athenaeum (periodical) 27–29, 149, 171, 215, 355
Atterbom, Per Daniel Amadeus 193
Auden, W. H. 26, 109
autobiography 2, 26, 83, 351

Bach, Johann Sebastian 268
Bacon, Francis 344
Barry, James (painter) 68
Bartels, Johann Heinrich 25
Basedow, Adelheid 195
Basedow, Johann Bernhard 195
Baudissin, Wolf von 251, 361
Baur, Ferdinand Christian 349
Beethoven, Ludwig van 82, 255, 260, 267
Befreiungshalle (monument) 249
Begas, Reinhold 257
Bellotto, Bernardo 246–247
Benecke, Georg Friedrich 191
Bengel, Johann Albrecht 349
Benjamin, Walter 175
Béranger, Pierre Jean de 183, 199
Bernhardi, August Ferdinand 356
Bertuch, Friedrich Justin 301
 Naturgeschichte 301
Bible, the 8, 12, 14, 17, 306
Biedermeier 179, 181, 185, 187, 190, 195, 293–294, 298
biography 79–84, 86–88, 91, 185–186, 212, 224, 230, 263, 340, 354
Bismarck, Otto von 124–125, 163, 245, 248–249, 257–258
Bläser, Gustav 254, 265
Blomberg, Alexander von 361
 Hinterlassene poetische Schriften 361
Blücher, Gebhard Leberecht von 260, 267
Boccaccio, Giovanni 150, 254, 256

Böckh, August 188, 190, 192
Böcklin, Arnold 163
Bodenstedt, Friedrich von 225, 240
Bodmer, Johann Jacob 11, 64, 190, 273, 279
Böhme, Jacob 114, 149, 348–349
Boisserée, Melchior 30, 267
Boisserée, Sulpiz 30, 267
Bopp, Franz 358, 362
Borchardt, Rudolf 317
Bosch, Hieronymus 157
Böttiger, Karl August 358
Boydell, Josiah 68
Braque, Georges 314
Braun, Volker 274
Breitinger, Johann Jacob 11, 279–281
  Critische Dichtkunst 280
Brentano, Clemens 149, 190, 192, 195, 210, 352, 359–360
  Der Goldfaden 359
  Des Knaben Wunderhorn 148, 189, 295, 300, 302, 339–340
  Die Gründung Prags 359
  Gockel Hinkel Gackeleia 148
Brentano, Peter 5
Brion, Friederike 4
Brockes, Barthold Heinrich 282
Brockhaus, Friedrich Arnold 182, 196, 203–204
Brockhaus, Heinrich 196
Bruford, W. H. 129
Bruno, Giordano 346
Brydone, Patrick 25
Büchner, Georg 1, 214, 293–294
Büchting, Adolph 239
Buff, Charlotte 4
Bunsen, Karl Josias von 340–341, 362
Burckhardt, Jacob 161, 163, 167–168, 171, 225, 232
Bürger, Gottfried August 85, 182, 191, 209
Burke, Edmund 277
Büsching, Johann Gustav 357
  Das Lied der Nibelungen 357

Byron, Lord 1, 82, 168, 182–185, 187, 189, 197, 199, 203–205
  Cain 184
  Manfred 184

Calandrelli, Alexander 257
Calderón de la Barca, Pedro 118, 155, 175, 212, 252, 358
Camerer, Clemens Christian 275
Camões, Luís de 171
Campe, Julius 212
Canaletto 246
Carl August, Duke 134–135, 137, 341
Carlsbad Decrees 133, 137–138, 183
Carlyle, Thomas 80–81, 123, 151, 168, 171, 209, 341–342
  Life of Friedrich Schiller, The 81, 209
Carmer, Johann Heinrich von 262, 268
Carus, Carl Gustav 251, 361
Cassirer, Ernst 104–105
catharsis 67
Catholicism 29, 33, 124–126, 197, 211, 231, 267, 295–296, 343, 350, 359
Cervantes, Miguel de 84, 171, 212, 214–215, 251
Charlottenhof villa 254–256
childhood 19, 73, 88, 106, 147, 357
Cicero 264, 278
  De officiis 264
Classicism 27–29, 31, 33, 37, 42–43, 46, 62, 91, 96–99, 101, 104–105, 126, 187, 191, 195, 211, 228, 233, 237, 254, 256, 278–279, 281, 286, 322, 324, 340–341, 343, 345, 348, 357–358
  Neoclassicism 59, 69, 88, 96, 98, 258, 350
Clauren, Heinrich 196
Cocceji, Samuel von 262
Coleridge, Samuel Taylor 45, 63, 173–174, 209, 236, 340–341, 344, 346–348, 350–351, 362
Collins, William 274
Colosseum, the 39–40
Columbus, Christopher 85–86, 227
comedy 214–215

Constant, Benjamin 1, 45
Contessa, Carl Wilhelm Salice 361
Cook, James 85–86
Copernicus, Nicolaus 86
Corneille, Pierre 175
Correggio, Antonio da 28
Cotta, Johann Friedrich 60, 196, 226, 294–295
   Morgenblatt für die gebildeten Stände 196
Creuzer, Georg Friedrich 104–105, 352, 358
   Symbolik und Mythologie der alten Völker 104, 352
Cysarz, Herbert 170

Dach, Simon 198
Daguerre, Louis 301
Dahlmann, Friedrich Christoph 353
Dante Alighieri 60, 63–70, 74–75, 84, 162–163, 171, 203, 249, 251–252, 254–255, 260, 326, 343, 361
   Divine Comedy 64, 249
      Inferno 60, 64, 66, 70
      Paradiso 70
   German reception of 63–67
Däubler, Theodor 317
death 1, 12–14, 16, 20–21, 28, 74–75, 103, 108, 116–118, 293, 301, 305, 313–314, 316–318, 320, 325–326, 330–331, 333, 335
Delaunay, Robert 314
Dessau 179, 187–188, 194, 196, 202
Deutsche Shakespeare-Gesellschaft 212, 226, 236
De Wette, Wilhelm Martin Leberecht 137, 349
Dickens, Charles 240
Dickinson, Emily 307
Dictys 99
Die Horen (periodical) 60, 64–66
Diepenbrock, Melchior 296
Dilthey, Wilhelm 47, 167, 170
Dingelstedt, Franz 225–226, 230
Distad, N. Merrill 340
   Guessing at Truth 340

Docen, Bernhard Joseph 347, 357
   Museum für Altdeutsche Literatur und Kunst 357
   Ueber die Ursachen der Fortdauer der lateinischen Sprache 347
Döllinger, Ignaz von 125–126
Donne, John 317
Döring, Heinrich 354
Dresden 113, 185, 194, 196–197, 202, 244–248, 252–253, 255, 259, 262, 265, 347, 351, 356
Droste-Hülshoff, Annette von 169, 293–296, 299–300
   Das geistliche Jahr 296, 299, 301
   'Der Dichter—Dichters Glück' 83, 201, 296, 298–300, 307
   Die Judenbuch 296
   Heidebilder 301
   'Im Grase' 298, 303
   'Lebt wohl' 295, 303
   'Spätes Erwachen' 303
Droysen, Johann Gustav 80–81, 126, 233, 353
Duller, Eduard 259
   Die Geschichte des deutschen Volkes 259
Dumas, Alexandre 220
Dürer, Albrecht 84, 91, 154, 255, 260

Eckermann, Johann Peter 2, 339, 354
Eichendorff, Joseph von 188, 210, 335
Eichhorn, Karl Friedrich 124, 342
Eliot, George 349
Eliot, T. S. 109, 319
   Waste Land, The 314, 324
Elisabeth Ludovika of Bavaria, Queen of Prussia 254
Elze, Karl 236
Emmerick, Anna Katharina 295, 300, 359
   Das bittere Leiden unsers Herrn Jesu Christi 359
   Das letzte Abendmahl unsers Herrn Jesu Christi 359
Empfindsamkeit (cult of feeling) 10–14, 20, 32, 53
Enlightenment 263

Erinnerungsorte. See places of memory
Ernest Augustus, King of Hanover 133, 140, 358
Ernesti, Johann August 349
Eschenburg, Johann Joachim 6, 345, 357
  Denkmäler altdeutscher Dichtkunst 357
Euripides 42, 59, 96, 98–101, 104–105, 111
  Bacchae 100, 104–105, 111
Eversmann, Eduard 347
  Reise von Orenburg nach Buchara 347

fairytale. See Märchen (fairytales)
Fauriel, Claude Charles 199
female writers 293, 296
Feuerbach, Ludwig 318, 349
Fichte, Johann Gottlieb 124, 129–136, 138–139, 267, 343
  Reden an die deutsche Nation 267
Fiedler, H. G. 363
Finck von Finckenstein, Carl Wilhelm 261
Flaxman, John 69–70
Fleming, Paul 198
Fohr, Philipp 192–193
folksong 187, 197
Fontane, Theodor 171, 212, 226–227, 237, 239–243
  Aus England 242
  Ein Sommer in London 242
  Jenseit des Tweed 242
  Wanderungen durch die Mark Brandenburg 242–243
  'Zum Schillerfest des "Tunnel"' 238
Förster, Friedrich 191, 197
  Die Sängerfahrt 191, 194
Forster, Georg 138, 251
Förster, Karl 197
Foscolo, Ugo 1
Foucault, Michel 83
Fouqué, Friedrich de la Motte 183, 188, 190, 343, 360–361
  Der Zauberring 361
  Siege of Ancona. A Romantic Idyll, The 360

Sintram 361
François, Étienne 245–247, 253
Franco-Prussian War 249
Frazer, James 210, 346, 352
Frederick II (the Great), King of Prussia 87, 188, 245, 247, 249, 253, 256–259, 261–265, 342
Frederick William III, King of Prussia 189, 253, 260, 265–266
Frederick William II, King of Prussia 128, 268
Frederick William I, King of Prussia 128
Frederick William IV, King of Prussia 249, 253–258, 260, 265
Freiligrath, Ferdinand 199, 212, 225, 229, 231, 240, 295
French Revolution 48, 130, 265
Freud, Sigmund 83, 107, 318
Freytag, Gustav 229, 233
Friedrich, Caspar David 149
friendship 13, 42, 88, 90, 181, 187, 190, 274–275, 278–279, 284–285, 287, 303, 307

Gadamer, Hans-Georg 323
Garve, Christian 262, 264
Gellert, Christian Fürchtegott 11, 259, 262, 264
  Praktische Abhandlung von dem guten Geschmacke in Briefen 11
Genée, Rudolph 225
Gentz, Friedrich von 97
George, Stefan 82, 162–163, 166, 170, 184
  circle around 162, 170
  Der siebente Ring 163
Gerstenberg, Heinrich Wilhelm von 65
  Briefe über Merkwürdigkeiten der Literatur 65
  Ugolino 65
Gervinus, Georg Gottfried 173, 229, 233, 236, 241, 252, 256
  Neue Geschichte der poetischen Literatur der Deutschen 252
Gesellschafter, Der (periodical) 192
Gilbert, Ludwig Wilhelm 114

Annalen der Physik 114
Gleim, Johann Wilhelm Ludwig 189, 191, 262, 264, 284–285
Goeckingk, Günther von 202
Goedeke, Karl 185, 204
Goethe, Johann Caspar 4
Goethe, Johann Wolfgang 1–16, 18, 22, 25–34, 36–43, 45, 47, 51, 59, 62–64, 72, 82, 88–91, 96–99, 102–105, 107, 118, 133–139, 141, 150, 154–155, 162–163, 165–166, 168–169, 171–172, 182, 184, 187, 191, 193–194, 197–199, 208–209, 213, 215, 224–225, 227, 230–231, 235, 238–239, 245, 253–256, 260, 263, 275–276, 281–282, 286–287, 295, 298–299, 301, 339, 341, 343, 347, 350, 354, 356
  Achilleis 98
  'Der Fischer' 299
  'Der Wandrer' 37
  Dichtung und Wahrheit 2, 7, 18, 26
  Die Leiden des jungen Werthers 1–5, 7–10, 12–22, 32, 43, 286
  Die Wahlverwandtschaften 29
  Faust 15, 99, 103, 245
  Götz von Berlichingen 3
  Iphigenie auf Tauris 41–43, 96–99, 103, 105, 107
  Italienische Reise 25–27, 29–30, 32, 37, 40, 43, 182, 193–194
  Pandora 97, 103, 105
  [Roman in Briefen] 3–4
  Römische Elegien 64
  Shakespeare und kein Ende! 172, 213, 215
  Skizze zu einer Schilderung Winckelmanns 88
  Torquato Tasso 255
  Ueber Kunst und Alterthum 43, 339, 354
  Unterhaltungen deutscher Ausgewanderten 64
  Wilhelm Meister 72
  Zum Schäkespear's Tag 3
Görres, Joseph 104, 157, 347–348, 351–352
  Aphorismen über Organonomie 351
  Die christliche Mystik 351
  Die teutschen Volksbücher 352
  Mythengeschichte der asiatischen Welt 352
  Rheinischer Merkur 352
  Teutschlands künftige Verfassung 347
  Teutschland und die Revolution 351
Gotter, Friedrich Wilhelm 4
Gotthelf, Jeremias 293–294
Göttingen Seven 133, 139–140
Gottschall, Rudolf 226, 233
Gottsched, Johann Christoph 209
Gozzi, Carlo 152
Grabbe, Christian Dietrich 213, 228
  Über die Shakespearo-Manie 213, 229
Grand Tour 25
Graun, Carl Heinrich 262–263
Graves, Robert 120
Gray, Thomas 274
Grey, George 353, 362
  Poems, Traditions, and Chaunts of the Maories 353, 362
Grillparzer, Franz 169, 172, 226, 233, 293–294, 298
  'Abschied von Gastein' 298
Grimm, Herman 80, 163
Grimm, Jacob 124, 128, 133, 139–141, 147, 191, 225, 232, 239, 295, 353, 357–358
  Kinder- und Hausmärchen 141, 147, 357
Grimm, Ludwig Emil 148
Grimm, Wilhelm 124, 133, 139, 141, 147, 191, 295, 353, 357–358
  Kinder- und Hausmärchen 141, 147, 357
Gruber, Johann Gottfried 87
Gryphius, Andreas 107, 175, 198
Guardini, Romano 323
Gubitz, Friedrich Wilhelm 192
Guizot, François 214, 246
Gundolf, Friedrich 82, 161–164, 166–176, 210, 227
  Romantiker 169, 210
  Romantiker-Briefe 161–164, 167, 169
  Shakespeare. Sein Wesen und Werk 168, 173–175

Shakespeare und der deutsche Geist 162, 165–166, 169–170, 172–173, 227
Günther, Johann Christian 198
Gutenberg, Johannes 255, 260
Gutzkow, Karl 217, 224–226, 354
   Über Goethe im Wendepunkte zweier Jahrhunderte 354

Hackert, Jakob Philipp 36–37
Hagedorn, Friedrich von 181, 284–285
Hagen, Friedrich Heinrich von der 191, 357
   Der Helden Buch 357
hagiography 28, 42, 83–84, 86, 88, 90, 183
Haller, Albrecht von 273–274, 285
Hamann, Johann Georg 342
Hamilton, Antoine, Count 155
Handel, George Frederick 242
Hardenberg, Friedrich von. See Novalis (Friedrich von Hardenberg)
Hardenberg, Karl August von, Prince 191, 267
Hare, Augustus 340
   Guesses at Truth 340, 346
Hare, Augustus J. C. 340, 343–344
   Memorials of a Quiet Life 340
   Story of My Life, The 340
Hare, Esther 345
Hare, Julius 123, 188, 338–364
   Guesses at Truth 340, 346
Harms, Claus 349
Hartmann, Ferdinand 356
Hatfield, James Taft 203
Hauff, Wilhelm 92, 182, 185, 196
Haym, Rudolf 165, 167, 210, 231, 267
   Die romantische Schule 210–211
Hazlitt, William 211, 213–214
Hebbel, Friedrich 218, 226, 233, 293
Hebel, Johann Peter 260
Hederich, Benjamin 98–100, 105, 112
   Gründliches mythologisches Lexicon 98–99
Hegel, Georg Wilhelm Friedrich 45, 124, 130, 132–133, 168, 171, 215, 219, 228–229, 267, 342, 350, 353

Heidegger, Martin 131
Heine, Heinrich 167–168, 180–186, 189–190, 199, 202, 207–220, 267, 293
   Buch der Lieder 189
   Reise von München nach Genua 182
   Shakespeares Mädchen und Frauen 207–208, 212, 215–220
   Zur Geschichte der Religion und Philosophie in Deutschland 214
Heinrich, Prince of Prussia 258
Heinse, Wilhelm 10, 102, 283
Hellingrath, Norbert von 162, 316
Hengstenberg, Ernst Wilhelm 349
Hensel, Luise 189
Hensel, Wilhelm 189–190, 195
Henze, Hans Werner 109
Heraclitus 164
Herder, Johann Gottfried 62, 65–66, 74, 129, 166, 172, 197, 210, 213, 215, 241, 254, 256, 342, 344, 353, 357
Hermannsdenkmal (monument) 249
Hermes (periodical) 182, 196, 199, 356
Herwegh, Georg 199, 212, 225, 231, 240
Hettner, Hermann 229, 233, 263
Heym, Georg 324
Heyne, Christian Gottlob 129, 141
Heyse, Paul 203, 225–226, 233
Heywood, Thomas 214
Hirzel, Georg 284
Hirzel, Johann Kaspar 280
historical drama 47–48, 54, 213, 218–219, 234
historicism 81, 167, 169
historiography 80, 167, 228, 237, 263
Hoffmann, E. T. A. 151, 162, 207, 340, 355, 360
   Die Elixiere des Teufels 355
   Die Serapionsbrüder 355
   Kater Murr 355
   Meister Floh 355
Hoffmann von Fallersleben, August Heinrich 230
Hofmannsthal, Hugo von 172, 184

Hölderlin, Friedrich 102, 162, 164, 169, 275–276, 282–283, 285, 287–288, 316–317, 319, 336, 354
  'Brod und Wein' 283, 316, 336
  'Der Rhein' 287
  'Mein Vorsaz' 275
  'Patmos' 287
Holy Roman Empire 4
Homer 84, 100, 105, 191, 227, 231, 326, 343
Horace 275, 281
Horn, Franz 212, 217, 346, 362
Houwald, Ernst von 361
Huch, Ricarda 167
Hugo, Victor 168, 214, 220, 246
Humboldt, Alexander von 132, 137, 191, 258–259, 267, 343
Humboldt, Wilhelm von 45, 90, 129–133, 136, 138–139, 267, 343, 358
Hyginus 99

iconography 34, 42, 91, 141, 147, 149, 246, 249, 251, 253, 300

Jacobi, Friedrich Heinrich 124, 343
Jäger, Oskar 232
Jahn, Friedrich 183, 190
Jahrbücher der Literatur (periodical) 356
Jahrbücher für Phiiosophie und Pädagogik (periodical) 356
Jahrbücher fur wissenschaftliche Kritik (periodical) 356
Jameson, Anna 206, 214, 217, 219
Jean Paul 1, 169, 208, 260, 342, 354–355
  Clavis Fichteana 355
  Dämmerung für Deutschland 355
  Titan 355
Jena 87, 129, 134–138, 152, 347, 350, 352
Jenkins, Roy 124
Jerome, King of Westphalia 139
Jerusalem, Johann Friedrich Wilhelm 7–8
Jerusalem, Karl Wilhelm 4–8, 13–14
John, King of Saxony 247–253, 255, 260, 262, 361
Johnson, Samuel 13, 73, 211, 213–214

Jones, William 341
Jordan, Charles-Étienne 262, 264
Joseph II (Holy Roman Emperor) 4, 87
Jung-Stilling, Heinrich 114, 351
  Theorie der Geisterkunde 114

Kafka, Franz 141
Kalckreuth, Friedrich von 183, 190, 197
Kannegiesser, Karl Ludwig Friedrich 251
Kanne, Johann Arnold 103, 110, 352
  Erste Urkunden der Geschichte, oder Allgemeine Mythologie 352
  Gianetta 352
  Mythologie der Griechen 103, 110, 352
  Romane aus der Christenwelt aller Zeiten 352
  System der indischen Mythe 352
Kant, Immanuel 46–47, 112, 124, 129–130, 166, 260–264, 268, 343
  Der Streit der Fakultäten 130
Karsch, Anna Louisa 265
Kayser, Christian Gottlob 359
Keble, John 302
Keller, Gottfried 96, 184, 225, 233, 239
Kerner, Justinus 182, 186–187, 197, 202–204
Kersting, Georg Friedrich 188
Kestner, Johann Christian 4–9, 13
Kinkel, Gottfried 231
Klages, Ludwig 170
Kleist, Ewald von 264, 280, 284–285
Kleist, Heinrich von 31, 92, 95–106, 110, 112–114, 118, 120, 169, 351, 354, 356, 360
  Amphitryon 95
  Das Erdbeben in Chili 101
  Das Käthchen von Heilbronn 100, 113
  'Der Schrecken im Bade' 100
  Der zerbrochne Krug 101
  Die Hermannsschlacht 95
  Die Verlobung in St. Domingo 101
  Marionettentheater 118
  Penthesilea 94–108, 110–114, 116–120
  Prinz Friedrich von Homburg 95, 118

Kleist, Marie von 113
Klemperer, Victor 246
Klingemann, Ernst August Friedrich 1
Klopstock, Friedrich Gottlieb 12, 14, 18, 20, 33, 39, 84–88, 90, 92, 95, 102, 108, 182, 238–239, 259, 273–288, 305, 343, 353
  'An Bodmer' 274
  'An Gott' 283
  'Auf meine Freunde' 102, 279, 281
  'Das Wiedersehn' 305
  Der Messias 84–86, 280
  'Der Zürchersee' 274–278, 282, 286–288
Kniep, Christoph Heinrich 36, 38
Knobelsdorff, Georg Wenzeslas von 262, 264
Knorring, Sophie von 358
  Flore und Blanscheflur 359
Koberstein, August 229
Kopisch, August 251
Köppen, C. F. 259
  Friedrich der Große und seine Widersacher. Eine Jubelschrift 259
Köppen, Peter von 348
  Die dreygestaltete Hekate und ihre Rolle in den Mysterien 348
Körner, Josef 354
Körner, Theodor 188, 267
Kotzebue, August von 137
Kreyssig, F. A. 236
Kugler, Franz 259, 264
  Geschichte Friedrichs des Großen 259
Kürenberger, the 190
Kurz, Hermann 203, 230
Kynosarges (periodical) 356

Lachmann, Karl 191, 358
Lamartine, Alphonse de 168
Lange, Samuel Gotthold 279
Laocoon 60, 62–63, 68–69, 71, 77
La Roche, Maximiliane von 5
La Roche, Sophie von 5
  Geschichte des Fräuleins von Sternheim 5
Lassberg, Joseph von 295

Leibniz, Gottfried Wilhelm 343
Leipzig 5, 8, 85, 194, 196–197, 230, 234–235, 259, 352, 357–358
Leistner, Bernd 204–205
Leistner, Maria-Verena 204–205
Lenau, Nikolaus 293–294
Lenné, Peter Joseph 254
Lenz, Jakob Michael Reinhold 12, 31, 62–63, 71, 284, 354
  Das Hochburger Schloss 61
Leopold, Prince of Anhalt-Dessau 188
Lessing, Gothold Ephraim 6, 53, 62, 65, 68, 80–81, 85–88, 90, 92, 209, 227–228, 230, 256, 260, 262–264, 283, 342, 354, 357
  Die Erziehung des Menschengeschlechts 264
  Emilia Galotti 6, 264
  Laokoon 65, 68
  Literaturbriefe 228
  Nathan der Weise 53, 264
Lessing, Karl 86
Lewes, George Henry 349
Liebermann, Max 314
lieux de mémoire. See places of memory
Lindau, Paul 226
literary canon 83–84, 86, 92, 171, 175, 204, 215, 224, 226, 233, 245, 255–256, 265, 267
literary criticism 176, 198, 209
literary history 183, 210, 259, 263, 294
literature
  national 61, 83, 92, 171, 186, 208, 213, 229, 239, 252, 255, 263
  travel 25, 182
  world 63, 197, 208–209
Lives of the Poets. See biography
loci memoriae. See places of memory
Loeben, Otto Heinrich, von 197
Lohenstein, Daniel Casper von 175
Lohre, Heinrich 203
Louis Philippe, King 219
Ludwig, Emil 82
Ludwig I, King of Bavaria 248–249, 361
Ludwig, Maximilian 238

Ludwig, Otto 46, 173, 226, 233
Luther, Martin 8, 84, 124, 260, 263, 273, 317, 346, 348–349

Majer, Friedrich 352
Malsburg, Ernst von der 197
Mann, Golo 83
 Wallenstein 83
Mann, Thomas 1, 55, 141, 161
Manning, Henry Edward 340
Märchen (fairytales) 142, 150–153, 155–156, 158
Marggraff, Hermann 225
Marlowe, Christopher 175, 191, 195, 199, 214
Mason, Eudo 174
Massow, Julius Eberhard von 129
materialism 49, 163, 169
Maupertuis, Pierre Louis 262, 264
Maurice, F. D. 123, 340
Maurois, André 82
Meidner, Ludwig 324
Meinecke, Friedrich 126–127
Meinhard, Johann Nicolaus 66
memory. See places of memory
Mendelssohn, Fanny 295
Mendelssohn, Felix 254, 296
Mendelssohn, Moses 86, 265
Menzel, Adolph 259, 264–265
Menzel, Wolfgang 362
metamorphosis 95–96, 99–100, 109–110, 112–113, 116, 118, 120, 319
metre (poetry) 42, 97, 249, 281–282, 298, 300, 304, 317, 321, 336
Metternich, Prince Klemens von 137, 186
Meyer, Conrad Ferdinand 171, 184, 223–224
Meyer, Heinrich 28, 30, 163
Michelangelo 80, 84, 163, 227
Michelet, Jules 219–220, 246
Mickiewicz, Adam 168
Middle Ages, the 30, 43, 152, 162, 171, 175, 357
Mill, John Stuart 123
Milton, John 61

Minor, Jacob 167
Möbius, Paul 234–235
Molière (Jean-Baptiste Poquelin) 95, 214
Mombert, Alfred 317
Mommsen, Theodor 125–126, 163, 168, 191, 233, 246
Monet, Claude 314
Montagu, Elizabeth 61
Montaigne, Michel de 278
Montesquieu, Charles de Secondat, Baron de 13
 Lettres Persanes 13
monument 86, 245, 246, 248, 249, 252, 253, 255, 257, 258, 259, 260, 263, 265, 267, 330, 331. See also places of memory
Moore, Thomas 199–200
Mörike, Eduard 169, 293–295
Moritz, Karl Philipp 36, 98, 103–104, 353
 Götterlehre oder mythologische Dichtungen der Alten 98, 103, 353
Möser, Justus 353
Müller, Adam 97, 118, 181, 347, 356, 362
 Die Elemente der Staatskunst 347
 Von der Idee des Staates und ihren Verhältnissen zu den populären Staatstheorien 347
Müller, Johannes von 124, 342, 353
Müller, Karl Otfried 358
Müller, Max 184, 186, 203
Müller, Wilhelm 92, 179–180, 182–193, 195–199, 201, 203–205, 208, 357, 362
 Askania 195
 Bibliothek deutscher Dichter des siebzehnten Jahrhunderts 198, 357
 Blumenlese aus den Minnesingern 190
 Bundesblüthen 189–190
 Debora 181, 189, 196, 203
 Die schöne Müllerin 179–181, 200–201
 'Die verpestete Freiheit' 200
 Die Winterreise 179–180, 188, 201–202
 Homerische Vorschule 195, 197
 Lieder der Griechen 189, 192, 199
 Lyrische Reisen und epigrammatische Spaziergänge 202

Neugriechische Volkslieder 199
Rom, Römer und Römerinnen 182, 193–194, 197, 203, 362
Sieben und siebzig Gedichte aus den hinterlassenen Papieren eines reisenden Waldhornisten 181, 193, 200
Müllner, Adolph 361
Musäus, Johann Carl August 152, 155
Volksmärchen der Deutschen 152
Musset, Alfred de 214
mysticism 17, 114
mythology 35, 60, 75, 96, 98–99, 104–106, 108, 194, 255, 286, 313, 317, 319, 348–349, 352–353, 362

Napoleon, Emperor of France 2, 4, 87, 188, 219, 357
National Socialism 126, 131, 141
Nazarenes, the 27, 29–30, 154, 192–194, 356
Nibelungenlied 357
Niebuhr, Barthold Georg 124, 191, 267, 340–341, 343, 346, 353
History of Rome 341, 343
Nienstädt, Wilhelm 119
Nietzsche, Friedrich 81, 102, 161–164, 168, 171
Nipperdey, Thomas 80, 249, 258
Nora, Pierre 245
Les Lieux de mémoire 245
Northcote, James 68
Novalis (Friedrich von Hardenberg) 31, 33, 91, 114, 149, 155–156, 158, 162, 168, 343, 354–356
Die Christenheit oder Europa 354
Geistliche Lieder 355
Heinrich von Ofterdingen 158
Novellenkranz 356

Odeonsplatz (Munich) 248
Oechelhäuser, Wilhelm 236
Oehlenschläger, Adam 360–361
Correggio 361
Oken, Lorenz 135–139, 301, 347, 351
Erste Ideen zur Theorie des Lichts 347

Grundzeichnung des natürlichen Systems der Erze 347
Isis (periodical) 137
Lehrbuch der Naturgeschichte 351
Ueber das Universum als Fortsetzung des Sinnensystem 347
Ueber den Werth der Naturgeschichte, besonders fur die Bildung der Deutschen 136, 347
Olivier, Ferdinand 188
Olliers Literary Miscellany (periodical) 360
Olshausen, Hermann 349
Opie, John 68
Opitz, Martin 175, 198, 204, 273
Ossian 20–21, 61, 84
Ovid 99–101, 108–109
Metamorphoses 100, 109, 111

Pabst, Johann Heinrich 359
Ein Wort über die Ekstase 359
Pange, Comtesse Jean de 82
Panizzi, Antonio 363
Panthéon (Paris) 245
Pantheon, the 39–40, 42, 85–86
Parthey, Gustav 358
Perrault, Charles 151, 154
Perry, Walter C. 125, 127–128
German University Education, or the Professors and Students of Germany 125
Persius, Ludwig 254
Perthes, Friedrich Christoph 350
Pesne, Antoine 262, 264
Phidias 343
Philalethes 249, 251, 252, 255, 256, 361. See also John, King of Saxony
philology 73, 81, 139, 167, 170, 172, 176, 191, 211, 341, 345, 348, 357–358
Phöbus (periodical) 97, 100, 113, 118–119, 356
Picasso, Pablo 314
Pindar 275, 279, 316
places of memory 245–247, 252–253, 256–257

Platen, August von 198, 293–294
Plato 33, 164
Plautus 95
Plutarch 102
Pope, Alexander 61–62, 101
positivism 79, 81, 169
Potsdam 246, 253, 255–256
Pound, Ezra 95, 109, 319
Prawer, S. S. 210
Preußische Jahrbücher (periodical) 167
Priebsch, Robert 363
Propyläen (periodical) 27–28, 43, 354
Prutz, Robert 362
Prynne, William 216
   Histriomastix 216

Raabe, Wilhelm 225
Rabelais, François 157
Racine, Jean 254
   Athalie 254
Ramler, Karl Wilhelm 262, 264
Ranke, Leopold von 80–81, 163, 167, 191, 233, 246, 353
   Ueber die Verschwörung gegen Venedig 353
Raphael 27, 30, 33, 41–43, 84, 89, 91, 227, 343
   cult of 27, 33, 41–43
Rauch, Christian Daniel 256–257, 268
Raumer, Friedrich von 353
   Das Brittische Besteuerungs-System 353
Raupach, Ernst von 361
Reck, Karl 354
Renaissance, the 40, 43, 85, 87, 154, 171, 175, 208, 211, 216, 220, 247, 286
Renoir, Pierre-Auguste 314
Reynolds, Joshua 62, 68–69
Rheims 245
Richardson, Samuel 3
Richter, Ludwig 259
Riedesel, Johann Hermann von 25
Riemer, Friedrich Wilhelm 339
Riepenhausen, Franz 148
Riepenhausen, Johannes 148
Rietschel, Ernst 231

Rilke, Rainer Maria 109, 313–314, 316–319, 321, 323–327, 330–332, 334–336
   'Alkestis' 326
   Duino Elegies (*Duineser Elegien*)
      I 316, 327
      IV 315
      V 313, 315, 323
      VI 313, 332, 334
      VII 313
      IX 313, 324
      X 313–336
   Malte Laurids Brigge 314
   Neue Gedichte 314
   'Orpheus. Eurydice. Hermes' 326
   Requiem. Für eine Freundin 327
Ritter, Johann Wilhelm 114, 152, 350
   Fragmente aus dem Nachlasse eines jungen Physikers 350
Robeck, Johannes 13
   De morte voluntaria 13
Robert, Ludwig 97
Robinson, Henry Crabb 344, 360
Roethe, Gustav 169
Romanticism 32, 91, 148, 161–163, 166–170, 176, 179, 181, 191, 212, 328, 354, 360
   German 91, 148, 162, 169, 176, 328
Rome 25–30, 39–41, 62, 89, 98, 192, 194, 265, 341, 343, 350, 356
Rosenkranz, Karl 167, 357, 362
Rossetti, Christina 306
   'A Birthday' 306
Rossetti, Dante Gabriel 184
Rötscher, Heinrich Theodor 229
Rousseau, Jean-Baptiste 274
Rousseau, Jean-Jacques 3, 8, 15, 101
   La Nouvelle Héloïse 15
Rückert, Friedrich 188, 198, 203, 267
Ruge, Arnold 362
Ruhl, August Sigismund 193
Rühs, Friedrich 188, 190
ruins 34, 37–39, 154, 247, 328
Rümelin, Johann Christoph Benjamin 275

Rumohr, Carl Friedrich von 192, 362
    Geist der Kochkunst 362
    Novellen 362
Runge, Philipp Otto 147–149, 156, 356

Sachs, Hans 357
Sack, Albert von 192
Sand, Karl 137
Sandrart, Joachim von 84
Savigny, Friedrich Carl von 124, 343, 356
    Zeitschrift für geschichtliche Rechtswissenschaft 356
Schanze, Helmut 233
Scharnhorst, Gerhard von 267
Schelling, Friedrich Wilhelm Joseph 104–105, 114, 124, 130–131, 135–136, 139, 233, 343, 349–351
    Philosophie der Kunst 233
    Philosophie und Religion 350
    System der Naturphilosophie 350
    Weltseele 350
Schenk, Eduard von 361
Schenkendorf, Max von 188, 267
Scherenberg, Christian Friedrich 239
Scherer, Wilhelm 126, 167, 233
Schiller, Friedrich 33, 45–49, 52–55, 59–60, 62, 64–65, 67, 72, 74, 77, 80–81, 85, 87, 90, 92, 97, 118, 124, 141, 171–173, 182, 185, 209, 223–232, 234–235, 238–241, 245, 253–256, 260, 263, 282, 284, 295, 300, 341, 343
    Briefe über die ästhetische Erziehung des Menschen 64
    centenary of 223
    cult of 238
    Demetrius 226
    'Der Taucher' 300
    Die Braut von Messina 96–97
    Die Räuber 46, 238
    Don Carlos 46
    Fiesco 46
    Geschichte des dreissigjährigen Krieges 47–48
    Maria Stuart 59
    Über naïve und sentimentalische Dichtung 64, 256
    Wallenstein 45–56, 59
    Wilhelm Tell 245
Schilling, Johannes 247
Schinkel, Karl Friedrich 254, 257
Schlabrendorff, Ernst Wilhelm von 261
Schlegel, August Wilhelm 27–29, 59–60, 63–66, 69, 71–72, 74–77, 82, 98, 105, 112, 124, 132, 168, 170–171, 173, 180, 191, 209, 211, 213, 215, 218, 228, 252, 267, 340–342, 352, 355, 357–360
    De geographia Homerica 358
    Die Gemählde 28
    Ion 98
    Vorlesungen über dramatische Kunst und Literatur 63, 72, 76, 82, 173, 209, 212
    'Zueignung des Trauerspiels Romeo und Julia' 75
Schlegel, Dorothea 358
    Florentin 358
Schlegel, Friedrich 27, 29–30, 32–33, 41–43, 63, 88, 92, 97, 105, 124, 149, 152–154, 156–157, 163, 168–171, 191, 209, 211, 215, 219, 340–342, 349, 352–355, 358
    Alarcos 97
    Concordia 29, 355
    Europa 355
    Geschichte der Jungfrau von Orleans 358
    Geschichte der Poesie der Griechen und Römer 105
    Gespräch über die Poesie 149
    Lucinde 161, 349
    Philosophie der Geschichte 353
    Philosophie des Lebens 358
    Über das Studium der Griechischen Poesie 105
    Ueber die Sprache und Weisheit der Indier 352
    Ueber Lessing 88
Schleiermacher, Friedrich 124, 130–131, 133, 136, 138–139, 267, 341–342, 346, 348–349

Vertraute Briefe über Fr. Schlegels Lucinde 349
Schleswig-Holstein crisis 227, 237, 241
Schlosser, Friedrich Christoph 353
Schlüter, Andreas 257
Schmidt, Erich 80–81, 101, 167, 169, 263
Schmidt, Fanny 283
Schmidt, Georg Philipp (von Lübeck) 187, 198, 201
Schmidt, Julian 223, 229, 233, 236, 241
Schnorr von Carolsfeld, Julius 192, 195
Schopenhauer, Adele 295
Schopenhauer, Arthur 233
  Die Welt als Wille und Vorstellung 233
Schubert, Franz 180, 183–184, 201
Schubert, Gotthilf Heinrich 113–114
  Ansichten von der Nachtseite der Naturwissenschaft 113–114, 351
Schücking, Levin 295
Schüddekopf, Carl 167
Schulze, Hagen 245–247, 253
Schumann, Clara (née Wieck) 296
Schumann, Robert 295–296
Schütz, Friedrich Karl Julius 354
  Goethe und Pustkuchen 354
Schütz, Wilhelm von 97, 359
  Anticelsus 359
  Der Garten der Liebe 359
  Der Graf und die Gräfin von Gleichen 359
  Dramatische Wälder 359
  Lacrimas 359
  Niobe 359
Schwab, Gustav 80, 90, 92, 183–186, 189, 202, 224, 230
Schwerin, Kurd Christoph von 268
Scott, Walter 200, 240–241
Semper, Gottfried 247, 253
Seneca, L. Annaeus 98
Sengle, Friedrich 83, 185
  Wieland 83
Seven Years' War 247
Severini, Gino 314
Seydlitz, Friedrich Wilhelm von 261

Shakespeare, William 3, 31, 46, 52–54, 59–67, 71–76, 82, 84, 92, 97, 111–112, 118, 154–155, 162, 165–166, 168–175, 196, 207–220, 225–230, 233–238, 240–243, 251–252, 342–343, 358
  As You Like It 72
  German reception of 59–61, 63, 65, 209, 212, 214, 217, 220, 240, 242, 252
  Hamlet 54, 71–73, 76, 112, 213, 229, 240–241
  Henry IV 46, 174, 219
  Henry V 174
  Henry VI 67–68, 72, 175, 219
  Henry VIII 72
  Julius Caesar 66, 72
  King John 67, 72, 249–250, 253, 260, 262
  King Lear 62–63, 68, 71–72, 77, 241
  Love's Labour's Lost 175
  Macbeth 46, 48, 51–55, 59, 72, 74, 77, 213
  Merchant of Venice, The 72, 215–217
  Midsummer Night's Dream, A 63, 72, 173, 240, 254
  Othello 54, 72, 76, 241
  Richard II 219
  Richard III 46, 67, 72
  Romeo and Juliet 46, 59–60, 66, 68, 71–73, 75–77, 241
  Tempest, The 66, 72
  translation of 64, 66, 71–72, 170, 172, 210–212, 230, 236, 240
  Troilus and Cressida 217
  Twelfth Night 72
  Winter's Tale, The 208
Sicily 25–26, 37, 39
Siegesallee 257–258, 268
Sinclair, Isaak von 283
Solger, Karl Wilhelm Ferdinand 105, 188, 193, 346, 362
solitude 8–9, 12, 22
Sophocles 46, 76–77, 97–98, 105, 118, 228, 254
  Antigone 77, 175, 254
  Oedipus at Colonus 76
  Oedipus Rex 76, 96

Spener, Jakob 349
Spinoza, Baruch 17, 348
Spitzweg, Carl 194
Spranger, Eduard 126
Staël, Madame de 82, 217, 343, 360
   De l'Allemagne 343, 360
Stägemann, August von 191–192
Stägemann, Elisabeth von 191
Stanley, A. P. 344
Steffens, Henrik 114, 130–131, 351, 359
   Die gegenwärtige Zeit 351
   Was ich erlebte 351
Steig, Reinhold 98, 140, 158, 167
Stein, Friedrich Karl, Freiherr vom 267
Sterling, John 123, 141, 342, 353
Stifter, Adalbert 294
Stolberg, Christian von 350
Stolberg, Friedrich Leopold von 24–27, 32–34, 36–43, 342, 350
   Geschichte der Religion Jesu Christi 350
   Reise durch Deutschland, die Schweiz, Italien und Sicilien in den Jahren 1791–92 26, 32–33, 37, 42
Storm, Theodor 182, 184
Strasbourg 3–4, 30, 245
Stratford 241–242
Strauss, David Friedrich 348–350
   Das Leben Jesu 349–350
Streckfuss, Karl 251
Streicher, Andreas 230
Sturm und Drang 1, 15, 61, 65, 85, 97, 215
sublime, the 59, 277–278, 283
Süvern, Johann Wilhelm 188
Swinburne, Algernon Charles 184

Tacitus 95
Tasso, Torquato 84, 157, 197, 203–204, 254, 256
Tennyson, Alfred 184, 346
Teutoburger Wald 246, 249
Thierry, Augustin 246
Thiersch, Friedrich 348, 358
   Ueber die Epochen der bildenden Kunst unter den Griechen 348
Thiersch, Heinrich Wilhelm Josias 349

Thirlwall, Connop 188, 341, 346
Thirty Years' War 47–48
Tholuck, August 349
Thomasius, Christian 129
Thorwaldsen, Bertel 230
Thümmel, Moritz August von 353
Thurn und Taxis, Princess Marie von 315
Tieck, Dorothea 295
Tieck, Ludwig 27–32, 41–43, 46, 73, 85, 91–92, 97, 105, 113, 118, 148–158, 161, 168–169, 171–175, 181, 191, 193, 196–197, 200–201, 211–215, 228, 230, 240, 251, 254, 256, 295, 340, 343, 345–346, 352, 354–358, 361–362
   Alt-Englisches Theater 358
   Buch über Shakespeare 174
   Deutsches Theater 357
   Dichterleben 214
   Dramaturgische Blätter 213
   Franz Sternbalds Wanderungen 149–150, 201, 356
   Frauendienst 357
   Genoveva 97, 146, 148, 152
   Herzensergiessungen eines kunstliebenden Klosterbruders 85, 150, 356
   Minnelieder aus dem Schwäbischen Zeitalter 148, 356
   Phantasus 31, 150–153, 155–156
   Poetisches Journal 352
   Shakspeare's Vorschule 358
   William Lovell 356
Tischbein, Johann Heinrich Wilhelm 36
Tolstoy, Leo 318
   Death of Ivan Ilyich, The 318
Tomlinson, Charles 319
Treitschke, Heinrich von 126, 233
Tropus, Karl 240

Ugolino della Gherardesca 60, 64–71, 74, 77
Uhland, Ludwig 182, 186, 197, 202–204, 295, 357
   Walther von der Vogelweide 357
Ulrici, Hermann 229, 236

universities 123–129, 131–132, 134, 140–141, 342
Urania (periodical) 196, 202, 356

Valéry, Paul 109
Vanvitelli, Luigi 40
Varnhagen von Ense, Karl August 362
Vasari, Giorgio 85
Veit, Johannes 29, 198
Veit, Philipp 29, 188
Velde, Carl Franz van der Velde 196
Versailles 248, 253
Victoria, Queen of the United Kingdom 140, 358
Vigny, Alfred de 214
Vilmar, August Friedrich 229
Virchow, Rudolf 125, 132
Virgil 36, 66, 255, 326
   Aeneid 99
   Georgics 36
Vischer, Friedrich Theodor 225, 229
Volkmann, Johann Jacob 25, 36
Volney, Constantin de 39
   Les Ruines, ou Méditations sur les Révolutions 39
Volpato, Giovanni 40
Voltaire, François Arouet de 61–62, 265, 278
Voss, Johann Heinrich 124, 191, 211, 343, 353

Wachler, Ludwig 252
Wackenroder, Wilhelm Heinrich 28, 31, 41–43, 85, 91, 150, 161, 356
   Herzensergiessungen eines kunstliebenden Klosterbruders 85, 150, 356
Wagner, Richard 82, 99, 162, 241
Waldberg, Max von 175
Walhalla (memorial) 246, 249, 260
Wallraf, Ferdinand Franz 267
Walzel, Oskar 166
Wars of Liberation 183, 188, 266, 267, 360
Wartburg 137, 246
Warton, Thomas 7
   'The Suicide' 7

Weber, Carl Maria von 196, 201
Weber, Max 127, 133
Welcker, Friedrich Gottlieb 358
Weltschmerz (melancholy) 1, 190, 201, 202, 294, 317
Wendt, Amadeus 195
   Taschenbuch zum geselligen Vergnügen 195
Wenzel, Gottfried Immanuel 362
Werner, Anton von 248
Werner, Zacharias 97, 118, 360
   Cunegunde 360
   Nachgelassene Predigten 360
   Wanda 360
Westminster Abbey 246
Wetzlar 4, 5, 8, 14, 232
Weygand, Christian Friedrich 5
Whewell, William 188, 341, 346
Wieland, Christoph Martin 33, 83, 87, 98, 124, 150, 154, 155, 254, 255, 256, 343
   Alceste 98
   Oberon 154
Wildenbruch, Ernst von 226
William I, German Emperor 257, 258
William II, German Emperor 253, 257, 268
William IV, King of Great Britain and Hanover 140
Wilson, Richard 40
Winckelmann, Johann Joachim 28, 29, 41, 42, 43, 62, 88, 89, 90, 91, 105, 262, 265, 343, 353
Wissenschaft (science) 35, 80, 81, 98, 127, 130, 131, 132, 168, 267, 341
Wittgenstein, Ludwig 318
Wolff, Christian 128, 138, 262, 264
Wolf, Friedrich August 124, 157, 188, 191, 192, 197, 343
Wolfskehl, Karl 162, 163, 170
Wöllner, Johann Christoph von 268
Wolzogen, Caroline von 87
Woolner, Thomas 338, 346
Wordsworth, William 276, 340, 341
World War Two 258
Wright, Aldis 348

Yeats, W. B. 319
Young, Edward 12, 33, 61, 85, 217, 229
    Night Thoughts 12, 33
youth. See childhood

Zeitung für Einsiedler (periodical) 347
Zelter, Carl Friedrich 2, 354

Zieten, Hans Joachim von 261
Zimmermann, Johann Georg 13
    Von der Einsamkeit 13
Zweig, Stefan 82

About the Team

Alessandra Tosi was the managing editor for this book.

Adèle Kreager performed the copy-editing, proofreading and indexing.

Andrew Corbett designed the cover.

Luca Baffa typeset the book in InDesign and produced the paperback and hardback editions. The text font is Tex Gyre Pagella; the heading font is Californian FB. Luca produced the EPUB, MOBI, PDF, HTML, and XML editions — the conversion is performed with open source software freely available on our GitHub page (https://github.com/OpenBookPublishers).

This book need not end here...

Share

All our books — including the one you have just read — are free to access online so that students, researchers and members of the public who can't afford a printed edition will have access to the same ideas. This title will be accessed online by hundreds of readers each month across the globe: why not share the link so that someone you know is one of them?

This book and additional content is available at:

https://doi.org/10.11647/OBP.0258

Customise

Personalise your copy of this book or design new books using OBP and third-party material. Take chapters or whole books from our published list and make a special edition, a new anthology or an illuminating coursepack. Each customised edition will be produced as a paperback and a downloadable PDF.

Find out more at:

https://www.openbookpublishers.com/section/59/1

Like Open Book Publishers

Follow @OpenBookPublish

Read more at the Open Book Publishers BLOG

You may also be interested in:

The Life of August Wilhelm Schlegel
Cosmopolitan of Art and Poetry
Roger Paulin

https://doi.org/10.11647/OBP.0069

Die Europaidee im Zeitalter der Aufklärung
Rotraud von Kulessa und Catriona Seth (Hg.)

https://doi.org/10.11647/OBP.0127

Hyperion, or the Hermit in Greece
Friedrich Hölderlin, translated and with an Afterword by Howard Gaskill

https://doi.org/10.11647/OBP.0160

www.ingramcontent.com/pod-product-compliance
Lightning Source LLC
Chambersburg PA
CBHW040746020526
44116CB00036B/2963